Karl Marx
and the Anarchists

Karl Marx and the Anarchists

Paul Thomas

Department of Political Science
University of California at Berkeley

Routledge & Kegan Paul

London, Boston and Henley

This book is for my Father and my Mother

First published in 1980
by Routledge & Kegan Paul Ltd
39 Store Street, London WC1E 7DD,
Broadway House, Newtown Road,
Henley-on-Thames, Oxon RG9 1EN and
9 Park Street, Boston, Mass. 02108, USA
Set in IBM Press Roman 10 on 11 pt
by Hope Services, Abingdon
and printed in Great Britain by
Redwood Burn Ltd
Trowbridge & Esher

British Library Cataloguing in Publication Data

Thomas, Paul
Karl Marx and the anarchists.
1. Anarchism and anarchists
2. Marx, Karl
I. Title
335'.83'0924   HX828   79 41564

ISBN 0 7100 0427 3

Contents

Preface

This book deals with Marx's disputes with and arguments against the anarchists, in the belief that knowledge of the issues involved in them can help us understand Marx's stature and importance as a theorist and as a revolutionist. Inevitably, and quite rightly, questions arise in books of this kind about the standing of Engels, who is not dealt with here. There are several reasons for his omission. It is important to distinguish between the two members of so celebrated an intellectual partnership, not in order to dismiss or diminish the contribution of Engels to the theory and practice of Marxism - he was an important theorist in his own right - but in order to acknowledge the specificity of the thought of Marx and Engels alike. The two were not interchangeable theorists, agreed about everything under the sun; the words of either one should not be used uncritically or incautiously to 'support' the opinions of the other. We should also admit at the outset - as Engels himself quite freely and indeed graciously admitted - Marx's pre-eminence in what was not, and what was not regarded as being, a partnership between equals. What Engels had to say about the anarchists (much of which may readily be encountered in the text I have used in what follows, *Anarchism and Anarcho-Syndicalism, Selected Writings by Marx, Engels, and Lenin*) does not add anything substantive to - nor does it significantly detract from - Marx's much more protracted and extensive attacks on anarchist doctrine and anarchism as a movement. Since it is these attacks that have not received the attention of scholars they deserve, and because Engels's comparatively brief forays into this particular field can be regarded at best as supplements rather than substantive additions, I feel justified in avoiding, in what follows, the needless repetition that would have resulted from the superimposition of Engels's views on to those of Marx.

Acknowledgments

This book has been some time in the making, and the number of friends, mentors, colleagues and students to whom my thanks are due is legion. To list all their names would be impossible; I am grateful to many whose names do not rise to the surface here. Some of those I do mention may be surprised at their inclusion, since not all of them have agreed with opinions I have expressed in the past; I nevertheless owe them a great deal.

Some of the thoughts that go into what follows first emerged in a doctoral dissertation for Harvard University in 1973, which benefited enormously from the advice, admonitions, cautions and criticisms of Judith N. Shklar and Michael Walzer. I am most grateful also to Miles Morgan for his extensive and sensitive comments on an earlier draft of this book, which helped me considerably in its revision. I should like to thank Terrell Carver, Hanna Pitkin and Norman Jacobson for their kind encouragement; Sir Isaiah Berlin, Reinhard Bendix, Michael Rogin, Martin Jay and Alan Ritter for their helpful comments on individual sections of the manuscript; and Bertell Ollman, Steven Lukes, David McLellan and Shlomo Avineri for planting ideas in my mind in the course of conversations – conversations which may have seemed inconsequential to them but which were to prove invaluable to me. My hope is that all those I mention, and those many more I fail to mention, will encounter traces of past conversation in what follows; responsibility for mistakes, omissions and drawbacks I insist upon claiming for myself alone.

This book was completed with the timely aid of a University of California Regents' Summer Faculty Fellowship; my thanks go also to the Department of Political Science at the University of California, Berkeley, and to its chairmen since I joined it (Norman Jacobson, Victor Jones and Chalmers Johnson) for their encouragement and aid. Connie Squires was a great help to me in revising Part 2, and Nancy Ruttenburg typed the bulk of the manuscript good-naturedly and cheerfully. My most heartfelt thanks go to my wife, Carolyn Porter, who I am sure thought it would never end and who deserves more thanks than she can know or I can possibly express.

viii

A note on sources

There is still no reliable, comprehensive edition of the writings of Marx - or for that matter of Proudhon, Stirner or Bakunin. In Marx's case two editions of the required type are promised, in the new *Gesamtausgabe: Editionsgrundsätze und Probestücke*, Berlin, Dietz, 1972 et seq., a monumental publishing project which by virtue of its scope is but barely under way; and in the English language Marx-Engels *Collected Works* (MECW), New York and London, International Publishers, 1975 et seq. Since ten volumes of this latter edition have appeared to date, I have used it alongside other easily available English language sources throughout, except for Chapter 4; the International Publishers' edition of *The Poverty of Philosophy*, New York, 1963, has the considerable merit of including within its covers Marx's important letters to Annenkov and von Schweitzer about Proudhon, so I have used it in preference to MECW, vol. vi, in which *The Poverty of Philosophy* is included (without the letters). Translations from the German and French are either my own or have been checked against the original. It would have been redundant for me to have repeated the Marx bibliographies that are readily enough available in English; the reader is referred, in particular, to David McLellan's 'Select Critical Bibliography' in his *Karl Marx: His Life and Thought*, London, Macmillan, 1973, and to Terrell Carver's more recent 'Guide to Further Reading' published as an appendix to the fourth edition of Sir Isaiah Berlin's *Karl Marx: His Life and Environment*, Oxford University Press, 1978, pp. 209-22. In my own List of works cited below, pp. 389-99, material included under Part 1 is not repeated under Part 2; I have included bibliographical notes on Stirner, Proudhon and Bakunin in the notes to Chapters 3, 4 and 5 respectively. Extracts from Marx-Engels *Collected Works*, vols 3, 4, and 5 are reprinted by permission of International Publishers, New York, 1975.

Introduction

We have not heard the last of the issues this book discusses. They are fundamentals of political thinking and organization alike. Ever since the French Revolution, the rise of the revolutionary Left, and the spread of its doctrines, has helped shape the contours of political life. The politics of our own times are simply incomprehensible if we fail to take this uneven rise into account, and there is no reason to suppose that its progress will be any smoother in the future than it was in the past. Marxism has by now assumed a variety of institutional as well as theoretical forms, but such predominance as it enjoys has never passed unchallenged. Marxism itself has never lacked critics, inside as well as outside the revolutionary Left, and it is not likely to lack them in any foreseeable future. Its critics within the revolutionary tradition may have interpreted the human brotherhood for which the Left is supposed to stand in the spirit of Cain and Abel (as Alexander Herzen once tersely put it), and the Marxists, for their part, have certainly responded in kind. This, however, should not blind us to the salutary reminder that Marxism's critics on the Left have provided: that it is a serious mistake to confuse Marxism with 'revolutionary doctrine', or 'socialism', or 'the Left'. To do so would be to confuse Marxism with its context, to take an overlap for a correspondence – or even an effect for a cause. These critical voices have never been stilled by the variety of Marxism's institutional accomplishments. On the contrary, attempts at institutionalizing Marxism – however successful they may seem to the uncritical – have stimulated and provoked, rather than dampened, criticisms from anarchists and others of Marxism's bearing and directionality.[1]

We are speaking, then, of an unfinished story. No matter how relevant Marxism may be to the world we live in and to the politics that animate it, this one particular sub-species of revolutionary socialism has never enjoyed an intellectual or institutional monopoly on the Left, and it is not likely to assume one. This point, indeed, can be made even more strongly, for it is precisely Marxism's successive pretensions to completeness that have drawn much of the fire from its revolutionary rivals; and their challenges have helped ensure that Marxism's purported monopoly of revolutionary thinking, action and 'truth' has remained an empty, fugitive ideal and not at all the *fait accompli* that some of its adherents – with no small degree of desperation – insist has been attained.

This book deals with some of the confrontations that belie Marxism's claims to completeness and finality, in the belief that such finality is (fortunately) unattainable. The particular challenges and responses that form the subject of this book raise issues which, like most political issues, defy final resolution. Marx may have got the better of his anarchist rivals, but he paid a heavy price for his success; even so, the bill was not presented in its entirety to Marx himself, and the final reckoning may still await settlement. It is certainly safe to predict that we have not heard everything from the anarchists; they, too, and the radical questioning they represent, have outlived the historical context in which their doctrine first came to light. This context overlaps significantly with that of the growth of Marxist doctrine; but such an overlap does not suggest the possibility of any future convergence, unless we assume, against all the evidence, a homogeneity of outlook within the Left, or an equally unlikely willingness to compromise of the type that neither Marxists nor anarchists have yet been eager to reveal.

Anarchists insist that the basic source of social injustice is the state. While they are not alone in wishing to overthrow the state – a fact that has led to some confusion of anarchism and Marxism – they distinguish themselves from Marxists by further insisting that all revolutions (in particular Marxist ones) which seek to replace one form of state by another will merely perpetuate or even extend tyranny. Freedom, they insist, is found by following the instincts of the masses, which lead them to organize themselves in communal institutions unsullied by power relations but galvanized by common interests. When the state, the main obstacle to communal life, is destroyed, the people, able to organize themselves without the need for any debilitating hierarchy, will form such communal associations and transform social existence. The removal of the state will suffice to restore man to his true nature, which has been whittled away and eroded by successive state-forms over the span of history.

Anarchism often shares with Marxism an indignation about the enervating effects of the division of labour in capitalist society. To both movements, the perfecting of industrialized economics and the reach of their economic tentacles into marginal, outlying areas has resulted in an increasing mechanization and quantification not only of productive activity *per se*, but also of human life itself so that mental and spiritual horizons are narrowed, injustice spreads like a cancerous growth, and the leisure produced by material progress becomes (for those fortunate enough to receive any of it) a vacuum, to be filled by mindless distraction and violence. Anarchism parts company with Marxism, however, in its insistence that Marxism itself has not provided, and by virtue of its theoretical limitations cannot provide, a solution to these very problems, for it worships the same gods as its enemies, without even recognizing that it does so. In this view, Marxism, just as much as capitalism, is a product of a soulless, rationalist faith in the supreme importance of material progress; it shares with capitalism a disconcerting overestimation of the significance of productivity, rationalization, quantification and mechanization.

The anarchists, in advancing this argument within Marx's lifetime, were undoubtedly prescient in their predictions (which sometimes even have a kind of 'Weberian' tinge) that pursuit of instrumental values would push capitalism and communism closer together, in certain respects, than either of these two supposedly bitter enemies would be comfortable believing. The distance between the 'alienation in the labour process' outlined so trenchantly and bitterly in Marx's 1844 *Manuscripts*, and Soviet Stakhanovism, they still remind us, may not be vast. And both capitalism and communism, the anarchists prophetically indicated even in the nineteenth century, would come to depend upon the progressive (if 'progressive' is the right word) incursion of bureaucracy into hitherto uncharted areas of human experience. Marx himself, of course, was no lover of bureaucracy – as we shall see – particularly when it proceeded from the autocratic state; but nineteenth-century anarchists, and their successors, have indicated that even deep insights into the nature of social evils like bureaucracy do not of themselves produce effective solutions to them. Faced with what they took to be the ambitious social blueprints of Marx, nineteenth-century anarchists were quite capable of being almost Burkean in their belief that such theorizing has an intrinsic tendency to mislead practice; and they could be almost Manichaean in their insistence that Marxists in power would repeat – or magnify – the mistakes of their capitalist and autocratic progenitors.

Anarchists – as their Marxist and non-Marxist antagonists have been made aware – have a way of asking awkward questions at inopportune moments, as part of an almost temperamental reluctance to accept doctrinal 'finality' on faith or on the authority of anybody (Marxists included). The unaccommodating and truculent manner in which these questions are advanced has engendered much criticism, proceeding from Marxist and non-Marxist alike, of anarchist doctrine in general. It may be true – and it happens to be my belief – that in the last analysis Marxism expresses more intellectual and human content, and has greater political sense, than its anarchist rivals have generally displayed. But the 'last analysis' has yet to be reached. It is not the intention of this study to say the last word about the issues separating Marx from the anarchists. These issues were manifestly not settled during the lifetimes of the protagonists I deal with; and, in any case, it is in the nature of the issues themselves that they could not be put to rest in a study like this one, even with the best will in the world. The issues are political ones, and political issues – fortunately enough – are not readily deadened either by academic discussion (with its inevitable aura of comfort and distance) or by polemical in-fighting (with its tendency to conceal issues even from the protagonists themselves). To wish to 'settle' finally the issues that separated Karl Marx and his anarchist inter-locutors would be to wish to stifle politics itself.

The dangers of adopting too foreshortened a perspective on the disputes that are the subject of this book can be indicated, in a pre-liminary and somewhat oblique sense, in two ways. In the first place, we can now see with the benefit of hindsight that books treating anarchism as an intellectual oddity having some curiosity value for the historian of ideas have themselves turned into intellectual curiosities; to some extent James Joll's valuable introductory study, *The Anarchists,*[2] was overtaken by events the likelihood of whose onset it did not suspect. Joll (all of whose books are concerned in one way or another with political failure) could hardly have predicted that the recrudes-cence of anarchist doctrine and the revival of even scholarly interest in it (which he played no small part in stimulating) would come as pre-cipitately as it did. (George Woodcock, the author of another valuable introductory study, *Anarchism,*[3] confessed in a 1950 biography of Kropotkin[4] that his subject, who died in 1921, was 'half-forgotten'; today many of Kropotkin's books have been reprinted by the MIT Press.)

The second danger is in some ways the obverse of the first. Interest – not all of it scholarly – in anarchism as the 'left-wing alternative' to 'obsolete communism' (to paraphrase the English language title of the Cohn-Bendits' *pièce de circonstance*)[5] was revived as part of the radical upsurge of the late 1960s. Much of the thinking behind this particular study of Marx's disputes with the anarchists was prompted and stimu-lated, if not caused, by this very upsurge; and to this extent it bears the imprint of what is still referred to in some quarters (and in hushed tones) as *les événements* surrounding May 1968. The events in question would not, I imagine, provoke anyone seriously to predict the onset of yet another anarchist revival, but the likelihood of similar upsurges can no longer simply be discounted or dismissed out of hand. It would be peremptory to dismiss May 1968 as an isolated example that is unlikely to repeat itself. Even isolated examples are examples of *something*; to write off the issues – issues which themselves have a history – as the preserve of 'extremists' would be short-sighted. Myopia in politics is itself a form of extremism. It remains true that anarchists can be im-patient people who tend to provoke impatient responses; Marx's own responses, to which I was led as a result of May 1968, were often impatient, and sometimes understandably so. Nevertheless, impatient responses are in real sense less than appropriate, or deserved. It may be

that anarchists' perspectives on political questions are themselves unduly foreshortened and 'absolute'. This is the way they were criticized
by Marx, among others. Yet foreshortened perspectives cannot be
blocked by perspectives that are foreshortened in a different way,
without leading into a chain of questions that is, in principle, endless.

As I write, we are at some distance from the late 1960s; and distance,
far from lending enchantment to the view - the view, after all, is one of
missed opportunities - perhaps enables us to begin to understand what
happened, and why. However theoretically unsophisticated they may
have been, anarchist alternatives to 'rigid', 'doctrinaire' Marxism held an
attraction to many participants - many of them thoughtful participants -
in the radical upsurge of that time. Whatever dust was then raised has
by now settled, but many of the questions raised at the same time
remain unresolved. What lay beneath the partisanship was often a real
desire to probe to the fundamentals of politics. (It is presumably no
accident that during the heyday of the student movement in the USA
there was a marked revival at Berkeley and elsewhere of interest in
orthodox political theory.) The claims of Marxism to represent radical
thinking in general were in the late 1960s given a much deserved jolt.
To many, Marxism seemed to resolve itself into an uneasy and unpro-
ductive amalgam - an admixture of elitism and deference to 'the masses'
conceived altogether abstractly. It seemed to provide a home - a home
that all too easily turned into a retreat - for esoteric theorists about
mass revolution, isolated in their scholasticism not only from 'the
masses' and from political action, but even from each other. It seemed
either divorced from political practice, in a refuge built on the basis of
increasingly esoteric and ethereal theorizing, or subsumed beneath an
ideologically dogmatic institutional communism of the type that is
singularly unlikely to tolerate independent theorizing of any persuasion.
The stultifying paradox - in Paris as well as Prague - was that independent
theorists could not be heard, or even survive, without a mass party; yet
the mass party had no more use for them than had anyone else. The
paradoxical eminence of intellectuals in what was ostensibly a 'workers''
party was simply one of the many unresolved problems brought out
into the light of day, however fleetingly, by other, younger, intellectuals;
but for these non-party militants, Marxism's much heralded 'unity of
theory and practice' might have continued to serve as a smokescreen,
behind which loomed the institutional monolith of 'the Party' at its
most hidebound and inflexible. Outflanked on its own left, institutional
communism responded by retreating into itself and proving its rivals'
every point against it; the self-appointed representatives of the working
class looked more self-appointed and less representative than ever; its
bureaucratic and ideological inflexibility looked more inflexible than
ever; its already stale phraseology looked more warmed over and inappropriate to the world outside the Party's confines than ever; and its

residual Stalinism was more apparent than ever. No amount of invocation of worn, hackneyed incantations about the 'class position' of its intellectual critics of the left, or about law-bound social regularities – all of them discredited phrases pulled from what looked like an increasingly remote, Victorian Eurocentrism – could redress the damage. It seemed, remarkably quickly, that, if spontaneity had anything to do with revolution, there was nothing even remotely revolutionary about orthodox Marxism.

Yet, spontaneity was not lacking – elsewhere – and those who lent exhilaration to the search for *la plage dessous les pavés* could not but be disdainful of 'authoritarian' Marxism. Radical disdain was bolstered in France among a variety of *groupuscules* by the conservative role that was played, just as they predicted, by the Parti communiste français and the trade union bureaucracy in their indifference to, or outright suppression of, any emergent radical currents within the French working class, or outside it. The remoteness of institutional communism from everything but the prevailing system – at a time when it looked as though it might not prevail – took on the character of a self-fulfilling prophecy as *les événements* proceeded with its encouragement or saction. They proceeded, too, in a spirit that was as antithetical to the joylessness of party orthodoxy as to that of everyday life. 'La grande fête de mai' seemed to one of its leaders, the irrepressible *bon enfant*, Daniel Cohn-Bendit, to be 'an irruption of the future into the present'; 'ayant vécu ces heures', he later said, 'je ne peux plus dire: c'est impossible'.

Yet even to Cohn-Bendit the exhilaration lasted a matter of 'hours', and his example testifies that the transformation of everyday life by spontaneous improvization, transitory and necessarily incomplete as it was, arrayed itself alongside the narcissistic, performing temperament of the movement's leaders. Cohn-Bendit's chutzpah made it easy for him openly to celebrate his notoriety, on the grounds that it was not to be taken seriously; he later said that 'j'ai eu le privilège *de me jouer moi-même* à grande échelle: la télé, la radio, les journaux'[6] (my emphases). Yet, particularly in France, where the long tradition of *épater le bourgeois* has always found its readiest customer *in* the hated bourgeois (witness the career of Sartre), revolutionary euphoria becomes as marketable a commodity as anything else. Today, all aspects of the so-called 'counter-culture' (including nostalgia for May 1968) can be bought and sold on the market.

Herbert Marcuse's *One-Dimensional Man*,[7] a book whose pessimism seems intended to justify yet another kind of self-serving retreat, indicates that society has again and again proved its ability to numb, absorb and (to use a word that was fashionable in 1968) 'co-opt' protest. Protest, for its part, knows this; cultural forms commonly become more and more extreme in their ultimately futile desire to shock (*épater*) the bourgeois. It is on the political front that bourgeois absorption of extremes remains much less likely. The attraction of discontented intellectuals to left-wing movements is not simply determined by the success and failure of the movement in question; it is also influenced by the peculiar tension between two forces – between solidarity and identification with more popular forces making for social change, on the one hand, and the desire for intellectual independence, on the other. The tension between wanting to feel *engagé* and needing to maintain one's own painstakingly trained critical distance – from society at large as well as from 'the movement' in particular – is a tension on which anarchists, whose *leitmotiv* is individual freedom, have thrived in the past. It may not be fanciful to suppose that they might thrive on it again.

Anarchists exemplify the radical tendency to question things established, to query received truth and dogma. There are many ways of answering the questions that they in turn pose; and Marx's responses, which form the subject of much of this particular study, do not displace or invalidate others. Nevertheless, Marx's responses have an importance for the study of politics that, thus far, has been oddly neglected. To understand what this importance may be, I have set myself the task of looking, or looking again, at what Marx said to, and said about, his anarchist rivals, and of examining the ways in which he countered their various arguments. Even if this examination should prove insufficient to settle the fundamental questions that underlie it – and this study entertains no pretensions to finality – it is hoped that it will bring into the open a controversy that has ill deserved its premature burial. The issues forming it have not died, and successive reports of its demise have been greatly exaggerated. To still discussion of these issues is, fortunately, beyond my powers; to stimulate further discussion, which is my hope, may not be.

Anarchism, Marx and theory

Anarchism, as David Apter has pointed out,[8] combines a socialist critique of capitalism with a liberal critique of socialism. Such a combination is bound to be tense and unsteady, and it is not surprising that anarchism, which grew up and emerged as a movement during the nineteenth century alongside socialism and Marxism, was not always – as we are about to see – in tandem with socialism and Marxism. Many of its doctrinal features point further back, through the Enlightenment of the eighteenth century into the liberal tradition. To say that anarchism is an outgrowth of certain features of the liberal tradition is not to suggest that the liberal tradition *necessarily* issues in anarchist conclusions, which would be to exaggerate wantonly. To scratch a Lockean liberal is not necessarily to touch, or galvanize, the anarchist lurking beneath his skin; Lockean minimal government *implies* anarchism as little (or as much) as the labour theory of value so presciently expressed in the fifth chapter of Locke's *Second Treatise on Civil Government* implies Marxist economics. Yet in either case the continuities are there. To see them, in the case of anarchism, we need remind ourselves only of some very basic features of liberal thinking about politics – of Locke's notion of government as a convenience, whose removal (for a while) by the governed may be no great inconvenience for them; of the 'night-watchman' state; of the 'self-regulating' economic sphere; of Adam Smith's disdain for politicians; and of the Actonian view of political power as being inherently corrupting. All these lead into the idea that power exists in order to be channelled, minimized, checked and balanced by countervailing power in what can take the form of a facile and mechanistic constitution-mongering.

Small wonder, then, that believers in minimal government, as Robert Nozick has recently and quite candidly admitted,[9] have to take and treat seriously the anarchist claim that the state is intrinsically immoral. It is for this reason, indeed, that the paradoxical phenomenon of resolutely *right*-wing neo-anarchist or libertarian thinking may be encountered readily enough, particularly in the USA. One basic point stands out. Anarchist convictions and doctrines are with rare exceptions based upon a negative view of liberty[10] – a view according to which freedom is to be understood in the first instance as freedom *from* some obstacle or impediment to its exercise, in this case the state and its various auxiliaries. All anarchist convictions can be summed up under the rubric not of the hindering of hindrances to but of the *removal of obstacles* from some vision of the good life. It is this imperative that links anarchism to the liberal tradition, and most particularly to the Enlightenment – the more so since the obstacles in question are seen, first and foremost, as *political* obstructions that need to be overthrown.

Anarchists believe that human affairs constitute *in potentia* an harmonious, naturalistic order, whose features are variously defined, or undefined, and which needs to emerge, uncontrived, by means of the removal (forcible if need be) of artificial impediments, chief among which is the state. Anarchists insist that once men are unfettered by an inappropriate political system that does violence to their individuality and commonality, they will at last fulfil their potentialities, become what they really are; artifice will have given way to nature, bad standards to good, and men will be reborn. The lineage here is clear. It was the *philosophes* of the French Enlightenment who had most markedly put forward the idea that 'all existing political and religious institutions were irrational, obsolete and [therefore]"unnatural" ', that they were 'designed to prevent an inherently self-regulating society from achieving universal felicity'. It was the French *Aufklärer* who believed that 'coercive institutions, especially the traditional state, were not only unnecessary; they actually prevented an orderly social life'.[11] It was the philosophers of the Enlightenment who insisted that bad, immoral legislation creates and sustains inharmoniousness in individuals and society alike, and that once these obstacles were removed, at their source, men would live together freely and harmoniously and prosper, individually, severally and socially.

Two points stand out here. The first is that these three for many *philosophes* exist on a single continuum; once the sources of oppression and injustice are removed, each one will simply and straightforwardly imply the others. The same assumption – that the social and the individual can, should and will dovetail neatly and tightly – informs anarchism, too, and does so at a very basic level indeed. Society to most *philosophes* and most anarchists is, like nature, inherently good once its operation is untrammelled; governments – along with their props and struts, particularly religious ones – prevent society from flourishing. The *Aufklärer*, like the anarchists, saw a conflict between state and society, and between conscience and power; but neither school envisaged a similar tension between the individual (once his various layers of prejudice and superstition had been stripped away) and society (once it, too, had sloughed off illegitimate political authority). In Shklar's well judged words, 'there was no suspicion of a necessary conflict between private and public interests, between individual freedom and social need'[12] among either group.

The second point about the confluence of individual and society that anarchist theories commonly proffer appears at first glance to derive from the fact that most anarchists, unlike most *philosophes*, are revolutionaries driven by despair and conviction to advocating violence; for what emerges from this advocacy is the dualistic proposition – very marked in Bakunin and some of his successors – that violence will bring about and turn into its opposite. Such dualism, variously expressed, is a characteristic feature of anarchism, and runs deep within anarchist doctrine. Hate will turn into love, chaos into harmony, violence into peace, desperation into hope and optimism. One example must suffice. Gerald Brenan recalls an experience during the Spanish Civil War.[13]

I was standing on a hill watching the smoke and flames of some two hundred houses in Malaga mount into the sky. An old Anarchist of my acquaintance was standing beside me.

'What do you think of that?' he asked.

I said: 'They are burning down Malaga.'

'Yes,' he said, 'they are burning it down. And I tell you not one stone will be left on another stone – no, not a plant, not even a cabbage will grow there, so that there will be no more wickedness in the world.'

The reader of literature by and about anarchists becomes accustomed to statements of this kind – so much so, that one of the striking features about them is too easily missed. The dualism involved, the belief that, to quote Bakunin, 'there will be a qualitative transformation, a new, living, life-giving revelation, a new heaven and a new earth, a new and mighty world in which all our present dissonances will be resolved into a harmonious whole',[14] is occasioned by immediate disruption. It is provoked by the violence and desperation that were a response to the unsettling and frequently disastrous irruptions of capitalism during the nineteenth century and beyond. But the form this response takes is not just one of desperation and violence; it involves a view of what comes in their wake, a vision of human perfectibility that can come about in no other way. Once the ground is cleared, once a *tabula rasa* is created, or regained, once the various successive layers or accretions of centuries of tyranny and prejudice have been reduced to rubble and cleared away from men's lives and spirits – then, and only then, will human perfectibility be placed on the agenda of history. The *philosophes*, whose idiom this is, were not themselves revolutionaries; yet their unparalleled emphasis on the clearing of the ground, on the removal of obstacles that alone prevent the emergence of men as they could and should be is one we encounter among anarchists again and again, in forms that would have surprised the *philosophes* themselves. Even the peaceable Proudhon – described so tellingly by Metternich as the illegitimate child of the Enlightenment – adopted with some flourish the motto *destruam et aedificabo*; and Jeremy Bentham, we may surmise, knew what he was about when he considered 'Anarchical Fallacies' to be implicit in the natural rights doctrines so beloved of the *philosophes* – the better, it is true, to combat each alike.

Anarchists, in Isaac Kramnick's words,[15] 'waver between a progressive, futuristic orientation with assumptions of perfectibility and endless improvement [on the one hand], and a nostalgic yearning for a simple, agrarian and pre-industrial existence' on the other; and while the latter was evidently provoked by nineteenth-century capitalism, it is too often overlooked that the former is an outgrowth of the Enlightenment. And while it may be true that the anarchist 'is forever torn between the liberal values of individuality, independence, autonomy, privacy, and self-determination, on the one hand, and the non-liberal values of community, solidarity and the encouragement of virtue through social pressure on the other',[16] we should remember that this tension also, and for many of the same reasons, characterizes the political theory of the Enlightenment.

Yet Enlightenment speculation about politics is not all of a piece. The aspect it turns towards anarchism, that of negative liberty and of a certain disdain for power – a project, that is, to limit its scope and to dispense with as much of it as is considered desirable – is not the only

face it has to present. There is also the very different approach epitomized by Rousseau, whose view of liberty was not negative but positive,
and whose desire was not to minimize power but to admit the need for
power legitimized as authority. Once it is legitimized, power is a promise,
not a threat. It is important to what follows in this book that we
recognize at the outset that it is Rousseau's perception of the problem
to which Marx, following Hegel, subscribes; and that there is a divide,
a watershed in Enlightenment thinking about power, authority and
politics. Marx is on one side of it, the anarchists on the other. The
difference is not simply genealogical but programmatic; it means that
while the distinction between Marxism and anarchism is in a sense
incomplete - both schools wish to abolish or overcome the state in its
present form the better to synthesize or make cognate the individual
and society - this area of agreement is in the nature of a penumbra, an
overlap, that is to say, and not a convergence. It is for this reason that
what on the face of it might appear to be a broad area of agreement
has done nothing to bring Marxism and anarchism any closer together,
in Marx's lifetime or since.

To describe this area as an overlap or penumbra is to recognize that
Marxists and anarchists approach it from different directions and draw
from it different conclusions. The conclusions in question have proved
to be irreconcilable ones, which should surprise nobody. The synthesis
of individuality and community that Marx proffered was not advocated
in the name of a natural harmony of interests; Marx - again following
Hegel (and not, in this case, Rousseau) - recognized that nature does
not provide standards in the required sense. What does provide standards
is society itself which in its various successive forms has shaped nature
to human purposes. It is in this sense that capitalism, for instance, may
be said to furnish preconditions as well as obstacles to emancipation,
and that the new science of economics - or, more exactly, of 'political
economy' - can be turned to good account. The distinction between
nature and artifice, which is so important and basic to anarchist thinking,
is subverted in and by the way in which Marx wishes to synthesize
individuality and community; and here, of course, Marx's itinerary
from Hegel is of crucial importance. We shall see that the distinction
Marx drew between individualism and individuality (not least in his
attack on Stirner) owes much to Hegel (and indeed to Rousseau).
Hegel's incisive portrait of modern civil society, as we shall also see,
has a great deal of relevance to Marx's depictions of capitalist society,
since what Hegel termed the 'system of needs' is the antithesis of
community to both of them. Yet because Marx's synthesis of Hegelianism and political economy takes a particular form, embodying as
it does a view of self-activity, a conception of the unity of theory and
praxis, and a revolutionary project that embodies what Ernst Bloch
termed 'futurity', we can see that the Marxist enterprise, unlike the

anarchist, far from being satisfied by the removal of obstacles and impediments to something that pre-dates them, is in the fullest sense a *political* enterprise. It is a creative endeavour; and whether or not we believe, or can afford to believe, with Marx, that the proletariat alone embody futurity and the possibility of community, it is important that we remember and acknowledge that the creation of community – *das Allgemeine*, the most important word in Hegel and in Marx alike – is a political task that goes against the grain of capitalist society.

Marx's task or enterprise is predicated to some extent on a theory of the production of new needs throughout human history, alongside the means to their satisfaction. This production of new needs involves a view of labour as anthropogenesis, but this is not all it involves; it also entails what can only be described as a political project, since one of the needs in question is the need for community. To look again at Marx's conception of class consciousness among the proletariat as the only possible embodiment of community is to recognize that Marx, unlike the anarchists, does not wish to dispense with politics. He wishes to re-cast politics, to extend its scope, to give it more meaning and greater depth. His view of politics is not restrictive but expansive. It is for this reason that the revolutionary unity of theory and practice is no mere empty phrase, is no merely rousing propaganda, and is not simply the unity of doctrine and method. It involves not a sloughing-off of politics but a substantive redefinition of what politics involves – a shift away from the increasingly foreclosed area of state action, towards the task of building a movement. We may – and I hope we will – differ about its outcome; but we must recognize that there is something heroic about the quest. Marx, in Sheldon Wolin's words, founded 'a new conception of politics, revolutionary in intent, proletarian in concern, and international in scope and organization'.[17] All three aspects had to be defended against anarchist attacks, as we shall see, and defended – sometimes against all the odds – they were; they were defended with the same kind of theoretical passion we encounter elsewhere in Marx, the passion that animated what Marx did as well as what Marx wrote. One example will have to suffice. 'I am working madly through the nights', we find Marx writing in 1857 to Engels, 'so that, before the deluge, I shall at least have the outlines clear.'[18] This may be one of the most extraordinary statements about theorizing ever made; it is small wonder that Prometheus to Marx was the most inspiring saint in the calender. Marx may not have been alone in devoting his life to a revolutionary cause or even in being galvanized by revolutionary urgency, as any look at the wonderland of nineteenth-century revolutionizing will show; but what is distinctive is his view of theorizing as an Archimedean lever with which to move the world. And it *did* move the world – if not immediately; rarely can the disparity between the immediate circumstances of theorizing* and the eventual effects of the theory have been wider than it was in the case of Marx. While my concern in this book is with the former rather than the latter, and indeed with some of the reasons for the gap between the two, this gap itself is no yawning chasm, as Marx himself somehow must have recognized. Marxism was and is a world-historical theory; the phrase is for once no euphemism. Sheldon Wolin has pointedly reminded us of

> the extraordinary fact that [Marx] succeeded in demonstrating the power of theory far beyond any of his predecessors. If it is proper to gauge a theorist's achievement by the extent to which his ideas survive and become common currency, by the number of his self-proclaimed followers and disciples, by the stimulus which his ideas have furnished to creative domains distantly removed from economics, politics or sociology, by the amount of criticism and vilification which has been dumped on his writings since his death and, above all, by the demonstrated impact of his theory on the lives of ordinary people and actual societies, then no other theorist – not Plato, Aristotle, Machiavelli, Locke, Smith or Ricardo – can be said to have equalled Marx's achievement. If Plato is the symbol of theory's eternal frustration, Marx is its triumphant hero.[20]

Marx against the anarchists: the problem posed

Marx's dislike of anarchist doctrine has often been misunderstood because of his forthright opposition to the bourgeois state. It has seemed to some commentators that because of the opposition to the state he 'shared' with his anarchist rivals, his doctrinal differences from them can safely be resolved into a difference in emphasis, about tactics. It has seemed that Marx and his anarchist competitors were in agreement about the desirable, or 'necessary', goal of revolution and disagreed merely about the means to be used to bring it about. But this is not the case. Neither Marx nor his anarchist interlocutors – particularly in the First International, where differences seemed more than purely theoretical in scope – were inclined to separate means from ends in so absolute a fashion; and there are good reasons for their reluctance.

Marx's attacks on the anarchists were not purely tactical or strategic; they did not treat of revolutionary means as though the revolutionary end could be taken as invariant or assumed as a 'given'. Neither side

*Marx once described himself to one of his daughters, Eleanor, 'as a machine condemned to devour books and then throw them, in a changed form, on the dunghill of history'.[19]

in the International was concerned to divorce revolutionary means from revolutionary ends. Future society, both sides recognized, is not, properly speaking, an end, but a *beginning*; how it would develop depended greatly on the character of, and decisions taken by, the revolutionary movement itself. Both sides acknowledged the very real stakes involved in any ostensible 'tactical' resolution about organization; they were the shape of future society. Both Marx and Bakunin saw the International not only as the embodiment of the revolutionary movement as it then existed, but also as a presentiment - quite possibly *the* presentiment - of future society which, like all societies, would be stamped by its origins. This joint perception was not a measure of their agreement, but the source of an increasingly bitter hostility, as Marx and Bakunin themselves were at pains to point out.

Marx's contemptuous dismissal of Bakunin was matched only by Bakunin's contemptuous dismissal of Marxism. The dispute between the two in the First International has its place not only in the history of socialism but also in the history of invective, a history that would not be stretched unduly if it also included Marx's earlier disputations with Max Stirner, in *The German Ideology*, and with Pierre-Joseph Proudhon, which culminated in *The Poverty of Philosophy*. The personal antagonism and pronounced tactical differences separating Marx from Bakunin were symptomatic of a far more fundamental division between Marxism and anarchism (which were *rival* ideologies, and were perceived as such by their bearers), a division which later historical events have done nothing to bridge.

To mention Marx's attacks on Stirner and Proudhon is not simply to point up the more famous dispute between Marx and Bakunin; it is also to emphasize the fact that Marx criticized, and criticized viciously, every anarchist with whom he came into theoretical or practical contact. All of Marx's objections reveal a method of social and political analysis that was fundamentally at variance with the anarchists' approach. The point here is not merely that Marx *had* a method, whereas the anarchists so often were inimical to method; it is also that the method in question has attributes and an intellectual lineage that separate Marx decisively and irreversibly from the anarchist tradition, whose attributes and lineage are quite separate.

Marx's lineage was Hegelian, but *how* Hegelian it was remains disputed among scholars. Marx's successive disputes with the anarchists cast light on the vexed issue of the extent of Hegel's influence on Marx's thought; the continuity that links together attacks on anarchism made at widely separated points in Marx's career is itself in significant respects Hegelian. Moreover, Marx's three main anarchist antagonists, Stirner, Proudhon and Bakunin, were themselves thinkers who in their various ways entertained 'Hegelian' pretensions, pretensions which Marx, for his part, was concerned to deflate. Stirner's historical schematization was broadly Hegelian; Proudhon claimed that his principle (or demi-urge) of 'contradiction' was based on the Hegelian dialectic; and Bakunin attempted to appropriate the same, Hegelian, base for his obsession with negativity, or destruction. Marx's main object, to be sure, was not to portray these anarchists as bad Hegelians – although the fact that he does succeed in doing this, if only *en passant,* should give pause, at least, to those who would de-emphasize the continued hold of Hegelian categories on Marx's thought. Marx, as we shall see, was no less successful in accomplishing what *was* his main goal: that of sharply distinguishing substantive theoretical difference between his approach and *any* anarchist alternative.

This task did not lack urgency. Marx was concerned to frame his successive arguments against the anarchists not for the sake of posterity, or even simply to hasten the advent of revolution; more immediately, his object was practical. Increasingly, as time went by, the emergent revolutionary movement needed to be shielded against rival revolutionary creeds. Within Marx's lifetime, after all, the theoretical and practical dominance of his own doctrine was never something that could be taken for granted; to confuse 'Marxism' with 'socialism' or even revolutionary 'communism' (the term Marx preferred) at this time would be an egregious error. Anarchism was not the only rival revolutionary creed that Marx (whose personal intolerance was notorious) felt the need to attack; but it was one of the most important, and its importance increased over time. With the emergence of the International, where revolutionary theory and revolutionary practice stood some chance of effectively being merged, the task of attacking anarchism took on an added importance.

Marx's conflict with Bakunin in the International brought to a head the issues raised in his earlier disputations with anarchists; continuity among these successive disputations can be shown, as we shall see. This is not to say that the International wrote the last chapter in Marxist-anarchist relations; the last chapter, presumably, has yet to be written. It may be that the issues involved in the International's duel of the Titans were, ultimately, left unresolved; indeed, it may be that these issues are unresolvable. We must content ourselves, for the time being, in delineating as clearly as possible what these issues *were* when they were so dramatically raised, bearing in mind throughout our investigation that neither side at the time regarded them as purely theoretical, or purely tactical.

What, then, in outline, *were* those issues? And how, in particular, do they concern Hegel? The answer need not be indirect. Hegel, the theorist of the modern, bureaucratic state and its ethical primacy over 'civil society', had priorities that Marx – particularly, and directly, in his earlier writings – took it upon himself to reverse. Marx awarded primacy over the bourgeois state to the capitalist economy and mode of production. The anarchists, for their part, made no such statement of primacy, and saw no need to do so; what they *did* see the need to do – at least in Marx's eyes – was habitually to exaggerate not only the oppressive nature but also the determining influence of the state, as a focus for revolutionary energies. They also made these excessive (to Marx) claims in the name of a similarly exaggerated and unrealistic 'anti-authoritarianism', an opposition to authority *as such* that Marx, manifestly, does not share. That Marx, unlike his anarchist enemies, saw fit to investigate forms of authority for the sake of distinguishing 'authority' from 'authoritarianism' suggests a point we find attested to in his writings taken as a whole. This is that Marx did entertain a distinction between power and authority. This distinction may not solve all our problems in the study of politics, but it is sufficiently sharp not only to cut through anarchist arguments but also the arguments of those who would confuse anarchist arguments with those of one of their most trenchant critics, Karl Marx himself. What I am suggesting, and proposing to bear out, is that the study of Marx and the study of politics are not inimical enterprises; and that this is so, not simply in the straightforward sense that Marx all too obviously provoked a revolutionary politics that shook the world, but in the additional sense that there is in Marx's writings a theory of the modern state, in its relationship with civil society, that has more substance than has often been credited to it.

We shall find that Marx's theory of what might be termed 'alien politics', adumbrated largely in his essay 'On the Jewish Question', raises analytical and political possibilities that cannot be resolved or satisfied by the anarchist panacea of abolition of the state, *tout court*. This means not only that the roots of Marxism are Hegelian whereas anarchism has no such lineage, but also something programmatic as well as genealogical. It means that Marx had in mind for future communist society not so much the outright abolition of *all* authority relations, but a possibly more drastic, and irreversible, alteration of the *form* of authority relations. Alien politics will be succeeded not by no politics but by authority relations that are re-integrated within society. This, of course, is exactly what Bakunin (who could be a prescient man) feared, and fought. It is also something that helps explain a number of questions that, without it, would seem rather unconnected: why Marx was so concerned about the practice of revolutionary politics in a pre-revolutionary context; why he always insisted, unlike the anarchists, on liberal rather than authoritarian allies; why, again unlike the anarchists, he insisted that class struggles are ultimately resolved not on the economic or cultural level, but on the *political* level.

When Marx described the modern state in terms other than those of the anarchists' 'Genghis Khan with telegraphs', when he said, unflatteringly,

of Bakunin, that 'this ass cannot even understand that any class movement, as such, is necessarily. . . a political movement', we may suppose
that he understood by the word 'political' something quite different
from the anarchist definition. Just how different it is my intention,
in this book, to demonstrate.

PART ONE

Foundations

CHAPTER 1

Hegelian roots

Hegel, even today, may be best known as an apologist for the nineteenth-century Prussian state. Because his complex arguments seem tailored to fit such a reactionary and unappealing political form, they have been discredited – and Hegel's political philosophy has appeared to bear little relevance to the modern world. While his influence on Marx (whose relevance is less in doubt) is sometimes admitted, it has often seemed wholly negative in character – the more so, since Marx himself is often too easily portrayed as the proponent of the kind of neo-anarchist stateless utopia that by its very nature owes nothing to a state-worshipper like Hegel.

The crucial point about these two interpretations – of Hegel the uncritical statist, and Marx the neo-anarchist – is not simply that they are mistaken, although the idea of Hegel's supposed servility to the Prussian state does not withstand close examination, and Marx was a bitter enemy of anarchist utopians. The crucial point is that these views are mistaken for much the same reasons. To see this, we should not be misled by the institution of the state – or, more nearly, by Hegel's 'statism' (which is statism of a most unusual kind) and by Marx's opposition to the Hegelian, or to the bourgeois, state (which, unlike that of the anarchists, does not imply a lack of belief in authority, as we shall see). What this suggests is a continuity between Hegel and Marx – a continuity that will seem unlikely only on the basis of an overdrawn polarization between the two. What then – from the point of view of Marx's disputes with the anarchists – are the elements of this continuity? To see them, we must probe beneath the purely institutional, to the deeper, conceptual level – much as Hegel and Marx themselves conducted their investigations. What emerges if we do this is a set of arguments about the nature of community – about what the notion of community means, about how it relates to the concept of individuality, about where on the historical spectrum it should, or can, be located, and about what threatens it. Hegel's depiction of the state and civil society is an attempt to answer these questions; and what is striking about Marx's disputes with the anarchists (which themselves did not proceed purely on an institutional level) is not only that these same questions were raised again as sub-themes in the course of the various polemics, but also that the positions Marx upheld against his anarchist interlocutors constantly indicate the extent and depth of his indebtedness to Hegel. What this means is that there is considerable substance to the claim that without understanding the Hegelian roots of Marxism, we fail to understand Marx; and that while hostility to anarchism is one of these roots, a specifically non-anarchist and anti-anarchist approach to the problem of community is another. A specifically Hegelian view of what is involved in this problem – of what sustains, and what threatens, community in the modern world – passes into Marx's writings and decisively separates Marx from anarchism.

To see this we must take our bearings. No one, I suspect, could be more remote from anarchism than Hegel, whose state-centredness is notorious; but it is striking that Marx, who was not at all state-centred in the same way, ran Hegel a close second. Marx's forthright and sustained opposition to anarchism is incomprehensible unless we take into account his Hegelian lineage. Marx disagreed with Hegel not because of Hegel's presentation of certain deep-seated (and apparently insoluble) social problems, but because he took exception to the political solution to these problems Hegel had put forward in *The Philosophy of Right.*

Marx's earlier writings, up to and including *The German Ideology*, sought to show that the modern state, as Hegel had portrayed it, instead of fulfilling, actually vitiated the professed aims of Hegelian philosophy. Marx operated with Hegel's basic duality of civil society and political state – of *bourgeois* and *citoyen* – but denied that they related in the manner Hegel had postulated; his denial, however, is not based on any substantive disagreement with Hegel's prescient (and surprisingly prophetic) presentation of the social tensions attendant upon the emergence of modern civil society. Marx considered that under modern conditions Hegel's state would be incapable of resolving these tensions, but this is not to say that they stood in no need of resolution; and while attempting to demolish Hegel's claims on behalf of the modern state – claims that it could be a mediating, ethical agency validated by historical understanding – Marx took the need for such an agency with all seriousness.

Hegel considered civil society (*bürgerliche Gesellschaft*) to embody a 'system of needs' and of 'universal self-interest', which the modern state would transcend by establishing and sustaining a system of law, and by integrating consciousness in such a way that the universal egoism animating civil society would be denied political relevance – without, however, being displaced within its own proper sphere. In Hegel's presentation, the modern state does not possess the wherewithal to *abolish* the individualistic self-assertion that characterizes civil society and poses political problems; instead, the estates (*Stände*) in *The Philosophy of Right* were intended to cleanse and purify particular interests of self-seeking, to deflect these particularistic interests (which of themselves will not intersect to produce any general good) towards more public ends. Subjective goals whose origin is in civil society are to be refracted through a complex series of intermediary institutions which, taken together, would according to Hegel provide an axis that would be altogether distinct from the subjective and 'arbitrary', but would not displace the subjective from its own, proper realm.

Marx agreed with Hegel that civil society poses - and is predicated upon - problems it is incapable of solving. But he was severely critical of Hegel's institutional solutions to these problems. Hegel's state was supposedly 'universal', while Marx came to recognize in the course of his tortured self-emancipation from Hegel that modern political institutions were so organized as to make the state the mere instrument of the interests dominating civil society and masquerading as general 'universal' interests. The state to Hegel was a different axis; to Marx it merely provided one more set of conduits. Legislation, Marx came to insist, was in practice dominated by particular interests originating in civil society, and not by any guiding principles of 'universal' applicability. Hegel's institutional mediations - the monarchy, the assembly of estates, the bureaucracy - were to Marx no more than mystifications, concealing behind their institutional façades powerful realities that needed to be brought out into the open by social, as well as political, investigations.

It is for this reason that while Marx's argument in his early critiques of Hegel proceeds largely at an institutional level, this should not distract us from why he was making it. What underlaid, and gave substance to, Hegel's institutional arguments was his fundamental belief that the state as a living ethical structure and the individual as a whole person presuppose and complement each other. Marx, on the other hand, considered that Hegel's exalted and exaggerated claims on behalf of the state are no real solution to a set of divisive social problems that not only remain in existence, crying out for a solution, but may also be given a new lease of life by virtue of any false, or incomplete, resolution at the level of political institutions. Only by abolishing the state as a particular institution could the aim of Hegel's political philosophy - cohesiveness and universality - become a reality. Yet Marx never disputed Hegel's arguments about the need for, and the features and prerequisites of, the kind of community that would resolve the atomistic tendencies of the modern economy. Indeed, Marx actually extended these arguments throughout his own writings, and it is at this level that the continuity between Marx's thought and that of Hegel emerges with greatest clarity. Both Marx and Hegel - to put the same point another way - are substantive theorists of community, and the reasons why this is so - which emerge, forcefully and dramatically, throughout Marx's disputes with the anarchists - indicate a marked continuity between the two thinkers.

If we suppose that political consciousness as Hegel portrays it cannot accomplish what Hegel thinks it can - or, if it is to do its job, *must* - accomplish, then we must look elsewhere for an analogue or a substitute for political consciousness. The unity of thought and action, as a regenerative principle, must be sought elsewhere - and, at base, it is this idea that underlies Marx's criticism of Hegel's *Philosophy of Right*, which indeed eventuates in Marx's identification of the poor and dispossessed (those cast out by Hegel) as the only possible source of political consciousness and genuine community alike. To some extent, Marx's identification of the revolutionary proletariat as the agency of social transformation - an identification that has never passed un-challenged, especially (as we shall see) by anarchists - follows from what Hegel had to say about the dialectics of labour, particularly when this discussion is laid alongside another, that of the insoluble problem of pauperism in *The Philosophy of Right*. But the lineaments of Marx's thinking owe more to Hegel than this. Hegel had fastened the idea of community on to the state, and Marx himself in his 'critique' of Hegel's *Philosophy of Right* focused his discussion on Hegel's 'institutional' paragraphs. He was endeavouring to meet Hegel on Hegel's own terms, in order to cast into sharp relief a central question Hegel had posed. If the distinction between state and civil society - a distinction which meant little enough to any anarchist theorist - is as Hegel portrayed it, and if it is not to be overcome by the various institutional mediations Hegel's *Philosophy of Right* outlines, then surely the need to overcome it still remains. Indeed, this can be put still more emphatically. The atmosphere of moral emergency - the belief that society has been deprived of ethical possibilities - that is present in Hegel's political writings extends much further in those of Marx. Many of the reasons why civil society points towards the antithesis of community had been indicated by Hegel himself; and Hegel's portrayal of civil society was of a system having its own dynamism. Its various characteristics - disruption, fragmentation, disunity - on Hegel's presentation have a momentum all of their own. What this means is that the longer civil society's problems - problems Hegel himself considers insoluble - remain in existence, the greater will be the need to solve them; and by the same token, there will be less and less chance of overcoming them by institutional or governmental means. The elements of this dilemma, it can be shown, are all present in Hegel's *Philosophy of Right*; what they point to is all too clearly a substantive notion about what it means to live in a community, about the nature of community, about the requirements that would satisfy it and the threats that would tear it apart. Marx was aware of these arguments, and was influenced by them throughout his career as a revolutionist. But they were not available in the same way to his anarchist interlocutors. Max Stirner regarded any community, any generality, any movement, as a threat to the sovereign individual; Marx's reading of Hegel enabled him to ridicule Stirner's argument. Pierre-Joseph Proudhon in a sense had his community – the pre-industrial workshop – ready-made; Marx, who operated with a Hegelian conception of the dynamism of human needs and productive techniques, regarded such a model for post-state society as austere and reactionary. Mikhail Bakunin threw historical continuity as well as caution to the winds in insisting that any worthwhile community would have to rise like a phoenix from the ashes of the destruction of society, and that it would in no way refer to even its proximate predecessor; Marx, by contrast, believed in studying capitalism in order to see what communism would look like. If we see that all of Marx's successive anti-anarchist arguments are of Hegelian lineage, we can also see that there is a good deal of substance to the claim that the roots of Marxism are Hegelian, while those of anarchism – despite the Hegelian pretensions of some of its spokesmen – are not.

Individualism and individuality

Hegel's extended and comprehensive critique of the French Revolution and of 'the maximum of frightfulness and terror'[1] it involved points up his central belief that the price paid for a strictly subjective individualism is incoherence and, in the case of the Terror, an unprecedented, morally chilling destructiveness. The 'absolute freedom' that underlay the Terror was seen by Hegel as a radical acting-out of the idea of the liberal self – that of having a supposed autonomy in the sense of being free of others, and engaging others abstractly and interchangeably – that itself can be traced back to the moral incompetence of the *philosophes*. What is often forgotten is that this radical individualism can also be traced forward; its ultimate avatar in many ways was Max Stirner, and its ultimate expression (or playing-out) Stirner's *The Individual and His Own*, a book Marx endeavoured to demolish in *The German Ideology*. In reading Marx's attack it is impossible not to be reminded of Hegel's point – which was directed at the German Romantics as well as what he called the French 'utilitarians' (i.e. the *philosophes*) – that to stress what was to be Stirner's *Eigenheit*, individual uniqueness and its irreducible originality, is to overlook the distinction between individualism and individuality; and that the Romantic emphasis on subjectivity for this very reason is best regarded as a reflex of, rather than a solution to, cultural alienation and social fragmentation. The integrity of the personality will become emphasized, in Hegel's view, only when, and precisely because, it had become a fugitive ideal.

This does not mean that Hegel dismissed German romanticism out of hand; there was much in its doctrines that he could adapt for his own purposes, without in any way accepting its precepts uncritically. He agreed with - and added to - the Romantics' critique of Enlightenment rationalism and instrumentalism, for example; and the Romantic critique of market society (which involved attacks on *Geldsklaverei*, disconnectedness, impersonality, fragmentation, and the loss of moral authenticity) was to have some part to play in Hegel's own, more searching examination of civil society (*bürgerliche Gesellschaft*). Yet Hegel's negative characterization of modernity had more content - and more futurity - than that of his Romantic precursors or than the rather backward looking solution to the problems of modernity Marx was to perceive, and attack, in the writings of Proudhon.

The *philosophes*, according to the Romantics, had rent asunder what was integral to the human personality; the Romantics wished to restore to man the unity that recent philosophy - including that of Kant - had dissolved: the unity of reason and experience, duty and inclination, imagination and ratiocination. Hegel himself was severely critical of the Kantian idea of duty as a purely rational imperative, divorced from and opposed to impulses, habits and instincts. The abstract Kantian 'ought' (*Sollen*), standing as it does outside the self, disregards what cannot be disregarded: the context of beliefs, habits, expectations and inclinations as Montesquieu had emphasized them. Only these enable the self to identify with what is outside its boundaries. The need for this identification was what the romantics (and Stirner) denied, and Hegel insisted upon. He, too, wishes to integrate and restore those integral features of human experience that had been shattered by modernity; but, unlike the Romantics, Hegel did not wish to do so within so incoherent a framework as that of subjectivity itself - a principle that could be stressed, and offered, only if the individual had ceased to be comprehensible to himself in the first place.

Hegel's real target whenever he took side-swipes at his Romantic contemporaries (as he did by name in *The Philosophy of Right*) was their distrust of reason as an integrative principle. Subjectivity and uniqueness were stressed by the Romantics in the name of some principle or sentiment that mere reason (which they confused with abstract rationalism) was said to be unable to grasp. This denial was to Hegel both anti-intellectual and whimsical. Moreover, the Romantics, aiming as they did to overcome dislocation, succeeded only in dislocating still further; self-assertion, taken as an end in itself, merely generalizes that same incoherence of the isolated, disconnected individual - the dislocated particular - that had created the need for self-assertion in the first place. The Romantics thus remain on the level of disruption, of fragmented immediacy; personal, self-defined moral autonomy in the Kantian sense - itself a deficient principle - was from Hegel's point of view bolstered, not subverted, by the Romantics' stress on subjectivity. The Romantics, too, have their place within the *Phenomenology*'s history of the displacement and evasions of egos, confronting (without recognizing) one another across the terrain of their own social creations.

Romantic subjectivism strikes at true selfhood because it is altogether lacking in social reflexivity; Hegel's very different notion of self-determination embodied both autonomy and interdependence, both being-for-oneself and being-for-another. The two qualities in question, according to Hegel, have to go together, have to interpenetrate, simply in order to be understood. Social reflexivity and selfhood, once they are properly defined, are different aspects of the same thing. To find, or to know, oneself is to discover the character of association with others. Solipsism, by contrast, is not the way to personal identity - as Marx was emphatically to reiterate, in his fashion, in his attack on Stirner. Personal identity requires access to others, as the ancient Greeks - whose polis and culture were so loved by the younger Hegel - knew full well.

Past and present

Hegel's conviction that what validated his belief in the integrative, expressive power of the state was the interplay of reason and history - his conviction that the state is the 'hieroglyph of reason', which needs deciphering - is a difficult argument. It is difficult not because it leads to conservatism of the traditionalist variety but precisely because it does not. In describing the state as the mediated, integrative (*einheimisch*) community, rendered habitable by thought, Hegel was not setting forth a justification for any current political form but offering a solution to a set of moral and philosophical problems. Indeed, what makes the centrality of the state as an integrative agency directly relevant to an understanding not only of Hegel - who endorsed such centrality - but also of Marx - who did not - is Hegel's argument about *why* this integration is necessary in the first place.

That Hegel's political philosophy was emphatically state-centred is well enough known. What is less well known, but equally important, is that the centrality of the state in Hegel's thought was predicated upon a sustained and incisive critique of all the social, political and philosophical sources of disintegration he could identify. Hegel was a relentless critic of all forms of moral individualism since Socrates. *The Phenomenology of Mind* and *The Philosophy of Right* were scathing in their criticisms of everything Hegel considered to have contributed to the disconnection and privatization of men in modern society, and thus to have obscured the prospect of a genuinely political community. Lack of connectedness, lack of cohesion, lack of a political public, lack of shared concerns and moral values – there are the themes, promulgated as a set of cross-cutting dilemmas in *The Phenomenology* (a study in moral and cognitive fragmentation), which *The Philosophy of Right* was to attempt to resolve at the level of political institutions. While any sustained examination of the themes that link *The Phenomenology* and *The Philosophy of Right* is beyond the scope of this study, one element in the continuity between them must be stressed. Hegel was concerned to account for, and come to terms with, the thought of the past before constructing philosophical and political systems that he considered valid for his own time and place. Yet it is of the essence of Hegel's philosophical method that these two tasks were kept separate only in a limited and provisional sense. Politics and philosophy were always intimately, and intricately, connected throughout Hegel's intellectual development. Hegel's passionately held concern – even as a young man – was for the establishment of a political life that would educate; from the outset, he believed that this task presupposed the restoration of intellectual, cultural and ethical unity. The task was a philosophical one, but Hegel's understanding of philosophy was expansive. He constantly stressed the social context, and political outcome, of apparently abstract ideas, and recognized that man's self-consciousness and intellectual progress are themselves social products with social and political consequences. In particular, the culture of a country or epoch – the form taken by Hegel's *Geist* – and the way it moulds men's minds – Hegel's *Bildung* (which was to Hegel a *political* enterprise) – strongly influence both the objective structures of political life, its laws and institutions, and the subjective sentiments and attitudes of men which sustain – or undermine – these structures.

The central point of Hegel's political philosophy is that self-determination needs an arena in which common (not uniform) values, interests and purposes can be elicited, formulated and sustained, and that this arena can be provided only by the modern state. What is striking about this prescription – and what makes it directly relevant to Marx's subsequent reflections – is the uncommonly acute sense Hegel possesses, throughout its explication, of the interpenetration of ways of thinking about the social and political world, and the forms taken by this social and political world. Even in *The Phenomenology*, which is concerned (as its title suggests) with the appearance of knowledge, Hegel's subject is the successive endeavours of consciousness to grasp (*begreifen*) the world and itself in relation to the world. The process is a reflexive one. Hegel never counterposed 'consciousness' as an external, transcendental corrective to the social and political world – as many of the utopian socialists and anarchists criticized in Marx's *Theses on Feuerbach* did; he portrayed consciousness – and indicated *whose* consciousness it was – as an immanent presence within the world. Instead of confronting 'the present' with 'the eternal' as two counterposed realms, it seemed necessary to Hegel to recognize that 'eternity' - if we must so character- ize it - is incomprehensible apart from the moments of its appearance and their historical, human character. Hegel here is resolute. To regard the itinerary of spirit, or consciousness, in the world as the path *to* the absolute, as Fichte did, is to leave out the world. Spirit is the path *of* the absolute, not *to* it. The 'beyond' (*Jenseits*) presenting itself to consciousness as a pure externality (*Anderssein*) is the enemy of philo- sophical self-awareness as Hegel conceived it - an enemy taking its cue from Kantian dualism and dividing the world arbitrarily into actuality on the one hand and potential on the other. This notion of infinity - infinity wrongly conceived - denies the finite, and is a form of vapid world-denial. Its effect is to make duty even more of an abstraction than it had been with Kant. What is necessary to redress the balance and rehabilitate the world, is Hegel's conception of *Vernunft*, or reason, as opposed to *Verstand*, or mere understanding. *Vernunft* signifies what Weber was to call 'this-worldliness', the inner connections linking apparently separate realities. It is too often forgotten that Hegel's 'spirit' (*Geist*) refers to the totality of attitudes, beliefs, rules, institutions and habits that make up the political culture of a country and epoch - and enable us to see how, and why, one political culture gives way to, or is displaced by, its successor. The concept is far less mystical than often has been supposed: its proximate mentor, as Hegel himself frequently and gratefully acknowledged, was Montesquieu, whose notion of the *esprit général* is a direct precursor of Hegel's 'spirit', which is in the first instance nothing but *human* spirit.[2] The term refers to the way a community knows and interprets itself, the way it gives itself form and coherence; and also to the way the individual personality knows itself through the community - that is, its identity, which is always integrally connected with the impact of society.[3] Knowledge itself - as always with Hegel - consists not in the accumu- lation of information but in moral transformation.

Hegel's historical psychology, which owes much more to Montesquieu than to Herder, is manifestly not relativist. Nor is his political theory at all complacent. He believed that to see morality and politics historically is to appreciate their failure. Culture (*Bildung*) is supposed to help its human constituents fulfil their potentialities; but it fails, and fails miserably, to do so in modern times. This is why Hegel, in *The Phenomenology*, speaks mainly of *ancient* politics; in comparison with these, modernity is characterized negatively, by what it lacks. On the other hand, as Lukács has pointed out,[4] Hegel's discussions of ancient society never involve its economic life, and always concentrate on its politics and religion. His discussions of modern society - as we shall see - are very different. Culture by its very nature shapes people; but in modern society, according to Hegel, it does so badly. The outcome is one of crisis, of moral emergency; the question became whether, in the face of what were to Hegel observably fragmenting tendencies permeating modern society, there was any possibility of a politics that would be either just or stable.

Despite his admiration for the polis, however, Hegel - by the time he wrote *The Philosophy of Right* - no longer shared in the prevalent, and somewhat escapist, Graecophilia of his age and nation; he recognized that the ancient polis had come to grief on the very principle - moral individualism - for which the modern age stood. Moral individualism, which Hegel criticized remorselessly, nevertheless cannot be wished out of existence; on the contrary, it has an integral place in modern society. This place, sharply demarcated though it is in modern times, was altogether lacking in the ancient city. Men in antiquity were not yet individuals; men in modern society run the risk of being nothing more. Yet men had to move beyond the naïve and spontaneous condition of the polis, where each man unreflectingly had seen every other in himself, and himself in them; movement beyond this unity is a clear historical advance, even though it is bought at a heavy - and inflationary - price; the ancient world, Hegel (unlike so many of his contemporaries) came to recognize, cannot be uncritically wrested out of its context to serve as a paradigm to his own times.

To see this emergence more clearly, according to Hegel, we should have recourse to history, considered broadly and philosophically. History to Hegel was a rational process; the human past exhibits an intelligible pattern of development, in the course of which men acquire an increasing awareness of themselves and their potentialities, creating institutions that reflect and give substance to their character as self-determining beings. The process is neither smooth nor uninterrupted, let alone unilinear; it has its setbacks, its false starts, its failures. These follow from the pattern Hegel depicts, in which the advances of one historical period become in their turn limitations which are to be overcome in the next. Men make their own history but can rarely predict the eventual outcomes of their own actions - actions which might be prompted by short-term selfish calculations or private interests, but whose consequences might prove momentous from a retrospective standpoint. And the only possible view of the route taken is a retro-spective one. The mind needs to recollect itself along the path taken. Reason in history should be understood as active *through* the individual not *over* him; our own comprehension of our own past - spread out, or *éloigné*, as the French say, like the self in psychoanalysis - is part of what history comports. 'Spirit' informs and infiltrates social reality by its purposive action in the world; history itself, that is to say, was to Hegel as much as to Marx the record of mankind's autonomous, self-created needs along with the successive means to their fulfilment. The language with Hegel as with Marx was that of self-validating emergence over time. (To describe social reality, Hegel constantly had recourse to the root verb *wirken* which describes or implies human action having concrete social effects, and which lacks the static, 'given' implications of the Latin *res*.) Social reality is both repository and realization of the finite, manmade past; what this means is that historical change is not only recognized as being fundamental to an understanding of normative problems (rights, duties, obligations) but also as the only vantage point from which the perennial problems of political theory could properly be viewed.

State and civil society

The path to freedom - in Hegel's sense of freedom as self-determination - runs *through* society, not outside it; there is no point outside society from which its progress can be judged. Hegel's notion of *das Allgemeine* (the universal, general, common, public) - the most important word in *The Phenomenology* and *The Philosophy of Right* alike - is not the enemy, but the expression, of freedom; and freedom, in Hegel's view of it, is the identity (not the correspondence) of the universal with the personal goals of the individual. Freedom, as the identification of subjectivity and objectivity is not a state or a condition, but an opportunity for action; it is an activity that has its conditions.

According to Hegel, the rationality that permeates the human, historical world becomes apparent and reveals itself by stages. At the level of the family, rationality is hidden behind feeling and sentiment; in civil society, it appears as the instrumentality of individual self-interest; but only at the level of the state does reason become 'conscious of itself'. Morality, which exists in the family and in civil society, reveals itself as thought only in the state. Hegel's state is meant to provide us with an opportunity. Only in the properly political realm can men's actions be at one with their intentions; only in the state may man, as a self-determining being, know what he wants and be able to act accordingly to bring it about. This requires that certain rather strict, ambitious requirements be met - not by men, but by the state - if the state is to be worthy of men's moral purposes. Hegel's state was to be free from the shackles of feudal absolutism, based on a complex, articulated network of institutions that would represent the various interests in society, served by a rationally ordered bureaucracy, and not to be based upon anything so 'accidental' as nationalistic, linguistic or ethnic ties. What justifies the state is its satisfaction of rational criteria; it should mediate, and strike a balance not simply among conflicting individual imperatives - this can be done within civil society - but among all the complex institutions and groups needing representation throughout the political community at large.

The picture is not an orthodox traditionalist one. Hegel distinguished himself from those who based their political constructions upon reason alone, and from those who were content to accept the *status quo* without enquiring too searchingly into its foundations. He certainly asserted the primacy of the modern state against, not alongside, the traditionalist notion of the German *Volk* as a political unity. In his forthright opposition to *grossdeutsch* nationalism, Hegel unequivocally dismissed Herderian attempts to revive the German *Ur-Mythos*; old German tradition, he had insisted, 'has nothing in our day to connect or adapt itself to; it stands as cut off from the whole circle of our ideas, opinions and beliefs, and is as strange as the imagery of Ossian or of India'.[5] Hegel decisively turned against the German nationalism of his day, largely because this movement had turned its back upon the *fait accompli* of the Napoleonic rationalization of law and politics, and had promulgated, in place of these needed reforms, an obscurantist and backward looking set of romantic chimeras. Hegel did not believe that mere survival over time conferred legitimacy on any state-form. As opposed to thinkers like Savigny, von Haller and Fries (or, for that matter, Burke) who – much to Hegel's disgust – would deny men even the capacity to legislate, Hegel set forth the belief that the legitimacy of the modern state has to meet requirements that do not involve any celebration of the customary of the kind paraded by the political theorists of German *Volksgemeinschaft*. It is, perhaps, no accident that the pietistic, romantic and pseudo-medieval Prussia of Frederick William IV – who went to the lengths of summoning the aging Schelling to Berlin University to stamp out the vestiges of Hegelianism – virtually ostracized Hegel. Hegel's Prussia – the Prussia in which and for which he wrote *The Philosophy of Right* – was the earlier, reformed and 'enlightened' Prussia of von Stein and Hardenburg. His servility to even this Prussia had its limits: the institutional structure of Prussia at its most reformed did not correspond to that which Hegel outlines in *The Philosophy of Right*. Far from having uncritically venerated or celebrated the Prussia of his day, Hegel, for all his pretensions, seriously misread the *Zeitgeist*, and underestimated the force of German nationalism.

In other respects, however, Hegel read the *Zeitgeist* all too well. The most relevant aspect of Hegel's theory of the state to Marx's response was Hegel's adamant insistence that the state should not be confused with, nor reduced to the level of, civil society. 'If the state is confused with civil society', Hegel emphasized, 'and its specific end is laid down as the security and protection of property and personal freedom, then the interest of the individual as such becomes the ultimate end of their association. But the state's relation to the individual is quite different from this.'[6] Hegel's statement is less illiberal than it sounds. In civil society, he tells us, ethical life (*Sittlichkeit*) is 'split up into its extremes and lost',[7] whereas the state has an altogether worthier and more integrative aim. The citizens of Hegel's state are united because they are conscious of the moral possibilities of acting together. All its institutional mechanisms are designed to encourage and facilitate such an advance in consciousness over the level it can attain in civil society, and the advance is moral and rational all at once. Hegel justifies the modern state because of the social self-understanding it permits, and which permits it. As modern men, Hegel admits, we appropriate the world subjectively - in the first instance; he adds that we may understand the world we appropriate only by paying attention to the appropriations of others. We understand them through ourselves, and ourselves through them, in a process (which can be a struggle) for recognition and acknowledgment. The state provides what is in modern times the only possible forum in which this acknowledgment can take place; it helps us focus on one another.

Freedom in Hegel's political philosophy consists in self-determination of the kind that specifically depends on the self-determination of others, and which presupposes an ethical community - the state - as well as the elements of moral autonomy and critical reflectiveness that emerge in civil society. Political self-determination contains within itself abstract self-assertion as one of its 'moments' but it cannot be satisfied by what self-assertion provides. It needs something altogether worthier: an arena where values, interests and purposes can be elicited, formulated and sustained. This arena - the state - makes provision (as civil society and its institutions cannot make provision) for the harmonization and synthesizing of private and public interests by means of the institutional and juridical structures that Hegel outlines, in all their complex articulation, in *The Philosophy of Right*. Ethical and political cohesion are achieved by means of an interpenetration of government, group representation and public opinion; this pattern of interaction, while it does not displace or annul the ethically less worthy pursuits of men in civil society, does provide an ethical content for men's lives that civil society, taken as a model, would be woefully incapable of furnishing.

The modern state Hegel outlined and defended is based on the rational and moral allegiance of the citizen as mediated by 'the spirit and art of political institutions' and not by social, nationalistic, linguistic or religious uniformities taken abstractly; all these could be regarded in Hegel's lexicon as 'accidental', although to more orthodox conservatives they were the mainstay of legitimacy. Hegel's concern that specifically political membership should be reduced to nothing outside itself is expressed most forcefully, however, in opposition to those who would make of the state, with its 'prodigious strength and depth'[8] a mere watchdog over men's pursuits in civil society. Properly political pursuits should on no account be confused with, or reduced to, economic pursuits. The state should not be regarded in instrumental terms. It works to its own end. In particular, not only is the state not a device for the protection of property (by its very nature it offends against property by levying taxes and waging war); it provides a system of moral integration specifically because economic life in civil society has particularized and atomized men so that they *need* the simultaneous higher membership the state provides. Hegel's state is said to overcome what Marx was to insist no state could overcome: it is to overcome the atomistic individualism of the economic sphere without in any way displacing or abolishing this individualism. It should be emphasized that Marx's opposition to Hegel's state is based more on what it *cannot* do than on what it does: as far as Marx was concerned, any state that does not abolish economic individualism is itself subsumed within - or beneath - such individualism. The need to abolish it is not postponed but strengthened if it is given a new lease of life by being validated and artificially kept alive by the state.

What Hegel and Marx share is very fundamental indeed: an opposition to the dissociative tendencies produced by modern civil society and the operation of the modern economy, and a profound recognition that modern economic life is the antithesis of community. The continuity between Hegel and Marx in this very respect - a continuity that has never been sufficiently emphasized - has as its outcome the demolition of what has been called 'the political theory of possessive individualism'. In Hegel's view, to regard the economy as a primary, inviolate realm - and the state as a mere regulatory agency, standing outside civil society and merely preserving the exterior conditions of civil society's supposedly automatic tendency to adjust and correct its own workings - is to get one's priorities reversed and to mistake cause for effect. Yet the 'hidden hand' of the classical economists would reduce the state to being the arbitrary political resultant of the play of social forces, and these social forces, the economists added, are in turn reducible to the clash of subjectivities in civil society. This reduction was to Hegel unconscionable. The clash of subjectivities can neither implement nor sustain a community of right. Indeed, the clash and clang of subjectivities according to Hegel is unlikely to produce anything more harmonious than the clamour of the market-place, which should on no account be allowed to drown out properly political discourse.

Over and above this objection, what was particularly bothersome to Hegel was the idea that contract between individual wills could stand as a model or paradigm for properly political relationships, as in social contract theories of the state. Social contract theory transfers 'the characteristics of private property into a sphere of a quite different and higher nature'.[9] The state is not a partnership. Nor is it something that anybody decides for or against. Political power cannot be dissolved into the assertion of private rights; it is not a matter of adjudicating conflicting individual claims. A state reduced to the level of doing so would become arbitrary in the sense that its basis, the individual human will, is arbitrary. Yet what was to Hegel the facile constitution-mongering of contractarian liberalism would reduce the state, which is 'exalted above the sphere of things that are made', to the level of an arbitrary political resultant of the play of social forces.[10] Hegel was happy to endorse Montesquieu's immanent critique of contractarian liberalism's mechanistic and artificial notion of a 'constitution' as a mere external juridical act. To Montesquieu and Hegel alike, the state is not an outcome but a presupposition; it is the basis, not the effect, of the individual's conscience and will.

Hegel, indeed, was at his shrewdest in disputing the claims not only of 'state of nature' theories of *government* but also of what generally were their basis, 'state of nature' theories of *property*. Such theories – Locke's would be an example – which endeavour to justify property in society on the grounds of its pre-social existence are, according to Hegel, deeply confused. All these theories can do is to establish or explain appropriation as a power or faculty, and not property as a right. Property *rights*, like all rights, depend for their existence on being recognized within a normative order; they are claims or entitlements and not the straightforward consequences of original appropriation. Locke – unlike Hegel – even presupposes original *self*-possession in the state of nature, which is from Hegel's point of view not only wrong but also ridiculous. The economic sphere to Hegel is not just a reflection of pre-existing needs and the struggle to satisfy them. It is a medium for their development, and 'political economy' itself, correspondingly, is not given but constituted within other aspects or areas of human life. Political economy does not stamp or dominate these areas – that power relations would collapse into relations of wealth was one of Hegel's greatest fears – but, instead, these areas make political economy comprehensible. Political economy was not with Hegel the master science, or even the basis for a general philosophical position, it was to be with some utilitarians.

Contractarian liberalism is 'abstract' to Hegel because it would build social and political relations on individual will and subjective self-assertion. If human relations are no more than relations among individual wills, then every individual would see in every other individual a rival, an obstacle, a limitation on his own purely personal freedom, and nothing or nobody outside the individual could express or embody that individual's freedom. At the level of civil society, each constituent can realize his own ends only in this way – either by disregarding those of everyone else, or by treating and encountering others abstractly and interchangeably. Contractarian liberalism, consequently, is based on deficient principle; specifically, two things are confused that at all costs, according to Hegel, should be kept apart – the merely social and the properly political. Contractarian liberalism, like economic life in civil society's 'system of needs', is reducible not to a genuinely moral principle of self-determination, but only to individual (hence 'abstract') self-assertion, which could provide no politically generative principle.

Hegel's criticism, though forthright, is not a blanket condemnation; he nowhere denies that the subjectivism and egoism that amount to deficient, incomplete political principles also have some salutary preliminary characteristics. Civil society is progressive in that its emergence signifies a break with the *ancien régime*, with all traditional legitimations – including that of religion – that might have restricted economic activity. Men in civil society are left free to do what they think fit, and this is an advance. Modern individualism corrodes traditional, ascriptive values, releases the individual from assigned, feudal status (a status the passing of which Hegel, like Marx, was not at all inclined to mourn), and makes possible – as well as necessary – individual participation in the state. For the first time individual satisfaction emerges from feudal circumscription as a human right, as one indispensable basis for membership in the state. Hegel never denied that critical, reflective subjectivity (however 'abstract' it may be) provides the basis of a higher morality than that of unthinking attachment to hallowed institutions and immemorial customs.

Subjectivity implies independence, self-sufficiency, autonomy and personal liberty, and all these have their part to play in modern society. Nevertheless, by their very nature they cannot provide unity, or provide for the cohesiveness that modern political life increasingly needs. Concatenation is a more likely outcome of the play of subjectivity than is unity. Relations of external dependence among isolated individuals – with their corollaries of egoism and conflict, both inner and outer – cannot produce or sustain properly political membership.

Hegel's portrayal of civil society (*bürgerliche Gesellschaft*) was predicated upon Adam Smith's – and Sir James Steuart's – depiction of modern society as, above all else, an institution of exchange. Within society so defined, self-interested persons separately pursue wealth, and their actions create, unintentionally, a minimal public interest. Thanks to Smith's 'hidden hand', separate private pursuits intersect into what is – to wrest a phrase from Kant – a kind of asocial sociability, one which results from the clash of subjectivities. Yet J.N. Findlay's claim that 'Hegel sees a deep affirmation of his own philosophy in the principles of Adam Smith and Ricardo, which connect the selfish pursuit of individual good with the realization of the collective good of all'[11] is unjustified. Hegel's limited arguments for 'the selfish pursuit of individual good' – which, as he recognized, was not a socially generative or integrative principle at all – were often defences against the aristocratic assertion that mere trade was base and ignoble. (Hegel's interpreter ignores the incisive portrait of bourgeois versus aristocrat in *The Phenomenology*[12] at his peril.) Men relate to one another in the commercial system of civil society, Hegel insisted, as the bearers of rights – in particular, of property rights and the rights of conscience; these may not have been fully recognized or sanctioned in the Germany of his day, but they are established as imprescriptible rights in *The Philosophy of Right*, long before Hegel deals with civil society as such. Men in civil society, that is to say, exhibit a self-certainty to which they are morally entitled; and they exteriorize themselves as the subjects of needs. In expressing and fulfilling these needs, men need some, minimal, measure of social co-operation. What Hegel calls 'the system of needs' provides this measure of co-operation, but in a wholly external manner. While at the level of the family the principle of social and moral unity is immediate, unreflective and inward, at the level of civil society people encounter other people reflectively, calculatingly, outwardly and indirectly. These encounters denote an advance in social self-consciousness over the level it attains within the family, and this advance makes of civil society a means to liberty (in the sense of self-determination) or a presentiment of liberty. But Hegel's civil society is an unsubstantiated version of liberty. It provides and can provide no real focus for individual or social identity; these need a specifically political, and not a merely social focus, as Rousseau had recognized.

Hegel's distinction here between the *bourgeois* and the *citoyen* is very much a distinction between individualism and individuality considered as animating principles, largely as the German Romantics had perceived it. Individualism may satisfy the requirements of the market economy, i.e. self-awareness and action (self-assertion) based upon it. Yet individuality requires more than civil society can provide. Men in civil society relate to one another through their own individual purposes which intersect, cross-cut and collide; civil society itself can best be seen as a force-field, its institutions taking the form of resultants rather than syntheses. Civil society exhibits some cohesion, but cannot supply integration; it operates as some sort of system – regularly and predictably – and it stimulates similar responses among its inhabitants, without in any way really uniting them. The network of individual purposes on which it is based enables the system to function predictably enough; but what is not needed for the *system* to function *is* needed by those human subjects whose activities make the system work. The analogy with Marx's portrayal of capitalism is striking; Hegel's civil society, and Marx's capitalist society, both operate, or function regularly and predictably, not despite but because of the moral and social reduction of their human constituents. But there is one crucial difference. According to Hegel, man is part of the system of civil society only in one of his aspects, only as a producer; he is integrated in no other sense. To Marx, it is precisely as a producer that man is most manifestly *not* integrated; the question of what else is left as a source of integration is quick to impose itself.

Sir James Steuart's conception of the 'statesman' (which really means 'form of government'), whose function is to superintend economic activity, points to conclusions very different from those of Adam Smith. The modern commercial economy in particular, according to Steuart, far from bringing into play some providential 'hidden hand', needs the kind of superintendence over its rate of growth that the 'statesman' can provide; only in this way, Steuart – and, following Steuart, Hegel – believes, can some of the more pernicious aspects of the growth of commercial relations be mitigated, and 'harm to any member of the commonwealth' be avoided. Steuart, who in this way was alien to Smithian *laissez faire*, was probably influenced by the German Cameralist tradition and in particular by Justi (Steuart's *Inquiry into the Principles of Political Economy* was composed in Tübingen where as a Jacobite he was exiled after the 1745 rebellion).[13] Hegel's 'police' (*Polizei*) – the controlling function over civil society's 'system of needs' – follows from Steuart's 'statesman'; each means the public authority making more secure the contingent and haphazard relationships dominating civil society. The problem – particularly in the case of Hegel – was that of securing and superintending civil society without stifling the freedom and autonomy that animate civil society in the first place. Hegel's solution is to restrict the authority of the 'police' very severely – so that it merely restores sufficient equilibrium to enable society to carry on – and to place it under some kind of representative control, without which it would appear as alien, as an intrusion. Marx, as we shall see, was to insist that the most 'representative' modern political authority, the liberal bourgeois state, must appear alien and intrusive in this very sense. What Hegel objected to in Adam Smith's depiction of civil society was not so much its accuracy – or indeed its character as what looked like the wave of the future – but its providentialism. On Smith's presentation, conflicting interests are balanced out by some 'hidden hand' so that harmony results. To Hegel, harmoniousness is exactly what is *lacking* in civil society. It has no principle of unity and it is incapable of producing any principle of unity. Smith had acknowledged the lack of any natural principle of equilibrium, and had sanctioned the removal of natural and supernatural validations for society and politics; the hidden hand is at least an intrinsic, artificial validation. As far as Hegel was concerned, however, artificial balance is no more morally worthy or integrative on Smith's presentation than is natural balance.

Hegel here is referring us to what it is that is being balanced. When individuals live ethically apart from one another, using or being used by other individuals, negotiating mutual use across a broadening spectrum of social existence, any real, morally generative rules can appear only as 'abstract', as distant, external, and partial; they would also have to be imposed. The rules that govern property, its acquisition, inheritance and exchange are moral rules – they are among the *first* moral rules. But there are severe limits to the content of the morality involved. The operation of property regulations establishes what Hegel calls 'abstract right' – the web or network of assurances and predictability (what the French call *prévision*) that underlies property relations. 'Abstract right' is exemplified in contractual relations, yet even these are to Hegel *minimal* relations among immediate persons – persons, that is, who are conceived of abstractly, and who are considered independently of all social relations, independently of the actual position in society that each of the contracting parties might hold. 'Abstract right' thus enjoins the notion of equality before the law – which in Hegel's lexicon is a presupposition of civil society, as well as of the more elevated state. The necessity for such legal fictions – which Hegel nowhere denies – nevertheless indicates the arbitrary, formal nature of contractual ties. Agreements about honouring contracts are arbitrary in the additional sense that they presuppose what they cannot create – the power that communal life and social expectations can give them. Contractual obligation, again, is morally unworthy in the sense that it brings about no change in the moral identity of the individuals who are engaged in contracting; these individuals start out as egoists, calculate accordingly, and emerge from the contract as egoistic as they were before (if not more so). There may be a bare-bones morality in keeping one's promises for the sake of maintaining the web of assurances made necessary by private property relations – it is not generally in one's long-term interests to break one's word – but this morality was to Hegel proximate not to significant morality but to criminality and cynicism (which passed for morality with Voltaire and the early political economists). Civil society, because it signifies the deprivation of ethical possibilities, creates requirements it cannot satisfy. In itself, it contains the germs of disillusion, hopelessness, cynicism and anarchy; it produces an ethical contagion it lacks the wherewithal to remedy.

Hegel considered wealth to be a purely instrumental category the pursuit of which cannot of itself inspire ethical ideals or educative values.[14] Wealth, indeed, is instrumental in the extremely limited sense that it can generate further wealth. But it leads nowhere beyond itself. Its limited character is pointed up by its obverse, aristocratic honour, as well as by its converse, pauperism; both wealth and honour breed arrogance and exclusivity, and both wealth and pauperism breed self-absorption. As an alternative to both aristocratic honour and the poverty of the 'rabble', wealth can provide power and independence, to be sure; but it is not power and independence that are lacking in the first place. They are components of the individual personality and will; but they are not its only components. Self-determination requires much more than power and independence taken (as Hegel thought they were being taken) as ends in themselves.

The individualism animating and exemplifying civil society is in Hegel's eyes sufficiently finite and restrictive to constitute what can only be, morally, a case of arrested development. In civil society one is simply not constrained to make choices. One does not decide how (or even whether) one should live in civil society: one does not reflect – nor does one *need* to reflect – what one's goals ought to be. Purely personal goals are of no account; and, sacrificing or bracketing them, one simply acts, or behaves, the way others act or behave. There is in civil society no conscious purpose, only given necessity. No agreement on the fundamentals of moral and social life – no properly political agreement – can arise there. It is because so little leeway is provided in civil society for the exercise of the rational will that Hegel insisted that this exercise is *political*.

The search for wealth fails the self. In pursuing it, the self engages others only abstractly; all encounters among individuals in their pursuit of wealth are blocked encounters, which point the way to a society of interchangeability. Market relations in civil society represent an uninterrupted self-existence which is necessarily disruptive and discontinuous, and which comes unhinged. Others are encountered, but only barely; everyone encountered has a use, but no one has a place. People think of themselves and others as dissociated beings; the prerequisite for an ethical order – intersubjectivity – is unavailable. People encounter others (and themselves through others) indirectly, if at all; self-understanding emphasizes the marginality of others in the conduct of everyday life; and any search for moral meaning is blocked off in advance. Consequently, moral meaning itself becomes elusive; access and recognition are reduced to the level of a blocked encounter; and moral horizons are foreshortened. Self-assertion, in short, turns into the negation of selfhood, for selfhood depends on the possibility of real moral transformation, which self-assertion, taken as an end in itself, must preclude. Civil society, the arena of self-assertion, the realm of the accidental, the contingent, the fortuitous, the arbitrary, the capricious, adds up to a system of universal dependence.

Failure: war

Small wonder, then, that the spheres of exchange, production, market relations and occupational hierarchy are for Hegel the most promising areas for the existence of self-estranged minds. Had Hegel attached any ultimate importance to the level of morality civil society exemplifies, his argument on war – to give one prominent example – would have taken a very different form. Hegel's argument as it stands amounts to a telling denial that war can be justified by the utilitarian motives of the defence of life and property. Hegel was one of the first political theorists to point out that it is absurd to demand that men sacrifice, in the act of war, the very things towards the 'preservation' of which it is waged - their lives and their property.[15] This absurdity would base war, not upon the states that actually wage it, but upon civil society. Hegel's justification of war not only identifies it, fairly and squarely, as the province of *state* action; it also puts forward the argument that war is ethical (*sittlich*) inasmuch as it exposes - not expresses - the accidental, the arbitrary, the contingent, the finite in everyday life. War, in other words, is politically integrative; it can *solve* the problem of fragmentation that civil society poses.

Hegel, however, puts the issue more forcefully; not only is war an integrative device, it is *the* fundamental integrative device that the state provides. However uncomfortable this may be to Hegel's liberal commentators, Hegel himself does not rest content with indicating that the state supplies the materials of integration; he also reminds us *how* states do so. The bureaucracy cannot of itself supply the moral and political integration men so desperately - and increasingly - need (except perhaps for the individual bureaucrat). War can supply it; it alone provides us with access to one another. Its effect of highlighting, of casting into sharp relief, the relativities of civil society is not an incidental by-product of its incidence. Force is a moment of right, as the master–slave dialectic in *The Phenomenology* reminds us. The internal order upheld and guaranteed by the state is connected to and dependent upon the likelihood of outer chaos. This outer chaos is not at all a sphere of irrationality defeating the solid achievements of reason in civil society. The opposite is the case. The possibility of war, says Hegel, serves to dry up potentially stagnant pools of irrationality in civil society; war, which 'preserves the ethical health of peoples', is compared to the 'blowing of winds preserving the sea from the foulness which would be the result of a prolonged calm.'[16] War does what the French Revolution wanted to do but failed to do until (with Brissot's curdling declaration of a 'revolution for export') it turned to war. Earlier French revolutionaries had thought - wrongly - that popular participation could conjure up the mutuality that in fact can be provided only by war, which gives the internal order upheld by the state something to define itself against.

Hegel's defence of war - like so much else in *The Philosophy of Right* - is a hit at Kant. It is perpetual *peace*, Hegel insists, that leads away from morality to corruption. Increasingly settled expectations in a liberal market society where not all injustices are obvious, but where pauperism and class differences are rampant, will lead to unjust privilege and abuse on the part of the rich; wealth might feed directly into political power - which was one of Hegel's greatest fears - an eventuality which the institutional structure outlined in *The Philosophy of Right* was designed, *inter alia*, to prevent. War should not be considered apart from this structure. Orderly expectations in civil society are undermined, and need to be undermined, by the 'ethical moment' in war. Hegel, on the surface of his argument, is criticizing the *Friedens-bund* of Kant – Kant who had believed force may accompany justice but has no power to create it, and that an internally just society is impossible unless the problem of war is solved. Yet Hegel in effect went much further than this, as can be seen from the evidence adduced by Albert Hirschmann in a recent study (which does not deal with Hegel), *The Passions and the Interests*. Theorists such as Hobbes, Locke and Kant – to name only the most prominent – all, in their various ways, contribute to a certain liberal vision of 'the sublimation of politics' (to use Sheldon Wolin's happy phrase). The argument, in broad terms, is that commerce is inherently peaceable; Schumpeter's idea that imperialism is nothing but the outcome of a residual, pre-capitalist mentality (while capitalism, being rational and calculating, is by its very nature averse to risk-taking on the scale that is implicit in heroic imperialist antics) is merely the argument's *ultima ratio*.[17]

Commerce, we are told (but not by Hegel), brings peace; the market is peaceable. Because of this the dilemmas of politics are solved. The state, standing in between the promise of justice and social order, on the one hand, and the menace of war, on the other, becomes integrated into a set of social relationships more comprehensive than the merely political – relationships based on the model (or the reality) of the peaceable market. A world governed by self-interest – not passion – is a world characterized by predictability and constancy. Expansion of domestic trade would create more cohesive communities, while expansion of foreign trade would help avoid wars among them. Love of gain – unlike the passions which are what Hobbes called 'divers', capricious, easily exhausted, suddenly renewed – is perpetual; it may be insatiable; but at least it remains constant. The pursuit of wealth is in this way rendered innocuous. Those who pursue it cannot, by definition, share in the heroic 'virtues' or violent passions of the aristocrat. 'The spirit of commerce', said Montesquieu (who was not uncritical of it), 'brings with it the spirit of frugality, of economy, of moderation, of work, of wisdom, of tranquillity, of order, and of regularity. In this manner, as long as this spirit prevails, the riches it creates do not have any bad effect.' Again, 'the natural effect of commerce is to lead to peace. Two nations that trade together become mutually dependent; if one has an interest in buying, the other has one in selling; and all unions are based on mutual needs.'[18] Sir James Steuart, like Montesquieu, considered that the regularity of commerce limits the arbitrary power of governments, and ultimately renders it useless; Adam Smith considered that economic progress was possible regardless of political (or *human*) improvement (thereby possibly overplaying his invisible hand). While earlier thinkers had pitted economic self-interest *against* the other passions – including the *libido dominandi*, the lust for power – Smith collapsed the distinction in his belief that the material welfare of 'the whole society is advanced when everyone is allowed to follow his own interests'. In Rousseauian terms, *amour propre* and the very different (because limitless) *amour de soi* are meshed into one by Smith; all non-economic drives – 'interests' and 'passions' alike – reinforce that of *enrichissez-vous.*

Smith – who was aware of the human costs this collapse involved – may have been more realistic than the author of a more recent passage which restates the more traditional view.

> Dangerous human proclivities can be canalized into comparatively
> harmless channels by the existence of opportunity for money-
> making and private wealth, which, if they cannot be satisfied in this
> way, may find their outlet in cruelty, the reckless pursuit of personal
> power and authority, and other forms of self-aggrandizement. It is
> better that a man should tyrannize over his bank balance than over
> his fellow-citizens; and whilst the former is sometimes denounced
> as being but a means to the latter, sometimes at least it is an
> alternative.[19]

What is striking about Hegel's response to this remarkably long-lived way of thinking – which those disinclined to mince words would call an ideology – is that he attacks it at its very foundation. Commerce cannot sublimate politics; the market simply is not peaceable, in the required sense, in the first place. It may be orderly, regular and systematic – though there are limits even to this – but order and regularity should not be confused with significant morality. Love of gain is anything but innocuous. What is required is *not* that dangerous political passions be sublimated by the provision of economic channels; what is required is *exactly the opposite.* The hypocrisy of the liberal model, Hegel is telling us, caricatures the moral possibilities of social existence. Commerce does not sublimate politics; it exemplifies conflict. It depends upon the moral and social fragmentation implicit in the exhortation to *enrichissez-vous.* Neither does politics in any everyday sense sublimate commerce. But war does. Commerce is shown up, and torn from its illusions of peace by war – war that is with Hegel (as class war was to be with Marx) a moral resource. It establishes – as commerce can never establish – the identity of a people, by indicating the relativity of life as it is lived. It serves the purpose of an integrative rationality; 'under its agency the ethical health of peoples is preserved in their indifference to the stabilization of finite institutions'. War undermines complacency. 'Property and life', says Hegel, 'should definitely be established as accidental. . . [in wartime] the rights and interests of individuals are established as a passing phase.' War 'deals in earnest with the vanity of temporal goods and concerns'.[20] Faced with it, we become present to one another.

It may be that morality deserves better than war; but Hegel's point is that in a world like this one, with its compacted tendencies towards fragmentation, anything more integrative than war is - to put it mildly - unlikely.

Hegel, like the ancients he so admired (and *ceteris paribus* like Marx), was sanguine about violence - force, to all of them, is a moment of right - on the straightforward grounds that it *is* part of our life, and cannot be wished out of existence. Relationships of economic dependency are not free from violence in this sense. As to war, a primary end of the state, its defence indicates forcefully that Hegel resolutely refused to make the state an expression of the interests of civil society.

Hegel's discussion of war, for all its sanguine 'realism' about the existence and avoidability of violence in our social and political existence, also indicates - presumably to anyone but Hegel himself - the moral failure that so often characterizes this kind of 'tough-mindedness'. The point here is not to sweep the discussion under the carpet, or to avert one's eyes from what is a central characteristic of Hegel's political philosophy; it is to admit its importance and to criticize it for the moral failure it exemplifies. It may be that, historically, 'force is a moment of right', just as it has proved true that men under arms display a rare comradeship; but to *justify* force, arms, violence and war, however carefully, because of the effects it might have in stimulating community is the merest dialectical trickery. This issue was joined by Marx, particularly in the course of his dispute with Bakunin - whose own justification of the most extreme and indiscriminate revolutionary violence has some specifically Hegelian roots. That is the subject of a later chapter.

Failure: poverty and pauperism

Hegel's picture of civil society is, above all, dynamic; it contains the seeds of its own dissolution unless it is complemented from above, by the state. These sources of dissolution prominently include the creation of what the English language translator of *The Philosophy of Right* calls a 'rabble of paupers'. The emergence of this mass of those deprived of all the benefits of civil society accompanies the concentration of wealth in a few hands. The two tendencies are directly related and reinforce each other: the more luxury, the more penury and dependence. Hegel's fear that wealth would breed political power was counterbalanced by his point that complete lack of wealth would breed powerlessness, lack of the barest personal autonomy, among the propertyless. The one process is the obverse of the other. The 'rabble of paupers' - Hegel's own term was *die Pöbel* - is not some accidental or coincidental by-product of civil society: it is the other side of the coin of luxury. Poverty, according to Hegel, is not a feature of civil society when it is in a state of decline or disintegration; it is a feature of civil society in its normal, everyday operation, when everything is running smoothly and 'civil society is in a state of unimpeded activity'.[21] Poverty is an endemic and ineradicable characteristic of civil society, and it means not simply the level of physical deprivation suffered by the poor but also the social attitudes of those who are deprived. The level of poverty in Hegel's presentation is not fixed by some neutral or objective standard; it is relative to what is needed to be a functioning, integrated member of society with a specific standard of living. Poverty in Hegel's strikingly modern characterization is relative deprivation, and there are social attitudes that characterize its onset and deepen its impact. Men become cut off from the various advantages of society – the acquisition of skills, education, the access to justice and to religion: all the mediating institutions and activities that link men to the social order, like work itself. In the absence of these mediations, men become estranged from this order. 'Poverty in itself does not make men into a rabble', says Hegel, 'a rabble is created only when there is joined to poverty a disposition of mind, an inner indignation against the rich, against society, against the government. . .'[22] Poverty – an inevitable by-product of the normal functioning of society – in this way feeds on itself, and is insoluble; organized charity or taxes levelled on the rich might alleviate physical deprivation but can do nothing to counteract the cast of men's minds, the loss of self-respect. Such measures are more likely to deepen the decline in self-respect; and public works would be ineffective, since Hegel considered that unemployment was caused by overproduction in the first place. Hence, 'despite an excess of wealth, civil society is not rich enough, in that its own resources are insufficient to check excessive poverty and the creation of a penurious rabble'.[23] Hegel even does more than toy with imperialism ('colonization') as a way of solving (or exporting) the problem of indigence based on overproduction;[24] but because of the psychology of the problem – it is Hegel to whom we owe the concept of the 'culture of poverty' – even this expedient could do little. The implications are far-reaching. The state cannot solve the problem: in other words it cannot provide a home for all its members. Yet the test of the Hegelian state is precisely its inclusiveness, its generality, its provision of community and the overcoming of alienation and estrangement. On all these counts the Hegelian state fails and Hegel himself fails as a social philosopher. Yet his portrayal of poverty is prescient in the extreme. Marx, when he insisted in 1843 that 'the class in need of immediate. . . concrete labour forms less a class of civil society than the basis on which the spheres of civil society rest and move',[25] was merely extending what Hegel had said about pauperism.

The numbers of the poor were enough to cause Hegel – and others – considerable concern. In Prussia alone the 'unincorporated poor' were beginning to constitute a numerical majority of the population.[26] 'Against nature', said Hegel, 'man can claim no right, but once society is established poverty immediately takes the form of a wrong done by one class to another. The important problem of how poverty is to be abolished is one of the most disturbing problems that agitate modern society.'[27] Hegel did not present poverty as a natural condition but as a social fact needing social redress; nor did he blame penury as a social problem upon the supposed fecklessness, or want of moral fibre, of the poor themselves. On the contrary, 'the formless mass' is brought into being, and its ranks filled and re-filled by the same social process that resulted in 'the concentration of disproportionate wealth in a few hands'.[28] While the poor cannot be held responsible for their own degradation, society, for its part, is in no position to redress what it must create and recreate. Hegel considered that any attempt to *solve* the problem of poverty – even within the institutional setting expounded in *The Philosophy of Right* – would merely compound and exacerbate the problem. Marx – who was led to his critiques of Hegel's *Philosophy of Right* by two articles, his earliest, that had investigated the plight of the propertyless – could not but concur. He had only to add the point that in modern society the poor alone might embody community to clinch an early stage of his argument. Marx, indeed, first identified the proletariat – which at the time he did not sharply distinguish from the unpropertied masses – as the agency of revolutionary change at the end of his second critique of Hegel's *Philosophy of Right* (1843–4).

> The proletariat is coming into being in Germany only as a result of the rising industrial development. For it is not the naturally arising poor but the artificially impoverished, not the human masses mechanically oppressed by the gravity of society but the masses resulting from the drastic dissolution of society. . .that form the proletariat. . . By proclaiming the dissolution of the hitherto existing world order the proletariat merely states the secret of its own existence, for it is in fact the dissolution of that world order. By demanding the negation of private property the proletariat merely raises to the rank of a principle of society what society has made the principle of the proletariat.[29]

By being deprived of all the benefits of civil society, the proletariat is outside and beyond civil society, even though civil society without the participation of the proletariat could not – and, Marx hastened to add, *would* not – persist.

> Where, then, is the positive possibility of a German emancipation?
> . . . In the formation of a class with radical chains, a class of civil

society that is not a class of civil society, an estate which is the
dissolution of all estates, a sphere which has a universal character
by its universal suffering and claims no particular right because no
particular wrong but wrong generally is perpetrated against it;
which can no longer invoke a historical but only a human title;
which does not stand in any one-sided antithesis to the consequences
but in an all-round antithesis to the premises of the German state;
a sphere, finally, that cannot emancipate itself without emancipating
itself from all other spheres of society; which, in a word, is the
complete loss of man and hence can win itself only through the
complete rewinning of man. This dissolution of society as a
particular estate is the proletariat.[30]

That the language of these well-known passages is Hegelian in the
extreme is evident; yet the content, too, amounts to what is mere
extension of Hegel's argument on the poor. Marx was meeting Hegel's
points.

Hegel, in dealing in *The Philosophy of Right* with the transfer or
alienation of property, says that

the reason I can alienate my property is that it is mine only in
so far as I put my will into it. Hence, I may abandon as a *res
nullius* anything that I have or yield it to the will of another and
so into his possession, provided always that the thing in question
is a thing external by nature.[31]

This proviso is extremely important. '[Those] goods or rather substantive characteristics, which consitute my own private personality
and the universal essence of my self-consciousness are inalienable and
my right to them is imprescriptible.'[32] That is to say, I can alienate
only what has been at some time not mine. Hegel immediately applies
this doctrine to labour.

Single products of my particular physical and mental skill and of
my power to act I can alienate to someone else and I can give him
the use of my abilities for restricted periods, because, on the
strength of this restriction, my abilities acquire an external
relation to the totality and universality of my being. By alienating
the whole of my time, as crystallized in my work, and everything
I produced, I would be making into another's property the
substance of my being, my universal activity and actuality, my
personality.[33]

This is precisely what Marx holds must happen under capitalism.
The entirety of the proletarian person becomes an object alien to that

person's being. Hegel himself had admitted that one can of one's own free will 'externalize' oneself and sell one's performances and services. 'Mental endowments, science, art, even. . .matters of religion. . .inventions, etc., all become objects of a contract; they are recognized and treated in the same way as objects for purchase.'[34] Such alienation (*Veräusserung*), Hegel continues, must have some limit in time, so that something remains of the universality (the personality) of the person. But if I were to sell 'the entire time of my concrete labour, and the totality of my produce, my personality would become the property of someone else; I would no longer be a person and would place myself outside the realm of right'. This, said Marx, is precisely what commodity production under capitalism involves and must involve; it is as though Marx were prompted by Hegel.

While this is not the place for any detailed analysis of Hegel's remarkably acute and prescient discussion of labour and the dialectics of labour, mention must be made of some of the elements in these discussions. Hegel believed that a man comes to a sense of self-consciousness and freedom not by merely consuming what is already to hand but by transforming what is at hand, by imposing his will on it and, in so doing, coming to know more about the world of objects which confronts him. At the same time he utilizes that knowledge to humanize the objective world. Hegel in making these points – which he did repeatedly – was not merely re-stating Vico's point that, as men, we can fully know only that which we have made; he was adding a certain kind of substance – of *social* substance – to Vico's perception, which Marx was to make programmatic. Hegel believed that labour is crucial to human history, labour *inaugurates* human history as the record of man's transformation of his environment, and that labour distinguishes man from animal and human history from the evolution of merely natural forms; and it is for this reason that he so contemptuously dismissed naturalistic explanations of human behaviour, whether these proceeded from French *philosophe* or from German Romantic.

What is particularly relevant for our purposes here about Hegel's discussions of labour is that in seeing it as the seed of personal autonomy, he specified that labour is the province of *some* men, not others. In what is probably Hegel's most celebrated depiction of the dialectics of labour, the 'master and slave' section of *The Phenomenology of Mind*,[35] Hegel's specification of where the historically generative principle lies is clear. It lies not with the master (*Herr*) but with the slave (*Knecht*). The slave's being is his work – his alteration and transformation of the *status quo*. While the master's ideal is necessarily preservative, the slave's is (equally necessarily) non-preservative. His relationship with the external world is that of reducing its externality; that to which he relates changes as a direct result of his activities. He transforms the world, and thereby the self which interacts with the world; and, ironically, the slave's structural and ontological superiority to the master consists in this dynamism, the momentum he is forced to sustain. The slave alone embodies the possibility of self-development. He is integral with his surrounding reality in a way the master cannot be. He can strive for an external embodiment which expresses him, as the master cannot. In this sense the slave has integrity and authenticity on his side.

There is no need to leap across the centuries and transform – crudely and illegitimately – 'slave' into 'proletarian' and 'master' into 'capitalist' to see the relevance of Hegel's set-piece on 'lordship and bondage' to Marx's subsequent emphases on alienation in the labour process and the fetishism of commodities. Hegel's paradigmatic emphasis on the world-transforming and self-transforming character of labour does not need to be overdrawn for us to see its striking relevance to Marx's thought. Indeed, Marx himself refers us to it. He described *The Phenomenology* as a whole as 'the true birthplace and secret of the Hegelian philosophy' and reserved his objections for the 'uncritical positivism and equally uncritical idealism' of Hegel's *later* works; he finds *elements* of these uncritical characteristics in *The Phenomenology*.[36] With respect to Hegel's treatment of labour, when Marx criticizes Hegel in the *Economic and Philosophic Manuscripts* of 1844 for perceiving labour 'only in an abstract way',[37] he does not mean that Hegel sees labour merely as contemplation, for it is clear from *The Phenomenology* that he does not. Hegel, indeed, regarded labour as man's 'universal activity' (*allgemeine Tätigkeit*); that he did so 'in an abstract way' implies – if we use the term 'abstract' to mean what Hegel meant by it, 'partial' or incomplete – that Hegel is afraid of the possible social consequences of his own analysis. Hegel's remarks about pauperism in *The Philosophy of Right* bear witness to such a backing-down; his analysis of lordship and bondage, similarly, all too readily raises the question of what would happen should the bondsman develop, from his self-awareness, self-*consciousness*. 'The outstanding achievement of Hegel's *Phenomenology*', wrote Marx,

. . .is. . .that Hegel conceives the self-creation of man as a process . . .that he thus grasps the essence of labour and comprehends objective man – true, because real, man – as the outcome of man's own labour. . . He grasps labour as the essence of man. . .[38]

In so doing, Marx goes on, Hegel has laid the groundwork for future theoretical developments.

Within the sphere of abstraction, Hegel conceives labour as man's act of self-genesis – conceives man's relation to himself as an alien being and the manifestation of himself as an alien being to be the emergence of species – consciousness and species – life.[39]

For Hegel and for Marx, labour is an activity in terms of which man succeeds in transcending his merely biological existence, and thus in becoming man in his true notion. Labour, in other words, is – or should be – a moment of freedom. If freedom consists in giving human form to inhuman objects, then labour (*ceteris paribus*) makes men free, even if men have yet to learn that this is so. To labour is to do away with the stubborn, intransigent independence of nature, of the conditions of life. It is to consciously transform these conditions in accordance with a preconceived purpose (even if this purpose is coerced, not spontaneous). In order to assert himself and to emerge from the realm of necessity, man has to transform the world in such a way that he can recognize himself in something that had been originally independent of him. The goal, for Hegel and for Marx, was that of self-realization by, for and of men; man, for both of them, was the outcome of his own labour. It is true that Hegel's paradigm furnished Marx with a prolegomenon altogether unwittingly (Marx ignored the specifically ancient placement of his 'struggle for recognition' – the outcome of which was the Stoicism shared by Marcus Aurelius and Epictetus); but such is the cunning of reason; and in any event, Hegel's attempted solution, according to Marx, amounted to something less than self-realization. Man in Hegel's civil society is not the outcome of his own labour, and cannot recognize himself in the world his labour creates, except in the inhumanly restricted sense Marx was to investigate throughout his life. Self-realization is inadequate if it depends on pauperization and war, together with the admittedly less extreme but also severe social and moral shortcomings that characterize even a smoothly running economic realm. Marx, even in his critiques of *The Philosophy of Right*, took issue not with the *aims* of Hegelian political philosophy, the ends of integration and community, which to Marx, too, were vital human needs. He took issue with Hegel's view that these aims could be provided for, and men in their social being satisfied, within the framework of a modern state that met Hegel's own specifications.

It is for this reason that Marx's criticisms of Hegel's *Philosophy of Right* – which raise several themes Marx was to take up again in his later writings on the state, as we shall see – are of vital importance to an understanding of the theory of the state Marx was to counterpose to those of the anarchists. Marx and the anarchists, it can be shown, are in the first instance answering different kinds of questions. What underlies Marx's investigations of various contemporary state-forms – investigations Marx undertook throughout his career – is a question posed originally (and starkly) by Hegel: what are the characteristics of the *modern* state, as opposed to earlier forms and as opposed to a specifically modern form of society, with specifically modern characteristics? The point here is not that anarchist theoreticians were necessarily unaware that the modern state differs from earlier state-forms, or that what helps characterize the modern state is its relationship with civil society - itself a product of relatively recent times. It is that the modernity of the state-form and the question of its relationship to civil society are questions that to an anarchist pale into insignificance alongside the presence of the state as the central enemy of freedom; to Marx, on the other hand, what makes a state-form identifiably modern, and how it relates to the civil society that underlies and penetrates it, are not incidental questions but central ones. Without answering them - as Hegel himself had recognized, whatever the shortcomings of his reconciliation may have been - we cannot, according to Marx, identify what the state *is*. To claim to understand the *nature* of the modern state without understanding the character of civil society - which is what Marx considered all his anarchist interlocutors to have claimed - is a futile and potentially dangerous pretension. *Awareness* of modernity and the existence of civil society is simply not enough; what is required is what Hegel himself had made possible and necessary: real investigation, that is to be speculative and empirical all at once, of what the state and civil society comport. Community - Marx's (and Hegel's) *Gemeinwesen* - is not simply something that can automatically replace an ill-investigated state; Marx recognized that after Hegel's investigation, community could in no sense be seen as automatic. Community, if it is to come about, must emerge from the structure of the present, its proximate forerunner; to know its shape we must know the contours of the present and of the threats to, as well as promises of, community it contains.

From the point of view of Marx's early essays - not to mention the way these are connected with his later writings on the state, which will be examined in the following chapter - we can see that Marx's standpoint differs from any anarchist standpoint not because Marx lays more *emphasis* on a commonly perceived problem, that of the contradiction between state and civil society, but because this contradiction is the *point d'appui* of *all* Marx's subsequent investigations - investigations that in all their breadth and depth would seem to an anarchist to be simply unnecessary. What matters to the anarchist, above all, is what the state *does*; what mattered to Marx is what no state *can* do. That no state, the Hegelian included, can embody community is a proposition the anarchist can take as read, or consider proven; to Marx, it was a working hypothesis, the basis of his subsequent investigations of the contours of capitalist society.

If Hegel's solution - which makes of citizenship in the modern state what Marx called 'the scholasticism of popular life'[40] - was, as Marx thought, a mystification, the problem it was supposed to resolve, the contradiction of state and society, of economic and political action, is real enough. Man's political significance, in his capacity as a citizen, is detached from his real private being, as an economic actor. Hegel had recognized this, in his own way, clearly enough; yet the mediating institutions that are supposed to ensure the resolution of the split between private and public being in *The Philosophy of Right* – the sovereign, the bureaucracy, the Estates, the Legislature – Marx demonstrates to his own satisfaction are incapable of effecting any meaningful reconciliation. Hegel's state, far from being exalted above the play of private interests, and far from representing any real general interest, is itself a false universal. Its claims to a kind of transcendence are demonstrably without substance.

Marx, in so characterizing the Hegelian state, makes a peculiarly deft and telling observation, since Hegel himself had constantly criticized Kant's *Rechtsstaat* for being an abstract universal which rests on the margins of civil life. Yet Marx was not concerned simply to hoist Hegel neatly on his own petard; there is a good deal of substance to his claim that a modern state that met Hegel's rather extreme conditions would nevertheless unavoidably correspond to an illusory 'citizenship' that itself would stay on the edges of everyday life. Worse still, its presence there effects in those men to whom it supposedly applies an 'essential schism' between man in his capacity as economic actor and man in his capacity as abstract citizen.

> In his political role, the member of civil society rids himself of his class, of his actual private position; by this alone does he acquire significance as man. . .his character as member of the state. . .appears to be his human character. For all his other characteristics in civil society appear to be unessential to man, the individual.[41]

Yet, if we ask what these supposedly 'unessential' characteristics are, the inventory that answers the question becomes disquietingly long. These 'unessential' characteristics are precisely *what make us individuals*, what distinguish each one of us from everybody else. This paradox, which is a monstrous one, is worth dwelling on, for it is one that any sensitive reader of Marx encounters again and again throughout his writings. It is clear from a reading of *The German Ideology* alone – as we shall see in considering Marx's attack on Max Stirner, which takes up the greater part of the book – that Marx was much more concerned to investigate what is involved in the concept of individuality (individuality as opposed to individualism, much as Hegel had distinguished the two) than is usually believed. Indeed it must be emphasized that Marx is much more concerned to synthesize individuality, so considered, and community than is often believed. It is because of these concerns that the question of Marx's itinerary from Hegel is so significant; for Marx was one of the very few people to recognize that Hegel's own investigation of what is involved in the notions of community and individuality had made all discussion in pre-Hegelian terms (such as that of the anarchists) irrelevant to the point of being nonsensical.

Returning to the question of citizenship in the modern state with the question of individuality (in its true notion) in mind, we can specify in what respects it falls short of any such individuality. Citizenship in the modern state abstracts those features of individual existence that distinguish one person from another; in its need to treat all men equally and indiscriminately, citizenship takes the form of a least common denominator rather than something that can be said to express human diversity – even though, or *precisely because*, this diversity under modern conditions is going to find *no other outlet*. Because 'civil society and state are separated', Marx writes in his 'Critique' of Hegel's *Philosophy of Right,*

> the citizen of the state is also separated from the citizen as the member of civil society. He must therefore effect a fundamental division within himself. . . [In] order to behave as an actual citizen of the state and to attain political significance and effectiveness, he must step out of his civil reality, disregard it, and withdraw from this whole organization [of civil society] into his individuality; for the whole existence which he finds for his citizenship of the state is his sheer, blank individuality, since the existence of the state as executive is complete without him, and his existence in civil society is complete without the state. . . The separation of civil society and political state necessarily appears as a separation of the political citizen, the citizen of the state, from civil society, from his own, actual empirical reality; for as a state-idealist he is quite another being, a different, distinct, opposed being. . .[42]

But even this is not all. Once the individual's 'sheer blank individuality' is separated or abstracted by citizenship from his 'actual empirical reality', we are still left with the question of what this reality ultimately can consist in under modern conditions. Marx's answer is still startling in its implications. The essence of a particular personality, he insists, 'is not its beard, its blood, its abstract physical character but its social quality';[43] but what remains of this 'social quality' if its ostensible arena, civil society, is as Hegel described it? That precious little remains can be seen if we examine so basic a feature of modern civil society as the division of labour. Adam Smith's well-known characterization of the division of labour in modern society differed from earlier accounts by virtue of the fact that with Smith production was emphasized at the direct expense of any personal differences in aptitude, character or talent, rather than being seen as an expression of these differences. To see what was distinctive about Smith's approach we need only indicate a rough comparison with Plato.

Plato, in his belief that each constituent of society should perform social tasks appropriate to his nature, shows the division of labour - the basis of society - to be a development following from the manifest needs and talents of the individual. Even if the talents and aptitudes are regarded one-sidedly, any production in Plato's *Republic* (production which will be severely restricted in scope) will be for the purpose of satisfying human needs - needs which, like the talents employed to satisfy them, are specific to determinate individuals. Plato's approach differs markedly from that of Adam Smith, to whom the division of labour was a means of increasing the quantity of 'wealth' - a much more abstract, less determinate category than needs - and speeding up the accumulation of capital. Smith meant two things by the division of labour - a phrase that seems first to have been used by Mandeville. Smith's division of labour means, *first*, the splitting up of the process of manufacture in a particular way - its segmentation into minute, regularized operations, into more or less identical, homologous cells. On the basis of this segmentation Smith employs the term 'division of labour' in its *second* signification as the separation of different trades and employments throughout society as a whole. But what is basic and problematic is the original segmentation which involves not different tasks' devolving on different people, but similar tasks' devolving on people who are likely to be different in skill, aptitude, personality, etc., but who for the purposes of production can be considered equal. In other words, whatever is specific to the individual worker - his personal, human qualities, his inclinations, aptitudes, and talents - is in Smith's division of labour not catered for but disregarded and abstracted, as irrelevant to the production of wealth.

Smith believed that people's similarities outweighed their differences, and that human nature is ultimately invariant and independent of historical and social context. He has as his starting-point an equalizing, non-specific and 'abstract' conception of human nature, of human labour, and for that matter of production, which is undertaken for the sake of an abstract 'wealth'. Marx recognized that the concept of labour, abstracted from any actual manifestations it may have, presupposes social conditions in which individuals are no longer identified with their social status - in contrast with earlier justifications of occupational inequality according to which one's place within the overall division of labour was said to correspond to an intrinsic personal quality - that of being 'slavish' or 'churlish', for example, in the case of slaves or churls. Under capitalist conditions, Marx was to point out in his essay 'On the Jewish Question', individuals are for the first time considered as equal *political* beings regardless of their actual *social* status; the same kind of abstracting of individual qualities and characteristics takes place at the specifically political level as takes place at the level of manufacture. Hegel, who did not subscribe to the ideology of 'the rights of man' and its homogenized notion of citizen, strove to avoid its political expression; and, even at the level of civil society, Hegel was concerned not to minimize but certainly to circumscribe the degree of 'abstraction' of personal qualities that could conceivably take place. He insisted – as though he was afraid of some of the consequences of his own (and Smith's) analysis – that man's most personal attributes, his skill, his knowledge, his beauty, are not alienable on the market. Marx in the *Economic and Political Manuscripts* was to insist that these very attributes under capitalism *do* and *must* become alienable commodities, services that can be bought and sold on the market just like everything else. Each person is relevant only as the seller or the purchaser of some commodity or commodities – and the notion of commodity, when applied to labour, implies a reduction from what is specific to a worker or an act of labour to what these all share, and to what can be measured along a common axis (that of the production of wealth).

This reduction or restrictiveness has political as well as economic implications. Relations in society from the point of view of production are not among men with various personal qualities but among producers and consumers – men, that is to say, who are formally 'free' and 'equal' and distinguishable only in what they have to offer or want to buy. The distinction between individuals that comes to be operative is one that manifestly disregards any *real* differences one from the other they may exhibit; it is reduced to a difference in the quantity of values, the difference in the amount of wealth, owned by each of them. The process, as Hegel was all too unhappily aware, was one of wilful abstraction; and it follows from the will to produce abstract 'wealth': quantities of value, that is to say, measured in terms of money and not by the desire to directly satisfy human needs (or, in the language of Marxist economics, to produce for the satisfaction of 'use-values'). Men in civil society act as dissociated beings, as disconnected singulars, not *despite* their reduction to the common level of producer but directly *because* of this reduction. What men have in common – their status as producers and consumers – does nothing to unite them or to forge bonds among them; on the contrary, it is an expression, a social manifestation of their separation one from another. One crucial prerequisite of community is not only lacking but is actually structurally prevented from emerging. Civil society, in other words, is not only 'ethically incomplete'; it must arrest the moral development of its human components.

CHAPTER 2

Alien politics

In freeing his thought from the direct imprint of Hegel, Marx, during the period beginning with his essays of 1842–3 and ending with *The German Ideology* of 1846, elaborated a theory of what we might call 'alien politics'. Marx's theory of alienation as it emerged at this time had a specifically political aspect that too often has escaped the attention of scholars, even though some of its main features preceded and set the tone of Marx's celebrated formulation of the concept of alienation in the labour process in the *Economic and Philosophic Manuscripts* of 1844. Marx's theory of alien politics also provides the background for his recurrent attacks on the anarchists, even though it was not until *The German Ideology* that he attacked an anarchist – Max Stirner – directly. While it varied from the abstract humanism and vacuous materialism of Feuerbach, through the state-worship and *étatisme* of Bruno Bauer, to the 'speculative idealism' of Edgar Bauer, young Hegelian thought – with the conspicuous exception of that of Stirner – was not at all anarchist; Marx's target in 'On the Jewish Question' (1843), Bruno Bauer, for instance, with his obsession with the secular state, seems as remote from anarchism as Hegel had been.

It may be wondered, then, what is the relevance of Marx's early critiques of such figures as Hegel and Bauer to his disputes with the anarchists; but to pose the question in these terms is to imply its answer. Over and above the fact that these critiques provide indispensable sources for various ideas Marx entertained and developed throughout his writings about the relationship of political life to social forms in bourgeois society, and besides the fact that these very ideas in turn form part of the continuity and unity of Marx's thought taken as a whole, Marx's essays of the early 1840s reveal yet another relevant continuity of outlook. Bauer, Proudhon, Bakunin and Stirner have rather more in common than initially might be supposed. From Marx's point of view, the *étatist* and the anarchist – like blind obedience and blind destruction – have in common a certain specific form of false consciousness. What Bauer and the anarchists shared was a type of idolatry. To all of them, in their different ways, the state bore almost religious credentials. Bauer, because of what he took to be the state's incorporation of the religious, saw all the more reason to idolize it; Proudhon, thinking that the state absorbed and expressed in a strengthened form everything (and there was a great deal) that was noxious to him, saw all the more reason to short-circuit its authority from below; Stirner, and the more collectivist Bakunin, saw all the more reason for the state's root-and-branch destruction. In this way, anarchism and *étatisme* are opposite sides of the same, idolatrous coin; the anarchist, in overestimating what Proudhon called the *puissance* of the state, wildly exaggerated what would be the effects, both immediate and ultimate, of its abolition. It was this kind of fundamental misapprehension that Marx attacked in the early writings under consideration; in particular, Marx's perception of the state as (in some sense) a religious entity external to the real life of man in capitalist society – a perception of Hegelian parentage which Marx outlined most fully in 'On the Jewish Question' – had an effect of pointing his thought in a specifically anti-anarchist direction.

Marx concluded that because Hegel was committed *a priori* to the idea that the empirical order was in the last analysis rational, because he 'conceives of the contradiction in appearance as being a unity in essence, i.e., the Idea', *The Philosophy of Right* failed to recognize that 'the claim that the rational is actual is contradicted precisely by an irrational actuality'.[1] Even though the Hegelian language and the occasional (democratic) state-worship of the *Critique of Hegel's Philosophy of Right* indicate that Marx's tortured auto-emancipation from the the hold of Hegel was in 1842 less than total, Marx did in this work take the methodologically interesting step of trying to separate *The Philosophy of Right*'s philosophical form from its empirical content, to strip away Hegel's 'mystical aura' from contemporary political institutions, which only then he believed would emerge as substantive realities open to direct, critical confrontation. Marx's procedure in the *Critique* involved a certain acceptance of Hegel's claims on behalf of his own philosophy – as having been the ultimate comprehension of reality and the highest point to which philosophical speculation – as speculation – could attain. On the one hand, given a deficient, contradictory structure of reality, Hegel's philosophy was indeed what Hegel claimed it was, the optimal speculative approach; in so far as it reflected and clearly expressed an 'irrational actuality', it was positively to be valued. On the other hand, Hegelianism on this very reckoning was part of the illusion of liberty which the modern state creates, upholds and requires. The 'illusion' in question, far from being fortuitous or arbitrary, was in a sense necessary: it signifies something real without itself being real. *The German Ideology* was, first and foremost, a frontal attack on the notion that we can speak of a system of ideas as being predominant within an historical epoch without reference to the social conditions of production characterizing that epoch. To abstract ideas from their social context, to isolate them, to attribute an independent existence to them, to take them at their own word, is to lend the *idées maîtresses* of an epoch a semblance of universality, and make them ideologically acceptable; it is to affix one's seal of approval on a defective social reality, a reality that because of such validation might be given a new, and undeserved, lease of life.

Hegel, however, had recognized something that Marx was to reiterate in 'On the Jewish Question'. Civil society (*bürgerliche Gesellschaft*), the creation of which he called 'the achievement of the modern world',[2] was to Hegel very much more than a conceptual category; in *The Philosophy of Right*, it emerged as an officially recognized sphere of activity with its own characteristic institutions. These institutions were, however, unlike political institutions such as the bureaucracy (which, to Hegel, was the 'universal class' needing no institutional structure outside itself to reconcile its particular existence with the common weal, because its aims as a particular group were, he claimed, identical with the universal aims of the state). The institutions of civil society – the corporations (*Stände*) and private property – unlike the bureaucracy, remained incomplete, in need of anterior institutional expression. The corporations – guilds, trade associations, professional and municipal organizations – were supposed to champion the multifarious interests of civil society against and towards the state, and to channel the egoism of the individual members of the group in question into co-operative endeavours, articulating their common aims in a way that would ensure their consideration in the process of legislative deliberation. Primogeniture, for its part, was supposed to provide an element of stability from generation to generation, shielding property from market fluctuations and arbitrary interference and encouraging a political independence for the property holder that allowed for the development of a disinterested political spirit. The Assembly of Estates was portrayed as a complex series of mediations synthesizing the several particularisms of civil society with the universality of the state, without antagonizing the Executive (the Crown) to which it remained complementary.

Marx, while he shared Hegel's perception of the problem of the separation of civil and political life, found much to criticize in the institutional mechanisms that Hegel believed had solved it. Hegel's institutional solutions represented, in effect, a wholly uncritical acceptance – or so Marx believed – of the estrangement of state and society in the ideological guise of its resolution. Marx's rejection of Hegel's categories was systematic: however unconnected they may seem at first glance, Marx's own agencies of emancipation, as they did emerge, were directly related to the Hegelian categories which they were designed to supplant. For the bureaucracy as the 'universal class' (*allgemeine Stand*) Marx (seemingly recognizing that in Hegel's political thought

the bureaucrat was in a real sense the only true citizen) was to some
extent to substitute the proletariat; for primogeniture and the corporations, he substituted the abolition of private property relations; for
war, Marx was to substitute class war; and in place of the Assembly
of Estates, Marx initially – and problematically – substituted universal
suffrage, which in the *Critique* and in his earliest journalism Marx
described as the medium *par excellence* for the abolition of the duality
between state and civil society, for the interesting reason that 'in true
democracy the political state disappears'[3] ('der politische Staat un-
tergeht'). Marx despairingly wrote to Arnold Ruge in 1843 that Prussia
was a despotism in which the monarch, ruling by caprice in a state
where men were despised and dehumanized, was the only 'political
person', properly so-called, and that, to combat this, a clearer critical
understanding of the operation of economic forces in society would
be necessary. Also,

> freedom, the feeling of man's dignity, will have to be reawakened
> . . . Only this feeling, which disappeared from the world with the
> Greeks and with Christianity vanished into the blue mists of heaven,
> can again transform society into a community [Gemeinwesen]
> of men to achieve their highest purpose, a democratic state.[4]

Although Marx was quick to drop his belief – which is also expressed
in the *Critique* – that men's highest purpose was a democratic state,
his corresponding ideal of *Gemeinwesen*, as embodying freedom, was
to play an important part throughout his thought.

Hegel had believed the Assembly of Estates could signify the abolition
of the duality of political state and civil society, yet Marx noted that
Hegel's own texts betrayed the Assembly's real character as the formal
illusion of popular participation in political affairs, affairs which in
fact were monopolized by bureaucratic officialdom. Hegel's machinery
of government served to indicate the real character of that government.
The 'political sentiment' of the legislative part of the Assembly, to give
one prominent example, was to be guaranteed, Marx noted with some
malicious glee, by independent, inherited land property. But, Marx
asked, how could entailed landed property form a principle of unity
synthesizing political and social life when it is itself nothing more than
'property whose social nerves have been severed, the epitome of private
rights freed from all political, ethical and social bonds'?[5]

The relationship of private property to the state, which as we have
seen had been a central concern of *The Philosophy of Right*, was
likewise a central concern of Marx. Discussing primogeniture, Marx
said (somewhat obscurely) that

> it appears [in Hegel's system] that private property is the

> relationship to the function of the state which is such that
> the existence of the state is something inhering in, or is an
> accident of direct private property. . . Instead of making private
> property a civil quality, Hegel makes political existence and
> sentiment a quality of private property.[6]

Worse still was the way he had done so. Hegel, paradoxically, had defended primogeniture on the grounds of the political disinterestedness it afforded the fortunate few, *and* had portrayed property as something subservient to and expressive of the will of its owner. This was the kind of contradiction on which Marx loved to pounce. And pounce he did. The essence of property, as Hegel had discussed it, was its alienability by the will of its owner; but, asked Marx, what was primogeniture if not property's becoming inalienable (i.e. non-property, on Hegel's definition) and subject, with the will of its so-called owner as predicate? The rule of property, as Marx repeatedly was to emphasize, means the predication of man. As primogenital property passes undivided from first-born to first-born, *it* becomes 'substance', its owner 'accident', and what is owned is the will of the supposed owner. Man does not inherit property, but property man. The original Hegelian relationship between the creative subject possessed of will and the objectification of his will is reversed. On the political level, this means that instead of the ownership of property's giving man the freedom to practice politics disinterestedly (which had been Hegel's starting-point), it is inanimate property that is *in principle* given the freedom to do with man what it will, without any political 'interference'.

The ultimate importance of Marx's far-reaching attack on Hegel's political defence of private property is, of course, that it was the prototype of his theory of alienation in the labour-process, and of the fetishism of commodities; when property is given the freedom to act, men are reduced to the status of mere objects. Men become the attributes of property – even though property is by definition the socially crystallized outcome of their own purposive creative activity. Reification, a concept which tolls like a minute bell through Marx's writings, was sounded in advance, as it were, in the *Critique*, where Marx first came to recognize that far from being the realization or objectification of human personality – which had been Hegel's original justification – private property actually negated human personality. Small wonder, then, that in *The Manifesto of the Communist Party* (1848) Marx was to sum up the communists' programme in the single phrase: abolition of private property; small wonder that in 'On the Jewish Question' (1843) and the *Economic and Philosophic Manuscripts* (1844) Marx specifically linked the possibility of human emancipation with the abolition of private property; and small wonder that Marx's initial, guarded praise of Proudhon in *The Holy Family* (1845) gave way to the hostility, with all stops out, expressed in *The Poverty of Philosophy* (1847).

Marx's *Critique*, having raised the question of the relationship of private property, civil society and the state, also attacked Hegel's theory of bureaucracy and discussed the central problem of the hiatus of civil and political life. The *Critique* also perceived all these issues in their connectedness. They all involve, at a fundamentally important level, the Rousseauian perception of the dualism of *homme privé* and *citoyen* together with the Rousseauian predicament: how can man be restored to a unified condition? One of the first works Marx examined and excerpted at Kreuznach, as he was writing the *Critique*, was Rousseau's *The Social Contract*, but in 'On the Jewish Question', the following year (1843), Marx was to become severely critical of the solution Rousseau had offered to this predicament. In 'On the Jewish Question' Marx insisted that man was no longer a generic social being; that men's powers were no longer apprehended as social powers; that the political existence of man, the realm of his social, collective and moral being, was alienated in relation to the demands of his concrete, immediate existence; and that there was, in human terms, an immense loss involved in the historical process that had brought about all these changes. Such sentiments have an obvious Rousseauian ring to them; but Rousseau, unlike Marx, had considered the isolated, autarchic existence of men to be 'natural', and as inhering in spontaneous qualities of human nature. To Marx such isolation was, by contrast, eminently social; and in indicating, by means of a (doctored) quotation from *The Social Contract*, that the isolation of individual members of civil society was an historical phenomenon, one which characterized a specific, transitory and oppressive phase of human history, Marx in effect turned Rousseau's own telling criticism of Hobbes against Rousseau himself. Rousseau had observed that Hobbes had ascribed to man in the state of nature qualities that could have been acquired only in society. Marx, in 'On the Jewish Question', says the same of Rousseau himself. Man's isolation from man takes place, said Marx, in a particular, contemporary setting, bourgeois society, yet Rousseau read it back into man's natural, primordial state. Worse yet, Rousseau's remedy had been purely political; Marx claimed that Rousseau had perceived only 'the abstraction of the political man'[7] instead of the real, individual man.

'In the real community', Marx was to write in *The German Ideology* (1846), 'individuals obtain their freedom in and through their association';[8] and while both Rousseau and Hegel in their very different ways would scarcely have dissented from such a statement, Marx, for his part, came to regard their views of freedom and association as anachronistic and retrospective. Hegel gave his backward glance a specific focus, as Marx recognized.

The peak of Hegelian identity, as he himself admits, was the Middle Ages. There, the classes of civil society in general and the Estates, or classes given political significance, were identical. The spirit of the Middle Ages can be expressed thus: the classes of civil society and the political classes were identical because the organic principle of civil society was the principle of the state. . . . The political state in distinction from civil society was nothing but the representation of nationality.[9]

The *Critique* went on to indicate the inappropriateness of medieval 'solutions' (such as the corporations and the Assembly of Estates in *The Philosophy of Right*) to what Hegel knew was a supremely modern problem, 'the separation of civil society and the political state as two actually different spheres, firmly opposed to each other'.[10] Marx was concerned to separate himself from those who advocated some kind of return to the Middle Ages, which he called 'the animal history of mankind',[11] and those who, like some French Revolutionary leaders, would appeal to classical models. These latter, said Marx, succeeded in being doubly misleading because 'with the Greeks, civil society was a slave to political society'[12] whereas in modern, bourgeois society the opposite is the case. Following Hegel, who had seen the classical Greek era as an 'undifferentiated substantiality', Marx characterized the polis as having been a political form where society is subsumed beneath the state. As Hegel himself had indicated, no specifically and exclusively political sphere existed apart from the daily conduct of life in the polis. Public life in this way was the 'real content' of individual life, and the person who had no political status was simply a slave, an *Unmensch*. 'In Greece', wrote Marx, 'the *res publica* was the real private concern, the real content of the citizen. . .and the private man was slave, i.e., the political state as political was the true and sole content of the citizen's life and will.'[13]

The Middle Ages offered a quite different spectacle. Here the 'private sphere' came to acquire political status. 'Property, commerce, society, man (i.e., private man, the serf) were all *political*: the material content of the state was fixed by reason of its own form; every private sphere had a political character or was a political sphere.'[14] Property was paramount in feudal society (and often primogeniture was its mode of transmission), to be sure, but it was so solely because its distribution was above all a political arrangement. Although the medieval period thus produced an integrated way of life in which 'the life of the people' was congruent with 'the life of the state', this was the case only because feudal man was unfree.

The old civil society [in the Middle Ages] had a directly political character; that is, the elements of civil life such as

property, the family and types of occupation had been raised, in
the form of lordship, caste, and guilds, to being elements of
political life.

If, however, in the Middle Ages 'man was the actual principle of the
state, he was an unfree man'; the medieval world to whose institutions
The Philosophy of Right had harked back was the 'democracy of
unfreedom, accomplished alienation',[15] and the feudal past had no
model to offer the future. What 'On the Jewish Question' called 'political
emancipation' (meaning, roughly, 'bourgeois revolution')

> released the political spirit, which had been broken, fragmented and
> lost, as it were, in the various culs-de-sac of feudal society. It
> gathered up this scattered spirit, liberated it from its entanglement
> with civil life, and turned it into the sphere of the community, the
> general concern of the people independent of these particular
> elements of civil life. A particular activity and situation in life
> sank into a merely individual significance, no longer forming the
> general relation to the individual as a whole.[16]

Whatever the loss might be in the process, the sequence is irreversible;

> all emancipation is restoration of the human world and the relation-
> ships of men themselves [and] political emancipation is a reduction
> of man to a member of civil society, to an egoistic independent
> individual on the one hand and to a citizen on the other.[17]

Marx insisted against those who would turn the clock back that 'the
abstraction of the state as such belongs to modern times because the
abstraction of private life belongs only to modern times'. Not only is
it true that, consequently, 'the abstract, reflected opposition [between
civil and political life] belongs only to modern times'; it also follows that

> [what] distinguishes the modern state from these states in which
> a substantial unity between people and state obtained [i.e. medieval
> and classical models] is not that the various moments of the
> constitution are formed into particular actuality, as Hegel would
> have it, but rather that the constitution itself has been formed into
> an actuality alongside the real life of the people [in civil society].[18]

Marx went on to claim that Hegel's defence of the modern state, on
the grounds that it had transcended the social and historical forces that
had brought it into being, was unwarranted and specious. Hegel presented
the state as the reconciliation of the very division in society – and of
every individual in society – of which the modern state was but a term.

The very emergence of the modern state, Marx insisted, presupposed the radical separation of politics from society for the first time in history. Not only do particular, oppressive and original interests parading under the banner of 'the general good' and the achieved universal (such as bureaucracy as celebrated by Hegel) reinforce the actual rule of private property and material process over human subjects and relationships, but the very institutional arrangements Hegel had insisted had abolished the new-found separation of the state from society were in fact themselves responsible for the maintenance of this unprecedented separation. The modern state, as Hegel had seen it, did not and could not liberate men from the disastrous effects of predatory social agencies (bureaucracy, private property, the division of labour, religion, money); the state's own inaction actually permitted them to flourish freely.

The state, far from subsuming the force of private property and exchange within itself, as Hegel had claimed, was in Marx's view not even insulated against the claims and encroachments of property and exchange - not to mention those of the bureaucracy (which Marx discussed in the *Critique*), those of religion (which Marx discussed in 'On the Jewish Question'), those of money (which Marx discussed in the 1844 *Manuscripts*) and those of the division of labour (which he discussed in the first part of *The German Ideology*). Moreover, even before he wrote *The German Ideology* and *The Manifesto of the Communist Party*, Marx had come to believe that the modern state, whatever its constitutional form, will in some way inevitably reflect the prevailing pattern of social determinations and relations; this is the least that is implied by his celebrated formulation of the state as the handmaiden, or surrogate, of the bourgeoisie. But in order to understand what this designation, and others like it, mean and do not mean, we need to turn for background from Marx's *Critique* to an even more important source for the emergence of his theory of alien politics, the essay 'On the Jewish Question', written in 1843 against Bruno Bauer.

Marx against Bauer: 'political emancipation'

Bruno Bauer, who had been a protégé of Hegel's, and an intellectual mentor to Marx (having supervised his doctoral dissertation in 1841), is best known as a radical critic of religion. Despite his corresponding championing of the claims of the secular state, his publication of religious views unpalatable to the Prussian government - which was anything but secular - lost him his professorial post at Bonn (thereby indirectly precluding an academic career for Marx). However, Bauer's pamphlet, 'The Jewish Question' (1843), which regarded the Jews much as Voltaire had regarded them - as reactionary - and which opposed the movement for their emancipation for this very reason, antagonized Marx, whose father had had to renounce his religion to keep his job, and who supported the granting of full civil rights to the Jews, as a measure that would be in accordance with the premises of bourgeois society and, as such, a necessary prerequisite of full, human emancipation. Marx was to express in *The Holy Family* (1845) as well as in 'On the Jewish Question' the belief that the degree of modernity achieved by a modern state-form could be measured by the political rights which the Jews living in it enjoyed. In his general advocacy of Jewish emancipation Marx was following Hegel, whose record in this respect, unlike Bauer's, was quite above reproach.

Bauer's pamphlet, 'The Jewish Question', had opposed the political emancipation of the Jews in Prussia and the Rhineland on the grounds that since their claim for equal treatment and participation could be granted only on the basis of a secular conception of society, the Jews would have to renounce their religion before being granted political rights. 'He requires', said Marx,

> on the one hand that the Jew renounce his Judaism and, in a general manner that man renounce religion in order to be emancipated civically. On the other hand, as a logical consequence, he considers that the 'political' suppression of religion is equivalent to the suppression of all religion. The state that presupposes religion is not yet a true and real state.[19]

Whereas Bauer wished to use the state to combat religious alienation, Marx considered that the secularization of the state – even if this were complete, as it manifestly was not in Prussia – would be quite insufficient either to loosen the hold of religious ideas or to free men from their real servitude. Marx's 'On the Jewish Question' indicated, along the lines laid down in the *Critique*, that the modern state – the state that Bauer, in Hegelian fashion, had presented as *the* solution to religious 'alienation' – was itself suffused with religious alienation. 'Since the existence of religion implies a defect', wrote Marx in a deceptively Feuerbachian manner, 'the source of this defect must be sought in the nature of the state itself. We no longer take religion to be the basis but only the manifestation of secular deficiencies.'[20] The split between the citizen and the adherent of a religion to which Bauer had drawn attention is in this way part of a more fundamental schism. 'The contradiction in which the adherent of a particular religion finds himself in relation to his citizenship is but one aspect of the universal secular contradiction between political state and civil society.' If religion, no longer officially sanctioned or promulgated by the modern state, is displaced so that it becomes a purely individual concern, this does not mean that the hold of religion on men is in any way loosened. Political emancipation from religion (in other words, the emergence of a secular state) leaves religion in existence; 'the emancipation of the state from religion is not the emancipation of actual man from religion'.[21]

In the same way, the abolition of property qualifications for the franchise, far from abolishing property, presupposes the continued importance of property and of distinctions among men based upon the amount of property held. 'Political emancipation', then, frees property from political restraint without freeing men from property itself. In its insistence that the amount of property, or the type of property, that is held by any particular person is politically irrelevant, property had become responsible to nothing outside itself, and its newly oppressive – because unrestrained – nature was, for the first time, clearly exposed and keenly experienced by those who in their everyday lives bore the brunt of its free play. Religiosity, like property, is consummated, not abolished, by the transition from medieval-theocratic to modern state-forms (a process which in Germany was far from complete, as Marx fully recognized). A theocratic state-form, using religion for its own purposes, obscures the human bases of religiosity. The modern state not professing any particular religious creed, on the other hand, is not the abolition but the realization of religion, which is displaced from the orbit of government to that of everyday life. This means that the emancipation of the state from religion, like its emancipation from property, will solve nothing for man: religion 'only begins to exist in its true scope when the state declares it to be non-political and thus leaves it to itself'.[22]

With the collapse of feudalism, civil society and the state become discontinuous in an unprecedented and radical way. Civil society and property relations become wholly emancipated from all political restraint or regulation for the first time in history. Private life, or indeed life in society, becomes independent of any consideration of the common good; all political limitations on economic activity give way, and the market becomes 'self-regulating'. Emancipation from feudal and communal restrictions (usury, guild regulations, sumptuary laws, censorship by ecclesiastical *fiat*) formally free civil society from state control. The removal of political limitations upon economic activity is, accordingly, decisive; it was signified most dramatically by (although it was not limited to) the French Revolution. The Declaration of the Rights of Man and the Citizen of 1789, which marked the emancipation of civil society from the purview of the state, is in this way doubly important. Just as the state became ideologically universal, out of the control of the aristocracy and the priesthood, proclamations of 'The Rights of Man' recognized the citizenship of the individual as such, be he rich or poor, Jew or Christian. Citizenship no longer depended upon birth, rank, status or occupation; all such attributes were to be not political qualifications or disqualifications, but were instead relegated to the level of purely individual concerns. This fundamental shift, Marx continued, had political and social implications which, although crucial, might not initially be apparent.

Marx believed that the emergence of bourgeois society had bifurcated men's lives in a fundamentally new way. Once bourgeois society had established itself, 'private' and 'public' were no longer in any sense contiguous realms, as they had been in the past. In the Middle Ages, for example, the dominant persons in society were *ipso facto* politically dominant also; the privileges of the feudal landowning aristocracy, for instance, linked the form of the state with the prevailing structure of society – which thus had had a 'directly political character' (albeit an unfree political character). Political emancipation, by contrast, detached man's political significance from his private condition. Citizenship and private life became mutually exclusive spheres of activity for the first time. A man was now a capitalist or worker *and* a citizen; vocation and political status were no longer linked organically. Instead, they coexisted uneasily alongside each other. Man, while he formally belonged to the state (as its citizen), actively participated only in civil society.

Not only did these two newly counterposed areas not overlap; their confrontation was expressed within each individual as a rigid distinction between his exclusive *roles*. The schism between state and society – a schism which in Hegelian terms opposed man's alienated universal essence to his everyday (*alltäglich*) activity – constantly reproduced itself in microcosm within each individual, in a distilled, concentrated form. Marx was to extend this particular aspect of 'political emancipation' in *The German Ideology*.

> In the course of historical evolution, and precisely through the inevitable fact that within the division of labour social relations take on an independent existence, there appears a division within the life of each individual, in so far as it is personal and in so far as it is determined by some branch of labour and the conditions pertaining to it. (We do not mean. . . that, for example, the rentier, the capitalist etc. cease to be persons; but their personality is conditioned and determined by quite definite class relationships and the division appears only in their opposition to another class, and, for themselves, only when they go bankrupt). In the estate, this is as yet concealed; for instance a nobleman always remains a nobleman, a commoner always a commoner, apart from his other relationships, a quality inseparable from their individuality. The division between the personal and the class individual, the accidental nature of the conditions of life for the individual, appears only with the emergence of the class, which is itself a product of the bourgeoisie.[23]

In 'On the Jewish Question' Marx indicated that the newly 'privatized' man, denied participation in the communal and universal, sought solace in a postulated realm of universality, a realm separate from the limited sphere of his mundane, finite life. This realm, though, was not religious, as Hegel and Feuerbach had thought; it was more nearly political.

The picture of political emancipation Marx drew in 'On the Jewish Question' nevertheless follows Hegel closely. Hegel, as we have seen, recognized and delineated the division of *homme* from *citoyen*, the self-validating distinction between the public role of the citizen and the private role of the person engaged in the mundane (and now politically untouchable) realm of needs, work and economic relations. Hegel had gone on to indicate that relations among men producing for the sake of their needs in an atomistic, competitive manner are 'ethically incomplete' and need for their substantiation that complement of rationality which only the state could provide. *The Philosophy of Right* had stressed that although man lives simultaneously in both realms, the satisfaction he derives from activity in the state is qualitatively different from that he derives from the pursuit of self-interested concerns in civil society; and it was against this Hegelian perception that Marx proceeded to indicate that 'political emancipation' was bound to have the effect of displacing and negating the very satisfactions that Hegel had valued most highly. In particular, what Hegel had put forward as man's need for the universal, or general (*das Allgemeine*), corresponding to the communal side of human nature, or to what Marx, in the 1844 *Manuscripts*, was to call 'species-being' (*Gattungswesen*), was bound to remain unsatisfied. Once civil society was emancipated, freed from political restraint, property relations were enabled to penetrate every crevice of the supposedly transcendent political realm.

Moreover, Hegel had portrayed the state as being both immanent and external to society, whereas to Marx only something ideal could stand above and beyond society in this way. This can only mean, as Marx deftly indicated in 'On the Jewish Question', that the state and the life of the citizen had become unreal, even religious, and that the state is thus eminently susceptible to the type of criticism Feuerbach (and Hegel) had levelled against religion. If the state was a realm of religious values in this way, Bauer's secularism was simply begging the question.

By its nature the perfected political state is man's species-life in opposition to his material life. All the presuppositions of this egoistic life remain in civil society outside the state but as qualities of civil society. Where the political state has achieved its full development man leads a double life, a heavenly and an earthly life, not only in thought or consciousness but also in reality. In the political community he regards himself as a communal being; but in civil society he is active as a private individual, treats other men as means, reduces himself to a means and becomes the plaything of alien powers. The political state is as spiritual in relation to civil society as heaven is in relation to earth . . . In the state where he counts as a species-being, he is the imaginary member of an imaginary universality, divested of his real individual life and endowed with an unreal universality.[24]

This 'abstract universality', however, is necessary. Despite the remoteness of political life from ordinary, profane individual pursuits – over which the state has relinquished control – universality and communality remain part of man's life in 'Feuerbachian' fashion if their attainment is impossible in reality. What men lack in fact they attain in fancy. If meaningful political participation is withheld or denied, man will participate abstractly, in the fantasy world of citizenship; the state itself becomes a kind of religious fetish. The division of man's social nature into separate, exclusive spheres of privacy and universality must mean that man's very 'universality' is fictitious. Worse still, the state is presented as 'universal' at the very historical moment when the relations of production begin to make the state, whatever its constitutional form, the surrogate of the bourgeoisie.

Marx goes on to stress the connection between the state's abstract, idolatrous universality and economic *laissez faire*. Political emancipation replaced the impact of personal power with the impersonal arbitrariness, the repressive anonymity, of the 'hidden hand'. The illusion of liberty which the modern state creates and sustains is necessary because the state does not and cannot liberate men from the disastrous effect of the predatory social agencies (private property and religion) it permits to flourish freely. The ideological expression and celebration of this state of affairs was none other than the doctrine of the 'Rights of Man' enunciated by the American and French Revolutions.

None of the supposed rights of man go beyond the egoistic man, man as he is, man as a member of civil society; that is, as an individual separated from the community, withdrawn into himself, wholly occupied with his private interest and acting in accordance with his private caprice. Man is far from being considered, in the rights of man, as a species-being; on the contrary, species-life itself, society, appears as a system which is external to the individual and as a limitation of his original independence. The only bond between men is natural necessity, need and private interest, the preservation of their property and their egoistic persons. . . The political liberators reduce the political community, to a mere means for preserving these so-called rights of man . . . The citizen is declared to be the servant of the egoistic man . . . The sphere in which man functions as a species-being is degraded to a level below the sphere where he functions as a political being . . . it is man as a bourgeois and not man as a citizen who is considered the true and authentic man.[25]

The 'rights of man' refer to men as though they were self-sufficient, self-motivated atoms closed to one another and thus lead by extension to a social system close to the Hobbesian *bellum omnium contra omnes*. 'This', says Marx,

is the liberty of man viewed as an isolated monad, withdrawn into himself. . . [which is] not based on the association of man with man but rather on the separation of man from man. . . The practical application of the right of liberty is the right of private property . . . it lets every man find in every other man not the reality but the limitation of his own freedom.[26]

In portraying the ideology and the reality of modern civil society as 'atomistic', Marx was not claiming that men were in fact reduced to the status of atoms, but that men's behaviour in certain respects was atomistic; he believed that to derive the former from the latter proposition would be to fall prey to the illusion of theorists such as Hobbes. Civil society was not, in Marx's view, a simple aggregate of human atoms unrelated to one another, as some British economists and utilitarians imagined, but a state of mutual dependence of all on all.

It is natural necessity, essential human properties, however alienated they may seem to be, and interest that hold together the members of civil society; civil, not political, life is their real tie. It is therefore not the state that holds together the atoms of civil society but the fact that they are atoms only in imagination, in the heaven of their fancy, but in reality beings tremendously different from atoms, in other words, not divine egoists, but egoistic human beings. Only political superstition today imagines that social life must be held together by the state whereas in reality the state is held together by civil life.[27]

'On the Jewish Question' was much more than a polemical *Streitschrift*, a mere reply to the essay by Bruno Bauer which had provoked and occasioned it; Marx extended the terms of the debate by incorporating into what is ostensibly an attack on Bauer a host of references not so much to Bauer as to Feuerbach, Hegel and others. As we have seen, Hegel, as well as Feuerbach, should be credited with having linked religion with human deprivation, with having refined the Enlightenment's view of religion as an agency that compensated men's perception of a world out of joint. Marx goes well beyond this kind of designation, however, in indicating that private, internalized religiosity signified a much more radical alienation than did official, institutionalized religion. Indeed, Marx's terrain was by now quite different from that of Feuerbach. He conspicuously does not rest content, as Feuerbach had, with dramatically uncovering and 'solving' deficiency as though it were merely a hidden secret. Instead, Marx offers an historical explanation based on an analysis of man's non-religious life; in particular, he emphasizes the part played there by property relations. Feuerbach's notion of alienation, when extended in this way from religion and contemplation to politics and society, is no longer Feuerbachian. Marx, in other words, shifted the grounds of alienation, making it something that could be not only outlined but *solved*, practically and socially.

> Only when the actual individual man takes back into himself the abstract citizen and in his everyday life, his individual work, and his individual relationships has become a species-being, only when he has recognized and organized his own powers as social powers so that social force is no longer separated from him as political force – only then is human emancipation complete.[28]

If citizenship is a religious phenomenon, the fantasy of universality, the reintegration of political powers to which Marx refers can be seen in one sense as the realization of the fantasy of citizenship, as a *genuine* secularization of the spiritual world. Yet 'On the Jewish Question' does not merely substitute some populist 'direct democracy' for a sham 'representative democracy'. Marx never believed that the state could be the agency or the instrument of its own reintegration. The state is an institutional expression of human alienation, and such alienation by its very nature cannot be overcome within the sphere of alienation. What this means is that the state (whatever its constitutional form), far from being insulated against the claims of property and exchange, will in some way reflect or express the prevailing pattern of property relations. What follows is that alienation can be overcome only by an agency which does *not* reflect property relations in this way. Civil society's animating principle, its *esprit général*, is private property; the proletariat, which is defined and given meaning by its propertylessness, might appear irrelevant to it; but, in fact, far from being marginal to civil society, as Max Stirner for example thought it was, the proletariat was its very basis. Without this basis bourgeois society could not – and Marx hastened to add, would not – persist. To invoke the spectre of Stirner is to be reminded that the overthrow of civil society does not correspond to the advent of anything resembling an anarchist utopia. What mattered to Marx is something very different – the re-integration of communal *control*, once 'political' has led to 'human' emancipation, into the realm of a society that is at present regulated only by the impersonal forces of the market. With 'political emanci-pation' there seems to be no *excess* of political rule at all. The forces dominating civil society are not political or communal forces, but the impersonal forces of private property and the division of labour. Since the consequences of the unimpeded domination of these mechanisms are inhuman and oppressive, what is required is some extension of rational, human control over them. This is a very different perception of the problem from the anarchists' complaints about the pervasiveness and deep-rootedness of the power of the state. Marx attributes to the state no real *autonomous* power at all, and advocates not more control *per se*, but more control of a certain type. Society stands in need of non-alien authority; without such an authority, it *can* operate as a system, or even as a self-regulating mechanism, but it can do so only in a destructive (and self-destructive) way.

The 'politically emancipated' state has abdicated control over the market. Society is left to its own devices; it operates as a system (and as such it is susceptible to analysis) but only to the extent that elements within civil society that are permitted to proceed blithely and destruc-tively, in their own manner, add up to a system. The elements in question are non-human and the results of their unrestrained operation – however 'systematic' they may be – are inhuman. If, in such circum-stances, citizenship is a fantasy, it is a fantasy that can and must be made real. That society has undergone a certain depoliticization says nothing, however, about the *kind* of reintegration of politics into society that Marx is advocating. There is no historical precedent for it, and Marx nowhere suggests that the state itself has the capacity to bring it about. Nevertheless, 'freedom', as Marx was some years later to put it,

> consists in converting the state from an organ superimposed upon
> society into one completely subordinated to it . . . instead of
> treating existing society (and this holds good for any future one)
> as the basis of the existing state (or of the future state in the case
> of future society) it [the German Workers' Party] treats the state
> rather as an independent entity . . .[29]

This statement, too, is nothing like any anarchist perspective: but it is remarkably akin to an earlier essay by the same writer, to 'On the Jewish Question' of 1843.

This similarity, spanning as it does some three decades of Marx's career, should not surprise us; *The Critique of the Gotha Programme* was to contain many direct echoes of Marx's attack on the *étatisme* of Bruno Bauer thirty-two years earlier. Both Bauer and the Lassalleans who helped draw up and clearly influenced the Gotha Programme indulged in their respective ways in the 'idolatrous' belief that the state could be dealt with in and of itself 'as an independent entity possessed of its own intellectual, ethical and libertarian bases'.[30] Marx never wavered in his contrary view that the state was not formative or determinant in this way, but instrumental and derivative. Statists like Bauer and Lassalle are guilty of arguing from the state to society – as though the state were capable of autonomously formulating the conditions of its own existence – as were anarchists like Proudhon in their facile and illegitimate overestimation of the primacy and effects of the removal of the state.

Marx was to castigate the Gotha Programme of 1875 because in it Lassalle's *epigoni* had made a first-order mistake similar to that of Bauer in 1843 in confusing political with human emancipation. Their Programme's demands, Marx insisted, were appropriate only to a democratic republic, which remained a distant prospect as far as their own 'present-day national state', the Prusso-German Empire, was concerned. From a confusion of political emancipation (the elusive 'free state' of the Lassalleans – or the supposedly secular state of Bauer) and human emancipation only defective theoretical formulations and meaningless demands could emerge. From such confusion the German Workers' Party could only fall prey to the illusion that accompanied political emancipation of the primacy and autonomy of the state, and fail to recognize that the Lassalleans' catch-all category, the 'present-day national state', was no more than an abstraction. The result in 1875 was the Party's programme: confusion worse confounded.

> . . . its political demands contain nothing beyond the old democratic litany familiar to all: universal suffrage, direct legislation, popular rights . . . They are demands which, in so far as they are not exaggerated in fantastic presentation, have already been realized. Only the state to which they belong does not lie within the borders of the German Empire but in Switzerland, the United States, etc. This sort of 'state of the future' is a present-day state, although existing outside the borders of the German Empire.[31]

Of the Programme's understanding of the relationship of democracy to socialism, Marx went on to say, archly, that

> even vulgar democracy, which sees the millennium in the democratic republic, and has no suspicion that it is precisely in this last form of state of bourgeois society that the class

struggle has to be fought out to a conclusion – even it towers
mountains above this kind of democratism [in the Programme]
which keeps within the limits of what is permitted by the police
and not permitted by logic.[32]

Marx's taunts, that the Lassalleans' lack of perspective on certain
elementary political realities would cause a supine attitude even towards
political reaction, did not lack for verification; and they apply also to a
certain kind of anarchist thinking which overvalues or is obsessed with
political power, as we shall soon see in discussing Proudhon.

Marx in *The Critique of the Gotha Programme*, as in 'On the Jewish
Question', presented what he had called in the earlier work 'political
emancipation' not as a solution to but as an index of men's degradation
in the face of impersonal market forces. Upon their 'political emancipation' individuals (whatever their real condition might be) were for
the first time officially and bureaucratically considered equal political
beings, or citizens; this formal consideration was supposed to pertain
whatever their social status or occupational category. The *Economic
and Philosophic Manuscripts* of 1844 specified (against Hegel) that in
bourgeois society men's most personal attributes – their skill, knowledge,
creative potential or even physical beauty – become alienable attributes
that can now be bought and sold on the market. It is of the utmost
importance for us to recognize, at this juncture, that these specifications
are linked. Each stresses that under capitalist conditions social relations
among individuals endowed with personal qualities and attributes
giving meaning to their lives had become impossible. Men, according to
the precepts of 'political emancipation' and Marxist economics alike,
are formally and in principle free and equal; but they are so only in an
inhumanly restricted sense. They are free at the level of bourgeois
citizenship and bureaucratic consideration; they are equal in the additional sense of being distinguishable only in what they buy or have to
sell. It is at this point in the argument that 'On the Jewish Question'
and the *Economic and Philosophic Manuscripts* come together; the
dehumanization of the distinctions among individuals the latter describes is the obverse and complement of the political and bureaucratic
homogenization of individuals required and defined by the former's
central concept of 'political emancipation'. The two are opposite sides
of the same coin. Without understanding alien politics, we fail to
understand alienation.

To recapitulate the argument of 'On the Jewish Question' is at this
point to better appreciate its resonance throughout Marx's later thought.
With the atomization of feudal, corporate society into *bürgerliche
Gesellschaft*, the behaviour of individuals in their everyday life fails to
transcend their self-defined, immediate goals. Because of this failure,
general regulative and ideological measures have to be imposed from

without. The manner of their imposition is as unprecedented as it is alien. The bourgeois state is grafted on to a realm of private self-interested activities, which nevertheless operate in such a way that the superimposition of the state does nothing to alleviate men's sub-jection to the conditions and relations of production. In so far as any real authority now exists, it is the impersonal authority of the market; the human control capitalism increasingly demands and denies is correspondingly projected upwards and outwards, on to the alien, fantastic level of the bourgeois state.

Yet this development is no mere ruse. Far from straightforwardly denying it, political emancipation presages human emancipation, blazes its trail, points the way forward – and parodies it in advance. Citizenship in the alien state is a cruel joke upon man, one which mocks the universality, the *Gemeinwesen*, the extension of real, social control he desperately and increasingly needs. It does so by presenting it to him in an alien, abstract form. Capitalism, which had had the positive and laudable effect of putting the whole world at the disposal of man and having 'created a world after its own image',[33] by the same token put men at the disposal of the material process of the impersonal market mechanism. Yet at the same time capitalism removed many of the obstacles to the emergence of man as he could be, man as the many-sided social individual; and it was precisely because capitalism had removed these obstacles that citizenship could so much as *appear* as a universal category. Capitalism, Marx believed, had more than one cutting edge; on the one hand its emergence and operation signalled 'real, human emancipation', towards which it was tending, and which was presaged and in a way promised, on the political level as citizen-ship, and on the economic level by capitalism's own expansionist, universalizing tendencies. On the other hand, it made man 'the play-thing of alien powers', powers which could not but stifle the 'universal' side of human nature that Marx and Hegel held so dear. Capitalism, in short, creates the need as it denies the need for emancipation; it plays with mankind, apparently granting as it substantively withholds signifi-cant, human emancipation. While it supplies preconditions for the emergence of man as man potentially could be, it can furnish these only in an alien (and tantalizing) form – that of the bourgeois state.

The continuity between one of Marx's earliest writings on the state, 'On the Jewish Question' (1843), and one of his last, *The Critique of the Gotha Programme* (1875), suggests that all of Marx's investigations of the modern state were predicated upon, and informed by, the theory of alien politics Marx developed in a series of writings leading up to *The German Ideology*. This common source, while it does not clear up all the ambiguities encountered throughout Marx's utterances, does help to put them into perspective. One of the most frequent objections to Marx's theory of the state has been that Marx did not comprehend the independent power of political institutions; yet we find that not only do Marx's more detailed essays address this very problem, and attempt to assess the degree of independence shown by political institutions, but also that they do so in a manner that unavoidably recalls the analysis found in 'On the Jewish Question'.

To see this is to begin to be able to deal with another frequently voiced objection to Marx's theory of the state. Most accounts emphasize its unfinished character. There are gaps in Marx's arguments which have bequeathed an ambiguous legacy; most notably, the third volume of *Capital* breaks off at the very point where Marx, according to his own admission, was about to embark upon an elaboration of the theory of the state and of class he had sketched out elsewhere. These sketches, which contain their fair share of cryptic, gnomic pronouncements – and of outright propaganda – are not, however, made up simply of isolated, fragmentary utterances. Marx wrote a great deal throughout his career about the various structures of the bourgeois state, about what distinguished modern bourgeois state-forms from their feudal forerunners, about the dangers of authoritarianism, and about the necessity for revolutionary struggle – which was to be a *political* struggle, as Marx never tired of insisting, not least against his anarchist interlocutors. All these features of Marx's theory of the state have a specifically anti-anarchist bearing and a discernibly Hegelian lineage; all of them proceed from the theory of alien politics first outlined in the course of his auto-emancipation from Hegel. These elements of continuity may not clear up all the ambiguities we encounter in what was an unfinished enterprise. Marx often wrote in a spirit of revolutionary urgency that only subsequently was proved by events to be unwarranted; *The Manifesto of the Communist Party*, a document that at the time of its composition was designed to push or shape events, is a case in point. But he was also no stranger to recollection in (enforced) tranquillity.

It is possible to distinguish between broad, theoretical formulations – such as those found in the *Manifesto* – and more detailed 'empirical' investigations, such as *The Eighteenth Brumaire of Louis Bonaparte*, where these broad formulations are, as it were, put to the test. Such a distinction – which indicates that what Marx discovers in the course of his specific historical investigations rarely bears out the broadest of his theoretical claims – is useful, even though it all too patently begs the question of whether Marx should be considered as a twentieth-century social scientist testing out 'empirically' his 'hypotheses'. This reservation to one side, however, the distinction between a theoretical Marx and an empirical Marx – a distinction that would have made little sense to Marx himself – is best complemented, not displaced, by the emphasis advanced here on Marx's early formulation of alien politics as a principle underlying whatever he had to say about the state.

To fail to include Marx's theory of alien politics - his idea of the state as a fake universal, based on men's alienated capacities - alongside his characterization of the state as an instrument of bourgeois predominance is to fail to see a significant connection between the two. Worse still, to exclude alien politics is to lay one's emphasis wrongly. To concentrate upon Marx's ruling-class theory of the state, as did Lenin, can easily enough be seen to be politically programmatic, for it leads directly into the notion of the dictatorship of the proletariat - a notion so disliked by anarchists. Yet Marx's own theory of the state has greater depth then Lenin saw fit (for good reasons of his own, perhaps) to plumb in *The State and Revolution*. Most importantly, we should recognize that what Marx has to say about politics and community is not exhausted by what he has to say about the bourgeois state; overemphasis on the latter might distract us from considering the former. The reason why such distraction is a danger best avoided is that Marx himself predicated even his most programmatic revolutionary message - the necessity for political action - not simply upon his ruling-class theory of the state, but also upon his notion of the modern, bourgeois state as the ideological representation of the alienated communal abilities of men, abilities which men as a result of revolutionary political activity can (and must) reappropriate.

Marx's theory of the state reconsidered

Marx's basic belief has been paraphrased quite accurately by Ralph Miliband: 'the state has only the illusion of being determinant, whereas in fact it is determined'.[34] The state in modern society may be instrumental to those who hold power in society, but it is none the less secondary and derivative, being determined in its operations and in its very existence by forces that are extrinsic to it - forces whose source is civil society. Marx, as we have seen, came to revolutionary maturity by disputing Hegelian and Young Hegelian claims that the state is autonomous, primary and formative; and he continued to denounce all attempts to argue from the state to society, whether these proceeded from Hegelians like Arnold Ruge and Bruno Bauer, from anarchists like Stirner, Proudhon and Bakunin, or from socialist politicians like Lassalle. Although these various figures would have agreed about very little, it is a point of the utmost importance that from Marx's point of view the heterogeneity of any list of them was more apparent than real; all of these figures, in their different ways, were inclined to consider the state as 'an independent entity, possessed of its own intellectual, ethical and libertarian bases'.[35] Marx, who considered any apparent independence of the state from society to be at best transitory and ultimately precarious - as we shall see - regarded it as an error of the first magnitude for anyone - particularly a revolutionist - to suppose that the state could be dealt with as an 'independent entity'.

In Marx's view, the modern state - as opposed to anarchist overestimations of what Proudhon called its powerfulness (*puissance*), as well as to Lassallean insistences on its character as 'free state' - was constrained by social forces and circumscribed by the balance of power in civil society. It can do, and may do, only what the prevailing mode of production, capitalism, permits. This provision permits it *some* free scope - from time to time, and from place to place - but any freedom it might enjoy is in the nature of a concession which might be revoked once the balance of forces in civil society alters, as it generally does, to the benefit of the capitalist class. In particular, the modern state is not free to establish or initiate social institutions or practices. It may - and commonly will - uphold them, but even if it does so, such action will not normally be independent action but action at the behest or instigation of powerful social forces. The state may pronounce and enunciate laws, but it cannot dictate or promulgate them to society in its own right. The state's role, even as lawgiver, is declaratory and expressive; legislation 'never does more than proclaim, express in words, the will of economic relations'.[36] The range of free play or autonomous activity any state may enjoy in modern society is, normally, severely circumscribed. 'Political conditions', Marx emphasized, 'are only the official expression of civil society'.[37]

Marx's acceptance of the Hegelian distinction between the state and civil society may immediately distinguish Marxism from anarchism; but Marx's sustained denial that the state and civil society can relate in the Hegelian manner nevertheless has the effect of making state action not so much second-hand as third-hand. Marx presents us, as it were, with three layers. There is economic activity, the root and foundation of civil society; there is civil society itself - the specific form taken by economic activity in the capitalist epoch, which has, and operates according to, its own rules, most importantly those relating to private property; and there is the state, which upholds and confirms these rules, which are established by the prevailing economic system. The priorities are clear: economic conditions do not vary according to the state's rules. The opposite is more likely. Law develops after economics, and the priority in question is logical as well as temporal.

The role of specifically political forces, then, is relegated; politics is no master science - it cannot even account for itself - and the crucial explanatory techniques about society are to be sought elsewhere. Politics is neither the moving force nor the binding force of history; and only specifically political illusions would have it otherwise. The notion - which might be termed a Hobbesian notion - that state action provides, and provides for, a predictable setting in which economic action is made possible (whereas in fact, according to Marx, the opposite might almost be said to obtain) is an illusion based upon an over-estimation of the power of the will. In opposition to consent theory, or to Hobbesian voluntarism, Marx - following Hegel - holds that society does not rest on the *will* or the consent of its constituents; individuals, rather, are said to be caught up in a system - a system that with remarkable frequency is in turn said to operate 'independently of their will'. If we overestimate the power of will - for example, if we overestimate the constitutive power of law - then the state will *appear* dominant; it may even be necessary for those who man the state's apparatus to believe that this apparent dominance is genuine. But, by the same token, it is necessary for those seeking its overthrow not to subscribe to this specifically political illusion; a proletariat that sees politics as an act of will, says Marx in an article written in 1844, because of its corresponding lack of social insight 'wastes its forces on foolish and futile uprisings that are drowned in blood'.[38] Marx amplified this warning in *The German Ideology*.

If power is taken as the basis of right, as Hobbes, etc., do, then right, law, etc. are merely the symptom, the expression of *other* relations on which the state power rests. The material life of individuals, which by no means depends upon their 'will', their mode of production and form of intercourse, which mutually determine each other - this is the real basis of the state and remains so at all the stages at which division of labour and private property are still necessary, quite independently of the will of individuals. These actual relations are in no way created by the state power; on the contrary they are the power creating it. The individuals who rule in these conditions, besides having to constitute their power in the form of the *State*, have to give their will, which is determined by these definite conditions, a universal expression as the will of the state, as law - an expression whose content is always determined by the relations of this class, as the civil and criminal law demonstrates in the clearest possible way. Just as the weight of their bodies does not depend upon their idealistic will or on their arbitrary decision, so also the fact that they enforce their will in the form of law, and at the same time make it independent of the personal arbitrariness of each individual among them, does not depend on their idealistic will . . . so long as the productive forces are still insufficiently developed to make competition superfluous, and therefore would give rise to competition over and over again, for so long the classes which are ruled would be wanting the impossible if they had the 'will' to abolish competition and with it the State and the law . . . it is only in the will of the ideologist that this

'will' arises before conditions have developed far enough to
make its production possible. After conditions have developed
sufficiently to produce it, the ideologist is able to imagine this
will as being purely arbitrary and therefore as conceivable at all
times and under all circumstances.[39]

That the power of those who man the state apparatus is severely
limited in practice can be seen, according to Marx, only if we step
outside the specifically political domain. From a non-political vantage
point, Marx tells us, we can see that political thinking is *inherently*
misleading and mistaken, because it contains a built-in bias in its own
favour. As Marx put it in 1844:

> The more powerful the state, and therefore the more political
> a country is, the less likely it is to seek the basis of social evils
> and to grasp the general explanation of them in the principle of
> the state itself, that is, in the structure of society, of which the
> state is the active, conscious and official expression. Political
> thought is really political thought in the sense that the thinking
> takes place within the framework of politics. The clearer and
> more vigorous political thought is, the less it is able to grasp the
> nature of social evils. The classical period of political thought is
> the French Revolution. Far from recognizing the source of social
> defects in the principle of the state, the heroes of the French
> Revolution looked for the sources of political evils in the
> defective social organization. Thus, for example, Robespierre
> saw in the coexistence of great poverty and great wealth only
> an obstacle to genuine democracy. He wished therefore to
> establish a universal Spartan austerity. The principle of politics
> is the will. The more partial, and the more perfected, political
> thought becomes, the more it believes in the omnipotence of the
> will, the less able it is to see the natural and mental limitations
> on the will, the less capable it is of discovering the source of
> social evils.[40]

The French Revolution, indeed, provided Marx with a storehouse
of examples of the way in which purely political consciousness, or a
state-centred perspective, inevitably distorts the view we might have of
social realities. Discussing, in the same article, the limitations on what
the state - what *any* modern state - can do to rectify the problem of
pauperism, Marx points out that, during the French Revolution, even
the Convention, which 'represented a maximum of political energy,
power and understanding', could do nothing about pauperism. 'What',
Marx asks, rhetorically, 'was the result of the Convention's ordinance?
Only that there was one more ordinance in the world, and that one

year later the Convention was besieged by starving weavers.'[41] (Marx was writing in the wake of the Silesian weavers' uprising in 1844.) To shore up his point that state action against pressing social evils is foredoomed to failure, Marx asks:

Can the state act in any other way? The state will never look for the cause of social imperfections 'in the state and social institutions . . .' Where there are political parties, each party finds the source of such evils in the fact that the opposing party, instead of itself, is at the helm of the state. Even the radical and revolutionary politicians look for the source of the evil, not in the nature of the state, but in a particular form of the state, which they want to replace by another form . . . The state and the structure of society are not, from the standpoint of politics, two different things. The state [from this standpoint] is the structure of society . . . In the last resort, every state seeks the cause [of pauperism] in adventitious or intentional defects in the administration, and therefore looks to a reform in the administration for a redress of these evils. Why? Simply because the administration is the organizing activity of the state itself.

The contradiction between the aims and good intentions of the administration on the one hand, and its means and resources on the other, cannot be removed by the state without abolishing itself, for it rests upon this contradiction. The state is founded on the contradiction between public and private life, between general and particular interests. The administration must, therefore, limit itself to a formal and negative sphere of activity, because its power ceases at the point where civil life and its work begin. In face of the consequences which spring from the unsocial character of the life of civil society, of private property, trade, industry, of the mutual plundering of the different groups in civil society, impotence is the natural law of the administration. These divisions, this debasement and slavery within civil society, are the natural foundations on which the modern state rests . . . If the modern state wishes to end the impotence of its administration it would be obliged to abolish the present conditions of private life. And if the state wishes to abolish these conditions of private life it would have also to put an end to its own conditions, for it exists only in relation to them.[42]

What is immediately striking about this quotation is not simply that the state, by its very nature, according to Marx, lacks the facility to 'put an end to its own conditions'; it is also that, by the same token, the state's wherewithal to undertake any positive action at all is severely limited - despite the dubious advantages of modern bureaucracy it might enjoy. Faced with so immediate and pressing a problem as that of pauperism, 'impotence is the natural law of the administration'; 'its power ceases at the point where civil life and work begin'. That Marx insisted on the state's impotence in this fashion - a point to which we shall return - indicates a difficulty with the ruling-class theory of the state that passed down into vulgar Marxism: in what sense, and to what extent, we must ask, can the purported ruling class be said to really *rule*? The notion that it does, and can, really rule or exercise power - let alone authority - would seem to stem only from a political perspective, a state-centred vantage point which can only distort, or even invert our view of social realities. Certainly, the rules that keep modern society in operation, while they might be enforced and upheld by the state, are in no way formulated or initiated by the state. On this point Marx is adamant. 'By the mere fact that it is a class and not an estate (*Stand*)', he says, 'the bourgeoisie is forced to organize itself no longer locally but nationally and to give a general form to its mean, average interest.' This, 'the form of organization the bourgeoisie necessarily adopts ... for the mutual guarantee of [its] property and interest',[43] is the state. Such passages, from *The German Ideology* (1846), provide the background and set the tone for Marx's most celebrated - and strident - depictions of the state, whose home is *The Manifesto of the Communist Party* (1848). Here, 'political power is but the organized power of one class for oppressing another' and 'the executive of the modern state is but a committee for managing the common affairs of the whole bourgeoisie'.[44]

This straightforward view of the state - whatever its crudity - is the one that passed into Marxism-Leninism. It is already clear, however, that Marx's theory of the state was at no stage of its elaboration as clear-cut and simplistic as the *Manifesto*'s succinct formulations, taken in themselves, might imply. (It might be added, indeed, that the conditional 'might imply' is used advisedly, as opposed to the definitive 'clearly state'; why is it that the *executive* - as opposed to some other branch - of the modern state manages the *common* affairs of the *whole* bourgeoisie? How likely is it that these common affairs will find expression?) We know that the *Manifesto* was a call to arms written under commission with a deadline - the supposedly revolutionary *annus mirabilis* of 1848 - in mind; the document was explicitly - indeed blatantly - a clarion-call in which overdrawn, pithy phrases might be expected. The point here is not to deny the effectiveness of the phrases at issue; such a denial would be ridiculous if we consider their power at the level of much later revolutionary propaganda. It is simply to indicate their character as distillations of the results of other, rather more searching, analyses of the role of the state. As such, the main drawback of the *Manifesto*'s dramatic and sweeping characterizations of the state is that, provocative though they may be, they tell us nothing about the way in which bourgeois revolution and the emergence of modern civil society had changed – decisively and irreversibly – the nature of the state and of political power, a shift that Marx discussed elsewhere (even within the *Manifesto*) at some length.

Over and above this shortcoming, the danger with Marx's more notorious slogans about the state is that if they are wrested out of context – and it is in the nature of a political slogan to be wrested out of context – they might suggest a rather crude conspiracy theory. There is a vulgar Marxist tendency to simply read, for 'the state', 'the bourgeoisie' as though these concerned themselves with providing palimpsests for each and every political proclamation. It is worth indicating that Marx himself (who could be as capable of vulgarity as anyone else) recognized this shortcoming for what it was. In his more considered passages Marx advanced views that did not express but actually precluded any such crude and reductive conspiracy theory.

> . . . if the bourgeoisie politically, that is, through the agency of its
> state power, maintains 'the injustice in the property relations', it
> does not create the latter which, conditioned by the modern
> division of labour, the modern form of exchange, competition,
> concentration, etc., does not proceed from the political rule of
> the bourgeoisie but, contrariwise, the political rule of the
> bourgeoisie proceeds from these modern relations of production,
> which are proclaimed by the bourgeois economists to be
> necessary and eternal laws.[45]

With bourgeois society, as we have seen, economic and political life are freed from feudal restraints and encumbrances in an altogether unprecedented way. The state's consequent withdrawal from interference within the market mechanism – a withdrawal urged by the classical economists – permitted the market mechanism freely to constrain its human objects; and, as part of the same process, state and society become separate and exclusive spheres of activity. Marx insisted that given this separation the state 'is based on the unhampered development of civil society [*bürgerliche Gesellschaft*], on the free movement of private interest'.[46] The assertion of these priorities – largely, if not entirely, against the very different and less historical priorities of the anarchists – is a *Leitmotiv* of Marx's theory of the state. Marx believed, as they did not, that the state is in modern times predicated as a false universal on the existence of antagonistic social relations, and that it is this predication that gives the modern state its specifically modern meaning and role. To fail to see this, to argue from the state to society, is to adopt an inverted perspective and, in overestimating the potency and initiative that the modern state exhibits, to mistake cause for effect; it is also to neglect a fundamental shift in the nature of the state in the capitalist epoch.

The paradox that emerges if we look at what Marx has to say about the state is that the theory of alien politics he adumbrated in response to Hegel – and not just in his earliest writings – on the face of it seems more substantive than, and irreducible to, the rather crude, reductionist ruling-class theory of the state we encounter, in its most strident and vivid form, in *The Manifesto of the Communist Party*. This more simplistic, if more straightforward, theory of the state has never lacked adherents; it passed through some of the writings of Engels, (notably *The Origin of the Family, Private Property and the State* of 1881, and that section of *Anti-Dühring* that appeared in 1887 as *Socialism: Utopian and Scientific*) to those of Lenin (most notably *State and Revolution*); and from thence it became ensconced and solidified as an official dogma of Marxism–Leninism. But the concept of the state as an 'engine of class despotism' all too clearly does not exhaust what Marx had to say on the subject; and, moreover, it raises a set of theoretical and practical problems.

In its purest form, any rigidly ruling-class theory of the state presupposes the possibility of unalloyed class rule, and the existence of an economic ruling class possessed of uniform common interests and which is, into the bargain, capable of asserting them. The various examples of the bourgeoisie that Marx encountered and analysed seem not to have met so monolithic a set of requirements. The state is a coercive instrument of a ruling class whose dominance is defined in terms of its ownership of and control over the means of production. Yet Marx did not invariably reduce class structure – the ultimate form of what he called the 'relations of production', which are relations among men – to the disposition of the forces of production (which are relations among men and things). Social and technological relations are rarely coterminous or interchangeable categories in Marx's writings. The picture becomes less mechanistic if we ask what a class is and allow ourselves to be reminded that class is a relationship, not a thing. This point has been well put by a distinguished Marxist historian. 'The notion of class', he reminds us,

> entails the notion of historical relationship. Like any other
> relationship, it is a fluency which evades analysis if we attempt
> to stop it dead at any given moment and anatomize its structure.
> The finest meshed sociological net cannot give us a pure specimen
> of class, any more than it can give us one of deference or love.
> The relationship must always be embodied in real people and in
> a real context. Moreover, we cannot have two distinct classes,
> each with an independent being, and then bring them *into*
> relationship with each other. We cannot have love without

lovers, not deference without squires and labourers. And class happens when some men, as a result of common experiences (inherited or shared) feel and articulate the identity of their interests as between themselves, and as against other men whose interests are different from (and usually opposed to) theirs. The class experience is largely determined by the productive relations into which men are born – or enter involuntarily. Class consciousness is the way these experiences are handled in cultural terms: embodied in traditions, value-systems, ideas and institutional forms. If the experience appears as determined, class-consciousness does not. We can see a *logic* in the responses of similar occupational groups undergoing similar experiences, but we cannot predicate any law. Consciousness of class arises in the same way in different times and places, but never in *just* the same way . . .[47]

A class on this definition, then, is not a solid bloc existing in isolation from other classes; on the contrary, what explains a class is other classes, its counterparts, and its context in the overall pattern of social relationships. These relationships – Marx's 'relations of production' – are not likely to exhibit any uniformity from country to country or from time to time, whatever their common features may be. The social context these relationships form will be an important part of the *meaning* of any class that helps make it up. In good Marxist analysis, classes are not treated as though they were undifferentiated units or homologous magnitudes that are capable of being isolated for the purposes of observation; in good Marxist analysis, classes are investigated *through* the pattern of the relations of production in a given society at a given time, a pattern which forms an important part of the meaning of any particular class.

Marx against Bonapartism: *The Eighteenth Brumaire* and beyond

It should come as no surprise that Marx's investigation of the chain of events leading up to Napoleon III's *coup d'état* is, as it were, a case study not only in Marx's theory of the state, but also of Marx's theory of class. The ruling-class theory of the state encountered in the *Manifesto* and elsewhere prepares us for the fact that in Marx's specific historical investigations the state, its position and placement, and the pattern of class relationships in society are here dealt with together, in tandem; but what it does *not* prepare us for is the degree of flexibility and sophistication Marx displays throughout this extended investigation. In *The Eighteenth Brumaire of Louis Bonaparte* (which is best considered as an emendation of *The Class Struggles in France*, which leads up to it both chronologically and analytically) we find that the degree of internal cohesion, the type and extent of unity within a class – and with it the possibility of collective self-assertion – is not at all a categorical postulate, but something that varies, and varies considerably, from one class to another. The various degrees of articulation of the interests of any particular class affect the opportunities of others; and there are, moreover, many and varied subdivisions *within* each class, subdivisions that make alliances across class lines possible and likely. The pattern is a complex one – being both articulated and reflexive – and the question (a loaded question) of the political representation of these various forces among and within classes makes the pattern more complicated still. The degree and kind of independence that may be exhibited by the political representatives – or by the institutional representatives – of social forces is outlined and investigated by Marx according to the structure and history of class relationships in French society; and we find something for which the ruling-class theory of the state does little to prepare us – the phenomenon of political powers' being exercised not *by* an autonomous, internally united bourgeois class, but *on behalf of* factions of a bourgeois class that is characterized by a severe lack of internal unity and autonomy.

The composite picture may be summarized as follows: there are, in French society in the middle of the nineteenth century, landowners; large landowners whose political representatives are the legitimists; these shade off, by degrees, into the small-holding peasants. These in turn shade off into the artisan class, and this *artisanat* in *its* turn shades off into an as yet undeveloped and not very numerous proletariat. Peasants, artisans and proletarians are also usually linked by virtue of their lack of political representation. As for the capitalists, these are divided into two factions, the finance capitalists and the industrialists, whose interests converge all too rarely. Different factions are politically dominant at different periods. The July Monarchy was a political expression of the interests of finance capital, 'a joint-stock company for the exploitation of France's national wealth . . . [of which] Louis-Philippe was the director . . . Trade, industry, agriculture, shipping, the interests of the industrial bourgeoisie, were bound to be continually endangered and prejudiced under this system'. As Marx goes on to put it,

> The bourgeois class fell apart into two big factions, which,
> alternately, the big landed proprietors under the restored
> monarchy and the finance aristocracy and the industrial
> bourgeoisie under the July Monarchy, had maintained a mon-
> opoly of power . . . the nameless realm of the Republic was
> the only one in which both factions could maintain with equal
> power the common class interest without giving up their
> mutual rivalry. If the bourgeois republic could not be anything

but the perfected and clearly expressed rule of the whole
bourgeois class, could it be anything but the rule of the
Orleanists supplemented by the Legitimists, and of the
Legitimists supplemented by the Orleanists, the synthesis
of the restoration and the July Monarchy? The bourgeois
republicans of the *National* did not represent any large faction
of their class resting on economic foundations. They possessed
only the importance and the historical claim of having asserted,
under the monarchy, as against the two bourgeois factions that
only understood their particular regime, the general regime of
the bourgeois class.[48]

The coalescence of interest between these two factions, moreover,
proves to be precarious; it may be 'the perfected and clearly expressed
rule of the whole bourgeois class', but the internal divisions within this
class are such that 'the nameless realm of the republic'[49] is the very
thing that did not, and according to Marx could not, last. No sooner
was the republic 'perfected' than it summarily collapsed.

Although Marx was concerned that his ruling-class theory of the
state should not collapse with it, the theory certainly seems dented.
Yet Marx succeeds - at least to his own satisfaction - in extricating
himself and salvaging his theory. 'The parliamentary republic', he
tells us, had been

no more than the neutral territory on which the two factions
of the French bourgeoisie, Legitimists and Orleanists, could
dwell side by side with equality of rights. It was the unavoidable
condition of their common rule, the sole form of state in which
their general class interest subjected to itself at the same time
both the claims of their particular functions and all the remaining
classes of society.[50]

In France Marx analysed what was not the united rule of an autonomous,
internally united, well-defined and class-conscious bourgeoisie but
rather a factional politics that played itself out to the extent of enabling
the 'grotesque mediocrity' of Louis Napoleon 'to play a hero's part';[51]
a factional politics as a result of which Bonapartists and bureaucrats
were enabled - momentarily but decisively - to hold the balance of
power, even though (or precisely because) they represented in the last
analysis none but themselves.

What Marx presents us with in his analysis of French politics is not
so much the state as a reflection of the forces in society, but, finally,
an instance of disjuncture of the state from society. Louis Bonaparte's
coup d'état was 'the victory of the executive. . . [the French nation] re-
nounces all will of its own and submits to the power of an alien will, to

authority'; 'the struggle seems to be settled in such a way that all classes, equally impotent and equally mute, fall on their knees before the rifle butt'. Even more unexpectedly, Marx goes on to say that 'under the second Bonaparte . . . the state seem[s] to have made itself completely independent';[52] 'bourgeois society, freed from political cares, attained a development unexpected even by itself'.[53]

Marx speaks of the 'executive power with its enormous bureaucratic and military organization, with its ingenious state machinery embracing wide strata, with a host of officials numbering half a million'; he refers to it as an 'appalling parasitic body which enmeshes the body of French society like a net and chokes all its pores'.[54] But how does the state attain such an independent and powerful position? Situations of balance, of unstable equilibrium, Marx explains, can occur among classes (and factions of classes) in civil society, and, in such a stalemate, no single class, whatever its social predominance, can gain *political* dominance. To resolve this stalemate, the state itself steps in to redress the balance. Acting in its own right, the executive power plays the part of umpire or moderator, and classes (or factions) might then see the state itself, and its administrative apparatus, as their ally or protector. This development is facilitated – though it is not exactly caused – by the growing strength and organization of the state apparatus. Every successive ruling group has an interest in improving the power of this apparatus, in increasing the coercive potential at the disposal of the state, with the result that the personnel manning the administrative apparatus itself becomes a powerfully placed faction having a vested interest in preserving and extending the scope of state action. Marx, in words that cannot avoid recalling what he had said about the Prussian bureaucracy, here speaks of a French political system

> where the executive power commands an army of officials
> numbering more than half a million individuals and which
> therefore constantly maintains an immense mass of interests
> and livelihoods in the most absolute dependence; where the
> state enmeshes, controls, regulates, superintends, and tutors
> civil society from its most comprehensive manifestations of
> life down to its most insignificant stirrings, from its most
> general modes of being to the private existence of individuals;
> where through the most extraordinary centralization this
> parasitic body acquires a ubiquity, an omniscience, a capacity
> for accelerated mobility and an elasticity which finds a
> counterpart only in the helpless dependence, in the loose
> shapelessness of the actual body politic. . .[55]

It is evident that Marx's depiction of the state in this passage – of a state power that is 'apparently soaring high above society'[56] – is one that recalls not the class-dominated instrumentality outlined in the *Manifesto* (and met with, apparently, nowhere in real life) but the alien universality and power described in 'On the Jewish Question', a universality that is 'parasitic' on society in much the same way. Only in the latter, and not at all in the former, view could the state be expected to 'enmesh, control, regulate, superintend and tutor' civil society. Marx proceeds to outline an unexpected paradox. He asks why the French National Assembly did not 'simplify the administration of the state, reduce the army of officials and . . . let civil society and public opinion create organs of their own, independent of the governmental power'. His answer to his own question betrays the fact that there is more than one way for the state to operate as the 'instrumentality' of the ruling class.

> . . . it is precisely with the maintenance of that extensive state machine in its numerous ramifications that the material interests of the French bourgeoisie are interwoven in the closest fashion. Here it finds posts for its surplus population and makes up in the form of state salaries for what it cannot pocket in the form of profit, interests, rents and honorariums. On the other hand, its political interests compelled it to increase daily the repressive measures and therefore the resources and the personnel of the state power, while at the same time it had to wage an uninterrupted war against public opinion and mistrustfully mutilate, cripple, the independent organs of the social movement where it did not succeed in amputating them entirely. Thus the French bourgeoisie was compelled by its class position to annihilate, on the one hand, the vital conditions of all parliamentary power, and therefore, likewise, of its own, and to render irresistible, on the other hand, the executive power hostile to it.[57]

The paradox is a monstrous one. On the one hand, 'never did the bourgeoisie rule more absolutely';[58] on the other hand, we have to ask in what does this purportedly absolute rule consist? Over and above the basic belief held by Marx that capitalism in general constrains conscious social power over the conditions of existence, in this particular instance bourgeois 'rule' expresses itself in what is nothing but a double bind having effects that are to prove fatal to its interests.

> The bourgeoisie confesses that its own interests dictate that it should be delivered from the consequences of its own rule; that, in order to restore tranquillity in the country, its bourgeois parliament must, first of all, be given its quietus; that, in order to preserve its own social power intact, its political power must be broken; that the individual bourgeois can continue to exploit

the other classes and to enjoy undisturbed property, family,
religion and order only on condition that their class be condemned
along with the other classes to like political nullity; that in order
to save its purse it must forfeit its crown, and the sword that is to
safeguard it must at the same time be hung over its head like the
sword of Damocles.[59]

In this unexpected way, France escapes the despotism of a class for
the despotism of an individual. Louis Bonaparte's *coup d'état* changes
the role of the state; 'as against civil society, the state machine has
consolidated its position so thoroughly that the chief of the Society of
Dec 10th [i.e. Louis Bonaparte] suffices for its head'.[60] The Bonapartist
state seems independent of any particular class, and it seems superior
to, set up against, society. But Marx adds an important qualification.
'And yet', he goes on, 'the state power is not suspended in mid-air.
Bonaparte represents a class, and the most numerous class of French
society at that, the small-holding peasants.'[61] Over and above Bonaparte's bribes to other sections of French society (his offer of tranquillity to the bourgeoisie, and a restoration of universal suffrage to
the workers), bribes which cancel each other out, his own class basis
is constituted by the peasantry. Indeed, the organization of so inherently
atomized a group as the French peasantry has to proceed from outside.
The peasants' lack of cohesion makes them 'incapable of enforcing
their class interests in their own name whether through a parliament
or a convention'. They therefore require a representative who

> must at the same time appear as their master, as an authority over
> them, as an unlimited governmental power that protects them
> against the other classes and sends them rain and sunshine from
> above. The political influence of the small-holding peasants,
> therefore, finds its final expression in the executive power
> subordinating society to itself.[62]

But what is the nature of the representation involved here? The
peasants want, hope or expect that Louis Bonaparte will 'represent'
their interests, but lack the wherewithal to oblige him to do so. Bonaparte's state is not the mere instrument of their will (if, indeed, they
can be said to have a common will at all). The peasants' hopes may
have the effect of limiting somewhat the executive's freedom of action;
but it is doubtful whether such limitation can be very severe, the
peasants themselves being hopelessly disunited. Moreover,

> as the executive authority which has made itself an independent
> power, Bonaparte feels it his mission to safeguard 'bourgeois order'.
> But the strength of this bourgeois order lies in the middle class.

He looks on himself, therefore, as the representative of the
middle class and issues decrees in this sense. Nevertheless, he is
somebody solely due to the fact that he has broken the political
power of the middle class and daily breaks it anew.

Nor is this all;

> as against the bourgeoisie, Bonaparte looks on himself at the same
> time, as the representative of the peasants and of the people in
> general, who want to make the lower classes of the people happy
> within the frame of bourgeois society . . . But, above all, Bonaparte
> looks on himself as the chief of the society of the 10th of December,
> as the representative of the *lumpenproletariat* to which he himself,
> his *entourage*, his government and his army belong. . .[63]

Small wonder, then, that Marx, faced with this confusing welter of
'representation', stresses the 'contradictory talk' of Louis Bonaparte
and the 'contradictions of his government, the confused groping about
which seeks now to win, now to humiliate first one class and then
another and arrays all of them uniformly against him'.[64] The point
remains that the Bonapartist state's power of initiative remains very
largely unimpaired by the wishes and demands of any one particular
class - or faction. On the other hand, however, the balance is delicate;
for Bonapartism is in no way neutral as between contending classes.
It claims to represent all classes and to be the embodiment of society
as a whole, but it was called into being and continued to exist for the
sake of maintaining and strengthening the existing social order - one
which is based on the domination of labour by capital. Marx was later
to write that Bonapartism was, above all else, a transitional form: 'it
was the only form of government possible at a time when the bourgeoisie had already lost, and the working class had not yet acquired,
the faculty of ruling the nation'. It was, again,

> at the same time the most prostitute and the ultimate form of
> the state power which nascent middle-class society had
> commenced to elaborate as a means of its own emancipation
> from feudalism, and which full-grown bourgeois society had
> finally transformed into a means for the enslavement of labour
> by capital.[65]

Ultimately, the Bonapartist state, however independent it may
have been politically from any given class in French society, remains
- and must remain in such a class society - the protector of an economically and socially dominant class. In this way, in the long run the
basic Marxist position reappears; the independence of the state, 'soaring

high above society', ultimately proves illusory as well as transitory. ᕁ
Politics is still explicable in the last analysis only in economic terms; ᕁ
ultimately, the social moorings of the Bonapartist state reveal themselves ('Bonaparte would like to appear as the patriarchal benefactor
of all classes. But he cannot give to one class without taking from
another'),[66] and economics determines political movements again.

> Driven by the contradictory demands of his situation and being
> at the same time, like a conjuror, under the necessity of keeping
> the public gaze fixed on himself. . .Bonaparte throws the entire
> bourgeois economy into confusion, violates everything that seemed
> inviolable to the Revolution of 1848, makes some tolerant of
> revolution, others desirous of revolution, and produces actual
> anarchy in the name of order, while at the same time stripping
> its halo from the entire state machine, profanes it, and makes it
> at once loathsome and ridiculous.[67]

Marx in such statements - and there is no shortage of them in *The
Class Struggles in France* and *The Eighteenth Brumaire* alike - may
(as Miliband thinks) or may not succeed in salvaging his original position
about the ultimate shaping of the political by the economic. Yet, over
and above this possibly contentious issue, what emerges from Marx's
studies of French politics and society in the middle of the nineteenth
century is something for which his ruling-class theory of the state,
taken in its purest (or crudest) form, cannot prepare us. What is revealed
is a striking continuity between what Marx said in 1850-2 and what he
had said in 1843.

> In periods when the political state as such comes violently to
> birth in civil society. . . political life seeks to stifle its own pre-
> requisites - civil society and its elements - and to establish itself
> as the genuine and harmonious species-life of man. But it can
> only achieve this end by setting itself in violent contradiction
> with its own conditions of existence. . . [The] political drama
> ends necessarily with the restoration of religion, of private
> property, of all the elements of civil society, just as war ends
> with the conclusion of peace.[68]

While the continuity such passages reveal will come as a surprise
only to those for whom Marx's theory of the state can have only one
face to present, or those who insist upon a rigid separation between
the 'early' and 'late' Marx (categories, incidentally, whose membership
tends to overlap), it is nevertheless a striking continuity. It is also one
to which insufficient attention has been paid in the literature on Marx's
theory of the state. Yet what is Bonapartism but an attempt 'to transform

the purpose of the state into the purpose of bureaucracy and the purpose of bureaucracy into the purpose of the state' – the very danger, implicit in 'political emancipation', Marx had warned against a decade earlier? Bonapartism signified that

> every common interest was immediately severed from society,
> counterposed to it as a higher, *general* interest, snatched from
> the activity of society's members themselves and made an object
> of government activity, from a bridge, a schoolhouse and the
> communal property of a village community to the railways, the
> national wealth and national university of France.[69]

This expropriation, to be sure, had its conditions. Every previous revolution, as Marx put it, had consolidated 'the centralized state power, with its ubiquitous organs of standing army, police, bureaucracy, clergy and judicature' so that the political character of the state had changed

> simultaneously with the economic changes of society. At the
> same pace at which the progress of modern industry developed,
> widened, intensified the class antagonism between capital and
> labour, the state power assumed more and more the character
> of the national power of capital over labour, of a public force
> organized for social enslavement, of an engine of class despotism.
> After every revolution marking a progressive phase in the class
> struggle, the purely repressive character of the state power stands
> out in bolder and bolder relief.[70]

All previous revolutions, in other words, had 'perfected this [state] machine instead of smashing it. The parties that contended in turn for domination regarded the possession of this huge state edifice as the principal spoils of the victors'.[71] Small wonder, then, that Marx was to insist in 1871 that 'the working class cannot simply lay hold of the ready-made state machinery, and wield it for its own purposes'.[72] Marx's address, *The Civil War in France*, insisted that 'the direct antithesis to the empire [of Louis Bonaparte] was the Commune' of 1871 because the Commune was the 'positive form' of 'a Republic that was not only to supersede the monarchical form of class rule, but class rule itself'.[73]

The most positive feature of the Paris Commune, according to Marx, was precisely that it de-institutionalized political power, and in so doing re-politicized society. 'Public functions ceased to be the vital property of the tools of the Central Government. Not only municipal administration, but the whole initiative hitherto exercised by the State was laid into the hands of the Commune.'[74] Society seized hold of the conditions of its own existence;

> the unity of the nation was not to be broken, but, on the contrary,
> to be organized by the Communal Constitution and to become a
> reality by the destruction of the State power which claimed to be
> the embodiment of that unity independent of, and superior to,
> the nation itself, of which it was but a parasitic excrescence. While
> the merely repressive organs of the old governmental power were
> to be amputated, its legitimate functions were to be wrested from
> an authority usurping pre-eminence over society itself, and restored
> to the responsible agents of society.[75]

Marx's characterization of the 'Communal Constitution' is all too
clearly couched in terms of, in the very idiom of, 'human' as opposed
to 'political' emancipation. 'The Communal Constitution', says Marx,
'would have restored to the social body all the forces hitherto absorbed
by the state parasite feeding upon, and clogging the free movement of,
society. By this one act', he continues, 'it would have initiated the
regeneration of France.' Marx's description of its attributes is far-
reaching.

> It was a thoroughly expansive political form, while all previous
> forms of government had been emphatically repressive. Its true
> secret was this. It was essentially a working-class government,
> the product of the struggle of the producing class against the
> appropriating class, the political form at last discovered under
> which to work out the economic emancipation of labour.
>
> Except on this last condition, the Commune would have been
> an impossibility and a delusion. The political rule of the producer
> cannot coexist with the perpetuation of his social slavery. The
> Commune was therefore to serve as a lever for uprooting the
> economical foundations upon which rests the existence of classes,
> and therefore of class rule. With labour emancipated, every man
> becomes a working man, and productive labour ceases to be a
> class attribute.[76]

Marx's praise of the Commune – his insistence that it was 'the true
representative of all the healthy elements in French society', 'the bold
champion of the emancipation of labour', and (most markedly) 'the
glorious harbinger of a new society'[77] – has seemed exaggerated as well
as fulsome to some commentators. We now know of Marx's private
reservations about the Commune's political pusillanimity, about its
social composition and about the shortcomings of its ideology. ('The
majority of the Commune was in no way socialist, nor could it be',
Marx wrote – not at all inaccurately – ten years later in the privacy of

a letter.)[78] Much – if not all – of the apparent inconsistency involved in Marx's successive responses can be explained not simply by Marx's evident desire to make political capital from the onset of a revolutionary movement that owed little enough to him, but also by Marx's concern to distinguish between what the Commune actually achieved – the practical measures it effected were, after all, negligible – and what the Commune *represented*. The draft manuscript of *The Civil War in France* defines the Commune as

> the reabsorption of the State power by society as its own living forces instead of as forces controlling and subduing it, by the popular masses themselves forming their own force instead of the organized force of their suppression – the political form of their emancipation, instead of the artificial force (appropriated by their oppressors) . . . of society wielded for their oppression for their enemies.[79]

That this idiom carries over into the somewhat firmer syntax of the address Marx eventually delivered should not surprise us; it is, very much, the idiom of Marx's earlier writings on the French state – and, by extension, of his earliest writings on the modern state in general, including 'On the Jewish Question'. The very concept of the bureaucratic state – which disfigures and distorts as well as reflects the society that gave it birth – signifies the separation between the citizens and the means to their common action, the progressive extension of the sphere of alien regulation of life in society. It is for this reason that Marx in *The Civil War in France* stresses the Commune's de-institutionalization of political power to the marked extent he does. This de-institutionalization cuts through the usurpation (and mystification) of men's conscious control over the social conditions of their lives; it is an act of re-appropriation of what had been alienated away. And it is this reappropriation that gives the Commune – for all its shortcomings – universal significance. The problem had been that of returning to society all the prerogatives usurped by the state so that socialized man – man as the subject of his own existence instead of an object worked upon by, and at the disposal of, alien forces – would freely associate with his fellows. Men associated in this way would control the totality of their social lives and become 'masters of their own movement'. Prior to the Commune this statement had to be written in the conditional tense; what lent the Commune general, universal significance is its character as exemplar, as prolegomenon. Working men had shown, had demonstrated practically that they *could* take control of their own conditions of existence – and it is for this, above all else, that Marx applauds them in his address.

What makes such action *political* – indeed, what makes it the prototype of the political action Marx had in mind for the proletariat – is its character as the re-capturing of alienated social capacities. What Marx acclaimed about the Paris Commune was that, unlike any previous social convulsion, it had sought not the consolidation of state power in different hands but its destruction. Whereas every previous revolution had merely consolidated 'the centralized state power, with its ubiquitous organs of standing army, police, bureaucracy, clergy and judicature' (so that 'after every revolution marking a progressive phase in the class struggle, the purely repressive character of the state power stands out in bolder and bolder relief'), the Commune would have 'restored to the social body all the forces hitherto absorbed by the state parasite feeding upon, and clogging, the free movement of, society'. Marx stressed the Commune's popular, democratic, egalitarian character and heartily approved also the way in which 'not only municipal administration but the whole initiative hitherto exercised by the State was laid into the hands of the Commune'. While the communal form of government was to apply even to the 'smallest country hamlet',

> 'the unity of the nation was not to be broken, but, on the contrary,
> to be organized by the Communal Constitution and to become a
> reality by the destruction of the state power which claimed to be
> the embodiment of that unity independent of, and superior to,
> the nation itself, from which it was but a parasitic excrescence.[80]

In Marx's notes the language, if more awkward, is even stronger:

> This was a revolution not against this or that legitimate,
> constitutional, republican, imperialist [Marx, as in *The Eighteenth
> Brumaire*, means by 'imperialist' Bonapartist] form of state power.
> It was a revolution against the *state* itself, of this supernaturalist
> abortion of society, a resumption by the people for the people of
> its own social life. It was not a revolution to transfer it from one
> fraction of the ruling class to the other, but a revolution to break
> down this horrid machinery of class domination itself . . . [The]
> Second Empire was the final form of this state usurpation. The
> Commune was its definite negation, and, therefore, the initiation
> of the social revolution of the nineteenth century . . . Only the
> proletarians, fired by a new social task to accomplish by them
> for all society, to do away with all classes and class rule – the State,
> the centralized and organized governmental power usurping to be
> the master instead of the servant of society. . . It had sprung into
> life against them. By them it was broken, not as a peculiar form of
> governmental (centralized) power, but as its most powerful,
> elaborated into seeming independence from society expression
> and, therefore, its most prostitute reality, covered by infamy

from top to bottom, having centred in absolute corruption
at home and absolute powerlessness abroad.[81]

In contrast to this, the Communal Constitution made of every man
a working man, so that labour ceased to be a class attribute, as did
political power itself. Each delegate to the National Delegation in Paris,
Marx emphasizes, under the Communal Constitution was 'to be at any
time revocable and bound by the *mandat impératif* [formal instruc-
tions] of his constituents'. Marx continues in a vein that cannot but
recall 'On the Jewish Question': 'the unity of the nation', he says,

> was not to be broken but, on the contrary, to be organized by the
> Communal Constitution and to become a reality by the destruction
> of the state power which claimed to be the embodiment of that
> unity independent of, and superior to, the nation itself, from which
> it was but a parasitic excrescence. While the merely repressive organs
> of the old governmental power were to be amputated, its legitimate
> functions were to be wrested from an authority usurping pre-
> eminence over society itself, and restored to the responsible agents
> of society. Instead of deciding once in three or six years which
> member of the ruling class was to misrepresent the people in
> parliament, universal suffrage was to serve the people, constituted
> in Communes, as individual suffrage serves every other employer
> in the search for the workmen and managers in his business.[82]

The more extensive original draft of *The Civil War in France* recalls
'On the Jewish Question' even more explicitly:

> Every minor solitary interest engendered by the relations of
> social groups was separated from society itself, fixed and made
> independent of it and opposed to it in the form of state interest,
> administered by state priests with exactly determined hierarchical
> functions.
>   This parasitical excrescence on civil society, pretending to be
> its ideal counterpart, grew to its full development under the sway
> of the first Bonaparte. . . but. . . received only its last develop-
> ment during the Second Empire. Apparently [it was] the final
> victory of this governmental power over society. . . the final
> defeat of the form of class rule pretending to be the autocracy
> of society by its form pretending to be a superior power in
> society. But in fact it was only the last degraded and the only
> possible form of that class ruling, as humiliating to those classes
> as to the working classes which they kept fettered by it.[83]

What is brought to mind by this passage and passages like it is not so much Marx's rigid ruling-class theory of the state but rather Marx's critical discussions of the modern bureaucratic state which were adumbrated originally in his writings of the 1840s, and which were to be extended programmatically in *The Critique of the Gotha Programme.* Marx's *Critique of Hegel's Philosophy of Right* had criticized the bureaucracy's tendency 'to transform the purpose of the State into the purpose of bureaucracy and the purpose of bureaucracy into the purpose of the State'. What the bureaucracy represents is, in Avineri's rather Hegelian words, 'the practical illusion of the universality of political life'; it 'exploits for its own ends the affairs of the community entrusted to it'.[84] Yet over and above the fact that the bureaucracy is favourably placed, indeed, uniquely placed to make affairs of state its own, private patrimony, there is more to the picture than what a bureaucracy in the modern, 'politically emancipated' state will tend to *do*. There is also what a modern bureaucracy *represents*. In this sense the bureaucratic state signifies an institutionalization of the topsy-turvy, inverted nature of the modern state, its character as embodiment and repository of society's 'general will' and communal potential, which it comes to express in an alienated and deceptive manner. What is at issue is less the bureaucratic state's character as *reflecting* the structure of civil society than the *way* it reflects civil society; it distorts and disfigures prevailing social relations – and, we might add, in effect gives these social relations a new lease of life by virtue of the wholly illusory reconciliation and commonality it represents. The claim to universality will itself distort and caricature universality wherever the chances of its genuine emergence are blocked off.

The fact that the bureaucracy is in this way the alienation of public life involves, according to Marx, the proposition that the revolutionary creation of a genuine public life must mean the root and branch extirpation of the bureaucracy. He saw in the elected magistracy of the Paris Commune a device that could render bureaucracy unnecessary. Basing itself, autonomously, on universal suffrage, the Commune approached the stage at which the distinction between the state and civil society began to disappear, and with it all need for the institutionalization of imaginary universality, or what Marx in his early *Critique* of Hegel had called *la république prêtre* of the bureaucracy. Marx praised the Commune's election and dismissal of public servants and the payment of workers' wages because of the deinstitutionalization and demystification of political power these measures involved, because the emergence of such a public magistracy itself implied the disappearance of the distinction between the state and civil society, and an insurance against the possibility of a re-emergence of a new, separate and alien sphere of political affairs. In this way government and administration are emptied of that kind of idolatrous power that makes them into forces independent of society.

Marx's position entails some theoretical implications that are worth discussing. One is that the Weberian critique - an implied critique, perhaps, but a critique none the less - of Marx for not having perceived any parallelism between bureaucracy and capitalism needs to be modified. Marx, it is true, discussed bureaucracy not in connection with the administration of industrial production but in connection with the state; at this level he may have missed or overlooked an important parallelism. It is also true that Marx approached the subject of modern bureaucracy indirectly - at least, from a Weberian point of view - and even obliquely. The explanation for the possibly oblique directionality of Marx's discussions of bureaucracy is, in a word, Hegel; for it is by no means fanciful to suppose that Marx, *whenever* he treated of bureaucracy, had at the back of his mind Hegel's powerful depiction of the modern bureaucratic state. Nineteenth-century European history was not short of examples that would bring Hegel's original presentation - and the necessity for meeting its points - to the fore. While there is little discussion of bureaucracy in *The Manifesto of the Communist Party* and *The German Ideology* (where Marx notes that because of the 'abnormal importance' acquired by German bureaucrats 'during the epoch of absolute monarchy', 'the state built itself up into an apparently independent force'[85] which proved to be not as 'transitory' in Germany as elsewhere), in this particular sense these works prove to be aberrations. French developments reminded Marx all over again that bureaucracy was no passing, 'transitory' political phase.

In dealing with its emergence, Marx's argument proceeds to some extent by indirection but is nevertheless an important and substantive one. What makes the emergence and irruption of capitalism and the bureaucratization of the state cognate in Marx's thinking is his notion of alien politics; the bureaucrat, the real *homme machine*, is the personification of alien politics - the same notion of alien politics that Marx, originally, adumbrated prior to the more famous notion of alienation in the labour process. Such 'priority' does not entail, however, that the two types of alienation can or should be considered separately. On the contrary, they overlap significantly and substantively. Not only do they arise in tandem and, once arisen, reinforce and supplement each other; not only is a process of apparently irreversible usurpation and subsequent mystification common to both; but there is a still more fundamental parallelism between these two types - or *levels* - of alienation. Just as capital, which is congealed labour, signifies and represents the collective character of labour in an alien and fetishistic form, the modern state - particularly in its bureaucratic manifestation - is a fetishistic and oppressive personification of the citizens' general will. Both capital and the state represent, in parallel and cognate ways, the real force of the members of society which opposes itself to them and is out of their control - even though it is *their* product, brought into being and sustained as the result of human (not naturalistic) agency. Both capital and the state represent the 'unintended consequence' of the human actions that create and sustain them; and they represent this unintended consequence with a vengeance. Before the capitalist – whose power is that of his capital – the individual worker (who produces this capital) is powerless, and lacks substance; before the alien state and its parasitic bureaucracy, society itself is powerless. It abdicates all will of its own and submits to the order of an alien will – that of political authority in general, and that of the bureaucracy in particular. This, indeed, is what Marx means in saying in *The Eighteenth Brumaire* that the executive power of the modern state expresses the heteronomy of the nation, in opposition to its autonomy; it represents what divides men one against another. Autonomy is precisely what is lost, and must be regained, by men in society.

But how can it be regained? Marx believed that workers' associations could provide the means; workers, by associating among themselves, could not only emerge from the fragmentation, the atomization, isolation and homogenization imposed upon them by capitalist society, but also, more positively, create new social bonds, and new social needs, among themselves. These new needs supply the cognitive basis for revolution; counterposed to capitalist society and its atomizing prerequisites, a new kind of social organization, according to Marx, was emerging. Its emergence is a kind of revolutionary act in and of itself, since it necessarily challenges the prevailing structure of rewards and expectations. It changes both external social reality and the workers themselves; association creates 'other-directedness', mutuality and community; *Gemeinschaft* (community) in this way emerges from and challenges the nature of *Gesellschaft* (association in the sense of mere external organization for the sake of accomplishing a task – the principle of capitalist society).

However true *in principle* it may be, however, the notion that the emergence of *Gemeinwesen* (communal being) and 'other-directedness' follows from the very nature of proletarian association can, and could, lapse into a dangerous romanticism – or even a purely categorical solution to the dissociative tendencies of capitalist production. Marx, by refusing to look to the past for corporative models of the future, guarded against this danger to some extent.

Marx's theory of the state: a recapitulation

The claim that this chapter has advanced is that while Marx's theory of the state in its most rigid and iron-clad manifestation – the theory that tells us that the modern state is no more than the handmaiden or surrogate of the economic ruling class – is not borne out to the letter by Marx's more detailed historical investigations, reconciliation of the two positions this difference implies is possible. It should proceed, not according to the ahistorical assumption that Marx was a social scientist investigating social reality to bear out his initial hypotheses – an assumption that seems not to square with what Marx himself thought he was doing – but according to the very factor this assumption neglects: the theory of alien politics that pre-dates Marx's ruling-class theory of the state and which informs (with a remarkable constancy) almost all of what Marx wrote subsequently on the subject of the state.

The point here is not simply that what I am calling 'alien politics' is an integral part of Marx's theory of the state; it is also that there are connections – connections important to an understanding of Marx's enterprise in general – between Marx's theory of the *state* and Marx's theory of *alienation*, a theory which is not, and was not intended to be, restricted to factory production in the machine age. Marx's theory of alienation, that is, has a resonance beyond the assembly-line; and much of this resonance is *political* as well as economic and social.

To see this more clearly we must take our bearings. Even though it was Hegel who in many respects posed the problem of alienation for Marx, as we have seen, Ludwig Feuerbach's concept of religious alienation had an important part to play in the evolution of Marx's response to Hegel. Feuerbach's influence can be discerned, readily enough, in the *Economic and Philosophic Manuscripts* of 1844 and in 'On the Jewish Question' (1843) alike. Yet, once Feuerbach's importance to Marx's self-emancipation from Hegel's influence is admitted, certain reservations need to be noted. In the first place, Hegel's discussion of religion – at least in *The Philosophy of Right* – has much more of a social bearing than Feuerbach's points about religious alienation displayed. It was *Hegel*, after all, who had indicated – to Marx, among others – that 'religion is principally resorted to in times of distress' (as Feuerbach had reiterated), and that 'man must venerate the state as a secular deity',[86] thereby setting up – and, in effect, cueing – the argument of 'On the Jewish Question'. This leads to a second reservation about Feuerbach's argument. Even though he perceived that what man lacks in fact he achieves in fancy, or fantasy, and that an opulent God is related to an indigent humanity, these points are in no way *politically* programmatic. Feuerbach even falls behind Hegel in the sense of not having penetrated beyond abstract categories like 'man' and 'humanity' – which means that Feuerbach's much-vaunted 'materialism' is itself abstract, as Marx pointedly made clear in his *Theses on Feuerbach*. The human essence (*Gattungswesen*) whose alienation accounts for religion can be reclaimed by men according to Feuerbach *at the level of conceptualization*. This solution to the problem of alienation is, in other words, a purely categorical solution of the kind Marx was to criticize trenchantly – as we shall see – in *The German*

Ideology. Marx, by contrast, regarded alienation as a social (and political) problem demanding a social (and political) solution. Whereas Feuerbach had presented the alienation of human essence as a *fait accompli*, and had not proffered any historical or social explanation for its incidence or persistence, Marx offered a very different kind of analysis. Marx set out to show that alienation is derived from a basic inadequacy in the structure of society and that it can be explained, accordingly, only by means of an investigation of people's (not 'man's') real, non-alienated, non-religious life.

One of Marx's earliest speculations, arrived at in the course of this investigation (an investigation best regarded as his life's work), can be found in his *Critique of Hegel's Philosophy of Right*, where Marx indicates the historical nature of his categories by contrasting medieval and modern relationships between the political and the social. In the Middle Ages, says Marx, all economic activity was simultaneously and by the same token political in character. 'In the Middle Ages property, commerce, society, man, are all political; the material content of the state was posited by its form. The life of the state and the life of the people are identical'; that this life is nevertheless *unfree* life is underscored by Marx's denigration of the Middle Ages as 'the democracy of unfreedom' and as 'the animal history of mankind'.[87]

Medieval times provide an explicit contrast, however, with modern times, times in which the state is abstracted from the world of 'property, commerce, society, man'. These categories are no longer 'political' in the sense they were. This abstraction of political relations, this separation of the state as a realm distinct from the social and economic arena is the outcome of the segmentation of modern social and political life which is expressed at the level of the individual, whose life becomes segmented into homologous roles that need not refer to each other. There arise in modern times private, sealed-off spheres of activity – free private commerce, trade unencumbered by medieval hindrances, manufacture untrammelled by guild restrictions and sumptuary laws. These spheres of activity are in no way functions or outgrowths of communal life; on the contrary, what *was* a kind of community fragments and shatters into them. They become separate, 'abstract' components of life at the general, social level *and* of life at the particular level – the life of the individual – alike. These roles can be discussed and explained – and commonly are discussed and explained – severally, apart from one another and apart from the social totality they nevertheless ultimately comprise.

At one level, the most pointed example of this fragmentation that is attendant upon the dissolution of the medieval type of integral unity is the separation of the state, of political activity as such, from society. What men do politically no longer involves, or is no longer coterminous with, what men do socially, and what men do productively, in the everyday conduct of their lives. Political action becomes its own sphere of activity. It seals itself off from social and economic activity. It is no longer cognate or coterminous with social and economic activity; the liberal theory of the night-watchman state, which stands aside from the self-interested economic pursuits of men in civil society, is an ideological expression of the social fact that politics no longer refers to, or has any real bearing upon, properly economic activity, which is said to be capable of regulating itself. Social and economic life have undergone depoliticization.

Marx constantly characterized the operation of the market mechanism as being unrestrained, and even anarchic. Far from being characterized by an excess of state regulation – as many an anarchist imagined that it was – society is left very much to its own devices, with disastrous effects on the lives of the human constituents who make it up, and whose activity sustains it. Depoliticization means that there is no real control over the division of labour in society, or over its process of production. Any adjustment among social needs and the imperatives of the productive process, any regulation of the various branches of production is consigned to, and effected by, the impersonal market mechanism – a mechanism over which even the most favourably placed capitalist occupying the most pivotal position has but a very limited effect. What is lacking is any conscious control over the operation of impersonal forces – the phenomenon of alienation in the labour process writ large. Individuals, whether we take them separately, one by one, or collectively, at the larger economic level, are powerless faced with the outcome of their own actions. Smith's 'hidden hand' deals out not harmoniousness but dislocation – as Hegel, in his manner, had recognized – and this dislocation is the real 'unintended consequence' of the nexus of economic activity. There follows the bitter paradox that increasingly socialized production increasingly eludes rational social control.

The dimensions of this outrageous and inhuman paradox, Marx wants us to believe, are purely historical in character; but this does not mean that its solution can be found in the past. Marx conspicuously does not preach a medieval type of organic society, the 'democracy of unfreedom'. It may be that in such a society political life is not divorced from but is identical with private life, life as it is lived; but it remains true that *neither* contiguous realm, neither political nor private life, gives any opportunity for self-determination. In the Middle Ages man is the real essence of the state, as Marx puts it, but he is an unfree man, just as the state itself awaits *its* freedom – the process of 'political emancipation' of 'On the Jewish Question'.

This political emancipation, as we have seen, assigns a two-fold set of roles to the individual. On the one hand, he is a member of civil society, an egoistical, independent, individual; on the other hand, he becomes a citizen, a moral and social being. The division can be traced back, through Hegel's distinction of state and civil society, to Rousseau's distinction between the *homme privé*, the bourgeois, and the *citoyen*, the man of public affairs; however, while with Rousseau the isolated, autonomous, self-sufficient existence of man is perceived as 'natural' and primal, and as corresponding to the inherent spontaneous qualities of human nature, in Marx this characteristic is historically specific. It corresponds to, and is the product of, modern civil society. The isolation of individual members of civil society one from another is required by the particular, transitory historical period it alone characterizes.

Yet, to follow Rousseau one step further, we can see that the political existence of man is the realm of his collective, social and moral existence. Marx added to this perception that it was precisely this realm that is alienated in relation to man's concrete, immediate existence once capitalism has taken root. Man under capitalism is not a generic social being; his personal attributes, characteristics and powers are not apprehended as social powers, and social power proceeds without regard to personal qualities. (To see this we can go beyond the well-known inversion of the proletarian, who becomes the object worked upon by the production process, and the machine, which becomes the subject; we can take the example of the capitalist. He possesses capital – the controlling power over labour and its products – not by virtue of any personal qualities he may exhibit but in his capacity as owner of capital. His power is the purchasing power of his capital; his mastery – rather like that of the master in Hegel's master-slave paradigm – is not illusory, but it is devoid of any real human content. There are even very real limits on its effectiveness in what is, at base, an impersonal system of production. Marx's emphasis on the emptiness and parasitism of the capitalist's role is, among other things, a riposte to Saint-Simon's misleading, because misplaced, distinction between *les industriels* and *les oisifs*.)

What is lacking, even at the level of the most favourably placed individual (or even at the level of the capitalist class *in toto*), is conscious social control. As a faculty, this becomes a fantasy, being projected on the remote and ineffective level of the alien state. By virtue of its own lack of content the state permits the dislocation of individual and social life to proceed unrestrained. The dichotomy of political and social life can be ended only by subjecting the latter to that degree of control which will *ipso facto* end the abstraction of genuine social regulation into the unreal realm of alien politics. 'Freedom', in the words of *The Critique of the Gotha Programme*, 'consists in converting the state from an organ superimposed upon society into one completely subordinate to it';[88] this, indeed, is much of the message of Marx's writings on nineteenth-century France, including *The Civil War in France*, which indicates how the conversion might be effected.

The duality that operates throughout these writings is that outlined originally in 'On the Jewish Question' - that of 'political' as opposed to 'human' emancipation. A society characterized by political emancipation splits human life in an unprecedented way into public and private roles; restricts man's social, collective life to the political realm, which is sharply demarcated and restricted; and makes this realm 'alien' as well as remote because it no longer corresponds to man's real, empirical life in civil society. *This* life, everyday life and action, is asocial and egoistic; man sees others as he is constrained to see them, as means of furthering his own ends, as obstacles to their attainment, as rivals and competitors. Man, in short, is debased, and becomes 'the plaything of alien powers', having no control over the powerful social forces engendered by his own activity.

All of these characteristics of 'political emancipation' are reflected in the modern state. The state becomes the abstracted, alienated general form of civil society, which must be separated from civil society because - and to the extent that - society does not form a moral and political whole in and of itself. It is dislocated, fragmented, split and torn by self-seeking individual and class interests. Since the orientation of the individuals who constitute this society does not transcend their selfish goals and egoistic ends, generality and sociality are projected upwards and outwards and take the form of the alien state. An alien structure is superimposed upon a realm of private, self-interested activity.

What is striking about the picture of 'political emancipation' first outlined in 'On the Jewish Question' is its similarity to what Marx, much later, had to say about the modern state in *The Class Struggles in France, The Eighteenth Brumaire of Louis Bonaparte, The Civil War in France,* and *The Critique of the Gotha Programme.* The independence of the state under Louis Bonaparte is very much the same conception of the alienated state we encounter in 'On the Jewish Question'. In each case, the state purports to represent and institutionalize, to embody and incorporate, all common interests. These common interests are transformed into a higher general interest, divorced from civil society and counterposed to it. This alien general interest is connected to the empirical structure of civil society, but it does not simply reflect this structure like a mirror. The myriad usages of the word 'represent' in *The Eighteenth Brumaire* indicate (among other complications) a far greater degree of complexity than that provided by the image of a static mirroring device. Distance, to be sure, is involved in the state's separation from civil society, but so is distortion.

One way of underscoring what this distortion entails is to note that the state-society dichotomy reproduces itself in microcosm within the life of the individual. The split between private and public, that is to say, reappears in microcosmic and internalized parallel form within each individual. The individual is the victim of a split personality in the specific sense that he is restricted to partiality, to incompleteness, to 'abstraction' in his occupational role, and that he acts 'universally' or communally only at the illusory level of citizenship in the alien state. The very language of Marx's designations of the modern bureaucratic state, apparently soaring high above society, signifies the separation between the citizenry and the means of their common action; it signifies the usurpation of the means of common control, and a kind of mystification into the bargain. The state becomes a fetishistic personification of political potential, very much as the concept of capital designates the separation between the conditions of labour and the producer. Both are the members of society's own, real force set up against them, opposed to them, out of their control. The same process of impersonal necessity which enriches society, multiplies productive potential and impoverishes the individual worker – the alienation of men's most personal attributes – reinforces the alien state and robs society of its substance. Once citizenship has become a purely formal category, men submit to the imposition of an alien will invested with authority. One theoretical conclusion suggested by this process is a parallelism between the bureaucratization of the state and the emergence of capitalism; another is the resonance of the concept of alienation once we see that it has a pronounced political bearing and aspect to it. There is, in this view, more than one set of 'expropriators' to be 'expropriated', more than one way of returning to society all the prerogatives usurped and mystified – in a cognate and parallel way – by the state and by capital. What the overcoming of the state means to Marx (but not to the anarchists) is that socialized man, man as the subject of his own existence instead of the object worked upon by alien political and economic forces, man freely associated with his fellows, could *control* the totality of his social existence, and become master of his own environment and activity.

It is a point of some importance that Marx also indicated how this could – and could not – be achieved. The adoption of a purely political standpoint by the revolutionary workers' movement would have been, to Marx, fraught with danger. In an article he wrote in 1844 against Arnold Ruge's belief that social reform could result from a purely political uprising, Marx argued that in a recent instance of uprising on the part of workers in Lyons, 'political insight deceived them about the origin of their social misery, distorted their consciousness of their real goal, and lied to their social instincts'. A real, social revolution, by contrast, Marx went on,

> takes place at the level of the totality, because even though it
> might be limited to one factory district, it is a protest of man
> against his dehumanized life, because its starting point is the
> one, real individual, because the communal nature from which
> the individual does not want to be severed is the true communal

nature of man. . . [on the other hand, the merely] political soul
of a revolution consists in the tendency of the politically powerless classes to put an end to their isolation from the state and its
authority. Its level is that of the state, an abstract totality, whose
whole being is to be separated from real life, and which is unthink-
able without the organized antithesis between the universal idea
and the individual existence of man. Hence a revolution of the
political soul also organizes, in accordance with the narrow and
split nature of this soul, a ruling group at the expense of society.[89]

Marx's position here was no early, immature sentimentalizing that
he was later, as a 'mature' thinker, to slough off and abandon. On the
contrary, Marx's reasons for applauding the lost cause of the Paris
Commune and for castigating the German Workers' Party in *The
Critique of the Gotha Programme* are very much the same as his reasons
for criticizing the Lyons workers in 1844. His further insistence that
'the working class cannot simply lay hold of the ready-made state
machinery and wield it for its own purposes'[90] in *The Civil War in
France* follows directly from his position in 1844. Thus while it is true
that the markedly Hegelian vocabulary of the 1844 essay – with its
reference to 'abstract totality', 'political soul', 'universal idea', and so
forth – was not carried over into Marx's later writings, the central
distinction Marx outlined in this and other writings between the 'merely
political' and the 'properly social' resounds through Marx's later writings
at a far deeper level than that of vocabulary. Picking up and extending
a point of Arnold Ruge's, Marx in 1844 went on to clarify the distinction in question.

Do not all uprisings without exception. . . break out in disastrous
isolation of men from the community? Does not every uprising
necessarily presuppose this isolation? Would the [French]
Revolution of 1789 have occurred without the disastrous
isolation of the French citizens from the community? Its aim,
after all, was to end this isolation. But the community from
which the worker is isolated is a community of a very different
order and extent than the political community. This community
from which his own labour separates him is life itself, physical
and spiritual life, human morality, human activity, human
enjoyment, human existence. Human existence is the real
community of man. As the disastrous isolation from this
existence is more final, intolerable, terrible and contradictory
than isolation from the political community, so is the ending
of this isolation. And even as a partial reaction, a revolt against
it means all the more, as man is more than citizen, and human
life more than political life. Hence, however partial the industrial

revolt may be, it conceals within itself a universal soul; no
matter how universal a political revolt may be, it conceals a
narrow-minded spirit under the most colossal form.[91]

Marx, as we shall see, was later in his career as a revolutionist to insist
(against Bakunin, among others) on the necessity for political action on
the part of the proletariat. There is, however, no real inconsistency
between what Marx said in the 1840s and his insistence (in the 1860s
and 1870s) that class action is political action, because what is involved
in both sets of claims is a common refusal. The proletarian movement,
Marx continues to believe, should not be misled by purely political
demands and imperatives, that is, by demands and imperatives that are
restricted within the political realm, and which bear no relation to –
and have no effect upon – the social and economic system. A purely
political movement, like a *coup d'état* on the part of a conspiratorial
elite, would be in Marx's view counter-productive from the social point
of view, since conspiratorial *Putsche* operate on the assumption that
a change in control at the helm would in and of itself be sufficiently
momentous to effect any necessary changes in the underlying social
and economic system. From Marx's point of view, such an assumption
cannot lead into substantial, fundamental revolutionary change because
any thoroughgoing revolutionary change has different priorities, just
as serious, worthwhile revolutionary doctrine proceeds (in Marx's eyes,
at any rate) from society to the state, and not vice versa.

   This does not mean that the political realm can be ignored, or left
to its own devices, by the conscientious revolutionary. On the contrary,
Marx was to remain adamant about the necessity to transform the
political realm by means of political action and struggle, although he
endeavoured to make it clear that such political action and focus was
not a substitute for social and economic transformation. Nor was it to
be undertaken at the expense of action in the social and economic
realm. It was to be *part of* such action – and a crucially important part
of such action into the bargain. Marx, in a letter of 1871, expressed
the kind of reasoning that was wont to send shivers down an anarchist's
spine. 'The political movement of the working class', said Marx,

   has, of course, as its final object the conquest of political power
   for this class, and this requires, of course, a previous organization
   of the working class developed up to a certain point, which itself
   arises from its economic struggles. But on the other hand, every
   movement in which the working class comes out as a class against
   the ruling class and tries to coerce them by pressure from without
   is a political movement. For instance, the attempt in a particular
   factory, or even in a particular trade, to force a shorter working
   day out of the individual capitalists by strikes etc. is a purely

economic movement. The movement to force through an eight-hour *law*, etc., however, is a *political* movement. And in this way, out of the separate economic movements of the workers there grows up everywhere a *political* movement, that is to say a movement of the *class*, with the object of achieving its interests in a general form, in a form possessing generally, socially coercive force. Though these movements presuppose a certain degree of previous organization, they are in turn equally a means of developing this organization.[92]

To see this may not solve all the problems of a Marxist politics, but it does cast light on these problems. Revolutionary action entails collective self-assertion on the part of a conscious proletariat; it means the recapturing of alienated powers through a process of social (not political) self-emancipation. That this self-emancipation is central to Marxism can be seen from Marx's *Theses on Feuerbach*. Marx recognizes that revolutionary social transformation must entail the transformation of men themselves, their attitudes, abilities and habits, and that without this more fundamental change, any institutional change at the political level – such as that of the French Revolution – will not be thoroughgoing. It will proceed merely at the level of the 'political emancipation' of 'On the Jewish Question', which would mean, *inter alia*, that the tension between human actuality and human potentiality (which had made transformation necessary in the first place) would remain in existence. Its form might change, its content would not. The need to bridge actuality and potentiality would remain strong. Everything hinges on how the process of reconciliation is to be conceived.

Attempts at reconciliation, that is to say, had been made; and all of them fell down at one particular kind of stumbling block. To take one rather well-known example, let us look briefly at Rousseau, a thinker for whom the difference between what men were and what they could be was palpable, and the task of their reconciliation an urgent one. Yet Rousseau's almost ruthless honesty testifies to his perception of the central difficulty.

For a new-born people to relish wise maxims of policy and to pursue the fundamental rules of statecraft, it would be necessary that the effect should become the cause; that the social mind, which should be the product of such institution, should prevail even at the institution of society; and that men should be, before the formation of laws, what those laws alone can make them.[93]

Rousseau was no revolutionary – although his iconoclasm inspired others who were revolutionaries – but the dilemma he specifies in this passage from *The Social Contract* is a particularly acute dilemma for revolutionaries; the more so since revolutionaries tend, broadly, to be materialists. Let us look at the dilemma more closely. Men, according to Enlightenment epistemology, are the products of their circumstances; they are unfit to found society anew so long as they are stamped and corrupted by imperfect institutions. They can recognize the need for, and acquire the ability to sustain, social change, only if they have already benefited from the influences of such change. They are caught in a vicious circle, which is broken, in Rousseau's case, by the Legislator, That this figure casts his shadow over subsequent revolutionary theorizing is clear from the writings of Buonarroti and Weitling. Buonarroti puts the matter starkly:

> The experience of the French Revolution. . . sufficiently
> demonstrates that a people whose opinions have been formed
> by a regime of inequality and despotism is hardly suitable, at
> the beginning of a regenerative revolution, to elect those who
> will direct it and carry it out to completion. This difficult task
> can only be borne by wise and courageous citizens who, consumed
> by love of country and love for humanity, have long pondered
> on the causes of public evils, have rid themselves of common
> prejudice and vice, have advanced the enlightenment of their
> contemporaries, and, despising gold and worldy grandeur, have
> sought their happiness. . . in assuring the triumph of equality.

Weitling is no less aware of the predicament. 'To want to wait', he wrote,

> as it is usually suggested one should, until all are suitably
> enlightened, would mean to abandon the thing altogether:
> because never does an entire people achieve the same level of
> enlightenment, at least not so long as inequality and the struggle
> of private interests within society continue to exist.[94]

Weitling – who used this point in his dispute with Marx – went on to compare the dictator who organizes his workers with a duke who commands his army.

There is no need to labour the point that revolutionaries – often for the reasons just outlined – often tend to elitism. But it is germane to this particular discussion to indicate that Marx attempted to cut through this dilemma. In 1879 Marx and Engels wrote a 'circular letter' that contained the following recollection:

> When the International was formed, we expressly formulated the
> battle cry: The emancipation of the working class must be the
> work of the working class itself. We cannot, therefore, co-operate

with people who openly state that the workers are too
uneducated to emancipate themselves and must first be freed
from above by philanthropic bourgeois and petty bourgeois.[95]

This sentiment was observed in the breach – as we shall see – at times
during Marx's disputes with Bakunin: yet the theoretical development
that underlies it is central to Marx's notion of proletarian politics and
praxis. 'The materialist doctrine concerning the changing of circumstances and upbringing', wrote Marx in 1845, 'forgets that circumstances
are changed by men and that it is essential to educate the educator
himself. This doctrine must, therefore, divide society into two parts,
one of which is superior. . .' The rider to the 'Third Thesis on Feuerbach' is no less significant: 'The coincidence of the changing of circumstances and of human activity or self-changing can be conceived and
rationally understood only as revolutionary practice.'[96]
 What Marx was attempting to do in 1845 was to shortcircuit the
predicament of the materialist revolutionary. His objections to the
various attempts to graft revolutionary action on to a resolutely materialist, determinist epistemology are readily enough listed. There is an
ethical objection to the notion of pursuing libertarian or emancipatory
ends by authoritarian means – a paradox we are to encounter again.
There are *epistemological* objections to the notion that the conditions
for a critical perspective on reality are denied most people, but that,
nevertheless, a few are (somehow) permitted a path to the truth.
Indeed, Enlightenment materialism proceeds to a bizarre combination
of the most mechanistic determinism (men are merely the effects of
their circumstances) with the most idealistic voluntarism (a few escape
this all-powerful conditioning to transform human circumstances at a
stroke). There are *political* objections to the idea that social reality is
inert, a closed system possessed of the power to shape its human objects
into acceptance or submission, and that nevertheless, against this
immense power, the force of a Rousseauian legislator, or Weitling's
'dictator', or of Buonarroti's 'wise and courageous citizens' can effectively prevail. But on top of all these objections is another – that whoever separates (even conceptually) 'circumstances' from 'men', counterposing and polarizing one to the other, acts in accordance with the
precepts and mechanism of bourgeois economy. The point, after all, is
that 'men' should *control* their 'circumstances' instead of vice versa.
 Marx's argument – which has more specificity than is often credited
– can be distinguished, and at this juncture *should* be distinguished,
from the arguments of many later Marxists. It is very different from
Lenin's short-lived but polemical (and influential) insistence in *What
is to be Done?* that the spontaneous movement of the working class
creates nothing more than the trade unionism which is 'precisely
working-class bourgeois politics';[97] it is very different from Althusser's

insistence that men, who are no more than the supports and effects of their social, political and ideological relations, can transform these relations only by means of knowledge ('theoretical practice') brought to them from without;[98] and it is very different from Marcuse's insistence upon a working class that is integrated, indoctrinated, manipulated and that is unable to see where its interests lie.[99]

Marx's argument about the cognitive basis of revolution was advanced, largely, in *The German Ideology*. Attacking Max Stirner's notion that 'a society cannot be made new as long as those of whom it consists and who constitute it, remain as of old', Marx points out that Stirner

> believes that the communist proletarians who revolutionize
> society and put the relations of production and the form of
> intercourse on a new basis – i.e. on themselves as new people,
> on their new mode of life – that these proletarians remain 'as of
> old'. The tireless propaganda carried out by these proletarians,
> their daily discussions among themselves, sufficiently prove how
> little they want to remain 'as of old', and how little they want
> people to remain 'as of old' . . . *In revolutionary activity the
> changing of self coincides with the changing of circumstances.*[100]

Marx is referring, in the first instance, to the fact of association among workers and the practical orientation this involves. Workers by associating create new social bonds – a different kind of social bond – and they emerge from the atomization, homogenization and isolation that would otherwise be imposed upon them by capitalist society. A new kind of organization is emerging, according to Marx; in and of itself, its emergence is a revolutionary act, changing both the individuals concerned and the external reality that they make and re-make. It is in this sense that an association (or an uprising) is 'universal', 'even though it might be limited to the factory district'. This association, in Avineri's words, 'creates other-directedness and mutuality, it enables the worker to become again a *Gemeinwesen* [communal being]. The act and process of association, by changing the worker and his world, offer a glimpse into future society',[101] because the activity involved creates the conditions for the realization of its own aims. In this sense the closed circle of alienation – and the social, political and epistemological dilemmas its involves – can be broken, as Marx makes clear in the *Economic and Philosophic Manuscripts*:

> When communist artisans form associations, teaching and
> propaganda are their first aims. But their association itself
> creates a new need – the need for society – and what appeared
> to be a means has become an end. The most striking results

of this practical development are to be seen when French
socialist workers meet together. Smoking, eating and drinking
are no longer simply means of bringing people together.
Society, association, entertainment which also has society
as its aim, is sufficient for man; the brotherhood of man is
no empty phrase but a reality. . .[102]

Yet the fact of association among workers is not in itself an *ultima
ratio*. Its significance, according to Marx, consists in its futurity, in
the way in which it points forward, in its character as a presentiment
of future communist society. In this sense workers' associations are
politically programmatic; they are instances of the reappropriation by
men of control over the conditions of their existence, and as such
cannot but point forward. Indeed, it is for this very reason that organizational questions were never treated by Marx as purely tactical, or
as being concerned purely with means towards some undefined revolutionary end; the organization of the revolutionary working class to
Marx - as his anarchist enemies in the International were to recognize
- *is* the revolutionary end *in statu nascendi*. Future society, as we shall
see in dealing with the International, is contained in embryo within
the kind of association that the working class was adopting. Future
society, after all, had nothing else from which it could grow. Marx
constantly stressed working-class organization as having a generative
character:

Both for the production on a mass scale of this communist
consciousness, and for the success of the cause itself, the
alteration of men on a mass scale is necessary, an alteration
which can only take place in a practical movement, a revolution:
this revolution is necessary, therefore, not only because the
ruling class cannot be overthrown in any other way, but also
because the class overthrowing it can only in a revolution succeed
in ridding itself of all the muck of ages and become fitted to found
society anew.[103]

Marx's position, as we shall see, is that political action on the part of
the proletariat is aimed at the state but cannot succeed at a purely
institutional level; general problems require general solutions, and not
partial solutions, or those that take the part for the whole. What is
crucially important to an understanding of Marx's conception of
politics - revolutionary and other - is that his theory of alienation and
his theory of the state cannot really be dealt with separately. If we
consider alienation, not as something restricted to the assembly-line
in the modern factory, but as a deeply rooted social (and political)
phenomenon, and as a social and political problem demanding a social

and political solution, we are closer to what Marx intended than are those who have emphasized the importance of the *Economic and Philosophic Manuscripts* at the expense of examining Marx's *other* writings of the same period. The *Manuscripts are* important, but we should not allow ourselves to become fixated on, or distracted by them if this means something it has meant in the past: that we can afford to ignore those writings where Marx made clear the specifically political dimension his concept of alienation embodies.

That 'man's own deed becomes an alien power opposed to him which enslaves him instead of being controlled by him' is not a perception Marx intended to limit to factory production (as an uncritical reading of the *Manuscripts* – and of nothing else – might suggest). Marx is not only pointing to but portraying alienation as a political problem that is specific to modern times, and that cries out for a political solution. What lies at the root of all forms of alienation is the unintended consequence of social action. Under capitalist conditions, Marx insisted, such unintended consequence is all-pervasive; it is practically systematic. Men are living in a world they cannot control, a world that eludes rational social control, a dynamic and progressive economic system that operates independently of the will of its human constituents and which appears to have its own momentum in riding roughshod over these constituents, who are more objects of a process of production than its subjects. The point here is not simply that in this topsy-turvy world objects are subjects and subjects objects, or that 'things' (to quote Ralph Waldo Emerson) 'are in the saddle and ride mankind', it is also that these very 'things' are human products. Under capitalism in particular, the material world is made by men, and external nature is humanized – however alien its form may be. As Marx puts it in a passage from *Theories of Surplus Value* defending Ricardo against Sismondi, even

> production for its own sake means nothing but the development
> of human productive forces, in other words the production of
> the richness of human nature as an end in itself . . . although, at
> first, the development of the capacities of the human species
> takes place at the cost of the majority of human individuals and
> even classes, at the end it breaks through this contradiction and
> coincides with the development of the individual; the higher
> development of individuality is thus only achieved by an
> historical process.[104]

Marx, as is well known, believed that the human mode of existence is inconceivable apart from the transformation of nature by productive activity; and that this transformation – the technology of labour – was *the* fundamental ontological determinant of human existence. Yet, what is often forgotten is that the realization of this teleology entails the transformation of reality into something that is (literally) realized, so that man can recognize himself in a world that he has himself created.

The goal recalls the German Romantics as well as Hegel; the aim is not to create men of a certain type but to enable men to create themselves. However, too much should not be made of these similarities; Marx adds specificity to his prescription by basing it on a careful analysis - one that is at once speculative and empirical - of the various manifestations of alienation (the denial of the 'free conscious activity' that is man's 'species-being') in capitalist society. The attainment of 'species-being' - the overcoming of alienation - is to Marx politically programmatic. The question, then, whether a stress on alien politics as an integral part of the overall pattern of alienation helps us specify what is involved in this overcoming of alienation, is quick to impose itself; and the question is particularly important in view of the fact that an apparent lack of specificity in Marx's notion of future communist society has bedevilled discussion in the past.

It is impossible to clear up all - or even many - of the ambiguities of Marx's position on future society, which he had good theoretical reasons not to wish to describe in detail. Given a choice between Hegel's insistence that philosophy is no crystal ball, that philosophical enquiry, properly so-called, consists in knowledge of the present in the light of retrospective knowledge of the past, and what Marx disparagingly called 'Comtist recipes for the cook-shops of the future',[105] it is clear enough that Marx opted for the former. Utopian socialists were, in general, anything but reluctant to specify, often in the minutest detail, what future society was about to look like; Marx, who ridiculed such pretensions, by contrast said very little about the shape of things to come. His reluctance was neither unprincipled nor indefensible, based as it was on an uncommon (at the time) recognition, one of Hegelian lineage, of the continuity of present and future. The present is, in this view, brought to bear on the future; the contours of future society, in so far as they are discernible at all, must be discerned within present-day society, for they have nowhere else from whence to emerge. Yet, even if this point is granted - and Marx's rather reserved, scholarly caution is compared favourably with the mania for prediction that characterized so many of his contemporaries - nagging doubts have persisted among sensitive readers of Marx. It has seemed paradoxical - or inadequate - to these readers that Marxism, an enterprise characterized by futurity above all else, a theory geared to a vision of the future, had so little to say about what this future would bring.

A stress on alienation - in the expansive sense outlined in this chapter, and as specifically including alien politics - does something to remedy these shortcomings. The advent of future society consists in the overcoming of alienation; and the overcoming of alienation implies the overcoming of all its *mediations*. The abolition of private property, as Marx never tired of insisting, is the *sine qua non* of communism, as is well known; but what is less well known – if equally important – is that the abolition of private property, while it is necessary, is certainly not sufficient as a condition for the survival of communism. Taken as an end in itself, the abolition of private property (as Marx indicated in the *Economic and Philosophic Manuscripts*) can lead only to 'the re-establishment of society as an abstraction against the individual', to the erection of society as a 'universal capitalist' or as a 'community of work and wages'.[106] While this austere ideal commended itself to many other socialist thinkers during Marx's lifetime – among them Proudhon – it did not appeal to Marx.

It is a point of some importance to Marx's disputes with the anarchists that his vision of future society, unlike theirs, was neither 'reactionary' nor 'utopian', at least in his own eyes. But is there any content to Marx's claim to have gone beyond the 'reactionary' and 'utopian' character of rival socialist, communist and anarchist creeds? It is certainly true that Marx constantly lampooned those, on the left and on the right, who fought capitalism on behalf of the traditional values it was corroding. Marx, indeed, seems never to have accepted the Romantic attitude that capitalism had disrupted a pre-industrial idyll; and this alone makes him unusual, if not unique, among his revolutionary contemporaries. Marx was aware that artisanship denoted the engulfment and absorption of the artisan within the confines of a narrow trade, that the artisan's mental horizon is restricted within the confines of his occupation. The proletarian, in Marx's view, is very different; his 'alienation' takes a more radical form, to be sure, but the independence, detachment, disengagement and indifference displayed by the modern worker – which can be taken as indices of his alienation – are nevertheless not unmitigated curses.

The proletarian's conceptual rejection of his occupation and its standards, in Marx's view, is progressive; it is so at least in the sense that the worker of pre-capitalist modes of production could not even conceive of the possibility of rejecting the conditions of his life. He understood himself as part of them, not them as part of himself. To put the same point another way: wage-workers, modern proletarians, stand in an alienated, 'abstract', detached relation to their conditions of life; but *it is a relation*. Formerly, there was none. It is for this reason that 'the subjection of the [modern] producer to one branch exclusively . . . is a necessary step in the development' of the human productive faculty; 'the new modern science of technology' resolves each aspect of production 'into its constituent movements, without any regard to their possible execution by the hand of man'.[107] That this development is oppressive is obvious enough: what Marx added to this point was another, that this very oppression liberates. The sacrifice of his 'organic' unity with the process of production entails a potential growth in the autonomy of the worker.

But even if this point - which Marx was wont to make in even stronger terms in the case of the peasantry - is admitted, what does it tell us about the character of future communist society? In the course of his lectures on *Wages, Price and Profit* Marx goes some way towards providing an answer. The early development of capitalism, says Marx, takes the form of

> a series of historical processes, resulting in a decomposition of the original union existing between labouring man and his instruments of labour. . . The separation between the man of labour and the instruments of labour once established, such a state of things will maintain itself and reproduce itself on a constantly increasing scale, until a new and fundamental revolution in the mode of production should again overturn it, and *restore the original union in a new historical form.*[108]

The succession Marx is referring to, here and elsewhere, is nothing if not a Hegelian one; the process starts with a simple, *undifferentiated unity* of producer with instrument of production, develops into a relationship involving *differentiation without unity*, and eventuates as a *differentiated unity* corresponding to the development of manifold human talents and attributes. Undifferentiated unity refers to feudal society and artisan production; differentiation without unity to the division of labour under capitalism; and differentiated unity to future communist society. Each stage denotes an advance in freedom; and what is striking about the dialectical sequence itself is that it corresponds to that which we encounter in Hegel's *Philosophy of Right*, where undifferentiated unity characterizes the family, differentiation without unity characterizes civil society, and differentiated unity characterizes the state.

While this is not the place to investigate in detail what this marked parallelism between Hegel and Marx may ultimately comport, it is germane to an understanding of Marx's conception of alienation and de-alienation to indicate that the sequence of categories involved implies *futurity* as well as historicity. Capitalism, as Marx often repeated, socializes the production process, collectivizes labour, and develops the capacities of the human species even if these capacities make only an alienated appearance under capitalist conditions. The process by which they come to present themselves to (or against) men in this way is, of course, akin - and indeed *directly parallel* - to the process of 'political emancipation' at the level of the state's relation to civil society. Political emancipation's immediate impact is oppressive: yet without it 'human emancipation' would be inconceivable. Differentiation without unity - which is just another way of describing the defining feature of capitalist production, the separation of the producer from ownership of or disposition over the means of production – has a similar immediate impact, one that is directly oppressive; yet it too, in Marx's view, is an oppression that liberates, or *can* liberate. Here, it is important to get the sense of Marx's perception.

> The fact that the particular type of labour employed is immaterial is appropriate to a form of society in which individuals pass easily from one job to another, the particular type of labour being accidental to them and therefore irrelevant. Labour, not only as a category but also in reality, has become a means to create wealth, and has ceased to be tied as an attribute to a particular individual.[109]

He who performs this labour is not dominated or even stamped by the form it takes; and because the division of labour in capitalist society entails a diminution of specialization *for the workers* (several of whom do the same thing) – if not for society at large – man as proletarian becomes labour in general, labour *sans phrase*. This is an oppression that can liberate because it raises the possibility of developing abilities in general.

In the case of artisan labour, only a few artisanal abilities are created; and because of this inherent limitation, there is no possibility of the transcendence of the conditions of life. 'Rural life' and its 'idiocy', under feudalism, similarly defines and limits its participants in such a way that, for example, the growth of successful class consciousness (at least according to Marx's celebrated depiction of the French peasantry in *The Eighteenth Brumaire*)[110] is precluded and blocked off in advance. Capitalism signifies an advance over this: the 'automatic workshop', as *The Poverty of Philosophy* tersely puts it, 'wipes out specialists and craft idiocy';[111] the mobility of labour, as it becomes called, presupposes a release from the various bonds that had restricted the artisan, and his horizons, under feudal conditions; and even capitalist manipulativeness has a positive side to it.

> . . . capital first creates bourgeois society and the universal appropriation of nature and of social relationships themselves by the members of society. Hence the great civilizing influence of capital: its production of a stage of society compared with which all earlier stages appear to be merely local progress and idolatry of nature. Nature becomes for the first time simply an object for mankind, purely a matter of utility; it ceases to be recognized as a power in its own right; and the theoretical knowledge of its independent laws appears only as a strategem designed to subdue it to human requirements. . . Capital has pushed beyond national boundaries and prejudices, beyond

the deification of nature and the inherited, self-sufficient
satisfaction of existing needs confined within well-defined
bounds, and the reproduction of the traditional way of life.
It is destructive of all this, and permanently revolutionary,
tearing down all obstacles that impede the development of
productive forces, the expansion of needs, the diversity of
production and the exploitation and exchange of natural and
intellectual forces.[112]

This passage, from the *Grundrisse*, parallels others that are rather
better known; the point of Marx's paeans to capitalism and its *mission
civilisatrice* is that even 'the extreme form of alienation. . . in which the
worker . . . is opposed to his own conditions and his own product is a
necessary transitional stage'. Any organic bonds between the worker
and 'his own conditions and his own product' are broken, rent asunder;
Marx had no illusions about what this meant, economically and humanly.
'[The] complete elaboration of what lies within man appears as his
total alienation, and the destruction of all fixed, one-sided purposes as
the sacrifice of the end in itself to a wholly external compulsion.'[113]
Yet the implications of this development point forwards, not back-
wards: Marx was the last person in the world to wish to put the clock
back. At 'early stages of development', as Marx put it, again in the
Grundrisse,

the single individual appears to be more complete, since he has
not yet elaborated the abundance of his relationships and has not
yet established them as powers that are opposed to himself. It is
as ridiculous to wish to return to that primitive abundance as it is
to believe in the continuing necessity of its complete depletion.
The bourgeois view has never got beyond opposition to this
romantic outlook and thus will be accompanied by it, as a
legitimate antithesis, right up to its blessed end.[114]

What, then, is involved in going beyond opposition to the 'romantic
outlook'? If Marx never envisaged reversion to a pre-industrial idyll
as a viable historical alternative to the depredations of capitalism,
where does his dismissal of the 'reactionary utopia' (advocated by
Proudhon and others) lead? The answer to these questions – and one
can be given, within limits, without doing an injustice to the textual
evidence – is cognate with, and parallel to, the answer to another: in
what way is 'human' an advance on 'political' emancipation? Or: in
what ways is 'political emancipation' a foretaste of real, 'human emancipation'? For what is implied throughout is reappropriation of control over the conditions of existence – the real meaning of the overcoming of alienation in all its manifestations. This solution, it should be

emphasized, is no more categorical than the predicament that prompts it; what it involves for men is, above all else, an opportunity. The well-known injunction 'from each according to his ability, to each according to his need' is less complacent than sometimes has been assumed. What it presupposes is that both 'ability' and 'need' *can be fully developed*. Their development is a human task, that men are prevented from undertaking under capitalism (or, of course, any earlier mode of production) except in an alienated manner. Capitalist society restricts the exercise and the scope of human abilities, and it disfigures the very nature of human needs - indeed, of human *senses* themselves. Only with the appropriation of what men produce by the men who produce it will enable these men either to contribute according to their abilities or to consume according to their needs. It is clear from the *Economic and Philosophic Manuscripts* that both abilities and needs will change and develop once they are free to do so. The 'productive forces', as *The Critique of the Gotha Programme* puts it, increase 'with the all-round development of the individual', and not in opposition to this development.

The scenario - dimly sketched as it admittedly (and, Marx would presumably add, necessarily) is - amounts to something very ambitious indeed. The *Manuscripts*, in all seriousness, envisage the liberation of the senses. Socialized man is one whose senses have been fully developed. 'The eye has become a human eye, just as its object has become a social, human object, derived from and for man. . . The senses of social man differ from those of the unsocial.'[115] This may seem surprising, coming from a theorist who prides himself on not being utopian, but it is not historically senseless. Much of what Marx means has been well put by Avineri:

> What the artist creates for himself is being created at the same
> time by others as well; what one person gains in creative
> experience is not at the expense of another person, in other
> words, there exists no zero-sum relationship between the
> artist's enjoyment of his creativity and that of his public.[116]

The scenario is not one that can be satisfied even by its *sine qua non* - the abolition of private property. By this category, Marx meant the abolition of private property *relations* (the existence of social classes defined by the amount and kind of property held) as well as private property as a brute social fact. Its abolition, or overcoming, is required; yet Marx believed that what was also needed was the simultaneous abolition of *other* mediations - of exchange (and of social relations based on exchange); of the division of labour (in its restrictive and monstrous Smithian form); of money (the alien mediation between labour and property) as well as wage-labour; and of the state. Looking at all these, it is of the utmost importance to see them as constituting an interlocking, articulated system, or structure. To single out any one of its components for destruction would be futile. *All* must go. Total problems require total solutions. All these mediations, all these components of alienation, are not symbols but manifestations, and they reciprocally imply, and depend upon, one another. To absolutize any one of them, to single out any particular instance at the expense of dealing with the reciprocal system they all comprise, is to make of the task of revolution a search for a panacea, to deflect one's revolutionary energies into one particular category.

Bearing this in mind, if we proceed to ask not what the overcoming of alienation entails, but what does *not* constitute 'de-alienation', we find, once again, a set of interlocking categories. To begin with, a change in 'control' at the helm is insufficient; to tinker about with the personnel manning the state apparatus, or to believe (with Marx's contemporary Louis-Auguste Blanqui) in the efficacy of a conspiratorially organized *coup d'état*, is to fall far short of what Marx meant by the 'dictatorship of the proletariat', and to remain within the confines of a purely political approach to revolution. It is to remain spellbound by 'political emancipation' and by its consummation, the French Revolution. But we can go further. Even the abolition of the state *per se* – the *Leitmotiv* of the anarchists – would be insufficient, since it might eventuate in the 're-establishment of society as an abstraction against the individual'. Again, mere reformism with wage-rates might institute 'society as a universal capitalist', and, as Marx indicated in the course of his polemics against Proudhon, any 'community' predicated upon even the *equality* of wages would be no more than a community of labour – of wage-labour counterposed to a universal capitalist called society. Alienation here, too, would survive in a different form. Even nationalization of the instruments of production in itself would prove insufficient or misleading, since *relations* as well as forces of production are involved in alienation. The collective appropriation of capital, that is to say, is a means to the overcoming of alienation, to be sure, but it cannot be taken as an end in itself. This point, too, can be put even more strongly. What Marx's warning against re-establishing society as an abstraction against the individual means is that wherever the public sphere is set against the private sphere, alienation still exists. Where the collectivity is counterposed to the individual and his pursuits, community in the sense of *Gesamtpersön-lichkeit* or intersubjectivity – which is the only real sense in which we can identify community – is denied. This, indeed, is the main point of Marx's attack on Max Stirner in *The German Ideology*, as we shall see. The opposition of public and private roles or spheres of activity, of community and individual, is the measure of alien politics, which will flourish if even a changed 'society' is elevated to a fantastic plane.

It seems that this latter point, in particular, has proven to be rather too close to the bone for the so-called 'people's democracies'.[117] If under capitalist conditions individuals reproduce themselves as isolated individuals, as Marx insisted, then under the bureaucratic communism of our times – an 'abstract collectivity' in Marx's terms if ever there was one – they cannot reproduce themselves as individuals at all. It is no accident, perhaps, that in the 'people's democracies' the early Marx (in so far as he is really studied there) is written off as an immature moralist with 'ideological' (non-scientific) concepts, or as a 'youthful idealist'. The extent to which his writings are not only incompatible with the practice of politics in the 'people's democracies', but also provide an immanent critique of them, has been recognized all too rarely.

PART TWO

Disputations

CHAPTER 3

Marx and Stirner

Few persons familiar with Marx's writings would deny the importance of *The German Ideology*. Yet even though its prominence may be readily admitted, this work has rarely been considered (or read) in its entirety; its belated publication[1] and translation into English has had the effect of obscuring the major part of its contents. In particular, the most lengthy section of *The Germany Ideology*, 'Saint Max', the section Marx devoted to a detailed examination of Max Stirner's book *The Individual and his Own* (*Der Einzige und sein Eigenthum*), has been almost completely ignored.[2] Roy Pascal's long-standard English language translation of *The German Ideology*[3] completely omitted Marx's sustained attack on Stirner, and largely because of this omission the assumption gained currency – almost, as it were, by default – that 'Saint Max' is at best of marginal importance to an understanding of *The German Ideology* as a whole, let alone anything outside its covers. This assumption is not supported by an examination of its text. The themes that emerge from such an examination prove to be central to an understanding not only of *The German Ideology* but also of Marx's thought taken in its entirety.

It may be unsurprising that many of the most important arguments that have long been associated with *The German Ideology* should find their fullest expression in 'Saint Max', its longest single section (which takes up fully three-quarters of the manuscript). Examples are not hard to come by; 'Saint Max' contains Marx's most extended arguments about why German liberalism was so pallid, about why German philosophical speculation was so irredeemably idealist, about why Kant's *Critique of Practical Reason* was in Marx's opinion so appropriate to the retarded development of German liberalism and of the German bourgeoisie alike.[4] While these strictures, and the connections among them, are on any reckoning integral to the general argument of *The German Ideology*, we cannot rest content with merely indicating that 'Saint Max' contains the fullest exposition of these and other themes; for 'Saint Max' indicates not only why Marx put forward the arguments of *The German Ideology* in the way that he did, but also why he saw the need to put them forward at all. 'Saint Max' is no mere satellite to a parent body, *The German Ideology*, that can be discussed apart from it; 'Saint Max' is its core.

The shortcomings of Max Stirner's peculiarly individualist brand of anarchism - shortcomings which, as we shall see, were in no way lost upon Marx - should not blind us to the importance of Stirner's *The Individual and his Own* in affording Marx the inescapable opportunity of settling accounts with the Young Hegelians and, by extension, with his own 'philosophical' past. What has been overlooked about 'Saint Max' is that it was Marx's first extended critique of an anarchist theory and also that Marx considered the theory in question to be the consummation of Young Hegelian theorizing, embodying its worst features and exemplifying them to the point of caricature. Marx's unflattering characterization of Stirner explains much about *The German Ideology* that has hitherto passed unnoticed. The very opening words to the 'Preface' amount to an ironic, but not at all unjust, paraphrase of Stirner's argument:

> Hitherto men have constantly made up for themselves false
> conceptions about themselves, about what they are and what
> they ought to be. They have arranged their relationships
> according to their ideas of God, of normal man, etc. The
> phantoms of their brains have got out of their hands. Let us
> liberate them from the chimeras, ideas, dogmas, imaginary beings
> under the yoke of which they are pining away. Let us revolt
> against the rule of thoughts.[5]

The very fact that this opening salvo serves both as a précis of Young Hegelian theorizing in general and of Stirner's argument in particular can tell us much: it tells us what 'the German ideology' is, it tells us why this phrase was used as the title of the book, and it tells us why Marx considered Stirner to be its touchstone. Yet because most commentators (unlike Marx himself) have regarded Stirner as being unworthy of critical attention, they have failed (again unlike Marx himself) to notice Stirner's distinctively Young Hegelian lineage. Nevertheless, it was the Young Hegelian provenance of Stirner's anarchism that prompted Marx to attack it as frontally and brutally as he did and that enabled Marx to signify by this attack his public, unequivocal rejection of Young Hegelianism in general.

Stirner's *The Individual and his Own* did not lack for attention, or even applause, among his fellow Young Hegelians upon its appearance in 1844; and largely for this very reason, the myth that Stirner merits an easy dismissal on the grounds that he moved 'merely on the fringes of Hegelian circles'[6] badly needs putting to rest. William Brazill's recent, painstaking study of the Young Hegelians, seeking in the interests of accuracy to distinguish this school, properly so-called, from the more amorphous Left Hegelians, awards the nomenclature of Young Hegelian to only six people other than Stirner.[7] Brazill's distinction has much to commend it. Stirner was in reality a characteristic, if eccentric, member of the Young Hegelian ginger group in Berlin who delighted in the name of 'the free' (*die Freien*). For all his carefully cultivated character as an *enfant terrible*, Stirner's Young Hegelian credentials were never called into question as the result of his book's appearance – least of all by Marx. Indeed, *The Individual and his Own* enjoyed on its appearance a certain *succès de scandale* in the Young Hegelian circle. Arnold Ruge commended Stirner for having given up Fichtean metaphysics and the Feuerbachian 'theology of humanism' – Stirner had indeed relinquished both – and proceeded to insist that '[Stirner's] book must be sustained and propagated. It is liberation from the stupidest of stupidities, the "social artisans' dogma" . . . which preaches . . . the salvation of *absolute economics*'. Ruge's pinpointing Stirner's opposition to revolutionary socialism may be the most significant part of his response; he also thought for a time (and with doubtful consistency) that *The Individual and his Own* was the ultimate in Young Hegelian thought – Marx *mutatis mutandis* was to agree – and that its very appearance signalled a decisive shift in human history from thought to action.[8] Moses Hess argued, less apocalyptically and rather more coherently, that Stirner had earned his place among those who had expressed the opposition of individuality and collectivism in its most extreme form. The theoretical impasse to which this tension has led, Hess went on to argue, could be resolved not by Ruge's 'action' but only by his own 'socialism', the communal organization of society[9] – a conclusion with which Sitrner, an arch-individualist, would never have agreed.

Ruge and Hess, however, were not the only writers who attempted to appropriate the undoubted *éclat* and shock-effect of Stirner's book of purposes of their own. The initial reaction of Engels is particularly striking. While he considered Stirner's egoism to be 'merely the essence of present-day society and of present-day men brought to the level of consciousness', Engels was nevertheless quick to insist (in a letter to Marx) that this very egoism 'can be built upon even as we invert it'. He went on to compare Stirner to Bentham, only to argue that Stirner's egoism must forthwith be transmuted into communism (*gleich in Kommunismus umschlagen*); and in the same breath Engels ventured the opinion that 'only a few trivialities' needed to be stressed against Stirner 'but what is true in his principles we have to accept.'[10] Marx's reply from Paris to Engels's surprisingly favourable first impression of Stirner's book has not been preserved, but we have more than the central part of a major book written by Marx to indicate that he disagreed; in a later letter Engels was to say that he had come round to Marx's viewpoint and that Hess had done so also.[11]

The responsiveness of the various members of the Young Hegelian circle (other than Marx) to Stirner's arguments indicates that Marx was not wrong in identifying this milieu as Stirner's true setting. Marx considered that the issues Stirner had raised, and the way in which he had raised them, were extreme but characteristic examples of the shortcomings of Young Hegelian 'theoretical bubble-blowing'. Young Hegelian thought in all its various manifestations tended in Marx's opinion to issue in the injunction that 'people have only to change their consciousness to make everything in the world all right'.[12] Such a remonstrance can indeed be levelled against Stirner, among others; but this tells us nothing about the specific arguments of *The Individual and his Own*, or about why Marx, for his part, saw fit to devote the lengthiest portion of a major work to their demolition. Stirner's arguments first of all demand to be outlined if we are to appraise Marx's phrase-by-phrase dissection of them, and to adjudicate the issues dividing the two.

The main lineaments of the argument of *The Individual and his Own* have been expertly traced by Sir Isaiah Berlin. 'Stirner believed', he says,

> that all programmes, ideals, theories as well as political, social and economic orders are so many artificially built prisons for the mind and the spirit, means of curbing the will, of concealing from the individual the existence of his own infinite creative powers, and that all systems must therefore be destroyed, not because they are evil, but because they are systems, submission to which is a new form of idolatry; only when this has been achieved would man, released from his unnatural fetters, become truly master of himself and attain to his full stature as a human being.[13]

What distinguishes Stirner both from other anarchists and from other egoists is the Young Hegelianism that underlies these beliefs – his Young Hegelian notion that men throughout history have been whoring after false gods was counterbalanced by its equally Young Hegelian corollary: that all we need do to change reality is to master our thoughts, instead of letting them master us.

Egoism and anarchism

Max Stirner may be best known as 'the egoistic anarchist'; yet both terms, egoism and anarchism, admit of much elasticity. Engel's immediate comparison of Stirner and Bentham might serve as a reminder of how supple a term 'egoism' can be. Indeed, Stirner's particular brand of egoism is distinct from most other variants. It seems very different, for example, from the argument of Mandeville (and by extension the early political economists) that 'private vices' add up to 'public benefit', if only because Stirner regarded the notion of public (as opposed to private) benefit as nonsensical. Stirner's egoism, again, seems irreducible to Romantic notions of subjectivity if only because Stirner was a forthright foe of all teleological categories – of goals, purposes, ends, even if these are imposed upon the individual by the individual himself. Stirner's aggressive egoism superficially might seem closer to the assertiveness propounded by theorists like Spinoza and Hobbes than to Romantic striving; but even this resemblance is more apparent than real. Stirner denied the possibility of any autocratic (or even political) outcome of the free play of personal, self-defined forces, and in any case did not share the psychological determination of a Spinoza, a Hobbes or an Helvétius. These theorists had maintained that the assertive ego could act only on its own behalf, whereas Stirner – a Young Hegelian to the last – despairingly maintained that quite to the contrary men throughout history had submitted themselves voluntarily to what he calls 'hierarchy' – a sequence of oppressive, outside belief-systems and institutions. All such systems and structures, Stirner insisted, had struck at men's uniqueness, originality and singularity.

David McLellan has pointed out, aptly, that Stirner's 'analysis of the modern age is a sort of demonology of the spirits to which humanity has been successfully enslaved';[14] *The Individual and his Own* takes the form of a diatribe against the effects of these successive *idées fixes*, against what Stirner's translator called 'wheels in the head' (Stirner's own term had been *die Sparren*), against beliefs that had worked successfully and remorselessly to prevent the ego from working on its own behalf. Stirner's aim was to tear away the veils, to remove the blinkers from men's eyes; the autonomous individual was in his conception not a descriptive category but a hoped-for goal of future human endeavour – a goal that is presaged only among the outcasts of modern society, only among its criminals and paupers. The obstacle to the final emergence of individual autonomy according to Stirner has proved to be consciousness – consciousness conceived in the Young Hegelian manner as being alien, oppressive and imposed.

Stirner has much more in common with his fellow Young Hegelians than with those who have (always loosely) been termed egoists, and if we fail to see this we are likely to misconstrue his argument, as have several of his anarchist admirers. *The Individual and his Own* takes the form of an inventory of obstacles to the free play of the ego, obstacles grounded in consciousness, which are attacked so broadly that the theories of most other 'egoists' would not escape condemnation. The 'absolute ego' of Fichte is a case in point; Stirner attacks it frontally because it is a postulated goal that might dominate individuals and feed on their autonomy, and because the goal in question was said to consist in the realization of rational universality, a project Stirner regarded as senseless. If Stirner's egoism were to be made operative, he never tires of telling us, it would not 'realize' anything; it would destroy all known forms of society once and for all.

This does not mean that Stirner considered himself a revolutionary or his doctrine a revolutionary doctrine. He saw revolution – as Arnold Ruge perceived – in the same, unsparing light in which he saw religious faith, moral duty, political organization and social institutions. All such beliefs, all such insititutions Stirner regarded as demands upon the individual self which displace its 'particularity' (Stirner's *Eigenheit*) with various conceptions of the purportedly 'true' self to which the real, empirical self must first aspire and subsequently adhere. Stirner aimed to undermine all such demands for self-sacrifice by spelling out their inadmissible implications, and the demands of revolutionaries were not excepted. Stirner believed that what most needs to be safe-guarded is the core of irreducible individuality or singularity (*Eigenheit* again) on which all known forms of society and state, and all kinds of revolutionary organization, had fed. Only the association (*Verein*) of egoists, which was to be the outcome not of revolution but of a very different form of uprising – which Stirner termed 'rebellion' – would not have the individual model himself upon some formative principle that is supposed to be greater than himself. The association of egoists which Stirner rather puzzlingly proffers was to come into being specifi-cally in order to preserve, and not to usurp, the self-defined privileges and prerogatives of the sovereign individual. According to Stirner, indeed, the association will somehow positively preserve and enlarge the individual's self-assertive particularity, which is to be untrammelled. Assertiveness and particularity stand in no need of mediation; Stirner was resolute in his concern to attack any mentality, revolutionary or not, that relied on moral postulates or depended in any way on the use of the word 'ought' (*sollen*). He believed that evil resided in the very notion of such ideals or 'vocations'.

The constraints against which Stirner's polemic was directed may be internal, external or both at once. Enslavement to the dictates of consciousness involves a loss or alienation of the individual self that may be as severe or demeaning as that entailed by regulation from without, by external moral codes. To follow commands is to allow one's actions to be determined: in Stirner's unorthodox lexicon, to 'find oneself' in thought, or in 'spirit', is to 'lose oneself' in 'reality'.

The loss of self involved is not uniform. It has taken different successive forms at different historical stages, stages which Stirner lists in a curious but paradigmatic opening section, 'The Life of a Man' (*Ein Menschenleben*), with which he sets the tone of *The Individual and his Own*. In the elaboration of this part of his argument – which has some interesting ontogenetic and phylogenetic implications that cannot concern us here – Stirner has recourse to a muted, Hegelian theory of history. The 'spirituality' he so detested, the way in which thought, by determining human action from without, had dominated history in successive stages, had served a potentially progressive and liberating function. The dominance of successive waves and consciousness had made the individual master of his natural environment, for instance, even if consciousness or spirit had done so not for the benefit of the individual but for its own sake. The culmination of the process of history according to Stirner was to be not the perpetuation of the reign of spirit but its utter subversion; it was to consist in the supremacy of the assertive ego. Even so, Stirner considered the historical process up to that point in Hegelian terms, as the autogenesis of man propelled by spirit or consciousness. Whatever his understanding of Hegel – which was to be called into question by Marx – it remains true that Stirner did appropriate a broadly Hegelian approach to history. While he may have been 'very weak on history',[15] he did allow for the development of spirit and self-consciousness; and while it may be true, as Marx thought, that Stirner had 'cribbed' his history from Hegel, Stirner himself aimed to turn his evident borrowings from Hegel to what he considered good account.

> I receive with thanks what the centuries of culture have acquired
> for me; I am not willing to give up anything of it; *I* have not
> lived in vain. The experience that I have power over my nature
> and need not be the slave of my appetites need not be lost upon
> me; the experience that I can subdue the world by culture's means
> is too dearly bought for me to be able to forget it. But I want
> still more.[16]

Young Hegelian theories of the dominance of concepts in history normally emphasize religion in general and, following Strauss and Feuerbach, Christianity in particular as exemplars of the process. Stirner's account is no exception. Stirner, indeed, gives an altogether original twist to the notion that 'Christianity begins with God's becoming man and carries on its work of conversion and redemption through all time to prepare for God a reception in all men and everything human, and to penetrate everything with the Spirit'.[17] The Christian *Sollen*, he insists, denigrates the individual in an unusually forceful way. Disdain for the world and devaluation of the individual were in Stirner's eyes the *idées maîtresses* of Christian spirituality. One characteristic expression of this disdain (at least according to Stirner's unorthodox view of the matter) was the belief of Descartes that only as mind is man alive. In loving the spiritual alone the Christian can love no particular person. The concern of Christianity 'is for the divine', and while 'at the end of Heathenism the divine becomes the extramundane, at the end of Christianity it becomes the intramundane'.[18]

What brings about Stirner's intramundane divinity is, of course, Protestantism. Whereas the Catholic according to Stirner is content with carrying out commands proceeding from an external, authoritative source, the Protestant is his own *Geistlicher* using his own 'internal secret policeman', the private conviction of conscience and its inward imperatives, to watch over every motion of his mind and to stifle every natural impulse.[19] Stirner perceives that the shift to Protestantism is political and religious all at once; liberalism considered as a characteristically modern political form entails the absence of intermediaries between citizen and state just as Protestantism involves their absence from the individual's relationship to the deity. The individual, as Stirner proceeds to put it, becomes a political Protestant in relation to his God, the modern state, the state which Hegel himself had called a 'secular deity' which 'men must venerate' as such.[20]

The section of *The Individual and his Own* that deals with political liberalism clearly bears the imprint of Marx's essay 'On the Jewish Question', an article which Stirner cites;[21] he repeats Marx's argument that just as religious freedom means that religion is free, and freedom of conscience that conscience is free, political freedom means that the state (not man himself) is free. Stirner, however, twists this argument in a direction that is all his own. 'Liberalism', he declaims, 'simply [introduced] other *concepts* – human instead of divine, political instead of ecclesiastical, scientific instead of doctrinal, real conflicts instead of crude dogmas.' What these shifts all mean is that 'now nothing but mind rules the world';[22] political liberalism according to Stirner accentuates and institutionalizes the 'Christian' depreciation of the individual. 'The rights of man . . . have the meaning that the man in me entitles me to this and that. I as individual am not entitled but "man" has the right and entitles me.'[23] After all, as far as Stirner was concerned, *any* general concept, task or 'vocation' demeans and tyrannizes over the individual; its liberty is (and is paid for by) his slavery. With the advent of modern citizenship (*Bürgerthum*), Stirner argued, 'it was not the individual man – and he alone is man – that became free, but the citizen, the *citoyen*, the political man, who for that very reason is not man'. Although what Stirner called *Bürgerthum* requires an impersonal (*sachliche*) authority, the 'Protestant' absence of intermediaries between state and individual citizen that this requires has the effect not of diminishing but of increasing individual submissiveness.[24] Without the denigration of the individual for the sake of what is an abstract *Sollen*, the state cannot subsist. This is why, on Stirner's logic, the uprising of the enraged individual would suffice to destroy the state, root and branch. Denigration of the individual is the principle of the state, its *raison d'être*. The kernel of the state, like the kernel of 'morality', was in Stirner's view the abstraction 'man'; every corrective category or concept respects and validates only the 'man' in the individual.

Stirner's anarchism pays a kind of back-handed tribute to Hegel's conception of the state as the historical embodiment of morality; by rejecting both the state and morality on the same grounds – both are to be overturned by 'rebellion' – Stirner underscores the connection between the two. The state to Stirner at one and the same time exercised domination and remained an *idée fixe*, an 'apparition', as he was wont to put it, by which men are 'possessed'. It is in his portrayal of the state, indeed, that Stirner is at his most Young Hegelian; his frankly contradictory view of the state recalls nothing as much as Feuerbach's view of the way Christianity oppresses mankind although – or because – its content is illusory. The Young Hegelianism of Stirner's discussion makes his critique of the state *per se* rather less forceful than those of most other anarchist theoreticians. His critique, compared with those of other anarchists, lacks specificity; while he presents the state throughout his argument as an agent or agency of sacredness and morality, he presents society and religion (not to mention revolution) in almost identical terms. Indeed Stirner never distinguishes state from society very clearly, although he does provide some rather incoherent pointers: while society denies the liberty of the individual, the state denies his peculiarity or uniqueness (*Eigenheit*); whereas society rests content with making the individual the bondsman of another, or of itself, the state can be maintained only if the supposedly valueless individual is made the bondsman of himself; society, which is as it were man's state of nature, man's natural condition from which man must nevertheless escape by asserting his *Eigenheit*, is not an illusion in the way the state is said to be one; society, unlike the state, is never linked with pauperism; and nothing in society is said to correspond to the internalization of the commands of law or to the total surrender of man that the state requires – the taking over, that is to say, by the Protestant-liberal state of the 'whole man' with *all* his attributes and faculties.

Stirner, similarly, says very little about forms of the state, beyond the propositions that any state is a despotism even if all men who belong to it despotize over one another, and that the liberal state reinforces the coercive power of conscience. That it is able to do so, indeed, is what accounts for its power; in itself the liberal state, Stirner insists, is no more than a mechanical compound. The state machine moves the clockwork of individual minds, the wheels in people's heads, but only so long as none of them move autonomously. An upsurge of *Eigenheit*, which will remove and undercut the individual's destitution of will, would destroy the mechanism, once and for all. This is to be the task – although Stirner would not have called it a 'task' – of 'rebellion'.

As part of this upsurge of individual rebellion, which we are to encounter again in the writings of Bakunin, who in a sense collectivized it, Stirner insisted that men would discover for themselves that the state is, in the last analysis, an illusion; and as an authority for this assertion he was emboldened to cite (of all people) Marx. Stirner, who had absorbed Marx's message in 'On the Jewish Question' that the state considered as a community was illusory and that citizenship considered as a measure of community was likewise more apparent than real, proceeded to go one better than Marx and assert that the state, not as a collective moral force, but as an alien physical force – as the repressive embodiment of the police, military and bureaucracy – was likewise an illusion. To Marx such a conclusion was preposterous. The idea that men obey the state because they are deluded does not lead to the proposition that the state itself is a delusion. Marx in 'On the Jewish Question' had seen the difference very clearly and drawn the line with some care; but Stirner, who had read and gained much from Marx's article, still believed that the rule of the state was a blatant, paradigmatic case of men's being ruled by their own illusions. His argument, which leads into his assertion of 'rebellion' as opposed to 'revolution', is that since man is by nature not a political animal, not a *zoon politikon*, and that since only the political in man is expressed in the state, political life is a fabrication. This leads to the further proposition that law embodies no coercive force except in the minds of those who obey it – a proposition rightly ridiculed by Marx. 'In every institution in our society', writes one of our own contemporaries, wittingly or unwittingly echoing Stirner,

> people must be helped to realize that the power of the ruling elite
> and its bureaucracy is *nothing*, nothing but their [people's]
> refusal and externalized power. Then it is a matter of
> recuperation of this power, and the recuperative strategy is
> quite simple; act against the rules, and the act itself converts
> the illusory power in them into real power in us.[25]

That such a Stirnerian argument can be trotted out again does nothing, however, to make it any less ridiculous.

Stirner, Feuerbach and Marx

It has rarely been recognized in recent literature about Stirner that *The Individual and his Own* was designed, *inter alia*, as it was received upon its first publication in 1845, as an attack on Feuerbach's *The Essence of Christianity*. Yet the very structure of Stirner's argument allows of no other explanation; the division of his book into 'theological-false' then 'anthropological-true' sections (which Stirner labels 'Man'

– *Der Mensch* – and 'Myself' – *Ich* – respectively) is intended to indicate its target by mirroring it. So is its subject-matter. Both *The Individual and his Own* and *The Essence of Christianity* are concerned with men's alienated attributes and their reappropriation, and both arguments are cast in terms of the task of recapturing human autonomy.

This comparison is not one that can be pressed too far; whatever the overlap between the two books, Stirner was convinced that the ultimate expression of the oppressive spirituality he so detested was the very book, *The Essence of Christianity*, in which Feuerbach had laid claim to having neutralized spirituality once and for all. Stirner regarded Feuerbach's theoretical *coup* as a mere 'theological insurrection', Feuerbach himself as a religious thinker *malgré lui*; his accusation should detain us, in spite of the familiarity of charges of this kind among the Young Hegelians. It is true that in the bitter and remarkably well publicized controversies that animated the Hegelian Left throughout its brief florescence it became commonplace to accuse one's opponent of remaining trapped within the insidious coils of a religious way of thinking or a theological cast of mind. (Feuerbach made this kind of accusation against Hegel, Bauer against Ruge and Marx, Ruge against Bauer and Marx, Marx against Bauer and Stirner, as well as Stirner against Feuerbach.) Nor is it beside the point that most of these accusations were quite justified; the radical critique of religion (which according to Marx in 1843 was 'the prerequisite of every critique') was regarded not so much as the contribution of Feuerbach – whose importance in this respect Engels was to exaggerate – but as part and parcel of the legacy of Hegelian philosophy. Hegel himself had indicated that 'religion is principally sought and recommended for times of public calamity, disorder and oppression', that 'people are referred to it as solace in the face of wrong or as hope in compensation for loss', and that religion 'may take a form leading to the harshest bondage'.[26] Bruno Bauer used the authority of Hegel to justify his public break with Christianity, and suffered the consequences; the activity of the Prussian censors, as well as that of the Young Hegelians themselves, attests to the connection both sides believed to exist between the radical critique of religion and that of politics. Marx's essay 'On the Jewish Question', to give one by now familiar example, had as its terrain the penumbra where religious and political critiques overlap; and it may be that what really distinguishes Feuerbach from his Young Hegelian confederates is not that he introduced them to a radical critique of religion (Engels's claim that Feuerbach did so is in David McLellan's words 'completely at variance with the facts')[27] but that he alone discussed religion without also discussing the state.

Stirner, whose central concern was domination, not religion, was on the other hand quick to perceive a connection between the critique of religion and the critique of politics. He believed that all claims emanating from outside the individual, whatever their designation, are attempts to annihilate the self, that with the advancement of such claims 'our essence is brought into opposition with *us* – we are split into an essential and an unessential self'. The outer 'man' is ranged against the real individual. Stirner's basic point against Feuerbach, accordingly, was very much the same as his basic point against everyone else; what Feuerbach called 'sense experience' was in Stirner's view by no means the actual experience of real, individual men, but instead an 'essence', an abstraction to which Feuerbach had given the name 'sensuousness' but which in reality, like all abstractions and essences, is likely to come to dominate real men. For this reason Feuerbach, according to Stirner, is an abstract philosopher like all the rest. More specifically, the weakness in Feuerbach's position that Stirner seized upon was his conception of man's 'divinity' not as something man had to build or create but as something that could be regained at the level of consciousness. Because man must by implication give way before his newly found 'divinity' once it is regained, Stirner believed that this very category would be as oppressive and burdensome a taskmaster as any other spirit or collectivity to which individuals historically had succumbed.

What this means, according to Stirner, is that Feuerbach's self-proclaimed and much vaunted atheism was at best half-hearted – and there is a certain truth in Stirner's accusation. Faith in an eternally present divinity does seem to be compatible with atheism on Feuerbach's definition: 'a true atheist', Feuerbach himself admitted, 'is one who denies the predicates of the divine being, not one to whom the subject of these predicates is nothing'.[28]

Stirner's *The Individual and his Own* challenged Feuerbach on the grounds that his celebrated reversal of subject and predicate ('all we need do is always to make the predicate into the subject . . . to arrive at the undisguised, pure and clear truth'),[29] his substitution of 'man' for 'God' as the agent of divinity, changes nothing for men. The relocated divine is no less burdensome and no less divine because of a mere change of position. 'Man' or mankind considered as a collectivity is no less oppressive and sacred than 'God' so long as the individual continues to be related to this collective divinity in a religious manner. Feuerbach had failed in Stirner's view to deal adequately with the oppression and indigence which had made men turn to religion in the first place; Feuerbach had achieved nothing more than an abstract change in the object of self-renunciation. What he had considered to be a radical clarification of the issue of religious alienation Stirner regarded as an exercise in obfuscation; Feuerbach, as Stirner put it, was just a 'pious atheist', and Feuerbach found it difficult to disagree. In his reply to Stirner he admitted that his statement 'There is no God' was only the negative form of the 'practical and religious, i.e. positive statement' that 'man is the God', which was precisely Stirner's point.[30]

Feuerbach's bombastic claims to have solved the problem of self-renunciation leave it more firmly entrenched than ever in human consciousness, and give self-renunciation a new lease of life by obscuring what Stirner considered to be the fundamental need to transcend or do away with *all* self-renunciation, before *any* 'higher' power, be it religious, social or political. Feuerbach's relocation of divine essence within a naturalistically conceived humanity means only that some categorical, collective human essence continues to be brought into opposition to the real individual, who remains split into 'essential' and 'non-essential' spheres of being. Stirner conceived his task to be that of overcoming all such divisions, on the grounds that if the individual makes an essence (Feuerbach's 'species-being' or Hegel's *Geist*, for example) or a moral imperative (such as the Kantian *Sollen*) the centre or goal of his being, he must bifurcate himself, exalting the 'better' spiritual or moral part of his nature over the paltrier residue.

The characteristic conclusion Stirner draws from his critique of Feuerbach is that Feuerbachian humanism is the *ne plus ultra* of man's self-renunciation, of his enslavement to the categories he has himself created; and that the adumbration of such humanism accordingly signals the imminence of the advent of Stirner's 'association of egoists' which is to rise like a phoenix from the ashes of 'spirituality'. But we need not follow Stirner's footsteps down this particular path, a tortuous and meandering one indeed, to appreciate the force of his argument against Feuerbach. Nor need we accept the very Young Hegelian polemical gloss Stirner gives his argument – the notion that because the distinguishing feature of Christianity since its inception is its location of divine essence within the individual, who is then said to be its vessel, Feuerbach's *The Essence of Christianity* expresses a distinctively Christian principle in the most extreme possible form. Feuerbach in this view is not just one more, but also the ultimate, Christian philosopher.[31]

What is crucial with respect to Marx's response to him is that Stirner, in the course of excoriating Feuerbach's notion of 'species-being' (*Gattungswesen*) as an example of empty but ominous humanitarianism, singled out Marx's use of the term in 'On the Jewish Question' in a manner that suggested that Marx himself was a Feuerbachian, subject to all Stirner's criticisms of Feuerbach. Whether or not Marx was personally stung or piqued by this criticism, as seems likely, Stirner's accusation, made though it was in passing, can be seen to have had sufficient force to elicit from Marx an extended response.

Marx's most obvious line of defence – one which he in effect adopted throughout *The German Ideology* – was that of asserting his credentials as a communist revolutionary and of identifying himself with other communist revolutionaries. This defence, which separated him decisively from Feuerbach, who disavowed social revolution, placed upon Marx the burden of disproving Stirner's insistence that revolutionary tasks and goals were as burdensome and anti-human as any other goal or essence; and this, as we shall see, is indeed one of the projects Marx did adopt in *The German Ideology*. To adjudicate whether or not Marx succeeded, we must stand back and take our bearings.

To begin with, there was much in Feuerbach's compensatory theory of religion in general and Christianity in particular with which Marx never disagreed. There is no reason why Marx's otherwise remarkable silence - remarkable, that is, for a nineteenth-century theorist - about religion throughout the body of his writings should not be taken to denote agreement with the main lineaments of Feuerbach's critique. Marx took exception to Feuerbach's social quietism and to his resolutely Young Hegelian belief that religious alienation could be abrogated at the level of consciousness:[32] but Marx nevertheless took over wholesale the Feuerbachian ideas that the attributes of man are in religious life projected, upwards and outwards, on to the man-made figure of the Divine; that what man lacks in fact he accordingly attains in fancy; that the vacuity of the real world accounts for the plenitude of God; and that only an indigent humanity needs an opulent God - a God who is defined by the real, empirical exigency from which he emerges. If God's in 'His' Heaven, all is manifestly *not* right with the world, its real counterpart. All of these prepositions imply beliefs that Marx and Feuerbach shared; all of them, too, are involved, as we have already seen, in Marx's essay, 'On the Jewish Question'.

What Stirner overlooked when he accused Marx of being a Feurbach-ian humanist, however, is that Marx differed from Feuerbach in significant ways. Even with respect to religion Marx distinguished himself quite uncompromisingly from Feuerbach in at least one crucial respect. Taking his cue, apparently, from the earlier (pre-1843) writings of his erstwhile mentor, Bruno Bauer, Marx never entertained the Feuer-bachian belief that all men had to do, in the face of the expropriation which had given rise to the need for religion in the first place, was to reclaim their alienated human essence at the level of consciousness. What Feuerbach refused to admit was something Marx, following Bauer, adamantly insisted upon: the point that any such consciousness must be as distorted, as dissonant, and as unworthy of human purposes and dignity as the image of God projected in the first place. As Marx himself put it:

> The foundation of irreligious criticism is this: man makes
> religion; religion does not make man. Religion is, in fact, the
> self-consciousness and self-esteem of man who has either not
> yet gained himself or has lost himself again. But man is no
> abstract being, squatting outside the world. Man is the world
> of man, the state, society. This state, this society, produce

religion, which is an inverted world-consciousness, because they
are an inverted world. Religion . . . is the fantastic realization
of the human being because the human being has attained no true
reality. Thus, the struggle against religion is indirectly the struggle
against that world of which religion is the spritual aroma . . .
Religion is the illusory sun about which man revolves only so
long as he does not revolve around himself.[33]

Feuerbach's mistake, from Marx's vantage point, had been to portray
God as harmonious, proportioned and superhuman. Bauer's God had
been very different; and Marx, following Bauer, hinged his argument
not on harmoniousness but on dissonance, a dissonance arising (in
Marx's case) from a destructive and self-destructive form of society.
It is largely for this very reason that Marx was driven to insist – in his
Theses on Feuerbach as well as in his essay, 'On the Jewish Question'
– against Feuerbach that an act of consciousness *per se* can change
nothing unless consciousness itself has undergone a prior change. In
Marx's own words, the 'critique of religion ends in the doctrine that
man is the supreme being for man; thus it ends in the categorical
imperative to overthrow all conditions in which man is a debased,
enslaved, neglected, contemptible being'.[34] Because this is a conclusion
Feuerbach refrained from drawing, Stirner's attack on Marx's use of the
Feuerbachian sounding phrase, 'species-being', is disingenuous, since
Marx's usage of this term in 'On the Jewish Question', or for that
matter the *Economic and Philosophic Manuscripts* of 1844, is no
longer Feuerbachian. In the former essay alone, as we have seen, Marx
extends Feuerbach's notion of alienation into the political and social
realm in a way that makes it incompatible with Feuerbach's theory;
once shifted and extended in this way alienation no longer requires
a mere adjustment of consciousness if it is to be transcended. A reality
like the state cannot be abrogated merely by revealing at the level of
consciousness its unsound position – although Stirner, as we are about
to see, thought that it could – and Marx, in indicating that alien politics
can be abolished only by actively transforming the real world, was in
effect revealing himself as much less Young Hegelian than either Feuerbach or Stirner. Marx did not share Stirner's typically Young Hegelian
belief in the oppressive force of Feuerbach's relocated divinity; but he
did share with Stirner a desire to assault Feuerbach's vapid anthropocentrism, the abstract love for an abstract 'Man' at the expense of any
concern for real, individual men. Marx maintained in *The German
Ideology* that Feuerbach

only conceives [man] as an object of the senses, not as sensuous
activity, because he still remains in the world of theory . . . [and]
stops at the abstraction 'Man' . . . [He] never manages to conceive

the sensuous world as the total, living, sensuous activity of the individuals comprising it.

Later in *The German Ideology*, in the course of his attack on the 'True Socialists', we find Marx maintaining that they, too, by casting their arguments in terms of an abstraction, 'Man', return from 'the realm of history' to 'the realm of ideology'.[35]

What underlies all such statements in *The German Ideology*, a book which is full of them, is something that emerges only from a careful analysis of its most lengthy single section, 'Saint Max'. Stirner's accusation that Marx, with his talk of 'species-being', was a Feuerbachian, however exaggerated and insensitive it may have been, nevertheless had enough bite to impel Marx to redefine his own position. In rejecting Feuerbachian humanism with all its shortcomings, Marx perforce had to avoid aligning himself with the extreme individualism that Stirner had propounded; and it is Marx's perception of the need to avoid the horns of this dilemma that does much to account for the argumentation, and the very structure, of *The German Ideology*. While Marx's attack on Feuerbach in the first section of *The German Ideology* has been contrasted, quite rightly, with his earlier near adulation of Feuerbach, it has rarely been recognized that it was none other than Stirner who impelled Marx into taking this new position as publicly and dramatically as he did.

Revolution and rebellion

Stirner's portrayal of successive stages of human submission issues in an injunction, which he intended as a call to action: 'my own will is the state's destroyer' ('der eigener Wille meiner ist der Verderberer des Staats'). While this sentiment, expresses an anarchist position, to be sure, Stirner was the first to deny that it could in any way be termed a revolutionary one. On Stirner's interpretation of it, revolution, like the state, and like all anterior social and moral systems, appeals, and must by its very nature appeal, to collectivity and self-sacrifice – principles from which an anarchist like Bakunin did not shrink, but which according to Stirner must at all costs be avoided by the assertive egoist. Social revolution of the type advocated most notably by Wilhelm Weitling (who, along with Feuerbach and 'the French Feuerbach', as the Young Hegelians were wont to label Proudhon, can be numbered among Stirner's *bêtes noires*) was a game not worth the candle. Stirner considered revolution to be just one more variant of faith, morality and domination, one more creed or *Sollen* displacing and feeding upon the uniqueness, particularity and singularity (*Eigenheit*) of the individual. Any submission to any revolutionary task, agency or body must rest according to Stirner on some prior belief in what he called the 'sacred-ness' of some precept or other, however ostensibly subversive such a precept may be; and it is belief in the sacredness of precepts that men most need to overcome, once and for all. Revolutionary organization may appear to go against the grain of established forms of society, but such appearances are deceptive; for all its disruptive claims and pre-tensions, revolutionary organization is after all a form of organization. What this fatal drawback means for Stirner is that men, in espousing revolutionary ends or even in succumbing to revolutionary fervour, are simply trading one form of submissiveness and self-sacrifice for another.

Revolution was to Stirner an agency of 'fanaticism', or morality, another imposed 'vocation' involving a prima facie devaluation of the individual; he did not hesitate to claim that the militant communism of Weitling and what came to be termed the 'mutualism' of Proudhon (who was not a revolutionary in the same sense, as we shall see) were alike 'religious' forms of doctrine because of the demands on the individual they made. Stirner saw no need to distinguish Weitling's revolutionary creed, which did embody certain residual elements of Christian millenarianism, from Proudhon's avowed and brash anti-clericalism. Stirner, whose individualism and anarchism were unremit-ting, insisted against all revolutionaries and utopians that freedom, which they claimed as the goal of their endeavours, was something that had to be taken, self-assertively; if it were simply 'received' it would amount in Stirner's unorthodox vocabulary to mere 'emanci-pation'. While revolution was no more than yet another 'human act', an act predicated on some normative vision of humanity, what Stirner called 'rebellion' (*Empörung*) was to be a rising of individuals who would be reacting to nothing outside themselves and relying on nobody but themselves. Such an uprising would take place spontaneously and without regard to future arrangements; its object would be less the overthrow of some established order than the elevation of the auton-omous individual above all established orders. Whereas revolution, if we are to believe Stirner, aims at new arrangements of one sort or another, rebellion aims at our no longer allowing ourselves to be arranged at all.

The incoherence of Stirner's distinction between revolution and rebellion is evident – Marx regarded it as 'comic' – but the anti-revolution-ary cast of his argument is unmistakable. Stirner's principle of 'rebellion' was specifically intended and advanced in order to avoid the need for the tyrannical regimentation that he thought necessarily characterized revolutionary (and non-revolutionary) organization. 'Rebellion' was to be an upsurge, an unleashing of individual passions, energy and anger against every social and political tie, which would be destroyed; the outcome of this expression of individual self-assertion and outrage was to be not a new kind of political or social form, but the non-systematic 'association' (*Verein*) of egoists, which Stirner characterized (rather than defined) in contradistinction to the state and its deficiencies.

Of all forms of organization, if we are to believe Stirner, only his own projected 'association' would exert no moral influence and exercise no legal constraint. It alone would not displace or feed upon the individual's distinguishing feature, his *Eigenheit*; the individual, indeed, according to Stirner would be and remain 'more than' the *Verein*. Stirner urges us to aspire not to the chimera of community but to our own 'one-sidedness'; we should combine with others purely and simply in order to multiply our own powers, and only for the duration of any given task.[36] To lapse into Stirner's own distinctive terminology, if the state 'consumes' the individual, the individual will 'consume' the 'association' in his turn. In view of such characterizations of the association of egoists, which Stirner himself portrayed as a 'free for all' in which everyone should have as much as he could appropriate, it is perhaps small wonder that Marx saw fit to regard it as an 'ideal copy' of capitalist society, of Hegel's 'civil society' and its 'system of needs'.[37] Stirner's 'egoistical property', said Marx (with considerable justification), 'is nothing more than ordinary or bourgeois property sanctified'.[38]

In Stirner's association, Marx went on,

> every relation, whether caused by economic conditions or
> direct compulsion is regarded as a relation of 'agreement' . . .
> [and] all property belonging to others is relinquished to
> them by us and remains with them only until we have the
> power to take it from them.

What this means is that

> in practice the 'Association' reaches agreement with Sancho
> [Stirner] with the aid of a stick. . . This 'agreement' is a mere
> phrase, since everyone knows that the others enter into it with
> the secret reservation that they will reject it on the first possible
> occasion.

Moreover, Stirner's conception of 'unique' property - his idea that private property would not only be retained in the 'association' but also actually perfected there because it would no longer need any legal guarantees - leads him into a contradiction on which Marx was quick to pounce. Marx paraphrases Stirner's egoist, the better to reveal his Young Hegelian pretensions: 'I see in your property something that is not yours but mine; since every ego does likewise, they see in it the *universal*, by which we arrive at the modern-German philosophical interpretation of ordinary, special, and exclusive private property.'[39]

What little Stirner says about the form of his 'association', indeed, lends support to Marx's accusation that Stirner in effect 'lets the old [civil] society continue in existence ... [and] strives to retain the present state of affairs'; for Stirner 'retains in his association the existing form of landownership, division of labour and money'. Marx adds that 'with such premises Sancho [Stirner] cannot . . . escape the fate of having a special "peculiarity" [Eigenheit] prescribed for him by the division of labour'.[40] (The resonance of this last point, in particular, will become apparent presently.)

Marx, indeed, at one level has little trouble disposing of Stirner's argument not only about the 'association' but also about the 'rebellion' that is supposedly to bring it into existence. Stirner, in attempting to make of 'rebellion' a means without an end, lapses into obscurity and incoherence. Even his advocacy of violence is muted, in effect, by the Young Hegelianism that tinges it. According to Marx it should not surprise us that Stirner

> waxes indignant at the thought of atheism, terrorism, communism, regicide, etc. The object against which Saint Sancho [Stirner] rebels is the Holy; therefore rebellion does not need to take the form of . . . action for it is only a sin against the 'Holy.'[41]

Yet there is another level to Marx's response which indicates that Stirner had, as it were, touched a nerve. Stirner insisted that the ideologies of liberation proferred by his 'progressive' contemporaries, in particular Feuerbachian humanism and the revolutionary communism with which Marx aimed to identify himself, were no solutions to the problem he was concerned to outline. Such 'liberation', he argued with some force, was simply not worthy of the name; its self-styled avatars, Feuerbach and Marx, are deceptive thinkers who deliberately refuse to acknowledge that their doctrines incur an irredeemable loss for the individual.

What concerns us here most pointedly is Stirner's accusation that revolutionary communism involves and must involve the violation of individuals. In advancing this accusation Stirner raised for Marx a spectre (however maladroit its conjuring up) that had to be put to rest, an issue (however badly raised it may have been) that demanded settlement. The point here is not that Stirner succeeded in convincing Marx that what passed for revolutionary enthusiasm among the Young Hegelians was bogus; Marx by 1845 stood in no need of being convinced of this. Yet Stirner did raise a question of some seriousness: whether there is any distinction not between revolution and 'rebellion', but between revolution, considered as a collective act requiring the possibility of self-abnegation and self-sacrifice on the part of the committed revolutionary, and other forms of subjection. The question was whether men in espousing revolutionary goals were (to steal a phrase from Rousseau) walking headlong into their chains. The importance of this question need not be laboured; but the fact that Marx, prompted by Stirner, was concerned to respond to it in 'Saint Max' and by extension throughout *The German Ideology* has often been overlooked.

It is no coincidence that Marx, faced with Stirner's anti-communist diatribe, took issue with it most vehemently and archly, no longer simply ridiculing Stirner's learning, logic and skill in argument with all the scorn and heavy-handed irony he could muster, but also outlining at great length the dangers inherent in such a false view of revolution. The question whether men, in succumbing to revolutionary ideals and revolutionary forms of organization, were simply replacing one form of subjection with another, at the immense and increasing cost of their own individuality, is, after all, a question of sufficient importance and moment to outweigh the particulars of scholarship and argumentation marshalled in its support; and it was a question, posed directly and bluntly by Stirner, to which Marx, for his part, responded at great length and in great detail not only in 'Saint Max' but throughout *The German Ideology*. When Marx wrote in one of its most central, and typical, passages that 'communist society is the only society in which the creative and free development of the individual is no mere empty phrase'[42] it is important to recognize that he had Stirner, who was responsible for having raised this issue, in his sights.

Pauperism, criminality and labour

Stirner's solution to the denigration of the individual by the collectivity and its various forms of consciousness was that of pinning his hopes not on political man in any of his forms but on the man held most in contempt by the respectable, upright citizen, the man despised because he 'lacks settlement' and has 'nothing to lose': the pauper. Whether or not pauperism is to some degree inevitable in modern society, as Hegel had thought it was, state and citizen according to Stirner regard the pauper as shiftless, immoral and at least potentially criminal; and these are precisely the reasons why Stirner positively values the pauper as exemplar of what man, freed from ties and guarantees, might be. Although Stirner in the course of his advancement of the pauper as paradigm uses the (French) word *prolétariat* to designate the pauper, his pauper has nothing in common with Marx's proletarian, which is one reason why the idea that 'the theory of the alienation of the proletarians was enunciated by Stirner at least one year before Marx'[43] is an exaggeration. Stirner included criminals and free-wheeling intellectuals among his *prolétariat* of paupers which, in the indignant but accurate words of Marx, 'consists of ruined bourgeois and impoverished proletarians, a collection of ragamuffins, who had existed in every epoch. . . Our Saint [Stirner]', Marx continues, 'has exactly the same notion of the proletariat as the "good comfortable burghers" '[44] – that they may be despised as riff-raff (*canaille*). Stirner, however, admired his paupers for this very reason; he thought that they alone could be free of the adverse, debilitating effects of Christianity. While Marx, for his part, agreed that 'the social principles of Christianity preach cowardice, self-contempt, debasement, subjugation [and] humility', he insisted against Stirner that these various indices of demoralization were 'properties of the *canaille*' and that the proletariat properly so-called 'which does not want to be treated as *canaille*, needs its courage, its consciousness of self, its pride and its independence far more than its bread'.[45]

Stirner, it is true, fails to distinguish the pauper from the proletarian just as he fails to distinguish the *citoyen* from the bourgeois; the opposition he specifies between the proletarian-pauper on the one hand and the citizen-bourgeois on the other is drawn largely according to the principles each confused composite is supposed to represent or embody: the principle of criminality as opposed to that of respectability. This polarization is the setting for Stirner's celebrated defence of crime, a defence which emphasizes not the acquisition of external goods so much as the assertion of the individual self of the criminal against the legal code of the state. This defence of crime makes sense only if we assume with Stirner – and without most other people, including Marx – that the law has binding force *as a matter of fact* largely because men believe it to be binding. Paul Eltzbacher points out that Stirner's constant preoccupation was with undermining such beliefs by spelling out their implications; in this he is quite correct, although his explanation neglects Stirner's own markedly Young Hegelian belief in the material power of thought, of conceptual schemes, of belief-systems. Another commentator, Henri Arvon, who by contrast with Eltzbacher is well aware of the Young Hegelian context of Stirner's thought, puts forward the argument that ordinary criminal activity undertaken in ignorance of the need to assert individuality against established moral and legal codes is not necessarily covered by Stirner's defence of crime; the trouble with Arvon's argument is, however, that nowhere does Stirner disapprove of *any* crime undertaken for *any* reason.[46] What he took to be important is what all crimes share, the assertion – however informed or conscious this assertion may be – of the self against a system of rules.

Stirner believed that paupers (and criminals) were in effect maintained by the 'respectable classes'; the continued existence of pauperism and criminality serves as a backhanded but prima facie justification of the socially and morally superior position of the 'good, comfortable burghers', a position typified by Stirner's phrase, a characteristic play upon words, 'das Gelt gibt Geltung'. (What he means is that the bourgeoisie, like the property and the money that defines it as such, rests on a legal title given by the state, and that 'the bourgeois is what he is by the grace of the state'; to Marx, the state, by contrast, rests on a legal title given by the bourgeoisie.) As far as Stirner was concerned, the corollary of the proposition that the state exists (*inter alia*) in order to repress paupers, should these become unruly, is that the pauper has no need of the state; since he has nothing to lose, 'he does not need the protection of the state for his nothing'. The denial of individuality that is the principle of the state is epitomized by the state's inability or refusal – here Stirner follows Hegel – to alter the condition of the pauper. Pauperism, as we have had occasion to see, confronted even the Hegelian state in all its majesty with an impasse; but the conclusions Stirner draws from this are once again all his own. 'Pauperism', he declaims

> is the valuelessness of me, the phenomenon that [*sic*] I cannot realize value [Geltung] from myself. For this reason state and pauperism are one and the same. The state does not let me come to my value, and continues in existence only through my valuelessness; it is forever intent upon getting value from me, i.e. exploiting me, turning me to account, using me up, even if the only use it gets from me consists in my supplying a *proles*. It wants me to be its creature.[47]

One of the faults of Stirner's argument at this juncture is that it slides from this set of propositions to the completely different idea that because *labour* is exploited (*ausgebeutet*) as a spoil (*Kriegsbeute*) of the enemy, the possessing classes, 'if labour becomes free, the state is lost'. The least that can be said about the abruptness and incoherence of this shift – and Marx's criticism is not characterized by restraint – is that because pauper and proletarian are not distinguished from each other, neither are poverty and labour. The ellipses in his argument, which on any reckoning (let alone Marx's) emerges as less than firm, enable Stirner to conclude, at least to his own satisfaction, that labour has an egoistic character and as such points the way to freedom. This made Marx indignant. 'Freedom of labour', he insisted with some archness, means 'free competition of workers among themselves. Saint Max is very unfortunate in political economy, as in all other spheres. Labour is free in all civilized countries; it is not a matter of freeing labour but of abolishing it'[48] – an injunction which raises problems all of its own.

These to one side, however (for the moment), the point remains that for Stirner the labourer too had become the egoist, even – for he does not shrink from this claim – the prototypical egoist. Marx was not slow to criticize, in this and other instances, the way in which Stirner's fervent and uncritical belief in the material power of reflective categories all too frequently led him to suppose that various disparate elements of social reality – paupers, after all, *lack* labour as well as 'settlement' – are intrinsically linked because they express some 'principle' or other. 'The road to the unique', said Marx, 'is paved with bad concluding clauses.' He criticized Stirner's notion of the egoistic character of labour on these very grounds; but it is significant, as we are about to see, that Marx's criticism of Stirner on this particular point goes very much further.

The division of labour

One of the most important themes of *The German Ideology* is one that points forward to the *Grundrisse* and *Capital*: the analysis of the division of labour in capitalist society. Marx in *The German Ideology* was concerned to extend the discussion of the labour process he had begun in the *Economic and Philosophic Manuscripts* by linking it with the discussion of individualism and individuality we may find in his earlier *Critique of Hegel's Philosophy of Right*. To see that Marx was concerned to outline and identify the fetters on selfhood and self-activity that were germane and specific to capitalist society is to see that Stirner played a much more important part than has generally been recognized in impelling Marx to construct the argument of *The German Ideology* in the way he did. Stirner's rather forced portrayal of labour as egoistic had overlooked the fact that labour, with the development of capitalism, had undergone certain well-marked changes: Stirner thought labour was egoistic at a time when according to Marx it could no longer even be personal.

The critical point that has been neglected in previous discussions of *The German Ideology* is not only that it was Stirner who had forced the issues of labour, individualism and individuality on to Marx's attention, but also that Marx need have framed his argument in the way he did only in response to Stirner. To Feuerbach, who has often been taken to be Marx's only important target in *The German Ideology*, but who tended to cast his arguments in terms of large-scale abstractions ('species', 'consciousness', 'nature'), labour, individualism and individuality were not important issues; Stirner alone among the Young Hegelians had attempted, however incoherently and wrongheadedly, to connect them. Marx's analysis in *The German Ideology* of the division of labour and its destructive effects on the individual in capitalist society is a barbed, pointed analysis; it is pointed, in the first instance, fairly and squarely at Stirner, for it was Stirner who had fatally misprized the obstacles to the emergence of the individual as he could be.

To give one prominent example, the passage in *The German Ideology* outlining Marx's belief that 'in communist society, where nobody has one exclusive sphere of activity, but each can become accomplished in any branch he wishes' so that the individual would be able to 'hunt in the morning, fish in the afternoon, rear cattle in the evening, criticize after dinner, just as [he has] a mind', is well enough known. But what is not well enough known is whose points this passage is designed to meet. It may be found in the 'Feuerbach' section of *The German Ideology* but has no real reference to Feuerbach; nevertheless the notion which has recently gained currency that Marx intended this passage as a 'parody of Stirner'[49] is wide of the mark indeed. It has nothing of parody about it; Marx, for better or for worse, took this passage, which comes in the middle of a sustained critique of the capitalist division of labour, with the utmost seriousness.

This passage is nevertheless often singled out – by virtue, one suspects, of its attractiveness – for ridicule on the grounds of its supposedly 'utopian' character. To write it off as utopian serves the additional function of making Marx's criticisms of utopian socialism appear disingenuous. But this is too easy. Accusations of visionary tendencies and of the unrealizability of the vision in question need to be tempered by a recognition that any utopian elements in this picture – elements that in Marx's opinion do not lend themselves to a derogatory construction – derive not from the agrarian character of the categories Marx used, for he used them *illustratively*, but from their expansive and forward looking implications. (Their source is probably Fourier, whose imaginative presentiment of a new society Marx admired, and whom he carefully distinguished from those he called 'philistine utopians'.) Marx of all people had no interest in putting the clock back. In this passage he is not at all advocating a reactionary rustic arcadia but instead predicating his prescription for future society on the emergence of new needs for the individual and on what is another expression of the same thing, an expansion of social wealth. The passage advocates an unprecedented expansion in the scope and scale of individual life-activity – the back-reference to Fourier is in this sense clear – which means that more people would be able to experience fuller and more varied forms of activity in their everyday life, forms of activity that heretofore had been not so much unreal or utopian as restricted to certain well-placed, favoured individuals in society, who were not reluctant to describe them.*

Marx's passage in *The German Ideology* was concerned to point up the existence, and to outline the ominous consequences of what he called the 'fixation of social activity' that is engendered and required by the division of labour in capitalist society, and its 'consolidation

---

*Witness, for instance, one of many possible examples, from the diary of John Adams, aged twenty-three 'Rose about sun-rise. Unpitched a load of Hay. Translated two Leaves more of Justinian, and in the afternoon walked to Deacon Webbs, then round by Millpond Home. Smoaked a pipe with Webb at the Drs and am now again about reading over Gilberts section of feudal tenures.'[50]

of what we ourselves produce into an objective power above us, growing out of our control and thwarting our expectations'.[51] Marx intended his passage about exclusive spheres of activity to indicate a decisive shift in the nature of the division of labour that had been inaugurated and was being maintained by the capitalist mode of production – a shift which, together with its implications, had passed unnoticed by Stirner. Stirner was not alone in his blindness, which was shared by the entire Young Hegelian circle; but Stirner was alone in his curious insistence on the 'egoistic' character of labour and the labourer, an insistence he put forward at a time when, according to Marx, 'the domination of material conditions over individuals and the suppression of individuality by chance [had] assumed its sharpest and most universal form', at a time when the division of labour required by the capitalist mode of production had come to entail the most complete dependence of worker upon worker as well as his dependence upon the objects and conditions of production. Labour, that is to say, had become anything but 'egoistic': it had 'lost all semblance of life activity and only sustains life by stunting it'. Marx insists that individuals

> must appropriate the existing totality of productive forces not
> only to achieve self-activity but also merely to safeguard their
> very existence. . . The appropriation of the totality of the
> instruments of production is, for this very reason, the
> development of a totality of capacities in the individuals
> themselves.[52]

These are ambitious claims, and Marx's reasons for advancing them need to be examined. We need to ask what the relationship is between the modern capitalist division of labour and what Marx calls 'self-activity'; and we must ask why Marx insists, against Stirner in the first instance, that the forms taken by labour in capitalist society deny and do not express this same 'self-activity'. These questions are complicated; to answer them we must stand back briefly from Stirner.

The pronounced shift in the character of the division of labour inaugurated by capitalism to which Marx wishes to draw our attention may best be appreciated by means of a comparison, admittedly a rough one, between Adam Smith and Plato (a comparison touched upon briefly in Chapter 1). Speculation about the division of labour in society – about who should do what tasks – was by no means unknown to pre-capitalist societies (although the actual expression 'division of labour' was not used before Mandeville); but the character of the division of labour that was outlined in pre-capitalist writings differed dramatically from the kind of division of labour that came to be defended, often eloquently, in the course of the eighteenth- and nineteenth-century discussions. To enter properly into the history of the concept would take us too far afield here. Instead, Plato has been selected – as Marx himself selected him – as a foil to Adam Smith for illustrative purposes. Their juxtaposition has the effect of highlighting something quite extraordinary. The shift in the character of the division of labour, and in the character of speculation about the division of labour, to which Marx and others wished to draw our attention, has been so marked that it might seem odd to consider Plato's *Republic* as containing an argument about the division of labour at all. Yet it could plausibly be argued that if we take a broader view, the *Republic* not only *advances* such an argument but actually *is* such an argument.

The *Republic* is concerned to prescribe the assignment or deployment of necessary tasks among various categories of the members of society in such a way that each member might best carry out the task (not 'perform' the 'role') that is best suited to his nature. Plato, that is to say, outlines a social division of labour that assigns different tasks to different people on the basis of their intrinsic differences one from another; his division of labour is in this way an expression and development of the particular talents, gifts, aptitudes, needs and other characteristics of the individuals concerned. Social harmony and political justice, he believed, could have no other foundation. It may be that Plato considers these needs and talents, gifts and aptitudes in a one-sided manner, but the point remains that the division of tasks the *Republic* outlines is devised as a means of putting to good effect specifiable human attributes that vary, often markedly, from one individual to another. What this means is that the individualized labour of each and every constituent member of Plato's *Republic* is deployed for the sake of satisfying human needs; it amounts (in the language of the economic theory Marx was to develop after completing *The German Ideology*) to production for use, not production for exchange. 'Use-value', we might say, completely displaces 'exchange-value'.

To use these categories of Marxian economics to point up the essential character of the Platonic division of labour is to point up how very different it is from the Smithian. According to eighteenth- (and nineteenth-) century arguments the division of labour in society has as its object something very different from, and quite irreducible to, what Plato had had in mind. The division of labour was seen as a mechanism for the production of wealth, as a means for increasing the quantity of goods produced and of expediting the accumulation of capital. The axis of the modern division of labour, if again we may use the language of Marxist economics, is not production for use but production for exchange. Adam Smith meant by 'the division of labour' not only the separation of different tasks, trades, and employments throughout society at large (or what Marx was to call 'the division of labour in society') but also the splitting up of a particular process of manufacture into minute, and if possible regularizable, operations (or Marx's 'division of labour in the workshop').

What underlies both meanings was a view of the nature not just of labour but also of the labourer, a view which in at least one crucial respect was radically at variance with Plato's conception; Smith had to assume as his *point d'appui* an equalizing, non-specific and 'abstract' conception of the nature of the worker. From the point of view of production, that is to say, similarities among workers *must* come to outweigh their individual differences one from another; whereas Plato, for all his evident disdain for manual labour, at least thought of it (and its products, which did not admit of reduction to the abstraction 'wealth') in specific, particular, terms.

While Plato believed that the particular characteristics of the individual *qua* individual (his attributes, aptitudes, gifts, talents, inclinations and needs) were qualities worthy of immediate social expression, of realization in, by and through the division of labour in society, Smith did not. While Plato believed that the carrying out of society's most necessary tasks, the production of objects and services that would maintain it in existence as a just society, should in some way express the individual characteristics of each and every one of society's constituent members, Smith did not. Adam Smith's concept of labour is a generalization; labour considered (as Smith manifestly *did* consider it) as an economic category is in no way reducible to, and may not be explained by reference to, the characteristics or qualities of the individual labourer. What concerns Smith in his 'science' of the 'production' of 'wealth' is what all men share; and what his invariant conception of human nature implies, in this particular respect, is that what men share is likely to be very basic indeed. Smith, unlike Marx for example, saw little reason to lament this development (at least not in *The Wealth of Nations*); indeed, it was the hard-boiled view of most of the early theorists and practitioners of 'political economy' that if what all men considered as labourers (or 'hands') share *is* very basic indeed, if, that is, what they share is in the nature of a lowest common denominator, so much the better; at least their 'output' – the outcome of the expenditure of their energies – will be measurable and quantifiable.[53] (Marx was later to call this expenditure 'labour-power', a category which tells us no more about any individual labourer than 'horse-power' would tell us about any particular horse.)

There is a world of difference between the creation by a particular person of a particular object (or the provision of a particular service) that will express and tell us something about that person's qualities and characteristics, on the one hand, and the subjugation of the producer to the imperatives of the productive process on the other. For what the latter is likely to involve is precisely what Smith found himself forced to advocate: that individuals who are likely to be very differently endowed in a variety of ways should none the less all do

the same thing, all perform the same kind of role, as part of the production process of a commodity.

The difference between these two kinds of division of labour was to
Marx less of a conceptual distinction than an historical fact.[54] The shift
to the Smithian division of labour had by 1845 long been taking place,
even if people like Stirner failed to notice. Stirner, we have seen,
regarded labour as 'egoistic'; but what such a view overlooks is that the
concept of 'labour' abstracted from any particular kind of labour
presupposes that the placement of individual workers in the productive
process that employs them is no longer considered to be connected
with or expressive of any personal qualities the individual worker
himself might possess. Stirner, in other words, could not be more
wrong. As Marx puts it in *The German Ideology*:

> Through the inevitable fact that within the division of labour
> social relationships take on an independent existence, there
> appears a division within the life of each individual, in so far
> as it is personal and in so far as it is determined by some branch
> of labour and the conditions pertaining to it. . . In the estate,
> this [division] is as yet concealed; for instance, a nobleman
> always remains a nobleman, a commoner always remains a
> commoner, apart from his other relationships, a quality
> inseparable from their individuality. The division between the
> personal and the class individual, the accidental nature of the
> conditions of life for the individual, appears only with the
> emergence of the class, which is a product of the bourgeoisie.[55]

It is important to see that the 'impersonal character' of labour which
Marx was concerned in passages like this one to outline has not existed
from time immemorial; it is specific to capitalism. Slaves in ancient
society were regarded as slavish, churls in feudal society as churlish;
nobles in medieval times were regarded (and regarded themselves) as
noble. Prior to capitalism, that is to say, a person's place within the
overall social division of labour appeared as an intrinsic personal quality;
people were held to relate to one another as the bearers of various
social *and* personal qualities, various productive *and* individual characteristics. More is involved here than nomenclature alone; the actual
assignment of characteristics to individuals in pre-capitalist epochs on
the basis of presumed occupational skills, and vice versa, was no doubt
unjust in the extreme – yet these characteristics, and their congruence
within the individual concerned, were supposed to exist, and to matter.
Under modern capitalist conditions, by contrast, standardization and
homogenization, not only of the commodities that are produced but
also in a real sense of the people producing them, takes place; and from
the point of view of production – sooner or later we have to personify

production - this is no mere metaphor. Differences in individual gifts, aptitudes, talents and inclinations that might once have been put to good use in the production of goods (and which might be again) do not cease to exist; but they do cease -*pace* Stirner - to matter. The distinctions that characterize individuals, the qualities that distinguish individuals one from another - what Stirner designated as the 'peculiarity' (*Eigenheit*) of each individual - may once have found expression of a sort; they can do so no longer.

Small wonder, then, that Marx in *The German Ideology* was so concerned to excoriate and ridicule Stirner's 'egoistic' view of labour and the labourer. What Stirner improvidently failed to see was that 'the individual' in all his irreducible uniqueness, the emergent egoist on whom he built all his hopes, had undergone and was still undergoing a decisive and momentous shift - a shift that applied to the powerful as well as the powerless, to the capitalist as well as the proletarian. If capital is - as Marx by 1845 believed - the controlling power over labour and labour's products, the capitalist possesses this power not at all by virtue of his personal human qualities which are of little, if any, account; he possesses it by virtue of the capital he owns. His power - even, if we are to believe the *Manuscripts*, his personality - is reducible to the purchasing power of his capital, and in this sense (though certainly not in any other) it is illusory and devoid of content. The emptiness of even the capitalist's power in this respect may point back to a certain emptiness in the power of the master in Hegel's 'master–slave' dialectic in *The Phenomenology of Mind*, as well as to Saint-Simon's mistaken inclusion of the capitalists among *les industriels* rather than *les oisifs*; but these back-references are not our main concern here. What is of central importance to Marx's critique of Stirner, however, is something that in turn makes Marx's critique of Stirner of central importance to Marx's thought in general: his perception that 'the individual', in the sense that Stirner had extolled him, has but a purely conceptual existence.

It is important at this juncture that we get the sense of Marx's argument, which is that in modern capitalist society some occupational categories, let us say the most important, crucial, central or typical ones, take the form of slots into which the individual -*any* individual, no matter who he is or what features he may possess - may in principle be inserted. Marx is not suggesting that *all* occupational categories take this form to the same extent; but he is suggesting that even those that are less standardized, and depend instead apparently directly on the creativity or gifts of the individual occupant, are in reality in no way exempt from the effects of the general social process. Even the giftedness of the individual artist, the exemplar of the Romantic stress on individuality, is expressed in a kind of forced contradistinction to the social division of labour and its restrictive effects upon everyone else.

Marx insists in *The German Ideology* that

> The exclusive concentration of artistic talent in particular
> individuals and its repression in the broad masses is the result
> of the division of labour . . . With a communist organization
> of society there disappears the subordination of the artist to
> local and national narrowness, which arises entirely from [the]
> division of labour, and also the subordination of the artist to
> some definite art, thanks to which he is exclusively painter,
> sculptor, etc., the very name of his activity adequately
> expressing the narrowness of his professional development and
> his dependence on the division of labour. In a communist
> organization of society there are no painters but at most
> people who engage in painting among other activities.[56]

Because the division of labour in its modern form had transformed
what were personal powers into material powers, the history of the
development of the productive forces of individuals could no longer
be equated with the history of these individuals themselves. Only in
Germany, a country which was according to Marx industrially under-
developed and where *idéologues* inhabited their own peculiar world
of airy fantasy, would this development not be obvious. Labour, if
we are to believe Marx, who has Stirner in mind, *can* become the
reappropriated power of the individual, the expression and outgrowth
of his individuality; but not under capitalism.

> The all-round development of the individual will only cease to
> be conceived as ideal, as vocation etc. when the impact of the
> world which stimulates the real development of the abilities of
> the individual comes under the control of the individuals them-
> selves, as the communists desire.[57]

It is important that we recognize that in this passage and passages like
it – *The German Ideology* is peppered with them – Marx is not dismissing
individuality as a principle but defending it against Stirner's miscon-
ceptions about its character and likelihood. One of the most important
features of *The German Ideology*, indeed, is Marx's attempt to demonstrate that communism and individuality, properly understood, are not
at all incompatible, despite Stirner's blunt conviction that the two
were necessarily incommensurate.

Individualism and individuality

We have seen that according to Marx the capitalist division of labour
entails an unprecedented 'fixation' of occupational roles; these roles

become 'material forces' oppressing their individual occupants, whose personal attributes and aptitudes they are not designed to express or fulfil. Because occupational categories in modern capitalist society are a denial, not an expression, of whatever particular features might characterize an individual occupant, Stirner's stress on the 'unique', 'peculiar' or 'egoistic' character of labour and the labourer is misplaced and inappropriate. Marx's perception, of course, has a wider and deeper application; to give but one prominent example, it is radically at variance with the point of view expressed in Durkheim's *The Division of Labour in Society* that 'the activity of every individual becomes more personalized to the degree that it is more specialized'[58] in modern society. Marx claimed, on the contrary, that specialization and 'personalization' of labour are not of a piece, and that capitalism should be seen as having separated the social determinations of men's lives from the individual qualities and characteristics of men themselves.

As the result of this separation, indeed as part of its meaning, 'the individual' might well be seen as being ranged against 'society' in certain senses, as Stirner in his own singular manner had perceived. Yet 'the individual' and 'society' are categories that can with an almost alarming ease turn into abstractions, which is what had happened according to Marx in the course of Stirner's exposition. There is what might be termed in Hegelian language a 'bad infinite' involved in Stirner's argument; and while it might be unsurprising to find Marx excoriating solipsism, the way in which he does so in the course of his attack on Stirner is instructive. Marx asks how Stirner's assertive, asocial 'ego' is ultimately to be characterized. In posing the question Marx hoists Stirner on his own petard: because 'the ego of Stirner's is not a "corporeal individual"' but 'a category constructed on the Hegelian method', Stirner in effect undermines his own argument. Marx proceeds to indicate why:

> Since every individual is altogether different from every other, it is by no means necessary that what is foreign, holy for one individual should be so for another individual; it even cannot be so . . . Saint Sancho [Stirner] could at most have said: for me, Saint Sancho, the state, religion, etc. are the alien, the Holy. Instead of this, he has to make them the absolutely Holy, the Holy for all individuals. . . How little it occurs to him to make each 'unique' the measure of his own uniqueness, how much he uses his own uniqueness as a measure, a moral norm to be applied to other individuals, like a true moralist, forcing them into his Procrustean bed . . . is already evident.[59]

Stirner's mistake in Marx's view was that of taking opposition between a postulated but ultimately undefined 'individual' and an unspecified 'society' of no determinate type as a datum to be applied, categorically and across the board, to the necessary relationship of *all* individuals to *all* societies, which are said to operate, by definition, at their expense and to their detriment. The trouble with this approach, as Marx indicated with some glee, is that individuality or 'uniqueness' then becomes an essence that is in no way dissimilar to those Stirner had set out to attack in the first place. Marx, early in 'Saint Max', reminds the reader of the opening paragraph of *The Individual and his Own* where Stirner had declaimed with a flourish that just as God is said to be by definition His own cause, *causa Sui*, so 'the individual' should be *his* 'own cause'. 'We see', says Marx,

> what holy motives guide Saint Max in his transition to
> egoism . . . had [he] looked a little more closely at these
> various 'causes' and the 'owners' of the causes, e.g. God,
> mankind, truth, he would have arrived at the opposite
> conclusion: that egoism, based on the egoistic mode of
> action of these persons, must be just as imaginary as those
> persons themselves.[60]

Nor is this all. Since Stirner's historical stages and conditions are nothing more than the mock-Hegelian embodiments of successive *idées fixes*, the success of his egoist according to Marx is reduced to consisting in the 'overcoming' of 'ideas', and his victories can take no more than a hollow, conceptual form. Marx insists that 'for Stirner, right does not arise from the material conditions of people and the resulting antagonism of people against one another but from their struggle against their own concept which they should "get out of their heads" '[61] – without ever touching the world itself. Stirner, that is to say, 'canonizes history' (hence his 'sainthood' according to Marx), transforms historical conditions into ideas, 'seizes everything by its philosophical tail' and takes

> as literal truth all the illusions of German speculative philosophy:
> indeed, he has made them still more speculative. . . For him, there
> exists only the history of religion and philosophy – and this exists
> for him only through the medium of Hegel, who with the passage
> of time has become the universal crib, the reference source for all
> the latest German speculators about principles and manufacturers
> of systems.[62]

Stirner's history is in this way, according to Marx, falsified and mystified; 'individuals are first of all transformed into "consciousness" and the world into "object", and thereby the manifold variety of forms of life and history is reduced to a different attitude of consciousness'. Worse still, Stirner is 'a clumsy copier of Hegel', one who 'registers ignorance of what he copies' in the manner of the worst of amanuenses.[63] The shortcoming in this respect of the successive stages of consciousness Stirner outlines in 'The Life of a Man' and elsewhere in *The Individual and his Own* is that each successive stage of what Stirner calls 'consciousness' (and what is in reality awareness) confronts a world that owes nothing to previous confrontations but is to all intents and purposes ready-made. Such an approach, Marx quite correctly indicated, for all its Hegelian pretensions, was radically at variance with Hegel's own approach, which at least had had the virtue of admitting, and attempting to account for, historicity. Marx himself, as we shall see, followed Hegel much more closely when he insisted, not just against Stirner, that the social world is not something *found* but something *made*; yet it was Stirner who had indicated in its most pointed and exaggerated form the danger that arises from all Young Hegelian attempts to account for historical change by ascribing constitutive power to consciousness. Because for Stirner

> the holy is something alien, everything alien is transformed into
> the Holy; and because everything Holy is a bond, a fetter, all
> bonds and fetters are transformed into the Holy. By this means
> Saint Sancho [Stirner] has already achieved the result that
> everything alien becomes for him a mere appearance, a mere
> idea, against which he frees himself merely by protesting against
> it.[64]

This is precisely the charge Marx levels, *mutatis mutandis*, against Feuerbach: that his ersatz notion of alienation, from which Marx was no less concerned to dissociate himself, invites no more than a supine, contemplative response. While Stirner was justified in criticizing, *sans phrase*, Feuerbach's dependence on generalities with no meaning, like 'man', Marx indicates that Stirner was nevertheless himself dependent upon such abstractions in very much the same way. Stirner, that is to say,

> constantly foists 'man' on history as the sole *dramatis persona*
> and believes that 'man' has made history. Now we shall find the
> same thing recurring in Feuerbach, whose illusions Stirner
> faithfully accepts in order to build further on their foundation.
> . . . If Stirner reproaches Feuerbach for reaching no result because
> he makes the predicate into the subject and *vice versa*, he himself
> is far less capable of arriving at anything, for he faithfully accepts
> these Feuerbachian predicates, transformed into subjects, as real
> personalities robbing the world . . . he actually believes in the
> domination of the abstract ideas of ideology in the modern world,
> he believes that in this struggle . . . against conceptions he is no
> longer attacking an illusion but the real forces that rule the world.

Stirner, in other words, like the Sancho Panza to whom Marx likens him, believes 'Don Quixote's assurances that by a mere moral injunction he can, without further ado, convert the material forces arising from the division of labour into personal forces'; 'the practical moral content of the whole trick', as Marx indignantly puts it, 'is merely an apology for the vocation forced on every individual' by the division of labour.[65] Stirner's belief, moreover, is not Hegelian but a typically Young Hegelian debasement of Hegelian doctrine.

Hegel himself had believed that selfhood is not given to the individual as an automatic or definitional attribute but that it must be created by that individual. The importance of Hegel's concept of selfhood as self-activity was not lost upon Marx, although it does seem to have escaped the attention of Stirner. Marx believed that Hegel's concept of self-activity had as an important part of its meaning not only a notion of potentiality beyond the given, but also a notion of creative work – work, moreover, of the very kind that the capitalist division of labour subverts and denies. Marx meant what he had said in the *Economic and Philosophic Manuscripts*, in a passage whose implications strike remarkably deeply into his thought taken as a whole. 'The outstanding achievement of Hegel's *Phenomenology*', Marx insisted, had been that 'Hegel grasps the self-creation of man as a process, . . . and that he therefore grasps the nature of *labour*, and conceives objective man (true, because real man) as the result of his own labour'. Even though labour as a source or form of self-realization was more important to Marx than it had been for Hegel, it remains true that the theme of the transformation of self-consciousness into self-realization that is effected by labour, labour seen as self-activity, runs through the *Phenomenology* and greatly influenced Marx. The idea that 'by working on the world, a man gives his own individuality an external, objective and enduring form' has as its best-known expression the 'Master and Slave' ('Herr und Knecht') section of Hegel's *Phenomenology of Mind*, but it may be encountered elsewhere in Hegel's writings. One illustrative example, which sounds as Marxist as it is Hegelian, may be found in his *Lectures on Aesthetics*:

> Man is realized for himself [für sich] by practical activity,
> inasmuch as he has the impulse, in the medium which is directly
> given to him, to produce himself, and therein at the same time
> to recognize himself. This purpose he achieves by the modification
> of external things upon which he impresses the seal of his inner
> being, and then finds repeated in them his own characteristics.
> Man does this in order as a free subject to strip the outer world
> of its stubborn foreignness, and to enjoy in the shape and fashion
> of things a [n] . . . external reality of himself.[66]

This means that the individual according to Hegel can attain self-knowledge only in and through what he has done and what he has made. Selfhood is a process, a capacity, not a Stirnerian datum; it is a development, not a state or a stage; and it validates itself over time. What this means is that selfhood implies self-activity and involves the mind's capacity to situate itself according to its own activity. The process in question is largely (but not entirely) retrospective; selfhood arises from the mind's ability to comprehend itself in its own emergence and development, along the path that it itself has taken. But the self can no more be reduced to this itinerary than it can be accounted for by whatever happens to surround and impinge upon it; it cannot be reduced to its social setting. The one aspect of the philosophy of the Enlightenment that Hegel rejected completely and unreservedly was Lockean sensationalism and its various materialist offshoots, all of which share a static, constricting conception of human nature, together with a tendency to dwell upon what is least significant to selfhood, its susceptibility to outside influence. As Marx's *Theses on Feuerbach* were also to recognize, to see men as passive, supine products of their environment is to fail to do justice to their creative capacities and potential and to fail to take into account anything that *characterizes* anyone – whatever, in Stirner's lexicon, is peculiar or unique to any particular person. People in Hegel's view are their experiences, deeds, thoughts, actions and potential combined; each person makes something different out of the situation in which all persons find themselves. Each person is an indissoluble ensemble, and all persons are their own creators, actualities and potentialities combined. They are not at all the objects of external necessity; and this, indeed, is why only a retrospective teleology can encompass and contemplate men's completed lives.

These Hegelian ideas form the background to Stirner's *The Individual and his Own* and to Marx's thought alike; both Stirner and Marx in their very different ways perceived that what had been in principle indissoluble to Hegel was in fact dissolved. Here, however, the resemblances between the two (resemblances which are in the nature of an overlap, not a convergence) end; if we ask what is the nature of the ensemble that is dissolved, when its dissolution takes effect, and by which agency, differences of some substances are quick to emerge.

To Stirner, what was in principle indissoluble had yet to make its appearance, since individual uniqueness had been obscured and occluded throughout human history by successive systems of thought and morality, of organization and self-denial, all of which had worked, seriatim, to devastating effect. In present-day society, according to Stirner, we meet with nothing more than hints and suggestions of individual uniqueness, and these are encountered only among society's outcasts and marginalia – the dispossessed: paupers, criminals, labourers. Stirner regarded these figures as exceptions to a general rule, to his trans-historical maxim of the denial of individual uniqueness. Marx's approach was very different; he admitted that 'individuals have always started out from themselves, and could not do otherwise';[67] he had admitted (in his 1844 Notebooks) that 'the greater and more articulated the social power is within the relationship of private property, the more egoistic and asocial man becomes', a point with which Stirner, *mutatis mutandis*, might have agreed (and which he would have celebrated). Stirner, however, would have found outrageous the clause Marx immediately added: the more egoistic and asocial man becomes, 'the more he becomes alienated from his own nature'.[68] For while Marx could write, in the *Economic and Philosophic Manuscripts*, that 'man is a unique individual – and it is just his particularity that makes him an individual', his conception of what it means to be an individual differs radically from that held by Stirner. To be an individual, Marx continues in the same passage, is to be 'a really individual communal being [Gemeinwesen]'.[69] Marx saw no contradiction in using the word *Gemeinwesen* to refer both to the individual and to society (though not to *capitalist* society). It is not hard to imagine what Stirner would have made of some of Marx's characteristic utterances (which are not all from his earlier writings): 'The individual is the social being [gesellschaftliches Wesen]'; 'individual human life and species-life are not different things'; man 'is in the most literal sense a *zoon politikon*, not only a social animal but an animal that can develop into an individual only in society'.[70] We may presume that the Aristotelian reference in this statement, with its familiar implications of purposiveness and teleology, was quite intentional (and, of course, for this very reason would have been no less horrifying to Stirner).

These statements, and statements like them, demand some explanation, coming as they do from a theorist who is commonly supposed – not least by Stirner, but also by more reputable opponents – to have been the enemy of the individual or to have subsumed 'the individual' beneath 'the collective' or 'the class'. Advocates of this commonly held view have never been characterized by their reticence; yet its advocacy should at least be tempered by a recognition that Marx derived, most proximately from Hegel, a more complex position than is generally ascribed to him. The hinge of Marx's argument is a distinction between individualism and individuality that he used most dramatically and forcefully in his polemic against Stirner. The neglect of 'Saint Max' has had the untoward effect of obscuring our understanding of Marx's position, a position which, while it is unlikely to still or conclude discussion of the issues surrounding individualism, individuality and society, deserves to be better known by those who might take up the cudgels for or against Marx in future. As an example – there are many more – of what needs to be overcome in future discussion, reference might be made to one recent commentator who regards Stirner's book, 'the testament of a dissenting intellectual', as 'a sociological document of the first order', and who ventures the opinion that 'Marx, who was well aware that "revolution begins in the mind of intellectuals", did not accord this credit to Stirner because at the time [1845-6] he was already thinking in terms of classes and not of individuals'.[71] In fact, Marx, who did not think that revolution begins in the *mind* of anyone, far from neglecting 'the individual' for 'the class', was attempting throughout *The German Ideology* to examine their relationship in capitalist society – thanks in no small measure to Stirner himself.

What this means is that Marx, far from evading the issue of the individual versus the collectivity that had been raised, pointedly, by Stirner, knew perfectly well how important it was; it means that Marx met Stirner's extreme presentation of the issue point by point, and dealt with it by re-casting Stirner's polarization in terms that clearly recall Hegel. Individualism, said Marx, is one thing, individuality another; the difference is akin to the distinction in Hegel between self-assertion (in civil society and its 'system of needs') and self-determination (which is political, and takes place only at the more elevated level of the state). Individualism and individuality are conceptually distinct, and historically they have come to work at cross-purposes. Individualism animates capitalist society and *by the same token* does violence to individuality; indeed it cannot do otherwise, since the distinguishing feature of labour in capitalist society is its negation and discounting of self-activity, properly so-called. Not only is this denial of self-activity fertile soil for alienation; alienation is alienation *of* self-activity, and, as we have seen in the last chapter, it takes two forms that reinforce each other. The domination of the product over the producer in the process of production – with all the monstrous paradoxes this implies – is one of them; the way in which men's social relations and communal potential take on an alien existence independent of men themselves is the other. One of the consequences of alien politics is that the division between civil society and state is reproduced in microcosm within the individual, whose powers, whether we consider them productively or politically, are expressed as something alien; because the outcome of activity in either realm stands opposed to the actor, the system is enabled to reproduce and reinforce itself at the expense of the individual.

Marx's use of the term *Gemeinwesen* to refer to the individual (*ein Gemeinwesen*) *and* society (*das Gemeinwesen*) indicates that quite unlike Stirner, he refused to separate individual and society *categorically* at all. As we have seen, Marx had insisted against Bruno Bauer, in 'On the Jewish Question', that the separation of bourgeois and *citoyen* entailed by 'political emancipation' was a denial, an alienation, of man's quintessentially social character; Marx insisted, in the same year, against Hegel that 'the nature of the particular person is not his beard, his blood, his abstract *physis*, but rather his social quality . . .'.[72]

It is a point of some importance that these claims are linked. To get the full sense of the links we need to examine 'Saint Max'; yet some of the main features of Marx's position have been well outlined by Joseph O'Malley in his 'Editor's Introduction' to Marx's *Critique of Hegel's Philosophy of Right*:

> What governs these discussions [Marx's 1842 and 1843 critiques] is a special notion of the relationship between the individual social being on the one hand, and society on the other: society is the *sine qua non* for the humanization of the individual man; and the character of the individual member of society will be a function of the character of society itself. At the same time, however, the character of society will be an expression of the character of its members, for society itself is the actual social or communal nature of its members. Such a conception of the nature of the relationship of the individual and society underlies Marx's use, in the *Critique*, of the term *Gemeinwesen* (communal being) to signify both the individual and . . . the social complex within which he lives and acts . . .[73]

– unless of course this 'social complex' is a capitalist one. The double-edged use of the term *Gemeinwesen* implies that the denial of one meaning is *ipso facto* the denial of the other; or to put the same point another way, that when the social and individual qualities of men have not yet been separated, man is both an individual *and* a social representative of the human species. The modern capitalist division of labour offends against *both* meanings of the word *Gemeinwesen* and sunders what had been a substantial unity.

In discussing representativeness in the *Critique*, Marx had observed that 'every function' in society can be regarded, prima facie, as a representative function, provided that the unity between individual and community, itself a prima facie unity, has itself not been broken.

> For example, the shoemaker is my representative in so far as he fulfils a social need, just as every definite social activity, because it is a species-activity, represents only the species; that is to say, represents a determination of my own essence the way every man is the representative of the other. Here, he is representative not by virtue of something other than himself which he represents, but by virtue of what he is and does.[74]

It is striking that by the time Marx investigated the modern division of labour in *The German Ideology* he recognized that in modern society it is manifestly no longer the case that every function in society can be taken as being representative in anything like the same sense. This means that while individual and society for Marx are not categorically separable, they *are separated* in capitalist society in a way that does violence to man's human, social character. What Hegel in his discussion of civil society had called 'the system of needs' - the realm of production, distribution and exchange - was to Marx as well as to Hegel the antithesis of community. Marx had expressed this belief prior to *The German Ideology*, in a rather less pointed form; in a passage whose argument strikingly recalls that of 'On the Jewish Question', Marx had indicated that

> [as] human nature is the true communal nature or communal being of man, men through the activation of their nature create and produce a human communal being, a social being which is no abstractly universal power opposed to the single individual but is the nature or being of every single individual, his own activity, his own life, his own spirit, his own wealth. . . Men as actual, living particular individuals, not men considered in abstraction, constitute this being. It is, therefore, what they are. To say that man alienates himself is to say that the society of this alienated man is the caricature of his actual common life, of his true generic life. His activity, therefore, appears as a torment, his own creation as a force alien to him, his wealth as poverty, the essential bond connecting him with other men as something unessential so that the separation from other men appears as his true essence.[75]

That 'separation from other men' takes on the aspect of an 'essence' is precisely Marx's accusation against Stirner in *The German Ideology*, as we have seen. Marx consequently indicated that Stirner's truculent 'ego' enjoyed but a hollow, conceptual existence; that the egoism Stirner asserted led him into solipsism, solipsism of a peculiarly Young Hegelian kind according to which the vaunted principle of 'peculiarity' could not avoid becoming one more 'essence' of the sort Stirner had taken it upon himself to attack; that his insistence on the egoistic character of labour overlooked the fact that in modern society proletarians, and individuals in general, 'are entirely subordinated to the division of labour and hence are brought into the most complete dependence on one another',[76] a dependence they could, and would have to, turn to good account in revolutionary organization.

What lies at the heart of Marx's attack on Stirner also lies at the centre of *The German Ideology* taken as a whole: the analysis of the division of labour and of the consequent need for emancipation, by means of revolution, from its disastrous effects. The forces of production (*Produktionskräfte*) were no longer in any significant sense the forces of the individual but forces of private property that were chillingly indifferent, or actively hostile, to the individual; and the individual in question has nothing in common with Stirner's egoist, since his life-activity has nothing distinctive or personal about it; he exists as the producer of products over which he has no control, products which are made, distributed and used without any regard to *any* 'peculiarities' the individual involved in their manufacture or use may possess or embody. The individual in this sense is – and here the Hegelian language Marx uses is appropriate – an 'abstract individual'; the only attributes he may possess that are relevant, or that 'count', are those each man has in common with others. These amount to a kind of lowest common denominator, one to which men and their labour were, daily, being reduced; all that matters is that which can be measured, an alienation indeed – their generalizable labour, their buying power, their selling power, and not what gives or could give them any individuality.

Self-activity and communism

Capitalism in Marx's opinion offends against community, individuality and selfhood alike; owing to the character of its division of labour as the exploitation, rather than the expression, of the diversity of human activity, capitalism subordinates individuals to production, which comes to exist 'externally to them, as a kind of fate, but social production is not [on the other hand] subordinated to individuals . . . Their own production [stands] in opposition to individuals as a thing-like relationship which is independent of them'. Under its domination 'labour itself can only exist on the premise of [the] fragmentation' of society and of the individuals of which it is composed.

> The productive forces appear as a world for themselves, quite independent of and divorced from the individuals, alongside the individuals; the reason for this is that the individuals, whose forces they are, exist split up and in opposition to one another. . . Thus we have a totality of productive forces which have taken on a material form and are for the individuals no longer the forces of the individuals but of private property. . . Never in any earlier period, have the productive forces taken on a form so indifferent to the intercourse of individuals as individuals, because their intercourse itself was previously a restricted one. . . Standing over against these productive forces we have the majority of the individuals from whom these forces have been wrested away and who, robbed in this way of all real life-content, have become abstract individuals. . . The only connection which still links them with the productive forces and with their own existence – labour – has lost all semblance of life-activity and only sustains their life by stunting it.[77]

The axis of Marx's discussion is self-activity, the emergence of a 'totality of powers' within each and every individual as opposed to the playing out of a restrictive and exclusive role. It is the notion of self-activity that links together Marx's sustained critique of the capitalist division of labour, in *The German Ideology* and elsewhere, for the narrowness and 'fixation of social activity' it brings forth and requires, on the one hand, and his fervent espousal of revolutionary communism on the other; and it is the notion of self-activity that undergirds the concept of individuality that Marx, prompted by Stirner, distinguished forcefully from the individualism that animates capitalist society. Individuality and self-activity are linked, and offended against by the capitalist division of labour; individuality, according to Marx, is thus not at all what Stirner had made of it, a raw datum, or a kind of core or heart existing beneath (but not within) successive layers of consciousness and 'vocations'. It is not something that is found or uncovered in this way – by peeling away layers – at all; it is something that is made, and something that cannot, or can but rarely, emerge under capitalist conditions. Only if individuality were to be seen in this way, as a potential or an expansive capacity, would it not turn into yet another Young Hegelian 'essence', as had Stirner's 'ego'. The implications of this point are directly political ones. Stirner, says Marx,

> believes that the communists were only waiting for 'society' to 'give' them something, whereas at most they only want to give themselves a society. . . He transforms society, even before it exists, into an instrument from which he wants to derive benefit, without him and other people by their mutual social relations creating a society and hence this 'instrument'. . . He believes that in communist society there can be a question of 'duties' and 'interests,' of two complementary aspects of opposites that exist only in bourgeois society (under the guise of interest the reflective bourgeois always inserts a third thing between himself and his mode of action – a habit seen in truly classic form in Bentham, whose nose would have to have some interest before deciding to smell anything). . . [Stirner] believes that the communists want to 'make sacrifices' to 'society' when they want at most to sacrifice existing society; in this case he should have described their consciousness that their struggle is the common cause of all people who have outgrown the bourgeois system as a sacrifice that they make to themselves.[78]

Stirner's analysis of the threats to individuality was in Marx's opinion vitiated by his ignorance of economics which had led him to overlook the most important, self-sustaining threat of all: the capitalist division of labour. Marx's criticism of Stirner on this particular score did not stop at this point, however; nor indeed could it have stopped here, in view of the other side of Stirner's argument, which raised an issue of considerable importance.

Whatever the shortcomings of Stirner's discussion – shortcomings to which Marx was in no way blind, as we have seen – it did raise the issue of the supposed threat to the individual posed by the communists, whom Stirner included prominently among the moralists and task-masters he was concerned to attack. The crucial point here is not only that Stirner had forced this issue on to Marx's attention; it is also that Marx need have framed his arguments – not only about the division of labour, individualism and individuality, but also about communism and revolution – only in response to Stirner. It is Stirner's presentation of individuality – a theme central to the argumentation of *The German Ideology* – that Marx was meeting. Private property and the division of labour, according to Marx,

> can be abolished only on condition of an all-round development
> of individuals, because the existing character of intercourse and
> productive forces is an all-round one, and only individuals who
> are developing in an all round way *can* . . . turn them into the
> manifestations of their lives.

It is a point of some importance that 'abstract individuals . . . are by this very fact [i.e. the fact of their "abstraction"] put into a position to enter into relations with one another as individuals'. Stirner

> believes that communist proletarians who revolutionize society
> and put the relations of production and the form of intercourse
> on a new basis – i.e. on themselves as new people, on their new
> mode of life – that these proletarians remain 'as of old.' The
> tireless propaganda carried on by these proletarians, their daily
> discussions among themselves, sufficiently prove how little they
> want to remain 'as of old,' and how little they want people to
> remain 'as of old'. . . . They know too well that only under changed
> circumstances will they cease to be 'as of old' and therefore they
> are determined to change these circumstances at the first
> opportunity. In revolutionary activity the changing of self
> coincides with the changing of circumstances.

What this means is that, far from being fundamentally similar or re-ducible to them,

> [communism] differs from all previous movements in that it
> overturns the basis of all earlier relations of production and

intercourse and for the first time treats all natural premises as the creatures of hitherto existing men . . . and subjects them to the power of united individuals. . . The reality which communism is creating, is precisely the true basis for rendering it impossible that anything should exist independently of individuals, insofar as reality is only a product of the preceding intercourse of individuals themselves.[79]

It is for this reason that Marx insisted that the communists' revolutionary injunctions and calls to action are in no way reducible to or comparable with moralistic imperatives and tasks of the kind that Stirner had set out to attack. Instead, they were, according to Marx, in the fullest sense of the word *historical* imperatives, the need for the realization of which was based not only upon the observably debilitated condition of individuals under capitalism but also upon the wherewithal for emancipation capitalism nevertheless provides. As Marx puts it,

> Communism is not for us a *state of affairs* which is to be established, an ideal to which reality [will] have to adjust itself. We call communism the *real* movement which abolishes the present state of things. The conditions of this movement result from the premises now in existence.[80]

What is distinctive about, and crucial to, Marx's depictions of capitalism is his awareness of its double-edged character, his perception that the dependence it produces, if complete, is also and by the same token universal or general (*allgemein*). 'All-round dependence', which Marx defined in *The German Ideology* as 'this natural form of the world-historical cooperation of individuals', will be transformed by 'communist revolution into the control and conscious mastery of these powers which, born of the actions of men on one another, have till now overawed and governed men as powers completely alien to them'.[81] Men's actions in capitalist society are not self-directed because they are no more than reactions to external necessity; yet they are universal in scope and scale, and this universality, Marx was to insist against many of his more past-oriented contemporaries – including, as we shall see, Proudhon – did denote progress, progress of a radically unsubstantiated kind, but which by virtue of its unsubstantiated character could be turned to good account. As Marx was to put it in the *Grundrisse*:

> Universally-developed individuals, whose social relationships are subject, as their own communal relationships, to their own collective control, are the product not of nature but of history. The extent and universality of the development of capacities

that make possible this individuality presuppose precisely
production on the basis of exchange-values. The universal nature
of this production creates an alienation of the individual from
himself and others, but also for the first time the general and
universal nature of his relationships and capacities. At early
stages of this development, the single individual appears to be
more complete since he has not yet elaborated the abundance
of his relationships, and has not yet established them as powers
and autonomous relationships that are opposed to himself. It is
as ridiculous to wish to return to that primitive abundance as it is
to believe in the continuing necessity of its complete depletion.[82]

Marx went on to argue, fatefully, that the individual, as a member of
the revolutionary proletariat properly so-called, would in no way have
his individuality diminished, since the collectivity in question becomes
the *sine qua non* for individual freedom and self-activity alike.

Modern universal intercourse can be controlled by individuals
. . . only when controlled by all. . . Only at this stage [at the
stage of the organization of the revolutionary proletariat] does
self-activity coincide with material life, which corresponds to
the development of individuals into complete individuals. . .
The transformation of labour into self-activity corresponds to
the transformation of the earlier limited intercourse into
the intercourse of individuals as such.[83]

It is for this reason that Marx insists against Stirner that the communists 'do not put egoism against self-sacrifice, nor do they express
this contradiction theoretically'. Instead, 'they demonstrate the material
basis engendering' this contradiction, 'with which it disappears of
itself'. The communists, again, 'by no means want to do away with the
"private individual" for the sake of the "self-sacrificing man" '; and the
communists 'do not preach morality at all, such as Stirner preaches so
extensively'.[84] The 'individual' and the 'collectivity' are exclusive and
opposed categories, as Stirner considered they were, only if the individual is considered mystically, as 'man' or as 'ego', and history as the
record of his self-estrangement, conceived spiritually.

Marx does not rest content, then, with painting an entirely negative
picture of capitalism, its division of labour and the alienation it brings
forth; it is when we ask how individuals, reduced as they are according
to Marx to such a debilitated state, are to emancipate themselves that
(to put matters mildly) doubt is cast on the entire Young Hegelian
perspective. Many lines of discussion are brought together in Marx's
argument; his direct references to Stirner's fervent objections to revolutionary communism enabled Marx not only to place 'Saint Max'

firmly within his Young Hegelian context, indeed to attack Stirner as the surrogate of the Young Hegelian outlook in general, but also to advance an argument about freedom – not, to be sure, the negative, individualistic freedom 'to buy, sell and otherwise contract' that is associated with capitalism, but the positive freedom associated with self-activity that is not bought by some and paid for by others, the freedom that is not antithetical to, but expressive of, community properly so-called. Marx's argument, finally, is as *political* as Stirner's is anti-political; and for good reason. For the proletarians, Marx insists against 'Saint Max', 'owing to the frequent opposition of interests among them arising out of the division of labour . . . no other "agreement" is possible but a political one directed against the whole present system'.[85] Marx had already indicated that while, 'in imagination, individuals seem freer under the domination of the bourgeoisie than before . . . in reality, of course, they are less free, because they are more subjected to the violence of things'.[86] This, indeed, is the reason why

> the transformation through the division of labour of personal
> powers into material powers cannot be dispelled by dismissing
> the general idea of it from one's mind but can only be abolished
> by the individuals' again subjecting these material powers to
> themselves and abolishing the division of labour. This is not
> possible without the community. Only in community with others
> has the individual the means of cultivating his gifts in all directions;
> only in the community, therefore, is personal freedom possible. . .
> In the real community, the individuals obtain their freedom in
> and through their association. . . The [earlier kind of] communal
> relationship into which the individuals of a class entered, and
> which was determined by their common interests over against
> a third party, was always a community to which these individuals
> belonged only as average individuals, only in so far as they lived
> within the conditions of existence of their class. . . With the
> community of revolutionary proletarians, on the other hand,
> who take their conditions of existence and those of all members
> of society under their control, it is just the reverse; it is as
> individuals that the individuals participate in it. It is just this
> combination of individuals which puts the conditions of the free
> development of individuals under their control – conditions which
> were previously abandoned to chance and which won an indepen-
> dent existence over against individuals just because of their
> separation as individuals. Combination up till now . . . was an
> agreement upon these conditions, within which the individuals
> were free to enjoy the freaks of fortune. . . This right, to the
> undisturbed enjoyment, within certain conditions, of fortuity
> and chance has up till now been called personal freedom.[87]

Marx's argument, however problematic it may be, is a powerful one, and has long been so regarded; yet most evaluations have been advanced in the absence of any adequate understanding of *why* he made it, and whose points he was meeting. A re-examination and re-evaluation of Stirner's argument has proved to be in order, since the significance of his egoistic anarchism – which itself proved to have few and isolated adherents – in provoking and shaping a detailed and theoretically significant response from Marx has for too long been overlooked. A more detailed examination of the evidence amply bears out Nicolas Lobkowicz's point that it was Stirner who impelled Marx to take the position he did in *The German Ideology* against Feuerbach and against the entire Young Hegelian school (whose worst faults are according to Marx embodied in and exemplified by Stirner's poaching of 'snipe existing only in the mind').[88] Yet in one way Lobkowicz goes too far, in another he goes not far enough. The point that needs to be stressed about Marx's response, a direct and extended series of rejoinders, to Stirner is not that Marx had occasion to regard Stirner as a threat.[89] Too much can be made of such an interpretation; we need consider not only Stirner's theoretical incoherence (not necessarily a setback to the influence of an anarchist theoretician), but also the justice of Marx's successive accusations that Stirner's entire argument, inconsistencies and all, remains entrapped within a purely theoretical framework (like Hobbes's 'bird in lime twigs' – 'the more he struggles, the more belimed') and makes no effort to ensure his maxims' translatability into a practice that would have to be political. Stirner's hostility to social or revolutionary movements and his disdain for political concerns were no news to Marx. Whether or not the growth of a mass anarchist movement in an uncertain future would have surprised Marx in 1845, Marx, one suspects, would not have been surprised one whit to learn that this movement was to play a far greater part in keeping Stirner's book in print (the date of the second edition, 1882, is significant) than Stirner's ideas were to play in fuelling an anarchist movement which he would doubtless have disowned.

Lobkowicz is quite right in suggesting, however, that it was Stirner who indicated to Marx some of the pitfalls of Feuerbachian humanism, forcing Marx to define his position not only against Feuerbach, but also against Stirner himself. That Marx's attack on Feuerbach in *The German Ideology* was something of a volte-face in view of his earlier near-adulation of Feuerbach has often been noticed – although the suddenness of the transition has been exaggerated – and Lobkowicz is, again, quite right in recognizing that it was none other than Stirner who had impelled Marx into taking this new position. But to account for the importance of 'Saint Max' *merely* along these lines will not do. More is involved than just the indication of pitfalls; more is involved, indeed, than 'Saint Max' itself (or 'Saint Max' himself). The important point is that Marx, seeing the need to dissociate his position from that (or those) of the Young Hegelians as a group, and in so doing to confront and reject the excesses of his own philosophical past, did much more in *The German Ideology* than fully appreciate the force of Stirner's argument against the vapid anthropocentrism of Feuerbach. Marx's declaration of independence from Feuerbach's influence was under way, as we have seen in the last chapter, before *The German Ideology* was embarked upon. Marx, it is true, was stung by Stirner's accusation that he was himself 'Feuerbachian' foe of the individual; this accusation was based not only on Marx's use of Feuerbachian terminology ('species-being' in particular) in 'On the Jewish Question' but also, much more importantly, upon Marx's assumption of what Stirner considered the Feuerbachian mantle of 'liberator of humanity'. To disavow Feuerbach was one thing; to reply to this charge was something else again, since the issue it brings in its train is one that on any reckoning transcends Feuerbach's presentation: that of individuality and communism. In dismissing revolution and communism on the grounds that they involved yet one more tyrannical, systematic form of regimentation, Stirner had raised a spectre that had to be laid to rest.

Marx met Stirner's accusation that communism as a means and as an end is by its very nature irredeemably opposed to the individual and his individuality by advancing several counter-arguments, not all aimed merely at discrediting Stirner. He was driven to deny that his position was in any way similar or reducible to those that any of the Young Hegelians had put forward, to immunize, in other words, his position against the accusations Stirner levelled against everyone else; and what this denial entailed was another – a denial that the revolutionary injunctions he was concerned to put forward were resolvable into earlier, purely moral or moralistic imperatives. Marx aimed in *The German Ideology* not only 'to debunk and discredit the philosophic struggle with the shadows of reality, which appeals to the dreamy and muddled German nation', but also to demonstrate that his own critique, far from condemning the present or its Young Hegelian vindicators in the light of some abstract categories or principles, did so on historical grounds – history serving to transcend and undercut the pretensions of all purely philosophical critiques and abstract standards. This means that Stirner's own criticisms of 'fanaticism' and the empty moralism he associated with the school have some force as applied to the Young Hegelians, whose revolutionism was indeed bogus; this indeed is why it was important for Marx to distinguish himself from them, publicly, brazenly and once and for all.

Marx was thus driven to insist in no uncertain terms that his own critical analysis of capitalism and individuality, far from being abstract or conceptual, was on the contrary embodied in what he called the 'real movement' of history. This is, of course, a large claim; the fullest substantiation Marx gave it is not restricted within the pages of *The German Ideology* but expanded upon throughout Marx's later writings. Yet the importance of *The German Ideology* in sketching out the themes and setting the tone and terms of these later writings - and indeed of raising many of their problems - ought not to be discounted. Not the least important of these themes sounded for the first time in *The German Ideology* were two connected themes that were to resound through Marx's later writings: the critical analysis of the division of labour in capitalist society and the advancement of revolutionary activity - *political* activity - as the only possible antidote to its unprecedented and deleterious effects on the individual.

What has often been overlooked in earlier discussions is the fact that it was Stirner who had forced both the issues, and the connection between them, on to Marx's attention, and that it was Stirner's presentation of them that Marx - in the first instance, at least - set out to meet. To begin with, Stirner had attacked 'revolution' as a 'vocation' and had asserted a kind of primordial, individual 'rebellion' in its stead. That Stirner's distinction is incoherent - as it surely is - constitutes the least of Marx's criticisms, since Stirner, carried away by his hatred of 'vocations' and tasks, had overlooked something very basic indeed, not only about revolution and communism but also about 'vocations' themselves.

> ... if ... the workers assert in their communist propaganda
> that the vocation, destiny, task of every person is to achieve
> an all-round development of all his abilities ... [Stirner] sees
> in this only the vocation to something alien, the assertion of
> the 'Holy.' He seeks to achieve freedom from this by taking
> under his protection the individual who has been crippled by
> the division of labour at the expense of his abilities and
> relegated to a one-sided vocation ... which has been *declared*
> his vocation by others. What is here asserted [by Stirner] in
> the form of a vocation, a destiny, is precisely the negation of
> the vocation that has hitherto resulted in practice from the
> division of labour ...[90]

particularly, as we have seen, from the division of labour in its modern, capitalist form which amounts to the 'fixation of social activity', the negation and alienation of self-activity, properly so-called.

Here a difference of some substance emerges between Marx and Stirner (and the Young Hegelians in general). What concerns Stirner above all about revolution as a 'vocation' is what it has in common with the state, *inter alia*; like the state, like all earlier systems of legality and morality, like all anterior forms of political and social organization, and like all tasks, vocations and ideologies that can be said to be collective (in the sense of supra-individual), revolution devalues the individual and appeals in the name of collectivity to self-abnegation and self-sacrifice. Marx's points against this perception are that it is too broad; that Stirner's argument by virtue of its broadness lacks specificity, and fails even to distinguish the state from civil society; that in view of this failure Stirner's state-centredness is unwarranted and specious; and that it misprizes the nature of revolution anyway. Marx's account for its part emphasizes not the political, moral and spiritual processes of self-bondage, but the forcible denial of self-activity, conceived expansively, that is engendered and sustained by the division of labour in capitalist society; if individuality is denied, what denies it in the first instance is not the state but the labour process, not the prospect of revolutionary change but the division of labour whose effects communism as an end and as a means would overcome once and for all.

> The difference between revolution and Stirner's rebellion is not, as Stirner thinks, that the one is a political and social act while the other is an egoistical act, but that the former is an act while the latter is no act at all. . . If Stirner had studied the various actual revolutions and attempts at revolution . . . [if,] further, he had concerned himself with the actual individuals . . . in every revolution, and their relations, instead of being satisfied with pure Ego . . . then perhaps he would come to understand that every revolution, and its results, was determined by these relations, by needs and that the 'political and social act' was in no way in contradiction to the 'egoistical act.'[91]

Marx's point here is not just the more or less familiar one that 'in revolutionary activity the changing of self coincides with the changing of circumstances' (though it certainly involves this belief); what underlies it, however, is a *way of conceptualizing the individual self* that is radically at variance with Stirner's. Marx's is expansive and dynamic, while Stirner's is restrictive and static. At the root of Marx's criticisms of Stirner's Young Hegelian variant of all the shortcomings of solipsism we find a conception of individuality that differs radically not only from the individualism that animates capitalist society but also from Stirner's 'ego' which is, finally, nothing but a kind of residuum, what is left after various layers of consciousness have been stripped away. Marx's accusation that on Stirner's logic the 'ego' must be nothing more than a conceptual category, and the truculent egoist must have but a hollow, purely conceptual existence, was not advanced simply to score a point, but as part of a more general argument. Stirner's assertion of 'peculiarity' (*Eigenheit*), by turning into yet another essence, has the effect of catapulting him back among the Young Hegelians, whose milieu is where he really belongs; but this is the least of it. Stirner's assertion of the peculiarity of the individual, besides being abstract and solipsistic, is also quite literally beside the point if it is put forward at a time when what might really distinguish one person from another or others is in the process of being cut from under him, at a time when personal powers are not, and cannot be, apprehended as social powers. The forces that oppose individuality – once individuality is conceived properly, as a potential, a capacity that has its conditions of emergence – are not conceptual forces opposing some fictitious core of being (or 'essence') but the real ones that, by striking at self-determination and self-activity, strike by the same token at freedom. As Marx was later to put it, in language that strikingly recalls that of *The German Ideology*,

> although at first the development of the capacities of the human species takes place at the cost of the majority of human individuals and even classes, at the end it breaks through this contradiction and coincides with the development of the individual: the higher development of individuality is thus only achieved by an historical process.[92]

What lies behind this characteristic Marxian claim is a set of issues and themes, developed initially in *The German Ideology* and with greatest resonance in its unjustly neglected central section, 'Saint Max': individualism, individuality, vocation, labour, self-activity, freedom, self-determination, communism. All are key words in the Marxian lexicon; all were raised in the course of Marx's attack on Stirner. What makes 'Saint Max' central to *The German Ideology* also makes it central to Marx's writings as a whole; Stirner, despite himself, takes us to the heart of the Marxian enterprise.

CHAPTER 4

Marx and Proudhon

Proudhon: the excommunicant of the epoch

To be *governed* is to be kept under surveillance, inspected,
spied upon, bossed, law-ridden, regulated, penned in,
indoctrinated, preached at, registered, evaluated, appraised,
censured, ordered about by creatures who have neither the
right, nor the knowledge, nor the virtue, to do so. To be
governed is to be at each operation, at each transaction, at
each movement, marked down, recorded, listed, priced, stamped,
measured, assessed, licensed, authorized, sanctioned, endorsed,
reprimanded, obstructed, reformed, rebuked, chastised. It is,
under the pretence of public benefit and in the name of the
general interest, to be requisitioned, drilled, fleeced, exploited,
monopolized, extorted, squeezed, hoaxed, robbed; then at the
slightest resistance, the first word of complaint, to be squelched,
corrected, vilified, bullied, hounded, tormented, bludgeoned,
disarmed, strangled, imprisoned, shot down, judged, condemned,
deported, sacrificed, sold, betrayed, and to top it off, ridiculed,
made a fool of, outraged, dishonoured. That's government, that's
its justice, that's its morality!

Proudhon, *Idée générale de la révolution au XIXe siècle*[1]

The writings of Proudhon (by far the most intelligent explorer of
the idea of 'anarchy' in modern times) are a prolonged condemnation of a state understood in terms of purposive association,
which he identifies as 'une uniformité béate et stupide, la
solidarité de la sottise.' He describes his concern as 'Trouver un
état de l'égalité sociale qui soit ni communauté, ni despotisme,
ni morcellement, ni anarchie, mais liberté dans l'ordre et
indépendance dans l'unité' . . . not a bad specification of the
civil condition.

Michael Oakeshott, *On Human Conduct*[2]

175

Pierre-Joseph Proudhon (1809-65) was an anarchist theoretician of a very different stripe from his near contemporary Max Stirner (1806-56). The theoretical differences between the two centre around something to be discussed at greater length in due course: they stem from Proudhon's obsessive desire for order in society, an order which he believed the state, an illegitimate, factitious and self-styled monopolization of the means of violence, undercut rather than expressed. That Proudhon and Stirner would abolish the state for opposite reasons makes it virtually certain that Proudhon would have disagreed with Stirner even more fervently than he disagreed with (apparently) everyone else. But the fact that he never bothered to do so underlines more than Proudhon's lack of concern for most things beyond the borders of France; it also indicates a more obvious difference, one of bearing, between his doctrine and Stirner's thought. Like his fellow Young Hegelians, with their somewhat misleading talk of the 'French Feuerbach', Stirner was acquainted with Proudhon's ideas (which he criticized in passing); Proudhon, who could have heard about Stirner from Marx, from Bakunin, or from Karl Grün at the height of whatever reputation Stirner enjoyed during his lifetime, never discusses his ideas, even to refute them.

This points to a considerable difference in reputation and influence. Stirner is best known for one book, *The Individual and his Own* (though he wrote others that remained obscure). Proudhon, on the other hand, was a voluminous writer. His collected works run, in various editions, into a bewildering number of volumes, to which it is today customary to add fourteen volumes of correspondence as well as five volumes of notebooks (the *Carnets*); he was an accomplished, if long-winded, publicist and controversialist as well as the author of a series of well-known books on more general themes.[3] Stirner lived a life of obscurity, punctuated only once by the kind of flare-up of notoriety that attended the appearance of *all* of Proudhon's best-known books. During Stirner's lifetime he had almost no followers – he was, as Daniel Guérin says, a *sans-famille*,[4] and attracted little subsequent attention after the Young Hegelian flurry that greeted his book in 1845; even his posthumous disciples were (in a sense appropriately) few and far between. Proudhon was very different. He was celebrated to the point of notoriety throughout most of an eventful life, the main incidents of which Proudhon, an able if self-dramatizing publicist in his own cause, made sure were well known. Even though humility was alien to his nature, Proudhon admitted his temperamental inability and unwillingness to lead a movement and he left in his wake no established body of followers; yet his wake was considerable and his influence, indirect as well as direct, enormous. He was, in the fullest sense of the word, a public figure, a status in which he gloried. His doctrine had many adherents, even though – or perhaps precisely because – it was sometimes incoherent and always open-ended, to the point, at times, of sheer inconsistency. Any linear application of so resolutely unprogrammatic a corpus as Proudhon's untidy doctrine would be impossible; yet his doctrine has connotations as well as denotations that were nothing if not effective in speaking to generations of French working men in an idiom that seemed, and was, authentic and powerful.

Proudhon himself influenced these working men by his example as well as his precepts; he was not, and did not seek to be, a spell-binding orator capable of moving masses, but he was an exemplar, the symbol and prototype of the 'free man', as his friend Herzen recognized. Proudhon did not always act admirably, but he was nevertheless enormously, if not universally, admired. Herzen, as ever, does much to explain why; he characterized the year 1849 in France as follows:

> The year which has passed, to end worthily, to fill the cup of
> moral degradation, offered us a terrible spectacle: the fight of a
> *free man* against the *liberators of humanity*. The words, the
> mordant scepticism, the fierce denial, the merciless irony of
> Proudhon angered the official revolutionaries no less than the
> conservatives. They attacked him bitterly, they defended their
> traditions with the inflexibility of legitimists, they were
> terrified of his atheism and his anarchism, they could not
> understand how one could be free without the state, without
> a democratic government. In amazement, they listened to the
> immoral statement that the republic is for man, not man for
> the republic . . .[5]

Proudhon's marked hostility to even (or sometimes especially) revolutionary political action, a hostility expressed in the name of freedom, could not, one suspects, be better put – except by Proudhon himself. It is in this hostility that Proudhon's *persona* and the resilience of his doctrine come together. What Proudhon stood for, and what Proudhonism – which was never a school of thought, like Marxism, nor yet merely a temperamental affinity or cast of mind among those looking to Proudhon as an exemplar – meant, was above all else an attitude to politics that conspicuously included revolutionary politics, an insistence, which could be steadfast and imperturbable or truculent and exasperating, on abstention from the political fray, from the dogmas and doctrines and in-fighting, from the party lines and creeds, shifts and alliances of those who took it upon themselves to personify *la Nation*, the Revolution, or progress. Political activity is class collaboration, pure and simple; to resort to electioneering is fatally to accept the rules of a game that need to be changed, the game itself scrubbed out.

Proudhon believed fervently – all Proudhon's beliefs were fervent

The State

- in the salvation of working men, by their own efforts, through economic and social action alone. He urged that the state, whatever its form or pretensions, be defeated, hands down, but not on its own ground, not (usually) by means of any kind of activity that could be termed political. To fight on the terrain of the state is to cede advantage to the state and those who would use it; instead, Proudhon advocated, and to a considerable extent inspired, the undercutting of this terrain from without, by means of autonomous working-class associations and organizations of the kind that owed nothing to the state. The point was not to conquer political power but to deny it its medium of existence, for political power in Proudhon's eyes corrupts and contaminates those who use it, or are fixated by or upon it. Working-class separatism from the prevailing system of rewards and expectations leads in Proudhon's thought to the reconstitution of social order by non-political means – not according to any political instrumentalities or means but instead according to the organization of labour.

Proudhon's thought is notoriously difficult to summarize, but it is possible to identify themes that were developed with some consistency from book to book, and which were to give Proudhonism its immense resiliency even after the death of Proudhon himself, in the French labour movement. His central idea was that society should be organized not for politics and war but for work; for only work, considered as a kind of *esprit général*, could and would make possible a moral order in society that would sustain itself without coercion and without the kind of parasitism on the efforts of others that Proudhon thought dominated present society, in political and economic life alike. What he thought most needed to be overcome was what today would be called a conjuncture, a conjuncture between the unlimited accumulation of capital, on the one hand, and the accumulation and monopolization of political power, on the other. The two processes were linked since the state could then be used as an instrument to deprive the many of their property for the sake of the few into whose hands it fell. Proudhon believed this process of concentration and monopolization to be self-sustaining, unless checked; and it could be checked only by extra-political means. Social order may be constituted, in Proudhon's view, not according to any political instrumentality – political power and government were always the enemy – but according to an altogether different and separable social principle, on the basis, that is, of labour. The reconstruction of society along 'industrial' lines is an idea that may owe something to Saint-Simonism, but there is a crucial difference not only of personnel (Proudhon would conspicuously not include the methodical capitalist among the industrious classes, *les industriels*) but also of scale: the agency of social regeneration was to be the small workshop, the *atelier*, and the face-to-face relationships among men it involved, relationships which were to provide what Proudhon in his later writings termed the 'mutualist' paradigm for social and moral renewal. The 'federalism' that according to Proudhon was to be built upon this mutualist base meant that free, decentralized initiative would be the condition as well as the result of the social and moral cohesion that were to sustain the new order. Such federalism was, indeed, ultimately to apply not only to relations within the French nation but also to international relations (not, of course, to relations among states).

What runs through these various Proudhonian themes and gives them a certain consistency is a marked hostility to determinism. Proudhon believed in a code of practical morality according to which the emergence of future society and its new principle of order was not at all a matter of ineluctable historical necessity but, instead, altogether a matter of moral awakening. Proudhon's animus against historical necessity and determinism was such that most of his writings contain nothing that could be termed a philosophy of history at all; perhaps sensing its lack, Proudhon did eventually endeavour to provide one in his later works, but this effort was in the nature of an *ex post facto* manoeuvre to bind together elements that originally owed nothing to any philosophy of history, and everything to a set of ideas about morality. Proudhon does not reject morality as a prejudice men would best slough off, in the manner of Stirner (or, sometimes, Bakunin); nor does he pin his hopes for morality on to the emergence of some 'new', post-revolutionary man. Proudhon's morality is more straightforwardly a ripening of what is best in men as they are, the permanent sub-stratum of values that includes self-respect, honesty, decency, rectitude and individual responsibility. Not all men, of course, exhibit these moral qualities; capitalists, proprietors, monopolists and their political lackeys, indeed, cannot exhibit them. The only people in society who can embody these characteristics in their day-to-day intimate activity are those who do not depend upon expropriating others: the workers. From this proposition Proudhon infers, somewhat shakily, that work of a direct and non-exploitative kind itself has a moral character; indeed Proudhon steadfastly refused to characterize work negatively, even under capitalist conditions. It is always, even under the least promising of circumstances, in and of itself an act of moral affirmation.[6]

What this means is that workers, in undertaking their long-term task of seceding from capitalism and bourgeois democracy, according to Proudhon enjoyed at the outset one pronounced advantage: that of simply being workers, able to exclude non-workers from their ranks. What underlies Proudhon's unrelenting advocacy of working-class separatism is not just the fact of social division; he was not simply attempting to make a virtue out of the necessity this enforced separation implied. What also underlies it is the value of labour itself. Proudhon, who even coined the term *démopédie* to signify its educational value, believed fervently in the expansive potential as well as the redemptive value of labour, to the point of holding that anything unconnected with it was somehow evil. If power corrupts, labour ennobles. Proudhon's *System of Economic Contradictions* – which Marx was to attack in *The Poverty of Philosophy* – defined work as 'the great matrix of civilization' ('la grande matrice de la civilisation');[7] work was indeed, in the words of James Joll, Proudhon's 'basic ethical standard'[8] which Proudhon himself was not above describing as 'une volupté intime'[9] – an interesting choice of words for one who was the first to condemn luxury and leisure because they lead, inexorably, to idleness and vice. His followers were in this respect no different: the strongly Proudhonist Paris delegates to the Geneva Congress of the First International in 1866, the year after Proudhon died, brought with them to Switzerland a programme the second article of which began, 'le travail est grand et noble, c'est la source de toute richesse et de toute moralité'.[10]

It is on the basis of this kind of thinking that Proudhon himself urged the view, against the Saint-Simonians as well as against Louis Blanc, that collective productive action, of the type denied to all but the worker, the *ouvrier*, and collective productive action alone carries within itself the principle necessary for the recasting, the root-and-branch reconstitution, of society's order. This recasting of an order that, though latent, was by the same token potential, would have to proceed from below and from within to be legitimate. This new but implicit principle of order would not exist and thrive as the state and capital most assuredly do exist and thrive, at the expense of the individual, at the cost of decentralized individual initiative. What Proudhon advocated in the name of anarchy was very different from what Stirner had advocated in the name of resurgent egoism. Proudhon urged not absence of authority but a 'recomposition of authority' that would sometimes by-pass and always undercut the state and capital without destroying order in society. Proudhon's last book, *The Political Capacity of the Working Classes* (*De la capacité politique des classes ouvrières*)[11] argued at length that the state could not generate any social order worthy of the name and for this reason was by its very nature degenerative rather than regenerative. The argument that the state was not and could not be a *cause génératrice* was a summation of much that Proudhon had said before, not least in opposition to the Jacobin formula 'everything *for* the people, but everything *by* the state' ('tout pour le peuple mais tout par l'état'), a formula that was itself, not surprisingly, powerful among the nineteenth-century French Left, particularly in the hands of Louis-Auguste Blanqui, another of Proudhon's *bêtes noires*. The argument Proudhon advanced against Blanquism, Jacobinism and state socialism of all persuasions was that the state existed at one remove from the society it had set itself up to regulate and superintend; that its existence and perpetuation were borrowed and supernumary; and that the forces sustaining and multiplying its inauthentic power (*puissance*) could only be reinforced by any Jacobin uprising, any 'revolutionary' *coup de main* or *émeute*. The point was to undercut these forces once and for all. Not only Jacobinism but *any* properly revolutionary movement would in Proudhon's opinion merely prolong the action, accelerate what he called the *mouvement*, of the state – the state which, whatever its form or credentials, always became the instrument of the propertied and, as such, always remained external to social forces (as 'la constitution extérieure de la puissance sociale') and was always an alienation of collective forces ('aliénation de la force collective'),[12] forces which in its absence would breathe life, justice and order into society.

Any resemblance between Proudhon and Marx on this point is more apparent than real. What those who regard Proudhonism as even a debased form of Marxism overlook in this connection is the fact that the state according to Proudhon is not only by its very nature bound to maintain hierarchy, multiply laws, suppress liberties and deprive people of their property but is also uniquely favourably placed to do so. It is no mere instrument; it can dictate to society so long as society itself refrains from sweeping it out of existence. 'Liberty' and 'government' were to Proudhon quite simply zero-sum alternatives, posed starkly for men (ou point de liberté, ou point de gouvernement').[13] The state was necessary to the accumulation of capital by virtue of its character as

> an instrument designed to dispossess the majority for the benefit
> of a small minority, a legalized form of robbery, which
> systematically deprived the individual of his natural right to
> property by giving to the rich sole control of social legislation
> and financial credit, while the *petite bourgeoisie* was helplessly
> expropriated.[14]

Proudhon's outrage at the paradox that this entire process took place under the *aegis* of free, liberal institutions sanctified by the French Revolution perhaps accounts for his own taste for paradoxical formulations (property is theft, God is evil, citizenship denotes deprivation of rights) which pepper his writings and given them an arresting, provocative character. But be this as it may, the reader does not encounter in Proudhon's writings anything approaching Marx's perception, outlined in 'On the Jewish Question' and elsewhere, that capitalism, for all its negative features, nevertheless denotes progress; that 'political emancipation', for all its deceptiveness, is nevertheless a precursor – in a radically unsubstantiated form – of 'human emancipation'. As far as Proudhon was concerned, matters were very much more straightforward. The modern state, whatever its 'revolutionary' credentials, is the unambiguous enemy of justice and order alike; claims that it might be used to effect justice and order were simply insidious, and to be rejected on principle.

The question remains how, given the polar opposition that obtains between the two, 'liberty' is to be made to succeed 'government', how *le régime propriétaire* is to be undercut. Proudhon's answer is to stress the need for and nobility of voluntary individual effort by members of the proletariat who should set up and sustain their own, autonomous counter-institutions, instead of allowing themselves fatally to be misled by Jacobins, republicans and revolutionaries of various stripes (not to mention reformist state socialists like Louis Blanc). These authentic, spontaneously generated institutions, which were to include mutual aid funds and workers' credit societies, but not trade unions (since Proudhon regarded strikes as violent and barbarous), would work as it were against the grain of bourgeois society, in opposition to its *esprit général* of the accumulation of capital and political power, because work itself as a redemptive agency can bind together workers in an organic manner that is denied in principle and in practice to members of the bourgeoisie who cannot by the very nature of their class even aspire to such an organic unity. The bourgeoisie in this view, unlike the working class, can be no more than an agglomeration of disconnected singulars, each of whom works in his own, self-defined interest and relates to his 'fellows' only by competing with them. Despite the uniquely proletarian principle of social collectivity, Proudhon believed that only moral renewal at the level of the individual could provide the impetus, the wherewithal, for social renewal. The necessity – a moral necessity – for voluntary individual change, a kind of singular moral resurgence, underlies all Proudhon's central, practical proposals. His at times fanatical voluntarism and fierce egalitarianism stand behind his advocacy of free, mutual exchange as the animating principle of a self-sustaining, pluralist system having no need for the state or the capitalist, the functionary or the financier.

The individual self-moralization that this task presupposes and is to sustain must be of a type that would exclude all outside, doctrinaire, collectivist regimentation of the emergent labour movement; the movement must, according to Proudhon, carve out for itself its own morality, its own identity. It must use and rely upon its own resources and must contaminate itself as little as possible with any resources that have been used (or could be used) by its enemies. The resources thus declared out of bounds on principle include not only economic resources – trade unionism of the type that might lead to strikes, for example – but also all manner of *political* instrumentalities – those having to do with the state as well as the Stock Exchange, with government as well as the banks, with parliamentarism as well as proprietorship, and, not least, with revolution as well as most versions of reform. What is normally to be a politically abstentionist, and is always to be a separatist, workers' movement is to progress along, and cleave to, its own lines to the final goal – a goal to be understood not as an end but as a beginning – of justice, order, mutualism and federalism.

Proudhon was above all else a moralist, as Max Stirner in his bizarre but acute way had recognized; indeed, in his capacity as moralist – a moral man to his admirers, a moralistic man to his detractors – Proudhon would happily have admitted to being one of Stirner's 'taskmasters' outlining a 'vocation' to the individual, a vocation, moreover, of a distinctly non-revolutionary kind. Stirner, had he been better acquainted with it, would have found much to object to in Proudhon's concept of justice, a concept as central to his thought as it was many-sided. His discussions of justice, like his discussions of so much else, are often confusing as well as complicated, although some, at least, of the confusion these discussions engender can be cut through, if not entirely dissipated, if we remember that the root and foundation of justice according to Proudhon is a moral force inherent in the individual from which a 'natural' balance of forces in society can emerge, under the right conditions. These conditions are of two kinds. The first is that obstacles to the emergence of justice – particularly, of course, the state – be removed; the second concerns the manner of their removal, which is to be neither violent nor revolutionary. Instead, what is a moral necessity – that of making order in society legitimate – demands moral means. The moral force within the individual, if it has not already been rendered inoperative by the accumulation of capital or the pursuit of political power, is to issue in what might best be described as a personal and social stock-taking, in what Proudhon himself called a 'prise de conscience'[15] – Proudhon was no determinist – since this outcome is to result from each individual's sense of right and wrong, his good faith (*bonne foi*), provided of course that these qualities had not been eroded by capitalism, parasitism or politics. There is an important sense in which, his own later protestations to the contrary notwithstanding, Proudhon's notion of 'justice' is not really 'metaphysical' at all. It is immanent, not transcendent; it implies, in social terms, a modest, non-exploitative, frugal existence, an *aisance*, for everyone, on the basis of which would arise mutual self-respect and recognition of the dignity of the other. This more attractive side of Proudhon's thought – and in fairness it must be said that there are other sides – calls to mind the thought of writers (Camus, Orwell) who in other respects are quite unlike him. One of the reasons why Proudhon disliked the state, the church, the banks, capital and other 'extrinsic' agencies of control is that all of them deny and feed upon the self-respect and mutuality on which justice in society would have to be based.

Only when the spontaneous balance of authentic economic and

social forces had replaced property, hoarding, monopoly and parasitism ('l'accaparement propriétaire', as Proudhon, sounding like the *sans-culottes* of the French Revolution, sometimes called it) would the inherent order of society make political, economic, financial and religious institutions of this type redundant. The point is that these should come to seem unnecessary and outmoded, that they should appear even to those manning their various apparatuses to have been rendered superfluous, to have been overtaken by events; this means that Proudhon's programme, whatever other problems it may encounter, is certain to take some time. This prospect left Proudhon generally unperturbed; if the goal is distant and long-term, if the means to it are protracted and (again generally) unimpeachably gradualist, the advantage is – or so Proudhon fondly believed – firmly on the side of the workers. Work, after all, implied and contained within itself the unique, aboriginal and organic principle of individual as well as collective life, whereas the state, capital, the banks and the church expressed only the mechanical, the formal, the inessential and the unnecessary. The power of these institutions, Proudhon insisted, not always too hopefully, can be undercut and circumscribed, but not by institutional means; what is crucial is that those doing the undercutting should in no way be tempted to take their cue from their enemies. They should act as an example to others, and not let others act as an example to them.

The state, in particular, cannot be uprooted, even once its branches have withered, if it is challenged on its own, authoritarian grounds. Political power and that of capital, these two being cognate and increasingly inseparable, cannot be used to emancipate labour; any worthwhile 'organization of labour', declaimed Proudhon (thinking no doubt of Louis Blanc) should be autonomous and bring about the downfall of political power and capital from without ('Quiconque, pour organiser le travail, fait appel au capital et au pouvoir, a menti parce que l'organisation de travail doit être la déchéance du capital et du pouvoir').[16] Proudhon's opposition to politics was apparently all-embracing; all politics, of whatever persuasion, corrupt their practitioners. 'Give power to a St Vincent de Paul', he once protested, 'and he will become a Guizot or a Talleyrand.'[17] Such protestations – 'to indulge in politics is to wash one's hands in dung'[18] – speak to a marked obsessiveness about politics, which did not pass unnoticed by Proudhon's contemporaries. They also speak to a certain lack of consistency, since Proudhon, as we shall see, was in practice prepared to suspend (if not reject outright) his belief in political abstentionism, often with surprising results.

What he was never prepared to suspend, however, was his forthright anti-communism and fervent opposition to revolutionary doctrine. This steadfastness helps account for George Sand's characterization of

Proudhon as 'socialism's greatest enemy'.[19] Sand had in mind more than Proudhon's opposition to communism, however; her characterization, which, while it was unkind, was no more unkind that Proudhon's characterizations of those he considered his enemies, referred also to Proudhon's well-marked truculence, arrogance and (at times) sheer bloody-mindedness – qualities he was prepared to bring to bear on his rivals, who were according to his own accounts legion, in apparently any available fray. Proudhon's willingness to enter the lists against these rivals was tinged with a certain vanity – the obsessive vanity of the autodidact, his rivals were wont to term it, jealous to the point of spitefulness and pettiness of anyone who so much as appeared to chip away at Proudhon's own originality as a thinker and a public figure. Proudhon, indeed, as George Sand recognized, did not always cut an admirable figure. His contemporaries – those, that is, who were not inclined to worship at the shrine – were well aware of a dark side that Proudhon often openly displayed. His thought has a frankly reactionary, prejudicial aspect, and his unsavoury prejudices would have been difficult to ignore, thanks to his well-marked taste for controversy and talent as a controversialist.

There are several senses in which Proudhon might appear to have provided Marx with an easy target (although Marx, as we shall see, indulged in attacks that misfired and had frequent occasion to regret Proudhon's influence – which was considerable – throughout his career as a revolutionist). Putting to one side Proudhon's tendency to write more voluminously than coherently, a tendency that was not unlimited, we are faced in his writings with an untrammelled hostility to hierarchy, and an always marked, sometimes cloying nostalgia for a society of small peasant proprietors and artisans, of masters and journeymen and apprentices, a society whose paradigm was the face-to-face contract and the 'good faith' it required. Nostalgia – which is so often the understudy of utopianism – in Proudhon's case often takes centre stage. Proudhon's undoubted radical individualism – a 'social individualism',[20] as George Woodcock quite rightly calls it, quite unlike the egoistic individualism of Stirner – was certainly radical in the sense of being drastic (though there are limits even to this qualification); but it was also tempered by an equally marked emphasis on values that are normally considered the mainstay of conservatism, even reaction. His emphasis on order, family, labour (*ordre, famille, travail*) actually brings to mind the Vichy slogan; only *patrie* is absent (and even this, if it were to be interpreted with reference to language, nationalism and culture, and not with reference to the state, could readily enough be included). 'Respect to [Proudhon's] memory', apologizes Daniel Guérin, disingenuously, 'inhibits all but a passing reference to his "salute to war," his diatribes against women, or his fits of racism.' Guérin's inventory is less than exhaustive – more hostile commentators have been less restrained – but even he admits that the conclusion to Proudhon's *Justice in the Revolution and the Church* (1858) is 'far from libertarian'.[21] James Joll's timely admission that 'Proudhon is hard to fit into the tradition of "progressive" liberal political thought'[22] is understatement indeed. Marx himself, it transpires, was not quite right in saying, in *The German Ideology*, that Stirner 'takes as communism the ideas of a few liberals tending towards communism';[23] for Proudhon was anything but liberal. George Lichtheim concluded that

STAR-

Proudhon, with his tolerance for Louis Bonaparte, his Anglophobia and anti-Semitism, his defence of Negro slavery [Proudhon publicly sided with the South during the Civil War in the United States, on the grounds of opposition to 'centralization'], his contempt for national liberation movements, and his patriarchal notions about women and family life, does not make a suitable model for present-day liberations.[24]

Then

Proudhon, for these and other reasons (not the least of them being his own impatience), sometimes invites impatient responses. Lichtheim's inventory is impatient to the point of not even being exhaustive – he could have added Proudhon's beliefs that strikes were 'barbaric' and his opposition to national educational schemes on the grounds that education, like women, should be kept in the home. Lichtheim's slighting reference to Proudhon's attitude to movements of national independence is too glib; the reason why Proudhon opposed such movements in Italy, Poland and Hungary – apart from a tendency to judge foreign affairs quite uncritically, but equally guilelessly, from the point of view of France's national interest (Jaurès was to say in *L'Armée nouvelle* that Proudhon was so completely French that he wished to prevent the formation of new nations on France's frontiers) – is that he considered these movements to be led by centralizers like Mazzini, or aristocrats and financiers whose actions could scarcely be expected to benefit the peasant and the small proprietor.

As to Proudhon's other prejudices – apart, that is, from Marx's standard jibe that he was a 'petty bourgeois' which we shall have occasion to examine in its proper place – one point, in particular, does need to be made. Victor Considérant described Proudhon as 'that strange man who seemed determined that none should share his views';[25] his characterization is a telling one, but not because Proudhon's views and prejudices were not shared by others. Proudhon's attitudes on many questions, as Joll suggests, remained those of a 'puritanical' young man from the provinces let loose in Paris and shocked by the extravagance, luxury, decadence and corruption he found there. These, however, were the tip of the iceberg, as Proudhon himself was not slow to indicate; what existed beneath them were the false values of capitalists, state functionaries and financiers – all those who lived off the labour and property of others. In response to this corruption, Proudhon's writings are ridden with a certain backward looking regard and respect for the vanishing (and often imagined) virtues of a simpler society, although it is easy to make too much of his more reactionary side: the idea that this whole view of the world (a view which was, like most others, stamped to some extent by its origins) remained rural and agrarian is an exaggeration. And while Proudhon retained throughout his life some prejudices that were characteristic of his peasant forbears, we should allow that he expressed these sentiments most viciously in his private notebooks which were not published until after his death (as the *Carnets*). The really uncomfortable thought is that to the extent that they did surface or were implicit in his published writings, these prejudices (which fall somewhere between the *sans-culotte* and the Poujadist) may help account for Proudhon's popularity and influence.

The most significant of them for our purposes is, properly, not a prejudice but a characteristic – the very characteristic to which Considérant called attention. Proudhon's hostility to system was not restricted to his depictions of political authority and economic power but also permeated the very structure of his writings. While it is possible to discern themes that Proudhon developed throughout these writings – separatism, political abstentionism, *démopédie*, order, justice, mutualism, federalism, horror at all but verbal violence, and a distinctive anti-communism – no one would claim that these are developed according to any discernible intellectual system or method. Proudhon was never plagued by consistency. Denis Brogan observes, quite accurately, that 'Proudhon had always a weakness for analogy, not as illustration but as argument';[26] like Stirner, Proudhon also exhibited a weakness for *a priori* and syllogistic argumentation as well as for etymological or even philological plays upon words. He could write well, and even his critics tend to salute his taste for the arresting paradox, for ironies which he would insist were part of the world he was describing, not of the language he used to describe it. Yet he can be infuriating to read: he scorned intellectual system as a matter of principle and, rather than even trying to produce what could be considered a definitive, orderly statement of his main views on anything, 'presented the public with a running analysis of his mental processes [and] thought aloud in print, giving full rein to irony, invective, metaphor and every kind of passion, as his feelings dictated',[27] without hesitating to correct himself as he went along. One might even conclude that this very quality of intellectual free association characterizes not only every single book or polemic but even his writings as a whole. Each individual piece of writing tends to present an iconoclastic opening designed to jump out of the pages and catch the reader's attention – 'property is theft' (la propriété, c'est le vol') is an example – but this initial shock effect is then whittled down (Proudhon's writings are full of digressions, reservations, embroideries) until his peculiar idea of moderation and good sense comes to prevail at the end. As Marx's so-called 'obituary'[28] of Proudhon seems to imply, much the same could be said of Proudhon's works considered as a series; the iconoclasm, or eclecticism, of *What is Property?* (as well as its first paragraph) is not sustained throughout his subsequent writings, but gradually toned down and progressively abandoned.

What Proudhon meant by his much maligned formula that 'property is theft' is important to his economic theorizing, and demands some explanation. The obvious objection to it has been well put by Avineri: that property cannot be called theft unless a system of property exists prior to the occurrence of the thievery. Proudhon's aphorism thus 'either implies infinite regression or is a *petitio principi*. Proudhon seems to invalidate the legitimacy of property by an assumption of the legitimate existence of property'.[29] Indeed he does; his rejoinder would be that he was concerned to contrast in his formula one kind of private property with another, to polarize exploitative and non-exploitative types of property. Proudhon never really disapproves of personally acquired property that can be seen as a direct extension of the being of the property owner. Property to be legitimate should be an extension of the self of the owner that does not invalidate or make impossible similar efforts on the part of others. It should in other words be both cause and consequence of a rough equality among men, instead of being what it is, under what Proudhon called 'le régime propriétaire', an index and manifestation of inequality and exploitation. What needs to be remembered above all is that Proudhon's animus against property resolves itself in the last analysis into a hatred of unearned income, of 'revenus sans travail', of *loyer*, and *rentes* and *intérêts*, in all the multitudinous senses these terms could have in nineteenth-century France. It was 'le droit d'aubaine', the 'right', that is to say, which is given by property to the proprietor to levy tolls on others, that according to Proudhon made possible the 'theft' ('le droit de vol') he so loathed. Proudhon's understanding of 'le droit d'aubaine', which after the French Revolution had not passed away from the face of the earth – this statement is to be taken literally as well as metaphorically – was accordingly an expansive one; recourse to an historical Larousse is necessary as a guide through his definition of it ('le droit en vertu duquel le seigneur "prend, suivant sa circonstance, et l'objet, tour à tour les noms de rentes, fermage, loyer, intérêt de l'argent, bénéfice, aïgo, escompte, commission, privilège, monopole, prime, cumul, sinécure, pot-au-vin" ').[30] The important point is that all these are ways

of depriving people of their (legitimate) property and that their scope
and scale had increased, not diminished, in the nineteenth century not
so much despite the French Revolution as because of its sanctification
of the right to (illegitimate) property.[31] Proudhon, with his acute
sense of 'the Revolution betrayed' (but still, like justice, implicit)
regarded the post-Revolutionary *régime propriétaire* as being founded
on a *carte blanche* for expropriation and dispossession.

That these terms, expropriation, theft and the like are moral as well
as economic in their bearing gives us the essential clue to the nature of
Proudhon's economic theorizing. From a strictly economic point of
view, his theorizing lays itself open to the kind of harsh treatment
Proudhon received from Marx; yet Proudhon's own point of view was
never strictly economic, and always largely moral. We might say that
he let his well-marked sense of moral outrage run away with him, in
the realm of 'political economy' as elsewhere. When he writes about
exploitation, about contract, about value, he guilelessly makes use
of the double signification of these terms (and terms like them), and
fails clearly to distinguish economic value, for instance, from moral
worth. This might be a result of sheer *naïveté*, and it might also be a
matter of a none too carefully calculated, but none the less extremely
powerful, rhetorical effect. For however badly judged it may be as
economic theory, it was never intended to convince economists, whose
writings Proudhon regarded as exercises in obfuscation and deliberate
over-complication. It was aimed, fairly and squarely, at those who for
good reasons of their own would be inclined to believe, with Proudhon,
that only direct, personal labour is productive and that, consequently,
capital and finance (which lead only to centralization, monopolization,
expropriation – in short, to *l'accaparement propriétaire*) cannot be so.

Proudhon's theory of value is almost incredibly simple, in a disarming
way. The source of value, according to Ricardo (whose *Principles of
Political Economy and Taxation* had been translated into French in
1835) is labour; and the measure of labour, *ceteris paribus*, is time.
This means to Proudhon that what he calls the 'constituted value'
('la valeur constituée') of any product is quite simply an expression
of the amount of labour time embodied in it. Now if goods were to be
exchanged only according to the *valeur constituée* of each, they would
exchange justly; the distortion introduced in capitalist society by
supply and demand would simply evaporate, and labour would be the
measure of value once and for all. This in turn would mean that once a
price has been fixed for all products, according to the invariant standard
of value Proudhon thinks he has provided, the veils of mystification
and 'contradiction' which needlessly complicate the capitalist system
would fall away. Goods would then exchange straightforwardly according to the principle that their direct producers be rewarded in
proportion to the labour they had expended in their production; and

this in turn would mean that the principle of exchange would be an uncomplicated, self-evident equity and reciprocity. According to this standard, producers would be able to enter into free, non-exploitative contracts with one another and to exclude non-workers. Unearned income, together with the exploitation of wage-earners it implies, would at last lack its medium of existence. Producers would be able to obtain credit without paying interest, provided that workers' credit banks providing interest-free loans (*crédit gratuit*) were set up; these would finally free the producers from the tyranny of the banks, of the financial superstructure, and of interest payment (which was indeed a real problem in an industrializing society with large numbers of landless peasants and small proprietors, as Proudhon was acutely aware).

Proudhon, who attached great importance to the organization of credit, put forward as his major institutional initiative the foundation of agencies charged with the provision of *crédit gratuit*. Although the schemes he inspired or actually instigated misfired, Proudhon's belief in their necessity remained unimpaired, since they were to be the mainstay of justice in society. Once men were freed from authoritarian economic relationships, from the crushing burden of debt that was their outcome, they would no longer pursue purely selfish ends; instead, what Proudhon called the 'collective reason' would produce and undergird justice throughout society. Credit was Proudhon's panacea, but to write it off as such, instead of accounting for it, would be to overlook what was in certain respects its most important feature: the limits Proudhon places on what it can do. He believed that the moral regeneration of society and the individuals who make up society would not be effected but merely facilitated by the provision of *crédit gratuit*. Credit made available freely would make possible the reform of society from the bottom up, nothing more; it would remove material, financial obstacles to the recasting of human relationships, *de bas en haut*, but it would not in itself effect such a reconstitution. Everything depends on individual moral renewal, in the absence of which any of Proudhon's more institutional devices or mechanisms – contract as well as credit – would be of little avail.

With respect to contract, Marx, as we shall see, was to pounce with some glee on Proudhon's notion that free and equal exchange, of a synallagmatic and commutative kind, could become the economic and moral basis of a new and better society, and we shall examine his criticisms in due course. What concerns us more immediately is the contractual basis of Proudhonian mutualism. Proudhon's in some respects curious contractualism might be taken as an ironical footnote to the long and distinguished history of 'social contract' theories of the state, since according to Proudhon's version the outcome of the free imposition of mutual, equally and reciprocally binding obligations and engagements was to be not the state but its disappearance.

Proudhon believed that if contract, of a simple and direct kind, between two parties, were made the paradigm of human relationships in general, this move would be both cause and effect of the removal of illegitimate political, as well as property, relationships. Free mutual exchange - of goods that are free and equal in value, by people who are free and equal in value, would secure a balance of interests in society so long as neither state nor monopoly interfered. It has been pointed out that many passages in Proudhon's writings are hymns to contract excluding government, that 'not even Sir Henry Maine had a more lyrical conception of contract than had Proudhon';[32] he believed that contract by its very nature excluded government, just as government by *its* very nature - a factitious and implicitly feudal nature - was the denial of order in society. To Proudhon, whose 'whole programme was contained in the search for the union of anarchy and order',[33] justice and mutualism in society could be made manifest only by contractual means, only by means that would undercut and render superfluous the state, and would provide a genuinely moral as well as socially generative principle that would owe nothing to the state.

First encounters

Marx, who lived in Paris from October 1843 until December 1845, first met Proudhon, who returned there from Lyons only in September 1844, while he was working on *The Holy Family*. Of their first meetings, little is known; Proudhon referred, subsequently and in passing, to having met during this period 'a great many Germans who had admired my work and my accomplishments, my having reached on my own conclusions which they claimed as theirs',[34] and among these visitors, presumably, was Marx. For his part, Marx, while he was more explicit, had a radically different evaluation of the meetings. 'In the course of long discussions which sometimes went on all through the night', he later disclosed, 'I infected [Proudhon], to his great detriment, with a Hegelianism he could not go deeply into because he did not know German. . . What I had begun Herr Karl Grün continued after my expulsion from France.' The tutelary tone of Marx's recollection - 'I mention this here because to a certain extent I am . . . to blame for his "*sophistication*," as the English call the adulteration of commercial goods'[35] - which was explicitly intended to damage Proudhon's posthumous reputation (and which, like Marx's other attempts, signally failed to do so) is deliberately deceptive. By 1844 Proudhon was already a celebrated socialist theoretician with four well-known books to his name; Marx, like many other German theoreticians on the left of his generation, had freely admitted admiring him. Marx's later recall of their meetings was, like Proudhon's, less than total, and it seems likely that the impression it was meant to convey of Marx's magnanimous provision of subsequently misunderstood insights, *de haut en bas*, was the opposite of what really took place. Not even his admirers considered Proudhon a good listener.

It is probable that after their initial meetings Marx and Proudhon saw very little of each other in Paris. (They never met after Marx's expulsion and seem to have corresponded only once.) Proudhon, despite his notoriety, refused to contribute to the ill-fated publishing venture, the *Deutsch-französische Jahrbücher*, that had brought Marx to Paris, even though he was almost alone among his compatriots on the Left in being unable to refuse to participate on religious grounds. The only non-German (as opposed to expatriate German) to contribute to the first issue of the journal was, ironically enough, Bakunin. We also know that the Paris police file used to expel Marx from France in 1845 does not mention Proudhon,[36] although it is probable that any sustained contact between the two would have been duly noted in it.

Yet the first really significant discussions of Proudhon's ideas in Marx's writings, which may be found in *The Holy Family* and the *Economic and Philosophic Manuscripts*, date from this period, although Proudhon's ideas are mentioned elsewhere and earlier. All these need careful appraisal in the light of the most common interpretation of Marx's relationship with Proudhon, which would have it that Marx's initially favourable (or even 'enthusiastic') responses gave way dramatically to a vicious attack in *The Poverty of Philosophy* (1847) that was occasioned by, or was the direct outgrowth of, a personal altercation between the two that had taken place in 1846. The truth is not quite so simple. As Franz Mehring was later to indicate, to

> object that Marx glorified Proudhon in *The Holy Family*, only
> to attack him fiercely a few years later is a facile academic trick.
> In *The Holy Family*, Marx is defending Proudhon's real achieve-
> ments from being obscured and mystified by the empty phrases
> of Edgar Bauer. . . Just as Marx attacked Bauer's theological
> limitations, he also attacked Proudhon's economic limitations,[37]

before *The Poverty of Philosophy* was so much as conceived. Mehring's claim, its polemical tone notwithstanding, is largely accurate. If we examine what Marx said about Proudhon before 1846 – bearing in mind that not all this material was available to Mehring – we find that Marx's comments on Proudhon, far from being fulsome, do not praise him unreservedly or unstintingly at all. They are at least implicitly critical, though in no way hostile; they are sometimes commendatory, always conciliatory. What burned the bridges was not so much the exchange of letters in 1846, which in and of itself might have been quite inconclusive, but Proudhon's book, his *System of Economic Contradictions, or Philosophy of Poverty* (1846) which followed in short order. The hostility of Marx's response, *The Poverty of Philosophy* (1847), which had as a kind of prolegomenon a long letter to Annenkov in 1846,[38] was provoked by the economic, philosophical and political ideas that had been expressed, many of them for the first time, in Proudhon's book; but while this hostility outlived the occasion of its first expression, Marx's subsequent comments, at times, guardedly (or grudgingly) praise Proudhon's earliest writings.

What this means is that if we take into account Marx's comments on Proudhon that were made after *The Poverty of Philosophy*, as well as those made in it and before it, we can see that there is much more continuity among Marx's successive criticisms of Proudhon and Proudhonism than has often been admitted. The criticisms Marx levels so unrelentingly in *The Poverty of Philosophy* lack neither precedent nor subsequent amplification. Marx's discussions of Proudhon's ideas, while they are not as extended, and for that matter not always as venomous as those advanced in *The Poverty of Philosophy*, span almost the entirety of his career. Proudhon is discussed and criticized in the *Economic and Philosophic Manuscripts*, and *The Holy Family*, defended against misrepresentations but attacked on other grounds in *The Holy Family* and *The German Ideology*, and given short shrift as one of many utopians with reactionary leanings in *The Manifesto of the Communist Party* (work on which Marx interrupted in order to write *The Poverty of Philosophy*). All these, together with the celebrated flailing of Proudhon in *The Poverty of Philosophy* itself, are just the beginning. Marx wrote an article about Proudhon in the *Neue Rheinische Zeitung* in 1849, and in *The Class Struggles in France* (1850) he criticized, in passing, Proudhon's scheme for a 'people's bank'. In 1851 Marx sought a publisher for a pamphlet he planned to write attacking Proudhon's book, *The General Idea of the Revolution*, which was first published in that year (although Marx's pamphlet, if indeed it was ever written, seems not to have surfaced).[39] In *The Eighteenth Brumaire of Louis Bonaparte* (1851–2) Marx's criticism of 'doctrinaire experiments, exchange banks and workers' associations' which 'necessarily [suffer] shipwreck',[40] was a hit at Proudhonian schemes; and Marx's 'Preface' to the second edition of this work, which was written in 1869, after information and rumour about Proudhon's role in Louis Napoleon's *coup d'état* had long been circulating, indicates that Proudhon's book, *The Social Revolution as Demonstrated by the Coup d'État of the Second of December* (1852) is 'worthy of notice' although his 'historical reconstruction of the coup inevitably turns into an historical apology for its hero'[41] (as – 'inevitably' or not – indeed it does). As to Proudhon's economic ideas, these are discussed in a series of letters in the 1860s (in particular, those to von Schweitzer in 1865, Engels in 1866 and Kugelmann in 1866),[42] but most notably, and at greatest length, in the *Grundrisse* (1857-8). Marx criticizes Proudhon in passing in *A Contribution to the Critique of Political Economy* (1859); and many of the points he makes in all these works are repeated, and sometimes expanded, in *Theories of Surplus Value*, vols i and iii (1861-3), and *Capital*, vol. i (1867) and iii (published posthumously in 1894).

The length of this list is a tribute to the resilience of Proudhonism and to the strength of the example set by its founder. Marx's hope that he could put paid to Proudhon's influence once and for all by writing a book attacking him proved to be unfounded indeed; Marx was to have frequent cause to regret Proudhon's considerable influence. The arch tone Marx adopted in his successive dressings-down of Proudhon – it was always Marx's intention to portray Proudhon as a talkative little boy all entangled in Platonic metaphysics and anti-working-class sentiments – was forced and deliberate. In reading these attacks we should remember that intellectual superiority is one thing, actual political influence something else again; and that, at the immediate level, Proudhon enjoyed by 1840, and continued to enjoy until his death in 1864, the kind of notoriety that was to attach itself to Marx as a result not so much of the publication of the first volume of *Capital* in 1867 as of the Paris Commune in 1871. Although Marx, who became at this point 'the Red Terrorist Doctor' and (in his own words) 'the most calumniated man in London',[43] was commonly supposed to have masterminded the Commune by pulling the strings of the International, in reality the Commune owed precious little to Marxism and a great deal more, ironically enough, to the Proudhonists, who had already proved themselves thorns in Marx's side during the first four years of the International's existence, as we shall see. Ultimately, even though Proudhonism *per se* (in the form of programmatic mutualism) did not long survive the savage suppression of the Commune, the influence of Proudhon's ideas survived for a long time afterwards, particularly during the hey-day of anarcho-syndicalism in France, many of whose main features – that is, its code of practical morality based on work, its fierce *ouvriérisme* and fervent belief in 'le séparatisme ouvrier' ('pas des mains blanches, seulement les mains calleuses'), its desire to redefine property as 'copropriété en main commune' (though not its belief in the regenerative power of violence as expressed in its espousal of the revolutionary general strike) – bear the unmistakable imprint of Proudhon. Indeed, it is not fanciful to see residual elements of Proudhonism even today, in the strength in France of the Parti socialiste's emphasis on workers' control as *autogestion*.

In his 1842 article on 'Communism and the *Ausburger Allgemeine Zeitung*'[44] Marx singles out Proudhon's work as being 'penetrating' (*scharfsinnig*) and the following year, in a letter to Arnold Ruge that was to be published in the *Deutsch-französische Jahrbücher*, Marx made the following observation:

> I am not in favour of raising any dogmatic banner. On the contrary we must try to help the dogmatists to clarify their propositions to themselves. Thus *communism*, in particular, is a dogmatic abstraction; in which connection, however, I am not thinking of some imaginary and possible communism, but actually existing communism as taught by Cabet, Dezamy, Weitling, etc. This communism is itself only a special expression of the humanistic principle, an expression which is still infected by it antithesis – the private [property] system. Hence the abolition of private property and communism are by no means identical, and it is not accidental but inevitable that communism has seen other socialist doctrines – such as those of Fourier, Proudhon, etc. – arising to confront it because it is itself only a special, one-sided realization of the socialist principle.[45]

This passage raises issues that are to be expanded upon in later writings – the *Economic and Philosophic Manuscripts, The Holy Family, The German Ideology* and *The Poverty of Philosophy*. Not only is Proudhon's anti-communism admitted and recognized; his 'socialism' is interpreted as being in some sense a predictable and appropriate response or counterweight to the one-sidedness of the kind of communism advocated by Weitling and others; and this communism itself is in its turn seen as imperfect and unsubstantiated. The relationship between crude communism's centrepiece, the abolition of private property, and communism properly so-called, communism in its fuller and more expansive form, is not one of identity – a point Marx was later to flesh out in the *Manuscripts* and *The Poverty of Philosophy* by indicating that what crude communism (and, later, Proudhonism itself) lacks, is any sense of the creation of new needs as a principle of historical change. Marx was at this time (1844), however, fond of comparing Proudhon and Weitling and of doing so not always, or not unambiguously, in the latter's favour. (In 'The King of Prussia and Social Reform' Marx makes reference to 'Weitling's excellent writings' which 'frequently surpass Proudhon in regard to theory, though they are inferior in execution'.)[46] Marx's admiration for Weitling – which was to continue, though not for long – should not surprise us; he was to break with Weitling most reluctantly, even though Weitling recruited among skilled artisans rather than proletarians and refused even to recognize the role of an organized working-class movement. But he was a revolutionary communist; Proudhon was neither a revolutionary nor a communist, but enjoyed considerable influence in France. It may be for this reason that Marx's comments on his writings were as conciliatory as they were; but on the other hand Marx did attempt, even in 1844, to strike some sort of balance of praise and blame.

This balance is most noticeably struck in the *Economic and Philosophic Manuscripts*, a work some of whose passages about Proudhon Marx was to copy, more or less verbatim, into *The Holy Family* in 1845. In the *Manuscripts* Marx identifies Proudhon with 'advocates of piecemeal reform' not only because of his desire 'to raise wages and thereby improve the condition of the working class' but also, more specifically, because Proudhon regarded 'equality of wages as the aim of the social revolution'.[47] Equality as a political goal is, according to Marx, what distinguished Proudhon, and by extension French socialism in general, from other thinkers and theories, and, Marx goes on, 'Proudhon should be appreciated and criticized from this point of view'.[48] On the one hand, Proudhon sees the need to abolish capital 'as such' and has come down on the right side of a fundamental divide: 'political economy begins with labour as the real soul of production and then goes on to attribute nothing to labour and everything to private property. Proudhon, faced by this contradiction, has decided in favour of labour against private property'.[49] All to the good; but what Proudhon fails to see are the dimensions of this 'contradiction'. He does not appreciate that wages 'are only a necessary consequence of the alienation of labour'. Hence, what Proudhon advocates,

> an enforced increase in wages (disregarding the other difficulties, and especially that such an anomaly could only be maintained by force) would be nothing more than a better remuneration of slaves and would not restore, either to the worker or to the work, their human significance or worth.
>
> Even the equality of wages which Proudhon demands would only change the relation of the present-day worker to his work into a relation of all men to work. Society would then be conceived as an abstract capitalist.[50]

We shall find that this criticism of Proudhon, in particular, is wholly cognate with those that were to be advanced in *The Holy Family* and *The Poverty of Philosophy* alike, and that what Marx finds praiseworthy in Proudhon in *The Holy Family* (and *The German Ideology*) he nevertheless tempered with some real criticisms. Yet Marx never, before *The Poverty of Philosophy*, dismisses Proudhon out of hand, and the reasons for his restraint ought, briefly, to detain us. To begin with, Marx always defended Proudhon against his German critics – against Karl Grün and Stirner in *The German Ideology* as well as against Edgar Bauer in *The Holy Family*. Marx, in a letter to Feuerbach prior to *The Holy Family*, contrasts Bauer's 'sad and supercilious intellectualism' with Proudhon's doctrine, commenting that Bauer's approach one-sidedly fails to appreciate the 'practical needs' that are the point of departure for Proudhon's arguments, and which credit and fortify them. As to the arguments themselves, Marx found 'great scientific advance' in Proudhon's view that

> political economy moves in a continuous contradiction to its basic premise, private property, a contradiction analogous to that of the theologian who constantly gives a human interpretation to religious ideas and thereby contradicts his fundamental assumption, the superhuman character of religion.

Marx goes on to credit Proudhon, whose *First Memoir* (*What is Property?*) he describes in exaggerated terms as a 'scientific' manifesto of the French proletariat written by one who was himself a proletarian, with having made the important discovery that contemporary relations of production had nothing human about them as they actually operated. Marx praises Proudhon further for having advocated action and not reform as a remedy for this state of affairs.[51]

Such a summary should give us pause since, as Haubtmann points out, it scarcely does justice to the arguments of the *First Memoir*. To begin with, the action it advocates is not revolutionary action. *What is Property?* also propounds such notions as the material force of ideas and invokes 'Justice' as a kind of demiurge – less forcefully, it is true, than some of Proudhon's later writings – in the corresponding belief that sheer knowledge of moral laws could stimulate, invigorate and cause social progress of a distinctly non-revolutionary kind. Putting to one side the actual merit, or otherwise, of these notions, it is quite safe to say that they could hardly have commended themselves to Marx; yet *The Holy Family* largely ignores them. Marx – uncharacteristically, as it came to seem – held his fire and reserved his wrath for other targets, and did so, we must presume, because of what he considered to be the fundamental importance of Proudhon's achievement. In the light of this, Marx considered *What is Property?* to have marked a real step forward in social analysis, an evaluation to which he was subsequently to adhere, as we shall see.

What is crucial, according to Marx in 1845, to Proudhon's argument is its comprehensiveness; what makes Proudhon's work valuable is Proudhon's readiness to make connections and draw links. He

> takes the human semblance in economic relations seriously and sharply opposes it to their inhuman reality [*wirkliche Unmenschlichkeit*] . . . He is therefore consistent in representing as the falsifier of economic relations not this or that kind of private property . . . but private property taken in its entirety [*auf universelle Weise*].[52]

Proudhon's generalization of private property, as private property *relations* pervading society, is what commended his book to Marx; it had the effect of highlighting the political economists' uneasy vacillations between the human bearing and origin of their subject-matter and the deterministic, non-human objective laws which they used to describe and characterize its actual operation – a contradiction which Marx's own writings on economics were also to be concerned to investigate. Marx's conclusions, however, were to be very different; just how different we shall see presently. For the time being, it is important to recognize that Marx was in his early estimations – and even to a lesser extent in his later appraisals – of Proudhon not loath to give credit where credit was due. Proudhon, indeed, according to Marx, had not simply drawn connections between private property relations and wage-labour but had also characterized these connections as (in some sense) dialectical ones. Marx and Proudhon, again, were to differ on the nature and meaning of dialectical connections; but Marx in 1845 had no quarrel with Proudhon's consideration of private property relations and the growth of the proletariat as opposite sides of the same coin.

> Political economy proceeded from the wealth that the movement
> of private property was supposed to create . . . to considerations
> which were an apology for private property, whereas Proudhon
> proceeds from the opposite side which political economy
> sophistically conceals, from the property bred by the movement
> of private property, to his considerations, which are a negation
> of private property.[53]

This, the directionality of Proudhon's analysis (which was, of course, similar to that of Marx), together with the links Proudhon had perceived between private property, the system of social relations built on its foundation, and the growth of the proletariat as a loose antithesis to these relations, sufficed for Marx, who ignored what he would later regard as serious deficiencies in Proudhon's actual definitions of these social forces. On balance, the book's virtues seemed to Marx to outweigh its defects and he was happy to commend it on this basis; indeed, twenty years later we find Marx doing the same thing in a letter about Proudhon to J.B. von Schweitzer, the publication of which he had good reason to anticipate and sanction. Proudhon's

> first work, *What is Property?* is undoubtedly his best. It is
> epoch-making, if not from the novelty of its content, at
> least by the new and audacious way of coming out with
> everything. Of course 'property' had been not only
> criticized in various ways but also '*done away with*' in

the utopian manner by the French socialists and communists
whose work he knew. In this book Proudhon's relation to
Saint-Simon and Fourier is about the same as that of Feuerbach
to Hegel. Compared with Hegel Feuerbach is extremely poor.
All the same he was epoch-making *after* Hegel because he laid
stress on certain points which were disagreeable to the Christian
consciousness but important to the progress of criticism, and
which Hegel had left in mystic semi-obscurity.

Proudhon's still strong muscular style, if I may be allowed the
expression, prevails in this book. And its style in my opinion is
its chief merit.

Even where he is still reproducing old stuff, one can see that
Proudhon has found it out for himself, that what he is saying
is new to him and ranks as new. The provocative defiance laying
hands of the economic 'holy of holies,' the brilliant paradox
which made a mock of the ordinary bourgeois mind, the
withering criticism, the brilliant irony, and, revealed here and
there behind these, a deep and genuine feeling of indignation at
the infamy of the existing order – all these electrified readers
of *What is Property?* and produced a great sensation on its first
appearance. In a strictly scientific history of political economy
the book would be hardly worth mentioning. But sensational
works of this kind play their part in the sciences. . .

But in spite of all his apparent iconoclasm one already finds
in *What is Property?* the contradiction that Proudhon is
criticizing society, on the one hand, from the standpoint and
with the eyes of a French small peasant (later petty bourgeois)
and, on the other, with the standards derived from his inheritance
from the socialists . . .[54]

Marx's praise of Proudhon in this letter subsequently turns to scorn;
and even when it was originally advanced in *The Holy Family* it was
praise of a distinctly guarded variety. Proudhon, Marx makes clear,
fails to infer the right kind of conclusion from the connection he
quite rightly perceives between proletariat and property. Putting to
one side the question of how incompletely Proudhon defined the
proletariat (a question Marx dealt with much more fully and adequately
in *The Poverty of Philosophy*), it is clear that in *The Holy Family*
Marx recognized that Proudhon's admittedly expansive definition of
property was nevertheless defective. Proudhon, says Marx, sees property
not as the realization of the forces of one's own being ('meine eigenen
Wesenkräfte zu betätigen und zu verwirklichen') but as something
excluding the claims of others ('den Andern auszuschliessen').[55] Whether
or not this latter is a particularly French conception of property, as
seems likely, Marx recognized that what Proudhon, in particular,

built upon it, his solution to the problem of property, which amounts to untrammelled equality of opportunity to hold property in small, more or less equal and non-exploitative amounts, is a solution that remains firmly locked within an alien framework.

> Proudhon's desire to abolish non-owning and the old form of owning is exactly identical to his desire to abolish the practically-alienated relation of man to his objective essence, to abolish the political-economic expression of human self-alienation. Since, however, his criticism of political economy is still bound to the premises of political economy, the reappropriation of the objective world is still conceived in the political-economic form of possession. Proudhon indeed does not oppose owning to non-owning, as Critical Criticism [here, Edgar Bauer] makes him do, but [instead opposes] possession to the old form of owning private property. He declares possession to be a 'social function'. . . . Proudhon did not succeed [however] in giving this thought appropriate development. The idea of equal possession is a political-economic one and therefore is itself still an alienated [entfremdete] expression for the principle that the object as being for man, as the objectified being of man, is at the same time the existence of man for other men, his human relation to other men, the social relation of man to man. Proudhon abolishes political-economic estrangement within political-economic estrangement [hebt die national-ökonomische Entfremdung innerhalb der national-ökonomischen Entfremdung auf] .[56]

This somewhat abstruse passage requires some elucidation if we are to see how important it is. Marx's 'First Critical Comment' on Proudhon in *The Holy Family* describes *What is Property?* as 'a criticism of political economy from the standpoint of political economy' on the grounds that 'the first criticism of any science is necessarily implicated in the premises of the science it is criticizing'. It is in this sense that *What is Property?* 'is as important for modern political economy as Sieyès' *What is the Third Estate?* is for modern politics'. Each blazes a trail, opens up further possibilities for investigation by emblazoning a new concept; neither is in principle unsurpassable or likely to remain unsurpassed. Indeed 'Proudhon's work will be scientifically surpassed by criticism [on the part] of political economy, even of political economy as conceived by Proudhon. This task only becomes possible through Proudhon himself. . .'.[57] Marx proceeds to indicate that whereas 'all developments in political economy presuppose private property' which 'basic proposition is regarded as an unassailable fact needing no further examination', Proudhon subjects the basis of political economy, *private property*, to a critical examination, in fact the first resolute, ruthless and at the same time scientific examination. This is the great scientific advance he made, an advance revolutionizing political economy and making possible for the first time a real science of political economy.[58]

However, Marx continues, 'Proudhon does not grasp the wider forms of private property - for example, wages, trade, value, price, money etc. - as themselves forms of private property'. Instead he 'uses these economic premises against political economists'; and while 'this is entirely in keeping with his historically justified standpoint'[59] of acting as a catalyst making possible future change, it is not an approach that in and of itself is likely to supply answers to the problems posed by the ubiquity of private property relations. Because the inhumane realities of the capitalist system belie the innocent and humane protestations of the political economists, these are forced to take refuge in various face saving expedients

> they . . . tackle private property in some partial form as the falsifier of wages which are rational in themselves, namely in the conception they have formed of wages, or as the falsifier of value which is rational in itself, or as the falsifier of trade, rational in itself. Thus Adam Smith occasionally attacks the capitalists, Destutt de Tracy the bankers, Simonde de Sismondi the factory system, Ricardo landed property, and almost all modern economists attack the non-industrial capitalists who regard property as merely a consumer.[60]

Proudhon alone will have none of this. As a way of pointing up the contradiction between the humane presuppositions of the political economists (the 'free' labour contract, the determination of value by costs of production alongside the social utility of the object produced) and the inhumane outcome of their application, Proudhon takes the humane presupposition at its face value.

> He took seriously the humane appearance of economic conditions and sharply confronted it with their inhumane reality. He demanded that these conditions should be in actuality what they are in conception, or rather that their conception should be abandoned and their actual inhumanity be established.[61]

Proudhon's approach, while it does highlight contradictions, nevertheless is one that runs risks. His thought, which in one sense (as Marx admits) an advance on classical political economy, in another sense actually falls behind it. In his discussions of contract – contract, as we have seen, being a mainstay of his thought – he takes the notion more seriously than had the political economists themselves. 'Proudhon does not misuse this relation in the sense of political economy,' Marx charges; 'indeed, he takes as real what political economists admit is illusory and nominal – the freedom of the contracting parties.'[62] While such freedom had in fact long been supplanted by compulsion, a fact which is highlighted by Proudhon's argument, Proudhon's solution, as disarming as it is drastic, is simply that of its restitution, so that the freedom of the contracting parties, which had been revealed as a myth, would fulfil its promise by being made real. Plekhanov followed in Marx's footsteps when he indicated that 'politically, [Proudhon's] programme is only the application to public relations of a concept (the "contract") drawn from the domain of the private right of a society of producers of commodities';[63] what has often been overlooked, however, is that the footsteps in which Plekhanov was to tread trace out a path through *The Holy Family* as well as *The Poverty of Philosophy*.

Contract, despite its centrality in Proudhon's thought, is not, however, the whole story. Proudhon also took the political economists at their word – more seriously than they took themselves in a certain sense – in other respects. On the one hand by deriving the value of a product and the measure of wages from labour-time, Proudhon according to Marx 'makes the human side the decisive factor' instead of 'the ponderable power of capital and landed property' and in so doing reinstates man in his rights; but, on the other hand, he does so in a contradictory (*widerspruchsvolle*) manner. While all the essential definitions (*Wesenbestimmungen*) of human activity are recognized throughout Proudhon's formulations, they are nevertheless encountered there only in an alien form.[64] One of the reasons why this, according to Marx, is so is that Proudhon, in counterposing 'the human side' to 'the ponderable power of capital and landed property', is insufficiently drastic. He thinks that developments *within* capitalism have a tendency to mitigate its worst excesses, and thinks so on the scantiest of evidence; he has a tendency, in other words, to grasp at straws, to adopt panaceas that he thinks will bring about changes, without tracing these back to their root causes. Changes in interest rates are a case in point:

> The diminution in the interest of money, which Proudhon regards as the annulling of capital and as the tendency to socialize capital, is really and immediately . . . only a symptom of the victory of working capital over extravagant wealth – i.e. the transformation of all private property into industrial capital. It is a total victory of private property over all those of its qualities which are still

in appearance human, and the complete subjection of the owner of private property to the essence of private property – labour. . . . The decrease in the interest-rate is therefore a symptom of the annulment of capital only inasmuch as it is a symptom of the rule of capital in the process of perfecting itself – of the estrangement in the process of becoming fully-developed and therefore of hastening to its annulment. This is indeed the only way in which that which exists affirms its opposite.

The dispute between economists over luxury and saving is, therefore, only a dispute between that political economy which has become clearly aware of the nature of wealth and that political economy which is still burdened with romantic, anti-industrial memories.[65]

Marx's point, in the words of another passage from the *Economic and Philosophic Manuscripts* – that 'everything which Proudhon interprets as the growing power of labour as against capital is simply the growing power of labour in the form of capital, industrial capital, as against capital which is not consumed as capital, industrially'[66] – presages later attacks on Proudhon in the *Grundrisse* and *Theories of Surplus Value*, where Proudhon (whose attacks had now broadened into an advocacy of manipulation of interest rates, people's banks and credit associations) is again accused of mistaking the effect for the cause.

. . . the demand raised by M. Proudhon, that capital should not be loaned out and should bear no interest, but should be sold like a commodity for its equivalent amounts at bottom to no more than the demand that exchange-value should never become capital, but always remain simple exchange value; that *capital* [in other words] should *not exist as capital.* This demand, combined with the other, that wage labour should remain the general basis of production, reveals a happy confusion with regard to the simplest economic concepts. . . His chatter about considerations of fairness and right amounts only to this, that he wants to use the relation of property or of law corresponding to simple exchange as the measuring rod for the relation of property and law at a higher stage of exchange-value . . .[67]

Marx's tone had changed by 1859, but the tenor of Marx's accusations remained remarkably similar to that we encounter in 1844. The same is true of Marx's critical comments on Proudhon in *Theories of Surplus Value* (1861–3): 'wanting to preserve wage-labour, and thus the basis of capital, as Proudhon does, and at the same time to eliminate the "drawbacks" by abolishing a secondary form of capital, reveals the novice'.[68] What Marx is urging against Proudhon, in the 1860s and the 1840s alike, is that total problems demand total solutions, at the level of causes, not simply at the level of selected secondary epiphenomena; yet

> superficial criticism [Marx means Proudhonism] – in the same
> way as it wants to maintain commodities and combats money –
> now turns its wisdom and reforming zeal against interest-
> bearing capital without touching upon real capitalist
> production, but merely attacking one of its consequences.
> This polemic against interest-bearing capital, undertaken
> from the standpoint of capitalist production . . . today
> parades as 'socialism' . . .[69]

What emerges from these comments on Proudhon made on either side of the altercation that reached its apogee in *The Poverty of Philosophy* is that Marx's criticisms have a consistency and continuity that too rarely have been acknowledged as such. As Marx put it in *The Holy Family*, Proudhon's 'criticism of political economy is still captive to the premises of political economy' so that he 'abolishes economic estrangement within economic estrangement'. By the time of *The German Ideology*, Proudhon, 'from whom the communists have accepted nothing but his criticism of property', is defended by Marx against 'true socialist' misrepresentations of his thought, but is nevertheless criticized on different, but by now familiar grounds: he 'opposes the illusions cherished by jurists and economists to their practice' yet 'criticizes political economy from the standpoint of political economy and law from the legal standpoint'[70] (a reference, *inter alia*, to his notion of contract). Proudhon, according to Marx, considers private property expansively, as a system of private property relations pervading an emergent capitalist society, but he does not derive from this potentially far-reaching appraisal of the permeation of society by property relations the need for thoroughgoing revolutionary change. Instead he settles from the earliest for schemes that are less than appropriate, schemes that propose to mitigate some of the most conspicuous abuses of the system without proceeding to the heart of the matter. 'He has done all that a criticism of political economy from the standpoint of political economy can do' – an evaluation to which we shall have cause to return.

Entr'acte: the break

> Liberty recognizes no law, no motive, no principle, no cause,
> no limit, no end, except itself. . . Placing itself above everything
> else, it waits for a chance to escape . . . all laws but its own, to

insult everything but itself, to make the world serve its fancies
and the natural order its whims. To the universe that surrounds
it it says: no; to the laws of nature and logic that obsess it: no;
to the senses that tempt it: no; to the love that seduces it: no;
to the priest's voice, to the prince's order, to the crowd's cries:
no, no, no. It is the eternal adversary that opposes any idea and
any force that aims to dominate it; the indomitable insurgent
that has faith in nothing but itself, respect and esteem for
nothing but itself, that will not abide even the idea of God
except insofar as it recognizes itself in God as its own antithesis.

Proudhon, *De la justice dans la révolution et dans l'Église*[71]

Whatever admiration for Proudhon Marx retained after completing
The Holy Family did not long outlive Marx's expulsion from Paris in
1845. Yet in 1846 he still regarded Proudhon as a possible collaborator;
in May of that year he wrote to Proudhon from Brussels, the site of his
exile. Marx and Engels had launched a practical project, creating a
chain of international correspondence committees in order to acquaint
working men in various countries with socialist initiatives, proposals
and alternatives. The basic idea behind this project may have owed
something to similar methods already used by the German artisans
in the Workers' Educational Association in London (where Marx had
visited Engels in 1845); the idea was to solicit the support of prominent
socialists and labour leaders in establishing various national and regional
committees, and in preparing international reports and exchanges of
information. While the scheme, by virtue of its international scope, was
in effect a prototype of the later International Working Men's Association, which was to be founded in 1864, and while it suggests how
quick and far-sighted Marx was in seeing the possibilities of international
proletarian organization (with which he had only just become acquainted), it was none the less probably premature. The response to
Marx's initiative in 1846 was in general unenthusiastic and desultory;
some contacts, none of them really new, were made in Germany, and
one (with Proudhon) in France. Marx's hopes of circulating new developments in socialist theory and of exchanging views and airing differences
across national boundaries were, for the time being, doomed to disap-
pointment, so that Marx and Engels instead concentrated their energies
in the direction of a pre-existing body, the League of the Just. They
hoped to convert what was in 1846 still a secret, conspiratorial artisan-
communist *Bund* into a more open, democratic Communist League
which would, in the words of what was to be its international programme (*The Manifesto of the Communist Party*) disdain to conceal
its views or its existence from the world.

All this, however, was in the future when Marx wrote to Proudhon in 1846, although the letter presented itself as part of a much broader initiative. 'I have organized', says Marx to Proudhon

> a continuous correspondence with the German Communists and Socialists, which is to take up both the discussion of scientific questions and the supervision of popular publications as well as socialist propaganda, which can be carried on in Germany by this means. It will be the chief aim of our correspondence, however, to put the German socialists in contact with the French and English socialists; to keep the foreigners posted on the socialist movements that are going to take place in Germany, and to inform the Germans in Germany of the progress of socialism in France and in England. In this way, it will be possible to air differences of opinion. We can achieve an exchange of ideas and an impartial criticism. It will be a step forward for the socialist movement in its '*literary*' expression, a step towards shaking off *national* limitations. At the moment of action it is certainly of great importance for each of us to be informed on the state of affairs abroad as well as at home.
>
> Besides the communists in Germany our correspondence would also embrace the German socialists in Paris and London. Our connections with England have already been established; as for France, we are all of the opinion that we could not find a better correspondent there than you. As you know, the English and Germans have up till now appreciated you more than your own fellow countrymen.
>
> So you see, it is only a question of initiating a regular correspondence and of assuring it the facilities for following the social movement in the various countries. . .[72]

Proudhon reacted to Marx's initiative cautiously and guardedly. The reasons for his reservations are not hard to find. To begin with, Marx appended to an otherwise conciliatory letter a postscript tactlessly denouncing Proudhon's friend Karl Grün. The terms of Marx's intemperate denunciation (' . . . a literary swindler, a charlatan . . . the man is dangerous. . . Therefore beware of this parasite . . . ') can have done nothing to inspire in Proudhon a belief in Marx's good faith, and had the ill-judged rhetorical effect of undercutting the tone of Marx's letter, with its exhortations that we should all reason together. This postscript (which is omitted, incidentally, from the *Marx-Engels Selected Correspondence*) was on any reckoning a blunder; in view of it, we should wonder not at the reserved nature of Proudhon's reply, but that he replied at all, particularly since there was still more in Marx's 'feeler' to perturb him. Marx's reference, be it unguarded or deliberate, to 'national limitations' must have cut close to the bone, since Proudhon, of all people, was certainly subject to them (and was to remain so); but perhaps Proudhon was disarmed by Marx's subsequent, flattering (and inaccurate) mention of Proudhon's international reputation. Most seriously of all, Marx's reference to 'the moment of action' was - duly or unduly - provocative, and Proudhon seized upon it. The moment of action means, of course, *revolutionary* action, any reference to which could not fail to disturb Proudhon, who regarded his own earlier flirtation with it as something best forgotten and buried.

Accordingly, while he expressed a willingness to participate, in a limited way, in the correspondence (which on the face of it was all that Marx had requested), Proudhon agreed to do so in a manner that made clear his suspicions as well as his reservations. What he says - with much more care than Marx had seen fit to employ - in his reply has a prescient, almost prophetic ring (one which has missed some commentators in some respects); his response reveals, in embryo, the differences of principle which were to divide him and his followers (and, for that matter, Bakunin and *his* followers) from what they were to call 'authoritarian socialism'.

[Although] my ideas on matters of organization and realization are at the moment quite settled, at least as far as principles are concerned, I believe that it is my duty, as it is the duty of all socialists, to maintain for some time yet an attitude of criticism and doubt; in short, I profess an almost absolute economic anti-dogmatism.

By all means let us work together to discover the laws of society, the ways in which these laws are realized and the process by which we might discover them. But, for God's sake, when we have demolished all *a priori* dogmatisms, let us not think of indoctrinating the people in our turn. Let us not fall into your compatriot Martin Luther's inconsistency. . . Let us not make further work for humanity by creating another shambles. I applaud with all my heart your idea of bringing to light all opinions; let us give the world the example of a learned and far-sighted tolerance [une tolérance savante et prévoyante], but let us not, just because we are at the head of a movement, make ourselves the leaders of a new intolerance, let us not pose as the apostles of a new religion, even if it be the religion of logic, the religion of reason. Let us gather together and encourage all protests, let us get rid of all exclusivity and mysticism; let us never regard a question as exhausted, and when we have used our last argument, let us begin again, if necessary, with eloquence and irony. On that condition, I will gladly join your association. Otherwise - no!

I have also some observations to make about the phrase in

your letter, 'at the moment of action.' Perhaps you retain the opinion that no reform is at present possible without a *coup de main*, without what used to be called a revolution but which is really nothing but a shock. That opinion, which I understand, which I excuse and would willingly discuss, having myself shared it for a long time, my most recent studies have made me completely abandon. I believe we have no need of it if we are to succeed, and that consequently we should not put forward revolutionary action as a means of social reform, because that supposed means would simply be an appeal to force, to arbitrariness, in short a contradiction. I put the problem in this way: how do we bring about the return to society, by an economic combination, of the wealth which was withdrawn from society by another economic combination? In other words, through political economy we must turn the theory of property against property in such a way as to produce what you German socialists call community and which for the moment I shall restrict myself to calling liberty or equality. Now I think I know the way in which this problem may be very quickly solved. Therefore I prefer to have property burn little by little, rather than give it new strength by making a Saint Bartholomew's Day of property owners. . . This, my dear philosopher, is my present position. If it happens that I am mistaken and you give me a good caning [la férule], I shall submit with good grace while awaiting my revenge. I must add in passing that this also seems to be the feeling of the French working class. Our proletarians are so thirsty for knowledge that they would ill receive us if we gave them only blood to drink. In short, it would in my opinion be very bad policy to use the language of extermination. Rigorous enough measures will come; for this the people need no exhortation.[73]

Proudhon adds that he is engaged in writing a book that will explain in detail his plans for peaceable reform (which, in the event, *The System of Economic Contradictions* was conspicuously not to accomplish); that he sincerely regrets 'the minor divisions which would appear to exist already in German socialism of which your complaint against M. Grün gives me proof'; and that it would give him 'much pleasure' to see Marx reverse his judgment – 'for you were in an angry frame of mind when you wrote to me'. Proudhon finally presses home an advantage, in a confrontation not without its undercurrents, by asking Marx to help sell his forthcoming book, not so much for Proudhon's own sake, as for that of Grün, who wished to translate it.

Marx's response to Proudhon's book, which appeared the following year (though not in Grün's translation, which never materialized), was of course very different; the 'cane' (*la férule*) to which Proudhon had referred, in all apparent playfulness, descended with a vengeance. Marx's *The Poverty of Philosophy: Response to 'The Philosophy of Poverty' of M. Proudhon* drew blood, and was clearly intended to do so. It hurt in such a way that no gracious reply would have been humanly possible; Proudhon, in the event, did not reply publicly at all. This subsequent development (and, indeed, other subsequent developments) poses a real temptation to anyone who would take it upon himself to adjudicate the issues raised in what was, beneath the surface, a highly charged exchange of letters – particularly since this altercation provides the only exchange of letters between Marx and Proudhon that is available. The temptation is to overdramatize what was, admittedly, in its way a dramatic confrontation by arguing, with the benefit of hindsight, that Proudhon in his letter had indicated in advance, as it were, how intolerant, dogmatic and authoritarian Marx could be. But to do so would be to lapse into prolepsis; Marx's 'authoritarianism' (as opposed to his theoretical impatience and intolerance of doctrines he considered – often with good cause – to be deficient) in 1846 had yet to emerge. Marx was in 1847 to take up some of the themes – the ideas about political economy, and Proudhon's reformism – that Proudhon had touched on in his letter; but it is probable that he would have done so even if the exchange of letters had never taken place. Here, it is difficult to be definitive; but Proudhon's views of political economy, reform and violence were to be expressed clearly enough in his book, and it does need to be remembered that Marx in *The Poverty of Philosophy* (the only full-length work on economics Marx published before 1859) was concerned primarily to advance *economic* arguments against Proudhon, and *all* of these arguments, it can be shown, had been foreshadowed in Marx's earlier critical comments on Proudhon – comments that were in fact by no means as 'enthusiastic' as some have imagined. What this means is that the celebrated altercation of 1846 in reality played a much smaller role in setting up the eventual battle-lines than has, too easily, been assumed.

Nor indeed is it the only easy assumption it is possible to make. It is tempting to allow oneself to be carried away by Proudhon's profession of tolerance and open-mindedness. Yet to take this at its face value, to polarize the exchange between Proudhon and Marx by casting Proudhon as the personification of these virtues, is to prejudge later, more momentous confrontations in far too innocent a manner. The superiority of an open exchange of views over an authoritarian stifling of opinion need not be laboured; indeed, it was all that Marx (whatever his views of Grün) has pressed for in his letter. But it does need to be borne in mind that while Marx, no doubt tactlessly as well as inadvertently, gave Proudhon every opportunity of displaying tolerance in his letter back, no controversialist – and Proudhon was nothing if not a controversialist – could be more intolerant and dogmatic than Proudhon himself, as many a French socialist of some other persuasion could (and did) attest. Marx, for the most part, was not on the receiving end of Proudhon's celebrated rancour, since Proudhon's sights were set firmly within the French horizon; Proudhon's uncharacteristic silence in the face of Marx's published attacks on him was simply a recognition that Marx's assaults could make no real difference. Proudhon in the 1840s was a celebrated theoretician, and Marx was not; *The Philosophy of Poverty* was translated into German almost immediately on its appearance, and Marx's *The Poverty of Philosophy* was translated into German only after Marx's death, almost four decades after it first appeared. Proudhon could afford not to call attention to an obscure book by an obscure author; and Marx, as he emerged from obscurity, had frequent occasion to regret the influence of Proudhon. Marx's Proudhonist enemies in the International, as we shall observe, were by virtue of their Proudhonism to be no less 'dogmatic' or 'intolerant' than Marx himself. The historical and dramatic ironies were to run deep; but we shall not be able to plumb them unless we recognize that the International, which was never intended to be an ideologically monolithic, or univocal, body, turned into one partly because of Marx, partly because of his Proudhonist enemies and their heirs, and partly because of the outcome of successive confrontations that escaped the control of either side.

The Poverty of Philosophy and beyond

Marx's attempt to destroy Proudhon's reputation as a theorist, once and for all, by writing a book attacking him, in 1847, was in its way guileless as well as unseemly, ill-judged as well as venomous. The shortcomings of Proudhon's *System of Economic Contradictions*, which appeared in two volumes (running close to 1,000 pages) in 1846, struck him as being so blatantly outrageous as to demand an unkind, blistering response. Marx's patience, never foremost among his qualities, had been undercut; indeed it had reached its breaking point. It is no accident that *The Poverty of Philosophy* was the only book Marx wrote in French and had published in Paris; even so, what was in many ways an attempt at character assassination misfired; Marx failed to discredit Proudhon, at least among the latter's most immediate and important audience. As far as the development of French (and by extension European) socialism was concerned, Proudhon's influence seems to have been diminished or deflected not one whit by the undoubted intellectual power, and equally undoubted personal malice, of Marx's withering attack. It would be tempting (but peremptory) to conclude that Marx, by creating a backlash of sympathy for Proudhon in France, inadvertently succeeded in augmenting Proudhon's reputation. Such a conclusion would not be without a certain poetic justice. The truth of the matter, however, is more prosaic. Proudhon's reputation needed no enhancing; and Marx's book, unlike Proudhon's, failed to sell many copies.

Proudhon, even though he never replied in print to Marx's scornful attack, was, not surprisingly, cut to the quick by it. He described *The Poverty of Philosophy* (in the margins of his own copy) as 'a tissue of vulgarity, of calumny, of falsification and of plagiarism'. Fond, as ever, of accusing others of jealousy of his own intellectual achievements, Proudhon added that

> what Marx's book really means is that he is sorry that
> everywhere *I* have thought the way *he* does, and said so
> before he did. Any determined reader can see that it is Marx
> who, having read me, regrets thinking like me. What a man!

This comment is interesting in the light of claims that have been advanced to the effect that Proudhon, in his later ventures into economics, took cognizance (in his inimitable manner) of the criticisms Marx had levelled at the *System of Economic Contradictions*, but this is an issue we cannot enter into here. Proudhon's only subsequent comments (in writing) about Marx are contained, perhaps fortunately, in the privacy of notebooks that remained unpublished during Proudhon's lifetime; these are generally straightforwardly anti-Semitic in character. The exception proving the rule was Proudhon's (again private) characterization of Marx as 'the tapeworm of socialism' ('le ténia de socialisme')[74] – a reference to Marx's tendency to infiltrate socialist movements that in their origin owed nothing to his efforts.

Even this kind of comment was not, however, a response in kind to Marx's attack in *The Poverty of Philosophy*, the tone and bearing of which is in some respects difficult to adjudicate. Marx attacks Proudhon's claims to be either a philosopher or an economist at all, on the grounds of his sloppy dialectics and ridiculous economic theory. Marx's arch *avant-propos* sets the tone as well as the terms of what is to follow.

> M. Proudhon has the misfortune of being peculiarly misunderstood
> in Europe. In France, he has the right to be a bad economist,
> because he is reputed to be a good German philosopher. In
> Germany, he has the right to be a bad philosopher, because he
> is reputed to be one of the ablest French economists. Being
> both German and economist at the same time, we desire to
> protest against this double error.[75]

And protest he does, throughout some 200 pages. On the one hand,

Marx's actual criticisms of Proudhon can readily enough be documented; they are those of a rigorous and conscientious thinker attacking someone who has not done his homework, who does not exhibit the intellectual equipment appropriate to the task he was unwise enough to set himself, who – in a word – is intellectually *pas sérieux*. The indignation of a serious scholar who believes that a philosophy of action (or even of reform) can be based only on the firmest of theoretical grounds is not something that in and of itself invites accusations of dogmatism (and certainly not an accusation of jealousy, as Proudhon himself thought – unless it is jealousy of Proudhon's popularity as opposed to his intellect). On the other hand, plangent and bombastic attempts at character assassination are by their very nature unsavoury enough to rebound on their perpetrators; and this is the case quite apart from the fact that Proudhon had already proved himself equally capable of this kind of character assassination (as Étienne Cabet, Louis Blanc and Louis-Auguste Blanqui, to name but three, had occasion to find out), and quite apart from the intellectual content of the theoretical argument Marx brought to bear on Proudhon's book.

To frame the issue in this way is to recognize that we need to ask, at this juncture, what it was that prompted Marx to attack Proudhon's book at all. Far from being on the face of it aimed in Marx's direction, or in any way directly provocative, the *System of Economic Contradictions* does not even mention him by name. Proudhon's concerns and targets, here as elsewhere, were in the first instance French; yet they were by the same token anti-communist concerns and, often, communist targets. While Proudhon's anti-communism had not been far below the surface in *What is Property?*, where he had assailed the Babouvists, six years later his language was much more extravagant. Returning to the fray in 1846, Proudhon once again selected Babeuf as a whipping-boy, and attacked his *communauté des biens* as 'nothing but the exaltation of the state, the glorification of the police',[76] adding that

> mankind, like a drunkard, flounders and hesitates between two
> abysses, property on the one hand, community [i.e. community
> of goods of the type Babeuf had propounded] on the other. . .
> Capital and power – the subordinate organs of society – are the
> gods which socialism adores; if they did not exist, socialism
> would invent them.[77]

The intemperance of such a claim suggests that Proudhon was setting about raising the stakes, particularly since his target was not just communism of the Babouvist variety. He proceeded to argue against revolutionary communism and reformist state socialism (his bellwether for the latter being Louis Blanc) that 'the abolition of the exploitation of man by man and the abolition of government are one and the same thing'.[78] While bourgeois society and its theoretical expression, political economy, consummated egoism and theft, neither revolutionary communism nor state socialism provided any viable alternative, as each would in its own way consummate monopoly and collectivity. The socialism of Blanc and the communism of Cabet alike are denounced by Proudhon as dictatorial, subversive of personal freedom and the supremacy of the individual, and destructive of healthy family life. Proudhon's railing and flailing against socialism and communism is such that, in the words of Marx's letter of 1846 to Annenkov,

> he bursts into violent explosions of rage, vociferation and
> righteous wrath (*irae hominis probi*), foams at the mouth, curses,
> denounces, cries shame and murder, beats his breast and boasts
> before man and God that he is not defiled by the socialist
> infamies.[79]

This sounds exaggerated only to those unacquainted with Proudhon's *System*, a book which even his staunchest defenders find difficult to justify.

The Poverty of Philosophy itself pays relatively little attention to Proudhon's fervent and unrestrained anti-communism; even its final section on 'Strikes and Combinations of Workers', which leads up to an exhortation to revolutionary violence, is concerned in the main with stressing the political importance of militant trade unionism. Marx's restraint, which is not carried over into his comments on Proudhon as an economist and dialectician, can probably be explained by what he had said in 1846 to Annenkov: 'a man who has not understood the present state of society may be expected to understand still less the movement which is tending to overthrow it'[80] – the truth of which statement Marx regards as self-evident. Proudhon is most notably criticized in *The Poverty of Philosophy* not directly for his anti-communism but for his economics and dialectics; and the text has come down to us mainly as a classic and concise statement of Marxist economic theory.

Yet the political stakes in Marx's 'Anti-Proudhon' should be borne in mind, since they are not so much 'background' to a discussion taking place on some altogether different terrain as implied throughout the discussion itself. One reason why this is so was provided by Proudhon himself in the *System* when he argued that communism 'reproduces . . . all the contradictions of liberal political economy'.[81] Marx, who in the period since Proudhon's first criticisms of communism had publicly sided with the communists, and who could scarcely have been expected to remain aloof from Proudhon's revamped attack in the *System*, sought to establish the opposite claim: that communism alone does *not* reproduce all the contradictions of classical political economy, whereas Proudhon fails to understand them.

(1) *Dialectics*

> My aim is not to write a moral treatise, any more than a philosophy of history. My task is more modest: first we must get our bearings, then everything else will follow automatically.

> Proudhon, *De la Justice dans la Révolution et dans l'Église* (1858)[82]

The Poverty of Philosophy, true to Marx's *avant-propos* (and indeed to its very title), had as its aim the discrediting of Proudhon's dialectics as well as his economics. Like his subsequent attack on the very different Manichaean dialectics of Bakunin, the focus of Marx's attack on Proudhon serves to indicate the continued hold of Hegel on Marx's thought. Hegel himself does not escape lightly in the second half of *The Poverty of Philosophy* (though this cannot be our main concern here), but Proudhon's somewhat high-handed attempts to *correct* Hegel fare much worse. Marx's basic objection to Proudhon in this connection is that in his argumentation 'high-sounding speculative jargon, [that is] supposed to be German-philosophical, appears regularly on the scene whenever his Gallic acuteness of understanding fails him'.[83] The 'jargon' in question, as Marx went on to indicate in his letter to Schweitzer (1865) was not always even Hegelian. The relevant shift within the sequence of Proudhon's writings took place in 1846 when, in his *System of Economic Contradictions*, Proudhon 'attempted to present the system of economic categories dialectically. In place of Kant's insoluble "antinomies," the Hegelian "contradiction" was to be introduced as the means of development'.[84]

As part of Proudhon's argument in *What is Property?* (1840),

> in the passages which he himself regarded as the most important he imitates Kant's treatment of the '*antinomies*' – Kant, whose works he read in translation, was at that time the only German philosopher he knew – and he leaves one with the strong impression that to him, as to Kant, the resolution of antinomies is something '*beyond*' the human understanding, i.e. something about which his own understanding is in the dark.[85]

Marx, whose point here is that a mock-Hegelian dialectic was to be produced in the manner of an intellectual *deus ex machina* in order to 'resolve' this failure of the understanding, but who admits to Schweitzer that he did not have a copy of *What is Property?* at hand when he was writing this, was, if anything (and for once), too kind to Proudhon in so characterizing his use of Kantian antinomies. Marx, indeed, presumably did not have a copy of his own *The Holy Family* to hand when he wrote to Schweitzer, for he had used this book to recast Proudhonian antinomies within a dynamic, dialectical setting and drew from them revolutionary conclusions with which Proudhon would have disagreed fervently, but which foreshadow Marx's later arguments in *The Poverty of Philosophy*.

> Proletariat and wealth are antinomies; as such they form a single
> whole. They are both forms of the word 'private property'
> [Privateigenthum]. The question is, however, what place each
> occupies in the antithesis. It is not sufficient to declare them
> two sides of a single whole [which is all Proudhon had done,
> at least according to Marx] . . . The proletariat . . . is com-
> pelled as proletariat to abolish itself and thereby its opposite,
> the conditions for its existence, what makes it the proletariat,
> i.e. private property. That is the negative side of the contradiction,
> its restlessness within its very self. . . When the proletariat is
> victorious, it by no means becomes the absolute side, for it is
> victorious only by abolishing itself, and its opposite (private
> property, the 'positive side') . . . it cannot free itself without
> abolishing the conditions of its own life (as proletariat).[86]

Proudhon, who according to Marx in this passage and passages like it in *The Holy Family* had failed to infer the right kind of conclusion from the antinomy of proletariat and wealth, was fond of comparing his antinomies to those of Kant, but this comparison does not withstand examination. Proudhon regarded 'antinomy' in *What is Property?* and elsewhere much as he was to regard 'contradiction' in *The System of Economic Contradictions*: as an opposition inherent in some of the forces constituting society, which will tear it apart unless we understand them. There is nothing Kantian about this position. The antinomies in *The Critique of Pure Reason* have as their medium not *being* (let alone 'society') but *reason*; they served to indicate that the understanding was operating outside its own proper sphere. Proudhon by contrast regarded the opposition signified by 'antinomies' as ubiquitous, and was to regard 'contradiction' in the same way in 1846; economic and social, as well as logical 'oppositions' (or, *mutatis mutandis*, 'contradictions'), Proudhon considered identical or identifiable – which is about as far from Kant as one can get. Proudhon also believed 'le régime propriétaire' could be comprehended as a 'structured totality' (as we would say today), one that is intelligible without reference to its history, although it is not intelligible according to Proudhon without reference to the contradictions that pervade it. To regard contradictions as non-historical in this way is about as far from *Hegel* as one can get, as Marx was not slow to point out.*

Even so, Marx in *The German Ideology* guardedly praised Proudhon's dialectics:

> The most important thing about Proudhon's book, *The Creation of Order in Humanity*, is his serial dialectic, the attempt to establish a method of thought by which the thought *process* takes the place of self-sufficient [selbständigen] thought. Proudhon is searching from the French standpoint for a dialectic system such as Hegel has actually established. The relationship with Hegel is present here in reality, not through a fantastic analogy. Hence it would be easy here to give a critique of the Proudhonian dialectic, if one had finished with the critique of the Hegelian.[87]

In the event, however, Marx was to supply us with a critique of the Proudhonian dialectic without ever completing a critique of the Hegelian (although some of the elements of this latter are included not only in the *Economic and Philosophic Manuscripts* but also in the second part of *The Poverty of Philosophy* itself). Although Marx's appraisal of Proudhon's dialectic was in general extremely negative, he admitted in his letter to Schweitzer (1865) that 'Proudhon had a natural inclination for dialectics', making sure however that he added the rider that 'as he never really grasped scientific dialectics he never got further than sophistry'. This is the view of Proudhon's dialectics, together with the view that Proudhon 'hides his dialectical feebleness under a great show of rhetoric' that Marx develops at great length in *The Poverty of Philosophy* and the 1846 letter to Annenkov alike. The latter is an important source; in it Marx poses the question, 'Why does he [Proudhon] resort to feeble Hegelianism to give himself the appearance of a bold thinker?', and proceeds to answer it himself. 'M. Proudhon', we read, 'mixes up ideas and things' and fails to understand that 'economic forms in which men produce, consume and exchange, are transitory and historical'.[88]

---

*This is not a point that can be developed here, but Proudhon's stress on a kind of contradiction or opposition, which owes much less to either Hegel or Kant than he claimed, actually has a positivistic ring to it, since 'contradiction' often operates as the linking mechanism among the laws of nature, being and logic. *The Creation of Order in Humanity* (1843) professes a law of three stages strikingly similar to Comte's, although he links it in his later book on justice (*De la justice dans la révolution et dans l'Eglise*) with equality in a way that would have scandalized Comte and recalls – of all people – Leroux. More often, we encounter the notion that truth consists in eternal laws embedded in nature which the correct method of social enquiry will uncover and bear out by inaugurating corresponding social institutions. While this notion is positivistic in the sense that Fourier is positivistic, it also seems to add up to a certain kind of 'natural law' assumption.

M. Proudhon, incapable [as he is] of following the real movement
of history, produces a phantasmagoria which presumptuously
claims to be dialectical. He does not feel it necessary to speak
of the seventeenth, the eighteenth and the nineteenth century
for his history proceeds in the misty realm of imagination and
rises far above space and time. In short, it is not history but old
Hegelian junk, it is not profane history – a history of man – but
sacred history – a history of ideas. From his point of view man
is only the instrument of which the idea or the eternal reason
makes use in order to unfold itself. The evolutions of which
M. Proudhon speaks are understood to be evolutions such as
are accomplished within the mystic womb of the absolute idea.
If you tear the veil from this mystical language, what it comes
to is that M. Proudhon is offering you the order in which
economic categories arrange themselves inside his own head
. . . it is the order of a very disorderly mind.[89]

The 'evolutions' to which Marx refers are three-fold: the division of
labour, machinery and competition which according to Proudhon's
System work, progressively though at cross-purposes, in the trans-
historical interest of equality and justice; these demiurges, which
themselves are not always sharply distinguished from each other or
from a third, the Revolution, Proudhon at times believed he personified.
What this means, according to Marx, is that

M. Proudhon is therefore obliged to take refuge in a fiction in
order to explain development. He imagines that division of
labour, credit, machinery, etc., were all invented in order to
serve his fixed idea. His explanation is sublimely naive. These
things were invented in the interests of equality but unfortunately
they turned against equality. This constitutes his whole argument.
In other words, he makes a gratuitous assumption and then, as the
actual development contradicts his fiction at every step, he concludes that there is a contradiction. He conceals from you the fact
that the contradiction exists solely between his fixed ideas and
the real movement.
  . . . He has not perceived that economic categories are only
abstract expressions of [human] relations and only remain true
while these relations exist. He therefore falls into the error of the
bourgeois economists, who regard these economic categories as
eternal and not as historical laws which are only laws for a
particular historical development. . . Instead, therefore, of
regarding the political-economic categories as abstract expressions
of the real, transitory, historic social relations, M. Proudhon,
thanks to a mystic inversion, sees in the real relations only

embodiments of these abstractions. These abstractions themselves
are formulas which have been slumbering in the heart of God the
Father since the beginning of the world.

But here our good M. Proudhon falls into severe intellectual
convulsions. . .[90]

Marx proceeds, here as in *The Poverty of Philosophy*, to accuse Proudhon of confusing progress and providentialism. To synthesize the
individualism animating bourgeois society with the desire for social
justice underlying the communist reaction to it seemed quite unprob-
lematic to Proudhon, who blithely assumed, and expatiated at great
length throughout the *System* on the assumption, that the good,
progressive features of social institutions could be separated without
undue difficulty from their bad, regressive characteristics which could
be sloughed off and cast aside. As Marx quite rightly indicated, simply
to regard everything as being somehow Janus-faced, as presenting a
double aspect, *du côté du bien et du côté du mal*, is insufficient to
make a system dialectical in even the Hegelian sense; to then add a
dash of providentialism, however watered-down ('nevertheless, despite
continual oscillations, the good seems to prevail over the evil and,
taking it altogether, there is marked progress toward the better, as
far as we can see'),[91] is *not* going to make up the difference. Proudhon,
who hated historical determinism, as a result turned his back on anything Marx (and in truth many others too) would recognize as historical
analysis; the attainment of equality and justice was urged instead by
means of a sometimes disarming, ultimately unconvincing faith that
every apparent setback was purely temporary, and that the long-term
trend favoured 'progress' at every turn. (Of Proudhon's works, only
The Political Capacity of the Working Classes – which was published
posthumously in 1865 – is not optimistic in this peculiarly artless
sense.) In Marx's words,

> it seems obvious to [Proudhon] that there is within the bosom
> of God a synthesis . . . in which [for example] the evils of
> monopoly are balanced by competition and vice versa. As a
> result of the struggle between the two ideas only their good
> side will come into view . . . apply it, and everything will be
> for the best; the synthetic formula which lies hidden in the
> darkness of the impersonal reason of man must be revealed.
> M. Proudhon does not hesitate for a moment to come forward
> as the revealer.[92]

Marx proceeds at this point to write a passage of fundamental importance to an understanding not only of what he thought was wrong with
Proudhon's notion of the dialectic but also with his grasp of economic

categories. For Proudhon, says Marx,

abstractions, categories are the primordial cause. According to him they, and not men, make history. The abstraction, the category taken as such, i.e. apart from men and their material activities, is of course immortal, unchangeable, unmoved; it is only one form of the being of pure reason, which is only another way of saying that the abstraction as such is abstract. An admirable tautology! ... M. Proudhon does not directly state that bourgeois life is for him an eternal verity; he states it indirectly by deifying the categories which express bourgeois relations in the form of bourgeois thought. He takes the products of bourgeois society for spontaneously arisen eternal beings, endowed with a life of their own... So he does not rise above the bourgeois horizon... Indeed he does what all good bourgeois do. They all tell you that in principle, that is, considered as abstract ideas, competition, monopoly etc. are the only basis of life, but that in practice they leave much to be desired. They all want competition without the lethal effects of competition. They all want the impossible, viz., the conditions of bourgeois existence without the necessary consequences of these conditions... Mr. Proudhon is therefore necessarily doctrinaire. To him the historical movement which is turning the world upside down reduces itself to the problem of discovering the correct equilibrium, the synthesis, of two bourgeois thoughts [in this instance, of monopoly and competition]. And so the clever fellow is able by his cunning to discover ... the unity of two isolated thoughts – which are only isolated because M. Proudhon has isolated them... [In] place of [the] vast, prolonged and complicated movement [revolutionary communism] M. Proudhon supplies the whimsical motion of his own head. So it is the men of learning that make history, the men who know how to purloin God's secret thoughts. The common people have only to apply their evaluations. You will now understand why M. Proudhon is the declared enemy of every political movement. The solution of present problems does not lie for him in public action but in the dialectical rotations of his own mind.[93]

There are several reasons for quoting this passage at such length. In it, Marx ties together the two strands of his subsequent critique, *The Poverty of Philosophy*, in which he valiantly tries, but largely fails, to treat them under separate headings, 'A Scientific Discovery' (which could be an ironical reference not only to Proudhon's insight that workers cannot buy back the product of their labour, but also to Marx's own, earlier praise of Proudhon for having made a scientific discovery) and 'The Metaphysics of Political Economy'. That the separation cannot, finally, be a neat one reinforces Marx's point that sloppy dialectics and an uncritical adoption of the 'horizon' *if not the actual tenets* of political economy go together and reinforce each other, with dire results. Proudhon, after all, cannot be said to be a 'doctrinaire' follower of the political economists in any obvious sense, since he was severely critical of their concepts and definitions, and indeed of the capitalist society to which these were to apply. He contents himself, however, with substituting other definitions and concepts of his own, which he considers more satisfactory. If his definitions and concepts are less appropriate to capitalism than those they were intended to supplant, so much the better: their profession would serve to underscore Proudhon's hostility to capitalism. What gets thrown out at this point, however, as Marx was to reiterate, is any explanatory force the concepts of the political economists may once have carried. To argue on the basis of revamped but less appropriate concepts, as Proudhon does, is not to reinforce but to vitiate a critical perspective for this very reason.

This leads to a point of some importance. If we ask, as we must, what Marx means by the 'bourgeois horizon' (or had meant, *mutatis mutandis*, in *The Holy Family* by 'the standpoint of political economy') we find that he does not simply mean 'following political economy' in the sense of uncritically adopting its definitions and tenets; he also, and in fact more fundamentally, means using a certain (broader) kind of definition in a certain way. He is objecting to a mode of conceptualization that prominently includes but is not satisfied by the procedures of the political economists themselves. The characteristic feature of Proudhon's definitions and concepts is not that they are directly tainted by those of the political economists but that they are purely conceptual standards up to which the reality dealt with by the political economists fails to measure. This can mean only that Proudhon's standards, to which present social reality signifies a lamentable failure to conform, occupy a rarefied level, a level from which judgments can be made. To say, for example, that competition as it has developed is a betrayal of the original idea of competition which, if uncovered, will make us ashamed in its light of what we have come to in its name, is to refer back to a kind of social form that is obsolete, idealized or both. Because they are overtaken by events, by the actual process of social development which cuts their ground from under them, these concepts come to have little actual reference or relevance to a society whose worst features they are meant to rectify. This is what Marx means in *The Manifesto of the Communist Party* when he says, archly, that the communists had no need to abolish the form of property that Proudhon held so dear, as the development of modern industry was abolishing it daily.[94]

It is important that we recognize that Proudhon here is being accused not only of having backward looking standards, but of having standards of a certain kind at all: that he is being accused, in other words, of hypostatizing concepts, which is, at root, what the political economics themselves do. 'Economic categories are only the theoretical expressions, the abstractions of the social relations of production', according to Marx, whereas Proudhon, 'holding things upside down like a true philosopher, sees in actual relations nothing but the incarnation of these principles', so that 'what Hegel had done for religion, law etc., M. Proudhon seeks to do for political economy',[95] an attempt which is, in fact, redundant as well as mystificatory. Proudhon's procedure is to abstract 'the substance of everything' into mere logical categories and then, having hypostatized these abstractions into principles, to represent real social and historical developments as expressions or embodiments of them.

> If we abstract thus from every subject all the alleged accidents, animate or inanimate, men or things, we are right in saying that in the final abstraction, the only substance left is the logical categories. Thus the metaphysicians who, in making these abstractions, think they are making analyses, and who, the more they detach themselves from things, imagine themselves to be getting all the nearer to the point of penetrating to their core – these metaphysicians in turn are right in saying that things here below are embroideries of which the logical categories constitute the canvas. This is what distinguishes the philosopher from the Christian. The Christian, in spite of logic, has only one incarnation of the *Logos*; the philosopher has never finished with incarnations.[96]

What this means is that Proudhon sees any social problem in the light of conceptual problems; the referent of any concept, say 'competition', becomes *another* concept, say 'monopoly', instead of the actual forms assumed in society by either competition or monopoly. Problems, such as how competition and monopoly are related, come to reside not in society but in the concepts used to characterize society; dealing with these is a purely reflexive, definitional exercise. Proudhon devotes himself to solving conceptual problems: 'The economist's material is [properly] the active, energetic life of man; M. Proudhon's material is the dogmas of the economist'[97] – dogmas that are rendered more dogmatic by being treated as self-sufficient entities in a 'pure ether of reason'.[98] For Proudhon, 'the circulation of the blood must be a consequence of Harvey's theory';[99] 'instead of saying like everyone else: when the weather is fine, a lot of people are to be seen going for a walk, M. Proudhon makes his people go for a walk in order to be able to ensure them fine weather'.[100]

The problem is one of illegitimate abstraction and hypostasis: 'With all these changeless and motionless eternities, there is no history left, there is at most history in the idea, i.e. history reflected in the dialectic movement of pure reason.'[101] Proudhon's penchant for dialectics compounds this tendency, for these too must be purely conceptual. One of the reasons Marx dismisses them as expressing an adulterated (*frélaté*) Hegelianism is that their dichotomies or 'contradictions' were purely conceptual in a way that Hegel's never had been. 'M. Proudhon has nothing of Hegel's dialectics but the language' ('n'a de la dialectique de Hegel que son langage');[102] he succeeds in reducing them 'to the meanest proportions'.[103] If this is so, society, which is, according to Proudhon, ridden with 'contradictions', nevertheless remains fundamentally the inert recipient of insights about 'contradiction' and 'synthesis' which spring from the mind of the theorist like Minerva from the brow of Jove; to Marx, on the other hand, contradictions, to be contradictions, are the product not just of the theorist's mental agility but also of society itself.

There remains Proudhon's manner of resolving his contradictions so that 'equilibrium' ensues; there remains, that is, his untoward moralism and feckless providentialism. Marx was justified in indicating, with no small impatience, that according to Proudhon

> every economic category has two sides, one good, one bad. . .
> The good side and the bad side, the advantages and the drawbacks,
> taken together form for M. Proudhon the contradiction in every
> economic category. The problem to be solved: to keep the good
> side while eliminating the bad[104]

and that, for Proudhon, 'the dialectical movement is the dogmatic distinction between good and bad'.[105] Or, again in Marx's words,

> the good side of an economic relation is that which affirms
> equality; the bad side, that which negates it and affirms
> inequality. Every new category is a hypothesis of the social
> genius to eliminate the inequality engendered by the previous
> hypothesis. In short, equality is the primordial intention, the
> mystical tendency, the providential aim that the social genius
> has constantly before its eyes as it whirls in the circles of
> economic contradictions. Thus Providence is the locomotive
> which makes the whole of M. Proudhon's economic baggage
> move better than his pure and volatile reason.[106]

Thus Proudhon's undoubted radicalism is, in the event, vitiated, not only by his tendency to transform historical conditions and relationships into a 'dialectic' of abstract categories and pre-existing eternal ideas, but also by an arrant providentialism. Proudhon saw contradiction everywhere; his book is a welter of contradiction. He even ascribed a kind of propulsive power to negativity (such *négativité motrice* being, after all, a component part of dialectical thinking, albeit one for which Marx gives no credit to Proudhon). Yet his thought can be said to be truly progressive in only a very limited way – in much the same sense, as David Owen Evans has pointed out, that Romantic theories of history are progressive. That 'the true in all things, the real, is that which changes . . . while the false, the fictitious, is anything that presents itself as fixed and unalterable',[107] a characteristic Proudhonian sentiment, is a point of view akin not to Hegel but to Victor Hugo's 'Préface de *Cromwell*'. The Hegelian dialectic does not admit of the moral absolute of 'justice' (or 'equality' or 'equilibrium') which Proudhon shamelessly placed *hors de combat* as a goal towards which everything, despite itself, was tending. As Louis Dupré, paraphrasing Marx, damningly put it, 'economic systems come and go not according to the laws of their intrinsic evolution but according to the development of a super-economic and superhuman Idea until they reach the state where Proudhon wants them to be'.[108]

(2) *Political economy*

Political economy is not my strong point and it will be most unfortunate if I have not given it up by the time I am forty.

Proudhon, Correspondance[109]

From Paris [Paul] Lafargue, who was often in the company of the Blanquists, wrote to Marx that Blanqui himself had a copy of *La Misère de la Philosophie*, which he often lent to friends. . . 'He has found the best word I know for Proudhon, he calls him a hygrometer.'

Maximilien Rubel and Margaret Manale, Marx Without Myth[110]

Many of the questions Proudhon had posed to himself in the *System*, which he intended as a volume about economics, were the very questions that more orthodox political economists had also addressed – questions about the source and nature of value, the distribution of the social product, the price mechanism, and the character of exchange. Proudhon's valiant but unconvincing attempts to grapple with such problems were at least the proximate cause of Marx's first real venture into the territory he defined as that of his life's work, the 'critique of political economy', a criticism, that is to say, of the capitalist system alongside a criticism of the concepts most commonly used to explain and justify it. Marx occupied himself with questions that to many a more modern economist would seem either *political* questions (what is the most just and equitable distribution of social wealth?) or 'metaphysical' ones (what is the nature of value?). Marx and Proudhon were attempting to answer the same kinds of question, however different their answers may have been. Proudhon, attempting in the *System* to deal with the problems raised by the political economists, endeavoured to situate himself, provisionally and on his own terms, on their terrain. Marx's basic argument against him is that by venturing so innocently and unpreparedly onto this terrain Proudhon in effect seals off his own exits and forecloses the possibility of a genuinely radical critique because of the assumptions, several of them moralistic assumptions, he brings in his baggage.

Marx generally criticized political economists for their tendency to believe that the categories with which they operated were timelessly and universally true, and for their failure to see through or beyond the immediate facts they used as data. 'The error committed by orthodox economists', as he once put it, 'is in not being aware of the socially-conditioned character of general economic categories and relationships and hence in taking the given social arrangements as natural, harmonious and eternal.'[111] There is no immediately obvious sense in which this stricture can be applied to Proudhon, who did not take 'given social arrangements as natural, harmonious and eternal' at all; Marx's point is that Proudhon's refusal to do so, far from indicating his immunity to their influence, to the contrary points up how insidious it can be.

As we have already seen, Marx in *The Holy Family* had accused Proudhon of some serious economic faults.[112] According to Marx, Proudhon took the political economists' invocation of 'contract', for example, more seriously than they themselves had taken it; their profession of the free and equal standing of the parties to a labour contract had been in the nature of a gesture, a ceremonial genuflection, a fiction made necessary by the fact of compulsion; whereas Proudhon, with his belief in the *morally* regenerative power of contract, had taken these professions at their face value, and those professing them at their word. Proudhon's steadfastness (or gullibility) in this regard has the salutary effect of highlighting the difference between the political economists' protestations and the inhuman reality that actually obtained under the aegis of wage-labour.

Yet Marx's conclusion that Proudhon 'does all that a criticism of political economy, from the standpoint of political economy, can do' is not an indication of approval (or 'enthusiasm') but a way of damning with faint praise. This becomes clear if we ask ourselves, as we must at this point, what 'the standpoint of political economy' *is* – for Proudhon certainly did not *think* he was mired in it – and what it means to inhabit, or remain locked within, this standpoint. To answer this question is to see that Marx's attacks on Proudhon in *The Poverty of Philosophy* do not signify a change of mind about Proudhon the economist at all; they are best regarded, rather, as an extension, a fleshing out, of his earlier criticisms.

Proudhon's economic argument proceeds on the basis of his observation that the more of anything useful there is, the lower will be its price, the less it will fetch on the market. This commonplace observation Proudhon regards as a fundamental 'contradiction'; he thinks it means that use-value (or utility) and exchange-value (or price) are locked into conflict. Use-value according to Proudhon is constituted by the producer, exchange-value by the consumer who estimates the scarcity of the product. Now there are two problems according to Marx with this formulation. First, on what basis does the consumer estimate? What gives him a basis for comparability? The only possible answer must be one that entails the existence, and circulation, of *other* products whose several exchange-values the consumer can scarcely be expected to have computed all on his own; this means that there must be a system of exchange operating independently of his will, unless, of course, the economy is very primitive indeed. That Proudhon misprizes what any real consumer can and cannot reasonably be expected to do under modern conditions (even if we suppose that consumption is a full-time job) leads to the second difficulty. The consumer and the producer cannot in fact be what Proudhon would like to make of them, that is free agents able to make up their minds about the prices of what they produce and what they consume, and to act freely upon their decisions, for the good and simple reason that their respective positions are in large part determined by the existence of a market economy. The least that this means is that 'the producer' is not free *not* to produce (something), the consumer is not free *not* to consume (something); and this in turn must mean that producer and consumer, far from inhabiting separate islands within which their separate decisions hold sway, are in fact linked or joined together by their mutual involvement in the process of exchange, which, again, operates as an exchange mechanism independent of the will of either. The existence of this mechanism means that supply and demand, which Proudhon wished to dismiss as mystifications concealing the existence of value which is constituted by labour (*valeur constituée*), in fact criss-cross and operate in such a way that production and consumption are in a real sense brought together.

Proudhon's contractualism in economic terms entails that it is possible, indeed desirable, to argue from an archetype of simple exchange between two producers to the operation of a complex economic system like capitalism, applying the norms of simple exchange to an advanced and developing system of circulation, with the legal and property relations such a system requires. Marx, on the other hand, believed these norms to be inappropriate to any more developed system by virtue of their static quality, restricted scale and primitivism. More modern forms of property and exchange, as Marx was frequently to reiterate in contexts other than *The Poverty of Philosophy*, can no longer be described as anything like the ideologists' picture of hard won, personally acquired property forming the groundwork of personal freedom and independence as well as the outcome and representation of personal labour. The point is not that it had never existed, but that it had been superseded; kinds of property answering to this description had existed during the 'heroic period' of early capitalist competition, and out of them had emerged property in its more developed forms. In the course of his earlier polemic against Max Stirner in *The German Ideology*, Marx had made a passing comment that was to prove germane to his critique of Proudhon: competition, Marx had written,

> certainly began as a 'competition' of persons possessing 'personal means.' The liberation of the feudal serfs, the first condition of competition, and the first accumulation of 'things' were purely personal acts. If, therefore, Sancho [Stirner] wishes to put the competition of persons in the place of the competition of things [as he did in his 'association' of egoists] it means that he wishes to return to the beginnings of competition. . .[113]

In *The Poverty of Philosophy* we find Marx making very similar claims – that any desire to replace 'competition of things' by 'competition of persons' is, in effect, plainly reactionary. In particular, we find Marx, in *The Poverty of Philosophy* and the *Grundrisse*, following the lines of his earlier criticisms of Proudhon (and Stirner), ridiculing Proudhon's attempt to derive general conclusions about the determination of value in capitalist society from his 'scientific discovery' that overproduction could be deduced from the fact – which Proudhon again termed a 'contradiction' – that under capitalism the labourer could not 'buy back' anything he had produced. This contradiction Proudhon believed was the root of several others. The labourer cannot buy back *his* product; consequently 'labour' (here we have a particularly but characteristically slippery transition) is systematically deprived of disposition over *its* product – a contradiction that in its turn leads into the lack of 'equilibrium' that characterizes the 'proprietory' economy from bottom to top. The entire economic system is permanently and progressively de-equilibrating, although the process can be checked at the level of its root cause.

But according to Marx the spinning of such webs is literally without foundation, since Proudhon's original formulation tells us nothing about the determination of value in the first place. His model for the determination of value is the kind of simple, face-to-face bargain between equal contracting partners, which exists only in Proudhon's fertile imagination. Proudhon believed that since only labour creates value, interest and profit were in the nature of a supplementary charge, the price of any finished product being in this way surcharged over its 'real' value, that is, its *valeur constituée*. Marx argued that this formulation bore no resemblance to anything that actually could be observed to take place and that, *pace* Proudhon, face-to-face bargains provide no actual or workable model for the determination of value in society as a whole.

Producers in capitalist society cannot in Marx's view directly and equally exchange the products of their labour *as individuals* for the very good reason that their labour itself is effectively socialized by the process of production. What this means is that capital cannot be said to confront 'the individual' *qua* individual at all.

> Already the fact that it is *labour* that confronts capital as
> subject i.e. the worker only in his character as *labour* and not
> *he himself*, should open the eyes. This alone, disregarding
> capital, already contains a relation, a relation of the worker
> to his own activity which is by no means the 'natural' one,
> but which itself already contains a specific economic
> character.[114]

Capitalist society in Marx's view – and here his critique of Proudhon comes together with that of Stirner – cannot be said to comprise individuals *qua* individuals (either in the morally elevated way Proudhon saw them or in the morally bereft way Stirner had envisaged them) at all. It is composed of conditions and relationships of such a kind, and in such a way, that the true congruence of individual and society has yet to come about. What counts is not the individual as such, but his roles; because Proudhon overlooked the real conditions of exchange, he failed to recognize that the individuals he valued, and their work (which he also valued, without examining what had happened to it), were in fact inert, atomized and bounded. People are not free agents, as they were in the lore of the political economy that Proudhon takes over so uncritically, but persons distinguishable only by the roles they occupy, roles determined by the existence and operation of the market economy. These persons are, according to Marx, linked, but only by their mutual involvement in the exchange mechanism, a social process operating without regard to them as individuals, independently of their wills.

Marx accordingly believes that Proudhon 'carries abstraction to the furthest limits when he fuses all producers into *one single* producer, all consumers into *one single* consumer, and sets up a struggle between these two chimerical personages'.[115] Proudhon's foray into the realm of political economy results in

> the substitution for use value and exchange value, for supply and demand, of abstract and contradictory notions like scarcity and abundance, utility and estimation, one producer and one consumer, both of them *knights of free will.*[116]

Nor is this all. Marx went on to point out that Proudhon, speaking as he did of the labourer's 'right' to the product of his labour (and indeed making it a linch-pin of his entire system), was blithely engaged in applying moral categories and solutions to economic problems and relationships. This mode of procedure Marx, for all the undoubted force of his own moral indignation, considered quite unacceptable. Proudhon wished to eliminate social antagonism in a non-violent, non-revolutionary manner by replacing wage-slavery with a system based directly on the labour that went into the commodity, on its *valeur constituée*. The problem here resides in how this value is to be determined, estimated and measured. The measure or yardstick would have to be quantitative, thus, making possible comparison between one good and another; and labour is most readily measured, as all the political economists were aware, along the axis of time. From this, Proudhon derives his 'formula for the future', that goods shall be exchanged according to the labour-time embodied in them. Unfortunately, however, Ricardo, whom Proudhon had read (and criticized), had arrived at the same position by taking a different route. That goods exchange in proportion to the labour-time embodied in them (or according to what Proudhon termed their *valeur constituée*) was to Ricardo, moreover, not a prescription for a more golden future, but a straightforward description of what was actually taking place in the present – on the assumption, of course, of the validity of the labour theory of value.

Marx, for his part, readily accepted Ricardo's belief that products under capitalist conditions already exchange at prices proportionate to their values. The outcome of the process of exchange, thus defined, is not, to be sure, Proudhon's projected society of equals but instead the perpetuation of inequality; and there is a good reason why this is so. What Proudhon overlooks, according to Marx, is something very basic indeed; that the labour theory of value *applies to labour itself*, that in a capitalist system of commodity production labour itself is produced and reproduced as a commodity. It is valued and paid for like other commodities, as one commodity among others; it is measured along the same scale as they are; and this comparability, indeed, is a defining and distinguishing feature of wage-labour in capitalist society. Marx in putting it forward was, at one level, re-stating, in more strictly economic language, an important implication of his earlier discussion of the division of labour in *The German Ideology*, a discussion we have already encountered; but there is at another level a pointedness to his invocation of wage-labour as a commodity *against Proudhon*.

The application of the labour theory of value to labour itself means that it is not the value he *produces* but the value he *costs* that is the worker's 'due', all to which he can be said to have a 'right', under capitalist conditions, because under these conditions value is arrived at *socially*, and not, *pace* Proudhon, at the level of the individual worker. Value is expressed, in other words, not according to the number of hours expended by the *individual* producer but in terms of *socially* necessary labour-time (that is, of how long it would take an average producer to produce a commodity of a certain type, under normal – that is, average under capitalism – conditions). To express value in individual terms, after all, would make calculability unwieldy. If the labourer's value is thus defined, if his value is simply the cost of his labour with respect to socially necessary labour-time, as capitalists compute (and must compute) it, then the worker actually receives his value. The capitalist has the worker exceed his value, or produce more than he costs; the employer, to put the same point another way, proceeds to use the labourer to produce *surplus*-value, the excess being over the level of subsistence at which (give or take a few notches) the worker is remunerated.

Proudhon's fundamental error was to have confused two quite dissimilar things: the value of labour and the quantity of labour embodied in the finished product. The value of labour, as this is necessarily computed under capitalist conditions, is quite simply the price that labour commands in the market, its wage-level. This price, being determined (like all prices) by competition, will tend, *ceteris paribus*, towards the minimum permissible. Just as the price of all commodities is determined by the cost of their production, the labourer gets in wages what it costs to 'produce' him, what it costs to maintain him as a labourer capable of reproducing others of his kind.

> To put the cost of manufacture of hats and the cost of maintenance of men on the same plane is to turn men into hats. But do not make an outcry of the cynicism of it. The cynicism is in the facts and not in the words which express the facts.[117]

This position vindicates not Proudhon but Ricardo.

> Ricardo shows us the real movement of bourgeois production, which constitutes value. M. Proudhon, leaving this real movement out of account, 'fumes and frets' in order to invent new processes

and to achieve the reorganization of the world on a would-be
new formula, which formula is no more than the theoretical
expression of the real movement which exists and which is so
well described by Ricardo. Ricardo takes his starting point from
present-day society to demonstrate to us how it constitutes
value – M. Proudhon takes constituted value as his starting point
to construct a new social world with the aid of this value. For
him, M. Proudhon, constituted value must move around and
become once more the constituting factor of a world already
completely constituted according to this mode of evaluation. . .
Ricardo's theory of values is the scientific interpretation of
actual economic life; M. Proudhon's theory of values is the
utopian interpretation of Ricardo's theory.[118]

If the worker actually *receives* his value, his cost in terms of socially
necessary labour-time, under the capitalist wage-contract, if in other
words everything does exchange at its value, as this value must necessarily be computed under the prevailing system, then the system is not
unjust according to its own lights. The corollary of this belief is that
the rules that can be shown to be appropriate to capitalism are in and
by this very congruence inappropriate to any other social form. Proudhon, by contrast, believed that it was both possible and desirable to
take hold of concepts that are appropriate to capitalist society, turn
them round, and derive (or extract) socialist conclusions from them,
even though more rigorous classical political economists like Ricardo
had entertained such concepts as the labour theory of value without
deriving from them a single radical prescription.

Marx's conviction that the concepts of political economy, as they
had evolved alongside capitalist society, were appropriate to capitalist
society and capitalist society alone amounts to a recognition that
political economy, for all its undoubted insights into an historically
specific reality, is by the same token in no way a politically 'neutral'
discipline – a mode of enquiry, that is, that could be used or made to
yield socialist conclusions from liberal-bourgeois premises. Marx's
lifelong 'critique of political economy' (in which *The Poverty of
Philosophy* occupies a prominent position) should be seen as being
devoted to the propagation of the very opposite belief – that capitalism and political economy stand, or fall, together. This belief separates
Marx's thought not only from that of Proudhon (and the 'Ricardian
socialists' like John Bray whom Marx criticizes in similar terms in
The Poverty of Philosophy) but also from Rodbertus and Lassalle;
for all these theorists (Lassalle being very much more than a theorist,
as we shall see) believed in their various ways that it was both possible
and desirable to utilize or harness the new science of economics directly
in the service of the labour movement. Seen in this way Marx's argument

against Proudhon is very much a *political* argument, with *political* stakes; and, as such, it is strikingly similar to his later arguments in *The Critique of the Gotha Programme* against the German Workers' Party, which even in its inception bore the impress of Lassalle, for having taken certain present-day social and economic forms as absolute, for having abstracted them from their own process of historical development, and for having derived from these perversely misconceived abstractions various trans-historical prescriptions for action.

Marx's position was very different, and his successive criticisms of Proudhon do much to show us the reason why. The emancipation of the proletariat, to be genuine, must involve *inter alia* its emancipation from the categories of bourgeois thought, categories that can mystify and obscure that which they purport to explain, categories that can fatally mislead and bamboozle the intrepid critic no less than the shameless apologist, the expert as well as the novice.

Marx never denied that these categories in and of themselves embodied a certain descriptive force, so long as capitalist society persisted; but he consistently argued against their application, across the board, to any other social form. It is because he fails to escape their stranglehold that Proudhon's 'solution' that was to bring about a better society was no more than one of the worst features of established society warmed over. That Ricardo's perception of the equal exchange of labour-values can fatally mislead is brought out in *The Poverty of Philosophy*, not least in a passage which, though it is directly pointed at John Bray, was intended to include in its purview Proudhon.

> Mr. Bray does not realize that this egalitarian relationship, this corrective ideal which he wants to apply to the world is nothing but the reflex of the real world, and that in consequence it is altogether impossible to reconstitute society upon a basis which is merely its own embellished shadow. In the measure that this shade takes on corporeal substance, one perceives that this body, far from being the dreamed-of transfiguration, is the actual body of society.

According to Marx, '[in] a purified individual exchange, freed from all the elements of antagonism [Bray] finds in it, he sees an "equalitarian" relation which he would like society to adopt generally'. The trouble is that, again according to Marx, '[there] is no individual exchange without the antagonism of classes'.[119] In the course of one of his discussions of Proudhon in the *Grundrisse*, Marx points to

> the foolishness of those socialists (namely the French, who want to depict socialism as the realization of the ideals of *bourgeois* society articulated by the French revolution) who demonstrate

that exchange and exchange value etc. are *originally* (in time) or *essentially* (in their adequate form) a system of universal freedom and equality, but that they have been perverted by money, capital, etc. Or, also, that history has so far failed in every attempt to implement them in their true manner, but that they have now, like Proudhon discovered e.g. the real Jacob, and intend now to supply the genuine history of these relations in place of the fake. The proper reply to them is: that exchange value, or, more precisely, the money system is in fact the system of equality and freedom, and that the disturbances which they encounter in the further development of the system are disturbances inherent in it, are merely the realization of *equality and freedom*, which prove to be inequality and unfreedom. It is just as pious as it is stupid to wish that exchange-value would not develop into capital, nor labour which produces exchange value into wage labour. What divides these gentlemen from the bourgeois apologists is, on one side, their sensitivity to the contradictions included in the system; on the other, the utopian inability to grasp the necessary difference between the real and the ideal form of bourgeois society, which is the cause of their desire to undertake the superfluous business of realizing the ideal expression again, which is in fact only the inverted projection [Lichtbild] of this reality.[120]

One of the striking features of this passage is its parallelism with some passages in Marx's essay, written some sixteen years earlier, 'On the Jewish Question'. That Marx in this passage castigates the depiction by Proudhon and others of 'socialism as the realization of the ideals of bourgeois society articulated by the French revolution', and pinpoints the ideals in question as 'equality and freedom', indicates not just a parallelism but an overlap. Freedom and equality are situated in the penumbra of 'political emancipation' and 'political economy'; it is an important feature of 'political emancipation' and 'political economy' alike that men be, formally and in principle, free and equal. That this is freedom to buy and sell and otherwise contract with one another, freedom at the level of abstract citizenship, and equality of a similarly abstract kind means, of course, that these characteristics turn into their opposites, 'inequality and unfreedom'; but this happens not because the original promise they once embodied has been eroded and abandoned but because this promise depends for its fulfilment on the overcoming of 'political emancipation' and 'political economy'. Its substantiation, in other words, exists not in an imagined past but in a future that has to be worked for and brought about, a future in which political will have given way to human emancipation and political economy to the abolition of the class antagonism that is its current matrix. In the meantime, as Marx was to reiterate with a remarkable frequency, political emancipation and political economy alike can, and are likely to, mislead the unwary; an 'inability to grasp the necessary difference between the real and ideal form of bourgeois society' was to afflict Lassalle as well as Proudhon. The fundamental point Marx makes against Proudhon, that reform of capitalism, involving an implicit acceptance of some of its rules and norms, does not amount to emancipation but may distract us from the task of emancipation, is a point that has a certain applicability to Lassalle's reform from above as well as Proudhon's reform from below. The importance of this point is about to become apparent.

The politics of anti-politics

And then the revolution, the Republic, and socialism, one
supporting the other, came with a bound. I saw them; I felt
them; and I fled before this democratic and social monster. . .
An inexpressible terror froze my soul, obliterating my very
thoughts. I denounced still more the revolutionists whom I
beheld pulling up the foundations of society with incredible
fury. . . No one understood me. . .

Proudhon[121]

What baseness would you not commit to root out baseness?

Bertolt Brecht, *The Measures Taken*

Make Proudhon a Minister of Finance, a President – he will
become a sort of inverted Bonaparte.

Alexander Herzen[122]

In January 1865, immediately after the death of Proudhon, Johann Baptist von Schweitzer wrote to Marx asking him for 'a detailed judgment of Proudhon'. Marx was quick to compose in reply what he claimed was not the detailed judgment requested: 'Lack of time prevents me from fulfilling your desire. Added to which I have none of his works to hand. However, in order to assure you of my good will I am hastily jotting down a brief sketch', an unflattering sketch of some nine pages which Marx sent to Schweitzer apparently by return of post. There was more than one immediate reason for Marx's evident haste, as we shall see; but not the least important of these reasons was that Schweitzer had written in his capacity as editor of the *Sozial-Demokrat*, the organ of the Lassallean political party in

Prissoa - the General German Workers' Association or Allgemeiner Deutscher Arbeiterverein (ADA). Marx in his reply took care to allow for the publication of his letter, a letter which shows every sign of careful composition, for reasons that will shortly become apparent. 'You can complete it, add to it or cut it,' said Marx, 'in short, do anything you like with it'; he added to its ultimate paragraph the closing words, 'And now you must take upon yourself the responsibility of having imposed upon me the role of this man's judge so soon after his death.' Marx's letter was indeed judgmental, and any 'good will' it displays stops well short of anything that is recognizable as respect for the memory of Proudhon - about whose passing Marx seems not to have been overcome by grief. In the event, Schweitzer published Marx's letter in its entirety, as Marx no doubt anticipated he would, and added in an editorial note that 'we considered it best to give the article unaltered'. The letter, now article, gained some unsurprising notoriety in the International as well as in France and Germany, as Marx presumably intended that it should; it was republished as an appendix to the first German edition of *The Poverty of Philosophy* in 1884 (the year after Marx's death), Engels's introduction to which is at pains to emphasize that the 'obituary' 'was the only article Marx wrote for [Schweitzer's] paper'.[123]

The 'obituary' itself is on the face of it a summary and recapitulation of Marx's earlier arguments against Proudhon, unleavened by any kind words except those describing *What is Property?* Even these are under-cut by Marx's insistence that the style of Proudhon's only good book is its 'chief merit'. It is as though Proudhon's death were insufficient to satisfy Marx, who proceeds in short order to rub salt into the wounds he himself had caused with the 'cane' (*férule*) of his earlier criticism. Marx includes in his 'obituary' notice the following morsel from *The Poverty of Philosophy*:

> M. Proudhon flatters himself on having given a criticism of both
> political economy and communism: he is beneath them both.
> Beneath the economists, since, as a philosopher who had at his
> elbow a magic formula, he thought he could dispense with
> going into purely economic details; beneath the socialists,
> because he has neither courage enough nor insight enough to
> rise, be it even speculatively, above the bourgeois horizon. . .
>   He wants to soar as the man of science above the bourgeoisie
> and the proletarians; he is merely the petty-bourgeois, continually
> tossed back and forth between capital and labour, political
> economy and communism.

'Severe though the above judgement sounds', Marx adds in 1865, 'I must still endorse every word of it today.' (The words dropped in the ellipsis are: 'He wants to be the synthesis: he is a composite error.' Let he take comfort who can.)[124] Indeed, Marx adds to his already formidable battery of criticisms two more, which, while they are familiar enough to those who have perused his earlier attacks, might here be singled out for some special attention, since in the context of the 1865 letter they have a significance that goes beyond Proudhon; they concern Proudhon's idea of science, and his class background as a 'petty bourgeois'.

To begin with, Proudhon's 'dialectics' are once more paraded as being 'unscientific':

> he and the other utopians are hunting for a so-called 'science' by which a formula for the 'solution of the social question' might be excogitated *a priori*, instead of deriving their science from a critical knowledge of the historical movement . . . He even tries to use the utopian interpretation of Ricardo's theory of value as the basis of a new science.

In *The System of Economic Contradictions*, Marx goes on, 'the twaddle about "science," and sham display of it, which are always so unedifying, are continually screaming in one's ears'. Proudhon is 'a *parvenu* of science',[125] a point which once again is directed ostensibly against Proudhon but also – and not at all 'between the lines' of what was, after all, a Lassallean publication – at others. This is not the place to expound at any length upon Marx's differences from Proudhon (or Lassalle) on the subject of science, except to note in passing that Marx's concept of science embodied what was at least a claim not to reduce 'science' to a formulaic or abstractly 'systems-binding' enterprise. The problematic paragraph in *The Poverty of Philosophy* that comes immediately before the ones Marx quotes in his 1865 letter does something to tell us why:

> Just as the economists are the scientific representatives of the bourgeois class, so the Socialists and the Communists are the theoreticians of the proletarian class. So long as the proletariat is not yet sufficiently developed to constitute itself as a class, and consequently so long as the struggle of the proletariat with the bourgeoisie has not yet assumed a political character, and the productive forces are not yet sufficiently developed in the bosom of the bourgeoisie to enable us to catch a glimpse of the material conditions necessary for the emancipation of the proletariat and for the formation of a new society, these theoreticians are merely utopians who, to meet the wants of the oppressed classes, improvise systems and go in search of a regenerating science.

But in the measure that history moves forward, and with it the struggle of the proletariat assumes clearer outlines, they no longer need to seek science in their minds; they have only to take note of what is happening before their eyes and to become its mouthpiece. So long as they look for science and merely make systems, so long as they are at the beginning of the struggle, they see in poverty nothing but poverty, without seeing in it the revolutionary, subversive side, which will overthrow the old society. From this moment, science, which is a product of the historical movement, has associated itself consciously with it, has ceased to be doctrinaire and has become revolutionary.[126]

Yet, as Marx's description of Proudhon as 'the *parvenu* of science' might serve to remind us, what lies behind (and to some extent, according to Marx, explains) Proudhon's charlatanry in science, as in much else, is the confusion of the social class to which he belonged: the petty bourgeoisie. We shall have occasion to deal firmly with this accusation in due course; what concerns us more immediately is the *political* reference Marx gives to his accusations, since it is this that enables us to put all the pieces together in the rather important puzzle with which Marx's 'obituary' of Proudhon presents us. Let us look at what Marx says in 1865:

The petty bourgeois is composed of On The One Hand and On The Other Hand. This is so in his economic interests and *therefore* in his politics. . . He is a living contradiction. If, like Proudhon, he is in addition, a gifted man, he will soon learn to play with his own contradictions and develop them according to circumstances into striking, ostentatious, now scandalous, or now brilliant paradoxes. Charlatanism in economics and accommodation in politics are inseparable from such a point of view. There only remains one governing motive, the vanity of the subject, and the only question for him, as for all vain people, is the success of the moment, the attention of the day. Thus the simple moral sense, which always kept a Rousseau, for instance, far from even the semblance of compromise with the powers that be, is necessarily extinguished.[127]

We need to pay close attention to Marx's words here, since, appearing as they did in a Lassallean publication, they embody - not very far below the surface - a sub-text. On the face of it Marx is quite simply reminding his readers of Proudhon's ignoble coquetry with Louis (and Jérôme) Bonaparte.

His work on the *coup d'état*, in which he flirts with Louis
Bonaparte and in fact strives to make him palatable to French
workers, and his last work, written against Poland, in which for
the greater glory of the Tsar he expresses the cynicism of a
cretin, must be characterized as not merely bad but base
productions; of a baseness which corresponds, however, to
the petty-bourgeois point of view.[128]

The point here is not merely that this enables Marx to adopt a patron-
izing stance (though of course it does: 'even later on I never joined in
the outcry about his "treachery" to the revolution. It was not his
fault that, originally misunderstood by others as well as by himself,
he failed to fulfil unjustified hopes');[129] the point is, throughout these
accusations Marx is implying that Proudhon, because of his petty
bourgeois leanings, had a tendency to wish to resort to authoritarian
solutions. Marx here is doing more than replying in kind to Proudhon's
anti-communism. We need only look at the date of his obituary to
recognize that several of Marx's comments about Proudhon have a
more than passing reference to Lassalle.[130] Indeed many of these
comments – that he was a 'living contradiction' in morals, that he was
governed by vanity, 'and the only question for him, as for all vain
people, is the success of the moment, the sensation of the day' – might
seem puzzling unless we remember that it was Lassalle (to whom these
characterizations apply much more nearly) that Marx also had in his
sights.

The parallels between Proudhon and Lassalle should not be exaggerated, but should be pursued. Lassalle had died some three months
before the death of Proudhon, in 1864 (the year of the founding of the
International). Like Proudhon, he had attracted the kind of mass
personal following that showed some signs of becoming a posthumous
personality cult, and that Marx and others considered dangerous to
the working-class movement in general and to the nascent International
in particular. Lassalle, like Proudhon, had been mesmerized by economic
science and had succeeded to a considerable extent in fixing upon his
followers a belief in the possibility and desirability of harnessing the
new science of economics (which, he believed, could be made to yield
'proletarian' conclusions) directly to the service of the working-class
movement. Most pointedly of all, Lassalle, like Proudhon, because
of his charlatanry in science, was, according to Marx, an accommodator
in politics; because neither had superseded the categories of political
economy (which they accepted uncritically as a set of formulaic propositions owing nothing to the context of the society to which they
had proved themselves appropriate), Lassalle, like Proudhon, believed
these categories could be put to direct use by the workers' movement,
even at the cost of an alliance with autocratic, reactionary forces

against democratic and liberal forces. As far as Marx was concerned, this meant that Lassalle and Proudhon, lacking as they did a sense of economic realities, lacked by the same token a sense of the most basic political realities.

Marx in January 1865, the date of his obituary of Proudhon, had just received, from Wilhelm Liebknecht, confirmation of his suspicions that Lassalle was 'the Richelieu of the proletariat'. Liebknecht had just exposed Lassalle's schemes to sell out the ADA to the Prussian government. As a *Realpolitiker*, as Marx was to describe Lassalle to Kugelmann the following month, Lassalle had believed he could compromise the integrity of the movement he led, as well as his own, by dealing with Bismarck.[131] We need not to go into the tawdry details of Lassalle's absurd treachery – there is no reason to believe that Bismarck took this self-styled *Realpolitiker* seriously – to see that his shade lurks uneasily in Marx's 'obituary' of Proudhon, and that this memorial notice has a wider range than might seem apparent on an innocent first reading.

It is important that we recognize that Marx's accusation – a dual accusation, in effect – involved an issue of principle. Proudhon and Lassalle had not suffered momentary lapses; in neither case was the alliance with the forces of the right favoured as a purely hypothetical contingency; both Proudhon and Lassalle had actually initiated contact with the autocratic forces that held power in their respective countries. Proudhon, admittedly, after much soul searching,[132] had chosen to suspend his principle of political abstentionism (not, it is true, for the first time) and to ally not with liberal, democratic and socialist forces but instead to coquet with Louis and Jérôme Bonaparte. Not only did he actively seek support for his credit schemes and people's bank from these tainted hands, he also wrote a book putting forward a (limited) defence of Bonaparte's *coup d'état*.[133] In neither case did he receive anything in return for his pains. Lassalle, in return for what he fondly imagined would be state support of a limited kind for the co-operative movement, and in return for mumblings about universal suffrage, had been prepared to approach Bismarck. The details of the initiatives of Proudhon and Lassalle remain obscure and debated; we have no way of knowing how far either of them would have gone down the primrose path of collaboration, because in the event neither of them was granted the opportunity to find out. But we do know why Marx thought their actions unprincipled and unconscionable, why he thought they should never have set foot on so slippery a slope in the first place.

First of all, however, Proudhon's motivations need to be examined. He believed, as we have seen, that to act as a class, to *become* a class, workers had to secede from bourgeois democracy, its trappings and its temptations, in the name and under the banner of proletarian autonomy, *le séparatisme ouvrier*. He believed that politics was a form of indulgence and a source of contamination, and his own faintly bizarre experiences in the National Assembly did nothing to alter his views. (In 1848, as a member of the National Assembly – the 'Parliamentary Sinai', as he called it in his subsequent *Confessions* – Proudhon, who was expected to be on the socialist left with Ledru-Rollin and Louis Blanc, not least by those who elected him, astonished his associates by voting with the right against the constitution of the Second Republic, on the grounds that he did not believe in constitutions!)[134] Proudhon continued to believe that 'to indulge in politics is to wash one's hands in dung'. Political action is to be adjured in principle by the workers' movement; the measures to be taken are to be economic and social and quite unsullied by politics. Action might in this way be circumscribed in its scope and scale, but no matter: it will at least remain uncontaminated, its purity preserved. Yet neither this position, nor indeed the standard (and by no means exclusively Marxist) objection to it – that 'clean hands' might mean 'no hands' – explains why Proudhon chose to suspend his insistence on politically clean hands not in aid of French socialists and democrats (all of whom Proudhon continued after 1848 to attack for various reasons) but by playing court to Louis Napoleon. Yet if it is the case – as it was according to Marx – that Proudhon's unrequited courtship of Louis Napoleon prefigures nothing so much as Lassalle's approaches to Bismarck, some explanation is necessary.

Proudhon's repeated denigrations of the political realm bear all the hallmarks not just of intense distaste but of obsession; and obsessiveness about political power can in and of itself have untoward results. '[The] danger of any fundamentally anarchist position', it has been pointed out, is that 'when one is disgusted by any and all government, whatever its forms, one finishes by losing sight of certain elementary political realities'.[135] What this statement means is that the anarchist fails to see that there are sides and positions in politics, or that he fails to make distinctions or to discriminate among these positions because as an anarchist he feels no need to choose among them. The statement is thus of little use if it is applied to Proudhon who, after all, *did* discriminate and was in no way reluctant to specify his grounds for doing so; his opponents on the left knew this as well as Proudhon himself did. It is thus possible for us to be more precise.

It may be true that Proudhon's inability to regard political power in any but institutional, oppressive and contaminatory terms, his tendency to see the *fonctionnaire*, whatever his colours, as the main enemy, his disgust with bourgeois liberalism and the 'lottery' of parliamentarism – that all these brought Proudhon perilously close to favouring alliance with autocracy. Yet normally these characteristics – which were, we should remember, constant features of his thought – did not push him over the brink. What did so was the Revolution of 1848. Proudhon's particular scorn and wrath were henceforward directed against those he singled out as the betrayers of the Revolution – the revolutionary politicians of the Left, who had sold it out. Proudhon fastened upon revolutionary politicians for two main reasons. The first is that they were revolutionaries – prepared, that is, to countenance the violence from which Proudhon recoiled. (The events of 1848 caused him shudders of horror for years afterwards; the thought that he may have contributed to the violence by his own admission provoked in him the intensest feelings of guilt.) The second reason is that revolutionary politicians by the nature of their craft – the double meaning is intended – were deceptive, their ideals insidious. Proudhon, like most French radicals of his generation, had an acute sense of the Revolution (that of 1789 as well as 1848) betrayed; he differed from his contemporaries only in thinking that revolutionary violence, and the dishonesty of those professing it, were the agencies of its betrayal. Indeed, they would continue to betray revolutionary ideals unless their sclerotic progress could be halted by the influence of people like Proudhon himself, the living embodiment of the ideals of the Revolution. Revolutionary violence on this view of it pretends to emancipate the powerless; by virtue of the illusions its practitioners generate, it garners and marshals support among the deluded masses, goaded as they are by impatience and despair. These, for want of anywhere else to turn, put their lives on the line. Revolutionary movements that espouse violence are responsible for their fate. If the movements fail it is they who pay, with their lives, victims to the sacrificial process that claimed it could emancipate them; if they succeed, then like all political movements they turn around in their new-found mantle of the *régime* and enslave those on whom their success has depended.

Proudhon had a tremendous – indeed to all appearances limitless – capacity for moral outrage. But it is moral outrage of the kind that is most particularly incensed not at the persistence of outright evil (to which, in a way, it gets inured) but at hypocrisy – in this case at the gall of the self-styled 'liberators of humanity' who would, given half a chance, enslave mankind. Proudhon's avalanche of indignation and outrage found its readiest expression in the paradoxes and ironies that resound through his writings, but it also emerged, less obviously but no less forcefully, in his scorn for those masters of deceit, the revolutionary politicians who, he knew, would delude and sacrifice those innocent enough to take them seriously. The sincerity of their professions of concern is belied at every step by the outcome of their actions. That revolutionary politicians in particular by their very nature are deceptive, insidious, slippery, volatile and untrustworthy has as its corollary what amounts in Proudhon's case to a curious reversal or about-face; for these claims can slide over almost imperceptibly into the proposition that the revolutionary Left is by its very nature unprincipled and lacking in a stable set of values. To admit this is to be ready for the fatal next step, which is to think that those on the Right, by contrast, may be utterly unscrupulous but will nevertheless be predictable and consistent in their unscrupulousness. This means that they cannot deceive us in quite the same way; we know, we can have no illusions about where they stand; with them, at least, we know where *we* stand. These, after all, are people who are used to the exercise and the 'realities' of power; in their way, they are dependable and much less likely than the un-principled Left to lead us astray. Better, after all, perhaps, the devil you know...

It is important that we recognize at this juncture how deep-seated the opposition between Marx and Proudhon is on this point. While Proudhon always considered political power in institutional terms, as an evil that is to be (normally) shunned, and always considered demo-cracy and universal suffrage as *une vraie lotterie*, Marx did not. As Shlomo Avineri has recently reminded us,

> Marx with all his critique of bourgeois liberalism, always
> supports political liberalism against the traditional Right, not
> because of any deterministic attitude which sees history as
> moving constantly 'leftward' but for completely different
> reasons... For Marx, socialism grows out of the contradictions
> inherent in bourgeois society and political liberalism. A socialism
> that would grow, like Lassallean socialism, out of an alliance
> with the Right after both have overthrown political liberalism,
> will necessarily carry with it some of the characteristics of its
> authoritarian ally.[136]

Marx, that is to say, supported political liberalism not grudgingly but reservedly for a straightforward reason that far outweighed any desire he might have had to polarize society into two hostile, irrevocably antagonistic camps. To say, with Avineri, that socialism in Marx's view grows out of the contradictions that are inherent in its direct, proximate precursor, or to say in the words of Maximilien Rubel's arresting (but exaggerated) paradox that 'Marx was a revolutionary communist only in theory, while he was a bourgeois democrat in practice'[137] is to say that 'human emancipation', to employ once again the vocabulary of 'On the Jewish Question', presupposes 'political emancipation', which informs and *should* inform it in advance. The Lassallean-Proudhonian tactic of destroying bourgeois society and liberal democracy with the aid of an autocratic state (aid which would not be given freely) would necessarily have socialism carry with it into the future some of the characteristics of its authoritarian ally so that society would become a reactionary utopia[138] instead of what Marx wanted it to become, and thought it would become.

The dispute between Marx and Proudhon is at one level about 'reform versus revolution', between amelioration of a gradualist kind and wholesale revolutionary emancipation. Proudhon was exclusively and quite sincerely interested in discovering ways to ameliorate 'la condition physique, morale et intellectuelle de la classe la plus nombreuse et la plus pauvre' (as he put it in his covering letter to the Besançon Academy introducing *What is Property?*). Marx by contrast was concerned (if we may play upon the German title of his 'Anti-Proudhon') not with *Elend* but with *Verelendung*; and the difference goes much deeper. Proudhon envisaged low-level social and economic measures of a peaceable, non-drastic and decentralized kind which, he thought, could be so organized that the negative (though not the positive) features of a social system he found morally contradictory could be progressively eliminated and undercut. Marx's argument has to it an altogether different directionality. He would say that Proudhon dissolves the possibility of political (not instead of but *as well as* economic and social) action into utopian economics. Marx himself was concerned to apply economic analysis as the theoretical basis of an envisaged *political* action; and as István Mézáros has pointed out,[139] the very language Marx uses is significant. While he employed economic categories in the analysis of the existing social forms of productive activity, Marx, whenever he discussed the supersession of these forms used specifically *political* terms – liberation, emancipation, *Gemeinschaft* – all of which have a non-corporative, non-nostalgic, forward-looking application. More is involved here than the undoubted stasis and austerity of Proudhon's utopia, since, as we have seen in our examination of 'alien politics', from Marx's point of view the anarchy of Proudhon and the autocracy implicit in Bauer, Lassalle and others are opposite sides of the same coin. Each in its own way maximizes alienation, while the point is to abolish it. Marx pressed for neither the externality of all norms and sanctions, nor for their outright abolition; he stood for the programme we can trace back to 'On the Jewish Question', that of the positive reintegration of all norms and sanctions into human life as a reassertion of conscious social control by men over their own activity and creations which, in becoming alien and external, had escaped men's control. Men under capitalism are dominated by needs that are external to them, by alien requirements which coerce while (and because) they do not express. Proudhon was aware of certain features of what was, to Marx also, a systematic process, but in seeing symptoms in terms of other symptoms, he could not but fail, according to Marx, to diagnose the disease or prescribe the correct remedy. Proudhon saw freedom and authority as opposites, utterly inimical one to the other, and this, finally, was the rock against which all his various attempts to reconcile anarchy and order foundered.

That the difference between Marx and Proudhon is, *inter alia*, a difference between expansiveness and restrictiveness can be seen if we turn, by way of conclusion, to a brief recapitulation of some of Proudhon's economic assumptions.

According to Proudhon's economic theory, nothing has value that is not the outcome of the individual's own work, the work of the producer's own hands. Accordingly, no participant in the economy should be able to get out of the process of circulation more, or much more, than he put into it; this rough and ready equality is to be the basis and outcome of Proudhon's contract, which is there to regulate the exchange of goods of equal value. This can mean only that Proudhon, in seeking a measure of value that would be independent of supply and demand, was looking for a *stable, underlying proportional relation* which the prices of commodities would necessarily express. He also believed that he had found it. His proposal to establish direct relations among producers based on the immediate exchange of equivalent amounts of labour-time in order to assure workers of the full value of their work presupposes its discovery. But in what can it consist? It can only resolve itself into a kind of *juste milieu*, a golden mean, a principle of proportionality or equilibrium between needs and resources; and this equilibrium would have to be something that always needs restoring. The eminently restorative nature of this ideal means that what lies behind Proudhon's economic theory is not only a notion of the inelasticity of wealth but also a real stasis. Proudhon's utopia would be a static and austere place to live. He has no notion of production as being in any way expansive; the constitutive power he ascribes to labour is thus *re*constitutive and restorative. Labour can be ennobling and uplifting if and only if it is kept within very strict bounds; in particular, labour has nothing to do with the creation and satisfaction of new needs, which to Marx, after all, was its defining feature – albeit one that is denied and subverted by capitalism. Yet Proudhon had no real conception of alienation in the labour process; while Marx considered that under capitalism 'labour is only an expression of human activity within alienation, of expressing one's life by alienating it ['Lebensäusserung als Lebensentäusserung']',[140] this conception would have been unwelcome, if not actually inconceivable, to Proudhon, to whom all labour, in all circumstances (not excluding those of capitalism), embodied and expressed something ennobling and regenerative. Marx considered that Proudhon had extended a basically moral, and indeed rather poetic, vision of labour into his economic theory, with fatal results:

> The surplus-value which causes all Ricardians and anti-Ricardians so much worry is solved by this fearless thinker simply by mystifying it. . . . The fact that actual work goes beyond necessary labour is transformed by Proudhon into a mystical quality of labour.[141]

Yet Proudhon's conception of labour does more than simply vitiate his economic analysis, since it was, as we have seen, also the basis for the centrality of 'autonomous' working-class organization in his thought. Here too there are differences of some substance from Marx, whose conception of productive labour does not involve the rehabilitation of the labouring class *by means of work* in anything like Proudhon's sense. The issue is an important one, since Proudhon's concept of autonomous working-class (*ouvriériste*) organization, based squarely on a belief in the redemptive, morally uplifting character of manual labour, stands out historically not by virtue of its incoherence but by virtue of its exraordinarily influential nature. The French anarcho-syndicalists (and by extension revolutionary syndicalists elsewhere) took it over lock, stock and barrel, along with its corollary, political abstentionism; and while this is not the place to enter into the minutiae of the continuity between Proudhonism and anarcho-syndicalism, a continuity that cannot really be doubted, two points do need to be made in passing. First, despite Marx's efforts to discredit Proudhon (or, possibly, partly because of them), France, a country that was familiar with attempts at socialist organization before Marx wrote his first journalistic article, continued to have a socialist tradition that owed little to Marxism, and indeed grew up quite independently of Marxism, until the 1890s; and even then the credentials of a resurgent Marxism were to be challenged, not least by an equally and simultaneously resurgent anarcho-syndicalism. The point here is not only that anarcho-syndicalism owed much more to Proudhon than to Marx; it goes much deeper because the features that were to separate anarcho-syndicalists from Marxists in the 1890s were, *mutatis mutandis*, the very features that had separated Proudhon and Marx in the 1840s.[142] These prominently included autonomous working-class organization, its deliberate separatism on the basis of economic and social counter-institutions from the prevailing system, and a rigid political abstentionism; these in turn were based on an idea of the affirmative quality of labour *per se*, the direct inspiration for which was Proudhon. The ideal of a French working-class movement and consciousness, free from academic orthodoxy and doctrinaire, 'outside' regimentation, creating its own weapons of combat and spontaneously producing its own leaders, suspicious (at times to the point of paranoia) of party creeds and state socialism – this was an ideal above all of authenticity, that indicates the fertility of Proudhon's thought, which was strong enough to penetrate an anarcho-syndicalist movement some of whose features (particularly the notion of the revolutionary general strike and a certain penchant for violence that underlay its profession) would not have commended themselves to Proudhon himself.

This point leads into another. To say that the issues between Marx and Proudhon outlasted their immediate protagonists is to point up the practical resonance of theoretical differences, in this instance differences about how labour in capitalist society is to be appraised. The differences between Marx and Proudhon in this respect run very deep indeed. This is so not only because Marx was concerned, unlike Proudhon, to emphasize the deleterious effects of the division of labour in capitalist society which, as we saw in the last chapter as well as this one, has distinguishing features which do nothing to lend *labour itself* any emancipatory potential. Nor is it simply a matter of Marx's theory of alienation in the labour process and its connection with his theory of value. The differences ultimately reside in *how labour itself is conceptualized* by either theorist. Proudhon, as we have seen, in ascribing constitutive power to labour *per se*, espoused a labour theory of value of a sort which did not rigidly keep apart 'value' in a moral sense and 'value' in an economic sense, so that his economics is vitiated by his moralism. We need to remind ourselves only of Marx's accusations that Proudhon 'abolishes political-economic estrangement within political-economic estrangement' and that 'he does all that a criticism of political economy, from the standpoint of political economy can do'.

Postscript: on the use of the term 'petty bourgeois'

The accusation that Proudhon's various failings (his accommodation in politics, the drawbacks of his economic theories) can be attributed to his 'petty bourgeois' background, interests or mentality is a *Leitmotiv* of Marx's successive attacks on him; and the question that remains to be dealt with is not so much what kind of accusation or attribution this is, but whether it can properly be said to be an attribution at all. Let us take some illustrative examples. In his letter to Annenkov of 1846, Marx not only describes Proudhon's 'petty-bourgeois sentimentality' as consisting in his 'declamations about home, conjugal love and all such banalities'. He goes further.

> From head to foot M. Proudhon is the philosopher and
> economist of the petty bourgeoisie. In an advanced society
> the petty bourgeois is necessarily from his very position a
> socialist on the one side and an economist on the other; that
> is to say, he is dazed by the magnificence of the big bourgeoisie
> and has sympathy for the sufferings of the people. Deep down
> in his heart he flatters himself that he is impartial and has
> found the right equilibrium, which claims to be something
> different from mediocrity. A petty bourgeois of this type
> glorifies contradiction because contradiction is the basis of his
> existence. He is himself nothing but social contradiction in
> action. He must justify in theory what he is in practice, and

> M. Proudhon has the merit [das Verdienst] of being the
> scientific interpreter of the French petty bourgeoisie – a
> genuine merit, because the petty bourgeoisie will form an
> integral part of the impending social revolutions.[143]

The timely admission contained in the last sentence is conspicious by
its absence from Marx's later characterizations of Proudhon as a petty
bourgeois, characterizations which do not 'merit' Proudhon with anything. Later, Proudhon's specific arguments are dismissed in shorthand
form, at least to Marx's satisfaction, by the simple device of attaching
what to Marx was the unflattering adjective 'petty bourgeois' to them.
Thus, for instance, the 1865 'obituary': 'to regard interest-bearing
capital as the main form of capital, while trying to use a special form of
credit, the alleged abolition of interest, as the basis for a transformation
of society is a thoroughly petty-bourgeois fantasy'.[144] And thus (again
from a welter of possible examples) *Theories of Surplus Value*:

> In the same way as [Proudhon] wanted commodities to exist but
> did not want them to become 'money,' so here he wants
> commodities, money to exist but they must not develop into
> capital. When all phantastic forms has been stripped away, this
> means nothing more than that there should be no advance from
> small, petty-bourgeois peasant and artisan production to large
> scale industry.[145]

We must balk, not only at this last point (which happens to suggest
something that is largely untrue) but also at the way it and others like
it are put. It is perfectly possible to criticize Proudhon's economic ideas
without recourse to the epithet 'petty bourgeois'; Marx himself, indeed,
sometimes – but not often – did so. That the frequent use of the label
'petty bourgeois' in subsequent Marxist writing is frequently unsavoury,
ad hominem and unfair, as well as wearying to the critical reader, is a
point that does not need to be laboured. What does need to be pointed
out is that any such use is in reality *mis*use which disqualifies the status
of arguments employing the label *as arguments*, properly so-called,
at all.

To see this we should take our bearings. There is a sense in which to
characterize Proudhon as a 'petty bourgeois', or even to apply 'petty
bourgeois' to some of his ideas, may seem appropriate. Such a characterization (with which Proudhon himself might have agreed, with some
pride) may not seem altogether wide of the mark, if it were kept within
limits. In early nineteenth-century France, it might generally be agreed,
a relatively large proportion of the population were small property-
owners, small masters, small employers, and – sometimes down through
well-nigh imperceptible shadings – journeymen, craftsmen, apprentices,

landed and landless peasants. All these groups were threatened by the onset and expansion of a capitalism that represented in their eyes an intensified exploitation, expropriation and dispossession. The penetration of capitalism was real enough, and rapid and unsettling enough to pose a threat to members of these groups; the writing, as it were, was on the wall, and it spelt deprivation of property – property broadly conceived to include the kind of labour that was still a skill and not yet a commodity – and it spelt proletarianization. The threat, indeed, was double-edged, since those who had something to lose as a result of 'progress' could scarcely have been expected to turn for support to the revolutionary Left in so far as it was made up of collectivist socialists and communists, since these, too, given a free hand, would deprive them of a property which was the more valued as it was more threatened. These groups, 'the shock absorbers of the bourgeoisie' (to wrest an appropriate phrase from George Orwell), had proved their volatility and vitality in defence of their threatened rights during the French Revolution.[146] Proudhon, for his part, had undoubted connections with this peculiarly French *menu peuple*. He came from their ranks, spoke up for them, spoke to them, had their interests at heart, and enjoyed much support and admiration among them. There is nothing surprising about this. Proudhon, indeed, as Marx seemed grudgingly to be on the point of admitting in 1846, was well placed to perceive, and speak to, the real, basically non-proletarian (or pre-proletarian) character of 'la classe la plus nombreuse et la plus pauvre' – unlike Saint-Simon who, as an aristocrat *malgré lui*, saw them from afar.

Thus Marx, in attributing petty bourgeois characteristics to Proudhon and his thought, was not wrong. But this is not all that he did. He used 'petty bourgeois' as a term of abuse and opprobrium; he maintained that the confusions and contradictions in Proudhon's thought in some way represented or could be reduced to the confusions and contradictions in the placement of the non-progressive petty bourgeois class. The objections to this procedure, considered as a mode of explanation, are, at one level, fairly obvious. It is unwarranted, because reductive; it begs the question of whether, or to what extent or in what way, intellectual confusion may legitimately be reduced to social contradiction; it has little if any explanatory force because to use it is always to beg the question not only of what these connections may be, but how they are to be traced; and, in particular, to use the term 'petty bourgeois' as an adjectival epithet to be applied to a thinker, or a body of thought, is to *misuse* what at best can be applied within strict limits to explain the provenance or bearing of an idea. To use it to refer to relations among ideas (connections, contradictions, confusions) is indefensible because all the problems of reductiveness are multiplied in the attempt itself.

These objections are damning and might be conclusive in themselves.

Yet there is another objection that is even more damning, having to do with the way we use (and ought to use) words. Raymond Williams[147] has tellingly observed that in Marxist discourse 'analytic categories . . . almost unnoticed become substantive descriptions to which, as analytic categories, they are attempting to speak'. Marx's attempt to characterize Proudhon as a 'petty bourgeois' is not an example Williams uses; but it is nevertheless a case in point. The term 'petty bourgeois' is, or can legitimately be used as, an analytic category. Those persons belonging to it have certain characteristics – let us say of being threatened in various ways by 'progress', or of subscribing in various ways to what E.P. Thompson called a pre-capitalist 'moral economy'.[148] This means that if we fail to specify what these characteristics are, any use of the category of which these are characteristics makes no sense. This in turn means that use of the category, if it *is* to make sense, depends on the characteristics that make it up. But if we 'describe' Proudhon as a petty bourgeois, the better, perhaps, to try to discredit him, we are trying to use the term 'petty bourgeois' adjectivally to characterize him or something about him; and this we simply cannot do, since 'petty bourgeois' is not a designation or a characterization in the required sense. It exists not in order to characterize but in order to *be characterized*. If we attempt to explain or account for Proudhon, or anything about Proudhon, by saying that he is a petty bourgeois, we are using an analytic category as a descriptive term; but no analytic category can be used as a descriptive term without losing all its meaning. Our attempt would be no more than the verbal trickery involved in substituting connotations for characterizations; and it is we who would be tricked.

CHAPTER 5

Marx, Bakunin and the International

The most immediate difference between Marx's dispute with Bakunin and his earlier attacks on Proudhon and Stirner is that it took place within an institutional setting. It was not the only political dispute that animated the International, but it was the most fundamental dispute of its kind in the history of this body, since what was at stake in it was not just the doctrinal superiority of one or another set of propositions but the shape, and the future, of the International itself. Proudhonists as well as Bakuninists attempted to use the International as a platform, even though Proudhonism did not fare too well and had effectively burned itself out by the time of Bakunin's entry. The transition, if we may so characterize it, from Proudhonism to Bakuninism – the two, as we shall see, were very different forms of anarchism – raised the stakes of any possible conflict. The shift was from a form of doctrine having some vague and, as far as Marx was concerned, irksome appeal, mainly among some French Internationalists, to an anarchist *movement* having a considerable, and widespread, appeal across national boundaries.

Marx and Bakunin each joined the International, a body that was instituted by, and in the name of, neither of them, for broadly similar reasons. Each of them saw in the International a readily available platform and base of operations; and this – whatever the intentions of its non-Marxist, non-anarchist founders – is, *inter alia*, what it became. Marxism and Bakuninism alike were to owe a great deal to the International; it provided them both with a medium of existence, and a forum where points of doctrine could be set out and – as it happened – bitterly disputed. The doctrines in question were, in a word, no longer merely doctrinal; they came to have directly political implications and ramifications since the rivalry between them called into question the *raison d'être* of the International itself. Without Bakunin, it has rightly been pointed out, 'anarchism would have existed, but perhaps not an anarchist movement as such';[1] what needs adding is that without the International the anarchist movement might have taken a very different, and much less potent, form. Much as Marx used the International to create what we today know as Marxism, Bakunin succeeded in using the International to create Bakuninism and, by extension, to bring into being anarchism as a revolutionary social movement.

There is something extraordinary about the International's double service – both to Marx *and* to Bakunin; we know, with the benefit of hindsight, that no institutional setting, whatever its form, could long have survived as a vehicle for both Marxism and Bakuninism. We know, from our own vantage point, that 'the bubble', as Engels was to put it, after the event, 'was bound to burst'. Yet hindsight is not all benefit; it can mislead; and it might make us forget that the reasons why the 'bubble' burst and the reasons why Marx and Bakunin were at loggerheads are different. That each had a bearing on the other is not in dispute; but we should remember that the International was something more than a trampoline for Marx and Bakunin's various doctrinal gymnastics. This recognition suggests that it is too easy to explain the *de facto* demise of the International in 1872, eight years after its foundation, as being in some way the inevitable outcome of the Marx–Bakunin dispute – even though a remarkable number of subsequent accounts proceed on such an assumption of inevitability. The demise of the International, which really took the form of its fragmentation, was occasioned by events over which neither Marx nor Bakunin had any control, events which cannot be reduced to, or explained by, the hostility between the two.

The most important of these events, the Paris Commune of 1871, was neither a Marxist nor a Bakuninist initiative. Neither Marxists nor Bakuninists played any significant role in it – although both groups could scarcely have avoided claiming some subsequent credit for so celebrated and (as it seemed) so forward looking a revolutionary uprising. Marx, after all, was not alone in regarding the Commune as the 'glorious harbinger of a new society'.[2] Marx, Bakunin and others wished to glory in various ways in the Commune (a wish that was by no means shared by all their fellow Internationalists); yet they owed more to the Commune than the Commune owed to either of them. The extent of the Commune's debt to various Internationalists, in and out of Paris, is disputed; that the International was far less important to the Commune than was the Commune – and its defeat – to the International is, on the other hand, indisputable.

The wave of counter-revolutionary reaction that came in the wake of the savage repression of the Commune – a minor White Terror that was in no way restricted to France – was one that threatened to engulf the International; this threat to its continued existence came at a time when the International was already weakened by the divisive effects of the Marx–Bakunin dispute. That this dispute came to a head at the very time when the International was most threatened from without certainly made this newly beleaguered body less able to stand the strain. Yet the strain in and of itself was considerable; that the International would buckle under it was made more likely by the bitter dispute – a dispute about fundamentals – between Marx and Bakunin. This dispute, which does help explain why the International did not long survive the suppression of the Commune, did not lead inevitably and inexorably, however, to its collapse.

This said, it may be likely that an International run along Marxist lines and an International run along Bakuninist lines would be incompatible enterprises; and it may be legitimate to infer such a conclusion from the dispute between Marx and Bakunin (as did the disputants themselves). Yet any such inference must remain conjectural, since the International itself was neither 'Marxist' nor 'Bakuninist'. It contained a powerful Marxist tendency and a growing Bakuninist movement that threatened to displace it; but these groups existed alongside many others which were just as characteristic of the kind of organization the International was, but which by the same token were by no means reducible either to Marxism or Bakuninism. It is a point of some importance that what came later to be known as the First International was in one crucial respect quite different from subsequent Internationals: it was not, and was never intended to be, an ideologically monolithic body. It may seem disingenuous to insist upon this point since Marx in the course of his dispute with the Bakuninists came perilously close to making the International homogeneous and doctrinally monolithic, doing much in this way to ensure that future Internationals would be monolithic where the first was not. Yet this very qualification points to a real difficulty. It is all too easy to assume that because subsequent Internationals were ideological monoliths, what is important about the First International is whatever monolithic tendencies it exhibited. Yet this assumption is merely a variant of the *post hoc ergo propter hoc* fallacy, a confusion of the subsequent with the consequent; it can lead us to read back the present into the past, later outcomes into earlier developments.

What we need to do in order to understand the conflict between Marx and Bakunin, however, is to resist this easy assumption and attempt to respect the intentions of the actors involved, together with their own understandings of what they were doing and why they were doing it, rather than pre-judging them in the light of subsequent events. To say this is not to insist that we close our eyes to questions of where the dispute between Marx and Bakunin was to lead; to do so would itself be a disservice to these protagonists, who were themselves aware that the issues involved in their arguments would outlive them. The point is, however, that *our* awareness, at this remove, of the longevity of these issues, their continuity from the 1860s to our own time, should not be allowed to distort our view of how and why they came originally to be raised. Yet remaining on our guard is easier said than done in the case of this debate, because of the very nature of its issues. Bakunin's accusations about Marx's autocratic tendencies appear to have a certain prima facie validity because of the autocratic tendencies we all know existed in subsequent communist movements. To read these subsequent tendencies back into Marx's dispute with Bakunin is, however, to beg too many questions. Similar questions are begged by all too many commentaries on the dispute, which abound, in many cases, in ahistorical judgments of the most egregious kind. Commentators who take it upon themselves to applaud Bakunin's 'perception' of 'techno-bureaucratic' tendencies among the European proletariat[3] are a case in point – though admittedly an extreme one.

It may be true that Bakunin in a sense was remarkably prescient, or (if you will) prophetic about what might defuse revolutionary sentiment among proletarians, and what might undercut revolutionary potential in proletarian political organizations; his disputes with Marx provide the seeker with a veritable storehouse of quotations that can be used to point up this moral.[4] In similar vein, it may be true that Bakunin's comments about the International in some ways foreshadow later analyses of working-class political movements that were to stress 'the iron law of oligarchy'[5] and the like. Yet in appraising these comments we would do well to bear in mind that Bakunin himself was faced with a proletariat in the 1860s and 1870s that was not even united, let alone characterized by 'oligarchic' or, worse still, 'techno-bureaucratic' tendencies. Likewise, Bakunin's persistent, indeed obsessive, complaints about what he insisted were 'dictatorial' powers exercised by the General Council of the International, a 'pan-German agency', or so he would describe it 'guided by a brain like Bismarck's' – these protestations should not be torn from their context in order to provide a 'prophetic' critique-in-advance of Leninist democratic centralism, or what you will; they should be arrayed alongside the real powers the General Council can be seen to have enjoyed (which conspicuously did not include the power to stifle Bakunin). If this is done, many of Bakunin's most characteristic judgments will emerge not as remarkable prophecies but as wilful exaggerations, or even fantasies.

Even though the point here is not to declare any premature *parti pris* in the Marx-Bakunin dispute – Marx, too, was quite capable, and guilty, of wilful, malicious misapprehension of his antagonist's positions – some imaginary Bakuninist interlocutor might protest that Bakunin's objections to the General Council were, at base, objections to Marx's presence on it (as indeed they were, as the reference to Bismarck indicates) and that Marx did prove himself capable in the heat of battle of acting in a high-handed 'authoritarian' manner. This protest, as far as it goes, is true; but, unless we assume (with Bakunin) that Marx had an 'authoritarian' temperament that 'explains' his actions, and which, running up against Bakunin's 'anti-authoritarian' temperament, made 'conflict' inevitable – an assumption that begs so many questions it explains nothing at all – the question that arises is why Marx acted in an 'authoritarian' manner *when* he acted in an 'authoritarian' manner The point here is not a trivial one, for if we examine Marx's dispute with Bakunin with this question in mind, we discover something quite striking. Each party's perception of the other influenced the responses of the other in a certain way. As the dispute intensifies, Marx comes to entertain a view of Bakunin as someone capable *only* of wrecking the International because of his obstinate adherence to certain ill-founded beliefs about the kind of body it ought to become. Bakunin, conversely, comes to entertain a view of Marx as being someone capable *only* of arrogating to himself certain powers and of ruling the International in so dictatorial a manner that by its very 'command–response' structure the organization contradicts, and cannot avoid contradicting, its goal, which is that of emancipation from illegitimate demands of this, or any other, type.

Once the antagonists' opinion of each other is formed, and as the conflict between the two antagonists reaches its apogee, Marx tends to act just as Bakunin 'knew all along' he would act, and Bakunin, too, tends increasingly to act just as Marx 'knew all along' he would act. It is as though, in a confrontation having its dramatic aspects, each actor played out the role the other had in mind for him; or, along the lines of a psychodrama, it is as though each protagonist acted out the other's nightmare. Marx acted – or, what is more to the point, seemed to Bakunin to be acting – in such a way as to confirm and reconfirm Bakunin's worst suspicions and most horrible imaginings; in so doing he in a sense *became* what Bakunin suspected him of being all along. Bakunin, for his part, acted in such a way, or seemed to Marx to be acting in such a way, as to confirm – and in Marx's eyes to validate – Marx's worst suspicions of *him*, so that he too became, or turned into, his antagonist's version of him. In this way each side's misgivings about the other became progressively confirmed, in a kind of spiral of suspicion and confirmation. The effect of each twist in the spiral was to reinforce a *position déjà prise*; each antagonist acted or appeared to act in such a way as to validate his counterpart's view of him.

This view of the dispute is not designed to detract from the importance of the issues involved in it, but merely to help account for the way or ways these issues were seen by the protagonists. It also helps account for mistakes that they made. What runs through E.H. Carr's biography of Bakunin in its account[6] – an important source – of the debate with Marx is the idea, which is really an unexamined proposition, that each side in the dispute was at all stages quite straightforwardly, and deliberately, plotting against the other, plotting as though full foreknowledge of the outcome of each and every move could have been appraised. Yet neither antagonist had, or could have had, the kind of foreknowledge that Carr (who in this is not alone) in effect ascribes to them. Both made serious mistakes (which neither would subsequently admit). The idea that Bakunin's dealings with the International reveal a single-minded and 'Machiavellian' pursuit of power, with its concomitants of seizing the main chance and exquisitely timed treachery, is quite unwarranted (although it could be derived from some of Marx's comments about him, taken at face value). There seem to have been times when Bakunin presumably would have benefited from greater ruthlessness; yet even though he was an extraordinarily manipulative man – an 'operator', as we now say – with a marked taste for conspiracy, his conspiracies often failed ignominiously. Had Bakunin really been the arch-conspirator of legend he would not have voted, for instance, for an extension of the powers of the General Council at the Congress of Basel in 1869; he would not have permitted the Italian socialists to hold back all their delegates from the International's Congress at The Hague in 1872, an oversight he could have avoided which probably cost him his majority there; and he would not have stayed away from the Hague himself. All such examples, which along with similar blunders on Marx's part will be dealt with more fully in their proper place, should serve to remind us that the dispute between Marx and Bakunin – which can be reduced neither to the 'temperament' of the protagonists nor to ultimate effects of which they could have known nothing – was a political dispute, a dispute in which penalties were paid, in short order, for mistakes made and in which each main participant's way of viewing his rival played its part in helping along the eventual outcome.

Two points are important, then, in what follows – which is intended not as an adequate institutional history of the International[7] but as an interpretation of some of its main events. First, the International should be regarded as neither 'Marxist' nor 'Bakuninist' *tout court* but as something more than a mere framework for the Marx–Bakunin dispute. This dispute was in large part a dispute about the International; what was immediately at stake was the shape, form and future of the International itself. The protagonists in the dispute had something in common over and above their respective desires for power in, and influence over, the International; the protagonists became counterparts in that each acted like the other's version of him. These points might be taken to suggest that the Marx–Bakunin dispute was in some way symmetrical, but such a suggestion should be resisted vigorously. Both protagonists may have wanted to use the International in what were, at base, similar ways; but the International Bakunin was to confront in 1868-9 was an already established entity, and as such was very different from the International Marx had encountered, *in statu nascendi*, four years earlier. The point here is not simply that in 1864, unlike 1868-9, the International had yet to be given shape; it is that the shape the International was given – under the guiding influence of Marx – permitted and facilitated not only Bakunin's entry but also the creation of Bakuninism as a revolutionary doctrine and movement. We are dealing, then, with what was an unintended consequence and, in what follows, with whether it could (and should) have been avoided.

The International before Bakunin

O what a world of profit and delight,
Of power, of honour, of omnipotence,
Is promised to the studious artisan!

Marlowe, *Doctor Faustus*, I, 53–5

The International Working Men's Association was set up in 1864 by trade unionists, but not as a purely trade union body. The first point of its statutes attests:

This Association was founded in order to create a central means of unity and co-operation between the associations of workers which already exist in the various countries and aim at the same goal, namely, the protection, the rise, and the complete emancipation of the working class.[8]

It is a point of some importance that this goal was conceived as a *political* goal from the very beginning; it is likely that its political character, along with the International's non-sectarianism, was instrumental in persuading Marx to participate as actively as he did.

This means that to consider the International purely as a defensive trade unionist, or *ouvriérist*, association is to seriously misprize its nature. Proudhonist attempts to exclude non-workers were given short shrift; and it is easily pointed out that as a trade unionist body the International was neither representative nor particularly effective. The International, in Cole's words, 'gave some help in strikes both by collecting money and by preventing the transport of strike-breakers across national frontiers; but beyond this it could do little to guide the course of events'. It is true, too, that 'the course of trade union development in both Great Britain and France, and also Belgium, can be explained without much reference to the International'.[9] The reasons why this is so have to do with the International's working-class base. The French labour leaders who were to be important figures in the International, and whose broadly Proudhonist sympathies are not to be wondered at, Tolain, Limousin, Fribourg, Varlin and Dupont, were, respectively, a carver, a lace-works machinist, an engraver, a bookbinder and a maker of musical instruments;[10] Marx's closest associates, for a while, included Georg Eccarius, a German tailor, and Hermann Jung, who was - the irony will become apparent - a Swiss watchmaker; and even in England, 'the metropolis of capital' as Marx called it, the International's 'trade union support was to come largely from building unions and from such relatively backward industries as tailoring, clothing, shoemaking and cabinet-making. In mining, engineering and heavy industry generally, its strength was small or non-existent'.[11]

Something other than its industrial base, then, must have commended the International to Marx; indeed there was another, more political reason why the new International could scarcely have appeared forward-looking. The Association came into being as the outcome of a visit to the International Exhibition in London, in 1862, of a delegation of French workers. This delegation, though elected, was nevertheless subsidized by the government of Louis Bonaparte, no doubt

> with the idea that they would return [to Paris] impressed
> by the moderation and good sense of the New Unionists and
> Co-operators of the most advanced capitalist country in the
> world, and in a mood to discard the revolutionary traditions
> which still lived on in the underground sentiment of French
> working-class society.[12]

While these workers stole the march on their sponsors by exceeding their brief, they did so - immediately, at any rate - only up to a point: their English counterparts from the London Trades Council were themselves no firebrands. Yet the internationalist initiatives taken by the London Trades Council, initiatives taken in the direction of radical democracy rather than revolutionary socialism, meant that the boundaries between narrowly trade unionist and more broadly political activity and agitation had been crossed in England, and a precedent for the International had been set. That these developments had taken place in England gives us one essential clue to the nature of the International. The freedom of manoeuvre that was enjoyed by politically minded trade union leaders in London was a freedom enjoyed also by the numerous continental political refugees, *quarante-huitards* and others, who were languishing there, and who tended to be more radical (and less patient) than the English. Many of these *émigrés*, who had been marking time since 1848, were to find (at last) some focus for their energies in the new International.

Among these refugees was, of course, Marx; yet the point needs reiterating that the International at its inception in 1864 was in no way Marx's idea and (later accusations notwithstanding) not even his creation. Marx's commitment to the principle of international proletarian organization, ever since the days of the League of the Just, had been marked.

(The extent to which he had sought to sustain this commitment among what was a bewildering array of *émigré* political associations in London is, however, disputed.) As the former head of the Communist League and the co-author of *The Manifesto of the Communist Party*, Marx could certainly claim some share in the background to the International, although he did none of the ground-work setting it up. He was invited to join, and accepted with alacrity; he found himself almost immediately engaged in policy making. The reasons for Marx's eagerness are not hard to see; he was in no way blind to the limited working-class base of the Association or to the suspiciously Proudhonist leanings of its French avatars; what outweighed such unwanted features was something more than the opportunity for action. Having long been isolated from what he called the 'real "forces"' ('wirkliche "Kräfte"')[13] of the labour movement of any country, Marx applauded what he saw, rightly enough, as an independent, non-sectarian initiative in the direction of working-class internationalism; henceforward he was to devote a great deal of time and effort – which, interestingly, coincided with a tremendous burst of intellectual work on his part[14] – in its cause. He did so, as he wrote to Joseph Weydermeyer, because 'it involved a matter where it was possible to do some important work'.[15] Work that would be international in its scope always seemed important to Marx; the strength and depth of his commitment to international proletarian organization cannot be overemphasized. What pervades Marx's writings and career as a revolutionist alike is his recognition that any proletarian revolution confined within national boundaries would be doomed to failure if, as often seemed likely, surrounding or adjacent nations remained capitalist. This conviction of the impossibility of a restricted proletarian revolution, which, of course, had as its corollary a stress on the fundamental importance of international organization, explains why Marx set such great store by 1848, which looked like an international uprising if ever there was one; it also explains why Marx, later in his career, discounted the possibility of a purely Russian revolution. He did so for the same reason that he discounted the possibility of a purely French revolution in the nineteenth century: that the universalizing tendencies of the expansionist capitalist mode of production would make the survival of isolated revolutionary regimes unlikely. The beliefs Marx expressed at different stages of his career that an uprising in Ireland might spark off a revolution in England, or an uprising in Russia sound the tocsin for a revolution in Western Europe (which alone, he thought, could ensure the survival of a revolutionary regime in Russia) – these, too, are expressions of Marx's fundamentally internationalist beliefs, beliefs which all too rarely were permitted actual, institutional expression.[16]

To remind ourselves of these beliefs and their bearing is to see more clearly why Marx set such store by the International, even though not all its features could have augured well in his eyes. None of the groups who were responsible for setting up the International – all of which (with the exception of the Mazzinians) were to continue to coexist uneasily within it – set out to endear themselves to Marx; and the International itself was to founder, a mere eight years after its foundation, in the midst of the kind of sectarian strife Marx had hoped (perhaps unrealistically) it could avoid, or transcend. Yet the gamble seemed to Marx to be one worth taking. He anticipated that the International, however unlikely its form, might become the vehicle for, and the embodiment of, class consciousness among the workers. Events – events over which he could have had no real control – were to prove Marx wrong; yet however ill-founded Marx's hopes and expectations may have turned out to be, the fact that they were entertained, put forward and acted upon has much to tell us about what Marx meant by proletarian class consciousness. The authors of one of the few political biographies that pays adequate attention to his activities in the International lean rather too far, in their account, in Marx's direction; yet Nicholaevsky and Maenchen-Helfen's assessment – which is really a paraphrase – of the tasks Marx set himself in and around 1864 is of considerable interest, for it helps tell us what is involved in a Marxist politics. Marx, they say, aimed

> to help [the International], to bring it to awareness and
> theoretical comprehension of what it must do and the
> experiences through which it must pass. . . He avoided giving
> prescriptions. This does not of course mean that he let things
> take their own course. What he did rather was to help every
> movement to get clear about itself, to come to an understanding
> of the connections between its particular interests and the
> whole, of how its special aims could not only be realized by the
> realization of the demands of the whole class, by the complete
> emancipation of the proletariat.[17]

This estimation is an assessment of Marx's aims, not (as we shall see) of his accomplishments; as such, it differs radically from later Bakuninist accounts of Marx's motives – not least because it comes closer to recognizing the limits to what Marx could have been expected to accomplish – and it raises some key problems of a Marxist politics. What was at issue was the conversion – which cannot be reduced to indoctrination – of the proletariat from the status of *Klasse an sich* to the status of *Klasse für sich*. (It is too often overlooked that this distinction, made in *The Poverty of Philosophy*, can also be inferred from Marx's career as a revolutionist.) The assumption that the International stood at a point of juncture between the two, between the class *in* itself and the class *for* itself, may in retrospect seem a curious one; what needs to be remembered, however, is that this unlikely vehicle was the only one available, as Marx himself seems to have recognized.

What, then, does the conversion of a *Klasse an sich* to the status of a *Klasse für sich* actually involve? Marx had reasoned, prior to 1864, that mere numbers might be an insufficient criterion of revolutionary success. It is frequently forgotten that in the 1847-8 period Marx pressed not for capitalist industrialization in Germany (which would have swelled the ranks of the German proletariat) but for a proletarian uprising; even though the German proletariat was at the time not at all numerically strong, Marx argued in *The Manifesto of the Communist Party* that German workers could make up for their numerical insufficiency by their theoretical and organizational clear-headedness. What this means is that a social class, if it is to become a revolutionary class capable of undermining the conditions that constrain its existence and its development, must be more than an objectively determined class in itself (*an sich*), to be characterized by the sheer numerical strength of a head-count. It must become a class for itself (*für sich*) by attaining consciousness of itself, its history, its placement, its potential. Marx, arguing (not least in the *Manifesto*) on the basis of his assessment of the growth of the bourgeoisie within the feudal society it eventually outgrew and overthrew, believed that any properly revolutionary class must complement its objective placement within the overall line-up and deployment of social forces with a subjective understanding of itself: of its own position, background, strength and, above all, of the futurity it embodies.

Any social class can be said and shown to be objectively determined, up to a point, in its placement within the overall mode of production or within the balance (or imbalance) of forces within a given society. Such objective placement may not, however, be crucial to the chances of any revolutionary success. Mechanistic metaphors about the objective balance of forces cease to apply at a certain pivotal point in the case of a forward looking, well informed revolutionary class; objective placement needs to be complemented by subjective understanding if revolution is to be successful and thoroughgoing. The difference is between position and positioning. The objective position of a class may guarantee nothing about revolutionary success; its subjective positioning may make all the difference to its chances. To put the same point another way, at the point of transition between one form of society and another, at what Marx called in his letter to Proudhon the 'moment of action', conditions, however 'objective' they may be, have to be acted upon, and contradictions, however objective they may be, have to be perceived and appraised as such; these perceptions in their turn must be acted upon if revolutionary change of a thoroughgoing kind is to ensue.

What is involved in the transformation of the proletariat from being merely a *Klasse an sich*, defined 'objectively' as a group of persons sharing a certain position within the prevailing mode of production, to the status of *Klasse für sich*, is a certain collective self-transformation. This transformation entails a comprehension of the conditions of existence for the class, together with an appraisal of how they are to be changed; it entails an inner transformation, a drawing together, the creation of bonds among members of the class in such a way that communality of interest and concern – a communality that is not mechanistic or numerical but which is organic – can emerge, and can be put to work. All this is to say that the transformation in question is *political* transformation, and the task of helping bring it about – which is the task Marx set for himself in 1864 – is a political task. It is also a task that is subject to political limitations, since the change in question is not one that can be induced or dispensed from without. Later Bakuninist accusations that Marx 'indoctrinated' the General Council and from thence attempted, in an 'authoritarian' manner, to 'indoctrinate' the International as a whole can be shown to be, at best, insufficient as an account of what happened during the years of the International. They are also radically insufficient as an account of Marx's intentions, of what he thought he could do, when he joined the International. Marx took it upon himself to try and act as an agent of change, a catalyst, if you will; yet he was aware that the only change that might matter, the transformation of a class in itself to a class for itself, is the kind of change in attitudes, in beliefs, in convictions and in knowledge, that cannot be reduced to mere 'indoctrination' and that cannot be imposed from without.

As Marx himself put it in his 'Inaugural Address', efforts that were by 1864 being made in various countries 'at the political reorganization of the working men's party' possessed 'one element of success. . .numbers; but numbers weigh only in the balance if united by combination and led by knowledge'. This meant that the other elements or prerequisites of success were to be organizational or political:

> Past experience has shown how disregard of that bond of
> brotherhood which ought to exist between the workmen of
> different countries, and incite them to stand firmly by each
> other in all their struggles for emancipation, will be chastised
> by the common discomfiture of their incoherent efforts.[18]

As this statement from his 'Inaugural Address' indicates, Marx was under no illusions about the heterogeneity of the new International. Although this heterogeneity showed signs that it might develop into the kind of socialist sectarianism Marx abhorred, awareness of these dangers seems to have deterred Marx not one whit. He launched himself into busy, indeed feverish, activity; he was persuaded (and more than willing) to write not only the 'Inaugural Address' but also the Rules of the International, together with the 'Preamble' to them. All of these are important sources for an understanding of Marxist politics; and Marx, in composing them with the kind of dedication that was not to slacken during the existence of the International, to all appearances was under no illusions about some of the fellow Internationalists with whom he would have to deal. He admitted in the privacy of a letter to Engels that in the composition of these documents it was

> very difficult for [him] to phrase matters in such a way that our own opinions would be [put forward] in a form that is acceptable to the present point of view of the labour movement. In a few weeks these same people [the English Internationalists] will hold meetings with Cobden and Bright to obtain the right to vote. It will take some time before the re-awakened movement will be in a position to use the bold language of yore. What is needed here is *fortiter in re, suaviter in modo*. . .[19]

Engels, who as usual considered that the errant Marx would have been more gainfully employed completing his *Critique of Political Economy*, admitted in his reply that Marx's 'Inaugural Address' should be a veritable feat ('muss ein wahres Kunststück sein') and added that 'it is all to the good that we are once more in contact with people who at least are representative of their class'.[20]

Yet, of course, it was their very representativeness that created the difficulties. To see this, we need only look at who was being represented. The committee elected to draft the International's programme and statutes had all of fifty-five members: Chartists, Owenites, Blanquists, Proudhonists, Mazzinians and Polish radical democrats – people who could hardly have been expected to agree about anything. Marx contrived to have the task of drafting the Rules and the 'Preamble' referred to a sub-committee (and, eventually, to himself); they emerged in the form of a lowest common denominator. Indeed, the 'Inaugural Address' Marx delivered, as well as the Rules and their 'Preamble' he was instrumental in drawing up – the three are best considered together – were not attempts to set his own imprint on the nascent movement. Such a move would have been either impossible or self-destructive. They were exercises in accommodation and compromise, skills in which Marx (whatever his private convictions or 'temperament') was to become proficient, at least until the entry of Bakunin into the International. Marx's earliest written contributions to the International, which was the kind of body he could not have taken under his wing even if he had wanted to do so, took the form of attempts not to displease rather than efforts to please, let alone convince or indoctrinate. Any sentiments of superiority he may have had Marx was careful to restrict to his letters. ('I was obliged to insert two phrases about "duty" and "right" into the "Preamble" to the Rules, ditto about "truth, morality and justice" ', Marx confided to Engels, 'but these are placed in such a way that they can do little harm.')[21]

It should not surprise us that the 'Address' was indeed gentle in style (*suaviter in modo*). Marx was even successfully prevailed upon to delete from it a derogatory reference to 'profit-mongers'. It emerged as a measured, cautious delivery, making no mention of so contentious an issue as socialization of the means of production, an idea which 'hardly presented itself as an issue'. Marx, in Cole's well-judged words, 'could not have come out as a collectivist without wrecking the International at the very start';[22] indeed, he could not have got away with even 'centralization', a term that was anathema to the Proudhonists and which consequently was omitted from the 'Address' altogether. Its absence helps explain why even Bakunin later admitted admiring the 'Address'.[23] Marx privately described the 'Address' as containing 'a sort of review of the adventures of the working class since 1845'.[24] Its *point d'appui* was the uncontentious thesis of the 'ever-widening gap'[25] between the wealth produced by modern industry and the poverty of the working classes; Marx also brought into play what he called the 'solidarity of defeat' that had united the English and the Continental working classes, albeit negatively, after the dispersal following 1848. He took care to add that a victory of the British working class over the bourgeoisie had been embodied in the Ten Hours Act which 'was not only a great political success; it was the victory of a principle; it was the first time that in broad daylight the political economy of the middle class had succumbed to the political economy of the working class'. Moreover, 'there was in store a still greater victory of the political economy of labour over the political economy of property. . .the co-operative movement'. Co-operation foreshadowed the disappearance of 'a class of masters employing a class of hands' at the workplace. 'Hired labour', Marx went on, with no small flourish, 'is but a transitory and inferior form, destined to disappear before associated labour plying its toil with a willing hand, a ready mind, and a joyous heart.'

Yet no co-operative measure – and by extension no purely economic solution – would in and of itself be sufficient to emancipate the working class; there was need also for political action at the national (and international) level if any new industrial order were to be brought into being and kept in being. 'National means', Marx argued – fatefully, as it turned out – are necessary to develop co-operative labour to national dimensions; and because 'the lords of land and the lords of capital will always use their political privileges for the defence and perpetuation of their economical monopolies. . . [to] conquer political power has therefore become the great duty of the working class'. This was a conclusion the Bakuninists were bitterly to oppose, as we shall have ample opportunity to see; more immediately, however, it was a conclusion to a chain of reasoning that the Proudhonists were quick to resist. Marx, who knew full well that they would do so, was more immediately concerned with Lassalleanism; his official capacity was as representative of the German workers, and it was not yet clear how small a role the Germans were themselves to play in the International.[26] Marx's sidelong glances at Germany are evident throughout the 'Address'. In praising producers' co-operatives he took care to single out 'cooperative factories raised by the unassisted efforts of a few bold "hands" ' – a word to the wise – and to insist that trade union movements had a positive and indeed vital role to play as instruments of political education. Both positions were hits at the Lassallean 'iron law of wages' which entailed what Marx considered a dogmatic belief that trade union activity was a waste of time (since the level of real wages falls with every rise in money wages), and an equally dogmatic belief that producers' co-operatives, to survive, needed a heavy dose of state aid – regardless, of course, of the form taken by the state in question.

Marx's hostility, in the 'Address' as elsewhere, to Lassallean statism should remind us that his understanding of the conquest of political power – however deliberately ambiguous this phrase may have been in the context of the 'Address' – differed fundamentally from, and was much more expansive than, Lassalle's. Bakunin's later accusations – he was fond of comparing Marx with Bismarck – were intended to conflate the two; that such a confusion, be it deliberate or not, cannot withstand examination is an important point to be discussed in its proper place. What is of more immediate importance is that Marx's 'Address', emphasizing as it did the conquest of political power as 'the great duty of the working class', could not avoid alienating the Proudhonists (although it left the Blanquists *and* the English unruffled by virtue of its ambiguity). Similarly, Marx's spirited defence of trade unions of the kind that go on strike – which in a sense was made necessary by the fact that *all* of the English Internationalists belonged to such unions – was bound to antagonize the Proudhonists. Not all of them continued to share their master's belief that strikes were barbarous (though some did); few actually advocated such extreme measures, however, even after Louis Bonaparte finally legalized strikes in 1864. On the face of things, Marx's 'Address' seems to rub salt into Proudhonist wounds in emphasizing the wrongs suffered by the Poles at the hands of the Russians; but this emphasis, too, is something that could scarcely have been avoided in the presence of Polish delegates and in an atmosphere of widespread sympathy (except among the Proudhonists) for their cause, a sympathy which Marx quite genuinely shared.

It was impossible to please everybody, and predictable enough that if any single group was to be selected as whipping-boy it would be the Proudhonists, not simply because of Marx's pronounced contempt for Proudhon – initially, at any rate, he seems not to have despised individual French Proudhonists nearly as much – but also because of the peculiarity of some of their inherited positions. In the wake of the London Trades Council's spirited and influential defence of the Union in the American Civil War, for example, it would have been impossible for Marx not to have voiced similar anti-slavery sentiments, even though Proudhon had stretched his dislike of centralization to cover support of the slave South. Marx's 'Address' was well received among the English Internationalists, who were trade unionists to a man and proud – rightly proud, as Marx himself acknowledged[27] – of their internationalist record in progressive, democratic causes; but by the same token the Proudhonists were less captivated. Yet Marx, in David Fernbach's words, had 'proved himself a friend of the English workers, and this alliance provided the political centre of the International up to the split of 1871-2'.[28]

This alliance, central though it was, had its curious features. It could work, as ballast (so to speak) or as a base of operations from which other adherents – the Germans, the Swiss, the Belgians, the non-Proudhonist French – could be won only if Marx was correct in his belief that England represented to these other countries the face of the future. Yet this belief – that 'with local colours changed, and on a scale somewhat contracted, the English facts reproduce themselves in all the industrious and progressive countries of the continent' – was in fact, as Collins and Abramsky point out, 'a dangerous oversimplification for which Marx was to pay dearly'.[29] His own commitment to this predictive scheme was not in doubt; he repeated it in the 'Preface' to the first German edition of *Capital*, volume i;[30] yet it was this very proposition that the growth of Bakuninism in Switzerland, in France, in Italy and in Spain was to call into question, and indeed disprove.

Marx nevertheless made it the cornerstone of his strategy, which was one of working outwards from a secure, English base. This strategy rested, however, on an oddity in the International's organizational structure. The IWMA was not a federation either of political parties (as the Second International was to be) or of trade unions (attempts to exclude non-manual workers always met with resistance). Its basic unit was the individual member, whatever his class background or political or trade unionist connections, who would join a branch or section. These in turn were linked to the General Council, though usually not directly; in all countries except England, a National Federal Council operated as an intermediary, or as what Bagehot would call in another connection a 'buckle'. The English Internationalists believed that any such intermediary council would be redundant in England, as long as the General Council remained in London (which it did until

1872); so the General Council in effect served a dual role, that of co-ordinating centre for the International as a whole and as British National Federal Council. The importance of this organizational accident - in the maintenance of which Marx came to have a vested interest - can be illustrated by two controversies. At the Congress at The Hague in 1872 Marx and Engels were driven to destroy the International by the radically simple expedient of proposing that the seat of the General Council be shifted from London to New York. Slightly earlier, a dispute, about whether a National Federal Council should be set up for England - alongside the General Council - had served to indicate that Marx's hitherto trouble-free alliance with the English Internationalists was effectively at an end.[31] Until then, English trade unionists (and, to a lesser extent, *émigrés* like Marx himself) were represented disproportionately at the highest level of the International. It is unsurprising that such disproportion, which was reflected in policy making, became a politically charged issue, most particularly once the International had begun to expand into previously uncharted territory, by the agency of Bakunin.

Marx's English alliance, with doughty trade unionists of an unimpeachably reformist disposition, had its limits. Marx could count on their support, in large part because these Internationalists were interested only in an extension of the suffrage (abroad as well as at home) along with the bread-and-butter issues of straightforward trade unionism. It is only a slight exaggeration to say, with Raymond Postgate, that the English members of the General Council 'were prepared to vote for any political resolution, however, absurd; they regarded these debates as mere exercises, not to be taken seriously'. One of them, George Howell, wrote in a letter about the Inaugural Congress that 'one of the seeds of discord was sown at this first Congress, viz., the introduction of the religious issue by Dr. Karl Marx. From this moment the discussions have led to interminable debates on all kinds of abstract notions, religious, political and socialistic. . . Whatever tendencies the Association may now have,' added Howell, blithely, 'they did not form part of the original programme, which a Gladstone or a Bright might have accepted with a good conscience'.[32]

Marx, faced with this kind of response - as he often was - on the General Council, was constrained to work 'behind the scenes',[33] as he himself put it. He seems to have done so with considerable skill and patience; mentions of Marx at a congress - he attended only one - are few and far between, and it is safe to say that in most sections of the International his name was unknown. Yet he did exercise influence over the General Council, of a kind that could have been predicted, and was foreseen, by no one in 1864. In drafting many official documents Marx succeeded in giving them a slant that was recognizably his own, although all of them required the Council's approval before they could be published. The balance was in many ways a delicate one, and Marx succeeded in treading it (for a while) by drafting the kind of document that would get the maximum possible support but which would also (and not at all incidentally) inch forward acceptance of his own views. The 'Inaugural Address', the 'Preamble' and the Rules are examples; the programme of the London delegates to the first Geneva Congress in 1866 – to which we shall shortly have occasion to turn – was another.

To what, though, do these examples point? At one level, Marx simply and straightforwardly wished to help build up an organization of the working class that would be appropriate to its strength in the various countries represented, and if possible not to engage in doctrinal polemics of the kind that (by reinforcing sectarian tendencies that were very much in evidence) would short-circuit the whole enterprise. At this level, Marx's aims differed little, at base, from those of his fellow Internationalists on the General Council. At another level, however, Marx had aims of his own, about which he had to keep tight-lipped, since they were shared by very few of his fellow Internationalists; his prudent silence does betoken a certain manipulativeness, on which his enemies were to seize. Yet we should not exaggerate what all this restraint and *sub rosa* manipulation could have been expected to achieve; it seems in practice to have amounted to not much more than the insinuation of ambiguous phrases into policy documents. Such underhandedness as these moves involved is certainly not the same thing as indoctrination, which is something that could never have worked. What needs to be put in the balance against later, Bakuninist accusations of indoctrination is the fact that the General Council refrained from making any common or theoretical programme binding upon members and sections of the International before 1871, the year before its *de facto* demise, and that up until then it 'left complete freedom to its various national sections as to the form their organization might take, and refrained from prescribing any definite methods of conducting the struggle'.[34] Indeed, the International, which was anything but a tightly organized body, could have survived in no other way; its heterogeneity was its strength and its weakness. Nicholaevsky and Maenchen-Helfen point out that the International

> had no programme, if by programme is meant a single, concrete, detailed system. Marx had intentionally made the statutes so wide as to make it possible for all socialist groups to join. An announcement in the spring of 1870 declared that it was not the duty of the General Council to express a theoretical opinion on the programme of individual sections. Its only duty was to see that they contained nothing inconsistent with the letter and spirit of the statutes.[35]

- statutes which were themselves very broadly framed. One of the beneficiaries of this latitude, as we shall soon see, was Bakunin himself.

The point here, however, is not to commend Marx for his restraint (which is what Nicholaevsky and Maenchen-Helfen's account sets out to do) but to recognize that no other policy could have worked if the International was not to be stillborn, or to fizzle out in its infancy. Nicholaevsky and Maenchen-Helfen concede too much to Marx in insisting that 'the groundwork for all his labour was a profound belief in the sound instinct of the proletarian mass movement'[36] (a perusal of his letters of the period suggests a very different appraisal). Their notion, again, that Marx 'sought [the] basis [for agitation] in the forms of the movement which life itself created'[37] is the kind of frequently encountered partisan formulation that collapses under its own weight. Nevertheless, these inflated claims to one side, Nicholaevsky and Maenchen-Helfen are broadly right in their claim that Marx cast himself in the role of guide rather than layer down of the law, having 'become convinced that great workers' organizations, able to develop freely within their own country, associated with the class movement as a whole, would find the right way in the end, however much they might vacillate and go astray'[38] on the way there. The arrant providentialism of such an assessment was one that Marx evidently shared; the irony is that while it sounds as though it could have come from Proudhon, it was Proudhon who (albeit posthumously) put it to its first serious test.

The adventures of the working class: Marx and the Proudhonists

C'est une société d'étude, non une
nouvelle charbonnerie.

Henri-Louis Tolain on the International[39]

Marx's disputes with the Proudhonists in the earlier years of the International foreshadow his later disputes with Bakunin in more than any immediately obvious sense. The former dispute directly set the terms for the latter only to a limited extent, since Proudhon and Bakunin were very different kinds of anarchist, having very different kinds of appeal to very different kinds of individuals and groups. Those Internationalists who looked to the memory of Proudhon (who died in 1864) and to his voluminous writings for guidance and direction were remarkably distinct from those who looked to the presence of Bakunin as exemplar for their guidance and direction. We shall have occasion presently to draw out more adequately the differences between Proudhon and Bakunin as anarchist theorists, and between Proudhonism and Bakuninism as anarchist movements (this latter enterprise being by now more to the point); for the time being we must content ourselves with two contrasts between these movements which, when taken together, indicate that the dispersal of the Proudhonists, which in one sense cleared the ground for Marx's later battle with Bakunin, in another sense raised the stakes of victory and defeat in that confrontation.

In the first place, Proudhon's followers, like Proudhon himself, were 'social individualists' (to use George Woodcock's apt formulation) who perceived not individualism but collectivism as the enemy. They were opposed not so much to individualism, which they merely considered to have been perverted by capitalism, but to collectivist regimentation which, they reasoned, always accompanied authority. Bakunin and his followers, by contrast, were resolute collectivists, opposed in the first instance not only to political authority but also to individualism, the bourgeois principle they considered a mainstay of illegitimate authority relations.

In the second place, Proudhon's followers were, like their *maître* (as Marx called him), anti-revolutionary. They recoiled - again like Proudhon himself - from violence, from revolution, even from strikes; and, like most people, they were less prone to verbal violence than Proudhon had been. In all these respects, Bakunin could hardly have been more different. He was a convinced and fervent revolutionary, who espoused violence, not as a necessary evil but as something positively to be valued.

These differences mean that arguments arrayed against Proudhon cannot be stretched to cover Bakunin too. Marx, who tended to overstate the connections between the two, came to a recognition of this inapplicability, but rather too late. Marx's objections to Proudhonism did not serve him well, and could not have served him well, against Bakuninism, a movement that pointed elsewhere. Proudhonism in the late 1860s was something of a rearguard action; Bakuninism by its very nature was forward looking and anticipatory. The Proudhonist movement always gave the impression of glancing backward, as though it needed for its each and every act some posthumous imprimatur from the shade of Proudhon. This need had the effect of further restricting the movement, defensively, within its francophone limits. Bakuninists, by contrast, were to be rather better served not only by the apparent omnipresence of their leader but also by the beliefs they shared with him. The two beliefs that are here isolated, somewhat arbitrarily, for the purposes of argument - revolutionism and collectivism - are not just beliefs Proudhon detested, but are also beliefs, differently understood, that Marx and Bakunin shared. We should be careful, however, not to draw errant conclusions from what was not a convergence of belief or a substratum of agreement but a penumbra, an overlap. This apparent narrowing of the ground of dispute did nothing to make the dispute any less intense; if anything, it had the very opposite effect.

Yet the eventual disarray of Proudhonism (owing to certain shifts within the French labour movement as well as the thunderous sounding declamations and denunciations that came from the platforms of successive Internationalist Congresses) did help clear the ground for Marx's dispute with Bakunin. Marx's disputation with the Proudhonists in the International was something other than a mere re-run of his earlier, doctrinal dispute with Proudhon; the outcome of these disputations, within the forum of the International, goes beyond questions of doctrine. It has to do with the influence of political ideas on political action and with the nature and survival of a political movement whose fate has affected that of so many subsequent ones.

Marx, early in 1865, insisted on parading, all over again, his uncomplimentary, and less than charitable, views of Proudhon in J.B. von Schweitzer's *Sozial-Demokrat*, the house organ of the German Lassalleans.[40] That this 'obituary' was, between the lines, one of Lassalle also may not have been lost on German readers (though it crept past von Schweitzer); but such hidden messages were of little immediate interest to French Internationalists, most of whom, as Proudhonians, were still in mourning, and were (predictably enough) outraged by what they took to be an ill-judged lack of courtesy on Marx's part. Whether or not this 'obituary' of Proudhon was intended for French eyes, Marx's 'Inaugural Address' most certainly was; yet even in what was an otherwise diplomatically phrased 'Address' Marx had done little enough to palliate, or endear his presence to the Proudhonists. On the contrary, his emphasis on the conquest of political power, on the educational value of trade union activity, and on the wrongs suffered by the Poles, whatever their other justifications, could have been deliberately calculated to ruffle Proudhonist feathers; and this is the effect they immediately had. From this point onwards it was Marx, unsurprisingly enough, who did more to antagonize the Proudhonists than any other single member of the International. (The Poles and the Mazzinians competed as groups for second place, but the Mazzinians having been outmanoeuvred – also by Marx[41] – ceded the contest.)

This antagonism was reciprocated. The Proudhonists from the very beginning were in Marx's eyes, as he was in theirs, exasperating and truculent. To begin with, the strongly Proudhonist Paris Committee of the International, charged in January 1865 with translating the Rules drawn up in English the previous year (into the 'Statuts de l'Association Internationale des Travailleurs'), mistranslated Marx's 'Preamble'. They dropped three words of the kind that matter so much in politics; this deliberate mistake rankled, and was of more importance than might initially seem to be the case because it was to be the Paris translation (which the committee refused subsequently to correct)[42] that would circulate, as propaganda, in all French speaking countries. Marx's 'Preamble' reads (in part) as follows:

Considering:

> That the economical subjection of the man of labour to
> the monopolizer of the means of labour, that is, the sources
> of life, lies at the bottom of servitude in all its forms, of all
> social misery, mental degradation, and political dependence;

> That the economical emancipation of the working classes is
> therefore the great end to which every political movement
> ought to be subordinate *as a means*. . . [emphases added][43]

These formulations in themselves were, of course, deliberately ambiguous. They could be – and were intended to be – read according to the predilection of the reader, as implying (or 'meaning') the primacy of trade union activity at the workplace over political activity (variously defined); or the indispensability of political action (whatever this may mean) as a means of 'economical emancipation'. (There is no doubt that the English trade unionists read the second of these clauses as advocating extension of the suffrage – indeed, much to the chagrin of Marx and others, they acted upon this reading in the reform agitation leading up to 1867, to the detriment of Internationalist duties, which the Reform movement effectively upstaged.) The Paris Committee considered any possible meaning to be a provocation. The terseness of the translation of the first of these clauses – which is itself grounds for suspicion – prepares us for the change in the meaning of the second:

> Que l'assujetissement du travail au capital est la source de
> toute servitude: polique, morale, et matérielle;
> Que, pour cette raison, l'émancipation économique des
> travailleurs est le grand but auquel doit être subordonné
> tout mouvement politique.[44]

This rendering completely alters the sense of the original; by the lack of a 'comme moyen' ('as a means') to qualify it, the French 'subordination' of any political 'mouvement' is quite consistent with ruling out political movements altogether. Marx was furious at being piqued in this way, but his outrage and sense of betrayal was not simply a matter of wounded pride or pedantry. It is likely that the mistranslation of the 'Preamble' had the effect of misinforming people about the International – or at least about what Marx wanted the International to be. The Swiss Bakuninist James Guillaume (the author of a major history of the International, written from a strongly francophone-Swiss point of view) described his surprise when he first discovered that the English original contained the words 'as a means', in 1905![45]

Marx's private assessments of the Proudhonists seem quickly to have changed by 1865. In November 1864 Tolain is described to Engels as *'the real worker's candidate at the last election in Paris,* a very nice fellow (his companions too were quite nice lads)' (emphases in original); in January 1865 we have 'Tolain, etc., who are Plon-Plonists',[46] i.e. Bonapartists. By 1866 Marx writes to Engels about a meeting of 'this Babylon', the General Council, in the following manner:

The representatives of 'Jeune France'. . . came out with the announcement that all nationalities and even nations were 'antiquated prejudices.' Proudhonized Stirnerism. Everything is to be dissolved into small 'groups' or 'communes' which in turn are to form an 'association' but no state. And this 'individualization' of humanity and the corresponding 'mutualism' are to go on while history comes to a stop in all other countries and the whole world waits till the French are ripe for a social revolution. Then they will demonstrate the experiment to us, and the rest of the world, overwhelmed by the force of their example, will follow suit. Exactly what Fourier expected of his model phalanstery. Moreover, whoever encumbers the 'social' question with the 'superstitions' of the old world is a 'reactionary.'

The English laughed a lot when I began my speech by saying that my friend Lafargue, etc., who had abolished nationalities, had spoken French to us, i.e. a language which nine tenths of the audience did not understand. I also suggested that by the negation of nationalities he appeared, quite unconsciously, to assume their absorption into the model French nation.[47]

The trouble with such Proudhonist formulations was that they combined a French-centred approach to international revolution with a denial of the legitimacy of any other nationalism. The rest of Europe according to this recipe is breathlessly to await the outcome of certain confected French developments, in the light of which movements of national liberation are to be disparaged. 'The essential nerve of the polemic', Marx had already pointed out to Engels, 'is the Polish question. The [French] fellows have all tied up with the Proudhon–Herzen Muscovitism . . . The Russian gentlemen have found their newest allies in the Proudhonized portion of "Jeune France".'[48]

Yet Marx found much to reject in Proudhonist programmes even apart from their ethnocentrism. Reporting to Engels on their showing at the Geneva Congress of 1866, Marx sounds a familiar strain:

> The Parisian gentlemen had their heads filled with the emptiest
> Proudhonian phraseology. They babble about science and know
> nothing of it. They scorn all revolutionary action, that is to say,
> action arising out of the class struggle itself, all concentrated
> social movements, every social movement that is centralized and
> therefore [they oppose] all action that can be carried through by
> legal, political means (as, for example, the legal shortening of
> the working day). Under the pretext of freedom, and of anti-
> governmentalism or anti-authoritarianism, these gentlemen – who
> for sixteen years have so calmly endured the most miserable
> despotism, and still endure it – actually preach ordinary bourgeois
> science, only Proudhonistically idealized! Proudhon has done
> enormous mischief. His sham criticism and sham opposition to
> the utopians (he himself is a philistine utopian, whereas in the
> utopias of a Fourier, an Owen, etc. there is the presentiment and
> imaginative expression of a new world) attracted and corrupted
> the 'jeunesse brillante' [glittering youth] and the students, then
> the workers, particularly those of Paris, who, as workers in
> luxury trades, are strongly attached to the old muck, without
> knowing it [Die als Luxusarbeiter, ohne es zu wissen, 'sehre' dem
> alten Dreck angehören]. Ignorant, vain, pretentious, gossipy,
> emphatically arrogant, they were on the verge of spoiling
> everything, since they rushed to the Congress in large numbers
> which had no relation to the number of their members. In my
> report, I shall rap their knuckles.[49]

The arrogance of Marx's post-mortem is unmistakable; though his
public comments were (from all accounts) more restrained and measured,
his letter to Kugelmann is of considerable interest, not least because it
brings out into the open Marx's impatience. Many of his claims are
disingenuous as well as immoderate. The Proudhonists, after all, had
every right to rush to the Congress, even 'in large numbers which had
no relation to the number of their members'; disproportionate representation would have been a fatal argument for Marx to have openly
used against them. The Proudhonists, like the representatives of the
General Council, were well briefed for the Geneva Congress (indeed,
their programme, which contains quotations from Exodus and Lucan,
is by far the best piece of writing the International has to offer);[50]
the idea that they 'packed' the Congress is, however, quite false, particularly as it comes from someone who was not to be averse to similar
techniques in the future. To scan the attendance records of national
delegations at successive Congresses of the International is to see that
the French Proudhonists, in making a good showing at Geneva (and, as

we shall see, at Lausanne the following year, 1867), were acting no differently from any other group faced with a Congress in an adjacent country which could be reached with relative ease. (It is quite safe to surmise that had The Hague Congress of 1872 been held at Geneva or Lausanne its outcome, following from its composition, would have been quite different.)

What of the Geneva Congress itself? Marx subsequently was to indicate that he

> had great fears about the first Congress at Geneva. But in general it has come out well, beyond my expectations. Its effect in France, England and America was unhoped-for. I could not and would not attend myself but it was I who wrote the programme of the London delegates. I limited it on purpose to points which admit of an immediate understanding and common action by the working men, and which immediately give strength and impetus to the needs of the class struggle and to the organization of the workers as a class.[51]

The programme[52] is evidence of how meticulously the English delegation was briefed for its first real stand-off with the Proudhonists; indeed it is much more than this, since Marx's instructions amount to a concrete programme of action for the International. They emphasize the importance of winning reforms from the existing bourgeois state wherever this was possible – reforms which would include labour legislation of the kind that had been embodied in the Ten Hours Act. Marx's instructions, by also singling out the importance of trade union activity, insist in effect that worthwhile reforms can and should be won by the working class, if possible, before the attainment of socialism in its full notion. The only possible way of doing so, for the time being, was through '*general* laws, enforced by the power of the state'.

Two points are important here. First, an explicitly anti-Proudhonian one: that 'in enforcing such laws, the working class do not fortify government power. On the contrary, they transform that power, now used against them, into their own agency'. Second, an implicitly anti-Proudhonian point is made, that if state power is to be transformed by the workers in this way, 'into their own agency', it has to be state power of a certain type. States like 'imperialist' (Bonapartist) France, or Bismarckian Germany may be appropriate to Proudhonian and Lassallean socialism respectively, but they are for this very reason not appropriate to the kind of reforms the working class could use to turn the state into its own agency. Proudhonian and Lassallean socialism are in reality opposite sides of the same coin, because neither sees fit to distinguish between different kinds of state; Marx was attempting to make the distinction they had a certain vested interest in not making, by insisting – and here we cannot avoid recalling his early essay, 'On the Jewish Question' – that progress in the direction of liberal democracy, however 'bourgeois' it may be, really is progress; it signifies and embodies something the working class can make use of, on its own terms, to the general good of society at large. The reason why the working class, in putting to good use what is progressive about liberal regimes, will not 'fortify' governmental power but 'transform' it, is that the state power in question is quite simply less autocratic in the first place. Marx in framing this argument – an argument important to an understanding of his works and career, and one we have encountered before – was unavoidably leaning in an English direction, away from the unsavoury possibilities presented by France and Germany, Bonaparte and Bismarck; and this means, of course, that his instructions for the Geneva Congress lay themselves open to a straightforwardly reformist interpretation – an interpretation that they actually received when the German Sozialdemokratische Partei Deutschlands, after Marx's death, used them and suppressed (for a time) *The Critique of the Gotha Programme*. To appreciate the extent of the misapplication of Marx's position this interpretation was to involve (this being a point to which we shall have occasion to return) we need only remind ourselves of the context in which Marx's instructions were drawn up: a context not only of an imminent struggle with Proudhonists who believed that any concession wrested from any state would fatally compromise and contaminate the workers' movement, but also of a parliamentary reform movement in England the International had helped along and which by 1866 was actually up-staging the International itself.[53] The situation was complicated, the balance needed was difficult; Marx advocated extension of the suffrage without advocating bourgeois parliamentarism as either a necessary or a sufficient condition of working-class politics. Thus, while it is true that, in Fernbach's words, Marx failed in his instructions to 'make clear. . .to what extent the working class could transform the existing government power into [its] own agency',[54] it is hard to see what else Marx, cross-pressured as he was by the need to oppose Proudhonism with English reformists, could have done. In the end, of course, the Paris Commune had the effect of answering many of Marx's questions fof him – and for us; but this is to anticipate.

The English reformists who were in large part Marx's only available weapon against the Proudhonists were also, however, trade unionists; yet Marx, here as elsewhere in his advocacy of trade union activity, does not simply applaud the forms it had taken and was taking. The instructions insist, to the contrary, that while trade unions were both legitimate and necessary, they 'had not fully understood their power of acting against the system of wage slavery itself' and 'must learn to act deliberately as organizing centres of the working class in the broad interest of its complete emancipation'. Indeed, trade unions 'must aid every social and political movement tending in that direction'. Legitimate trade union activity, in other words, is not simply a matter of the improvement of working conditions at the level of the individual plant or industry, and the raising of wage levels; it is also, and more importantly, expansive and educative in its scope, its scope being that of the 'working classes' as a whole. Narrow, sectional activity – particularly that of the better-paid workers whose skills had not yet been eroded, whose labour had not yet been homogenized – will not fit the bill. The relatively privileged workers, Marx insists, must 'consider themselves and act as the champions and representatives of the whole working class'; they must 'convince the world at large that their efforts, far from being narrow and selfish, aim at the emancipation of the downtrodden millions'. Merely sectional activities, of the kind, let it be remembered, indulged in by most English Internationalists at the time, would counteract and work at cross-purposes with 'the whole activity of the International Association which aims at generalizing the till now disconnected efforts for emancipation by the working classes in different countries'. The trade unions, which had grown up as 'centres of organization of the working class, as the medieval municipalities and communes did for the middle class', had for this very reason nevertheless 'kept too much aloof from general social and political movements'; now, however, if 'the Trades' Unions are required for the guerilla fights between capital and labour, they are still more important as organized agencies for superseding the very system of wages labour and capital rule'.

There remains the question of co-operative labour, which Marx dealt with along the lines laid down in the 'Inaugural Address'. He acknowledges

the co-operative movement as one of the transforming forces of the present society based upon class antagonism. Its great merit is to practically show that the present pauperising and despotic system of the subordination of labour to capital can be superseded by the republican and beneficent system of the association of free and equal producers... Restricted, however, to the dwarfish forms into which individual wage slaves can elaborate it by their private efforts, the co-operative system will never transform capitalistic society. To convert social production into one large and harmonious system of free and co-operative labour, general social changes are wanted, changes of the general conditions of society, never to be realized save by the transfer of the organized forces of society, viz. the state power, from capitalists and landlords to the producers themselves.

Marx took care to preface all these remarks about co-operation with a disclaimer. Since it 'is the business of the International Working Men's Association to combine and generalize the spontaneous movements of the working classes, but not to dictate or impose any doctrinaire system whatever', Marx insisted that the 'Congress should, therefore, proclaim no special system of co-operation, but limit itself to the enunciation of a few general principles'. Marx, here at any rate, was not the dogmatist dictator of policy Bakunin was to make of – and in a sense to make – him.

The outcome of the Geneva Congress as well as Marx's instructions to the English delegates suggest that Marx (whatever his private comments about them) wished to avoid further alienating the Proudhonists. Questions about 'credit' and 'religious questions' were left up to them; and Marx deliberately did not attempt to put the question of strikes on the agenda, telling the London delegates not to discuss the usefulness or otherwise of strikes but instead to emphasize 'international assistance for the struggle of labour with capital' and, in particular, strikebreakers (who tended in the 1860s to be foreign) – an emphasis that, it was thought, would be harder for the Proudhonists to repudiate.

The Proudhonists' position at the Congress of Geneva has been admirably summarized by David Riazanov.[55] 'The French delegation', he says,

> presented a very painstaking report which was an exposition of the economic ideas of Proudhon. They declared themselves to be vigorously opposed to woman labour, claiming that nature herself [sic] designated woman for a place near the family hearth, and that a woman's place is in the home, and not the factory. Declaring themselves definitely opposed to strikes and to trade unions, they propounded the ideas of co-operation and particularly the organization of exchange on the principles of mutualism. The first conditions were agreements entered into by separate co-operatives and the establishment of free credit. They even insisted that the Congress ratify an organization for international credit, but all they succeeded in doing was to have a resolution adopted which advised all the sections of the International to take up the study of the question of credit [a victory for the General Council delegates] . . . They even objected to legislative interference with the length of the working day,

an issue on which they were defeated. Another issue the Proudhonists fought and lost concerned public education, which they opposed because it implied *state* education and thereby an increase in the *puissance* of the state. (Such characteristic lack of proportion has the effect of making Marx and the Council delegates look relatively enlightened;

what the 'Instructions' have to say – and indeed, what *The Critique of the Gotha Programme*[56] was to say – about child labour has rather the opposite effect.) These were important 'symbolic' victories for the General Council, since each of them committed Congress to political action and the use of state power as a means of enforcing social reforms – an implication by no means lost on the Proudhonists. In general,[57] the Geneva Congress gave the International a constitution by ratifying (with amendments) the draft constitution that had been adopted by the Inaugural Congress in 1864; it approved the Rules of the IWMA (a victory for the General Council); it adopted Marx's ally Becker's resolution on Poland, and six of the nine points of Marx's 'Instructions' (on standing armies, trade unions, co-operative labour, women's and child labour, working hours and international union). The Proudhonist 'memoire', which in many ways was better composed than Marx's 'Instructions', and was certainly equally systematic, was defeated (with minor concessions) largely by the Swiss delegates who, unsurprisingly, held the balance of power.

They also held the balance of power at the Congress of Lausanne the following year (1867); this was to prove important, since the Swiss, unlike the French Proudhonists, had no objection in principle to the presence in the International of non-manual workers. (There was a danger that the International in Paris might fall into the hands of radical republicans, Jacobins or Blanquists, which helps explain the fears entertained by Tolain and others about 'outside intellectuals' and *savants*;[58] Tolain, however, had expressly included 'citizen Marx' among the 'bourgeois intellectuals' he had moved, at Geneva, to formally exclude.) In other respects, however, the Proudhonists, at the Congress of Lausanne (1867) and Brussels (1868), continued to step in the footprints they had made at Geneva. They protested in the name of 'freedom of contract' against any legally enforceable standards governing hours and conditions of work on the grounds that it was improper for an international congress to interfere in the relations between an employer and a worker, and that legal standards would in any case enhance the *puissance* of the state; they continued to oppose the General Council's defence of trade union activity; and they continued to recommend that the workers concentrate instead on developing co-operative and credit associations in which they would enjoy the product rather than the wages of industry.

Even though the Geneva Congress had done nothing to commit the International to Proudhonist principles, and indeed had ratified rules for the Association he had drawn up, Marx remained adamant.

> I consider it of the highest importance [he wrote in a letter]
> to free the French from the false views in which Proudhon,
> with his petty-bourgeoisness, has buried them. At the Geneva

Congress, as well as in the connections which I, as a member
of the General Council of the International Working Men's
Association, have had with the French Branches, I have
repeatedly encountered the most repulsive consequences of
Proudhonism.[59]

He complained to Engels that 'the worst is that we do not have a
single person in Paris who could make contact with *anti*-Proudhonist
sections among the workers', adding in a parenthesis that these anti-
Proudhonists 'are in the majority'.[60] Whether or not this is true, shifts
were beginning to take place within the Proudhonist ranks, where a
real split was emerging. While orthodox Proudhonists were to continue
to oppose all anti-capitalist measures and motions advanced within the
International, others (who still called themselves mutualists) began to
move in the direction of collectivism. The shift was away from Tolain
(who by 1871 was sufficiently isolated from the workers' movement
to become, not a *communard*, but a senator in Thiers's Assembly) and
towards people like Eugène Varlin, and, outside France, towards the
extraordinary César de Paepe (an independent who was sometimes to
swing the Belgians behind Bakunin). Varlin, de Paepe and others, in
Max Nomad's words,

> combined Proudhon's rejection of the state with the idea of
> expropriation of the capitalists and collective ownership of
> the means of production. They had arrived at these non-
> Proudhonist heresies when they began to realize that the growth
> of large-scale industry left the workers little hope of economic
> independence, and that to defend their interests, the workers
> would have to organize in labour unions and strike for higher
> wages, two altogether non-Proudhonist concepts.[61]

Conditions in France (and French Switzerland) favoured the growth of
trade unionism – and with it the growth of the International – in the
later 1860s. That these were opportunities for trade union action
created real dissension in what had until then been a united Proudhonist
movement can readily be seen from the proceedings of the Congress of
Lausanne.[62]

This Congress managed to pass a series of confused, contradictory
and face-saving resolutions. It resolved, for instance, that the state
should become 'the proprietor of the means of transport and exchange'
without deciding whether the state should be considered 'the strict
executor of the laws voted upon and recognized by the citizens' or
'the collectivity of the citizens', and without adopting de Paepe's
amendment calling for public ownership of land (which would have
alienated the Proudhonists). Whether 'public' ownership of monopolies

implied 'state' ownership (as the Proudhonists feared) was never really decided; this and other obvious cracks were papered over with deliberately ambiguous, inconclusive and innocuous 'resolutions', since neither side appeared to anticipate any advantage in pressing the issue. It is arguable, however, that the Proudhonists made a mistake in not doing so, since their inaction in effect opened the floodgates: debates about 'collectivism', 'collectivization' and 'collective ownership', which were bound by their very nature to compromise the Proudhonists, dominated the proceedings of all subsequent Congresses. These debates served effectively to isolate those who did not, like Varlin (who was to become a martyr of the Commune) move leftwards.

The Lausanne Congress passed a resolution saying that 'the social emancipation of the workers is inseparable from their political emancipation' and that 'the establishment of political liberties' – Congress had in mind pre-eminently those of the press and assembly, which in France were still illegal – 'is a measure of absolute necessity',[63] an essential first step. Even though these resolutions were in Cole's words 'too vaguely worded to divide the delegates',[64] neither one strengthened the Proudhonists, particularly as Congress insisted that each of them be 'solemnly reaffirmed' at every subsequent Congress. For the rest, there were further gyrations – again inconclusive – around the questions of co-operation and Proudhonian credit banks, and another face-saving resolution on public education; and, last but not least, there was the question of how the International should respond to the League of Peace and Freedom's invitation to the Geneva Peace Congress. Marx had been opposed to any collaboration with those he called the 'Peace Windbags',[65] a group of well-meaning *bourgeois* notables opposed in principle to war; but Marx, who was engaged in 1867 in reading the proofs for the first volume of *Capital*, this time had played little part in committee work for the Lausanne Congress, and was overruled. (All Marx did in the preparation for the Lausanne Congress was to edit the French text that had been drafted by Lafargue of the General Council's 'Address', which came to differ radically from the English language text, and to contain some characteristically Marxian sentiments.)[66] Even so, Marx in the end got his way, but by the unlikely agency of Tolain, de Paepe and Guillaume, and with results he could never have foreseen. The resolution Congress carried committed the International 'fully and entirely to the Peace Congress' but 'with a view to arriving as speedily as possible at the emancipation of the working class and at its liberation from the power and influence of capital', since peace 'needs . . . to be constituted by a new order of things that will no longer know in society two classes, the one of which is exploited by the other'. Once it was decided to send a delegation to Geneva to present the address, Tolain, ever suspicious of collaboration with non-workers, moved an amendment which was, in Cole's words 'meant to put the cat among the pigeons' (or doves):

> The [Lausanne] Congress, considering that war has as its first
> and principal cause pauperism and the lack of economic
> equilibrium, and that, to achieve the suppression of war. . .
> [it is] necessary to modify social organization by ensuring
> more equitable distribution of production, makes its adherence
> [to the League of Peace and Freedom] subject to the acceptance
> by the Peace Congress of the declaration set forth above.[67]

The ultimate importance of Guillaume's stand when he presented this
declaration of the International in Geneva, in a form that guaranteed
the League would not endorse it, is not so much that it pushed the
International in the direction of something Marx regarded as an absurdity,
a workers' general strike for peace; it is that it had the effect of undercutting the position of Bakunin, who was already active in the League
as leader of its left wing. Bakunin's quest to persuade the League to
take a stand on 'the social question' no doubt would have turned out
to be forlorn in any case; but the League's entirely unpredictable
rebuff to Guillaume, which Tolain and de Paepe had, of course, engineered in advance, was at least the proximate cause of Bakunin's decision,
the following year (1868) to secede with his followers from the League
and throw in his lot, instead, with the International. The affairs of the
International at this point undergo a jolt, and in a sense it never returned
to the (relatively) even keel that had sustained its buoyancy up through
1868; before returning to its affairs, we must, by way of excursus,
attempt a sketch of this disruptive presence, Bakunin.

Bakuniniana

> I shall continue to be an impossible person so long as those
> who are now possible remain possible.[68]

M.A. Bakunin

> Notre ami Bakounine est un homme impayable le jour de
> la révolution, mais le lendemain il faut absolument le faire
> fusiller.[69]

Caussidière

The life of Mikhail Alexandrovich Bakunin (1814-76)[70] is most con-
veniently divided into four periods. Although only the fourth is central
to his dispute with Marx in the International, it does not lend itself to

any hard-and-fast separation from the others. We have, first, Bakunin's youth in Russia, his imbibing of Fichte and Hegel, his membership in the *cénacle* of Stankevich,[71] his departure for Germany in 1840 and his abandonment of philosophy (and *byronisme*) in 1842; second, the period of Bakunin's friendship with German radicals, of his earliest revolutionary agitation, of consecutive expulsions from successive countries, and of participation in serial uprisings – February 1848 in Paris, June 1848 in Prague (Bakunin having embraced the Slav cause), May 1849 in Dresden; third, the period from his capture and extradition to Russia, through his imprisonment in the Peter and Paul fortress in St Petersburg to his exile in Siberia; and fourth, the period of his escape, his forays into Italy and Switzerland, his elaboration of anarchist doctrine as an impetus to a burgeoning anarchist movement, there and in Spain – and, as part of this enterprise, his dispute with Marx in the International.

What this schematization conceals is a series of questions – questions that cannot be answered here – about the relationship of early influences to later positions. One bone of contention is whether the idea of freedom in Russia was from the first bound up with anarchism more tightly than in Western Europe; this would mean that the struggle between Marx and Bakunin acquires fresh significance as one between 'western' and 'eastern' views of revolution, which is certainly what Marx and Bakunin themselves thought. While this issue cannot yet be joined, we do need to bear in mind what complicates it: on Bakunin's side, the fact that he was above all else a cosmopolitan revolutionary who followed the star of revolution outside Russia, and the extent of whose influence within Russia is disputed; and the existence inside Russia of a veritable galaxy of politically radical positions (which changed) during Bakunin's lifetime. Yet at one level, Bakunin's Russian-ness is unmistakable. 'We may argue', he wrote in his *Political Confession* (the one composed at Olmütz), 'about the case for revolution in various countries, but in Russia there can be no doubt about it. In that country, whose whole life is organized immorality, revolt must be a moral action.'[72] This sentiment was nothing if not shared. In the words of a thinker whose hostility to Bakunin is a matter of record, Russians 'held the institution of the state in particular hatred, since to them it was at once the symbol, the result and the main source of injustice and inequality – a weapon wielded by the governing class to defend its privileges – and one that, in the face of increasing resistance from its victims, grew progressively more brutal and blindly destructive'.[73] The defeat in 1848 of liberal as well as radical forces in the West confirmed many such victims in their conviction that salvation could not lie in politics, parties, parliaments, which now seemed as much of a mockery to a brutalized Russian people as did the half-life of factories and proletarianization that seemed in the West to accompany them.[74]

The influence of these peculiarly, if not exclusively, Russian sentiments on Bakunin was profound - profounder, perhaps, than his influence on Russia; for while the Russian populists of the 1870s and 1880s looked to Bakunin (as did so many others) as an exemplar, there was no Bakuninist uprising of any kind in nineteenth-century Russia.

Our biographical sketch conceals more than one *Confession* of Bakunin's. The other one was that written in 1851 in the Peter and Paul fortress for the eyes of the Tsar. This *Confession*, the one blot on his record as a revolutionist, did not discredit Bakunin during his lifetime; it remained undiscovered until the twentieth century, although the existence of some such document proving complicity was not unsuspected - and not unhoped for - during the years of the International. The 1851 *Confession* would certainly have been grist to Marx's mill, had he but known about it. This document remains of interest as evidence less of perfidy on Bakunin's part than of the almost childlike guilelessness involved in his belief that the weight of past history and circumstance - his own, or that of civilization itself - could be cast to the winds by an act of faith, be it only sufficiently strong.[75] This in turn could be cast to the winds by another - as Bakunin's subsequent career indicates.

This episode, like so many others, leads us to Bakunin's extraordinary, larger than life personality, by dint of which he succeeded in talking his way across Siberia, the Pacific, the USA, the Atlantic, to appear on Herzen's doorstep in London. This is the stuff of which myths are made. Herzen, here as ever, gives us priceless descriptions. Bakunin, back in action,

> argued, preached, gave orders, shouted, decided, arranged, organized, exhorted, the whole day, the whole night, the whole twenty-four hours on end. In the brief moments which remained, he would throw himself down on his desk, sweep a small space clear of tobacco ash, and begin to write ten, fifteen letters to Semipalatinsk and Arad, to Belgrade, Moldavia and White Russia. In the middle of a letter he would throw down his pen in order to refute some reactionary Dalmatian; then, without finishing his speech, he would seize his pen and go on writing. . . His activity, his appetite, like all his other characteristics - even his gigantic size and continual sweat - were of superhuman proportions. . .
>
> At the bottom of this man's nature lies the seed of a colossal activity, for which he could find no employment. A Columbus without an America, without even a ship! He has within himself the potentialities of an agitator, a tribune, and apostle, a heretic priest, a tireless fighter. . .[76]

Bakunin's personality matters greatly in his dispute with Marx, not because the dispute can be reduced to a conflict of personalities, but precisely because it cannot. Bakunin's personality did not fit him to become the leader of a movement in any accepted sense of the term at all; as Herzen recognized, he was an exemplar, an embodiment and a symbol of the needs and expectations of those who rallied to him, and to men like him. Anarchism is too often treated as a product of anarchist 'leaders'; yet the cateogories we would use to account for leadership rarely apply. In the case of Bakunin, his considerable personal magnetism should be regarded not as an explanatory category in and of itself but as a focus. The point about magnetic force is that it attracts something. The sources of Bakunin's appeal lie less in his psychological make-up than in the felt needs of those who responded to it, for good reasons of their own. The form taken by Bakunin's dispute with Marx does not always help us to remember this; Marx tended to see the movement, Bakuninism, through the man, Bakunin, as though it were simply an expression of his personality. We, at our remove, should endeavour – with some difficulty – to avoid making the same mistake. To Marx, Bakunin represented some old, pre-given *bête noire* – Proudhonism in Russian clothing, or Russia itself. Yet in fact Bakunin represented much more than Marx's old bugbears. The extraordinary thing is that he could personify emancipation, revolt, revolution, that he could be *l'homme révolté* even to the distinctly non-revolutionary bourgeois of the League for Peace and Freedom, to those very people his views were shortly thereafter to shock. An eyewitness account of Bakunin's appearance at the Geneva Congress of the League in 1867 makes this clear:

> As with heavy, awkward gait he mounted the steps leading to
> the platform where the bureau sat, dressed as carelessly as ever
> in a sort of gray blouse, beneath which was visible not a shirt
> but a flannel vest, the cry passed from mouth to mouth:
> 'Bakunin!' Garibaldi, who was in the chair, stood up, advanced
> a few steps, and embraced him. This solemn meeting of two
> old and tired warriors of revolution produced an astonishing
> impression. . . Everyone rose, and there was prolonged and
> enthusiastic applause. . .[77]

Bakunin's reputation as hero of the barricades and, in Woodcock's words, as 'energumen of revolutionary enthusiasm'[78] should not mislead us, however. It was Thomas Masaryk who pointed out that for all his undoubted volatility, if 'the anarchists esteem Bakunin as a man of action, they are mistaken; he was a dilettante of action. His practical, like this theoretical, life was a patchwork of fragments'.[79] Bakunin lived for the moment. Revolutionary escapades and theoretical

treatises alike would be embarked upon fervently but seldom completed; a brief flare-up of intense devotion to the matter at hand
would give way soon enough to impatience, to unease at the prospect
of seeing through any project to its conclusion. Bakunin, who was
anything but introspective, admitted that

> there was a capital defect in my nature: love of the fantastic, of
> extraordinary and unheard-of adventures, of undertakings
> revealing unlimited horizons. . . I suffocated in a calm and
> ordinary existence, I felt ill at ease . . . my mind was in a
> continuous agitation, because it demanded life, action,
> movement.

Proudhon once wrote that hell for him would be a world where he was
conservative; Lampert suggests that hell for Bakunin was to succeed so
well that nothing remained to be done.[80] One of the few writings
Bakunin did complete was the *Confession*, composed in the enforced
idleness of the Peter and Paul fortress, where even Nechaev was to
suffocate.

Bakunin, who was in Franco Venturi's words 'born for spontaneous
action',[81] thought of himself as what would later be called a revolutionist
of the deed, 'not a philosopher and not an inventor of systems like
Marx'.[82] He rejected intellectual systems, theories, even constructs,
in principle. In a variety of ways he expressed his abiding belief that
men should be reduced to fit no Procrustean bed, no theoretical strait-
jacket, no causal treadmill explaining or purporting to explain their
actions. Men should be free to shape their own destinies; they should
not be squeezed or moulded into any set of rigid, abstract formulae.
There exist no '*a priori* ideals or preconceived, preordained laws'. In
particular, 'no theory, no book that has ever been written, will save
the world. I cleave to no system,' Bakunin added. 'I am a true seeker.'
He dismissed, rejected in principle, what he called the 'dictatorial'
concept of intellectual system. In *Federalism, Socialism and Anti-
theologism* he insisted that 'metaphysics [acts] according to the principle
of centralized states' and that 'cloudy and congested thoughts must
totally dissolve, to take shape in large and exuberant deeds'.[83] What
lies behind and informs all such declamations – Bakunin's writings are
peppered with them – is the belief, as basic as it is blunt, that theory
per se is to be opposed because it tells people what to do or how to
act. Any theory that is separate from action cannot but act as a brake
on action, which depends on spontaneity if it is to be action, properly
so-called, at all.

Bakunin's words to Skuryevski in 1849 were words he was to
repeat, and act upon, many times during his career as a revolutionist:
'Je renonçai. . .la science transcendentale – *denn grau ist alle Theorie* –

et je me jettai tête baissée dans la vie pratique.'[84] The contrast between a revolutionist like Bakunin (who turned into a revolutionary direction the Napoleonic watchword, 'on s'engage et puis . . . on voit') and a revolutionist like Marx could scarcely be more pronounced. Pavel Annenkov's *Souvenirs littéraires* recall a meeting in the 1840s at which Wilhelm Weitling's utopianism so exasperated Marx that he hurled at Weitling the remonstrance that 'to excite the workers without giving them reasoned arguments is quite simply to deceive them. To awaken fantastic hopes can lead only to disaster, not deliverance'.[85] Marx was attacking the first militant revolutionary Bakunin encountered, who took Bakunin to his first workers' meeting, and whose combination of messianism and conspiratorialism Bakunin was to reproduce on a far more dramatic scale. Yet Bakunin, who was part of the milieu of the Russo-German meeting Annenkov was to recall, became contempt-uous even of Weitling. 'This is not a free society,' said Bakunin, 'a really live union of free people, but a herd of animals, intolerably coerced and united by force, following only material ends, utterly ignorant of the spiritual side of life.'[86] No German revolutionary was exempt from Bakunin's Teutophobia; yet the matter goes rather deeper than this. For if Bakunin had no love for Weitling, he had even less for theory. It is a point of some importance that 'to excite the workers without giving them reasoned arguments' and 'to awaken fantastic hopes' was *precisely* what Bakunin set out to do. Fantastic hopes, not reasoned arguments, were to Bakunin the very breath of revolution. Theory was in his eyes a 'metaphysic'[87] which, by paralysing 'fantastic hopes', paralysed revolutionary action itself. It was a main-stay of Bakunin's revolutionism that where there was a doctrine, an ideology, an intellectual construction of any kind, there lurked in the wings centralization and the state. In 1872 Bakunin defended the *fédérés* of the Paris Commune of 1871 on the grounds that they were strong enough to dispense with theory altogether.

> Contrary to authoritarian communist belief – in my opinion wholly erroneous – that a social revolution can be decreed and organized . . . the socialists of Paris. . .believed that it could be effected and fully developed only by means of the incessant actions of the popular masses, groups and associations.
>
> Our Paris friends were a thousand times right. In fact, what mind, however brilliant or – if we want to consider a collective dictatorship, even one consisting of several hundred individuals endowed with superior faculties – what intellects are powerful enough. . .to embrace the infinite multiplicity and diversity of real interests, aspirations, wills, needs, whose sum constitutes the collective will of a people? What intellects are powerful and broad enough to invent a social organization capable of

satisfying everyone? Such an organization would only be a bed
of Procrustes on which violence more or less sanctioned by
the state would compel the unfortunate society to lie.[88]

The agency for reducing all men to one standard, we should note, is not
violence (which, differently sanctioned, Bakunin defended) but *theory
itself*, theory that cannot avoid stifling the revolutionary ardour every
oppressed man possessed by virtue of his oppression. This contention,
an article of faith from which nothing could shake him, was the basis
of Bakunin's belief that 'Russian idealism' (or something like it) could
and would rejuvenate the International, not despite but *because of* its
non-theoretical, anti-intellectual character. In this view, Marx's stress
on the relationship of revolutionary theory to revolutionary practice –
or indeed the idea that they were related at all – was doctrinaire and
dictatorial because it was systematic. In 1873 we find Bakunin remi-
niscing that 'the last nine years have seen a development within the
International of more ideas than are necessary for the salvation of the
world, if indeed the world can be saved by ideas. . . It is no longer a
time for ideas but a time for deeds and facts'.[89]

Bakunin in 1848 said to Herwegh that he would restlessly, cease-
lessly preserve 'the sacred spirit of revolt'; revolt to Bakunin had the
broadest of significations. 'What I preach', he wrote, 'is a revolt of
life against science, science which is but a . . . victimization of fleeting
but real life on the altar of eternal abstractions.'[90] Bakunin declaimed
in *The Knouto-Germanic Empire and the Social Revolution* (written at
the height of his dispute with Marx, in 1870–1) that 'the sole mission
of science is to light the way. Only life itself, freed from all governmental and doctrinaire fetters and given the full liberty of spontaneous
action, is capable of creation'.[91] Life, action, spontaneity and creation
lie on one side, then, of the great divide; theory, abstraction, ossified
dogma, authority, regimentation lie on the other. The two sides are
counterposed; each side can operate only at the expense of the other.
Because Bakunin was, above all else, a dualist in this sense, we should
exercise caution in characterizing his own thought. Sir Isaiah Berlin,
whose sympathetic understanding of nineteenth-century Russian
intellectual history is generally cause for delight, has ventured the
opinion that

Bakunin had a considerable element of cynicism in his character,
and cared little what the exact effect of his sermons might be on
his friends – provided only that it was powerful enough; he did
not ask whether they excited or demoralized them, or ruined
their lives, or bored them, or turned them into fanatical zealots
for some wildly utopian scheme. Bakunin was a born agitator
with sufficient scepticism in his system not to be taken in himself

by his torrential eloquence. To dominate individuals and to sway assemblies was his *métier*: he belonged to that odd, fortunately not very numerous class of persons who contrive to hypnotize others into throwing themselves into causes – if need be, killing and dying for them – while themselves remaining coldly, clearly and ironically aware of the effect of the spells which they cast.[92]

This unusually uncharitable (for its author) view, one which is shared in its broadest outlines by E.H. Carr in his biography of Bakunin, has in it some elements of truth but rests on a misconception. Bakunin *had* no system with which he sought coldly and dispassionately to impress others; he sought rather to teach others to reject all systems. To this end, he was manipulative, in political and personal affairs alike; he lived, in Venturi's words, 'like a *barin*, whose easy-going and impractical habits revealed the Russian provincial gentleman beneath the bohemian and the revolutionary'[93] – this indeed being the aspect of Bakunin's character used by Turgenev in his depiction of Rudin. Yet the consistency of private and public we find here is other than that for which Berlin (or Turgenev)* allows. Bakunin did not think before he acted; nor did he want anybody else to do so. Thoughts or words are either part of action, or they are meaningless. This has two immediate implications. First, despite the considerable element of fantasy that tended to inhabit Bakunin's bombast, he was in fact the *first* to be taken in by, and to act upon, his own words – and for that matter upon the words of others (provided that they were words, and these were others, of the right kind). His bamboozlement by Nechaev indicates how easily led, how impressionable, Bakunin could be, how easily the victim of the right kind of make-believe; in Pyziur's words,[94] 'parallel to his own talent for mystification was his inability to see through the abracadabra of others' – not all others, to be sure, but certainly those, like Nechaev, that Bakunin was predisposed to believe. Second, and perhaps more important, Bakunin did not believe that his frequent clarion-calls to insurrection embodied any causal force, in and of themselves. No 'theory' could. He regarded his calls to arms as no more than catalysts, acting upon the innate, if inchoate stirrings of the masses (taken singly or collectively). The latent fury of the masses – and the more inchoate this was, the more powerful – was not at all to be channelled by Bakunin's words but simply charged by them. (It is not fanciful to suppose that the faith Bakunin had in the masses, which was to all intents and

---

*A noteworthy feature of *Rudin*, which may be Turgenev's least political novel (in its original form), is the final page Turgenev tacked on, after it was first published; it depicts Rudin (who is based on Bakunin) dying on the Paris barricades in 1848. His heroism is wasted. If in his life Rudin is manipulative and empty, Turgenev – who was not without vindictiveness – makes his death (and his revolutionism) futile.

purposes unlimited, accounts in large measure for his appeal and influence over them, which did of course have its limits.)

Bakunin distrusted intellection, his own or anybody's else's; but we cannot simply take his consistent distrust of reason, doctrine, system, or theory, label it as mindless 'anti-intellectualism', and then move on. To do so would be to pass over how deep-seated and fervent his revolt – and that of those who listened to him – really was. One pointed illustration must suffice. The principle of reason in history, so precious to Hegel and Marx (and in different ways important to Proudhon and Stirner too), suggested to Bakunin something he could not abide: any notion of balance or harmonization that is said to be immanent or implicit in nature or in history seemed to him to be no more than religious providentialism *in statu seculari*. History to Bakunin had in common with nature only its dissonance, its oppression, its inherent violence (the contrast with the anti-Bakuninist communist anarchism of Kropotkin, who wrote about nature to disprove Thomas Henry Huxley,[95] could not be more marked). Neither history nor nature corresponds to the various providentialisms men use to make them palatable; history in particular provides no consolation, but is quite simply an unreasonable, irrational, unsystematic and potentially explosive set of events, just one thing after another, without rhyme or reason. Elemental forces always come to the fore or rise to the surface, prominent among them power and oppression (which legitimate themselves as authority, justice and the like); and the whole sorry story of human suffering, injustice and oppression could be redeemed only by the blind destructiveness which Bakunin, unlike most revolutionaries, never attempted to minimize or argue away. Nor indeed did he see any real need to justify revolutionary violence; he constantly celebrated the most ruthless, indiscriminate violence as a deliverance, as the only real deliverance from bourgeois society and from all the injustices, falsehoods and hypocrisies sustaining it. Without such explosions of indignation, as Bakunin put it in a letter to Herzen in 1867, 'one would despair of the human race'.[96]

Bakunin's espousal of violence went beyond individual acts of terror; he believed in the necessity of *liquidation sociale*, of the root and branch extermination of the prevailing society with its good and its bad and its civilization. The *Appeal to the Slavs* contains an exhortation that is in no way untypical.

We must overthrow from top to bottom this effete social world which has become impotent and sterile... we must first purify our atmosphere and transform completely the milieu in which we live; for it corrupts our instincts and our wills and contracts our heart and our intelligence. The social question takes the form primarily of the overthrow of society.[97]

Because what Bakunin called 'positive anarchy' could result only from the *nihilisme du combat*, destruction takes on the capacity to invert itself and to become an immanent life-force. Such an inversion is not dialectical but dualistic, Manichaean; as against even Proudhon's wish to embody synthesis, Bakunin above all wished to personify antithesis, negation, destruction. Berlin has pointed out that Russian revolutionaries of the same period other than Bakunin shared

> one vast apocalyptic assumption: that once the reign of evil, autocracy, exploitation, inequality, is consumed in the fire of the revolution, there will arise naturally and spontaneously out of its ashes a natural, harmonious, just order, needing only the gentle guidance of the enlightened revolutionaries to attain its proper perfection. . .[98]

Anarchists other than Bakunin, indeed, often issue the dualistic injunction 'to change our false, filthy, boring, hideous life into a just, clean, gay and beautiful life'.[99] Yet Bakunin succeeded in giving this more or less familiar dualism a twist all of his own. The article, 'The Reaction in Germany', which he wrote (under a pseudonym) for the *Deutsche Jahrbücher* in 1842 contains what might be his best-known exhortation:

> Let us put our trust in the eternal spirit which destroys and annihilates only because it is the unfathomable and eternally creative source of all life. The urge to destroy is also a creative urge [Die Lust der Zerstörung ist zugleich eine schaffende Lust].[100]

The form Bakunin gives this defence of the aspect of revolution that most other revolutionaries, less sanguine and obsessive than Bakunin, tend to de-emphasize, is one that brings to mind not so much Stirner (who advocated violence but whose extreme individualism prevented real revolutionism) as Russian nihilists like Pisarev.[101] 'What can be broken, should be broken,' Pisarev had said. 'What can be struck down, must be struck down unceasingly: whatever resists the onslaught, is fit for existence; whatever flies to pieces, is fit for the rubbish heap. Hew your way vigorously, for you can do no harm.' What was in the offing, to Pisarev and Bakunin alike, was the unconditional end of a compulsory and servile world, which needed cauterizing; 'our task', said Bakunin, 'is terrible: total, inexorable and universal destruction'.[102] Nothing less drastic, thorough and ultimate would do. In his *Letter to a Frenchman*, Bakunin exhorted his readers to 'unbridle that popular anarchy . . . let it loose in all its breadth, so that it may flow like a furious lava, scorching and destroying everything in its path. . . I know that this is a dangerous and barbarous way', he added, 'but without it there is no salvation. It is essential that [revolutionaries] should be *possessed by a demon*, and nothing but the anarchy of revolution can fill their bodies with this demon'.[103] What is noteworthy here is that any joy is the demonic glee of destruction; whenever Bakunin portrays future society – which, in truth, he does but rarely – he does so in sombre, pessimistic colours. Never do we find an emphasis on future joy; the only joy is in breaking the idols. This aspect of Bakunin's thought – which we cannot go into here – places him at the opposite end of the spectrum to Fourier; even Proudhon, in this respect, is much closer to Fourier than to Bakunin. Albert Camus claimed that his conception of revolution as 'une fête sans commencement et sans fin' is taken from Bakunin; it needs to be balanced against Nechaev's 'Revolutionary Catechism', which Bakunin at least approved, and which proclaims in its first sentence that 'the revolutionary is a doomed man'.[104]

There remains the propensity to destroy; and it is their propensity to destroy that led Bakunin to espouse first the Russian, then the Southern European peasants as agents of revolution. Much nonsense has been written about Bakunin's view of the Russian peasantry. Bakunin did say that 'if the workers of the West delay too long it will be the Russian peasant who will set them an example';[105] but to infer from this, as Lichtheim does, that Bakunin's collectivism was based upon 'the Slavophil worship of the village commune he shared with Herzen',[106] is to commit an egregious error. Bakunin was pan-Slav, not Slavophile; he advocated the complete destruction of the rural commune, the *mir*, and broke with Herzen largely on this issue.[107] He would have agreed with Herzen that 'centralization is contrary to the Slav genius. . . The historical form of the state has never answered to the national ideal of the Slavs',[108] but not because of the *mir* and its 'absolute slavery of custom, thought, feeling and will'. (Ironically, it was Marx, who detested Herzen's idea that Russia could rejuvenate the West, who came around to a view of the *mir* as a possible agent of Russian regeneration.)[109] Bakunin's views on the *mir* should be sharply distinguished not only from those of Herzen but also from those of Lavrov,[110] not least because Bakunin transferred his revolutionary hopes, as no Lavrist or Populist or Slavophile would have done, to Italy and to Spain.[111]

Bakunin entertained illusions about peasant communal institutions like the *mir* for only a brief period; it was not in his nature to pin his hopes on any institution, and what really attracted him to the peasants was their propensity to *Pougatovchtchina*, to unorganized, indiscriminate violence. Bakunin in this respect was close not to the Russian populists but to Weitling, who on one memorable occasion had horrified his listeners by advocating that the 'thieving proletariat' be turned loose on society 'to found the kingdom of heaven by unleashing the furies of hell'.[112] Bakunin considered the proletariat to be the least 'thieving' and least revolutionary of all oppressed groups, yet his sentiments were similar to Weitling's: his toast, 'I drink to the destruction of public order and the unleashing of evil passions',[113] is legendary. He believed that

> the 'evil passions' will [in turn] unleash the peasants' war, and this cheers me, because I am not afraid of anarchy but long for it with all my heart. Only this can uproot us from the accursed mediocrity in which we have been vegetating for so long.[114]

Bakunin, early in his career, did not discount the proletariat and the peasants. 'There will be a terrible revolution, a real flood of barbarians, which will wipe the ruins of the old world off the face of the earth. Then the fortunes of the good, amiable Bürger will be bad, terrible.'[115] The real trouble with the proletariat was that of all potentially revolutionary classes it was most likely to imbibe science and doctrine of the kind that would stifle its revolutionary will, and keep submerged whatever vestiges of anger and 'fantastic hopes' that remained in its memory. During his dispute with Marx in the International, Bakunin insisted that

> the great mass of the working class. . . is ignorant and wretched. Whatever political and religious prejudices people have tried to implant and even partly succeeded in implanting in its consciousness, it remains socialist without knowing it; it is basically and instinctively and by the very force of its position more seriously and more really socialist than all the bourgeois and scientific socialists put together. It is socialist through all the conditions of its material existence, through all the needs of its being, while the others are only socialists through the needs of their thoughts; and in real life, the needs of a man's being always exert a much stronger influence than those of his thought. Thought being here, as everywhere and always, the expression of being, the reflections of its successive developments, but never its moving principle.[116]

It is for this reason that Bakunin turned away from the proletariat and its scientific socialism and fixed his hopes on the 'socialisme primitif, naturel et beaucoup plus sauvage des campagnes',[117] of the peasant, the rural brigand and the bandit. As he himself put it,

> Brigandage is one of the most honoured aspects of the people's life in Russia. At the time when the state of Moscow was being

founded, brigandage represented the desperate protest of the people against the horrible social order of the time which was not yet perfected or transformed according to Western models. . . the brigand is always the defender, the avenger of the people, the irreconcilable enemy of the entire state regime, both in its civil and in its solid aspects, the life-and-death fighter against our statist-aristocratic, official-clerical civilisation. . . The brigand, in Russia, is the true and only revolutionary – the revolutionary without phrase-making and without bookish rhetoric. Popular revolution is born from the merging of the revolt of the brigand with that of the peasant. . . Such were the revolts of Stenka Razin and Pugachev. . . and even today this is still the world of the Russian revolution; the world of brigands and the world of brigands alone has always been in harmony with the revolution. The man who wants to make a serious conspiracy in Russia, who wants a popular revolution, must turn to that world and fling himself into it.[118]

Bakunin's views are of course exaggerated. Rural banditry has nothing automatically revolutionary about it, and the brigand is often the sheerest mercenary (Bakunin himself in his *Confessions* quotes the adage 'point d'argent, point de Suisse',[119] although he never thought of applying it to Russian bandits).

Bakunin's Russian brigands have little enough in common with the romantic *Räuber* of the young Schiller, and much more in common with the traditional (and legendary) Russian *homo viator*, homeless, outcast, adrift and senselessly destructive. Bakunin believed that the socially outcast, the marginal, the outlaw and the criminal shared with the oppressed an exemplary victimization and an exemplary desire for vengeance and propensity for violence. All these groups shared and embodied a more or less latent, more or less potentially explosive revolutionary demiurge that sought only an outlet and needed only the right spark. Bankunin accepted the notion of class war as a revolutionary strategy only in the light of the rebellious surge that he thought was somehow endemic, instinctive to *all* oppressed strata of the population. It is for this reason that he assigned a major role to disaffected students and marginal intellectuals, 'fervent energetic youths, totally *déclassé*, with no career or way out'[120] – to people, in fact, like Nechaev – who had nothing to lose. These alone, he insisted, could escape the fate of becoming 'slaves, playthings and victims of a new group of ambitious men' during and after the revolution, but could do so only by making their revolution themselves – ruthless, chaotic, unrestrained.

Bakunin's commitment to real and potential outlaws calls to mind Stirner's invocation of criminals and paupers as iconoclastic egoists-in-the-making; but such an obvious, and tempting, comparison has its immediate limits. The Nechaev episode* shows that Bakunin's pre-occupation with reckless, marginal, *déclassé* elements in society was no mere abstract, doctrinaire commitment but one which he actually tried to put into practice, with dire and sinister results that did much to discredit Bakuninism in the International. Nechaev, who was made famous by Bakunin, himself practised what he preached, thus catching Bakunin short; he is best regarded, perhaps, as Bakunin's Bakunin – the protégé or disciple who becomes *plus royaliste que le roi* and reveals to his mentor the unwelcome logic of his own position. As such, Nechaev might serve as the nemesis for Bakunin and Stirner alike.

The more immediately relevant comparison is, however, that of Bakunin and Proudhon, the founders of the two anarchist movements that played such important parts in the International. By the time of the Bakuninist flare-up, Proudhonism had largely burned itself out within the International; yet Bakuninism was to fan many of its embers. The two movements, which were geographically distinct, had much in common. The links between Proudhon, the first theorist to call himself an anarchist, and Bakunin, the creator of anarchism as an expansive, internationalist doctrine, were quite clear to Bakunin himself. He revered 'the illustrious and heroic socialist Proudhon, the only one who had the courage [in 1848] to defy and expose [the] rabid herd of bourgeois conservatives, liberals and radicals'[122] for what they were. Bakunin felt proud to be associated with Proudhon; and associated he was, by Marx and others. Marx's every attempt to dismiss Bakunin as a warmed-up Proudhonist – however wrongheaded they may finally have been – had the effect of making Bakunin more certain than ever of the correct-ness of his views, which he himself described as 'Proudhonism, greatly developed and taken to its ultimate conclusion by the proletariat of the Latin countries'[123] – an extension which implies the limits of the comparison, since Proudhon himself had entertained very little interest in the Latin countries. During Proudhon's lifetime, however, he and Bakunin (circumstances permitting) were, from all accounts, personally close; Bakunin, indeed, was one of the few to have been spared the force of Proudhon's verbal wrath. Of influence, there can be no doubt; Franco Venturi claims that it was reciprocal.[124] Bakunin described his

*Sergei Nechaev, having collaborated as a student in Moscow with Tkachev and incurred the suspicion of the authorities, left in 1869 for Geneva, where his ruthlessness and *braggadocio* won over Bakunin; the two collaborated,[121] and created a Secret Alliance, the Narodnaya Rasprava (People's Summary Justice). Nechaev, who was literal-minded as well as unscrupulous, once back in Moscow murdered a student, Ivanov – *pour encourager les autres* – who had threatened to quit the Alliance (this incident was used by Dostoevsky in *The Possessed*); and, having fled to Geneva, implicated Bakunin still further by threatening the Russian publisher of Marx's *Capital* (which Bakunin was to have translated) with a similar fate. Bakunin disowned him, but not before discovery of Nechaev's activities had provided his enemies with evidence galore linking the two, evidence that was used against Bakunin at The Hague Congress of the International in 1872.

own anarchism as 'Proudhon's system enlarged, developed and freed from all its metaphysical, idealist and doctrinaire decoration';[125] this characterization is significant, not because it provides anything like an accurate account of the differences that really did obtain between Bakuninism and Proudhonism, but because it indicates Bakunin's perception of what Proudhonism would need in order to become more appealing and effective. Bakunin was indeed quite perceptive about Proudhon's weaknesses and strengths.

> As I told him a few months before his death, Proudhon, in
> spite of all his efforts to shake off the tradition of classical
> idealism, remained all his life an incorrigible idealist, immersed
> in the Bible, in Roman law and metaphysics. His great mis-
> fortune was that he had never studied the natural sciences or
> appropriated their method. He had the instincts of a genius
> and he glimpsed the right road, but, hindered by his idealistic
> thinking patterns, he fell always into the old errors. Proudhon
> was a perpetual contradiction; a vigorous genius, a revolutionary
> thinker arguing against idealistic phantoms, and yet never able
> to surmount them himself. . .[126]

Bakunin's presentation of them gives us a pointer to what his differences from Proudhon were, and how they were expressed. Proudhonism was indeed metaphysical, idealistic and doctrinaire in a way Bakuninism was never to be; it was also rearguard, backward looking and exclusively French, whereas Bakuninism was expansive, forward looking and internationalist in its (and in its founder's) application. Yet beneath these, and other differences and discontinuities there are similarities and continuities which are not hard to find. The most important of these links is the most obvious. Bakunin's attitude towards political power and the state was of a piece with Proudhon's. In the 'Socialism' chapter of his *Federalism, Socialism and Anti-theologism*, Bakunin indicates that while

> in general, regulation was the common passion of all the socialists
> of the 1848 era. . . [who] were all more or less authoritarian . . .
> [the] exception is Proudhon. The son of a peasant, and thus
> instinctively a hundred times more revolutionary than all the
> doctrinaire and bourgeois socialists, Proudhon armed himself
> with a critique as profound and penetrating as it was merciless,
> in order to destroy their systems. Resisting authority with
> liberty, against those state socialists, he boldly proclaimed
> himself an anarchist; defying their deism and their pantheism,
> he had the courage to call himself an atheist. . .
> His own socialism was based upon liberty, both individual

and collective, and on the spontaneous action of free associations obeying no laws other than the general laws of social economy, already known and yet to be discovered by social science, free from all government regulation and state protection. This socialism subordinated politics to the economic, intellectual and moral interests of society. It subsequently, by its own logic, culminated in federalism. . .[127]

Bakunin, when he insisted that 'it is necessary to abolish completely, in principle and in practice, everything that might be called political power, for so long as political power exists, there will always be rulers and ruled, masters and slaves, exploiters and exploited'[128] – Bakunin in these frequent insistences was speaking in the authentic idiom of Proudhon, as he himself frequently and gratefully acknowledged. The implication that followed, that of political abstentionism, was equally Proudhonian.

The epoch of parliamentary life, of constituent and National Assemblies, is over. Anyone who squarely asks himself the question must confess that he no longer feels any interest, any forced and unreal interest, in these ancient forms. I do not believe in constitutions and laws; the best constitution in the world would not be able to satisfy me. We need something different: inspiration, life, a new, lawless and therefore free world.[129]

Bakunin, in constantly reiterating that political activity inevitably compromises the actor, and that the revolutionary movement should not set out to capture the state by political means, but should instead undermine and overthrow it, was treading in Proudhon's footprints. The revolutionary movement, Bakunin argued just as fervently as Proudhon, should not contaminate itself, should not impugn its own integrity and revolutionary authenticity by using the machinery or requiring the recognition of the state. This broad area of agreement, however, is just the tip of the iceberg. What Bakunin and Proudhon shared was a hard and fast opposition not only to the state but also to religion, capitalism, social hierarchy, parliamentarism, and state socialism ('the vilest and most formidable lie which our century has engendered',[130] according to Bakunin, who here even sounds like Proudhon); they shared a pronounced hostility to intellectual hierarchy in the form of congealed doctrine or dogma (particularly Marx's); and they shared what was not so much a readiness to countenance as an eagerness to embrace non-proletarians, pre-capitalist workers and peasants as *the* revolutionary agents *par excellence*. All these shared features can be reduced to a mutual sentiment about freedom.

Proudhon, in the words of Bakunin, 'understood and had a far greater feeling for freedom' than Marx;

> Proudhon, when he was not obsessed with metaphysical doctrine, was a revolutionary by instinct; he adored Satan and proclaimed Anarchy. It is likely that Marx could construct a more rational theory of freedom, but he lacks the instinctive feeling for it.
> As a German and a Jew he is authoritarian from head to foot.[131]

Yet the very fact that Bakunin, in this and other passages, would see fit to compare Proudhon and Marx might give us pause. Proudhon, who did not readily admit the influence of anyone, and who generally mentioned others by name only to attack them, would have been incapable of any such gesture. The point here is not to applaud Bakunin's generosity, however – Proudhon would make almost anyone else look warm-hearted – but to indicate that Proudhon and Bakunin (who were both very anti-Semitic) had very different views of Marx. Bakunin discusses Marx's ideas with remarkable frequency; Proudhon hardly mentioned his name. Bakunin fully recognized, and frequently acknowledged, the intellectual stature of Marx; Proudhon had regarded Marx as unimportant because he was foreign. Bakunin frequently took issue with Marx's ideas; Proudhon, who regarded Marx's attacks on *his* ideas as of little consequence, and as capable of doing him little damage, never bothered to respond, publicly, to Marx's attacks at all. Any such response he would have regarded as an irksome waste of effort. Bakunin's attitude towards Marx was, for want of a better term, more complicated. He commonly opened attacks on Marx by publicly paying homage to his 'scientific' achievements, a double-edged compliment if ever there was one, coming from Bakunin; and he constantly admitted Marx's superior standing as a theorist – again, a way (for Bakunin) of damning with faint praise – and responded to it with a mixture of envy and admiration. That this mixture was laced with a certain spiteful hostility does not mean that Bakunin's admiration was insincere; it is one of the paradoxes of their dispute that Bakunin's thought was actually influenced by that of Marx. He recalled in 1871 that during the 1840s

> as far as learning was concerned, Marx was, and still is, incomparably more advanced than I. . . Although younger than I, he was already an atheist, a conscious materialist, and an informed socialist. It was at that time that he was elaborating the foundations of his system as it stands today. We saw each other often. I greatly respected him for his learning and for his passionate devotion to the cause of the proletariat – though it was always mixed with vanity. I

eagerly sought his conversation, which was always instructive and witty when it was not inspired by petty hate, which, alas, was only too often the case. He called me a sentimental idealist, and he was right; I called him vain, perfidious and cunning, and I was right too.[132]

Bakunin's words – elsewhere he says of Marx that he had

established the principle that juridical evolution in history is not the cause but the effect of economic development, and this is a great and fruitful concept. . . to Marx belongs the credit for establishing it as the basis for an economic system[133]

– serve to remind us that he and Marx did have some basic points in common. Both believed in the primacy of economic 'base' over political 'superstructure'; both wished to overthrow capitalism and were engaged upon working as active revolutionists to this end; both were socialists and collectivists, opposed to bourgeois individualism; both were bitterly at odds with religion; and both had a veneration for natural science. Bakunin, for his part, freely allowed for Marx's superiority as a theorist, an attribute he could recognize without in any way valuing it; unlike Proudhon, he was unconcerned with questions about his own intellectual originality; and, most important, Bakunin was not the man to occupy himself with queries about the provenance, origin or credentials of any idea, provided it was grist to his mill. He cared only whether it could be put to good use in the spread of Bakuninism.

For these reasons, it should not surprise us that Bakunin, who quite freely borrowed what suited him from Marx's doctrine, had a rather higher estimation of Marx than Proudhon had had. This difference between Proudhon and Bakunin is symptomatic of many others. To begin with, there is the question of violence. Proudhon, as we have seen, favoured gradualist, incremental, institutional change from below, the slow, peaceful growth and imperceptible accretion of counter-institutions behind and within existing institutions. He tended to stand back from violent revolutionary action, since he associated violence with the state; he was refractory even about strikes, which he thought were violent enough to sully the mutualist movement and to contaminate it politically. Bakunin had no such inhibitions. He never concealed his taste for violence in his life or in his writings; he never associated violence exclusively with the state; and he never stopped agitating for sudden, violent elemental change. To this end, he threw himself with an almost unparalleled temerity into any convenient, or available, fray. This fundamental difference points to another – a difference in temperament. Unlike Bakunin, Proudhon was famous and revered because of the books he wrote, but always shunned the limelight; he disliked the public forum, and cut and thrust of open debate. He tended not only to recoil from violence but also to stand back from the kind of socialism that (in Oscar Wilde's words) takes up too many evenings. He was not a participant; he made converts from afar. Bakunin was always a participant, who made converts in person.

Proudhon's attachments were more limited, more distanced. He believed in labour as a redemptive agency, and this belief was the basis of his agencies for the peaceable reconstitution of society from below – the workshop (*l'atelier*) as an educative institution, proletarian self-help and *Bildung* (what Proudhon called *démopédie*), and class purity (*ouvriérisme*). While all these Proudhonian themes were to feed into later anarcho-syndicalism, Bakunin's influence on anarcho-syndicalism, which was to be just as pronounced as Proudhon's, took the form of a belief not in labour but in violence as the redemptive agency. Bakunin agreed with Proudhon that suffering and oppression were exemplary and ennobling, but parted company from Proudhon in insisting that only violence redeems oppression and suffering. Proudhon was obsessed with order, *aisance*, a modest sufficiency and quiet life for all; Bakunin, who was anything but a theorist of order like Proudhon, was obsessed with the kind of pan-destruction and *nihilisme du combat* that made Proudhon (and others) shudder. Proudhon defended the patriarchal family, the hearth and home; Bakunin did not. Proudhon finally defended private property (he wanted everyone to have some); Bakunin worked for its destruction. Even in the case of the hostility to religion the two anarchists shared, Bakunin's railings, which varied between the Promethean and the demonic, make Proudhon's sparrings look palely anticlerical by comparison.

These are differences of some substance; as so often happens, it was the heretical disciple, Bakunin, who carried on and transmitted the main body of the master's ideas into the rough and tumble of political life. They did not survive unshaken. Proudhon's permission had been needed for his followers – those who had composed the *Manifeste des 60* largely in order to obtain it – to participate in the International. Proudhon's permission was forthcoming, but with some reluctance; it involved modification of the doctrine of political abstentionism, which Proudhon somewhat grudgingly reformulated in his last book, *De la Capacité politique des classes ouvrières*. Bakunin shared none of Proudhon's aloofness, none of his reluctance to have his followers participate in a movement for many of whose principles he held no brief. Any movement was grist to Bakunin's mill – not only the International, but even, earlier, the unlikely forum of the bourgeois League for Peace and Freedom; any movement pointed in the direction of liberation of any kind – including the Italian and Polish movements the Proudhonists continued to oppose[134] – was good enough for Bakunin. As to the International, Bakunin was more than anxious to get his foot in the door; as E.H. Carr neatly puts it, 'the spirit in which Bakunin made this momentous move was one not of hostility but of patronage. Far from wishing ill to the International, he would take it under his wing'.[135]

There is one more characteristic difference between Proudhon and Bakunin. It has often been pointed out, more or less uncharitably, that

> for every 'anarchist' statement in Proudhon's voluminous writings, one can find an 'authoritarian' utterance, just as one can find him simultaneously on the side of revolutionary workers, conservative peasants, Louis Bonaparte. . .and the slave-holders of the American South, whose vile cause he espoused because they were fighting against 'centralization.'[136]

On this score, Bakunin's record is untarnished – with the possible exception of the *Confession* read by the Tsar. Yet the ambivalent relationship between anarchism and authoritarianism, which can almost always be found in an anarchist theorist, comes out in Bakunin's case. It comes out not so much in his *Confession* but in his obsessive conspiratorialism, a conspiratorialism Proudhon would certainly have abhorred. Proudhon's idea of a revolutionary conspirator was Louis-Auguste Blanqui, whom he detested; Bakunin's idea of a revolutionary conspirator was Sergei Nechaev, whose flattery threw him entirely off balance. Far from refusing to have anything to do with him – in the manner of Proudhon's aloofness from Blanqui – Bakunin adopted this urchin of the revolution. The difference can tell us a great deal. It can be exaggerated; the claim that Bakunin helped author Nechaev's chilling 'Catechism' has been disproved.[137] Yet Nechaev's paradox of demanding in the name of freedom a Jesuitical obedience *ac cadavar* from members of a revolutionary cell – the organization of which is the very antithesis of freedom – is a paradox that was familiar to Bakunin himself. It has often been pointed out that Bakunin would commonly argue the impossible: 'a spontaneous countryside rebellion, based on the people of the "lower depths," under the control of a secret society that was somehow not to be the kind of organization that consistent Jacobins like Tkachev favoured'; and that Bakunin, who was

> in theory a protagonist of absolute liberty, and ready to denounce in the bitterest terms the rigid discipline of communism. . . resorted, in organizing his revolutionary activities, to methods which were not only the precise contradiction of his own principles, but went far beyond the most extreme ambitions of the dogmatic and dictatorial Marx.[138]

Bakunin would commonly set up separate revolutionary cells, or even rival networks of cells, to spy on one another, keeping (or pretending to keep) the threads of conspiracy and control in his own hands. The web of alliances, bureaux, brotherhoods and directorates which Bakunin had set up by 1868 in order to worm his way into the International is of a complexity that all but defies description. No attempt will be made here to disentangle the web, which would be a forlorn quest. That the organizations in question seem often to have existed only in Bakunin's fertile imagination ought to give pause to those (Leninists included) who fondly imagine parallels between Bakunin - or even Nechaev - and Lenin.[139] Bakunin's successive schemes were generously larded with fantasy, and this is as true of his manipulations within the International as of any others. He was not a particularly successful conspirator, as the following sketch of his machinations in and around the International is about to show. He was, however, the kind of conspirator who is so adept (or maladroit) at weaving webs of intrigue that he succeeds in concealing the ineffectuality of his schemes not only from others but also from himself. His continuous inventions of competing but nebulous cabals should remind us that Bakunin's obsession was, finally, less with power than with personal influence; he simply could not tolerate rivals, and would prefer to command a small, select group which he could dominate by virtue of his considerable personal magnetism than to be prominent, but not predominant, in a larger, more impersonal organization - an organization, that is to say, like the International itself by 1868, the year of his entry.

Brotherhood, League and Alliance

> I will lay counter-mines against Mazzini in
> Florence through Bakunin.
>
> Marx to Engels, 1865[140]

Bakunin might seem a curious choice as Marx's *longa manus* in Italy, yet Marx renewed his acquaintance with him to this end in 1864. Few meetings can have augured less favourably. Bakunin's penchant for the violence of the lower depths, his taste for conspiratorialism, and his instability of temperament were, like Marx's Russophobia, well enough known; all of these were to be amplified as their dispute ran its course. Even apart from these there was a more particular bone of contention. Marx in 1848 had reported in the *Neue Rheinische Zeitung* the existence of documents proving that Bakunin, in his capacity as a Tsarist agent, had denounced some Polish insurgents who were subsequently executed by the Russian authorities. Even though Marx publicly retracted this irresponsible accusation,[141] the incident still rankled when

Bakunin wrote his *Confession*; and Marx, in making amends, seems not to have modified his private misgivings about Bakunin, who remained in his opinion as little to be trusted as any Russian with pan-Slav leanings. By 1864, however, Marx and Bakunin shared an interest in the character assassination of Mazzini, who still posed a threat to the fledgling International; and the meeting between the two passed off surprisingly amicably. Marx reported in a letter to Engels that would have its place in any compendium of famous last words that Bakunin 'will now take part only in socialist movements. . . I must say that I like him much better than before . . . he is one of the few people whom. . . I find directed not towards the past but the future'.[142] Bakunin, for his part, emphasized that Marx had taken the initiative toward reconciliation.

> He [Marx] swore that he had never acted against me, either
> in words or in deeds; that, on the contrary, he had always
> nurtured a sincere friendship towards me and a great respect
> for me. I knew he was not telling the truth, but I had never
> really harboured any resentment. I knew he had played a big
> part in the International: I had read the 'Inaugural Address' he
> had written. . . an important, serious and profound manifesto,
> like everything that comes from his pen when he is not
> engaged in a personal polemic.[143]

Bakunin, back in Italy, seems to have busied himself concocting nebulous libertarian associations – mainly, it seems, 'in the clouds of his tobacco smoke' (as his disciple Guillaume once put it). Bakunin's insistence on attacking the state made little sense in an atmosphere of unfulfilled nationalist aspirations, but he was never noted for his sense of occasion. Until he moved from Florence to Naples in 1865, Bakunin seems to have achieved little either for the International or for anybody else – Marx's letters (attempts, apparently, to direct Bakunin from London) went unanswered – and little more in Naples itself, except among disgruntled intellectuals.[144] The smallness of his following caused him little grief; the Christian religion, he reminded his readers in *Il Popolo d'Italia*, had needed only twelve apostles to conquer the world

> and they conquered it. . .because of their heroic madness, the
> absolute, indomitable, intractable character of their faith in the
> omnipotence of their principle and because, disdaining deception
> and cleverness, they waged open war, without transactions or
> concessions. . .

These words are no mere bluster; as Hostetter indicates, they anticipate 'the guiding principle of Bakunin's later revolutionary activity. . . that an heroic elite with a single-minded faith in the libertarian ideal, can carry the day by the very intransigence of their credo and by a spontaneous mass intuition of its validity'.[145] Not that Bakunin had become incapable of bluster; by July 1866 we find him boasting to Herzen and Ogarev that for the previous three years his sole occupation (whatever Marx might think) had been 'to organize a secret international socialist society' and that despite the 'detestable theory of bourgeois patriotism spread by Mazzini and Garibaldi' he had 'adherents in Sweden, Norway, Denmark, England, Belgium, France, Spain and Italy. We also have some Polish friends and we even count some Russians among us'.[146] Most of this was the sheerest fantasy, although Bakunin, we know, had produced a formal blueprint for a vast, intricate 'International Brotherhood'; we also know that Mazzini, as though to justify Marx's concern,[147] in September 1866 founded a Universal Republican Alliance to counteract the influence of the International and reaffirm the priority of republicanism over socialism. Yet Marx, who still perhaps believed in the effectiveness of his counter-mines, seemed more confident than perturbed. In 1867 he crowed to Engels:

> At the next Congress, in Brussels, I shall personally deal with
> these jack-asses of Proudhonists. I have managed the whole
> thing diplomatically and did not want to come out personally
> until my book was published [*Capital*, vol. i, had just appeared]
> and our Association had struck root. . . Meanwhile [the
> International] has made great progress. . . The swine among
> the English Trade Unionists, who thought we had gone 'too
> far,' now come running to us. . . *Les choses marchent*. In the
> imminent revolution, which is perhaps closer than it seems,
> we (that is, you and I) have this powerful engine in our hands.
> Compare this with the results of Mazzini etc. for the last thirty
> years! Furthermore, without financial means! With the intrigues
> of the Proudhonists in Paris, of Mazzini in Italy, of the jealous
> Odger, Cremer and Potter in London, with the Schulze-Delitsch
> group and the Lassalleans in Germany, we can be well content![148]

Things were indeed moving, but not in a direction to make Marx and Engels content. The intrigues of Bakunin, once they took corporeal form, were to prove more significant than those Marx lists in his over-confident letter, which estimates the success of the International not according to its own growing strength but according to the disunion and 'intrigues' among Marx's enemies – an unbalanced judgment if ever there was one.

September 1867 was the date of the Geneva Peace Congress which Bakunin attended, along with Victor Hugo, John Stuart Mill *et al.*; the

Congress set up the League for Peace and Freedom, into whose Central Committee Bakunin insinuated himself. In this capacity he *did* work for the International, seeking what he called a 'working entente' between it and the League, in the belief that if he could guide the latter, which had no mass following of its own, towards socialism – an unlikely prospect – *rapprochement* with the increasingly well-manned International might follow. Marx was contemptuous of 'the Peace Windbags' and spoke against the International's affiliation with them. 'The peace-at-any-price party', in the words of the relevant General Council minutes, 'would fain leave Russia alone in the possession of the means to make war upon the rest of Europe, while the very existence of such a power as Russia was enough for all the other countries to keep their armies intact.'[149] Marx wrote to Engels in October 1867 that 'the Russians, naturally, have set up the [Peace] Congress. . . and for this purpose they have sent their well-worn agent, Bakunin'.[150] In the event, contact between the International and the League was scotched, as we have seen, since the latter refused to go on record as favouring 'a new order . . . that will no longer know in society two classes, the one of which is exploited by the other'. Some Internationalists attended the League's Geneva Congress (1867) in a private capacity, however; and Bakunin, undaunted, tried again, this time persuading the League to invite the International to participate in its next Congress (which was to be held at Bern in 1868). The invitation went so far in identifying the aims of the League with those of the International, however, that it provided hostile Internationalists with all the ammunition they would need; the International's 1868 Congress in Brussels, accordingly, declared in response that it saw no good reason for the League's continued existence, and high-handedly suggested that members of this now superfluous body should, if they wished, enrol in their local sections of the International. This declaration from without that the League had no further *raison d'être* was regarded as an ignominious slight which its Council reproached Bakunin for having engineered.

Bakunin was further reproached at the League's Bern Congress for his political opinions; impervious to atmosphere, as ever, Bakunin had attempted to initiate a debate on the 'equalization of classes', thereby scandalizing the other delegates, who promptly accused him of communism. Bakunin defended himself eloquently.

> Because I press for the economic and social equalization of classes and individuals, because, along with the workers' Congress at Brussels, I have advocated collective property, I am now accused of being a communist. I am asked what distinction I would make between communism and collectivism. . . I hate communism because it is the negation of liberty and because humanity is for me unthinkable

without liberty. I am not a communist because communism
concentrates and causes all the powers of society to be
absorbed by the state, because it leads necessarily to the
concentration of property in the hands of the state, while
I want the abolition of the state - the radical extirpation of
authority and control by the state which, under the pretext
of moralizing and civilizing men, has, up to the present,
enslaved, oppressed, exploited, and depraved them. I want the
organization of society and collective or social property from
the bottom up, by way of free association, and not from the
top down by means of any authority whatsoever. Since I want
the abolition of the state, I want the abolition of individually
inherited property, which is only an institution of the state, a
consequence of the principle of the state. There you have the
sense in which I am a collectivist and not a communist.

Finding little support for these views among the bourgeois of the
League, Bakunin (who had already joined the Geneva section of the
International) withdrew, along with his entourage, from the League

considering that the majority of the members . . . have
passionately and explicitly declared themselves against the
economic and social equalization of classes and individuals,
and that any programme and any political action that does
not have as a goal the realization of this principle could
not be accepted by socialist democrats, that is, by
conscientious and logical friends of peace and liberty,
the undersigned believe it is their duty to withdraw from
the League.[151]

Bakunin and his followers - Russian, Swiss, Polish, French, Italian
and German - at this point founded the International Alliance of Social
Democracy, the 'social' in whose title was soon changed to 'socialist'
because the term 'social democracy' reeked of German authoritarianism. Its main difference from all the other alliances, brotherhoods and
directorates Bakunin was so adept at instituting, or inventing, was that
the Alliance from the outset considered itself a branch of the International, accepted its statutes, and, in short order, applied in December
1868 for formal membership. This means that dual membership in the
Alliance and the International was, presumably, countenanced from
the very beginning; but what this dual membership actually implied -
or was supposed to imply - has been disputed ever since. Some accounts
insist on the existence of an International Brotherhood whose 'only
country was universal revolution and whose only enemy [was] reaction';
this form of organization, which we know attracted Bakunin, at least in

the abstract, would have made the Alliance

> a secret society in the heart of the International, to give it
> a revolutionary organization, to transform it and all the
> popular masses which exist outside it into a power sufficiently
> organized to destroy the politico-clerico-bourgeois reaction,
> and the economic, juridical, religious, and political institutions
> of the state.[152]

Whether Bakunin's Alliance was an open 'front' for a clandestine brotherhood – as Marx and others in time came to believe – is impossible to establish definitively; what we do know is that the Alliance programme that was sent to the General Council of the International was considerably more radical than the International's own. It called for the collectivization of all instruments of production, for the abolition of the right of inheritance, and of all 'national states' in favour of 'a universal union of free associations, industrial and agricultural', for the equalization of individuals and classes, and for a militant atheism.

These views constituted no technical obstacle to the Alliance's admission to the International, whose rules defined as eligible for admission 'all workers' societies aspiring to ... mutual assistance [and] the complete emancipation of the working class'; that the Alliance's members were not workers was no obstacle either. Marx, however, was formidably suspicious, despite, or because of, the fact that Bakunin attempted personal blandishment on him.

> I am [your friend] more than ever, dear Marx, for better
> than ever I have come to understand how right you were in
> following and in inviting all of us to follow the great road of
> economic revolution, and in denigrating those of us who
> would have got lost in the byways either of purely national
> or of exclusively political undertakings. I am now doing what
> you began to do more than twenty years ago. Since the
> solemn and public adieux I bade the bourgeois of the Bern
> Congress, I have known no other society, no other milieu than
> the world of the workers. My fatherland now is the International,
> of which you are one of the principal founders. You see, dear
> friend, that I am your disciple, and proud of being so...

Marx, not too surprisingly, remained unconvinced by such protestations of fidelity – an *entrée sentimentale*, as he called it. He sent the Alliance's rules to Engels; 'Mr. Bakunin', he wrote in his accompanying letter, 'is kind enough to want to take the workers' movement under *Russian* control'.[153] Marx's own marginal comments on the copy of the Programme and Rules of the Alliance he was sent[154] (and sent Engels) have survived. They ridicule the notion of 'equality of classes', and dismiss 'abolition of the right of inheritance' as 'the old Saint-Simonist panacea'; the Alliance's rejection of 'rivalry between nations' occasions Marx's marginal comment: 'There is rivalry and rivalry, my dear Russian!'; and against the claim that the Alliance was 'established entirely within the International' Marx wrote, 'established within and established against!'. Marx was doing more than venting his private opinions (and Russophobe obsessions), however, in adding to his marginalia the observation that 'the International . . . does not admit any "International" branches'; for the General Council, evidently following Marx's lead, rejected the Alliance's application on these very grounds. Its resolution[155] (which was written by Marx) expresses the fear that if bodies like the Alliance were admitted the International would 'soon become a plaything [un jouet] for intriguers *of all race and internationality*' (my emphases). One wonders how international the International was supposed to be. Marx had a point in insisting that 'the presence of a second international body working within and outside the International . . . [would] be the most infallible means of its disorganization' – one could argue, indeed, that subsequent events were to bear out this interpretation – but the text he used in expressing this point had its limits. Marx was quick to add that a precedent for the rejection of the Alliance's application had been set by the treatment already meted out to the League, a measure for which several signatories of the Alliance's application had themselves voted (in their capacity as delegates to the Brussels Congress of the International).[156] Such a twisting of the knife was surely gratuitous; it certainly makes accusations about Marx's 'authoritarianism' more credible.

In February 1869 the Alliance put in a second bid for membership, agreeing to dissolve itself as an 'international' body if its sections in Switzerland, Italy and Spain were allowed to enrol as regularly constituted sections of the International – which was all that the General Council had had any right to ask of it. The General Council, despite Marx's continued misgivings, this time was obliged to agree, provided that the phrase 'equalization of classes' be stricken from the Alliance's programme. ('It is not the logically impossible "equalization of classes" . . . but the historically necessary "abolition of classes," the true aim of the proletarian movement, which forms the great aim of the [International] . . . however . . . that phrase, "égalisation des classes", seems to be a mere slip of the pen. . .' It was, in fact, to prove otherwise.)[157] The General Council, which was not in the business of vetting the phraseology of member associations' programmes on points of logic, once again had no right to insist on this; to have done so was foolish and shortsighted, since it needlessly created resentment and raised the stakes of a conflict which Marx knew was on its way. The General Council had given Bakunin the kind of foothold he needed to develop a real influence in the International; he was free to advance the cause of 'anti-authoritarian socialism' under the mantle of legitimacy that only the resolutely anti-anarchist General Council could confer. As Marx was uncomfortably aware, the General Council was powerless not to confer this legitimacy; he drafted the General Council's reply to the Alliance, as he put it in a letter to Engels,[158] with the following tactical considerations in mind:

> Bakunin thinks: if we approve his 'radical programme,' he can make a big noise about this and compromise us *tant si peu*. If we declare ourselves against it we shall be designated as counter-revolutionaries. Moreover: if we admit then he will see to it that he is supported by some of the riff-raff at the Congress in Basel...

More fundamentally, however, Marx failed to take the Bakuninists' programme seriously. 'Their "revolutionary programme" ', he wrote scornfully to Engels,[159]

> is supposed to have a greater effect in Italy, Spain etc. in a few weeks than that of the International in years. If we reject their 'revolutionary programme' we bring about a separation between the countries of 'revolutionary' workers' movements (these are...France, where they have two whole correspondants, Switzerland (!), Italy – where the workers, with the exception of those belonging to us, are a mere tail to Mazzini – and Spain, where there are more priests than workers) and [on the other hand] the countries of *slower* development of the working class (viz. England, Germany, United States, Belgium). Hence separation between the volcanic, Plutonic workers' movement on the one side, and the aqueous on the other... That the Swiss represent the revolutionary type is really amusing.

Marx's scorn, as we shall see, was to rebound on him soon enough.

Whether Bakunin actually did dissolve his Alliance – a question that was to become important – we may never finally know. E.H. Carr's biography of Bakunin claims not only that he did not dissolve it, but also that our conspirator plotted a set of Chinese boxes (Bakunin's directorate inside a secret International Brotherhood inside the Alliance inside the International), his aim being to dominate each in turn. This is the kind of claim that cannot really be supported; and so, for that matter, is Carr's assertion that Bakunin, earlier, had

> conceived the bold plan of concluding an alliance between the League and the International which would make him, the prime

mover in the League, co-equal with Marx, the directing spirit
of the International. The League would thus serve him as a
stepping-stone to that position in the International to which his
personality and record entitled him.[160]

The trouble with these claims is not only the absence of any direct
evidence; it is that the mixture of fantasy and reality in Bakunin's
various plots and machinations – whatever the evidence of what he had
in mind – is impossible to disentangle. The historical record appears to
show that Bakunin was if anything remarkably slow to reap advantage
from a new found position of strength, strength he may not have
known.

Of all the Alliance sections, only one, the Genevan, actually took
the trouble to enrol in the International. This in itself suggests either
the marginality of the others or Bakunin's lack of influence over what
they did (or both); but, the others to one side, Geneva itself was less
than ideal for Bakunin's purposes. The complication was that Geneva
was already the major Swiss centre of the International, the seat of
what was (under another name) the Swiss National Federal Council,
the Geneva Federation. Almost all the Geneva Internationalists – the
Fabrika, as they were known, solid, careful craftsmen all, whose fas-
tidious 'bourgeois' instincts repelled Bakunin – were hostile to Bakunin's
ultra-revolutionism; and the Geneva Federation refused to accept the
Geneva section of the Alliance as an affiliated body, even though the
London General Council had done so. Bakunin's Alliance was thus
obliged to fight on two fronts – against the Geneva Federation, in a
running battle that proceeded alongside the larger struggle between
Bakunin and Marx. The course of these fights can be traced out in
Bakunin's regular articles for the Geneva journal *L'Égalité* in 1868
and 1869.[161] By October of 1869 Marx was writing to Engels[162] that

> the secretary of our French committee in Geneva has had
> Bakunin up to his ears and complains that his 'tyranny' has
> ruined everything. In *Égalité* Bakunin announces that the
> German and English workers have no need for individualism
> and that they therefore accept our *communisme authoritaire*.
> In contrast, Bakunin represents *le collectivisme anarchique*.
> The anarchy is really in his head, where there's room for only
> one clear idea, that Bakunin must play first fiddle. . .

Prior to the Congress of Basel – which, as we shall see, marked the
turning-point in the history of the International – *L'Égalité* had relent-
lessly published articles by Bakunin which professed to explain the
principles of the International but which in reality presented the
Alliance's programme as the 'real' programme of the International and

the 'treason' of selected working-class politicians or leaders as the natural, inevitable issue of political action on the part of the working class.

Bakunin's initial support in Switzerland - like Marx's in England – came from resident aliens, political refugees from Russia, Poland, France and Italy; but he also gathered support among *Gastarbeiter* for whom Geneva was already a centre, where builders, carpenters and workers in heavy industry tended to be French or Italian. The Geneva builders' strike was one of many in 1868 that the International helped, and whose success helped buoy the International. Bakunin, helped by Guillaume, also marshalled considerable support among French speaking domestic workers and watchmakers in the Jura, who disliked the German Swiss almost as much as Bakunin disliked anything German (or Marx anything Russian).

From Basel to The Hague

In view of his advance preparations, which (for Bakunin) were assiduous, it is perhaps surprising that Bakunin was as slow as he was to press home his new found advantage. Yet at the first (and only) Congress of the International he attended, at Basel in 1869, only twelve out of seventy-five delegates could be called Bakuninists; and Bakunin himself actually voted and spoke in favour of *extending* (not diminishing) the powers of the London General Council[163] - which, if he was plotting as systematically as Carr and others suggest, would have to be counted as a grave tactical error. One of the reasons Bakunin did so is indicated by Cole: 'the General Council had accepted the affiliation of the Alliance . . . whereas the Geneva [Federation] had rejected it'.[164] Whatever other reasons he may have had for doing so, Bakunin pronounced in favour of giving the General Council wide powers - power to admit or refuse admission to the International (subject to ratification by the annual Congress) and power to suspend between Congresses any section suspected or accused of acting against the interests of the International (again subject to the offended section's appeal to the next Congress). The importance of these resolutions will become apparent.

The Basel Congress was the most representative yet (only The Hague in 1872 was to be more so); it even included a small German delegation. It was convened as the International was reaching a peak - indeed *the* peak - of its influence. Trade union membership and strike activity had increased throughout Western Europe in 1869, and almost every strike was attributed to the International's machinations; the Internationalists, in Cole's words, 'joyfully tried to live up to the role which their opponents assigned to them'.[165] Even so, the Basel Congress - two incidents, each of them connected with Bakunin, apart - had a retrospective, almost complacent air to it; its delegates concerned themselves with past business, and tying up the loose ends left by previous Congresses. Apart from the debate about the powers of the General Council, which was instigated by the Council itself, unsure as it was of its own competence, the Basel Congress occupied itself most prominently with a question that had already been voted on at the previous Congress at Brussels (1868) – that of landed property. Tolain and others insisted that the 1868 vote had been taken without adequate preparation; Congress agreed to reopen the matter, even though Tolain all too manifestly had an ulterior motive for his request: the Brussels Congress had decided that the land – as well as mines, quarries, canals, railways, telegraphs and other means of communication – should come under collective ownership, and passage of this measure – and another, in favour of strikes – was considered a defeat for the Proudhonists.

When the issue of landed property was raised again in 1869 at Basel, Bakunin distinguished himself (as was his wont) in debate, advocating – against the Proudhonists – not only the collectivization of land but also of all 'social wealth', and throwing in for good measure the abolition of the state, 'the only guarantee of existing property'. (He had already offended his hosts by vehemently opposing a German-Swiss proposal to place on the Congress agenda the question of 'direct legislation', or what we would call the referendum, which he regarded as a matter of bourgeois politics having nothing to do with the working class.) The most hotly disputed issue, however, was that of inheritance; this, above all, enabled Bakunin to steal the show. His Alliance, ever since its foundation, had considered the abolition of the right of inheritance to be a cornerstone of its strategy. Bakunin argued that the right of inheritance underlay private property and the state, and that its abolition would lead to the downfall of each. Eccarius, presenting the General Council's report, which had been written, somewhat tersely, by Marx,[166] argued that 'like all other civil legislation, the laws of inheritance are not the cause but the effect, the juridical consequence of the existing economical organization of society, based upon private property in the means of prduction'; the right to inherit slaves, after all, had not been the cause of slavery. He went on,

> The disappearance of the right of inheritance will be the
> natural result of a social change superseding private property
> in the means of production; but the abolition of the right of
> inheritance can never be the starting point of such a social
> transformation. . . To proclaim the abolition of the right of
> inheritance as the starting point of the social revolution
> would only tend to lead the working class away from the
> true point of attack against present society. It would be as
> absurd a thing as to abolish the laws of contract between

buyer and seller, while continuing the present state of exchange
of commodities.

Marx's impatience with the notion of abolishing the right of inheritance
is manifest. It carried over into Eccarius's inept defence of the General
Council report – he had not been well briefed – which, although, it had
the edge logically (Marx had pointed out that to abolish inheritance
alone would be to imply the legitimacy of non-inherited property), was
lackluster in comparison with Bakunin's spirited defence of the Congress
commission's proposal for 'complete and radical abolition'. In Carr's
words, Bakunin's 'tempestuous eloquence, and the straightforward
simplicity of his case made a powerful appeal'. In view of Eccarius'
ineptitude and Marx's complacency, it is not too surprising that first
the Commission, then Congress at large (once the closure was applied)
took Bakunin's part, and that the General Council's report – which
Wilhelm Liebknecht defended at his first appearance – went down to
defeat. Technically, the issue was undecided; symbolically it was a
clear victory for Bakunin, who claimed to have overheard Eccarius
mutter, 'Marx will be terribly annoyed' ('Marx wird sehr unzufrieden
sein'), as indeed he was.[167]

Two incidents at this point reinforced Bakunin's Teutophobia, and
Bakunin believed Marx was behind them both. Wilhelm Liebknecht
(whom Bakunin regarded as Marx's mouthpiece) had apparently denounced Bakunin as a Slavophile and a dangerous enemy of the International; even though he withdrew these charges at a Court of Honour
held at Bakunin's request during the Basel Congress – Bakunin melodramatically lit a cigar with the verdict to demonstrate that he had no
hard feelings, thereby destroying the evidence – they were immediately
repeated, this time by Moses Hess.[168] Hess's post-mortem of the Basel
Congress declared that

> between the collectivists of the International [the General
> Council and its allies] and the Russian communists [the
> Bakuninists] there was all the difference that exists between
> civilization and barbarism, between liberty and despotism,
> between citizens condemning every form of violence and
> slaves dedicated to the use of brutal force.[169]

What lurked in the background of Liebknecht's and Hess's accusations
alike was Marx's old belief, brought out and dusted off for the occasion,
that Bakunin was in reality a Tsarist agent. E.H. Carr believes, with
Liebknecht, that 'only Bakunin's abnormal sensitiveness. . . distorted a
criticism of his political activity into a slander involving his personal
honour', but this is too simple; Carr's formulation, which issues in the
belief that Bakunin's sensitiveness 'began. . .to assume the proportions

of a persecution mania',[170] begs too many questions – among them
whether we should be surprised that any revolutionist of Russian
nationality should take personal offence at even the suspicion of
Tsarist sympathies; and whether, indeed, Bakunin's post-Siberian
revolutionary activities were in any real sense 'Russian' or Russophile
at all. (The Nechaev episode could be regarded as a desperate attempt
to re-establish contact with Russia.)

These considerations do not justify the form taken by Bakunin's
response to Hess – which was not only a letter defending his own
revolutionary credentials against an ignominious slight, the long *Confession of Faith of a Russian Social Democrat,*[171] but also, by way of
a preface, 'A Study on the German Jews', the anti-Semitism of which
was virulent even by Bakunin's standards. Herzen, to whom Bakunin
sent this production, was appalled ('Why all this talk of race and Jews?'
he is reported to have said to Ogarev), but he interceded with the
editor of *Le Réveil* (which had published Hess's piece), Delescluze,
who had had no intention of publishing Bakunin's 'elucubrations', and
prevailed upon him to print a letter from Herzen himself in defence of
Bakunin. Bakunin, for his part, remained convinced that Marx 'was
the originator and instigator of all the filth that has been heaped upon
[him]', a belief which Herzen encouraged, probably because it was true.
In October 1869 Bakunin wrote to Herzen:

> I know as well as you that Marx is quite as much to blame as
> the rest. . . Why then have I spared him and even praised him as
> a great man? For two reasons, Herzen. The first is *justice*.
> Leaving on one side all his iniquities against us, one cannot
> help admitting. . . his enormous services to the cause of socialism,
> which he has served ably, energetically and faithfully throughout
> the twenty-five years I have known him, and in which he has
> undoubtedly outstripped us all. He was one of the first founders,
> almost the chief founder, of the International. That is in my eyes
> an immense service which I shall always recognize whatever he
> does against me.
> The other reason is *political calculation*, and in my opinion,
> perfectly sound tactics. . . Marx is unquestionably a useful man
> in the International. He has been hitherto one of the strongest,
> ablest and most influential supporters of socialism in it, one of
> the most powerful obstacles to the infiltration into it of any
> kind of bourgeois tendencies or ideas. I should never forgive myself
> if, from motives of personal revenge, I destroyed or diminished
> his undoubtedly beneficial influence. It may happen, and probably
> will happen, that I shall have to enter a conflict with him, not for
> a personal offence, but on a matter of principle, state communism,
> of which he and the party led by him, English and German, are

fervent supporters. Then it will be a life and death struggle.
But all in good time: the moment has not yet come.

I spared and praised him for tactical reasons, out of
personal calculation. How can you fail to see that all these
gentlemen together are our enemies, and form a phalanx which
must be disunited and split up, the more easily to destroy it.
You are more learned than I and therefore know better who
first said: *Divide et impera*. If I now declared war on Marx,
three-quarters of the International would turn against me,
and I should. . .lose the only ground on which I can stand. But
if I begin the war by attacking his rabble, I shall have the
majority on my side; and even Marx himself, who has in him,
as you know, a big dose of malicious satisfaction at other
people's troubles, will be very pleased that I have abused
and told off his friends.[172]

Herzen found this exculpation unconvincing. 'You will never make a
Machiavelli with your *divide*,' he told Bakunin, who had indeed apparently forgotton by its third paragraph who was attacking whom. Yet it
is evident from this letter that Bakunin foresaw a 'life and death struggle'
with Marx; and it is evident from his letters of the period that Marx,
too, was convinced by the General Council's defeat on the inheritance
issue that the International was being undermined by a deliberate
campaign on Bakunin's part.

It is for this reason that developments in Switzerland began to
attract his attention. Marx believed that a series of articles critical of
the General Council that appeared late in 1869 in *L'Égalité* and in *Le
Progrès* were the work of Bakunin. Sending a copy of the former to
Engels, Marx adds that

you will see how insolent Signor Bakunin is becoming. This
lad now has at his disposal four organs of the International. . .
He believes the moment has come to begin an open conflict
[öffentlichen Krakeel] with us. He poses as the guardian of
true Proletarianism [als Wächter des wahren Proletarianismus].
Still, he will wonder. . .[173]

Marx was seeing the movement, Bakuninism – he called Bakunin's
followers *Kosaken*! – through the man, Bakunin, who had in fact
unaccountably left Geneva for Italy the previous autumn, and had
not written the articles in question (though he certainly inspired them).
Marx was provoked to draft (in the name and with the sanction of the
General Council) a remarkably testy letter to the Federal Council of
Romance Switzerland about the articles – 'in accordance with decisions
of the last Congress, we can suspend them if necessary, [so] they will

think twice. . . As soon as a Russian creeps in, there is the devil to pay', as Marx put it to Engels.[174] Marx's letter foreshadows many subsequent missives by virtue of its arrogance and pulling of rank. 'The General Council', wrote Marx,

> does not know of any article, either in the rules or in the
> regulations, which obliges it to enter into correspondence or
> into polemic with *L'Égalité* or to provide 'answers' to 'questions'
> from newspapers. Only the Federal Council of Romance
> Switzerland represents the branches of Romance Switzerland
> *vis-à-vis* the General Council. . . *L'Égalité* joins *Le Progrès* in
> inviting *Le Travail*. . .to demand an explanation from the
> General Council. This is almost a *Ligue du bien publique.*[175]

Since even the notes to the Moscow edition of the *Documents* of the International tell us that the Ligue du Bien Publique was an association directed against Louis XI's policy of uniting France into a single, centralized state, we are entitled to wonder whether Marx quite knew what he was doing in using so ill-judged a comparison; that Marx was running the General Council in the manner of an autocratic, centralizing 'state' was a *Leitmotiv* of the articles in question, and was to be a theme sounded in many more. Marx's archness and hectoring were to rebound upon him; his enemies were not slow to note his tendency, under threat, to treat the General Council as a kind of private patrimony, to fulfil, in other words, the Bakuninists' worst suspicions of what he was like. Whether these suspicions could have been allayed, instead of reinforced, by the winter of 1869–70 we shall never know; it is safe to assume, however, that each move like this one on Marx's part lessened whatever chance he may have had of laying such suspicions to rest in the future.

While it could be argued that Marx's each and every move was specifically designed to bring matters to a head and to provoke the 'open conflict' he thought Bakunin wanted, this is unlikely, since it would have split the International. A much more likely hypothesis – one that takes into account the easily forgotten fact that no one could have known how protracted the dispute would become – is that Marx and Bakunin were both playing for time, Marx because he thought (or hoped) that Bakunin would succeed in out-manoeuvring himself, and Bakunin because only with more time at his disposal could he gain support. Each protagonist was engaged, of course, in anticipating the moves and cast of mind of the other, and interpreting these in the light of explanations of the other's behaviour that grew more and more rigid and inflexible; each protagonist was in this sense painting himself into a corner. Bakunin became Marx's Bakunin, Marx Bakunin's Marx; and each clutched at any available straw, the better to reinforce his view of the other. An example of how dangerously near-sighted such presumptions could become is that Marx, learning at last of Bakunin's quite unexpected *Italienreise* and abandonment of his Alliance in Switzerland (management of which was left in the less than capable hands of others), seems immediately to have believed that Bakunin's days as a trouble maker were over. In March 1870 he sent a confidential circular to the German sections summarizing Bakunin's activities[176] and, taking heart from his absence from Switzerland, claiming that 'the game of this most dangerous intriguer will soon be brought to an end'. Events almost immediately proved him wrong.

The events in question were initiated – in Bakunin's absence – in Switzerland. The Geneva section of Bakunin's Alliance, whose affairs Bakunin himself had lately neglected, and which had lost control of *L'Égalité* (a foolish move), applied for admission once again to its local Federal Council, the Fédération romande, which held its Annual Congress at Chaux-les-Fonds at the beginning of April 1870. The Congress voted to admit the Geneva Section of the Alliance to the Fédération romande in accordance with the rules of the International, which should have been the end of the matter; but it did so by a margin of three. The anti-Bakuninist minority immediately seceded from the Fédération and held its own Congress, separately from the pro-Bakuninist majority. Each claimed to be the true Fédération romande, and their claims had to be adjudicated by the General Council in London. This was too good an opportunity to miss. The General Council, acting on Marx's advice, ruled that the majority in question was only 'nominal' since the 'minority' represented more members than the majority did.[177] The General Council also opined that the original Fédération romande, now the minority, which had always acted justly in the past, should not be deprived of its title and that the organization of the majority should therefore adopt some other name.[178]

This reasoning was specious, at least in the sense that the representativeness criterion was never applied to other delegates or other sections of the International – to have done so would have turned up surprises galore. There is perhaps an element of poetic justice in the fact that very shortly the International was to prove capable of expanding its membership only at the behest of the Bakuninists; but this is to anticipate. There are two main reasons, prolepsis aside, why the General Council's ruling was badly judged. First, it had conspicuously exceeded its brief and taken an action that might legitimately seem to be not in accordance with its own rules – rules which were applied *literally* whenever the Bakuninists might suffer. The point here is not a purely legalistic one. The pedantic niceties of whether or not the General Council's decision was, or could be interpreted as being, legal, *stricto sensu*, is less important than what it seemed to people in Switzerland and elsewhere to have done, people who by now were on the lookout for

(real or imagined) slights of this kind. The second reason why the
General Council acted unwisely can be seen from the context in which
this decision was made; its date was June 1870, and three months
earlier the General Council had admitted to the International a Russian
section, which had been organized among Russian émigrés in Geneva as
a counterweight to Bakunin's Alliance. The instigator of this section
was Nicholas Utin, who was sufficiently suspicious of Bakunin to
spread the old rumour that he was a Tsarist agent,[179] and sufficiently
in awe of Marx to ask him to represent his section on the General
Council – to become, in other words, Corresponding Secretary for
Russia (a country having no other representation). Marx, incredibly,
agreed; as he wrote to Engels (this is best given in the trilingual original):

> Drôle de position für mich, als Repräsentant der jeune Russie
> zu funktionieren! Der Mensch weiss nie, wozu er es bringen kann
> und welche strange fellowship er zu untergehen hat. [A strange
> position for me to be functioning as the representative of
> young Russia! One never knows what one may come to or what
> strange fellowship one may have to submit to!][180]

For all these reasons, by the summer of 1870 it was beginning to look
as though the General Council would keep playing with loaded dice.
Its decisions about Switzerland simply reinforced the split that had
already taken place. The Geneva Section, the official Fédération
romande, supported the General Council and Utin, and, wasting no opportunity to discredit Bakunin, went through the motions of solemnly
expelling Bakunin and the other Alliancists from it; the Bakuninists
became the Jura Federation.[181] The battle-lines were set; the Bakuninists had succeeded in tapping a potent source of discontent. What was
already certain by the summer of 1870 was that the Jura Federation
and the General Council in London would continue to watch, and
eagerly interpret, each other's every move from now on.

Bakuninism had by 1870 proved itself much less 'Russian' than
Marx thought (or wished). It spread, chiefly in those countries – Spain,
southern Italy, parts of France and Switzerland – where large numbers
of newly restive peasants, domestic workers and artisans, all of them
threatened in various ways by what seemed to them to be the 'leap in
the dark'[182] of capitalism (which held out the certain prospect only of
proletarianization) were gaining a new political voice. Carr considers
that only the outbreak of the Franco–Prussian War prevented Bakunin's
Alliance from taking root in France; Bakuninism was certainly powerful
in Lyons, where a Congress of the French sections of the International
was held in March 1870. Only Germany, over whose labour movement
Marx himself had very little influence, and Britain, where some labour
leaders still maintained their curious, but by now beleaguered, alliance

with Marx on the General Council, were to remain unaffected by the blandishments of Bakuninism. Countries with established labour movements, that is to say, tended to be unreceptive to Bakuninism; this was true even of France, where Bakuninism spread in areas distant from Paris, a city Bakunin himself never visited after 1864. The neatness of any over-schematic separation between pre-industrial anarchism and capitalist socialism was broken most notably in Belgium, a country which, though poorer, was sufficiently industrialized by the 1860s to stand comparison with England. The highly developed Belgian labour movement was led by the extraordinary César de Paepe, who was conciliatory towards Bakuninism (and, earlier, Proudhonism) but who retained the respect of Marx. The identification of anarchism, in its Bakuninist form, with pre-capitalist elements in Southern Europe should not be overdrawn in any case; its appeal was to those on the brink of capitalism, to those faced with capitalism as a prospect, to those on the margins, to those to whom a capitalist mode of production was the writing on the wall, real enough to pose a threat and to call for a new kind of response. Franz Borkenau observed that 'the Spanish labour movement is based on a mentality directed against the introduction, not against the indefinite continuance, of capitalism', but also that 'were there no capitalist intrusion whatsoever, there would be no anarchism'.[183] To men on the margins the *élan* of Bakuninism and its exemplars,* their headlong assault on church and state, landlord and capitalist, parliament and bourse, seemed more immediately relevant and forceful than the less spectacular approach of Marx would have been.[185] Marx's approach, with its emphasis on gradualism and organization, on order and parliamentary procedure, on the need to build up, patiently if need be, the political as well as the industrial power of organized labour, seemed (to those who knew about it) plodding and irrelevant when compared with the verve and immediacy of Bakuninism. More to the point, perhaps, the Marxist alternative – which, we should remember, was not always presented – seemed (and

---

*Anselmo Lorenzo's description of Bakunin's lieutenant, Giuseppe Fanelli, who – this is no exaggeration – introduced anarchism into Spain, gives some idea of this. 'Fanelli', he writes,

> was a tall man with a kind and grave expression, a thick black beard and large black expressive eyes which flashed like lightning or took on the appearance of kindly compassion according to the sentiments which dominated him. His voice had a metallic tone and was susceptible to all the inflexions appropriate to what he was saying, passing rapidly from accents of anger and menace against tyrants and exploiters to take on those of suffering, regret and consolation when he spoke of the pains of the exploited, either as one who without suffering them himself understands them, or as one who through his altruistic feelings delights in presenting the ultra-revolutionary ideas of peace and fraternity. He spoke in French and Italian, but we could understand his expressive mimicry and follow his speech.

Twenty years later, Lorenzo could recall the very accent with which Fanelli had said, rolling his black eyes above his black beard, 'Cosa orribile! Spaventosa!'[184]

was) remote, geographically and economically as well as spiritually. It meant, for the most part, only opposition in principle to the kind of immediate or indiscriminate violence that to so many anarchist converts held out the only possibility for any hope. We should not be too surprised at the rapid spread of Bakuninism in view of what Gabriel Kolko (in another connection) has termed the 'original sin' of Marxism[186] – its insistence, that is, that nothing should stand in the way of the attainment of long-term goals, or of the maturation of objective conditions, if necessary over a span of generations. This, to men at the end of their tether, seemed irrelevant, a mockery, at a time when their livelihoods were *already* on the line. Bakuninism's appeal was direct and immediate; by 1869 alone there were journals in Geneva, Le Locle, Lyons, Naples and Barcelona, all of them busily disseminating Bakunin's ideas to a ready public, and to the evident, and increasing, dismay of Marx.

Marx, indeed, decided in the face of these 'counter-revolutionary intrigues', as he called them (a description which can serve as a reminder of the value he placed on the right kind of revolution, or as an indication of how out of touch he had become) – Marx decided to stage the fifth Congress of the International in Mainz, where the Germans could see to it that Bakunin would not dominate the proceedings. (Wilhelm Liebknecht duly suggested that 'the connection between political action and the social movement of the working class' be included on the agenda; the General Council complied.)[187] The Mainz Congress, however, thanks to the Franco–Prussian War, was never held; what Marx wanted to guard against there is best illustrated by the country where Bakuninism spread most quickly and struck deepest roots. Before Fanelli's mission to Spain in 1868, as Bakunin's legate, not only was the International not represented there, but to European socialists the country was *terra incognita.*[188] Fanelli, in Gerald Brenan's words,

> left behind him [in Madrid] copies of the statutes of the Alliance for Socialist Democracy, the rules of a Geneva working class society, a few numbers of Herzen's *Bell*, and various Swiss and Belgian newspapers containing reports of speeches by Bakunin. These were the sacred texts on which a new movement was to be constructed. . . . a movement that was to endure, with wave-like advances and recessions, for the next seventy years, and to affect profoundly the destinies of Spain.[189]

Fanelli, strictly speaking, made a mistake in setting up the whole International in Spain with the programme of the Alliance; but it was a mistake that endured, helping to give Spanish anarchism its distinctive, and extraordinarily resilient, form. In 1870 at a General Congress at Barcelona 150 societies from thirty-six regions constituted the Spanish

Regional Federation of the International and adopted as their statutes those of the Jura Federation, which had been drawn up by Bakunin. The combination of these with Fanelli's mistake could have been tailor-made for Spanish conditions. The disemination of anarchism in Spain, with such a programme, was, as Brenan puts it, 'an easy matter'. It was precisely 'this combination of federations of working men, forming. . .free pacts with one another with a small, secret revolutionary body that permeated and controlled them' that, again according to Gerald Brenan in 1942, 'has been the typical organization of Spanish anarchism down to the present day'.[190] This organization was well fitted to survive successive waves of repression, and able to recoup its losses and bounce back after each one.

This is not the place to enter into the chequered history of Spanish anarchism; the circumstances of its growth, however, do help us understand why 'the development of Marx's programme was impossible at that time in Russia, Italy and Spain, as was that of Bakunin in England, Germany and France'.[191] At root, this observation of Brenan's, which puts the matter in a nutshell, helps explain why Marx's obsessive fears about Bakuninism, and the Bakuninists' about Marx, turned so quickly into realistic predictions of how the other group (or individual) would act; but it does not tell *how* this pattern of cross-perception worked to the detriment of the International. It is to this question we now return, but not before insisting upon one crucially important point. Immediately before the Paris Commune of 1871, the International was experiencing a marked decline in membership and considerable apathy in the industrial countries.[192] Wherever the International was spreading, it was doing so under the mantle of Bakuninism. Marx's Address on the Commune, *The Civil War in France*, can be seen, at one level, as a calculated move aimed at re-unifying a disparate movement which could unite around the symbolism of the Commune; Marx's insistence on publishing it with the imprimatur of the General Council (it was an official address *to* the International) alienated several English reformist Internationalists, as Marx knew it would. But it was not their support that had become crucial, as the spread of Bakuninism was indicating. Whether or not Marx was, or could have been, aware of this, it remains true that wherever Bakuninism, and with it the International itself, was spreading by 1871 there was little awareness among converts of the doctrinal issues separating Bakunin from Marx. The doctrinal controversy that loomed so large in London and Geneva was of little concern wherever Bakuninism was making headway. Bakunin, who was now sustaining his literary output, knew this perfectly well and used it shrewdly to his own advantage. In Italy, for example, Bakunin was able to use his well-publicized dispute with Mazzini (who had condemned the Commune) to prosecute his feud with the General Council. Mazzini, says Bakunin in *To My Italian Friends*, 'wants the dictatorship of Rome, not of London; but we, who have no religion, who detest despotism in general, reject that of Rome, as we would reject that of London'. Mazzini's responses – which were always forthcoming – to accusations like this would have the desired effect of identifying Bakunin with the International. The General Council seemed not to have been *au courant*: Engels (who, when he moved from Manchester to London, actually became Corresponding Secretary for Italy) blithely assumed that Bakunin's gains were London's losses, but the General Council in reality had had no influence to lose in the first place.

By the time that the Conference of Delegates was convened in London – in September 1871, three months after the publication of Marx's philippic, *The Civil War in France* – it had become clear that Marx and the General Council could defeat Bakunin only by up-staging him, and that to up-stage him would involve acting in such a way as to confirm Bakunin's recurrent accusations of authoritarianism. Some sort of point of no return had been reached. The composition of the London Conference – held in lieu of a regular Congress and thus empowered to pass only administrative resolutions – alone was enough to incur suspicion. Only two delegates were invited from Switzerland, one of them Utin (who had assiduously investigated Bakunin's Russian activities and writings, the better to discredit him); the Jura Federation was not invited, on the grounds – a pretext – that it had never relinquished the title of Fédération romande. The Conference, in short, looked like a stage-managed affair, and indeed was little else; it consisted of the General Council and its selected (and voting) guests. It adopted resolutions – which were 'administrative' in name only, each one having ideologically charged implications – of an unprecedented rigidity, particularly since now they were made binding on all sections of the International. Resolution IX specified that political action, heretofore a subordinate instrument for social emancipation (it had been stressed in the Rules 'as a means' of social emancipation), was now linked 'indissolubly' to it. Resolution XV authorized the General Council to set the time and place of the next Congress, in view of the post-Commune Terror on the continent – which opened the possibility of the indefinite postponement of a proper Congress in favour of further cabals. Resolution XVI purported to accept in good faith the self-dissolution of Bakunin's Alliance in Switzerland – Bakunin's followers in his absence had reconstituted it under a new name – but refused to let it re-affiliate with the International. The General Council used the resolution that had been passed at the Basel Congress, which Bakunin had supported, specifying that 'the General Council has the right to admit or refuse admission to any *new* society or group, saving an appeal to the Congress'. But the General Council had now arrogated to itself the right to decide when (and where) the next Congress was to be, the better to pack it with favourably disposed delegates; and, worse still, Resolution XVI coupled a General Council *opinion* with a Congress *decision* in the interests of the Council. This was chicanery, and was rightly regarded as such. Hostetter sums up the outcome of the London Conference succinctly:

> Bakuninism is a heresy until Congress decides otherwise; the Council decides when a Congress convenes; therefore, Bakuninism is heresy until the Council decides otherwise... The anarchists naturally drew the conclusion that, failing all other measures, Marx had finally decided to play the game for ideological and political supremacy...with a stacked deck.[193]

In the immediate wake of the London Conference, a Congress of the Jura Federation, now dissident, was convened, in November 1871; it issued the Sonvilliers Circular (also known as the 'Circulaire des Seize'),[194] which was sent to all federations of the International and which claimed that the London Conference's decisions were invalid because of its unrepresentative character. The circular also claimed that the Conference had arrogated to itself unconstitutional powers; that the outcome of its deliberations was consequently invalid; and that a new Congress should be convened immediately to consider the divisions in the International the Conference had created. In the words of the Sonvilliers Circular:

> The functions of the General Council have come to be regarded as the private property of a few individuals... they have become in their own eyes a kind of government; and it was natural that their own ideas should seem to them to be the official and only authorized doctrine of the [International] while divergent ideas expressed by other groups seem no longer a legitimate expression of opinion equal in value to their own, but a veritable heresy...

Yet, in fact, the Rules of the International did not allow for this kind of 'secret conference' called at London, particularly when this conference proceeded to turn what had been 'a free federation of autonomous sections' into 'a hierarchical and authoritarian organization of disciplined sections' under the control of the General Council; and while this was no more than should be expected from those whose ideal was 'the conquest of political power by the working class', this ideal was itself no longer shared by those other members in whose name they had acted, *ultra vires*. The International must return to the principle of autonomy for its various sections; the General Council must revert to the status it was always intended to have, that of 'a simple correspondence and statistical bureau'. Last but not least, the circular sought to bring out into the open why all this mattered so much; lest it be thought that these were abstract proposals made simply to prove a point, with no practical import, the signatories insisted that

> future society should be none other than the universalization
> of the organization which the International has given itself. . .
> How can a free and equal society arise from an authoritarian
> organization? It is impossible. The International embodies
> future human society. . .

Marx replied to these charges, in what had by now become a kind of propaganda war, in a pamphlet issued by the General Council bearing its official seal, *Les Prétendues scissions dans l'Internationale* (*The Fictitious Splits in the International*).[195] The very title of this document was designed to suggest that the rifts existed only in the fertile imagination of certain dissidents in the Jura; that it was printed in Geneva but sent to all federations of the International[196] indicates, on the other hand, that the rifts were more real than apparent. The document is the first of several attempts on the part of the General Council to trace the history of 'persistent efforts of certain meddlers to deliberately maintain confusion between the International and a society [the Alliance] which has been hostile to it since its [this must mean the Alliance's] inception'. At a time when 'the International is undergoing the most serious trial since its foundation',[197] Marx insists that

> denunciations in the bourgeois press, like the lamentations of
> the international police, found a sympathetic echo. . .in our
> Association. Some intrigues, directed ostensibly against the
> General Council but in reality against the Association, were
> hatched in its midst. At the bottom of these intrigues was
> the inevitable International Alliance of Socialist Democracy,
> fathered by the Russian, Mikhail Bakunin.[198]

Marx endeavours to establish that Bakunin's each and every move had been intended 'to replace the General Council with his personal dictatorship'; that 'to this end he created a special instrument [the Alliance]. . . [which was] intended to become an International within the International';[199] and that the effect of all these manoeuvres was to divide the International from within at the very time when it was most threatened from without.

The General Council, Marx argued, 'ever since its origin' had been 'the executive delegation' of the International, charged by the Geneva Congress with publishing 'the official and obligatory text of the rules' without displacing the right of local sections 'to adapt the General Rules and Regulations "to local conditions and to the laws of their country"'. But

> who is to establish whether or not the particular rules [of a local section] conform to the General Rules? Evidently, if there would be no 'authority' charged with this function, the resolution [at Geneva] would be null and void. Not only could police or hostile sections be formed, but also the intrusion of declassed sectarians and bourgeois philanthropists into the Association could warp [dénaturer] its character and, by force of numbers at Congresses, crush the workers.[200]

Infiltration, at least by the police, was a real danger, as events were to show; yet the rest of Marx's argument presents equally real difficulties. The General Council had never acted in any earlier dispute as though its function were to see to it that particular *conformed to* general Rules; it had simply seen to it that nothing incompatible with the latter had appeared on a local level – or had tried to do so, since it lacked the means to enforce its rulings anyway. Moreover, the crucial point raised in the Sonvilliers Circular – that the General Council had in 1871 arrogated to itself certain powers *not* covered by its own original 'Rules' – is the one Marx blithely ignores altogether, although in what had become a crisis in the legitimacy of the General Council it is the one point that should have been met most immediately.

It is for this reason that Marx's more general arguments about freedom, authority, sectarianism and political action – arguments that are of considerable interest and importance, in and of themselves – sit oddly and awkwardly in a document whose tone and evasions vitiate their force. Marx argues against the Alliance that its members,

> these proponents of absolute clamour and publicity organized within the International, in contempt of our Rules, a real secret society directed against the International itself with the aim of bringing its sections, unbeknownst to them, under the sacerdotal direction of Bakunin.[201]

He argues that 'to them, the working class is so much raw material, a chaos into which they must breathe their Holy Spirit before it acquires a shape'; 'they seem to think that the mere fact of belonging to the General Council is sufficient to destroy not only a person's morality but also his common sense'.[202] Most importantly of all,

> The Alliance . . . proclaims anarchy in proletarian ranks as the most infallible way of breaking the powerful concentration

of social and political forces in the hands of the exploiters. Under this pretext, it asks the International, at a time when the old world is seeking a way of crushing it, to replace its organization with anarchy. The international police want nothing better. . .[203]

There is something in each and every one of these points, as we shall see; yet the fact remains that all of them are raised not in order to meet the charges levied in the Sonvilliers Circular, but to deflect attention away from them. One of the few arguments in the circular that *Les Prétendues scissions* does address directly was the argument that the International should in its organization prefigure future society. The Jura Federation had written that 'future society should be a universalization of the organization [of] the International'; Marx writes:

> In other words, just as the medieval convents presented an image of celestial life, so the International must be the image of the New Jerusalem, whose embryo the Alliance bears in its womb. The Paris Communards would not have failed if they had understood that the Commune was 'the embryo of the future human society' and had cast away all discipline and all arms, that is, the things that will disappear when there are no more wars![204]

Yet even this rejoinder is in a significant sense disingenuous, since if there is one belief that both sides shared in this dispute it is the belief that the International *was*, indeed, the organization of future society in embryo, and also that the Paris Commune gives an important clue to the character of future society. This argument about prefiguration had been implicit in the Marx-Bakunin dispute from the very beginning; but proper discussion of this point, too, must await its proper place, since the dispute itself developed further.

Bakunin's 'Response'[205] to *Les Prétendues scissions* (which opens with the words 'Dear companions in disgrace: the sword of Damocles that has threatened us for so long has, at last, just fallen on our heads. Yet it is not a sword, but the habitual weapon of Mr. Marx, a heap of filth [un tas d'ordures]') seems to recognize the unsatisfactory character of Marx's pamphlet, considered as a response to the issues the Sonvilliers Circular had raised. Carlo Cafiero, too, dismissed the General Council's pamphlet as merely 'washing dirty linen in public' (a reference to its publicizing several hitherto secret or private documents) instead of directly defending its position. Yet Bakunin's 'Response' buries the issues still further by treating *Les Prétendues scissions* as nothing more than a personal attack on him (which it was not). In their eagerness to bury the issues separating them and to engage instead in personal polemic, Marx and Bakunin were beginning to resemble each other. For what Marx thought, we must turn yet again to his correspondence of the period. In November 1871 we find him writing to Bolte a résumé of the whole contretemps.

At the end of 1868 the Russian, Bakunin, joined the International with the aim of forming inside it a second international under the name of Alliance of Socialist Democracy, with himself as leader. A man devoid of theoretical knowledge, he claimed that this separate body was to represent the scientific propaganda of the International, and that this propaganda was to become the special function of the second international within the International.

His programme was a mish-mash [ein Mischmasch] superficially scraped together from right and left – EQUALITY OF CLASSES (!), abolition of the right of inheritance as the starting point of the social movement (Saint-Simonist nonsense), atheism dictated as a dogma to the members etc., and as the main dogma (Proudhonist) abstention from the political movement.

This children's story found favour (and still has a certain hold) in Italy and Spain, where the real conditions of the workers' movement are as yet little developed, and among a few, vain, ambitious, empty doctrinaires in French Switzerland and Belgium. . .

For Mr. Bakunin the doctrine (the rubbish he has scraped together from Proudhon, St. Simon etc.) was and is a secondary matter – merely a means to his personal self-assertion. Though a nonentity theoretically, he is in his element as an intriguer.[206]

Marx goes on to indicate on the one hand that he was the victim of a conspiracy to paint the General Council 'pan-German' and on the other hand that publicity of the Nechaev trial 'will expose [Bakunin's] infamous . . . activities' in Russia, 'a country where they know how to estimate Bakunin, and where my book on Capital is just now being published'.[207] This kind of juxtaposition – and this kind of reasoning – is an instance (one of many) of how a theoretical dispute was being reduced to the level of a personal polemic. Yet Marx, prior to The Hague Congress, at another level estimated the balance of forces in the International accurately enough (if somewhat optimistically):

England, the United States, Germany, Denmark, Holland, Austria, the majority of the French groups, the Italians of the North, Sicilians and Romans, the overwhelming majority of the Swiss

Romande, all of German Switzerland, and the Russians in Russia (whom one has to distinguish from some Russians abroad who are tied to Bakunin) go along with the General Council.

On the other side, the Jura Federation in Switzerland (that is the men of the Alliance who hide behind this name), Naples, perhaps Spain, a part of Belgium, and some groups of French refugees. . .all constitute the opposition camp. Such a split, not too dangerous in itself, could become awkward at a certain point, as we must march against the common enemy with closed ranks. . .[208]

The ranks, however, were never to close. Instead, the General Council and the Jura Federation entered the lists against each other. Each accused the other of betraying the International; each campaigned actively for delegates at the forthcoming Congress. On the eve of The Hague Congress, Marx wrote to Kugelmann that he knew it would be 'a matter of life and death to the International; and before I die I want at least to preserve it from disintegrating elements'.[209] Since picking the site of a Congress, a task which could make all the difference to its outcome and proceedings, was now the prerogative of the General Council, Marx was able to benefit from the advantage this gave him; Geneva was carefully avoided and The Hague selected as the venue of the next Congress.[210] Yet it was in the selection of suitably disposed delegates to The Hague, particularly Italian delegates, that Bakunin jettisoned his own strength. The Bologna Congress of the Romagna sections, held in March 1872, carried Bakunin's anti-authoritarianism just one step too far; it resolved to recognize *both* the London General Council *and* the Jura Federation as mere 'offices of correspondence and statistics', thereby achieving the dubious distinction of horrifying both Marx *and* Bakunin – Marx because this move fragmented the International still further, Bakunin because the Italians had implied that the Jura Federation and the General Council were rivals, the very point Marx had been trying to establish in order to marshal support for Bakunin's expulsion from the International.[211]

But this was a mere foretaste. The first National Congress of Italian Socialism, which was held at Rimini in August 1872, resolved unanimously that the London Conference of 1871's 'special authoritarian doctrine', the General Council's 'slander and mystification', the 'indignity' of its circular, *Les Prétendues scissions*, all revealed its 'lust for authority'; it resolved that the General Council's decision to convene at The Hague was a deliberate move to exclude the delegates of the 'revolutionary' countries (as indeed it was); and it resolved that for these reasons

the Italian federation of the International . . . breaks all solidarity with the General Council of London . . . and proposes to all those

sections who do not share the authoritarian principles of the
General Council to send their representatives on September
2nd 1872 not to The Hague but to Neuchâtel in Switzerland,
for the purpose of opening. . . [an] anti-authoritarian
Congress.[212]

This, of course, was a disaster for Bakunin, who needed every vote at
The Hague he could get; it is possible that by this resolution - which
they proceeded to put into effect - the Italians, carried away by their
own (or Bakunin's) logic, cost him his majority there.

Yet even apart from this *malenttendu* the advantage lay throughout
with the General Council. The choice of venue, the composition of the
delegates, and indeed the absence at The Hague of much of the usual
conflict and haggling over the credentials of those who appeared there -
all these assured Marx of support. The General Council had won the
battle for delegates *sans mot dire*, before the Fifth (and in a way final)
Congress so much as convened. Marx even took the unprecedented step
of attending The Hague Congress himself, though Bakunin, unaccountably, did not. Bakunin, perhaps, sensed what would happen there; all
the resolutions the General Council sponsored carried comfortably,
even though one, at least, was dubious and another completely unexpected. The Congress handsomely defeated a Bakuninist proposal to
convert the General Council into a central office for correspondence
and statistics; instead, the Council won a motion incorporating Resolution IX of the London Conference into the Rules of the International.
Next, a committee of enquiry headed by Engels's former operative in
Italy, Theodor Cuno, reported that Bakunin had headed a secret
organization, the Alliance for Socialist Democracy, an *imperium in
imperio*, which had since its inception violated the spirit and the letter
of the International;[213] and, as the logical capstone to this report that
Marx had desired, Bakunin and Guillaume were expelled from the
International. (Their ally Schwitzguébel escaped condemnation narrowly
and left of his own accord.) It was resolved, on rather slender evidence,
that Bakunin's Alliance had aimed by its secret organization to impose
a sectarian programme on the International; and that this worked
against the very principles for which the International stood by virtue
of its division of Alliance sympathizers 'into two castes: the initiated
and the uninitiated . . . the latter designed to be led by the [former] by
means of an organization whose very existence is unknown to them'.
The report itself[214] finds 'insufficient evidence' for the existence of the
Alliance after 1869, yet manages to condemn Bakunin *et al.* for belonging to it. It seems that Marx swayed the committee by producing -
behind closed doors - a copy of a letter from Nechaev to a Russian
publisher who had advanced Bakunin money to translate Marx's *Capital*
(vol. i) into Russian, which threatened reprisals if he should ask Bakunin

to return the money. Marx, counting on foreknowledge of what Nechaev's idea of reprisals meant, had deliberately procured this letter (which Bakunin may not even have known about) and deliberately had held it back until it could be produced as the last straw in a campaign to discredit Bakunin once and for all.[215] Marx's underhanded action has been defended by Nicholaevsky and Maenchen-Helfen:

> The International must not be a screen for activities à la
> Nechaev. Even if Bakunin himself were incapable of drawing
> the practical consequences of his own teaching, as Nechaev
> had done, the Nechaev affair had demonstrated that people
> might always be found who would take his theories seriously.
> One crime like Nechaev's carried out in Europe in the name of
> the International would suffice to deal the workers' cause a
> reeling blow. The struggle against Bakunin had become a
> matter of life and death for the International.[216]

This seems accurate as a paraphrase of Marx's thinking; yet even though Marx for these reasons presumably considered any means justified in order to rid the International of Bakunin, the accusation he used to sway the committee was not shown to have had anything to do with the Alliance, and the committee, without doubt, exceeded its competence in including consideration of it.

It was at this point – the vendetta against Bakunin having been concluded – that Engels, backed by Marx, Longuet and (some) other members of the General Council, produced the bombshell of The Hague Congress, moving that the seat of the General Council be moved to New York. This motion, which was completely unexpected by the assembled delegates, was carried amid considerable (and understandable) confusion. Marx had destroyed the International in order to save it; why he did so has remained a matter of considerable controversy ever since.

Marx's motives to some extent can be reconstructed, but only on the assumption that his almost melodramatic move actually was what it appeared to be, a way of effectively killing off the International. The new American General Council, which in its earlier guise as the North American National Federal Council had already weathered a serious and divisive split, was valiantly to go through Congresses of the International in the USA, but these were fewer in number, and indeed less in importance, than those of the anti-authoritarian (anarchist) International in Europe, which functioned much more successfully. If Marx suspected that the transplanted International would atrophy in the USA, what caused him to produce his *coup de grâce*? The answer has several levels. To begin with, dissension within the General Council, which by 1872 was not at all the solid Marxist bloc the anarchists imagined it to be, played a part. One member, Hales, had long flirted with the Bakuninists; others, outraged at Marx's defence of the Paris Commune, had resigned *en bloc*; and Marx had felt obliged to make up the balance by co-opting Blanquist refugees from the Commune to sit on the General Council. Yet a choice between Blanquists and Bakuninists as bellwethers for the International was in Marx's eyes no choice at all, since both groups were conspiratorialists with a taste for 'barricadology' which Marx considered irresponsible. In any tug of war between London and Switzerland about the site of the General Council, the International itself would become discredited as a conspiratorial clique. Yet other locations were no more promising. Brussels and Paris could be ruled out because of the dangers of reaction in the wake of the suppression of the Commune, as indeed could Berlin. Madrid or Geneva would have meant Bakuninism regnant. New York at least would be safe from European governments and Bakuninists alike; so, at this level, Marx's dealing of his controversial death-blow can be seen to have been carefully calculated. There are other reasons, other levels, too. Marx, whose health was worsening, saw more point in completing *Capital* than in continuing to wear himself out in pursuit of what had become a lost cause. He described The Hague Congress in advance as 'the end of my slavery. Then I shall become a free man; I shall accept no further administrative function'.[217]

We are led, then, to consideration of the reasons why the International was by 1872 a lost cause. The reasons must be sought further back. The Hague Congress was preceded (and, in truth, succeeded) by a confused pattern of decline, not all of it reducible to the Marx–Bakunin dispute but much of it exacerbated by the conflict with the Bakuninists. Two points, in particular, need to be borne in mind. First, the Marx–Bakunin dispute was superimposed upon a pattern of repression following the Paris Commune. As Morgan has reminded us, 'the International's rival "Marxist" and "Bakuninist" factions might have left to fight out their struggle in complete obscurity if the International had not been suddenly and firmly associated with the Commune'[218] of 1871. This association – which both Marx and Bakunin encouraged – dealt the International a blow from which it never really recovered. Second, in considering the Marx–Bakunin dispute, we must in Raymond Postgate's words 'imagine this violent polemic accompanied by a continuous dwindling of the sections, [by] decay, and [by] the erection of false sections for election purposes. We are present at the death of a movement'.[219]

The International: a post-mortem

'We always knew the bubble would burst,' said Engels in 1873, in a celebrated *a posteriori* judgment;[220] and, knowing that this would happen,

it was not a matter of delaying the catastrophe but taking care
that the International emerged from it pure and unadulterated. . .
if we had come out in a conciliatory way at The Hague, if we
had hushed up. . .the split – what would have been the result?
The sectarians, especially the Bakuninists, would have had another
year in which to perpetuate, in the name of the International, still
greater stupidities and inanities; the workers of the most developed
countries would have turned away in disgust; the bubble would
not have burst, but, pierced by pinpricks, would have slowly
collapsed, and the next Congress. . .would have turned into the
most sordid personal row, because principles would have been
already abandoned at The Hague. Then the International would
have gone to pieces. . .

Engels (putting to one side the exculpatory confusion of foreknowledge
and hindsight that runs through this letter) was probably right; by
1872 a point of no return had been reached, and the character of the
International had changed irreversibly. In the industrialized countries
it had lost its muscle; in the areas where it could spread (and was
spreading) it could do so only under the aegis of Bakuninism – only at
the cost, that is, of decentralization and of Bakunin's obsession with
conspiratorialism.

Marx's worst fears, in other words, had been realized; the fight
against what he thought of as revolutionary sectarianism had proved
unsuccessful; the battle-lines, always beleaguered, had finally given
way. Yet Marx, who at first had had no choice but to keep the International open-ended, and to avoid brow-beating delegates, had himself
given way; he finally had converted the International into a dogmatic
forum in response to Bakunin, and had done so, indeed, in such a way
as to realize many of Bakunin's worst fears. By employing unsavoury
strategems worthy of Bakunin himself, Marx had by 1872 reinforced
the anarchists' belief that he had 'authoritarian' leanings, and – much
more importantly, in the long run – he had done much to guarantee in
advance that future Internationals would have to be either ludicrously
ineffective or more ideologically monolithic than the first. We may be
present at the death of a movement, as Postgate thought; yet, to use
an image of which Marx was perhaps inordinately fond, the death-throes
of one kind of movement may affect the birth-pangs of another.

Could all this have been avoided? The question can only be answered
with reference to the history of the International, and of the Marx-
Bakunin dispute within it, and this is so for two main reasons. First, the
idea that the International from its very inception somehow bore the
seeds of its final crisis is supportable only to a very limited extent, and
makes sense, as we shall see, only if applied to the fissiparous tendencies
that were apparent from the outset.[221] What concerns us here is the

way in which Marx endeavoured - vainly, as it turned out - to manage and control these tendencies; and this leads to our second point, that whatever doctrinaire tendencies Marx exhibited in the course of his Donnybrook with Bakunin were themselves not pre-ordained. Marx's prior experiences in and credentials from the Communist League had in no way marked him as doctrinaire in any obvious sense (although he was not of an amiable or tolerant disposition and his personal intolerance was notorious). He had resigned from the Central Council of the League for irreproachably gradualist reasons, and it is worth reminding ourselves of them since they were to be raised in another form in the course of his dispute with Bakunin.

> The minority [Marx had written] have substituted the dogmatic spirit for the critical, the idealist interpretation of events for the materialist. Simple will-power, instead of the true relations of things, has become the motive force of the revolution. While we say to the working people, 'You will have to go through fifteen, twenty, twenty-five years of civil wars, and wars between nations not only to change existing conditions but to change yourselves and make yourselves worthy of political power,' you on the other hand, say 'We ought to get power at once, or else give up the fight.' While we draw the attention of the German workman to the undeveloped state of the proletariat in Germany, you flatter the national spirit and the guild prejudices of the German artisans in the grossest manner, a method of procedure without doubt the more popular of the two. Just as the democrats make a fetish of the word 'people' you make one of the word 'proletariat.' Like them, you substitute revolutionary phrases for revolutionary action.[222]

It might have been expected from such a farewell to extremism that Marx would be if anything a moderating influence on the diverse sects that originated and animated the International; a voice of moderation was in 1864 certainly needed. Marx considered that the purpose of the International would be that of combating the kind of conspiratorialism and sectarianism that (in Marx's view) had rent apart and stymied the Communist League. Marx always thought of the International as a centrifugal force that existed in order to counteract the centripetal tendencies that in fact eventually helped break it apart; he had hoped - vainly, as it turned out by 1872 - that open workers' associations, working together and in tandem in the International, would eventually displace conspirators and sectarians (as Marx thought of them) once and for all. But by 1872 Bakuninists could be out-manoeuvred only with Blanquists: one set of conspirators and sectarians only by using another. The International had defeated its own purpose; having begun life in 1864 as an attempt at merging together labour movements (which were not necessarily socialist) and socialist political associations (which were not necessarily rooted in the working class), the International by 1872 had ceased to be the kind of forum where these (and other) divergent tendencies might be consolidated. To look at the International in this light is to see that *all* attempts at consolidation were thwarted, not just by the Bakuninists and 'Alliancists' (who were, after all, comparative latecomers) but also by the Proudhonists (who were not) and other groups – reformist trade unionists, Chartists, Owenites, positivists, freemasons, Lassalleans, co-operators of the Schulze-Delitsch type, Mazzinian democratic nationalists, Blanquist conspirators and all the rest. Freymond and Molnar's excellent summing up reminds us of

> how great a distance separated the Jura watch-maker. . . from the Parisian. . .disciple of Proudhon, the London trade-unionist from the Geneva bricklayer, and the Barcelona weaver from the Milanese follower of Mazzini. And an abyss separated all these workers from revolutionary communists such as Marx and Engels.[223]

The heterogeneity of these groups would have been the strength and the weakness of the International, Bakunin or no Bakunin; and it is raised here not as a way of minimizing the Marx–Bakunin conflict but simply as a way of recalling its context. One point is clear and fundamental. If, to Marx, the International was necessary, defensible and vindicated to the extent that it transcended working-class sectarianism and particularism, to Bakunin the International was 'authoritarian', therefore unconscionable to the same extent. Unity at the price of dictatorship was to Bakunin not worth striving for; it would either not hasten the revolution or bring about a revolution run on authoritarian lines. In either event it would run counter to the only goals – those of freedom and decentralization – that had ever justified revolution (or the International) in the first place.

Marx's point of view was not a new one; but it was very different. He believed, in the words of his letter to Bolte, that

> the development of socialist sectarianism and that of the real labour movement always stand in inverse relationship to each other. So long as the sects are justified (historically) the working class is not yet ripe for an independent historical movement. As soon as it has obtained this maturity, all sects are essentially reactionary.[224]

To point to the history of the International as something that vindicates this idea would be to accept too much on faith. One of the precipitating causes of the demise of the International, after all, was the Paris Commune; and it is the Paris Commune that reveals, dramatically, what is wrong with Marx's much too formulaic view of working-class organization. If the 'real movement' of the working class was embodied in or expressed by the International *vis-à-vis* what Marx called the 'sects', how could the most celebrated working-class uprising of the nineteenth century take place without much more than a sidelong glance at the International? The Commune put Marx in a difficult position, as he himself was aware; he was to admit in The *Critique of the Gotha Programme* that 'the International was no longer practicable in its first historic form after the fall of the Paris Commune'.[225] In truth the International was no longer practicable in this form after its *rise*. The further irony is that the International – every mention of which by the bourgeois press was followed by Marx, avidly – as a result of the Commune was regarded by the same press as the kind of underground terrorist organization *Bakunin* would have liked it to be. That this view could not have been less accurate is beside the point; and that Marx in fact had his private reservations about the Commune – he regarded it as foolhardy and incapable of surviving – is beside the point too, since its very arrival put Marx in a difficult position. He could not have avoided coming out, publicly and brazenly, in its defence (not least because of the de-institutionalization of political power the Commune represented); but he knew what defending the Commune would mean. The Civil War in France needed the imprimatur of the General Council, the very General Council that by now was restive and chafing at the bit; to obtain this imprimatur meant splitting the General Council and tearing apart even further the tattered remnants of unity in an International that was already beginning to split at the seams. Nor was this all. Marx's defence and sanction of the Commune earned him the very reputation as 'red terrorist Doctor' he feared would damage the International irreparably; and here, too, his fears turned out to be justified. Once the International, as a result of the Commune and Marx's defence of the Commune, had become tarred with the brush of conspiratorialism and terrorism, the wheel in a real sense had turned full circle, since Marx not only considered that conspiratorialism and terrorism should be eschewed in principle and in practice by the International, but also that to combat them was the very *raison d'être* of the International. The association between Internationalism, conspiracy and terrorism was made, moreover, just as Bakuninism looked most threatening, and at the very time when the sinister escapades of Nechaev were coming to light.

It is the convergence or coalescence of all these developments that helps explain what happened subsequently. The balance of forces in the Marx–Bakunin dispute shifted irreversibly, as indeed did the meaning of the terms used in the arguments, as a result of the Commune - an uprising which, ironically enough, had been instigated in the name of neither Marx nor Bakunin, and which owed very little to anything either of them had said or done. Its effect on both Marx and Bakunin was, however, enormous, in an unsettling kind of way. It was in the immediate wake of the Commune that the London Conference of the General Council imposed organizational (and ideological) measures of unprecedented rigidity on all sections of the International and arrogated to itself unprecedented powers. These measures, from Marx's point of view, were in the nature of a last-ditch attempt to create, or re-create, unity at a time when the International looked weak enough to succumb to external pressure; Marx's worst fear - that a once promising political movement of the working class would, after everything, buckle inwards and collapse - was on the point of being realized, and only emergency measures might save it. From Bakunin's point of view the measures Marx thought were called for amounted to proof positive of what he had suspected all along: the General Council's (and Marx's) 'authoritarian', 'dictatorial' tendencies. Marx's attempt to forestall the realization of *his* worst fears provoked and became the occasion of *Bakunin's* worst fears. Bakunin had had his suspicions confirmed; he could now feel that he had been right all along. When he acted on his perception, the measures taken had the by now unavoidable effect of confirming and reconfirming Marx's worst suspicions about him. From this point onwards, the controversy could only feed on itself.

To see that we are by now in the presence of what might be termed, in Hegelian language, a 'bad infinite' is to appreciate how a crucially important feature of the Marx–Bakunin dispute is to be interpreted. That each party caricatured the features of the other has often been noticed; that the mutual caricaturing had a certain pattern to it (as does all caricature), however, has but rarely been addressed. The pattern is not just one of wilful exaggeration, although this certainly played a part and has often been remarked; Bakunin's obsessive views of the General Council as a monolithic phalanx of authoritarian communists with an unshakeable, unreasoning belief in state centralization, or as a pedantocracy that concealed behind endless layers of theorizing its own *manque de volonté* is a case in point; Marx's portrayal of the Jura Federation as the unwitting tool of Bakunin's ubiquitous, sectarian, dictatorial and Jesuitical Alliance, which in turn because of its disruptive tendencies was an unwitting tool of the forces of reaction, is another. That both views are exaggerated is easily pointed out. (On hearing of his expulsion at The Hague, Bakunin characterized the General Council as 'a state, a government, a universal dictatorship! The dream of Gregory VII, of Boniface VIII, of Charles V and Napoleon is reproduced in new forms but ever with the same pretensions, in the camp of social democracy!')[226] In reality the General Council was no pan-German agency guided by a brain like Bismarck's; nor was it under Marx's thumb as much as Bakunin (or, at times, Marx himself) liked to imagine. Marx pointed out in the debate on the General Council at The Hague Congress that the Council had no army, no budget 'but only moral force' and that it would be impotent without 'the consent of the entire Association'[227] – consent the dispute had made impossible to get. The more monolithic Bakunin thought the General Council was, the more divided it was in reality; but this no longer mattered. Much the same is true of Marx's accusations of Bakunin, who in fact was a singularly inept conspirator, easily taken in, easily swayed and easily distracted. What Marx characterized as his campaign of disruption was in fact marked by numerous mistakes and blunders; Bakunin made himself an easy target.

In essence, each party in the dispute attributed to the other a group of followers who had a clear understanding of what was at stake in the confrontation (the Alliancists and General Council members respectively), yet neither group has any counterpart in reality. The point here, however, is not just that Marx and Bakunin, in making similarly exaggerated charges, came to resemble each other; it is that the beliefs of each about the other came to displace the realities. In politics, as in psychoanalysis, beliefs and feelings in a sense become facts, and 'objectivity' is breached. Bakunin's *belief* in the General Council as a disciplined 'pan-German' phalanx of authoritarians guided by a Bismarckian brain came to matter in this debate more than the reality did, just as Marx's belief in the existence of a ubiquitous conspiratorial Alliance masterminded by Bakunin and bent upon destroying the International from within mattered more in the debate than the reality did – although the reality in this case would be impossible to trace. Each party assumed the worst and acted on this perception; each party's view of the other sought (and found) its own confirmation. It is this, indeed, that lends a certain symmetry to the debate; sometimes the very arguments used in it feed on each other. (Bakunin would commonly refer to the Tsar of all the Russians as a German, or a Prussian import; Marx claimed that 'Prussianism as such has never existed and cannot exist other than in alliance and in subservience to Russia.')[228]

An approach to the Marx–Bakunin conflict that stresses each protagonist's changing perception of the other is more satisfactory, it seems, than the kind of approach that rests content with pointing out that each protagonist was making a calculated 'bid' for 'power', or that each wished to impress the International into his own mould, or that each made exaggerated – or similarly exaggerated – claims. The latter kind of approach begs too many awkward questions and finally explains very little; yet even the former approach, whatever its intrinsic superiority, is insufficient to explain the outcome of the conflict, however much light it may shed on its form. What needs to be explained is why the Marx-Bakunin dispute led to the break-up of the International, and why this happened *when* it happened. What translated a background cause of disunity into a precipitating cause of decline was the Paris Commune – not simply because of the repressive measures from various governments that were aimed, in the aftermath of the Commune, at the International, but also because the aftermath of the Commune refocused the debate between Marx and Bakunin. After the Commune, and after the 1871 London Conference, Marx and Bakunin's worst fears and horrible imaginings of each other, exaggerated as they were, appeared to have the ring of truth – not for the first time, admittedly, but nevertheless now more than ever they seemed to have been borne out. The General Council looked *more* 'authoritarian' and 'dictatorial' (and indeed was so); Bakunin's Alliance looked *more* threatening (and was so too). The Commune – albeit for all the wrong reasons – made the International famous, or notorious; but it also sounded the International's death knell.

Marx and Bakunin's *Statism and Anarchy*

Late in 1874 Marx read Bakunin's *Statism and Anarchy* to help teach himself Russian, and in doing so could not resist the temptation – fortunately for us – to copy into a notebook extracts (in Russian) from Bakunin's book, interspersing them with comments (in German) of his own. Marx's conspectus has survived, and is of considerable interest; it serves to sum up some of the issues dividing him from Bakunin, two years before Bakunin's death, and to distil, as in a concentrate, some of Marx's objections to Bakuninism.

Statism and Anarchy, one of Bakunin's longer works, is also one of his most important; it was published among the Russian colony in Geneva in 1873 with the subtitle 'The Struggle of the Two Parties in the International Working Men's Association',[229] although this subtitle does not adequately summarize its contents. *Statism and Anarchy* also expresses Bakunin's thoughts – with the numerous digressions to which the reader of Bakunin becomes accustomed – on contemporary Russian developments, particularly the growth of Russian populism, on which it was intended to have some influence. In this, Bakunin's book was largely successful; *Statism and Anarchy* was from all accounts very influential among the Russian *narodniki* of the 1870s, and Axelrod was to admit having been profoundly affected by its arguments.[230]

These arguments take the form of attempting to link Bakunin's struggle with Marx in the International with the struggle of the Slav peoples against German domination; each struggle symbolizes the movement of revolution against the obduracy of reaction. Germany had become the centre of reaction, not least in its authoritarian socialism;

pan-Germanism and statism are one and the same thing, since the Germans are impregnated with the spirit of obedience and *Obrigkeit*, of slavishness and docility; of all peoples, they are the least receptive to the spirit of liberty. Romance and Slavic peoples form the opposite end of the spectrum; they are the keepers of the flame, the guardians of the sacred spirit of revolt, and they alone can form the vanguard of those forces unalterably opposed to the forces of centralization which otherwise will 'pan-Germanize' Europe by means of conquest. The struggle between Bakunin and Marx in the International is to be interpreted in the light of this larger, polar contrast; Marx and his pan-German allies, who could not see beyond the need to centralize the forces of the proletariat in order to seize state power, are in effect the unwitting dupes of the larger historical tendency of centralization, to which the Slav genius stands opposed by its very nature. Its instincts need only to be galvanized by anti-authoritarian socialism if the process of centralization, authoritarianism, and Germanic systemization, which Marx had carried into the revolutionary camp, was not to inaugurate a period of official dictation and of despair and resignation. *Statism and Anarchy* is not one of Bakunin's more rousing works, however; on the contrary, the Slav genius is invoked as a kind of last-ditch line of defence against those forces Bakunin, by now, had come to believe were triumphant.

Yet several familiar themes are sounded in *Statism and Anarchy*, among them opposition to organization from top to bottom as a means of telling people – particularly those who stood in least need of such arrogant regimentation – how they ought to conduct themselves; and the idea that revolution will proceed not from those who were more 'advanced' on Marx's dehumanizing scale, the pan-German proletariat, but will proceed from the lower depths, from the downtrodden, the oppressed, the exemplary. Political action, Bakunin insists all over again, reeks of dictatorship; and political action on the part of revolutionaries reeks of revolutionary dictatorship, which, being a contradiction in terms, amounts in effect to no revolution at all. Marx's concept of the dictatorship of the proletariat (which Bakunin does not distinguish from that of Blanqui, or indeed from that of Lassalle) is singled out for scornful treatment. Bakunin believed that

> *former* workers. . .as soon as they have become rulers and representatives, *cease to be workers* . . . and look down on the whole common workers' world from the height of the state. They will no longer represent the common people but only their own claims to rule them.

Bakunin's argument can, of course, be traced back to Proudhon's 'homme élu, homme foutu'; and Proudhonist and Bakuninist alike would have been scandalized by Marx's response. Workers, said Marx, as representatives or governors, cease to be workers

> as little as a factory owner today ceases to be a capitalist if he becomes a municipal councillor. . . If our Bakunin were *au courant*, if only with the position of a manager in a workers' co-operative factory, all his nightmares about domination would go to the devil. He should have asked himself what form the administrative function can assume in a workers' state, if he wants to call it thus. . .[231]

Bakunin had posed the rhetorical question, 'What does it mean, the proletariat raised to the position of the ruling class?' and whether 'the proletariat as a whole' would be at the head of the government. Marx responds by asking whether

> in a trade union, for example, does the whole union form its executive committee? Will all division of labour cease in the factory, and will the various functions which correspond to this division of labour, cease? And, in Bakunin's constitution, *de bas en haut*, will all go to the top? In which case there will be no bottom.[232]

Bakunin accused Marx of wanting the domination of the people by a small number of elected representatives; Marx replies that such a view is 'asinine':

> This is democratic verbiage, political drivel! An election is a political form, which is present even in the smallest Russian commune and in the *artel*. The character of the election does not depend on this name, but on the economic basis, the economic relations of the electors, and as soon as the functions [in question] have ceased to be political ones, then there exists 1.) no governmental function, 2.) the distribution of general functions has become a business matter which does not result in anyone's domination, and 3.) election has nothing of its present political character.[233]

Bakunin had protested that

> the so-called people's state will be nothing but the despotic guidance of the mass of the people by a new and numerically very small aristocracy of genuine or sham scientists. Since the people are not learned or scientific they will be freed from the cares of government and entirely regimented into a common herd. A fine liberation!,

Marx points out in reply that 'the class rule of the workers over the strata of the old world with whom they have been fighting can only exist as long as the economic basis of class existence is not destroyed'. Bakunin asks, 'What does it mean, the proletariat raised to the position of the ruling class?'; Marx answers:

it means that the proletariat, instead of struggling in isolation against the economically privileged classes, has acquired sufficient strength and organization to employ general means of coercion in the struggle against them. But it can only use the kind of means that destroy its own character as a wage-earner [Marx uses the word *salariat*] and thus its own character as a class. Thus its domination ends with its complete victory, since its class character has disappeared.[234]

We shall return to this formulation, which is of a piece with those of 'On the Jewish Question' and the *Critique of Hegel's Philosophy of Right*, presently; for the time being we need note only that Marx, who had ridiculed the idea expressed in the Sonvilliers Circular that the International in and by its free federal organization could foreshadow the organization of future society, nevertheless believed that class-based action on the part of the revolutionary proletariat outlined in advance the proletariat's exercise of political power, for the sake of suppressing its enemies.

Since the proletariat, during the period of the struggle for the destruction of the old society still acts on the basis of the old society, and hence still gives to the movement political forms which more or less correspond to it, it has not yet reached its definite organization during its period of struggle. From this, Bakunin concludes that it would be better for the proletariat to do nothing at all, that it should await the day of *general liquidation*, the last judgment.[235]

The 'conspectus' is an important, if overlooked, source on what a Marxist politics involves, not least because of what it says about the relationship between proletarian dictatorship and the peasantry. If the peasant is to be won over for the revolution, Marx argues against Bakunin, the proletariat in power

must not hit the peasant over the head, as it would e.g. by proclaiming the abolition of the right of inheritance or the abolition of his property... Still less should small-holding property be strengthened, by the enlargement of the peasant allotment simply through peasant annexation of the larger estates, as in Bakunin's revolutionary campaign. . . .if [a radical social revolution] is to have any chance of victory, it must be able to do as much immediately for the peasants as the French bourgeoisie, *mutatis mutandis* did in its revolution for the peasants in France of that time. A fine idea, that the rule of labour involves the subjugation of land labour![236]

Conclusion

Marx, in the course of disputing Bakunin's *Statism and Anarchy* says of its author that

> he understands nothing about the social revolution, but only
> political phrases about it. Its economic conditions do not
> exist for him. As all hitherto-existing forms, developed or
> undeveloped, involve the enslavement of the worker (whether
> in the form of wage-labourer, peasant etc.), he believes that a
> radical revolution is possible in all such forms alike. . . . The
> will, and not economic conditions, is the foundation of his
> social revolution.[1]

This is an assessment with which Bakunin might have agreed; it can certainly serve as a *point d'appui* by which Marx's differences from the anarchists can begin to be appraised. Bakunin's extreme voluntarism takes the form of what is surely an overestimation of the potency of revolutionary will among society's lower depths and outcasts. It was more an act of faith than an appeal to evidence. In the International Bakunin opposed organization *de haut en bas*, as well as theorizing and generalization about the supposed preconditions for revolution, and did so with considerable success. He considered that the International was being used by Marx and his cohorts to impose a set of dogmas on those who stood least in need of any such arrogant regimentation; that such imposition reeked of Germanic *Obrigkeit* and encouraged servility; and that the imminent revolution would proceed from the downtrodden, the oppressed, the exemplary, the despairing and potentially violent, and not from those who were deemed to be more 'advanced' on Marx's scale.

Bakunin's conflict with Marx was a bitter and pointed one, not just because of what he said, which does raise many of the problems attendant upon a Marxist politics, but also because of how and where he said it. The conflict took place within the forum of the International, where each protagonist could observe the effect of his own, and his opponent's words and actions. The setting of the conflict magnified the issues involved; each protagonist, after a certain point, could scarcely avoid acting in such a way as to bear out the worst fears of his rival.

There was in this disputation a certain immediacy that was lacking in Marx's earlier attacks on Stirner and Proudhon, partly because the direction of a revolutionary movement – and eventually its very existence – was at stake, and partly because the linkage between the immediate and the ultimate, the short term and the long term, was lost neither on Marx nor on Bakunin. Everything having to do with the organization, allies and ideology of the International retained in the eyes of Marx and Bakunin alike a significance that transcended immediate tactical considerations. Both were sensitive to, and aware of, what might be the eventual outcome of even the smallest tactical decision; each protagonist considered in his own way that post-revolutionary society was presaged in and by the organization, allies and choices of the International itself. Marx disparaged the Bakuninists' claim in the Sonvilliers Circular that the International was a presentiment or the prefiguration in embryo of future society; yet in truth his own beliefs about the futurity embodied in and by the International were, *mutatis mutandis*, not so very different.

This point is of considerable importance, since it has been suggested, understandably but quite wrongly, that because of the opposition to the state Marx is said to have 'shared' with his anarchist rivals, his differences from them, even in the International, can safely and un-problematically be resolved into a difference about tactics, and that disagreements were merely about the means to be used to bring about the common end of the abolition of the state. The trouble with this oversimplified and overdrawn view is that the abolition of the state, in Marx's view and in Bakunin's, was not an end but a beginning, and that neither was inclined to treat revolutionary means and revolutionary ends separately. Neither Marx nor Bakunin, in other words, treated tactical means as though the end could be taken as invariant or simply assumed as a 'given'. The participants in the dispute believed in the necessity or desirability of revolution; but unless we bear in mind that they were also afraid that the wrong *kind* of revolution – the kind propounded by the other side – might ensue, the dispute itself makes no sense. The protagonists in the Marx–Bakunin dispute were agreed basically on one thing and one thing only: that the dispute itself mattered, since its outcome would affect the direction of future society. What explains the intensity of their debate is the hothouse atmosphere in which it was conducted; Marx and Bakunin alike believed that future society would be stamped by its origins, that it had nowhere from which to emerge but the organization of the revolutionary movement itself, and that each and every move made within the International embodied a real futurity.

Bakunin's emphasis on the primacy of revolutionary will recalls Stirner; Stirner's trade mark, *der eigener Wille meiner ist der Verderber des Staats*, could easily have been written by Bakunin, though not in the first person singular. To Stirner and Bakunin alike the source of revolutionary liberation was the will of the revolutionary, uncontaminated either by politics or theory; this will, once extended, is capable of destroying the state and its 'hierarchy'. Marx's words in *The German Ideology* against Stirner might apply equally well to Bakunin.

> So long as the productive forces are still sufficiently developed to make competition superfluous, and therefore would give rise to competition all over again, for so long the classes that are ruled would be wanting the impossible if they had the 'will' to abolish competition and with it the state and law . . . it is only in the mind of the ideologist that this 'will' arises before conditions have developed far enough to make its production possible.[2]

To argue from the primacy of will over 'real conditions' is, according to Marx, to fall into the same trap into which Stirner had so haplessly stumbled.

Bakuninism signified much more than the primacy of will, however; it also signified what Proudhon had called 'l'indifférence en matière politique' as a guiding conception for the revolutionary movement. Abstention from any revolutionary activity that could be called political was bitterly opposed by Marx, who remained untroubled by what seemed to his anarchist rivals to be an unbearable paradox: that of using political means in order to transcend what now passes for politics. Marx saw no reason why the proletariat should not 'use means for its liberation which become superfluous after its liberation';[3] the important point was not to abjure political action across the board, lest it contaminate the actor, but to be able to distinguish among different kinds of political action, the better to be able to use those that were appropriate to furthering the revolutionary cause. Politics, after all, does not stop just because some people think it unimportant or distasteful. Marx's 1872 speech on The Hague Congress[4] is adamant on this point: the International, Marx insisted, had finally proclaimed the necessity for political struggle and had repudiated once and for all the 'pseudo-revolutionary' principle of abstentionism from political struggles. The workers, Marx went on,

> must overthrow the old political system sustaining the old institutions. If they fail to do this, they will suffer the fate of the early Christians, who neglected to overthrow the old

system and who, for that reason, never had a kingdom of this world. I must not be supposed to imply that the means to this end will everywhere be the same. We know what special regard must be paid to the institutions, customs and traditions of various lands; and we do not deny that there are certain countries such as the United States and England (and, if I knew your institutions better, I would add Holland) where the workers may hope to secure their ends by peaceful means. If this is so, we have to recognize that in most of the countries of the continent force must be the lever to which it will be necessary to resort in due time if the domination of labour is at last to be established.[5]

The distinction Marx is concerned to draw here is crucial. It is a distinction that meant little enough to the anarchists, to whom 'the state', *any* state, was the main enemy, and politics was an unconditional evil; but to Marx, who regarded the category 'the state' as an abstraction – as *The Critique of the Gotha Programme* shows – it meant a great deal. Marx, far from denigrating the positive accomplishments that the emergence of the modern, liberal-bourgeois state had brought about, insisted that political reforms tending to make the state more liberal and more democratic were laudable and worthy of support. What Marx's early essay, 'On the Jewish Question', had termed 'political emancipation' – the freedom signified by the French and other bourgeois revolutions, which consisted in liberal democracy, formal freedoms and parliamentarism – may mark a radically unsubstantiated stage of freedom in its true notion, of real, 'human emancipation', the need for which it cannot satisfy, and the outlines of which it can but dimly discern. Yet it is a stage, and the gains denoted by 'political emancipation' are no less real by virtue of their incomplete character; they are not to be despised or ignored but recognized and, where appropriate, put to good use by those having an interest in revolutionary emancipation in its more substantiated form.

The distinction between an autocratic state, be it Bonapartist or Bismarckian, and the liberal bourgeois state may have meant nothing to the anarchists, to whom all these adjectives paled into insignificance alongside the monstrosity to which they all referred, from whose abolition all blessings would flow; the anarchists were not inclined to regard liberal democracy as a measure, hint or premonition of progress, as Marx did. From Marx's perspective, on the other hand, the anarchist argument that differences among state-forms were not differences at all but insignificant variations on a brute theme was simply statism inverted. The choice of allies, the selection wherever possible of liberal rather than autocratic allies may have mattered comparatively little to those who would turn, with impunity, to a Louis Bonaparte, a Bismarck, a

Tsar of all the Russians; but it mattered a great deal to Marx, who took it with a great deal of seriousness and invariably supported it against the right on the straightforward grounds that any future society brought into being with the help of autocratic allies, or by means of a conspiratorial or terrorist mode of organization, would be a reactionary utopia.

The corollary of Marx's position is that there is no reason why the workers' movement should not work within, enjoy recognition by, and extract reforms and concessions from the state – provided only that the state in question be liberal-bourgeois, like England, and not autocratic, like Bonapartist France or Bismarckian Germany. Marx's insistence that the workers' movement should under these circumstances on its own initiative engage in political activity, enjoying the legal protection and even using the electoral machinery of the democratic state, like his cognate insistence that the workers' movement be organized openly rather than conspiratorially, was greatly disliked by the anarchists – many of whom, like Bakunin himself, had an incurable taste for conspiracy, a kind of closet authoritarianism. Marx held to an increasingly unpopular position tenaciously, even though in so doing he had to tread a delicate balance, and treat political activity as a means towards emancipation, not an end worthy of pursuit for its own sake. Otherwise, the illusion would be fostered that social ties were determined by political relations – the very illusion Marx had always wished to counter.

Marx's position was sufficiently complicated not always to lend itself to straightforward defences, and is still often misunderstood. He considered, for example, in 1852, that

> the carrying of universal suffrage in England would...be a far more socialistic measure than anything that has been honoured with that name on the continent. Its inevitable result... [would be] the political supremacy of the working class.[6]

Yet Marx's argument is not the purely parliamentarist-reformist one it might seem to be; it is rather that suffrage would facilitate the articulation of common grievances and concerns, thus contributing to class consciousness and the class struggle. Parliamentary representation was valued not because it would subsume, replace or sublimate class conflict but because it would lend it one more forum. Parliamentarism cannot satisfy the requirements of working-class political activity; taken in and of itself, it might be a snare and a delusion, as Marx's reference in 1879 to the 'parliamentary idiocy'[7] of the German workers' movement should remind us. The point was not to pursue the franchise as though it were a Workers' Holy Grail but to transform it 'from the institute of fraud it has been up till now into an instrument of emancipation'.[8] Marx's insistence in the Resolutions of the London Conference of

1871 that were so infuriating to the anarchists, that the working class should transform itself 'into a political party distinct from, and opposed to, all old parties formed by the propertied classes . . . in order to ensure the triumph of the social revolution',[9] implies parliamentarism, but as a means, not an end. If we need reminding that the aims of the working-class movement pointed beyond the confines of the bourgeois state and its institutions, we need only remember that the resolutions of the London Conference appeared but a few months after that other official document of the General Council, *The Civil War in France*, with its emphasis on the overcoming of parliamentary limitations and the revolutionary de-institutionalization of political power.

Marx's 'Instructions' to the Geneva Congress of the International are consonant with this point of view, stressing as they do the importance of the struggle to win reforms from the existing bourgeois state, particularly those concerning conditions of labour. The 'Instructions' argue against the Proudhonists – and by extension later Bakuninist abstentionists also – that the working class can win valuable reforms prior to the attainment of socialism, and that the only method of doing so is through 'general laws, enforced by the power of the state'. Marx further believed that 'in enforcing such laws, the working class do not fortify governmental power. On the contrary, they transform that power, now used against them, into their own agency'.[10] This is a statement that is all too easily ripped from its context, as it was to be by the German SPD who used it to justify their belief that the working class could gradually take over the existing state and wield it for its own purposes; and while Marx countered such readings effectively enough in *The Civil War in France* as well as *The Critique of the Gotha Programme*, it remains true that, in David Fernbach's words, Marx 'did not make clear . . . to what extent the working class could transform the existing governmental power into their own agency, and what the limits of this transformation were'.[11]

The important point here is not simply that Marx during the years of the International propounded certain beliefs about political action which can be shown to be cognate with some of his earliest political speculations; it is the extreme lengths to which he was prepared to go in their defence, knowing full well that the merest suggestion of political action was anathema to important and growing sections of the International. Yet not only did Marx steadfastly refuse the compromise, or the playing down of the issue, which prudence might have dictated; he raised the stakes, quite deliberately stepping up his campaign on its behalf by having the principle of political action formally enshrined in the Rules of the International. The 1871 London Conference specified that social emancipation and political action were linked 'indissolubly'; and against those who ventured to disagree Marx descended to the kind of strategem and the kind of abuse that could have been calculated to make all subsequent accusations of 'authoritarianism' appear to many otherwise uncommitted, or *parteilos* Internationalists – De Paepe, Hales and Becker are cases in point – to have the ring of truth. Indeed, Marx was not content with converting the International into a dogmatic forum, thus bearing out Bakunin's worst suspicions; he jeopardized the future of the International itself by making the 1871 London Resolutions formally binding on all sections of the International. (That such a ruling was unenforceable, therefore futile, makes it even worse.) Finally, of course, once he was faced with a choice – a choice his own actions had done much to set up – between an International that in practice would abjure political activity and no International at all, Marx opted decisively for the latter.

Why was Marx prepared to go to such lengths in defence of the principle of political action? In 1871 he said of Bakunin, unflatteringly as usual, that 'this ass cannot even understand that any class movement, as such, is necessarily and always has been, a political movement'.[12] What Marx meant here is something to be elaborated more fully in his letter to Bolte in 1871.

> The ultimate object of the political movement of the working class is. . . the conquest of political power for this class, and this naturally requires that the organization of the working class, an organization which arises from its economic struggles, should previously reach a certain level of development. On the other hand, however, every movement in which the working class as a *class* confronts the ruling classes and tries to constrain them by pressure from without is a political movement. For instance, the attempt by strikes etc. in a particular factory or even in a particular trade to compel individual capitalists to reduce the working day, is a purely economic movement. On the other hand the movement to force through an eight-hour, etc., law is a political movement. And in this way, out of the separate economic movements of the workers there grows up everywhere a *political* movement, that is to say, a *class* movement, with the object of enforcing its interests in a general form, in a form possessing general, socially coercive force [die allgemeine, gesellschaftlich zwingende Kraft]. While these movements presuppose a certain degree of previous organization, they are in turn equally a means of developing this organization.[13]

This distinction should give us pause, since Marx's understanding of the term 'political' is very different from, and indeed ultimately incompatible with what the anarchists understood by the word. Politics is understood in this statement, and in statements like it, as being expansive, not restrictive; politics does not amount to the threat the anarchists always saw in it, but actually embodies promise and potential. Anarchists - we must here think of Stirner and Proudhon as well as Bakunin - always see power, authority, organization and politics itself in purely institutional terms, as though measure were *always* external measure, organization *always* imposed from without as what Stirner had called a 'task' or 'vocation', and as though regulation were *always* restrictive and intrusive. It is here that anarchists' links with the liberal tradition and its negative conception of liberty - as freedom *from* something external and exterior - are at their clearest.

Proudhon and Bakunin, unlike Stirner, each believed in organization of the kind that would go against the grain of the prevailing form of society. Proudhon, who was a theorist of order, believed in organization on the basis of the workshop and workplace, since such organization, he believed, contained within itself a socially regenerative principle. Bakunin, who was an advocate of disorder, believed in organization of clandestine, conspiratorial and decentralized cells, and that violence alone was redemptive and regenerating. In either case organization of the required type was valued because it was held *not* to be political; the organization in question was predicated upon rejection, across the board, of the political realm. Politics in its established form, no matter what this form is or how it was established, is conceived as an external threat or impediment, which is always, in principle, to be avoided as ominous and reprehensible. Freedom and authority are regarded as unalterably opposed, as polar opposites, as zero-sum categories.

Marx's point of view was very different. The anarchist notion of the rejection, across the board, of the reprehensible never endeared itself to him. It may have made the anarchists quick to spot 'contradictions' - Proudhon, in particular, saw contradiction everywhere - yet the contradictions, and the way they are seen, have nothing properly dialectical about them. Contradiction with the anarchist is a dualistic, almost Manichaean* principle, particularly in the case of Bakunin. To Marx, capitalism in some ways creates the preconditions of its own transcendence, preconditions that have to be acted upon; the 'political emancipation' that characterizes the emergence of the modern state both denies and creates the need for its own supersession, as well as the means by which this supersession might best be brought about. Yet neither process is uniform; evaluations and choices - that is political evaluations and political choices - need to be made. From this perspective, the trouble with any anarchist rejection on principle of all instances

---

*Lest it be thought that to invoke Manichaeanism is to suggest that anarchism is basically a pre-modern movement - which is quite false - Manichaean dualism should here be contrasted not just with the dialectic but also with the principle of plenitude Lovejoy[14] identified as a mainstay of medieval speculation. The principle of plenitude entails that different degrees of evil are to be valued for their ultimate contribution to the good; Manichaeans explain the counterpoint of good and evil in a directly opposite way, as agencies of two independent, co-equal principles, so that evil *as evil* is required if the good is to establish itself.

of 'the state', or anything else considered reprehensible, is that clean hands may mean no hands. What good is revolutionary purity without a revolution? As Plekhanov once, almost bitterly, put it, 'the utopian negation of reality by no means preserves us from its influence'.[15]

Let us take an example by way of arriving at how deep-seated the opposition between Marx and any anarchist perspective ultimately is. Marx considered that the British Ten Hours Act of 1846 'was not only a great practical success; it was the victory of a principle; it was the first time that in broad daylight the political economy of the middle class succumbed to the political economy of the working class',[16] because it raised the prospect of the social control of economic relations – control, that is, over the operation of an inhuman and dehumanizing market mechanism, 'the rule of dead matter'. The operation of this mechanism is blind, purposeless, uncontrolled, alien to those who are its victims; against it, Marx advocated not the abolition or diminution of control but the extension of a certain kind of control, not the abolition of all norms and sanctions but their reintegration into areas of human life that under capitalism evade conscious social control. What is aimed for it not at all the disappearance of anything that might be termed authority but, on the contrary, the reassertion of conscious social control by men, associated one with another, over their own lives, creations and relationships. Marx wrote in *The German Ideology* that

> with the community of revolutionary proletarians the advanced
> state of modern productive forces. . .puts the conditions of
> free development of individuals under their own control,
> conditions which were previously abandoned to chance and
> won an independent existence over against the separate
> individuals precisely because of their separation as individuals.[17]

Revolutionary politics is for the sake of overcoming such separation, and is itself a means of overcoming it. The goal of revolutionary politics as Marx described it in 1874 is that the working class, 'instead of struggling in isolation against the economically-privileged classes, [would acquire] sufficient power and organization. . .to use generalized means in the struggle against them'.[18] The anarchists' fears that Marxist revolutionary politics pointed towards and would lead to proletarian dictatorship were well-founded; Marx's advocacy of the dictatorship of the proletariat was as central to his doctrine and, more to the point, to his activity in the International, as they thought it was, and more recent attempts to play down its significance are unconvincing. Shlomo Avineri claims that 'Marx does not use the term more than two or three [*sic*] times . . .and then always in what is basically a private communication'.[19] Marx's anarchist interlocutors would have taken some convincing of this. In one of these private communications

(Marx's 1852 letter to Weydermeyer),[20] he describes the dictatorship of the proletariat as one of his three basic discoveries; another 'communication' was *The Critique of the Gotha Programme*, which should not, properly, be regarded as 'private' at all; and in any case, Marx used phrases *like* 'proletarian dictatorship' frequently. It may be that part of what he meant by it was dictatorship in its Roman sense: an assumption of power for a limited period for the sake of carrying through tasks specified in advance. A glance at the Oxford English Dictionary reveals that the use of the term 'dictatorship' to signify absolute power without even a time limit was only just gaining currency during Marx's lifetime, although this is the sense in which Bakunin used it.

Yet the dictatorship of the proletariat, whatever its connotations, should not be regarded as an institutional panacea for what was not a purely institutional problem. To the anarchist he who says 'politics' says 'the state'; but this is palpably untrue of Marx. The goal of a Marxist politics is the Hegelian goal that man recognize himself in and through his own creations, this being (as Hegel had recognized) the only possible basis for intersubjectivity and thereby for community; the goal in other words is a political goal, the means to its attainment political means. Marx's starting-point is the Hegelian perception that 'ethical order' and community are impossible in modern civil society, to which alien politics alone is appropriate. When individuals live apart from one another, negotiating mutual use in a condition of what Hegel had called 'mere isolated subjectivity', moral rules and political regulations can appear only as alien, abstract and distant. Yet the solution to alien politics cannot be no politics, but only politics of a different kind; it cannot be further depoliticization, but only repoliticization of the required type. Anarchism is not the solution to alienation but the maximization of a certain kind of alienation – alienation from the future prospect of genuine community.

Marx's starting-point was that of an Hegelian distinction between the state and civil society, and it is significant that no anarchist perceived this distinction in anything like the same way. Stirner conflated the two and thought that the state and society alike would fade away once men began imperturbably to ignore their existence. Proudhon urged his readers to undermine and undercut the state but from the standpoint of the very civil society whose rules, those of political economy, he accepted as having a timeless validity.* Bakunin, who like Proudhon awarded a certain primacy to the state in wildly overestimating the

---

*Albert Hirschmann has wryly pointed out that 'the modern political argument for capitalism that is today associated with such authors as [von] Mises, [von] Hayek and Milton Friedman was originally put forward by none other than Proudhon. . . [who] fearful of the enormous power of the state. . . in his later writings conceived of the idea of opposing to this power a similar "absolutist". power – that of private property'.[21]

social effects of its abolition (Marx's words about Proudhon, that 'he thinks he is doing something great by arguing from the state to society', certainly apply to Bakunin too), also confused the state with civil society, at least to the extent of urging the simultaneous violent destruction, *la liquidation sociale*, of both.

Marx, however, was party to none of these confusions. He awarded no primacy to the state, his break with Hegel having dictated quite different priorities; he rejected the rules of political economy as having an inhuman application and a purely provisional validity; and he regarded the state as illusory only in its capacity as community, not in its capacity as an agency of the means of violence. This means that the continuity among Marx's successive attacks on the anarchists, which this book has been concerned to trace, can readily enough be demonstrated. Marx did not simply trot out the same arguments again and again as the occasion demanded, as though he were merely applying an invariant formula; different, successive issues demanded different, successive responses, all of which, taken together, reveal a continuity of outlook and approach that can tell us much about the continuity of Marx's thought as a whole. Marx used the same kind of argument, which is not easily separated from invective, against Bakunin in the International, as he had already used earlier in his career in his attacks on Proudhon and Stirner; throughout them he emerges at his least appealing and at his most hectoring and heavy-handed.

Anarchism does indeed have the 'broad back' that Octave Mirbeau attributed to it.[22] Stirner, Proudhon and Bakunin each raised different issues that demanded different successive responses from Marx, responses which played an important part in the elaboration and evolution of his thought. Yet anarchism, largely under the aegis of Bakuninism, became not just a doctrine but also, much more importantly, a movement, and this shift has important implications. The Marx-Bakunin dispute was unlike Marx's earlier disagreements with anarchists because its protagonists were actually agreed upon two basic fundamentals: revolution as opposed to reform, and collectivism as opposed to individualism, be this the truculent egoism of Stirner or the no less truculent 'social individualism' of Proudhon. Moreover, the battle for collectivism – much more than the battle for revolutionism – had largely been won within the ranks of the International itself, to the evident disarray of the Proudhonists. Yet all these areas of convergence did nothing to push Marx and Bakunin any closer together, but instead exacerbated their remaining differences, which quickly came to seem more irreconcilable than ever. Marx's earlier disdain for anarchism was exacerbated, not repressed, by his encounter with Bakuninism. This leads us to a point of some importance. Merely to counterpose those issues on which Marx and Bakunin could (for different reasons) come to some residual agreement – that is, revolutionism and collectivism – to those that still awaited settlement – the role of the proletariat, of secrecy, conspiratorialism and violence, of capitalism, of the state, of politics itself – would be much too schematic an approach. The point is, rather, that the way in which Marx had confronted the earlier issues, and for that matter the way in which he had confronted earlier anarchists, led him to try to bring to bear a similar approach to his dealings with Bakunin.

Anarchism's transformation from the status of a doctrine to the level of a movement took place within and *as part of* Marx's career as a revolutionist; yet Marx did not adjust his arguments against anarchism accordingly. To examine the anti-Bakuninist documents written by Marx and issued under the imprimatur of the General Council is to be struck time and time again by their similarity, even in the archness of their tone, to Marx's earlier anti-anarchist expostulations. Bakunin simply reminded Marx of all the nonsense he had already encountered and (at least to his own satisfaction) put to rest. Marx saw in Bakuninism even at its most expansionist little more than something he was already familiar with – 'Proudhonized Stirnerism' or Proudhonism warmed over and *mis à la Russe*. Such designations tell us nothing about what is distinctive about Bakuninism, the existence and spread of which indicates that Bakunin himself was much more than one more thorn in Marx's flesh. Besides misjudging Bakuninism's nature and expansive potential, Marx failed to recognize that doctrinal impatience, heavy-handed irony and withering scorn, which had never been effective in disposing of Proudhonism, would be counter-productive if brought to bear in so similar a way against Bakunin in the context of an organization like the International. Marx's armoury of abuse served mainly to reinforce accusations that he was dogmatic and 'authoritarian'; he became in this way the victim of his own earlier arguments. Even though these arguments are vital to our understanding of Marx's thought and career as a revolutionist, the continuity among them that may readily enough be traced is not one that worked to Marx's advantage – or for that matter to ours.

For we are led once again to Marx's *coup de grâce* at The Hague in 1872: the climax and upshot of a long series of anti-anarchist arguments and manoeuvres which did so much to ensure that 'proletarian internationalism' would turn into the dogma it need (and should) never have become, and that future Internationals would be ideologically monolithic in a way the First International was never originally intended to be. The doctrinal rigidity of future Internationals is on no account to be defended. It reinforced tendencies within Marxism we would all be better off without; it is a sorry story of hidebound inflexibility, bureaucratization and the stifling of questioning and initiative from below. These tendencies have never lacked for defenders – defenders whose bluff was called in May 1968; lovers of the idea of 'poetic justice', or perhaps of Hegel's 'cunning of reason', will be quick to point out that Bakunin was more right, so to speak, than he could possibly have known.

Yet the issues Bakunin addressed go beyond dogmatism, just as they go beyond their immediate setting. They have to do with whether a transition to socialism is possible without bourgeois society's having already attained an advanced stage of development with high levels of production and strongly established democratic practices which would provide a reliable foundation for an extension of human freedom. The point here is not simply that this question has not yet adequately been answered, but that it has to it certain dimensions we would all do well to ponder. On the one hand, if we regard history as an automatic, causal process and the socialist movement, correspondingly, as a 'necessary', determined phenomenon – this is still the received view of Marxism in some quarters – then the transition to a socialist society will be, likewise, an inevitable development. If all this is true, then moral impulses and aims would be of no account and socialist politics could be represented (as they were by Kautsky, for example) as an ethically neutral technology based on a science of society. Politics would become supernumerary, the government of persons the administration of things. This picture of Marxism is not compelling; my hope is to have shown that it is also radically incomplete.

There is another dimension to our problem. As Barrington Moore has (somewhat melodramatically) put it,

> The chief basis of radicalism (in modernizing countries) has been the peasants and the smaller artisans in the towns. . . .the wellsprings of human freedom lie not where Marx saw them, in the aspirations of classes about to take power, but perhaps even more in the dying wail of a class over whom the wave of progress is about to roll.[23]

There is much here that is well-founded, particularly after a hundred years or so of *chercher le prolétariat* among committed Marxists. Yet even to agree with Moore that the proletariat is the *fata morgana* of Marxism should not blind us to deeper questions: whether we can trace the lineaments of a free and decent society from the voice-prints and 'dying wails' of those who were faced with 'progress' – here the record of the anarchists does not uniformly inspire confidence – and whether freedom (which Moore does not define) and progress are in fact antithetical. It is because there is at least a strain in Marxism that tells us they are not antithetical but cognate that I find myself in agreement with the words of Charles Taylor, that 'the line from Hegel to Marx remains in many ways the most clear and intellectually structured theory of liberation in the modern world'.[24]

Notes

Introduction

1 See Anthony Arblaster, 'The Relevance of Anarchism', in *The Socialist Register*, ed. Ralph Miliband and John Saville, London, Merlin Press, 1971, pp. 157–84.

2 London, Eyre & Spottiswoode, 1964.

3 Harmondsworth, Penguin, 1962.

4 George Woodcock and Ivan Avacumović, *The Anarchist Prince: A Biography of Peter Kropotkin*, London, Boardman, 1950.

5 Daniel and Gabriel Cohn-Bendit, *Obsolete Communism: The Left-Wing Alternative*, trans. Arnold Pomerans, Harmondsworth, Penguin, 1969.

6 See Daniel Cohn-Bendit, *Le Grand Bazar*, Paris, Belford, 1976.

7 Boston, Beacon Press, 1966.

8 David Apter, 'The Old Anarchism and the New', *Government and Opposition* (London School of Economics), vol. v, no. 4, autumn 1970, pp. 397–8.

9 Robert M. Nozick, *Anarchy, the State, and Utopia*, New York, Basic Books, 1974, p. xi. Nozick's index contains the interesting entry, 'Anarchism: *see* State of Nature'.

10 On this, see Isaiah Berlin, 'Two Concepts of Liberty', in *Four Essays on Liberty*, Oxford University Press, 1970, pp. 118–72.

11 Judith N. Shklar, *After Utopia*, Princeton University Press, 1957, pp. 8–10.

12 Ibid.

3 Gerald Brenan, *The Spanish Labyrinth*, Cambridge University Press, 1972, p. 189.

14 Quoted in Woodcock and Avacumovic, *The Anarchist Prince*, p. 12.

15 'On Anarchism and the Real World: William Godwin and Radical England', *American Political Science Review*, vol. lxvi, 1972, p. 128.

16 Ibid.

17 Sheldon S. Wolin, review of David McLellan, *Karl Marx: his Life and Thought* (New York, Harper & Row, 1973) in the *New York Times Book Review*, 13 January 1976, pp. 23–4.

18 *Marx–Engels Werke*, Berlin, Dietz vol. xxix, 1966, p. 225.

19 McLellan, *Karl Marx*, p. 334.
20 Wolin, review of McLellan.

1 Hegelian roots

1 *Hegel's Philosophy of Right*, trans. with notes by T.M. Knox, Oxford, Clarendon Press, 1962, § 258, p. 157. Cf. G.W.F. Hegel, *The Phenomenology of Mind*, trans. with an introduction by J.B. Baillie, New York and Evanston, Harper & Row, 1967, pp. 599–610; and, for discussions, Judith N. Shklar, *Freedom and Independence: A Study of the Political Ideas of Hegel's 'Phenomenology of Mind'*, Cambridge University Press, 1976, pp. 173–9, and Charles Taylor, *Hegel*, Cambridge University Press, 1975, pp. 185–8, 403–27.

2 On the usually unremarked links between Montesquieu and Hegel, cf. Michael Mosher, 'The Spirit that Governs Cities: Modes of Human Association in the Writings of Montesquieu and Hegel' (doctoral dissertation, Harvard University, Cambridge, Mass., 1976), *passim*. My indebtedness to this manuscript is considerable.

3 *Hegel's Philosophy of Right*, §279A, p. 288.

4 Georg Lukács, *The Young Hegel: Studies in the Relations Between Dialectics and Economics*, trans. Rodney Livingstone, London, Merlin Press, 1975, p. 40. See also J. Glenn Gray, *Hegel and Greek Thought* (originally published under the title *Hegel's Hellenic Ideal*), New York and Evanston, Harper & Row, 1968, *passim*.

5 G.W.F. Hegel, *Early Theological Writings*, trans. T.M. Knox, with an introduction by Richard Kroner, Philadelphia, University of Pennsylvania Press, 1971, p. 149. Cf. Shlomo Avineri, 'Hegel's Nationalism', *Review of Politics* (Notre Dame, Ind.), vol. xxiv, no. 4, 1962, pp. 461–84, and in general, Avineri's *Hegel's Theory of the Modern State*, Cambridge University Press, especially ch. III (pp. 34–61).

6 *Hegel's Philosophy of Right*, §258, p. 156.

7 Ibid., §184, p. 123. George Armstrong Kelly characterizes the state's relation to the individual, cryptically but sensitively, as follows:

> The problem of life is purpose, order, fulness – *lebendiges Leben*; the problem of philosophy is justification through comprehension – the *Sichwissen des Geistes*. Life actualizes; thought eternalizes; they do this to each other. The state is the amniotic protection for the exchange. Where the political community is impotent, fragmented or 'accidental' to its role, thought retreats to subjectivity and life is cleaved into private wish and public act, into 'chimera' and prejudice. (*Idealism, Politics and History: Sources of Hegelian Thought*, Cambridge University Press, 1969, p.348)

In accordance with this ambitious demarcation of the political, Eric Weil points out that the purely private world of action and work, civil society, constitutes 'un monde qui se fait sans vouloir se faire'; men need not understand what their actions are perforce bringing about. The state provides the opportunity and wherewithal for such understanding. (Cf. Eric Weil's valuable *Hegel et l'état*, Paris, Presses Universitaires de France, 1950, p. 46.)

8   *Hegel's Philosophy of Right*, §260, p. 161.

9   Ibid., §75, p. 59; cf. §75A, p. 242; §294, p. 191.

10 Ibid., §273, p. 178.

11 J.N. Findlay, *Hegel: A Re-examination*, New York, Collier, 1962, p. 324. Hegel believed to the contrary that individuals quite simply 'do not live as private persons for their ends alone' (*Hegel's Philosophy of Right*, §260, p. 161).

12 Hegel, *The Phenomenology of Mind*, pp. 520 ff.; Shklar, *Freedom and Independence*, pp. 152–63.

13 Raymond Plant, 'Hegel's Social Theory', *New Left Review* (London), no. 103, May–June 1977, p. 85.

14 Shklar, *Freedom and Independence*, p. 156.

15 *Hegel's Philosophy of Right*, §324, pp. 209–10. Cf. Shlomo Avineri, 'The Problem of War in Hegel's Thought', *Journal of the History of Ideas* (Chicago), vol. xxii, no. 4, pp. 463–74; Avineri, *Hegel's Theory of the Modern State*, pp. 194–207; Paul Thomas, 'Hegel: Civil Society and War', *Proceedings* of the 4th Biennial Meeting of the American Hegel Society (Villanova University, Philadelphia, November 1976), Philadelphia, State University of Pennsylvania Press, 1978.

16 *Hegel's Philosophy of Right*, §324A, p. 295.

17 Albert O. Hirschmann, *The Passions and the Interests: Political Arguments for Capitalism Before its Triumph*, Princeton University Press, 1977, *passim*; Sheldon S. Wolin, *Politics and Vision*, Boston, Little, Brown, 1960, ch. X, pp. 352 ff.; Joseph A. Schumpeter, 'The Sociology of Imperialisms' (1917) in *'Imperialism' and 'Social Classes'*, New York, Kelly, 1951.

18 Montesquieu, *L'Esprit des lois*, X, 7; XX, 2; cf. Hirschmann, *The Passions and the Interests*, pp. 71, 80.

19 John Maynard Keynes, *The General Theory of Employment, Interest and Money*, London, Macmillan, 1936, p. 374; cf. Hirschmann, *The Passions and the Interests*, p. 134.

20 *Hegel's Philosophy of Right*, §324, pp. 209–10.

21 Ibid., §243, p. 149.

22 Ibid., §244A, p. 277.

23 Ibid., §245, p. 150.

24 Ibid., §246, p. 151.

25 Karl Marx, *Critique of Hegel's Philosophy of Right*, trans. Annette Jolin, ed. and with an introduction by Joseph O'Malley, Cambridge University Press, 1970, p. 81; for the same text, *Marx–Engels Collected Works* in English, New York and London, International Publishers, 1975, vol. iii, p. 80. Henceforward these texts are cited as O'Malley and MECW iii respectively.

26 Heinz Lubasz, 'Marx's Initial Problematic: The Problem of Poverty', *Political Studies* (Oxford), vol. xxiv, no. 1, March 1976, p. 27.
27 *Hegel's Philosophy of Right*, §244A, pp. 277-8.
28 Ibid., §244, p. 150; cf. §195, p. 128.
29 O'Malley, p. 142; MECW iii, p. 187.
30 O'Malley, pp. 141-2; MECW iii, p. 186.
31 *Hegel's Philosophy of Right*, §65, p. 52.
32 Ibid., §66, pp. 52-3.
33 Ibid., §67, p. 54.
34 Ibid.
35 Hegel, *The Phenomenology of Mind*, pp. 228-40. Cf. Alexandre Kojève, *Introduction à la lecture de Hegel*, Paris, NRF, 1947, especially pp. 52 ff., for an influential interpretation; and G.A. Kelly, 'Notes on Hegel's "Lordship and Bondage"', *Review of Metaphysics* (Chicago), June 1966, pp. 780-802, for a criticism of Kojève.
36 Karl Marx, 'Critique of Hegel's Dialectic and Philosophy as a Whole', in T.B. Bottomore, ed., *Karl Marx: Early Writings*, New York, McGraw-Hill, 1964, pp. 198-9, 201; MECW iii, pp. 329, 332.
37 Marx, "Critique", p. 203; MECW iii, p. 333.
38 Marx, "Critique", p. 202; MECW iii, p. 332.
39 Marx, "Critique", pp. 213-14; MECW iii, p. 342.
40 O'Malley, p. 32; MECW iii, p. 31.
41 O'Malley, p. 81; MECW iii, p. 80.
42 O'Malley, pp. 77-8; MECW iii, p. 77. Cf. Herbert Marcuse, *Reason and Revolution: Hegel and the Rise of Social Theory*, Boston, Beacon Press, 1968, p. 208.
43 O'Malley, p. 22; MECW iii, p. 21.

2 **Alien politics**

1 Marx, *Critique of Hegel's Philosophy of Right*, trans. Annette Jolin, ed. and with an introduction by Joseph O'Malley, Cambridge University Press, 1970 (henceforward cited as O'Malley), pp. 91, 64; to be found also in *Marx-Engels Collected Works* (henceforward cited as MECW), vol. iii, New York and London, International Publishers, 1975, pp. 91, 63.
2 *Hegel's Philosophy of Right*, trans. with notes by T.M. Knox, Oxford, Clarendon Press, 1962, §182A, p. 266.
3 O'Malley, p. 31; MECW iii, p. 30.
4 Marx to Arnold Ruge, May 1843, in MECW iii, p. 137.
5 O'Malley, p. lvi; cf. pp. 98-101 (MECW iii, pp. 98-100).
6 O'Malley, p. 111; MECW iii, p. 111.
7 Marx, 'On the Jewish Question', in T.B. Bottomore, ed., *Karl Marx: Early Writings*, New York, McGraw-Hill, 1964 (henceforward cited as Bottomore), p. 30; MECW iii, p. 167.
8 Marx and Engels, *The German Ideology*, trans. Clemens Dutt,

ed. Salo Ryazanskaya, London, Lawrence & Wishart, 1965, pp. 91–2; MECW v, p. 78.

9   O'Malley, p. 72; MECW iii, p. 72.
10 Ibid.
11 O'Malley, p. 82, cf. p. 106; MECW iii, p. 81, cf. p. 106.
12 O'Malley, p. 73; MECW iii, p. 73.
13 O'Malley, p. 32; MECW iii, p. 32.
14 Ibid.
15 Bottomore, p. 128; MECW iii, p. 165; O'Malley, p. 32; MECW iii, p. 32.
16 Bottomore, p. 28; MECW iii, p. 165.
17 Bottomore, p. 31; MECW iii, p. 168.
18 O'Malley, p. 32; MECW iii, p. 32.
19 Bottomore, p. 7; MECW iii, p. 149.
20 Bottomore, pp. 9–10; MECW iii, p. 151.
21 Bottomore, p. 21; MECW iii, p. 159–60.
22 Marx and Engels, *The Holy Family,* in MECW iv, p. 117.
23 *The German Ideology,* p. 93.
24 Bottomore, pp. 13–14; MECW iii, pp. 153–4.
25 Bottomore, p. 26; MECW iii, p. 164.
26 Bottomore, pp. 24–5; MECW iii, pp. 162–3.
27 *The Holy Family,* in MECW iv, pp. 120–1.
28 Bottomore, p. 31; MECW iii, p. 168.
29 Marx, *The Critique of the Gotha Programme,* in *Marx–Engels Selected Works,* Moscow, Foreign Languages Publishing House, 1962 (henceforward cited as MESW), vol. ii, p. 32.
30 Ibid.
31 MESW ii, p. 33.
32 Ibid., pp. 33–4.
33 Marx and Engels, *The Manifesto of the Communist Party,* in MESW i, p. 38.
34 Ralph Miliband, 'Marx and the State', in R. Miliband and John Saville, eds, *The Socialist Register, 1965,* New York, Monthly Review Press, 1965, p. 280. This pioneering article has now been extended: cf. R. Miliband, *Marxism and Politics,* Oxford University Press, 1977, *passim.*
35 *The Critique of the Gotha Programme,* in MESW ii, p. 32.
36 Marx, *The Poverty of Philosophy: Response to 'The Philosophy of Poverty' of M. Proudhon,* New York, International Publishers, 1963, p. 83.
37 Ibid., p. 174.
38 Marx, 'Critical Marginal Notes on the Article "The King of Prussia and Social Reform." By a Prussian', in MECW iii, p. 204.
39 *The German Ideology,* pp. 357–8; MECW v, pp. 329–30.
40 'Critical Marginal Notes', in MECW iii, p. 199.
41 Ibid., p. 197.
42 Ibid., pp. 197–8.
43 *The German Ideology,* p. 78; MECW v, p. 90.
44 *The Manifesto of the Communist Party,* in MESW i, pp. 54, 36.

45 Marx, 'Die moralisierende Kritik und die kritisierende Moral.
    Beitrag zur deutschen Kulturgeschichte. Gegen Karl Heinzen'.
    Original in *Marx-Engels Gesamtausgabe*, Moscow, 1932 et seq.,
    I/6. Partial translation in H.J. Stenning, ed., *Karl Marx: Selected
    Essays*, New York, International Publishers, 1926; this
    quotation is from Stenning, pp. 136-7.
46 *The Holy Family*, in MECW iv, p. 113.
47 E.P. Thompson, *The Making of the English Working Class*, New
    York, Vintage, 1966, pp. 9-10.
48 Marx, *The Class Struggles in France, 1848-50*, in MESW i, pp. 142,
    189-90.
49 Ibid., p. 189.
50 Marx, *The Eighteenth Brumaire of Louis Bonaparte*, in MESW i,
    p. 312.
51 Marx, 'Preface' to the second edition of *The Eighteenth Brumaire*,
    in MESW i, p. 244.
52 *The Eighteenth Brumaire*, in MESW i, pp. 331-2.
53 Marx, *The Civil War in France*, in MESW i, p. 518.
54 *The Eighteenth Brumaire*, in MESW i, p. 332.
55 Ibid., p. 284.
56 *The Civil War in France*, in MESW i, p. 518.
57 *The Eighteenth Brumaire*, in MESW i, pp. 284-5.
58 Ibid., pp. 285-6.
59 Ibid., p. 288.
60 Ibid., p. 333.
61 Ibid., p. 333.
62 Ibid., p. 334.
63 Ibid., pp. 340-1.
64 Ibid., pp. 340-1.
65 *The Civil War in France*, in MESW i, p. 518.
66 *The Eighteenth Brumaire*, in MESW i, p. 342.
67 Ibid., pp. 343-4.
68 'On the Jewish Question', in Bottomore, p. 16; MECW iii, p. 356.
69 *The Eighteenth Brumaire*, in MESW i, p. 333.
70 *The Civil War in France*, in MESW i, pp. 516-17.
71 *The Eighteenth Brumaire*, in MESW i, p. 333.
72 *The Civil War in France*, in MESW i, p. 516.
73 Ibid., p. 519.
74 Ibid., p. 519.
75 Ibid., p. 520.
76 Ibid., pp. 521-2.
77 Ibid., pp. 526, 542.
78 Marx to Ferdinand Domela-Nieuwenhuis, 22 February 1881, in
    Marx-Engels Selected Correspondence, Moscow, Foreign
    Languages Publishing House, 1975, p. 318; cf. Shlomo Avineri,
    The Social and Political Thought of Karl Marx, Cambridge
    University Press, 1970, pp. 239-49.
79 The first draft may be read in English in its entirety in the *Archiv
    Marksa i Engelsa* (Marx-Engels Archives), Moscow, 1934, iii (viii).

This quotation is from p. 324. Cf. Miliband, 'Marx and the State', pp. 280–1, 296, n. 79.

80   *The Civil War in France,* in MESW i, pp. 516, 517, 521, 519, 520.

81   *Archiv Marksa i Engelsa,* p. 324.

82   *The Civil War in France,* in MESW i, p. 520.

83   *Archiv Marksa i Engelsa,* pp. 320–2; cf. Avineri, *The Social and Political Thought of Karl Marx,* pp. 50–1.

84   Avineri, *The Social and Political Thought of Karl Marx,* p. 23.

85   *The German Ideology,* p. 208, MECW v, p. 195.

86   *Hegel's Philosophy of Right,* §272A, p. 285.

87   O'Malley, pp. 32, 82; MECW iii, pp. 32, 81.

88   MESW ii, p. 32.

89   Marx, 'Critical Marginal Notes', in MECW iii, pp. 204, 205.

90   *The Civil War in France,* in MESW i, p. 516.

91   'Critical Marginal Notes', in MECW iii, pp. 204–5.

92   Marx to Friedrich Bolte, 23 November 1871, in MESW ii, pp. 466–7.

93   Jean-Jacques Rousseau, *The Social Contract,* trans. and with an introduction by Maurice Cranston, Harmondsworth, Penguin (Classics edn), 1968, Book II, Chapter 7, pp. 86–7.

94   Buonarroti and Weitling, as quoted in Michael Löwy, *La Théorie de la révolution chez le jeune Marx,* Paris, Maspero, 1970, pp. 85, 90–1. For these references I am indebted to Norman Geras's excellent short article, 'Proletarian Self-Emancipation', in *Radical Philosophy* (London, Radical Philosophy Group), no. 6, winter,1973, pp. 20–2.

95   Marx and Engels to Bebel, Liebknecht, Bracke and others, 17 September 1879, in MESW ii, p. 485.

96   Marx, 'Third Thesis on Feuerbach', in *The German Ideology,* p. 646; MECW v, p. 4.

97   V.I. Lenin, *What is to be Done? Burning Questions of our Movement,* Moscow, Foreign Languages Publishing House (paperback edn), n.d., p. 160.

98   Cf. Louis Althusser, *For Marx,* trans. Ben Brewster, New York, Vintage, 1970, and Louis Althusser and Etienne Balibar, *Reading Capital,* London, New Left Books, 1972, *passim*; this position is largely unchanged in Althusser's *Essays in Self-Criticism,* trans. G. Looke, London, New Left Books, 1976.

99   In particular, cf. Herbert Marcuse, *One-Dimensional Man, Studies in the Ideology of Advanced Industrial Society,* Boston, Beacon Press, 1966, *passim.*

100 *The German Ideology,* pp. 229–30; MECW v, p. 214.

101 Avineri, *The Social and Political Thought of Karl Marx,* p. 141.

102 Bottomore, p. 176; MECW iii, p. 313.

103 *The German Ideology,* p. 86; MECW v, pp. 52–3.

104 Marx, *Theories of Surplus Value,* vol. ii, Moscow, Foreign Languages Publishing House, 1972, pp. 117–18.

105 Marx, 'Postface' to the second (German) edition of *Capital,* vol. i; in the Penguin/New Left Book edn, trans. Ben Fowkes, Harmondsworth, 1976, p. 99.

106 Bottomore, pp. 158, 154, 132; MECW iii, pp. 299, 295, 280.
107 Marx, *Capital*, vol. i, ch. 15, section 9; trans. Fowkes, p. 616.
108 Marx, *Wages, Price and Profit*, lecture no. 7; in MESW i, p. 424.
109 Marx, *A Contribution to the Critique of Political Economy*,
     Moscow, Foreign Languages Publishing House, 1971, p. 210;
     cf. G.A. Cohen, 'Marx's Dialectic of Labour', *Philosophy and
     Public Affairs* (Princeton, N.J.), no. iii, spring 1974, pp. 253–61.
110 *The Manifesto of the Communist Party*, in MESW i, p. 38; *The
     Eighteenth Brumaire*, in MESW i, pp. 333 ff.
111 *The Poverty of Philosophy*, p. 111.
112 Marx, *Grundrisse*, trans. Martin Nicolaus, Harmondsworth,
     Penguin, 1973, pp. 409–10.
113 Ibid., p. 488.
114 Ibid., p. 162. Marx's concept of 'labour power' extends this; cf.
     p. 151 above.
115 Bottomore, p. 116; MECW iii, p. 300.
116 Shlomo Avineri, 'Marx's Vision of Future Society and the
     Problem of Utopianism', *Dissent* (New York), summer 1973,
     p. 330. For an exchange, cf. David Resnick, 'Crude Communism
     and Revolution', *American Political Science Review*, vol. lxx,
     no. 4, December 1976, pp. 1136–45; Avineri, 'Comment', ibid.,
     pp. 1146–9; Resnick, 'Rejoinder', ibid., pp. 1130–5.
117 This point has been ably put by István Mézáros, *Marx's Theory
     of Alienation*, London, Merlin Press, 1970.

3 Marx and Stirner

1 During Marx's lifetime only the fourth chapter of the 'Saint
   Bruno' section of *The German Ideology* was published as the
   'Obituary to M. [Moses] Hess' (the original chapter title) in
   the *Westphälischer Dampfboot*, August–September 1847.
   Engels published a version of Marx's *Theses on Feuerbach* as
   an appendix to *Ludwig Feuerbach and the End of Classical
   German Philosophy* in 1888, but *The German Ideology* itself
   was first published in the Soviet Union only in 1932 (in
   German) and 1933 (in Russian).
2 Sidney Hook's pioneering work, first published in 1936,
   From Hegel to Marx, New York, Humanities Press, 1950,
   devoted a chapter (pp. 165–85) to Stirner and Marx which
   does not explain why Marx devoted the best part of a major
   work to attacking Stirner. ('Saint Max' was composed by
   Marx, not Engels.) Of more recent books, R.M. Tucker's
   Philosophy and Myth in Karl Marx, Cambridge University
   Press, 1967, does not mention Stirner, and Shlomo Avineri's
   The Social and Political Thought of Karl Marx does not discuss
   Stirner. The best outline accounts of the dispute in English
   are those of Nicolas Lobkowicz in *Theory and Practice:
   History of a Concept from Aristotle to Marx*, Notre Dame,
   Ind., University of Notre Dame Press, 1967, pp. 401–26;

R.W.K. Paterson in his *The Nihilistic Egoist: Max Stirner*,
Oxford University Press, 1971, pp. 101-25; and Jerrold
Siegel in *Marx's Fate*, Princeton University Press, 1978,
pp. 154-69.

3   Marx and Engels, *The German Ideology*, trans. Roy Pascal,
London, Lawrence & Wishart; New York, International
Publishers, 1938. The first complete English translations
appeared only in 1965 and 1976. Cf. *The German Ideology*,
trans. Clemens Dutt, ed. Salo Ryazanskaya, London, Lawrence
& Wishart, 1965; and a different rendering (the order of the
pages in Part 1 differs significantly), also by Clemens Dutt, in
the *Marx-Engels Collected Works*, New York and London,
International Publishers, 1976, vol. v. Both translations, which
will be referred to hereafter as *The German Ideology* and
MECW v respectively, make use of the textual discoveries of
S. Bahne. Cf. his ' "Die deutsche Ideologie" von Marx und
Engels. Einige Textergänzerungen', *International Review of
Social History* (Amsterdam and Assen), vol. 7, part 1, 1962,
pp. 93-104.

4   *The German Ideology*, pp. 206 ff., esp. pp. 207-11; MECW v,
pp. 193 ff., esp. pp. 193-5.

5   *The German Ideology*, p. 23; MECW v, p. 23.

6   James Joll, *The Anarchists*, London, Eyre & Spottiswoode,
1964, p. 171.

7   William Brazill, *The Young Hegelians*, New Haven, Conn., Yale
University Press, 1970, pp. 13-14. The others were Strauss,
the brothers (Edgar and Bruno) Bauer, Feuerbach, Vischer and
Ruge.

8   Paul Nerrlich, ed., *Arnold Ruge: Briefe und Tagebuchblätter*,
Leipzig, Weidmann, 1886, vol. 1, pp. 388-90; Arnold Ruge,
Zwei Jahre in Paris: Studien und Erinnerungen, Leipzig, Jurani,
1846, Part II, chs 13-14, esp. pp. 117-34.

9   Moses Hess, *Die letzten Philosophen*, Darmstadt, Leske, 1845,
pp. 6-7.

10 Engels to Marx, 19 November 1844, in *Marx-Engels Werke*,
Berlin, Dietz (hereafter cited as MEW), vol. xxvii, pp. 11-12.

11 Engels to Marx, 20 January 1845, in MEW xxvii, pp. 14-18.
Cf. Paterson, *The Nihilistic Egoist*, p. 103.

12 *The German Ideology*, pp. 52, 304; and MECW v, pp. 56, 282.

13 Isaiah Berlin, *Karl Marx: His Life and Environment*, 4th edn,
Oxford University Press, 1978, p. 106.

14 David McLellan, *The Young Hegelians and Karl Marx*, New York,
Praeger, 1969, p. 121.

15 Ibid., p. 119.

16 Max Stirner, *Der Einzige und sein Eigenthum*, 2nd edn, Leipzig,
Wigand, 1882, pp. 344-5. Most libraries catalogue this volume
under Stirner's real name, Johann Kaspar Schmidt. For a
translation, cf. John Carroll, ed., *The Ego and his Own*, London,
Cape, 1971, pp. 238-9. Unhappily, Carroll's edition is today the
most accessible in English: it sits oddly among the other volumes

in the Roots of the Right Series (series editor George Steiner);
and Carroll selects sparingly from the standard but sloppy
translation of Steven T. Byington (*The Ego and his Own*,
London, Fifield, 1912), a rendering which is sufficiently
defective, for instance, to translate *Nationalökonomie*
(political economy) as 'national economy', which is meaningless. Carroll's introduction should be complemented by a
reading of John P. Clark's *Max Stirner's Egoism*, London,
Freedom Press, 1976, a short and thoughtful critique from
a non-egoist anarchist viewpoint. The most comprehensive
Stirner bibliography is at the end of Hans G. Helms's
fascinating attempt to deal with Stirner from a Marxist
perspective, *Ideologie der anonymen Gesellschaft: Max
Stirners 'Einzige' und der Fortschritt des demokratischen
Selbstbewusstseins vom Vormärz bis zur Bundesrepublik*,
Cologne, DuMont, 1966, pp. 510-600.

17 Stirner, *Der Einzige*, p. 375.
18 Ibid., p. 375.
19 Ibid., pp. 91-2; cf. MECW iii, p. 182, for a rare instance of
    agreement (or convergence) on the part of Marx.
20 Stirner, *Der Einzige*, pp. 107-9; cf. *Hegel's Philosophy of
    Right*, trans. and with an introduction by T.M. Knox, Oxford,
    Clarendon Press, 1962, §272A, p. 285.
21 Stirner, *Der Einzige*, p. 179; cf. pp. 109-10.
22 Ibid., p. 99; Carroll, ed., *The Ego and his Own*, p. 88.
23 Stirner, *Der Einzige*, p. 325.
24 Ibid., pp. 112-14.
25 David Cooper, *The Death of the Family*, New York, Pantheon,
    1970, p. 78; Stirner, *Der Einzige*, pp. 315-16, 200, 232, 238;
    Carroll, ed., *The Ego and his Own*, pp. 211, 132, 150, 115-6.
26 *Hegel's Philosophy of Right*, §270, p. 165.
27 McLellan, *The Young Hegelians and Karl Marx*, p. 93; cf. pp. 94-5.
28 Ludwig Feuerbach, *Sämmtliche Schriften*, ed. F. Boline and
    W. Jodl, Stuttgart, Frommann, 1959, vol. vi, p. 26; cf. *The
    German Ideology*, p. 256, or MECW v, p. 237.
29 Feuerbach, 'Preliminary Theses for the Reform of Philosophy'
    ('Vorläufige Thesen zur Reform der Philosophie'), 1842: 'Wir
    dürfen nur immer das Prädikat zum Subjekt und so als Subjekt
    zum Objekt und Prinzip machen – also die spekulative Philo-
    sophie nur umkehren, so haben wir die unverhüllte, die pure,
    blanke Wahrheit.' Ludwig Feuerbach, *Anthropologischer
    Materialismus: Ausgewählte Schriften*, ed. Alfred Schmidt,
    Munich, Europa, 1957, vol. i, p. 83. Cf. *The Fiery Brook:
    Selected Writings of Ludwig Feuerbach*, trans. and with an
    introduction by Zawar Hanfi, New York, Anchor, 1972, p. 154;
    and Feuerbach, *The Essence of Christianity*, trans. George
    Eliot, New York, Harper & Row, 1957, p. 189.
30 Feuerbach, *Sämmtliche Schriften*, vol. vii, pp. 294-310;
    Stirner, *Der Einzige*, pp. 351-2.

31   Stirner, *De Einzige*, pp. 34–6.
32   Cf. Nathan Rotenstreich, *Some Basic Problems in Marx's Philosophy*, New York, Bobbs-Merrill, 1965, p. 14.
33   Marx, *Critique of Hegel's Philosophy of Right*, trans. Annette Jolin and ed. Joseph O'Malley, Cambridge University Press, 1970 (henceforward cited as O'Malley), p. 131; MECW iii, p. 175.
34   O'Malley, p. 137; MECW iii, p. 182.
35   *The German Ideology*, pp. 58–9, 502; MECW v, pp. 40–1, 456.
36   Stirner, *Der Einzige*, pp. 318, 332; Carroll, ed., *The Ego and his Own*, pp. 214, 168. Cf. *The German Ideology*, pp. 448–9; MECW v, p. 409.
37   *The German Ideology*, p. 224; MECW v, pp. 208–9.
38   *The German Ideology*, p. 400; MECW v, p. 367.
39   *The German Ideology*, p. 445, cf. p. 224; MECW v, p. 406, cf. pp. 208–9.
40   *The German Ideology*, pp. 439, 437; MECW v, pp. 400–1, 399.
41   *The German Ideology*, p. 325; MECW v, p. 300.
42   *The German Ideology*, p. 483; MECW v, p. 439.
43   Isaiah Berlin, *Karl Marx*, p. 11.
44   *The German Ideology*, pp. 216–17; MECW v, p. 202.
45   MEW iv, p. 200.
46   Paul Eltzbacher, *Anarchism*, trans. Steven T. Byington, London, Fifield, 1908, p. 100; Henri Arvon, *Aux sources de l'existentialisme: Max Stirner*, Paris, Presses Universitaires de France, 1950, p. 108.
47   *The German Ideology*, p. 217, MECW v, p. 202; Stirner, *Der Einzige*, p. 261, Carroll, *The Ego and his Own*, p. 163.
48   *The German Ideology*, p. 220; MECW v, p. 205; Stirner, *Der Einzige*, p. 119.
49   *The German Ideology*, pp. 44–5; MECW v, pp. 47–8; McLellan, *Young Hegelians*, p. 132.
50   Carl Bridenbaugh, 'The Conservative Revolutionist' (a review of *The Papers of John Adams*), *Times Literary Supplement* (London), 12 May 1978, p. 527.
51   *The German Ideology*, p. 45, cf. pp. 247–8; MECW v, p. 48, cf. pp. 229–30.
52   *The German Ideology*, p. 83; MECW v, p. 87.
53   Cf. Albert O. Hirschmann, *The Passions and the Interests: Political Arguments for Capitalism Before its Triumph*, Princeton University Press, 1977, *passim*.
54   *The German Ideology*, p. 87; MECW v, p. 81.
55   *The German Ideology*, p. 93; MECW v, p. 78.
56   *The German Ideology*, pp. 431–2; MECW v, p. 394.
57   *The German Ideology*, pp. 315–16; MECW v, p. 292.
58   Émile Durkheim, *The Division of Labour in Society*, quoted in Anthony Giddens, ed., *Émile Durkheim: Selected Writings*, Cambridge University Press, 1972, p. 140.

59 *The German Ideology*, pp. 205, 307; MECW v, pp. 192, 284-5.
60 *The German Ideology*, pp. 123, 279-81; MECW v, pp. 120, 258-60; Stirner, *Der Einzige*, pp. 5-8; Carroll, ed., *The Ego and his Own*, p. 39.
61 *The German Ideology*, p. 345, cf. pp. 205, 142; MECW v, p. 318, cf. pp. 192, 137.
62 *The German Ideology*, pp. 296, 182; MECW v, pp. 275, 171.
63 *The German Ideology*, pp. 196, 180, 183-7; MECW v, pp. 184, 170, 172-6.
64 *The German Ideology*, pp. 132, 304, cf. 132-4; MECW v, pp. 128, 282, cf. pp. 128-9.
65 *The German Ideology*, pp. 255-6, 252-3, 315; MECW v, pp. 237, 232, 291-2.
66 *Karl Marx: Early Writings*, ed. T.B. Bottomore, New York, McGraw-Hill, 1964 (henceforward cited as Bottomore), p. 202; MECW iii, pp. 332-3; G.W.F. Hegel, *On Art, Religion, Philosophy*, ed. J. Glenn Gray, New York, Harper & Row, 1970, p. 58. Cf. Richard Norman, *Hegel's Phenomenology: A Philosophical Introduction*, Brighton, University of Sussex Press, 1976, p. 53.
67 *The German Ideology*, p. 481; MECW v, p. 437.
68 MECW iii, p. 220.
69 Bottomore, p. 158; MECW iii, p. 299. Cf. O'Malley, p. xliv.
70 Marx, *Grundrisse*, trans. and with an introduction by Martin Nicolaus, Harmondsworth, Penguin, 1973, p. 84.
71 Eugène Fleischmann, 'The Role of the Individual in Pre-revolutionary Society', in Z.A. Pelczynski, ed., *Hegel's Political Philosophy*, Cambridge University Press, 1971, p. 225.
72 Bottomore, p. 22; MECW iii, pp. 21-2.
73 O'Malley, p. xliii.
74 O'Malley, pp. 119-20; MECW iii, p. 119.
75 MECW iii, pp. 216-17.
76 *The German Ideology*, p. 82; MECW v, p. 86.
77 *Grundrisse*, p. 159; *The German Ideology*, pp. 82-3; MECW v, pp. 86-7.
78 *The German Ideology*, p. 281, cf. pp. 82-3; MECW v, p. 213, cf. pp. 86-7.
79 *The German Ideology*, p. 49, cf. pp. 229-30, 86-7; MECW v, pp. 51-2, cf. p. 213, 81.
80 *The German Ideology*, p. 47; MECW v, p. 49.
81 *The German Ideology*, pp. 66-7; MECW v, p. 66.
82 *Grundrisse*, p. 162.
83 *The German Ideology*, p. 84; MECW v, p. 88. Cf. Theo Ramm, 'Die künftige Gesellschaftsordnung nach der Theorie von Marx und Engels', *Marxismusstudien* (Tübingen), vol. ii, 1957, pp. 77-179, *passim*.
84 *The German Ideology*, p. 482; MECW v, p. 438.
85 *The German Ideology*, p. 405; MECW v, p. 371-2.
86 *The German Ideology*, pp. 93-4; MECW v, pp. 78-9.

87   *The German Ideology*, pp. 91–2; MECW v, pp. 77–8.
88   *The German Ideology*, p. 470; MECW v, p. 427.
89   Lobkowicz, *Theory and Practice*, p. 402; Carroll, ed., *The Ego and his Own*, p. 14.
90   *The German Ideology*, p. 315; MECW v, p. 378.
91   *The German Ideology*, pp. 412–13; MECW v, p. 378.
92   Marx, *Theories of Surplus Value*, Moscow, Foreign Languages Publishing House, 1972, vol. ii, pp. 177–8.

4   Marx and Proudhon

1   *Oeuvres complètes de P.-J. Proudhon*, ed. Célestin Bouglé and H. Moysset, Paris, Marcel Rivière, vol. ii, 1924, p. 344. Proudhon's description of himself as 'l'excommunié de l'époche' may be found in *Correspondance de P.-J. Proudhon*, Paris, Lacroix, 1875 et seq., vol. vii, p. 265.
2   Michael Oakeshott, *On Human Conduct*, Oxford, Clarendon Press, 1975, p. 319n. The quotation is from *De la célébration du Dimanche, Oeuvres complètes*, vol. iv (1926), p. 61: 'to find a state of social equality which is neither community [Proudhon means a Babouvist *communauté des biens* or indeed a Fourierist community whose individual members are repressed by the whole], nor despotism, nor fragmentation, nor anarchy, but liberty in order and independence in unity'.
3   Proudhon published twenty-six volumes in his lifetime; twelve appeared posthumously. The most important include *Qu'est-ce que la propriété?* (1840); *De la création de l'ordre* (1843); *Système des contradictions économiques, ou philosophie de la misère* (1846); *Confessions d'un révolutionnaire* (1849); *L'idée générale de la révolution* (1851); *Philosophie de progrès* (1853); *De la justice dans la Révolution et dans l'Église* (1858); *La Guerre et la paix* (1861); *Du princip fédératif* (1863); *De la capacité politique des classes ouvrières* (1865, posth.). Of these, only the 1840, 1846 and 1851 works have been translated into English. There is no definitive edition of Proudhon's writings. Bibliographical complications are best avoided by recourse to the extensive (if unselective) bibliography in Robert Hoffman, *Revolutionary Justice: The Social and Political Theory of P.-J. Proudhon*, Urbana, University of Illinois Press, 1972, pp. 359–418; cf. also pp. xi–xii. Of the two comprehensive but incomplete editions of Proudhon's works, I have generally used the Rivière *Oeuvres complètes*, as cited above in n. 1 (15 vols, 1923–59), as this is more generally available. The Rivière volumes are unnumbered and require identification by the date of publication of each; I have followed Hoffman (*Revolutionary Justice*, pp. 359–60) in numbering them in the order of their appearance and adding the dates in parentheses. Proudhon's writings as he composed them sometimes

run into more than one volume; these are classified *within* a
Rivière volume, as in n. 71 below (the third volume of
Proudhon's *De la justice* appears, with the others, within the
eighth volume (1930) of the Rivière edition). The other
edition of Proudhon is the Lacroix edition (*Oeuvres*, 26 vols,
Paris, Lacroix, 1867–70). Proudhon's *Correspondence* (Paris,
Lacroix, 1875 et seq.) runs to 14 volumes, and his notebooks
are still in the course of making their appearance in print, as
the *Carnets*, ed. Pierre Haubtmann, Paris, Rivière, 1960 et seq.
For the respective biases of Proudhon's French language
interpreters, see Alan Ritter, *The Political Thought of
Pierre-Joseph Proudhon*, Princeton University Press, 1969,
ch. 1, pp. 3–25.

4 Daniel Guérin, *Ni Dieu ni maître: anthologie de l'anarchisme*,
Paris, Maspero, 1974, vol. i, p. 9.

5 Alexander Herzen, *From the Other Shore*, trans. Moura Budberg,
with an introduction by Isaiah Berlin, London, Weidenfeld &
Nicolson, 1956, pp. 132–3. See also *My Past and Thoughts: The
Memoirs of Alexander Herzen*, trans. Constance Garnett, revised
by Humphrey Higgins, with an Introduction by Isaiah Berlin,
New York, Knopf, 1968, vol. II, ch. 41, pp. 805–22. 'The
masses', Proudhon wrote in 1858, 'do not read me but without
reading me they hear me' – a far from ridiculous claim. 'In the
1860s the cobbler Rouillier always carried a volume of Proudhon in his pocket: its pages were uncut, but he considered
himself a Proudhonist all the same' (Maxime Vuillaume, *Mes
Cahiers rouges au temps de la Commune* (1910), p. 313, quoted
by Theodore Zeldin, *France, 1848–1945*, vol. i: *Ambition,
Love and Politics*, Oxford, Clarendon Press, 1973, p. 465; cf.
pp. 459–66, *passim*).

6 Cf. in particular *L'idée générale* (Rivière, vol. ii (1924);
Lacroix, vol. x) and *De la justice* (Rivière, vol. viii (1930);
Lacroix, vols xxi–xxvi), *passim*.

7 Proudhon, *Système des contradictions économiques*, ed. Roger
Picard, in Rivière, vol. i (1923), p. 405; cf. pp. 378 ff.

8 James Joll, *The Anarchists*, London, Eyre & Spottiswoode,
1964, p. 66.

9 Proudhon, quoted by Georges Weill, *Histoire du mouvement
sociale en France*, Paris, Alcan, 1924, p. 75.

10 Jacques Freymond, ed., *La Première Internationale: Recueil
de documents*, Geneva, Droz, 1962, vol. i, pp. 87–8; cf. Jules
L. Puech, *Le Proudhonisme dans l'Association Internationale
des Travailleurs*, Paris, Alcan, 1907, *passim*.

11 In Rivière, vol. iii (1924). Introduction and notes by Maxim
Leroy.

12 Rivière, vol. ii (1924), pp. 367–9, 365.

13 Ibid., p. 89.

14 Isaiah Berlin, *Karl Marx: His Life and Environment*, 4th edn,
Oxford University Press, 1978, p. 83.

15 The 'prise de conscience' Proudhon characterized in 1858 as 'the act by which men, declaring themselves to be essentially producers, abdicate all claims to govern one another' ('l'acte par lequel l'homme et l'homme, se déclarant essentiellement producteurs, abdiquent l'un à l'egard de l'autre toute prétention au gouvernance'.) Cf. *De la justice*, Paris, Librairie Internationale, 1868, vol. ii, 4th Étude, p. 267. Also in Rivière, vol. viii (1930).

16 'Whoever appeals to power and capital for the organization of labour is lying, because the organization of labour should be the overthrow of power and capital.' *Système*, in Rivière, vol. i (1923), p. 310; cf. Joll, *The Anarchists*, p. 63.

17 Quoted in Daniel Guérin, *Anarchism*, trans. Mary Klopper, New York and London, Monthly Review Press, 1970, p. 22.

18 Quoted by George Woodcock, *P.-J. Proudhon*, London, Macmillan, 1956, p. 180.

19 George Sand, *Correspondence*, Paris, Calmann-Lévy, 1882, vol. iii, pp. 340–1; David Owen Evans, *Social Romanticism in France*, Oxford, Clarendon Press, 1961; Henri de Lubac, *The Un-Marxian Socialist*, trans. R.E. Scantlebury, London, Sheen & Ward, 1948.

20 George Woodcock, *Anarchism*, Harmondsworth, Penguin, 1962, p. 99.

21 Guérin, *Anarchism*, p. 6.

22 Joll, *The Anarchists*, p. 73.

23 Marx and Engels, *The German Ideology*, trans. Clemens Dutt, Moscow, Foreign Languages Publishing House, 1965, p. 222; also in *Marx–Engels Collected Works* (henceforward cited as MECW), New York and London, International Publishers, 1975, et seq. vol. v, p. 207.

24 George Lichtheim, *A Short History of Socialism*, New York, Praeger, 1970, p. 58.

25 Quoted by Woodcock, *P.-J. Proudhon*, p. 60.

26 D.W. Brogan, *Proudhon*, London, Hamish Hamilton, 1934, p. 32.

27 William Pickles, 'Marx and Proudhon', *Politica* (London School of Economics), vol. iii, no. 13, September 1938, pp. 236–60.

28 Marx to Johann Baptist von Schweitzer (24 January 1865), original text in *Marx–Engels Werke* (henceforward cited as MEW), Berlin, Dietz, 1956 et seq., vol. xvi, pp. 25 ff.; trans. as an appendix to *The Poverty of Philosophy*, New York, International Publishers, 1973, pp. 193–202. See below, n. 35.

29 Shlomo Avineri, *The Social and Political Thought of Karl Marx*, Cambridge University Press, 1968, p. 83.

30 Quoted by Maxim Leroy, *Histoire des idées sociales en France*, Paris, NRF, 1950, vol. ii, p. 470.

31 For an incidental illustration of the complexity of property titles in nineteenth-century France, cf. Michel Foucault, ed., *I, Pierre Rivière. . .A Case of Parricide in the Nineteenth Century*, trans F. Jellinek, New York, Pantheon, 1975, *passim*.

32 Brogan, *Proudhon*, p. 60; cf. Woodcock, *P.-J. Proudhon*, p. 171; George Plekhanov, *Marxism and Anarchism*, trans. Eleanor Marx Aveling, Chicago, Charles Kerr, 1918, p. 73.

33 F.F. Ridley, *Revolutionary Syndicalism in France*, Cambridge University Press, 1970, p. 270; Leroy, *Histoire des idées sociales*, vol. ii, p. 492.

34 Proudhon, *Correspondence*, vol. ii, p. 176 (letter of 19 January 1845); cf. Édouard Dolléans, *P.-J. Proudhon*, Paris, Gallimard, 1948, p. 95; Dolléans, *Histoire du mouvement ouvrier*, Paris, Colin, 1936, vol. i, p. 209.

35 Marx to Schweitzer: *The Poverty of Philosophy*, p. 196.

36 Pickles, 'Marx and Proudhon', p. 241. For further details, cf. Hoffman, *Revolutionary Justice*, pp. 87-118, and Erich Tier, 'Marx and Proudhon', *Marxismusstudien* (Tübingen), vol. ii, 1957, pp. 120-50, *passim*.

37 Franz Mehring, *Karl Marx, the Story of his Life*, trans. Edward Fitzgerald, New York, Covici, Friede, 1935, pp. 129-30.

38 Marx to Pavel V. Annenkov, 28 December 1846. Original in MEW xxvii, pp. 451-63; trans. as an appendix to *The Poverty of Philosophy*, pp. 177-93.

39 Maximilien Rubel and Margaret Manale, *Marx Without Myth*, Oxford, Blackwell, 1975, p. 101.

40 *Marx-Engels Selected Works* (henceforward cited as MESW), Moscow, Foreign Languages Publishing House, 1962, vol. i, p. 254.

41 Ibid., p. 244.

42 These may be found in *The Poverty of Philosophy*, pp. 194-202; Marx, Engels and Lenin, *Anarchism and Anarcho-Syndicalism*, New York, International Publishers, 1974, pp. 41-2; ibid., pp. 43-4 (or MESW ii, pp. 459-60), respectively.

43 See Eric Hobsbawm, 'Dr. Marx and the Victorian Critics', in *Labouring Men*, New York, Doubleday, 1967, pp. 283-93; Rubel and Manale, *Marx Without Myth*, p. 267.

44 MECW i, p. 220.

45 MECW iii, p. 143.

46 Ibid., p. 201.

47 Ibid., p. 241.

48 Ibid., p. 313.

49 Ibid., p. 280.

50 Ibid., p. 280.

51 Ibid., p. 356; MECW iv, pp. 32, 41, 36.

52 MECW iv, p. 33.

53 Ibid., p. 34.

54 *The Poverty of Philosophy*, pp. 194-6.

55 MECW iv, p. 42.

56 Ibid., pp. 42-3.

57 Ibid., pp. 31-2.

58 Ibid., pp. 31-2.

59 Ibid., p. 32.

60   Ibid., p. 33.
61   Ibid., p. 33.
62   Ibid., p. 50.
63   Plekhanov, *Marxism and Anarchism*, p. 73.
64   MECW iv, p. 49.
65   MECW iii, p. 316.
66   Ibid., p. 317.
67   Marx, *Grundrisse*, trans. and with an introduction by Martin Nicolaus, Harmondsworth, Penguin, 1973, p. 319; cf. p. 311.
68   Marx, *Theories of Surplus Value*, Moscow, Foreign Languages Publishing House, 1972, vol. iii, p. 525.
69   Ibid., p. 456; cf. vol. i, pp. 323–5.
70   MECW iv, p. 216; *The German Ideology*, pp. 232, 584, or MECW v, pp. 216, 530.
71   Rivière, vol. viii (1930), 3, p. 424.
72   The full texts of Marx's and Proudhon's letters may most readily be found in Stewart Edwards and Elizabeth Fraser, *Selected Writings of P.-J. Proudhon*, New York, Doubleday, 1969, pp. 147–54. (Proudhon's letter was published as an appendix to the first edition of his *Confessions* in 1849; see Rivière, vol. vii (1929), pp. 432–7. For Marx's letter, see also *Marx-Engels Selected Correspondence*, Moscow, Progress Publishers, 1975, pp. 24–5).
73   Edwards and Fraser, *Selected Writings of P.-J. Proudhon*, pp. 150–4.
74   Proudhon, letter of 19 September 1847 to Guillaumin, in *Correspondance*, vol. vii, pp. 415–23; cf. Dolléans, *Histoire du mouvement ouvrier*, vol. i, p. 211; 'Appendix', ed. Roger Picard, to Rivière, vol. i (1923), pp. 267–8, for Proudhon's marginal comments on *The Poverty of Philosophy*; Proudhon, *Carnets*, vol. v, p. 109.
75   *The Poverty of Philosophy*, p. 29. The original (French) text, worth consulting because of the flatness of the standard English translation, may be found in *Marx-Engels Gesamtausgabe*, vol. 1, Abt. vi, Moscow, 1932, pp. 117 ff.
76   Proudhon, *Système*, vol. i, in Rivière, vol. i (1923), p. 284. See also George Lichtheim, *The Origins of Socialism*, New York, Praeger, 1969, p. 92.
77   Proudhon, *Système*, vol. ii, in Rivière, vol. i (1923), 2, pp. 258, 266. Cf. Lichtheim, *The Origins of Socialism*, p. 92.
78   Proudhon, quoted by Leroy, *Histoire des idées sociales en France*, vol. ii, p. 492; cf. Paul Louis, *Histoire du socialisme en France*, Paris, Rivière, 1937, p. 148.
79   *The Poverty of Philosophy*, p. 192.
80   Ibid.
81   Proudhon, *Système* in Rivière, vol. i (1923), 2, p. 258.
82   Rivière, vol. viii (1930), 1, p. 239.
83   *The Poverty of Philosophy*, p. 199.
84   Ibid., p. 197.
85   Ibid., p. 195.

86   MECW iv, pp. 35-6.
87   *The German Ideology*, p. 584; MECW v, p. 530.
88   *The Poverty of Philosophy*, pp. 202, 180, 181.
89   Ibid., pp. 182-3.
90   Ibid., pp. 186-7.
91   Proudhon, *The General Idea of the Revolution in the Nineteenth Century*, trans. John Beverley Robinson, London and Berlin, Freedom Press, 1923, p. 41.
92   *The Poverty of Philosophy*, p. 187.
93   Ibid., pp. 189-91.
94   Marx and Engels, *The Manifesto of the Communist Party*, in MESW i, p. 47.
95   *The Poverty of Philosophy*, p. 107.
96   Ibid., p. 106.
97   Ibid., p. 105.
98   Ibid., p. 114.
99   Ibid., p. 150.
100 Ibid., p. 60.
101 Ibid., p. 116.
102 Ibid., p. 112.
103 Ibid., p. 108.
104 Ibid., p. 111.
105 Ibid., p. 112.
106 Ibid., p. 119.
107 Proudhon, *Philosophie de progrès* (introduction and notes by Theodore Ruyssen), Rivière, vol. xii, (1946), pp. 50-1.
108 Louis Dupré, *Philosophical Foundations of Marxism*, New York, Harcourt, Brace, 1966, p. 183.
109 Proudhon, *Correspondance*, vol. vi, p. 313. Alan Ritter, who quotes this passage from Proudhon, adds wryly that 'his foreboding came true . . . he dabbled confusingly in economics all his life' (*The Political Thought of Pierre-Joseph Proudhon*, p.14).
110 Rubel and Manale, *Marx Without Myth*, p. 243.
111 Quoted by David Horowitz, 'Introduction' to his *Marx and Modern Economics*, New York, Random House, 1968, p. 14.
112 Cf. n. 56, above.
113 *The German Ideology*, p. 409; MECW v, p. 375.
114 *Grundrisse*, p. 310. Cf. above, ch. 2, pp. 147 ff.
115 *The Poverty of Philosophy*, p. 42.
116 Ibid., p. 43; cf. *Grundrisse*, pp. 424-5.
117 *The Poverty of Philosophy*, p. 51.
118 Ibid., p. 49; cf. *Grundrisse*, pp. 265-6.
119 *The Poverty of Philosophy*, p. 79.
120 *Grundrisse*, pp. 248-9.
121 *Oeuvres* (Lacroix), vol. xviii, p. 6.
122 Herzen, *From the Other Shore*, p. 34.
123 Engels, 'Introduction' to first German edition of *The Poverty of Philosophy* (1884); reprinted in the 1973 English edition, p.7.
124 Ibid., pp. 198, 127.

125   Ibid., pp. 198–9.
126   Ibid., p. 125. For a discussion, cf. Paul Thomas, 'Marx and
       Science', *Political Studies* (Oxford), vol. xxiv, no. 1, March
       1976, pp. 1–24.
127   *The Poverty of Philosophy*, p. 202.
128   Ibid., pp. 201–2.
129   Ibid., p. 199.
130   This point is sketched with remarkable brevity by Rubel and
       Manale; see *Marx Without Myth*, pp. 204–5. On Marx and
       Lassalle, cf. George Lichtheim, *Marxism: an Historical and
       Critical Study*, New York, Praeger, 1971, pp. 92 ff.
131   Rubel and Manale, *Marx Without Myth*, pp. 204–5.
132   Thus Proudhon in 1852: 'I understand that this work can only
       compromise me seriously without compensating advantages. It
       involves participating in the crime to a certain extent, by
       breathing some life into it. . . To find a way out of a nest of
       thieves, an explanation for an ambush! a meaning for perjury!
       an excuse for cowardice! a point to imbecility! a rationale and
       a cause for tyranny! To do this is to prostitute reason, it is to
       abuse one's powers to think, observe and judge.' *Carnet* entry
       of 13 April 1852, cited in Édouard Dolléans and Georges
       Duveau, 'Introduction' to Rivière, vol. ix (1936), p. 71. The
       ellipsis is in the original.
133   See Proudhon, *La Révolution sociale démontrée par le coup
       d'état de deux decembre* (1858) in Rivière, vol. ix, 1936.
134   On this incident, cf. Woodcock, *P.-J. Proudhon*, p. 129; Artur
       Desjardins, *P.-J. Proudhon*, Paris, Perrin, 1896, vol. i, p. 210;
       Édouard Droz, *P.-J. Proudhon*, Paris, Pages Libres, 1909, p. 163.
135   Georges Duveau, 'Introduction' to Rivière, vol. ix, pp. 12–13.
136   Avineri, *The Social and Political Thought of Karl Marx*, p. 183.
137   Maximilien Rubel, 'Notes on Marx's Conception of Democracy',
       New Politics (New York), vol. i, no. 2, winter 1962, p. 79.
138   See István Mézáros, *Marx's Theory of Alienation*, London,
       Merlin Press, 1970, pp. 126–30.
139   Ibid., p. 129.
140   MECW iii, pp. 331–3; cf. Avineri, *The Social and Political
       Thought of Karl Marx*, p. 80.
141   *Grundrisse*, p. 641.
142   Cf. Annie Kriegel, 'Le syndicalisme révolutionnaire et
       Proudhon', in *Le Pain et les roses: Jalons pour une histoire
       du socialisme*, Paris, Presses Universitaires de France, 1968,
       pp. 33–50, *passim*.
143   *The Poverty of Philosophy*, p. 193.
144   Ibid., p. 201.
145   *Theories of Surplus Value*, vol. iii, pp. 526–7.
146   See in particular Barrington Moore, Jr, *Social Origins of
       Dictatorship and Democracy: Lord and Peasant in the Making
       of the Modern World*, Boston, Beacon Press, 1966, pp. 70–110;
       Albert Soboul, *Les Sans-culottes parisiens en l'an II*, Paris,

Éditions de Seuil, 1968, *passim* (the severely shortened English translation, *The Sans-Culottes: The Popular Movement and Revolutionary Government 1793-94*, trans. Remy Inglis Hall, New York, Doubleday, 1972, is, shamefully, out of print); and Gwyn A. Williams, *Artisans and Sans-Culottes: Popular Movements in France and England during the French Revolution*, New York, Norton, 1969, pp. 19-58.

147 Raymond Williams, *Marxism and Literature*, Oxford University Press, 1977, pp. 80-1.

148 For the notion of 'moral economy' cf. E.P. Thompson, *The Making of the English Working Class*, New York, Vintage, 1966, *passim*.

5 Marx, Bakunin and the International

1 Stuart Christie, quoted in Anthony Masters, *Bakunin, the Father of Anarchy*, New York, Saturday Review Press, 1974, p. 262.

2 Marx, *The Civil War in France*, in *Marx-Engels Selected Works* (henceforward cited as MESW), Moscow, Foreign Languages Publishing House, 1962, vol. i, p. 542; and in *The First International and After*, ed. with an introduction by David Fernbach (henceforward cited as Fernbach), Harmondsworth, Penguin (Karl Marx Library, vol. iii), 1974, p. 233.

3 On this, see the exchange between John P. Clark ('Marx, Bakunin and the Problem of Social Transformation') and Paul Thomas ('Marx's Response to Anarchist Theories of Social and Political Change'), *Proceedings* of the 73rd Annual Meeting of the American Political Science Association, Washington, DC, 1-4 September 1977.

4 See Clark, 'Marx, Bakunin and the Problem of Social Transformation'. Also cf. Michel Bakounine, 'Articles écrits pour le journal *L'Égalité*' in *Oeuvres*, ed. Max Nettlau and James Guillaume, Paris, Stock, vol. v, pp. 13 ff., especially 'Politique de l'Internationale', pp. 169-99; *L'Empire Knouto-Germanique et la révolution sociale*, in *Oeuvres*, vol. ii, pp. 287-455; 'Trois conférences faites aux ouvriers du Val de Saint-Imier', *Oeuvres*, vol. v, pp. 299 ff.; 'Lettre au journal *La Liberté* de Bruxelles', *Oeuvres*, vol. iv, pp. 341-90, or in Arthur Lehning *et al.*, *Archives Bakounine*, Leiden, Brill, vol. ii (1965), pp. 145-68; 'L'Allemagne et le communisme d'état', in *Archives*, vol. ii, pp. 107-19.

5 See Robert Michels, *Political Parties, a Sociological Study of the Oligarchic Tendencies of Modern Democracy*, trans. Eden and Cedar Paul, New York, Dover, 1959, esp. pp. 377 ff.

6 E.H. Carr, *Michael Bakunin*, New York, Vintage, 1961, pp. 341-457.

7 There is no adequate institutional history of the International, though many of what would be the sources for such a history

are readily enough available. Jacques Freymond, *La Première Internationale: Recueil de documents*, Geneva, Droz (Publications de l'Institut Universitaire de Hautes Études Internationales, no. 39), 2 vols, 1962 (cited hereafter as Freymond), contains minutes of the Congresses, which sometimes can be supplemented usefully with the material in James Guillaume, *L'Internationale: documents et souvenirs 1864-1878*, 2 vols, Paris, Cornély (Société nouvelle de librairie et de l'édition), 1905-7 (cited hereafter as Guillaume). Guillaume was present as a delegate at some of the Congresses he recalls from a French–Swiss anarchist viewpoint. The only Congress minutes available in English are those of The Hague Congress, in two editions. Hans Gerth, ed. and trans., *The First International, Minutes of The Hague Congress of 1872 with Related Documents*, Madison, University of Wisconsin Press, 1958 (henceforward cited as Gerth), needs complementing with the fuller compendium, *The Hague Congress of the First International, Sept. 2-7, 1872: Minutes and Documents*, trans. Richard Dixon and Alex Miller, Moscow, Progress Publishers, 1976. Discrepancies between these sources are generally indicated in the footnotes of the latter, which is in general the better documented of the two. *Documents of the First International, 1864-72* (henceforward cited as *Documents*), trans. Nina Nepomnyashchaya, Molly Pearlman and Lydia Belyakova, 5 vols, Moscow, Progress Publishers, 1974, contain General Council documents and minutes, together with most of what came from the pen of Marx (except letters, an invaluable source). Selections of these documents may also be found in Fernbach, and in *Karl Marx and the First International*, ed. and trans. Saul K. Padover (henceforward cited as Padover), New York, McGraw-Hill (Karl Marx Library, vol. iii), 1973; also in *Karl Marx und die Gründung der 1. Internationale: Dokumente und Materialen*, Berlin, Dietz, 1964. The most useful English language accounts of the International are G.D.H. Cole, *Marxism and Anarchism, 1850-1890*, London, Macmillan (A History of Socialist Thought, vol. ii), 1969; Julius Braunthal, *History of the International, 1864-1914*, trans. Henry Collins and Kenneth Mitchell, London, Nelson, 1966. Less general but still useful are Henry Collins and Chimen Abramsky, *Karl Marx and the British Labour Movement: Years of the First International*, London, Macmillan, 1965, and (despite the inaccuracy of some of its citations) Richard Hostetter's *The Italian Socialist Movement, 1, Origins (1860-1882)*, Princeton, Van Nostrand, 1958, which contains a wealth of information. Of political biographies of Marx the most useful in adequately covering the International are David Riazanov, *Karl Marx and Friedrich Engels, an Introduction to Their Lives and Work*, trans. Joshua Kunitz, London and New York, Monthly Review Press, 1973; Otto

Rühle, *Karl Marx*, trans. Eden and Cedar Paul, New York, Viking, 1929, and Boris Nicholaevsky and Otto Maenchen-Helfen, *Karl Marx, Man and Fighter*, trans. Gwenda David and Eric Mosbacher, Harmondsworth, Penguin, 1976.

8 For the text of the Rules, see *Documents*, vol. i, pp. 288–91.
9 Cole, *Marxism and Anarchism*, pp. 103, 102.
10 Ibid., p. 90.
11 Collins and Abramsky, *Karl Marx and the British Labour Movement*, p. 80.
12 Cole, *Marxism and Anarchism*, p. 88.
13 Marx to Engels, 4 November 1864, in *Marx–Engels Werke* (henceforward cited as MEW), Berlin, Dietz, vol. xxxi, pp. 10–16; also in *Marx–Engels Selected Correspondence* (henceforward cited as MESC), Moscow, Foreign Languages Publishing House, 1965, pp. 146–9; and Padover, pp. 367–70.
14 For a thought provoking examination of the relationship between Marx's 'productivity' as a writer, his political activity and his personal life, cf. Jerrold Siegel, *Marx's Fate: The Shape of a Life*, Princeton University Press, 1978, *passim*.
15 Marx to Joseph Weydermeyer, 29 November 1864, in MEW xxxi, p. 428; also in Padover, p. 372, and in Marx and Engels, *Letters to Americans 1848–95*, New York, International Publishers, 1969, p. 65.
16 Cf. the little known (partly because misleadingly titled) study of Marx's internationalism by Solomon F. Bloom, *A World of Nations*, New York, Columbia University Press, 1941, *passim*; and, for a much briefer discussion, Paul Thomas, 'The Mao–Marx Debate: A View from Outside China', *Politics and Society*, vol. vii, no. 3, 1977, pp. 331–41.
17 Nicholaevsky and Maenchen-Helfen, *Karl Marx, Man and Fighter*, p. 284.
18 Marx, 'Inaugural Address of the Working Men's International Association' (1864), in *Documents*, vol. i (1864–6), p. 286; also in MESW i, p. 385.
19 Marx to Engels, 4 November 1864, MEW xxxi, p. 16; MESC, pp. 139–40; Padover, p. 370.
20 Engels to Marx, 7 November 1864, MEW xxxi, p. 17.
21 Marx to Engels, 4 November 1864, *ibid*.
22 Cole, *Marxism and Anarchism*, p. 95.
23 Bakunin to Nabruzzi, 23 January 1872, quoted in Hostetter, *The Italian Socialist Movement*, p. 248.
24 Marx to Engels, 4 November 1864, MEW, xxxi, p. 17.
25 For the text, cf. *Documents*, vol. i, pp. 277–87; Padover, pp. 5–12; Freymond, vol. i, pp. 3–9.
26 On the role of the German movements, the definitive work in English is Roger P. Morgan, *The German Social Democrats and the First International, 1864–72*, Cambridge University Press, 1965.
27 Marx to Weydermeyer, 29 November 1864, MEW xxxi,

pp. 428-9, Padover, p. 372; Marx to Lion Philips, 29 November 1864, MEW xxxi, pp. 431-33, Padover, p. 371.

28 Fernbach, p. 15.

29 *Documents*, vol. i, pp. 281-2; Collins and Abramsky, *Karl Marx and the British Labour Movement*, p. 46.

30 Marx 'Preface' to the first German edition of *Capital*, vol. i, trans. Ben Fowkes, Harmondsworth, Penguin (Pelican Marx Library), 1976, pp. 91-2.

31 Cf. *Documents*, vol. ii, p. 346, n. 67; *Documents* vol. iii, pp. 401-2. For further developments, see Nicholaevsky and Maenchen-Helfen, *Karl Marx, Man and Fighter*, pp. 361-2, 379; Cole, *Marxism and Anarchism*, pp. 197-8, 207-8; and Henry Collins, 'The English Branches of the First International' in Asa Briggs and John Saville, eds, *Essays in Labour History in Memory of G.D.H. Cole*, London, Macmillan, 1960, pp. 242-75.

32 Raymond Postgate, *The Workers' International*, London, Swarthmore Press, 1926, pp. 33, 23-4.

33 Marx to Kugelmann, 9 October 1866, MEW xxxi, 529-30, cf. Padover, p. 423, and Nicholaevsky and Maenchen-Helfen, *Karl Marx, Man and Fighter*, p. 281. Cf. also Marx to Engels, 5 March 1869, MEW xxxii, pp. 273-4, and in MESC, pp. 219-21, and Padover pp. 466-7; and Engels's reply, 7 March 1869, MEW xxxii, p. 276.

34 Nicholaevsky and Maenchen-Helfen, *Karl Marx, Man and Fighter*, p. 283.

35 Ibid., p. 287.

36 Ibid., p. 283.

37 Ibid., p. 284.

38 Ibid.

39 Quoted in E.-E. Fribourg, *L'Association Internationale des Travailleurs*, Paris, Le Chevalier, 1871, p. 33. Cf. Jules L. Peuch, *Le Proudhonisme dans l'Association Internationale des Travailleurs*, Paris, Alcan, 1907, p. 112.

40 Marx, letter to Schweitzer, 24 January 1865, in *The Poverty of Philosophy*, New York, International Publishers, 1973, pp. 194-202. Cf. Marx to Engels, 25 January 1865, MEW xxxi, p. 42; Padover, pp. 377-8.

41 Cf. Cole, *Marxism and Anarchism*, pp. 89-90; Nicholaevsky and Maenchen-Helfen, *Karl Marx, Man and Fighter*, pp. 281-3, 287-9; *Documents*, vol. i, pp. 170, 374-7; Collins and Abramsky, *Karl Marx and the British Labour Movement*, pp. 40-4; Hostetter, *The Italian Socialist Movement*, pp. 50-69; Padover, pp. 22, 386-7.

42 *Documents*, vol. ii, p. 342.

43 *Documents*, vol. i, pp. 288-9; Padover, pp. 13-14; Fernbach, p. 82.

44 For the French text, see Freymond, vol. i, pp. 3-9; Guillaume, vol. i, pp. 11-21, usefully lists English and (successive) French

texts alongside one another in a table. See also *Documents*,
vol. iii, pp. 405-6, and Cole, *Marxism and Anarchism*,
pp. 101-2.

45 See Guillaume, vol. i, p. 12n; Riazanov, *Karl Marx and
    Friedrich Engels*, p. 160.

46 Marx to Engels, 4 November 1864, MEW xxxi, pp. 10-16;
    Padover, p. 367; Marx to Engels, 25 January 1865, MEW xxxi,
    pp. 42-3, Padover, p. 377.

47 Marx to Engels, 20 June 1866, MEW xxxi, pp. 228-9; also in
    Padover, pp. 418-19, and *Anarchism and Anarcho-Syndicalism,
    Selected Writings by Marx, Engels and Lenin*, ed. N.Y. Kolpinsky,
    New York, International Publishers, 1972, pp. 41-2.

48 Marx to Engels, 5 January 1866, MEW xxxi, p. 169; Padover,
    p. 403.

49 Marx to Kugelmann, 9 October 1866, MEW xxxi, pp. 529-30;
    Padover (pp. 422-3) gives 'attacked' for 'attracted': this is a
    mistake. See also Guillaume, vol. i, pp. 26-7; *Anarchism and
    Anarcho-Syndicalism*, pp. 43-4; MESC, pp. 183-4.

50 For the text, cf. Freymond, vol. i, pp. 85-107.

51 Marx to Kugelmann, 9 October 1866, MEW xxxi, pp. 529-30;
    MESC, pp. 183-4; Padover, pp. 422-3.

52 For the text, cf. *Documents*, vol. i, pp. 340-51; Padover,
    pp. 23-32; (in French) Freymond, pp. 25-36.

53 On this, see Marx to Engels, 6 April 1866, MEW xxxi, pp. 304-5;
    Padover, p. 412, Also Marx to Engels, 26 December 1865,
    MEW xxxi, pp. 162-4; Padover, p. 402. Cf. Collins and
    Abramsky, *Karl Marx and the British Labour Movement*,
    pp. 63-5.

54 Fernbach, p. 17.

55 Riazanov, *Karl Marx and Friedrich Engels*, pp. 171-2.

56 See Marx, *The Critique of the Gotha Programme* in MESW ii,
    p. 36.

57 For the proceedings at Geneva, cf. Freymond, vol. i, pp. 27-57;
    Guillaume, vol. i, pp. 4-27.

58 Max Nomad, 'The Anarchist Tradition' in Miloran M.
    Drachkovitch, ed., *The Revolutionary Internationals 1864-1943*,
    Stanford University Press, 1966, p. 61.

59 Marx to Büchner, 1 May 1867, MEW xxxi, pp. 544-5; Padover,
    p. 425.

60 Marx to Engels, 12 September 1867, MEW xxxi, pp. 346-7;
    Padover, p. 429.

61 Max Nomad, 'The Anarchist Tradition', pp. 61-2.

62 Cf. Freymond, vol. i, pp. 231-3.

63 Freymond, vol. i, p. 234; *Documents*, vol. iii, pp. 322-4.

64 Cole, *Marxism and Anarchism*, p. 113.

65 Marx to Engels, 4 September 1867, MEW xxxi, pp. 337-9;
    Padover, p. 426.

66 The English and French texts may be consulted in *Documents*,
    vol. ii, pp. 285-7 and 288-91, respectively.

67   Freymond, vol. i, p. 235; Guillaume, vol. i, p. 37; Cole, *Marxism and Anarchism*, pp. 114–15.
68   Bakunin, quoted by Eugene Pyziur, *The Doctrine of Anarchism of Michael A. Bakunin*, Chicago, Gateway, 1968, p. 11.
69   Quoted by Carr, *Michael Bakunin*, p. 157. (Caussidière was the revolutionary Prefect of Police in the Paris of 1848.) See also Alexander Herzen, *My Past and Thoughts: The Memoirs of Alexander Herzen*, trans. Constance Garnett, revised by Humphrey Higgins, with an Introduction by Sir Isaiah Berlin, New York, Knopf, 1968, vol. iii, p. 1353.
70   I am following the scheme laid down in Benoît-P. Hepner, *Bakounine et le Panslavisme révolutionnaire, cinq essais sur l'histoire des idées en Russie et en Europe*, Paris, Rivière, 1950, p. 57. This fine study is of broader application than its title might suggest. Hepner's is one of the best books on Bakunin. The most accessible biographies are those of E.H. Carr (*Michael Bakunin*) and of H.-E. Kaminski, *Michel Bakounine, la vie d'un révolutionnaire*, Paris, Aubier, 1938. Each is more reliable than Anthony Masters's *Bakunin, the Father of Anarchy*; Carr's is more scholarly, Kaminski's more lively and sympathetic. Of other sources, Franco Venturi's *Roots of Revolution, a History of the Populist and Socialist Movements in Nineteenth-Century Russia*, trans. Francis Haskell, with an introduction by Isaiah Berlin, New York, Knopf, 1964, is a valuable source, R.M. Hare, *Portraits of Russian Personalities*, Oxford University Press, 1959, is a useful source, and E. Lampert, *Studies in Rebellion*, London, Routledge & Kegan Paul, 1957, is an invaluable one. Pyziur's *The Doctrine of Anarchism of Michael A. Bakunin* is a useful, well-documented interpretive essay which contains a good (but not exhaustive) bibliography; see note 83 below for further bibliographic details.
71   See Isaiah Berlin, 'A Marvellous Decade (ii) 1838–48: German Romanticism in Petersburg and Moscow', *Encounter* (London), November 1955, pp. 24 ff.; Hepner, *Bakounine*, pp. 74–103; Venturi, *Roots*, pp. 40 ff.; Herzen, *My Past and Thoughts*, vol. ii, pp. 397 ff. The best study of Bakunin's early intellectual development is Peter Scheibert, *Von Bakunin zu Lenin*, vol. i, Leiden, Brill, 1956.
72   Quoted by Hare, *Portraits of Russian Personalities*, p. 32.
73   Isaiah Berlin, 'Introduction' to Venturi, *Roots*, p. ix. See also Berlin's essay, 'Herzen and Bakunin on Liberty', in *Continuity and Change in Russian and Soviet Thought*, ed. and with an introduction by Ernest J. Simmons, Harvard University Press, 1955, pp. 473–99.
74   Berlin, 'Introduction', to Venturi, *Roots*, p. x; *The Confessions of Michael Bakunin* (with the marginal comments of Tsar Nicholas I), trans. Robert C. Howes, with an introduction by L. D. Orton, Ithaca, Cornell University Press, 1977, pp. 39–40.

75 Bakunin, *Confession*, pp. 79-80; Hepner, *Bakounine*, pp. 144-5;
   Venturi, *Roots*, p. 52.
76 Quoted in Murray Bookchin, *The Spanish Anarchists: The
   Heroic Years 1868-1936*, New York, Harper & Row, 1977,
   p. 22. See also Carr, *Michael Bakunin*, pp. 254-5; Lampert,
   Studies in Rebellion, pp. 117-19; Pyziur, *The Doctrine of
   Anarchism*, p. 5; Herzen, *My Past and Thoughts*, vol. ii, p. 951,
   vol. iii, p. 1358.
77 Vyrubov, quoted by Carr, *Michael Bakunin*, p. 343, and
   James Joll, *The Anarchists*, London, Eyre & Spottiswoode,
   1964, p. 98.
78 George Woodcock, *Anarchism*, Harmondsworth, Penguin, 1962,
   p. 135.
79 Thomas Masaryk, *Russland und Europa*, Jena, Fischer, 1913,
   vol. ii, p. 34; quoted by Pyziur, *The Doctrine of Anarchism*,
   p. 10.
80 Bakunin, *Confession*, p. 92; cf. Kaminski, *Michel Bakounine*,
   p. 18; Hostetter, *The Italian Socialist Movement*, p. 177, n. 41;
   Lampert, *Studies in Rebellion*, p. 133.
81 Venturi, *Roots*, p. 36.
82 Quoted by Paul Avrich, *The Russian Anarchists*, Princeton
   University Press, 1967, p. 21.
83 Hare, *Portraits of Russian Personalities*, p. 24. The quotation is
   from Michel Bakounine, *Oeuvres*, vol. i, p. 69. The *Oeuvres* are
   in five volumes (out of a projected seven); volume i was edited
   by Max Nettlau, the other four by James Guillaume; these,
   together with M. Dragomanov, ed., *Correspondance de Michel
   Bakounine: lettres à Herzen et à Ogareff*, trans. from the
   Russian by Marie Stromberg, Paris, Perrin, 1896, provide what
   are still the most important primary sources for Bakunin, at
   least for the reader who does not know Russian. Ignorance of
   Russian is not a crippling disadvantage in any case, since
   Bakunin tended to write in French. The *Archives Bakounine*,
   ed. Arthur Lehning, A.J.C. Rüter and Peter Scheibert for the
   Internationaal Instituut voor Sociale Geschiedenis at
   Amsterdam, Leiden, Brill, 1965 et seq., will displace these
   sources in time. The *Archives* provide a mine of information,
   authoritatively documented and presented in French and
   Russian. To date, four volumes of a projected fifteen (vol. i
   being in two parts) have appeared. Of these, vol. ii, *Michel
   Bakounine et les conflits dans l'Internationale*, is most
   directly relevant to our present concerns. (Some puzzles about
   the chronology of the volumes that thus far have appeared are
   cleared up in the 'Introduction' to vol. iv, p. x; Lehning's
   introductory essays must be read cautiously, since they
   editorialize shamelessly on Bakunin's behalf.) The closest
   approximation to the limited comprehensiveness of the
   Oeuvres in German is Michael Bakunin, *Gesammelte Werke*,
   3 vols, ed. with an introduction by Max Nettlau, Berlin, Der

Syndikalist, 1921-4. In English, the problem is worse. Only
the *Confession, Marxism, Freedom and the State,* and *God and
the State* have been translated in their entirety. G.P. Maximoff's
The Political Philosophy of Bakunin: Scientific Anarchism,
Chicago, Free Press, 1953, which is an unrepresentative set of
ahistorically selected snippets, should be complemented with
Michael Bakunin, *Selected Writings,* trans. Steven Cox and
Olive Stevens, with an introduction by Arthur Lehning,
London, Cape, 1976, and with Sam Dolgoff, ed., *Bakunin on
Anarchy,* New York, Vintage, 1971, to whose excellent
selected bibliography (pp. 401-5) – which is much fuller than
Pyziur's for the non-Russian sources – the reader is referred for
further details.

84   Bakunin, quoted by Hepner, *Bakounine,* p. 180.
85   Annenkov, quoted by Hepner, *Bakounine,* p. 205.
86   Quoted by Venturi, *Roots,* p. 45.
87   See Hepner, *Bakounine,* p. 180.
88   Bakunin, *The Paris Commune and the Idea of the State,* quoted
     by George Lichtheim, *A Short History of Socialism,* New York,
     Praeger, 1970, p. 129.
89   Quoted Hare, *Portraits of Russian Personalities,* , p. 65.
90   *Oeuvres,* vol. i, pp. 76, 91; cf. vol. iii, pp. 88-9, 92-5, 98-9, and
     Lampert, *Studies in Rebellion,* pp. 140-1.
91   Bakunin, in Maximoff, *The Political Philosophy of Bakunin,*
     p. 76.
92   Berlin, 'A Marvellous Decade', pp. 26-7.
93   Venturi, *Roots,* p. 37.
94   Pyziur, *The Doctrine of Anarchism,* p. 7; Lampert, *Studies in
     Rebellion,* p. 122; Herzen, *My Past and Thoughts,* vol. iii,
     p. 1357.
95   Peter Kropotkin's *Mutual Aid: A Factor of Evolution* (1902)
     was an attack on Huxley's 'The Struggle for Existence: A
     Programme', *The Nineteenth Century* (London), vol. xxiii,
     February 1888, pp. 161-80.
96   Bakunin to Herzen, 23 June 1867, in Dragomanov, *Correspon-
     dance,* p. 273.
97   Bakunin, quoted in Joll, *The Anarchists,* p. 86.
98   Berlin, 'Introduction' to Venturi, *Roots,* pp. xiii-xiv.
99   Alexander Blok, 'The Intelligentsia and the Revolution', in
     Russian Intellectual History: An Anthology, ed. Marc Raeff,
     with an introduction by Isaiah Berlin, New York, Harcourt,
     Brace, 1966, pp. 366-7.
100 Pyziur, *The Doctrine of Anarchism,* p. 27; Lichtheim, *A Short
     History of Socialism,* p. 123; Carr, *Michael Bakunin,* pp. 115-16.
101 Cf. Benoît-P. Hepner, 'Nihilisme: mot et idée', *Synthèses*
     (Brussels), January 1949; and, on Stirner and Bakunin, the
     pointed words of Thomas Masaryk, *The Spirit of Russia,* trans.
     Eden and Cedar Paul, London, Allen & Unwin, 1955,
     pp. 73-4.

102 Bakunin, *Secret Statutes of the Alliance*, London, Darson and Hamburg, Otto Meisner, 1873, p. 65.

103 *Oeuvres*, vol. ii, pp. 233-4. The obvious Dostoevskian parallels are usefully discussed in Lampert, *Studies in Rebellion*, pp. 125-8.

104 Albert Camus, *The Rebel*, trans. Anthony Bower, Harmondsworth, Peregrine, 1962, p. 127; cf. Philip Pomper, *The Russian Revolutionary Intelligentsia*, New York, Crowell, 1970, p. 95, and Nicolas Berdaiev, *Les Sources et le sens du communisme Russe*, trans. from the Russian by L.J. Cain, Paris, Gallimard, 1951, p. 129.

105 *Oeuvres*, vol. v, p. 252; cf. Venturi, *Roots*, pp. 59-60, 436.

106 George Lichtheim, *The Origins of Socialism*, New York, Praeger, 1969, p. 127.

107 Bakunin to Herzen and Ogarev, 19 July 1866, in Dragomanov, *Correspondance*, pp. 212-41. See also Pyziur, *The Doctrine of Anarchism*, pp. 60-1, Venturi, *Roots*, pp. xviii and 54-5.

108 Alexander Herzen, *From the Other Shore*, trans. Moura Budberg, with an introduction by Isaiah Berlin, London, Weidenfeld & Nicolson, 1956, p. 175; cf. pp. 183-6, 203.

109 See MEW xix, pp. 242-3, 296, 384-406; MESC, pp. 339-40; P.W. Blackstock and B.F. Hoselitz, eds, *Karl Marx and Friedrich Engels: The Russian Menace to Europe*, Chicago, Free Press, 1952, pp. 218-26; and, for interpretations, Maximilien Rubel, 'Marx et le socialisme populiste russe', *Revue Socialiste* (Paris), May 1947, and Paul Thomas, 'The Mao–Marx Debate: A View from Outside China', *Politics and Society*, vol. vii, no. 3, 1977, pp. 331-41.

110 See Pyziur, *The Doctrine of Anarchism*, pp. 60-1, n. 62; A.P. Mendel, *Dilemmas of Progress in Tsarist Russia*, Cambridge, Mass., Harvard University Press (Russian Research Center Studies, no. 43), 1961, p. 108, cf. p. 121; Samuel H. Baron, *Plekhanov, the Father of Russian Marxism*, Stanford University Press, 1963, pp. 13-14, n. 39. See also Turgenev to Herzen, 8 November 1862, quoted in Isaiah Berlin, 'Fathers and Children: Turgenev and the Liberal Predicament', published as an 'Introduction' to Ivan Turgenev, *Father and Sons*, trans. Rosemary Edmonds, Harmondsworth, Penguin, 1977, pp. 18-19.

111 *Oeuvres*, vol. iv, p. 32; *Archives Bakounine*, vol. iii, pp. 206-7; Joll, *The Anarchists*, p. 92; Hepner, *Bakounine*, p. 287.

112 See Carl Wittke, *The Utopian Communist: A Biography of Wilhelm Weitling*, Baton Rouge, Louisiana State University Press, 1950, p. 44.

113 Bakunin, quoted by Postgate, *The Workers' International*, p. 48.

114 Quoted in Venturi, *Roots*, p. 57. Such sentiments were later to be held against Bakunin; see *The Hague Congress of the First International*, p. 573.

115 Venturi, *Roots*, pp. 53-4.

116   *Oeuvres*, vol. v, p. 180.
117   *Oeuvres*, vol. ii, p. 92.
118   Bakunin, quoted by Venturi, *Roots*, pp. 368-9 and Carr,
       Michael Bakunin, p. 395. See also Franz Borkenau, *The Spanish
       Cockpit*, London, Faber & Faber, 1937, pp. 21-2, 14-15; and
       E.J. Hobsbawm, *Primitive Rebels: Studies in Archaic Forms of
       Social Movement in the Nineteenth and Twentieth Centuries*,
       New York, Norton, 1965, p. 28, n. 1. Cf. Venturi, *Roots*, p. 506;
       Hare, *Portraits of Russian Personalities*, p. 66; Carr, *Michael
       Bakunin*, p. 497.
119   *Confession*, p. 111; cf. *Oeuvres*, vol. iv, p. 37: 'If the human
       race were on the point of extinction, the Swiss would not
       resuscitate it.'
120   Berlin, 'Herzen and Bakunin', p. 495.
121   Cf. n. 137 below; and, for further details, Venturi, *Roots*,
       pp. 354-88; Carr, *Michael Bakunin*, pp. 390-409; *The Hague
       Congress of the First International*, pp. 366-480, 567-610;
       Archives Bakounine, vol. iv (1971), *Michel Bakounine et ses
       relations avec Sergej Nečaev* (1870-2), *passim*; Lampert, *Studies
       in Rebellion*, pp. 151-4. For an English translation of the
       Catechism of the Revolutionary, see Max Nomad, *Apostles of
       Revolution*, Boston, Beacon Press, 1939, pp. 228 ff.
122   Bakunin, 'Politique de l'Internationale' in *Oeuvres*, vol. v, p. 188.
123   *Oeuvres*, vol. iv, p. 252.
124   Venturi, *Roots*, pp. 46-7; see also *Archives Bakounine*, vol. ii,
       p. 199n; Dolgoff, *Bakunin on Anarchy*, p. 314; and Herzen,
       My Past and Thoughts, vol. ii, pp. 812, 423.
125   Venturi, *Roots*, pp. 46-7.
126   Quoted by James Guillaume, 'Michael Bakunin: A Biographical
       Sketch', in Dolgoff, *Bakunin on Anarchy*, p. 26.
127   *Oeuvres*, vol. i, pp. 39-40; in English, Dolgoff, *Bakunin on
       Anarchy*, pp. 116-17.
128   *Oeuvres*, vol. ii, p. 49.
129   Bakunin, quoted in Joll, *The Anarchists*, pp. 86-7.
130   Bakunin, quoted in Hare, *Portraits of Russian Personalities*, p. 50.
131   Bakunin, quoted by Max Nettlau, 'Bakunin und die Inter-
       nationale in Italien bis zum Herbst 1872', *Grünbergs Archiv für
       die Geschichte der Sozialismus und die Arbeiterbewegung*,
       vol. ii, 1911-12; cf. Venturi, *Roots*, pp. 46-7, and Avrich, *The
       Russian Anarchists*, p. 26. Guillaume's 'Biographical Sketch'
       omits the final sentence (see Dolgoff, *Bakunin and Anarchy*,
       p. 26), though this is quite characteristic of Bakunin's thinking.
132   Quoted in Dolgoff, *Bakunin and Anarchy*, p. 25; cf. *Archives
       Bakounine*, vol. i, part 2, pp. 122 ff.
133   Dolgoff, *Bakunin and Anarchy*, p. 26.
134   Cf. ibid., p. 314.
135   Carr, *Michael Bakunin*, p. 359.
136   Lichtheim, *A Short History of Socialism*, p. 58.
137   See Michel Confino, 'Bakounine et Nečaev, les débuts de la

rupture', *Cahiers du monde russe et soviétique,* vol. viii, October–December 1966, pp. 581–699; and his *Violence dans la violence: Le débat Bakounine–Nečaev,* Paris, Maspero, 1973, *passim.*

138 Lichtheim, *A Short History of Socialism,* p. 135; Carr, *Michael Bakunin,* p. 193.

139 See, for example, Hostetter, *The Italian Socialist Movement,* pp. 251–3. Lehning's 'Introduction' to the *Archives Bakounine,* vol. iv, *Michel Bakounine et ses relations avec Sergej Nečaev,* p. xxix, attributes Marxist and Blanquist ideas to Nechaev, which is insupportable.

140 Marx to Engels, 11 April 1865, MEW xxxi, p. 105; Padover, p. 386.

141 For the details, cf. Guillaume, in Bakunin, *Oeuvres,* vol. ii, pp. xvi ff.; Herzen, *My Past and Thoughts,* vol. iii, pp. 1161 ff.; Nicholaevsky and Maenchen-Helfen, *Karl Marx, Man and Fighter,* p. 469, n. 4. See also Hostetter, *The Italian Socialist Movement,* p. 78, n. 35, and David Riazanov, 'Marx als Verleumder', *Die Neue Zeit,* 2 December 1910.

142 Marx to Engels, 4 November 1864, MEW xxxi, p. 16; MESC, pp. 139–40; Padover, p. 370.

143 This was Bakunin's recollection in 1871. See *Archives Bakounine,* vol. i, part 2, p. 128 (the whole fragment, pp. 121–30, is a valuable source). See also Hostetter, *The Italian Socialist Movement,* p. 78 (although he mistranslates this passage), and Guillaume, vol. i, p. 292, n. 2, for part of the fragment.

144 Hostetter, *The Italian Socialist Movement,* pp. 79–85; David Riazanov, 'Bakuniniana', *Grünbergs Archiv für die Geschichte der Sozialismus und die Arbeiterbewegung,* vol. v, 1915, p. 187; Hobsbawm, *Primitive Rebels,* pp. 93–4.

145 Hostetter, *The Italian Socialist Movement,* p. 90.

146 Dragomanov, *Correspondance,* pp. 214–15.

147 See Marx to Engels, 24 March 1866, 17 May 1866, in MEW xxxi, pp. 193–5, 219; Padover, pp. 409–11, 417.

148 Marx to Engels, 11 September 1867, MEW xxxi, pp. 342–3; Padover, pp. 427–8. Cf. David McLellan, *Karl Marx: his Life and Thought,* London, Macmillan, 1973, pp. 380–1.

149 Marx to Engels, 4 September 1867, MEW xxxi, pp. 337–9; Padover, p. 426; *Documents,* vol. ii, p. 152.

150 Marx to Engels, 4 October 1867, MEW xxxi, pp. 352–6 (passage omitted from Padover); Hostetter, *The Italian Socialist Movement,* p. 113.

151 Guillaume, vol. i, pp. 74–5.

152 These are the words of a letter of Bakunin's written in 1872; see Gerald Brenan, *The Spanish Labyrinth,* Cambridge University Press, 1972, p. 137. On the foundation of the Alliance, see Guillaume, vol. i, pp. 132–3.

153 Bakunin to Marx, 22 December 1868, Guillaume, vol. i, p. 153;

Padover, p. 460; Hostetter, *The Italian Socialist Movement*,
p. 119; Joll, *The Anarchists*, p. 102. Marx to Engels, 15
December 1868, MEW xxxii, p. 234; Hostetter, *The Italian
Socialist Movement*, p. 119, Padover, p. 459.
154   See *Documents*, vol. iii, pp. 379–83; Padover, pp. 157–61.
155   *Documents*, vol. iii, pp. 299–301 (in French), pp. 387–9
(in English); quoted (in part) in Guillaume, vol. i, pp.
103–4.
156   *Documents*, vol. iii, p. 50; cf. p. 389n.
157   *Documents*, vol. iii, pp. 310–11; Guillaume, vol. i, pp. 140–1.
158   Marx to Engels, 5 March 1869, in MEW xxxii, p. 273; MESC,
pp. 219–21; Padover, p. 466.
159   Marx to Engels, 14 March 1869, MEW xxxii, p. 279; Padover,
p. 467.
160   Carr, *Michael Bakunin*, pp. 364, 352.
161   See *Oeuvres*, vol. v, pp. 13–218. Some are translated in Dolgoff,
Bakunin on Anarchy, pp. 160–74. For *four* of the articles in
Progrès, see *Oeuvres*, vol. i, pp. 207–60.
162   Marx to Engels, 30 October 1869, MEW xxxii, p. 380; Padover,
p. 478.
163   On this, the best source is Guillaume, vol. i, p. 208.
164   Cole, *Marxism and Anarchism*, p. 131.
165   Ibid., p. 128; cf. the General Council's crowing report, in
Documents, vol. iii, pp. 326–42.
166   *Documents*, vol. iii, pp. 322–4.
167   Guillaume, vol. i, p. 194.
168   Hess's article, 'Communists and collectivists at the *Bâle Congress*'
appeared in *Le Réveil*, 2 October 1869. See Guillaume, vol. i,
pp. 220 ff.; Carr, *Michael Bakunin*, pp. 383–4; Nicholaevsky and
Maenchen-Helfen, *Karl Marx, Man and Fighter*, p. 312.
169   Quoted in *Oeuvres*, vol. v, p. 223.
170   Carr, *Michael Bakunin*, p. 383.
171   See *Oeuvres*, vol. v, pp. 239–94.
172   *Oeuvres*, vol. v, pp. 232–5; Guillaume, vol. i, pp. 220–1; Carr,
Michael Bakunin, p. 385.
173   Marx to Engels, 17 December 1869, MEW xxxii, pp. 421–2;
Padover, p. 486. The articles are summarized in MEW xxxii,
p. 785, n. 483.
174   MEW xxxii, pp. 622–3; Padover, pp. 486–7.
175   *Documents*, vol. iii, pp. 354–63, 399–407; cf. p. 195.
176   MEW xvi, pp. 409–20.
177   *Documents*, vol. iii, pp. 226, 469; cf. Miklós Molnár, *Le déclin
de la première internationale: la conférence de Londres de 1871*,
Geneva, Droz, 1963, Annex I, pp. 199–204; Guillaume, vol. ii,
pp. 3 ff.
178   *Documents*, vol. iii, p. 412; Guillaume, vol. ii, pp. 55–6; Carr,
Michael Bakunin, p. 431; *Archives Bakounine*, vol. i, part 2,
p. 361.
179   Guillaume, vol. ii, p. 10.
180   Marx to Engels, 24 March 1870, MEW xxxii, p. 466; Padover,

p. 497; *Archives Bakounine*, vol. ii, p. xviii.

181 See Guillaume, vol. ii, pp. 13–17.

182 This phrase is wrested from Karl Polyani's fine study of the industrial revolution in England, *The Great Transformation, the Political and Economic Origins of Our Time*, Boston, Beacon Press, 1957. See, especially, part ii, pp. 33 ff.

183 Borkenau, *The Spanish Cockpit*, pp. 21, 24.

184 Quoted in Brenan, *The Spanish Labyrinth*, pp. 139–40.

185 Borkenau, *The Spanish Cockpit*, pp. 18–19, 20–1. See also Nicholaevsky and Maenchen–Helfen, *Karl Marx, Man and Fighter*, p. 355; Guillaume, vol. i, p. 285, n. 3.

186 Gabriel Kolko, *The Triumph of Conservatism, a Reinterpretation of American History 1900-1916*, New York, Free Press, 1963, pp. 288 ff.

187 See *Documents*, vol. iii, pp. 268–70, 477, 372.

188 Brenan, *The Spanish Labyrinth*, p. 138.

189 Ibid., p. 140. On Spanish anarchism the reader is also referred to Bookchin, *The Spanish Anarchists*, 1977; Temma Kaplan, *Anarchists of Andalusia, 1868-1903*, Princeton University Press, 1977; and (for a detailed account of a shorter period) Max Nettlau's monumental *La Première Internationale en Espagne (1868-1888)*, trans. with an introduction and notes by Renée Lamberet, Dordrecht, Reidel (for the Internationaal Instituut voor Sociale Geschiedenis), 1969.

190 Brenan, *The Spanish Labyrinth*, pp. 137–43.

191 Ibid., p. 136.

192 For details, see Henry Collins, 'The International and the British Labour Movement', *Bulletin* no. 9 of the Society for the Study of Labour History, London, Autumn 1964, pp. 26–39.

193 Hostetter, *The Italian Socialist Movement*, p. 213.

194 For the text, see Freymond, vol. ii, pp. 261–5; Cf. *Archives Bakounine*, vol. i, part 2, pp. 401 ff.; vol. ii, pp. 269–96; *Oeuvres*, vol. ii, pp. xlix–l; and Nicholaevsky and Maenchen–Helfen, *Karl Marx, Man and Fighter*, p. 368.

195 *Documents*, vol. v, pp. 356–409; Freymond, vol. ii, pp. 266–96.

196 *Documents*, vol. v, p. 572, n. 313.

197 Ibid., p. 356.

198 Ibid., p. 360.

199 Ibid., p. 361.

200 Ibid., p. 393.

201 Ibid., pp. 398–9.

202 Ibid., pp. 398, 390.

203 Ibid., p. 407.

204 Ibid., p. 399.

205 *Archives Bakounine*, vol. ii, pp. 123–5; *Oeuvres*, vol. ii, p. 1; cf. Joll, *The Anarchists*, pp. 106–7.

206 Marx to Bolte, 23 November 1871, MEW xxxiii, p. 329; Padover, pp. 544–5; MESC, p. 254.

207 MEW xxxiii, pp. 330–1; Padover, pp. 545–6 (dropped from MESC).

208   Marx to de Paepe, 24 November 1871, MEW xxxiii, p. 339; Padover, p. 549.
209   Marx to Kugelmann, 29 July 1872, MEW xxxiii, p. 505; Padover, p. 569.
210   *Documents*, vol. v, pp. 418–19; 437–8.
211   See Hostetter, *The Italian Socialist Movement*, pp. 245–6.
212   Ibid., p. 284; Nicholaevsky and Maenchen-Helfen, *Karl Marx, Man and Fighter*, p. 381; *The Hague Congress of the First International*, p. 555; *Archives Bakounine*, vol. ii, pp. 313 ff.
213   See Guillaume, vol. ii, pp. 345–7; cf. *Archives Bakounine*, vol. ii, pp. 321 ff.
214   See Gerth, pp. 225–7; Freymond, vol. ii, p. 365.
215   For details, see Marx to Danielson, 15 August 1872 and 12 December 1872, MEW xxxiii, pp. 516, 548; Nicholaevsky and Maenchen-Helfen, *Karl Marx, Man and Fighter*, pp. 373–4; *Archives Bakounine*, vol. ii, p. xlix.
216   Nicholaevsky and Maenchen-Helfen, *Karl Marx, Man and Fighter*, p. 377.
217   Marx to de Paepe, 28 May 1872, MEW xxxiii, pp. 479–80; to Danielson, 28 May 1872, MEW xxxiii, pp. 477–8.
218   Morgan, *The German Social Democrats and the First International*, p. 203.
219   Postgate, *The Workers' International*, p. 74; cf. Drachkovitch, *The Revolutionary Internationals*, pp. 14–15.
220   Engels to August Bebel, 20 June 1873, MEW xxxiii, pp. 590–1; MESC, pp. 266–7.
221   See Jacques Freymond and Miklós Molnár, 'The Rise and Fall of the First International', in Drachkovitch, *The Revolutionary Internationals*, pp. 3–35, for an excellent discussion of this point.
222   Marx, Speech to Central Committee of the Communist League, 15 September 1850, in MEW viii, pp. 412–13; also in Marx, *The Revolutions of 1848*, ed. and introduced by David Fernbach, Harmondsworth, Penguin (Pelican Marx Library, vol. i), 1973, p. 341, and in Marx and Engels, *The Cologne Communist Trial*, trans. with an introduction and notes by Rodney Livingstone, London, Lawrence & Wishart, 1971, pp. 62–3.
223   Freymond and Molnár, 'The Rise and Fall of the First International', p. 15.
224   Marx to Bolte, 23 November 1871, MEW xxxiii, pp. 329 ff.; (in part) MESC, pp. 253–5.
225   Marx, *The Critique of the Gotha Programme*, in MESW ii, p. 28.
226   *Archives Bakounine*, vol. ii, p. 147; also in *Oeuvres*, vol. iv, p. 342.
227   *The Hague Congress of the First International*, p. 154; Gerth, p. 212.
228   Marx to Sorge, 1 September 1870, MEW xxxiii, pp. 139–40; Padover, pp. 516–17.
229   For the text, cf. *Archives Bakounine*, vol. iii (1967), pp. 201–380.

230 See Lehning, 'Introduction', ibid, pp. xxv–xxvi.
231 Marx's conspectus of Bakunin's *Etatisme et anarchie* may be
     found in MEW xviii, pp. 630–6. The two English translations
     are those of Fernbach (in Marx, *The First International and
     After [Political Writings, vol. iii,]* Harmondsworth, Pelican
     Marx Library, 1974, pp. 333–8) and Mayer ('Marx on
     Bakunin: A Neglected Text', *Études de Marxologie* (Paris,
     Cahiers de l'ISEA, 2nd series, no. 2, October 1959, pp. 107–17).
     This quotation may be found in Mayer, 'Marx on Bakunin',
     pp. 112–13; Fernbach, pp. 336–7.
232 Mayer, 'Marx on Bakunin', pp. 110–111, Fernbach, p. 335.
233 Mayer, 'Marx on Bakunin', p. 112; Fernbach, p. 336.
234 Mayer, 'Marx on Bakunin', pp. 114, 110. Fernbach, pp. 337,
     335.
235 Fernbach, pp. 333–4 (omitted from Mayer).
236 Mayer, 'Marx on Bakunin', pp. 114–15; Fernbach, p. 338.

Conclusion

1 Marx, 'Conspectus of Bakunin's *Statism and Anarchy*' in *The
   First International and After,* ed. with an introduction by
   David Fernbach (henceforward cited as Fernbach), Harmondsworth, Penguin (Pelican Marx Library, vol iii), 1974, p. 334;
   also in H. Mayer, 'Marx on Bakunin: A Neglected Text',
   Études de Marxologie (Paris, Cahiers de l'ISEA, 2nd series,
   no. 2, October 1959, pp. 109–10.
2 Marx and Engels, *The German Ideology*, trans. Clems Dutt, ed.
   Salo Ryazanskaya, London, Lawrence & Wishart, 1965, p. 358.
3 Fernbach, p.338; Mayer, 'Marx on Bakunin', p. 114.
4 See Boris Nicholaevsky and Otto Maenchen-Helfen, *Karl Marx,
   Man and Fighter*, trans. Gwenda David and Eric Mosbacher,
   Harmondsworth, Penguin, 1976, pp. 387–8.
5 *Marx–Engels Werke* (henceforward cited as MEW), Berlin, Dietz,
   vol. xviii, pp. 159–61.
6 Marx, 'The Chartist Movement', *New York Daily Tribune*, 25
   August 1852; quoted in Solomon F. Bloom, *A World of Nations*,
   New York, Columbia University Press, 1941, p. 91.
7 Marx to Sorge, 19 September 1879, in *Marx–Engels Selected
   Correspondence* (henceforward cited as MESC), Moscow,
   Foreign Languages Publishing House, 1965, p. 328.
8 Marx, 'Introduction to the Programme of the French Parti
   Ouvrier' (1880) in Fernbach, p. 377.
9 *Documents of the First International 1864–72* (henceforward
   cited as *Documents*), trans. Nina Nepomnyashchaya, Molly
   Pearlman and Lydia Belyakova, Moscow, Progress Publishers,
   vol. iv, p. 445; Fernbach, p. 270.
10 *Documents*, vol. i, p. 345; Fernbach, p. 89.
11 Fernbach, p. 17.

12   Marx to Lafargue, 19 April 1870, MEW xxxii, p. 675; *Anarchism and Anarcho-syndicalism, Selected Writings by Marx, Engels and Lenin*, ed. N.Y. Kolpinsky, New York, International Publishers, 1972, p. 46. The entire letter is a valuable source.

13   Marx to Sorge, 23 November 1871, MEW xxxiii, pp. 332-3; MESC, pp. 254-5.

14   On the principle of plenitude, see Arthur O. Lovejoy, *The Great Chain of Being*, Cambridge, Mass., Harvard University Press, 1957, chs 1 and 2.

15   George Plekhanov, *Marxism and Anarchism*, trans. Eleanor Marx Aveling, Chicago, Charles Kerr, 1918, p. 73.

16   *Documents*, vol. i, p. 284.

17   Marx, *The German Ideology*, pp. 93-4.

18   Marx, 'Conspectus', in Fernbach, p. 355; and Mayer, 'Marx on Bakunin', p. 110.

19   Shlomo Avineri, *The Social and Political Thought of Karl Marx*, Cambridge University Press, 1968, p. 204.

20   Marx to Weydermeyer, 5 March 1852, in MESC, p. 60.

21   Albert O. Hirschmann, *The Passions and the Interests: Political Arguments for Capitalism Before its Triumph*, Princeton University Press, 1977, p. 128.

22   Octave Mirbeau, quoted by Noam Chomsky, 'Introduction' to Daniel Guérin, *Anarchism: From Theory to Practice*, trans. Mary Klopper, New York and London, Monthly Review Press, 1970, p. vii.

23   Barrington Moore, Jr, *Social Origins of Dictatorship and Democracy: Lord and Peasant in the Making of the Modern World*, Boston, Beacon Press, 1966, p. 505.

24   Charles Taylor, 'Feuerbach and the Roots of Materialism', *Political Studies* (Oxford University Press), vol. xxvi, September 1978, p. 421.

Works cited

Part One

Althusser, Louis, *Essays in Self-Criticism*, trans. Grahame Locke, London, New Left, 1976.

Althusser, Louis, *For Marx*, trans. Ben Brewster, New York, Vintage, 1970.

Althusser, Louis, *Reading Capital*, trans. Ben Brewster, London, New Left, 1975.

Apter, David, 'The Old Anarchism and the New', *Government and Opposition* (London School of Economics), vol. v, no. 4, autumn 1970, pp. 397–8.

Arblaster, Anthony, 'The Relevance of Anarchism', in *The Socialist Register,* ed. Ralph Miliband and John Saville, London, Merlin Press, 1971, pp. 157–84.

Archiv Marksa i Engelsa (Marx–Engels Archives), Moscow, 1934, iii (viii).

Avineri, Shlomo, 'Hegel's Nationalism', *Review of Politics* (Notre Dame, Ind.), vol. xxiv, no. 4, 1962, pp. 461–84.

Avineri, Shlomo, *Hegel's Theory of the Modern State*, Cambridge University Press, 1972.

Avineri, Shlomo, 'Marx's Vision of Future Society and the Problem of Utopianism', *Dissent* (New York), summer 1973, pp. 323–31.

Avineri, Shlomo, 'The Problem of War in Hegel's Thought', *Journal of the History of Ideas* (Chicago), vol. xxii, no. 4.

Avineri, Shlomo, *The Social and Political Thought of Karl Marx*, Cambridge University Press, 1968.

Berlin, Isaiah, *Karl Marx: His Life and Environment*, Oxford University Press, 4th edn, 1978.

Berlin, Isaiah, 'Two Concepts of Liberty', in *Four Essays on Liberty*, Oxford University Press, 1970, pp. 118–72.

Bottomore, T.B., ed., *Karl Marx: Early Writings,* New York, McGraw-Hill, 1964.

Brenan, Gerald, *The Spanish Labyrinth*, Cambridge University Press, 1972, p. 189.

Carver, Terrell, ed., *Karl Marx: Texts on Method*, Oxford, Blackwell, 1975.

Cohn-Bendit, Daniel, *Le grand bazar*, Paris, Belford, 1976.

Cohn-Bendit, Daniel and Gabriel, *Obsolete Communism: The Left-Wing Alternative*, trans. Arnold Pomerans, Harmondsworth, Penguin, 1969.

Easton, Lloyd D., and Guddat, Kurt H., *Writings of the Young Marx on Philosophy and Society*, New York, Doubleday, 1967.

Findlay, J.N., *Hegel: A Re-examination*, New York, Collier, 1962.

Geras, Norman, 'Proletarian Self-Emancipation', *Radical Philosophy* (London), no. 6, winter 1973, pp. 20–22.

Gray, J. Glenn, *Hegel and Greek Thought*, New York and Evanston, Harper & Row, 1968.

Hegel, G.W.F., *Early Theological Writings*, trans. T.M. Knox, with an introduction by Richard Kroner, Philadelphia, University of Pennsylvania Press, 1971.

Hegel, G.W.F., *The Phenomenology of Mind*, trans. with an introduction and notes by J.B. Baillie, New York and Evanston, Harper & Row, 1967.

Hegel's Philosophy of Right, trans. with notes by T.M. Knox, Oxford, Clarendon Press, 1962.

Hirschmann, Albert O., *The Passions and the Interests: Political Arguments for Capitalism Before its Triumph*, Princeton University Press, 1977.

Joll, James, *The Anarchists*, London, Eyre & Spottiswoode, 1964.

Kelly, George Armstrong, *Idealism, Politics and History: Sources of Hegelian Thought*, Cambridge University Press, 1969.

Kelly, George Armstrong, 'Notes on Hegel's "Lordship and Bondage"', *Review of Metaphysics* (Chicago), June 1966, pp. 780–802.

Keynes, John Maynard, *The General Theory of Employment, Interest and Money*, London, Macmillan, 1936.

Kojève, Alexandre, *Introduction à la lecture de Hegel*, Paris, NRF, 1947.

Kramnick, Isaac, 'On Anarchism and the Real World: William Godwin and Radical England', *American Political Science Review*, vol. 66, 1972, p. 128.

Lenin, V.I., *What is to be Done? Burning Questions of our Movement*, Moscow, Foreign Languages Publishing House (paperback edn, n.d.).

Lovejoy, Arthur O., *The Great Chain of Being*, Cambridge, Mass., Harvard University Press, 1957.

Löwy, Michael, *La Théorie de la révolution chez le jeune Marx*, Paris, Maspero, 1970.

Lubasz, Heinz, 'Marx's Initial Problematic: The Problem of Poverty', *Political Studies* (Oxford), vol. xxiv, no. 1, March 1976, pp. 24–42.

Lukács, Georg, *The Young Hegel: Studies in the Relations Between Dialectics and Economics*, trans. by Rodney Livingstone, London, Merlin Press, 1975.

McLellan, David, *Karl Marx: His Life and Thought*, London, Macmillan, 1973.

Marcuse, Herbert, *One-Dimensional Man: Studies in the Ideology of Advanced Industrial Society*, Boston, Beacon Press, 1966.

Marx, Karl, *Capital,* vol. i, trans. Ben Fowkes, Harmondsworth, Penguin (Pelican Marx Library), 1976.

Marx, Karl, *Critique of Hegel's Philosophy of Right,* trans. Annette Jolin, ed. and with an introduction by Joseph O'Malley, Cambridge University Press, 1970.

Marx, Karl, *Grundrisse,* trans. and with an introduction by Martin Nicolaus, Harmondsworth, Penguin, 1973.

Marx, Karl, *The Poverty of Philosophy: Response to 'The Philosophy of Poverty' of M. Proudhon,* New York, International Publishers, 1973.

Marx, Karl, *Theories of Surplus Value,* 3 vols, Moscow, Foreign Language Publishing House, 1972.

Marx, Karl, and Engels, Friedrich, *The German Ideology,* trans. Clemens Dutt, ed. Salo Ryazanskaya, London, Lawrence & Wishart, 1965.

Marx–Engels Collected Works (MECW), New York and London, International Publishers, 1975 et seq.

Marx–Engels Selected Works (MESW), 2 vols. Moscow, Foreign Languages Publishing House, 1962.

Mézáros, István, *Marx's Theory of Alienation,* London, Merlin Press, 1970.

Miliband, Ralph, 'Marx and the State' in R. Miliband and John Saville, eds, *The Socialist Register, 1965,* New York, Monthly Review Press, 1965.

Miliband, Ralph, *Marxism and Politics,* Oxford University Press, 1977.

Mosher, Michael A., 'The Spirit that Governs Cities: Modes of Human Association in the Writings of Montesquieu and Hegel', unpublished doctoral dissertation, Harvard University, Cambridge, Mass, 1976.

Nozick, Robert M., *Anarchy, the State and Utopia,* New York, Basic Books, 1974.

Plant, Raymond, 'Hegel's Social Theory', *New Left Review,* no. 103, May–June 1970, p. 85.

Ramm, Theo, 'Die künftige Gesellschaftsordnung nach der Theorie von Marx und Engels', *Marxismusstudien* (Tübingen), vol. ii, 1957, pp. 77–179.

Resnick, David, 'Crude Communism and Revolution', *American Political Science Review,* vol. lxx, no. 4, December 1976, pp. 1136–45.

Schumpeter, Joseph A., *'Imperialism' and 'Social Classes',* New York, Kelly, 1951.

Shklar, Judith N., *After Utopia,* Princeton University Press, 1957.

Shklar, Judith N., *Freedom and Independence: A Study of the Political Ideas of Hegel's 'Phenomenology of Mind',* Cambridge University Press, 1976.

Stenning, H.J., ed., *Karl Marx: Selected Essays,* New York, International Publishers, 1926.

Taylor, Charles, *Hegel,* Cambridge University Press, 1975.

Thomas, Paul, 'Hegel: Civil Society and War', *Proceedings* of the 4th Biennial Meeting of the American Hegel Society, Philadelphia, State University of Pennsylvania Press, 1978.

Thompson, E.P., *The Making of the English Working Class*, New York, Vintage, 1966.

Wolin, Sheldon, *Politics and Vision*, Boston, Little, Brown, 1960.

Woodcock, George, *Anarchism*, Harmondsworth, Penguin, 1962.

Woodcock, George, and Avacumović, *The Anarchist Prince: A Biography of Peter Kropotkin*, London, Boardman, 1950.

Part Two

Anarchism and Anarcho-Syndicalism, Selected Writings by Marx, Engels and Lenin, ed. N.Y. Kolpinsky, New York, International Publishers, 1972.

Arvon, Henri, *Aux sources de l'existentialisme: Max Stirner*, Paris, Presses Universitaires de France, 1950.

Avrich, Paul, *The Russian Anarchists*, Princeton University Press, 1967.

Bahne, S., '"Die deutsche Ideologie" von Marx und Engels. Einige Textergänzungen', *International Review of Social History* (Amsterdam and Assen), vol. vii, part 1, 1962, pp. 93–104.

Bakounine, Michel, *Oeuvres*, 5 vols, ed. Max Nettlau and James Guillaume, Paris, Stock, 1895–1911.

Bakunin, Michael, *Gesammelte Werke*, 3 vols, ed. with an introduction by Max Nettlau, Berlin, Der Syndikalist, 1921–4.

Bakunin, Michael, *Secret Statutes of the Alliance*, London, Darson, and Hamburg, Otto Meisner, 1873.

Bakunin, Michael, *Selected Writings*, trans. Steven Cox and Olive Stevens, with an introduction by Arthur Lehning, London, Cape, 1976.

Baron, Samuel H., *Plekhanov, the Father of Russian Marxism*, Stanford University Press, 1963.

Berdaiev, Nicolas, *Les Sources et le sens du communisme Russe*, trans. from the Russian by L.J. Cain, Paris, Gallimard, 1951, p. 129.

Berlin, Isaiah, 'Herzen and Bakunin on Liberty', in *Continuity and Change in Russian and Soviet Thought*, ed. and with an introduction by Ernest J. Simmons, Cambridge, Mass., Harvard University Press, 1955, pp. 473–99.

Berlin, Isaiah, 'A Marvellous Decade (ii) 1838–48: German Romanticism in Petersburg and Moscow', *Encounter*, (London), November 1955.

Blackstock, P.W., and Hoselitz, B.F., eds, *Karl Marx and Friedrich Engels: The Russian Menace to Europe*, Chicago, Free Press, 1952.

Bloom, Solomon F., *A World of Nations*, New York, Columbia University Press, 1941.

Bookchin, Murray, *The Spanish Anarchists: The Heroic Years 1868–1936*, New York, Harper & Row, 1977.

Borkenau, Franz, *The Spanish Cockpit*, London, Faber & Faber, 1937.

Braunthal, Julius, *History of the International, 1864–1914*, trans. Henry Collins and Kenneth Mitchell, London, Nelson, 1966.

Brazill, William, *The Young Hegelians,* New Haven, Conn., Yale University Press, 1970.

Brogan, D.W., *Proudhon,* London, Hamish Hamilton, 1934.

Camus, Albert, *The Rebel,* trans. Anthony Bower, Harmondsworth, Penguin, 1962.

Carr, E.H., *Michael Bakunin,* New York, Vintage, 1961.

Clark, John P., *Max Stirner's Egoism,* London, Freedom Press, 1976.

Cohen, G.A., 'Marx's Dialectic of Labour', *Philosophy and Public Affairs* (Princeton, N.J.), no. iii, spring 1974, pp. 253–61.

Cole, G.D.H., *Marxism and Anarchism, 1850–1890,* London, Macmillan, 1969.

Collins, Henry, 'The English Branches of the First International' in Asa Briggs and John Saville, eds, *Essays in Labour History in Memory of G.D.H. Cole,* London, Macmillan, 1960, pp. 242–75.

Collins, Henry, 'The International and the British Labour Movement', *Bulletin* no. 9 of Society for the Study of Labour History, London, autumn 1964.

Collins, Henry, and Abramsky, Chimen, *Karl Marx and the British Labour Movement: Years of the First International,* London, Macmillan, 1965.

The Confessions of Michael Bakunin (with the marginal comments of Tsar Nicholas I), trans. Robert C. Howes, with an introduction by Lawrence D. Orton, Ithaca, Cornell University Press, 1977, pp. 39–40.

Confino, Michel, 'Bakounine et Nečaev, les débuts de la rupture', *Cahiers du monde russe et soviétique,* vol. vii, October–December 1966, pp. 581–699.

Confino, Michel, *Violence dans la violence: Le débat Bakounine-Nečaev,* Paris, Maspero, 1973.

Cooper, David, *The Death of the Family,* New York, Pantheon, 1970.

Desjardins, Artur, *P.-J. Proudhon,* Paris, Perrin, 1896.

Documents of the First International, 1864–72, trans. Nina Nepomnyashchaya, Molly Pearlman and Lydia Belyakova, 5 vols, Moscow, Progress Publishers, 1974.

Dolgoff, Sam, ed., *Bakunin on Anarchy,* New York, Vintage, 1971.

Dolléans, Édouard, *Histoire du mouvement ouvrier,* Paris, Colin, 1936.

Dolléans, Édouard, *P.-J. Proudhon,* Paris, Gallimard, 1948.

Drachkovitch, Miloran M., ed., *The Revolutionary Internationals 1864–1943,* Stanford University Press, 1966.

Dragomanov, M., ed., *Correspondance de Michel Bakounine: lettres à Herzen et à Ogareff,* trans. from the Russian by Marie Stromberg, Paris, Perrin, 1896.

Droz, Édouard, *P.-J. Proudhon,* Paris, Pages Libres, 1909.

Dupré, Louis, *Philosophical Foundations of Marxism,* New York, Harcourt, Brace, 1966.

Edwards, Stewart, and Fraser, Elizabeth, *Selected Writings of P.-J. Proudhon,* New York, Doubleday, 1969.

Eltzbacher, Paul, *Anarchism,* trans. Steven T. Byington, London, Fifield, 1908.

Evans, David Owen, *Social Romanticism in France*, Oxford, Clarendon Press, 1961.

Feuerbach, Ludwig, *Anthropologischer Materialismus: Ausgewählte Schriften*, ed. Alfred Schmidt, Munich, Europa, 1957.

Feuerbach, Ludwig, *The Essence of Christianity*, trans. George Eliot, New York, Harper & Row, 1957.

Feuerbach, Ludwig, *Sämmtliche Schriften*, ed. F. Boline and W. Jodl, Stuttgart, Frommanns, 1959.

Foucault, Michel, ed., *I, Pierre Rivière. . . A Case of Parricide in the Nineteenth Century*, trans. Frank Jellinek, New York, Pantheon, 1975.

Freymond, Jacques, *La Première Internationale: recueil de documents*, 2 vols, Geneva, Droz (Publications de l'Institut Universitaire de Hautes Études Internationales, no. 39), 1962.

Freymond, Jacques, and Molnár, Miklós, 'The Rise and Fall of the First International', in Miloran M. Drachkovitch, ed., *The Revolutionary Internationals 1864-1963*, Stanford University Press, 1966.

Fribourg, E.-E., *L'Association Internationale des Travailleurs*, Paris, Le Chevalier, 1871.

Gerth, Hans, ed. and trans., *The First International, Minutes of The Hague Congress of 1872 with Related Documents*, Madison, University of Wisconsin Press, 1958.

Giddens, Anthony, ed., *Émile Durkheim: Selected Writings*, Cambridge University Press, 1972.

Guérin, Daniel, *Anarchism: From Theory to Practice*, trans. Mary Klopper, New York and London, Monthly Review Press, 1970.

Guérin, Daniel, *Ni Dieu ni maître: anthologie de l'anarchisme*, 2 vols, Paris, Maspero, 1974.

Guillaume, James, *L'Internationale: documents et souvenirs 1864-1878*, 2 vols, Paris, Cornély, 1905-7.

Hague Congress of the First International, Sept. 2-7, 1872: Minutes and Documents, The trans. Richard Dixon and Alex Miller, Moscow, Progress Publishers, 1976.

Hanfi, Zawar, ed., *The Fiery Brook: Selected Writings of Ludwig Feuerbach*, New York, Anchor, 1972.

Hare, R.M., *Portraits of Russian Personalities*, Oxford University Press, 1959.

Hegel, G.W.F., *On Art, Religion, Philosophy*, ed. J. Glenn Gray, New York, Harper & Row, 1970.

Helms, Hans G., *Ideologie der anonymen Gesellschaft: Max Stirners 'Einzige' und der Fortschritt des demokratischen Selbstbewusstseins vom Vormärz bis zur Bundesrepublik*, Cologne, DuMont, 1966.

Hepner, Benoît-P., *Bakounine et le Panslavisme révolutionnaire, cinq essais sur l'histoire des idées en Russie et en Europe*, Paris, Rivière, 1950.

Hepner, Benoît-P., 'Nihilisme: mot et idée', *Synthèses* (Brussels) January 1949.

Herzen, Alexander, *From the Other Shore*, trans. Moura Budberg, with an introduction by Isaiah Berlin, London, Weidenfeld & Nicolson, 1956.

Herzen, Alexander, *My Past and Thoughts: The Memoirs of Alexander Herzen*, trans. Constance Garnett, revised by Humphrey Higgins, with an Introduction by Sir Isaiah Berlin, New York, Knopf, 1968.

Hess, Moses, *Die letzten Philosophen*, Darmstadt, Leske, 1845.

Hobsbawm, E.J., *Labouring Men*, New York, Doubleday, 1967.

Hobsbawm, E.J., *Primitive Rebels: Studies in Archaic Forms of Social Movement in the Nineteenth and Twentieth Centuries*, New York, Norton, 1965.

Hoffman, Robert L., *Revolutionary Justice: The Social and Political Theory of P.-J. Proudhon*, Urbana, University of Illinois Press, 1972.

Hook, Sidney, *From Hegel to Marx*, New York, Humanities Press, 1950.

Hostetter, Richard, *The Italian Socialist Movement 1. Origins (1860-1882)*, Princeton, Van Nostrand, 1958.

Huxley, Thomas Henry, 'The Struggle for Existence: A Programme', *Nineteenth Century* (London), vol. xxiii, February 1888, pp. 161-80.

Kaminski, H.-E., *Michel Bakounine, la vie d'un révolutionnaire*, Paris, Aubier, 1938.

Kaplan, Temma, *Anarchists of Andalusia, 1868-1903*, Princeton University Press, 1977.

Karl Marx and the First International, ed. and trans. Saul K. Padover, New York, McGraw-Hill (Karl Marx Library, vol. iii), 1973.

Karl Marx und die Gründung der 1. Internationale: Dokumente und Materialen, Berlin, Dietz, 1964.

Kolko, Gabriel, *The Triumph of Conservatism, a Reinterpretation of American History 1900-1916*, New York, Free Press, 1963.

Kriegel, Annie, 'Le Syndicalisme révolutionnaire et Proudhon', in *Le Pain et les roses: Jalons pour une histoire du socialisme*, Paris, Presses Universitaires de France, 1968, pp. 33-50.

Kropotkin, Peter, *Mutual Aid: A Factor of Evolution*, Harmondsworth, Penguin, 1939.

Lampert, E., *Studies in Rebellion*, London, Routledge & Kegan Paul, 1957.

Lehning, Arthur, Rüter, A.J.C., and Scheibert, Peter, eds, *Archives Bakounine*, 5 vols, Leiden, Brill, 1965 et seq.

Leroy, Maxim, *Histoire des idées sociales en France*, Paris, NRF, 1950.

Lichtheim, George, *Marxism, an Historical and Critical Study*, New York, Praeger, 1971.

Lichtheim, George, *The Origins of Socialism*, New York, Praeger, 1969.

Lichtheim, G., *A Short History of Socialism*, New York, Praeger, 1970.

Lobkowicz, Nicolas, *Theory and Practice: History of a Concept from Aristotle to Marx*, Notre Dame, Ind., University of Notre Dame Press, 1967.

Louis, Paul, *Histoire du socialisme en France*, Paris, Rivière, 1937.

Lubac, Henri de, *The Un-Marxian Socialist*, trans. R.E. Scantlebury, London, Sheen & Ward, 1948.

McLellan, David, *The Young Hegelians and Karl Marx*, New York, Praeger, 1969.

Marx, Karl, *A Contribution to the Critique of Political Economy*, Moscow, Foreign Languages Publishing House, 1971.

Marx, Karl, *The First International and After*, ed. with an introduction by David Fernbach, Harmondsworth, Penguin (Pelican Marx Library, vol. iii), 1974.

Marx, Karl, *The Revolutions of 1848*, ed. and introduced by David Fernbach, Harmondsworth, Penguin (Pelican Marx Library, vol. i), 1973.

Marx, Karl, and Engels, Friedrich, *The Cologne Communist Trial*, trans. with an introduction and notes by Rodney Livingstone, London, Lawrence & Wishart, 1971.

Marx, Karl, and Engels, Friedrich, *The German Ideology*, trans. Roy Pascal, London, Lawrence & Wishart; New York, International Publishers, 1938.

Marx, Karl, and Engels, Friedrich, *Letters to Americans 1848-95*, New York, International Publishers, 1969.

Marx-Engels Selected Correspondence (MESC), Moscow, Foreign Languages Publishing House, 1965.

Marx-Engels, Werke (MEW), 39 vols, Berlin, Dietz, 1956 et seq.

Masaryk, Thomas, *Russland und Europa*, Jena, Fischer, 1913.

Masaryk, Thomas, *The Spirit of Russia*, trans. Eden and Cedar Paul, London, Allen & Unwin, 1955.

Masters, Anthony, *Bakunin, the Father of Anarchy*, New York, Saturday Review Press, 1974.

Maximoff, G.P., *The Political Philosophy of Bakunin: Scientific Anarchism*, Chicago, Free Press, 1953.

Mayer, H., 'Marx on Bakunin: A Neglected Text', *Études de Marxologie* (Paris, Cahiers de l'ISEA, 2nd series, no. 2, October 1959), pp. 107-117.

Mehring, Franz, *Karl Marx, the Story of his Life*, trans. Edward Fitzgerald, New York, Covici, Friede, 1935.

Mendel, A.P., *Dilemmas of Progress in Tsarist Russia*, Cambridge, Mass., Harvard University Press, 1961.

Michels, Robert, *Political Parties, a Sociological Study of the Oligarchic Tendencies of Modern Democracy*, trans. Eden and Cedar Paul, New York, Dover, 1959.

Molnár, Miklós, *Le Déclin de la première Internationale: la conférence de Londres de 1871*, Geneva, Droz, 1963.

Moore, Barrington, Jr, *Social Origins of Dictatorship and Democracy: Lord and Peasant in the Making of the Modern World*, Boston, Beacon Press, 1966.

Morgan, Roger P., *The German Social Democrats and the First International, 1864-72*, Cambridge University Press, 1965.

Nerrlich, Paul, ed., *Arnold Ruge: Briefe und Tagebuchblätter*, Leipzig, Weidmann, 1886.

Nettlau, Max, 'Bakunin und die Internationale in Italien bis zum Herbst 1872', *Grünbergs Archiv für die Geschichte der Sozialismus und die Arbeiterbewegung*, vol. ii, 1911-12, pp. 283-4.

Nicholaevsky, Boris, and Maenchen-Helfen, Otto, *Karl Marx, Man and Fighter*, trans. Gwenda David and Eric Mosbacher, Harmondsworth, Penguin, 1976.

Nomad, Max, *Apostles of Revolution*, Boston, Beacon Press, 1939.

Norman, Richard, *Hegel's Phenomenology: A Philosophical Introduction*, Brighton, University of Sussex Press, 1976.

Oakeshott, Michael, *On Human Conduct*, Oxford, Clarendon Press, 1975.

Oeuvres complètes de P.-J. Proudhon, ed. Célestin Bouglé and H. Moysett, 15 vols, Paris, Rivière, 1923–59.

Paterson, R.W.K., *The Nihilistic Egoist: Max Stirner*, Oxford University Press, 1971.

Pelczynski, Z.A., ed., *Hegel's Political Philosophy*, Cambridge University Press, 1971.

Pickles, William, 'Marx and Proudhon', *Politica* (London School of Economics), September 1938, vol. iii, no. 13, pp. 253–4.

Plekhanov, George, *Marxism and Anarchism*, trans. Eleanor Marx Aveling, Chicago, Charles Kerr, 1918.

Polyani, Karl, *The Great Transformation, the Political and Economic Origins of Our Time*, Boston, Beacon Press, 1957.

Pomper, Philip, *The Russian Revolutionary Intelligentsia*, New York, Crowell, 1970.

Postgate, Raymond, *The Workers' International*, London, Swarthmore Press, 1926.

Proudhon, P.-J., *Carnets*, 5 vols (to date), ed. Pierre Haubtmann, Paris, Rivière, 1960 et. seq.

Proudhon, P.-J. *Correspondance*, 14 vols, Paris, Lacroix, 1875 et. seq.

Proudhon, P.-J., *The General Idea of the Revolution in the Nineteenth Century*, trans. J.B. Robinson, London and Berlin, Freedom Press, 1923.

Proudhon, P.-J., *Oeuvres*, 26 vols, Paris, Lacroix, 1867–70.

Puech, Jules L., *Le Proudhonisme dans l'Association Internationale des Travailleurs*, Paris, Alcan, 1907.

Pyziur, Eugene, *The Doctrine of Anarchism of Michael A. Bakunin*, Chicago, Gateway, 1968.

Riazanov, David, 'Bakuniniana', *Grünbergs Archiv für die Geschichte der Sozialismus und die Arbeiterbewegung*, vol. v, 1915, p. 187.

Riazanov, David, *Karl Marx and Friedrich Engels, an Introduction to Their Lives and Work*, trans. Joshua Kunitz, London and New York, Monthly Review Press, 1973.

Riazanov, David, 'Marx als Verleumder', *Die Neue Zeit* (Berlin), 2 December 1910.

Ridley, F.F., *Revolutionary Syndicalism in France*, Cambridge University Press, 1970.

Ritter, Alan, *The Political Thought of Pierre-Joseph Proudhon*, Princeton University Press, 1969.

Rotenstreich, Nathan, *Some Basic Problems in Marx's Philosophy*, New York, Bobbs-Merrill, 1965.

Rubel, Maximilien, 'Marx et le socialisme populiste russe', *Revue Socialiste* (Paris), May 1947.

Rubel, Maximilien, 'Notes on Marx's Conception of Democracy', *New Politics* (New York), vol. i, no. 2, winter 1962.

Rubel, Maximilien, and Manale, Margaret, *Marx Without Myth*, Oxford, Blackwell, 1975.

Ruge, Arnold, *Zwei Jahre in Paris: Studien und Erinnerungen*, Leipzig, Jurani, 1846.

Rühle, Otto, *Karl Marx*, trans. Eden and Cedar Paul, New York, Viking, 1929.

Russian Intellectual History: An Anthology, ed. Marc Raeff, with an introduction by Isaiah Berlin, New York, Harcourt, Brace, 1966.

Sand, George, *Correspondance*, vol. iii, Paris, Calmann-Lévy, 1882.

Scheibert, Peter, *Von Bakunin zu Lenin*, vol. i, Leiden, Brill, 1956.

Siegel, Jerrold, *Marx's Fate: The Shape of a Life*, Princeton University Press, 1978.

Soboul, Albert, *Les Sans-culottes parisiens en l'an II*, Paris, Éditions de Seuil, 1968.

Stirner, Max, *The Ego and his Own*, trans. Steven T. Byington, London, Fifield, 1912.

Stirner, Max, *The Ego and his Own*, ed. John Carroll, London, Cape, 1971.

Stirner, Max, *Der Einzige und sein Eigenthum*, 2nd edn, Leipzig, Wigand, 1882.

Thomas, Paul, 'The Mao–Marx Debate: A View from outside China', *Politics and Society*, vol. vii, no. 3, 1977, pp. 331–41.

Thomas, Paul, 'Marx and Science', *Political Studies* (Oxford), vol. xxiv, no. 1, March 1976, pp. 1–24.

Tier, Erich, 'Marx und Proudhon', *Marxismusstudien* (Tübingen), vol. ii, 1957, pp. 120–50.

Tucker, Robert M., *Philosophy and Myth in Karl Marx*, Cambridge University Press, 1967.

Turgenev, Ivan, *Fathers and Sons*, trans. Rosemary Edmonds, Harmondsworth, Penguin, 1977.

Venturi, Franco, *Roots of Revolution, a History of the Populist and Socialist Movements in Nineteenth-Century Russia*, trans. Francis Haskell, with an introduction by Isaiah Berlin, New York, Knopf, 1964.

Weill, Georges, *Histoire du mouvement sociale en France*, Paris, Alcan, 1924.

Williams, Gwyn A., *Artisans and Sans-Culottes: Popular Movements in France and England during the French Revolution*, New York, Norton, 1969.

Williams, Raymond, *Marxism and Literature*, Oxford University Press, 1977.

Wittke, Carl, *The Utopian Communist: A Biography of Wilhelm Weitling*, Baton Rouge, Louisiana State University Press, 1950.

Woodcock, George, *P.-J. Proudhon*, London, Macmillan, 1956.

Zeldin, Theodore, *France, 1848–1945*, vol. i, *Ambition, Love and Politics*, Oxford, Clarendon Press, 1973.

Index